ECONOMICS AND METHODOLOGY

This is IEA conference volume no. 126

Economics and Methodology

Crossing Boundaries

Proceedings of the IEA Conference held in Bergamo, Italy

Edited by

Roger E. Backhouse

Daniel M. Hausman

Uskali Mäki

and

Andrea Salanti

in association with the
INTERNATIONAL ECONOMIC ASSOCIATION

First published in Great Britain 1998 by
MACMILLAN PRESS LTD
Houndmills, Basingstoke, Hampshire RG21 6XS and London
Companies and representatives throughout the world

A catalogue record for this book is available from the British Library.

This book is published in the *International Economic Association* series
General Editor: Michael Kaser
Series Standing Order ISBN 0–333–71242–0 (*outside North America only*)

ISBN 0–333–67458–8

First published in the United States of America 1998 by
ST. MARTIN'S PRESS, INC.,
Scholarly and Reference Division,
175 Fifth Avenue, New York, N.Y. 10010

ISBN 0–312–21099–X

Library of Congress Cataloging-in-Publication Data
Economics and methodology : crossing boundaries : proceedings of the IEA conference held in Bergamo, Italy / edited by Roger E. Backhouse . . . [et al.].
p. cm. — (IEA conference volume ; no. 126)
"In association with the International Economic Association."
"Originally presented at the IEA conference on 'The nature of economics: case studies in economy methodology', held at the University of Bergamo on 17–19 June 1996"—Ackn.
Includes bibliographical references and index.
ISBN 0–312–21099–X (cloth)
1. Economics—Methodology—Congresses. I. Backhouse, Roger. II. International Economic Association. III. Series: I.E.A. conference volume ; no. 126.
HB131.E2574 1998
330–dc21 97–40288
CIP

This book is printed on paper suitable for recycling and made from fully managed and sustained forest sources.

10 9 8 7 6 5 4 3 2 1
07 06 05 04 03 02 01 00 99 98

Printed in Great Britain by
The Ipswich Book Company Ltd, Ipswich, Suffolk

Contents

The International Economic Association

A non-profit organisation with purely scientific aims, the International Economic Association (IEA) was founded in 1950. It is a federation of some sixty national economic associations in all parts of the world. Its basic purpose is the development of economics as an intellectual discipline, recognising a diversity of problems, systems and values in the world and taking note of methodological diversities.

The IEA has, since its creation, sought to fulfil that purpose by promoting mutual understanding among economists through the organisation of scientific meetings and common research programmes, and by means of publications on problems of fundamental as well as of current importance. Deriving from its long concern to assure professional contacts between East and West and North and South, the IEA pays special attention to issues of economics in systemic transition and in the course of development. During its nearly fifty years of existence, it has organised some hundred round-table conferences for specialists on topics ranging from fundamental theories to methods and tools of analysis and major problems of the present-day world. Participation in round tables is at the invitation of a specialist programme committee, but eleven triennial World Congresses have regularly attracted the participation of individual economists from all over the world.

The Association is governed by a Council, composed of representatives of all member associations, and by a fifteen-member Executive Committee which is elected by the Council. The Executive Committee (1995–8) at the time of the Bergamo Conference was:

President:	Professor Jacques Drèze, Belgium
Vice-President:	Professor Anne Krueger, USA
Treasurer:	Professor Erich Streissler, Austria
Past President:	Professor Michael Bruno, Israel (deceased 26 December 1996)
Other Members:	Professor Anthony B. Atkinson, UK
	Professor Vittorio Corbo, Chile
	Professor Karel Dyba, Czech Republic
	Professor Jean-Michel Grandmont, France

	Professor Yujiro Hayami, Japan
	Professor Seppo Honkapohja, Finland
	Professor Valery Makarov, Russia
	Professor Luigi Pasinetti, Italy
	Professor Hans Werner Sinn, Germany
	Professor Rehman Sobhan, Bangladesh
	Professor Alan D. Woodland, Australia
Advisers:	Professor Kenneth J. Arrow, USA
	Academician Oleg T. Bogomolov, Russia
	Professor Mustapha Nabli, Tunisia
	Professor Amartya Sen, India
	Professor Stefano Zamagni, Italy
Secretary-General:	Professor Jean-Paul Fitoussi, France
General Editor:	Professor Michael Kaser, UK

Sir Austin Robinson was an active adviser on the publication of IEA conference proceedings from 1954 until his final short illness in 1993.

The Association has also been fortunate in having secured many outstanding economists to serve as President: Gottfried Haberler (1950–53), Howard S. Ellis (1953–56), Erik Lindahl (1956–59), E.A.G. Robinson (1959–62), Ugo Papi (1962–65), Paul A. Samuelson (1965–68), Erik Lundberg (1968–71), Fritz Machlup (1971–74), Edmund Malinvaud (1974–77), Shigeto Tsuru (1977–80), Victor L. Urquidi (1980–83), Kenneth J. Arrow (1983–86), Amartya Sen (1986–89). Anthony B. Atkinson (1989–92) and Michael Bruno (1992–95).

The activities of the Association are mainly funded from the subscriptions of members and grants from a number of organisations, including continuing support from UNESCO, through the International Social Science Council.

Acknowledgements

Essays and comments collected in this volume were originally presented at the IEA conference on 'The Nature of Economics: Case Studies in Economic Methodology', held at the University of Bergamo on 17–19 June 1996. The editors would like to thank the other members of the programme committee as well as all the participants for their valuable contributions, and, last but not least, Ms Laura Capelli and Ms Paola Bortolotti of the secretarial staff of the Department of Economics of the University of Bergamo for their invaluable help. Financial support from CNR (the Italian National Research Council), the *Pro Universitate Bergomensi* Foundation and the Department of Economics of the University of Bergamo is also gratefully acknowledged. The editors wish to thank Michael Kaser for his assistance with the production of this volume.

List of Participants

Professor Roger E. Backhouse, University of Birmingham, UK
Dr Pierluigi Barrotta, University of Pisa, Italy
Professor Andrea Boitani, Catholic University of Milan, Italy
Professor Nancy Cartwright, LSE, UK
Dr Marina Colonna, University of Naples, Italy
Professor Sergio Cremaschi, University of Turin, Italy
Professor Michel De Vroey, Université Catholique de Louvain, Belgium
Dr David Gay, University of Arkansas, USA
Dr Francesco Guala, LSE, UK
Professor D. Wade Hands, University of Puget Sound, USA
Professor Daniel M. Hausman, University of Wisconsin–Madison, USA
Professor Kevin D. Hoover, University of California, Davis, USA
Professor Leonid Hurwicz, University of Minnesota, USA
Professor Michael Kaser, University of Birmingham, UK, IEA General Editor
Professor Maarten Janssen, Erasmus University, Rotterdam, The Netherlands
Professor Maurice Lagueux, Université de Montréal, Canada
Professor Axel Leijonhufvud, University of Trento, Italy
Professor Bennett T. McCallum, Carnegie Mellon University and NBER, USA
Professor Thomas Mayer, University of California, Davis, USA
Professor Uskali Mäki, Erasmus University, Rotterdam, The Netherlands
Professor Philip E. Mirowski, University of Notre Dame, USA
Professor Philippe Mongin, CNRS and Université de Cergy-Pontoise, Paris, France
Dr Matteo Motterlini, University of Milan, Italy
Dr Stephen Nash, University of Sydney, Australia
Professor Ariel Rubinstein, Tel Aviv University, Israel
Professor Andrea Salanti, University of Bergamo, Italy
Professor Pierre Salmon, Université de Bourgogne, France
Professor Nancy J. Wulwick, Binghamton University, USA
Professor Stefano Zamagni, University of Bologna, Italy

Abbreviations

AMA	American Medical Association
CDC	Centers for Disease Control
CNRS	Conseil National de la Recherche Scientifique
ESS	evolutionary stable strategies
FOMC	Federal Open Market Committee
FPPE	Finnish Postgraduate Programme in Economics
GDP	gross domestic product
GNP	gross national product
GT	game theory
HHC	Harold Hotelling Collection (Columbia University)
IEDS	iterative elimination of dominated strategies
II	institutional individualism
JPE	Journal of Political Economy
MI	methodological individualism
NE	Nash equilibrium
OLS	ordinary least squares
PI	psychological individualism
PIR	principle of insufficient reason
POC	principle of coordination
RE	rational expectations
SSK	sociology of scientific knowledge
SSRC	Social Science Research Council

Introduction

Daniel M. Hausman and Uskali Mäki

The symposium on economic methodology that occupies this volume was originally conceived by Stefano Zamagni. In conversations with both of us during the summer of 1992 he pointed out that the International Economic Association had never sponsored a conference specifically devoted to methodology. Given the increasing volume and sophistication of work in the field, he believed that such a conference was long overdue, and he urged us to organise one. We then put together a prospectus for a symposium on methodology and invited Nancy Cartwright, Philippe Mongin and Stefano to join us as members of a programme committee. After the International Economic Association decided in autumn 1993 to offer its sponsorship, we began soliciting proposals for papers. These were screened by the Programme Committee, which was also involved in deciding on whom to invite as commentators. But the conference would never have taken place without the efforts of the other two editors of this volume, Roger Backhouse and Andrea Salanti, who joined us later as organisers and members of the Programme Committee. Not only did they play a critical role in the Committee, but they also did the hard organisational work that made the symposium a reality. Andrea was also instrumental in securing funding for the symposium.

Interest in the methodology of economics has increased rapidly since the late 1970s. Although many economists regard discussions of methodology with suspicion (or worse), the amount written on methodology both by practising economists and by economists who specialise in methodology has grown rapidly. In the introduction to the first edition of his anthology, *The Philosophy of Economics* (1984), Hausman listed nineteen books on the subject published in the previous decade. In the second edition in 1994, Hausman lists fifty published since 1984.

The methodology of economics is rapidly establishing itself as a separate interdisciplinary subdiscipline. For the first time, studies in the conceptual and methodological foundations of economic science constitute a collective and cumulative endeavour. During the past fifteen years there have been three new journals (*Research in the History of Economic Thought and Methodology, Economics and Philosophy,* and the *Journal of Economic Methodology*), and an annotated bibliography (Redman, 1988). Both informal and formal networks have been established: the last decade has seen the formation of the International Network for Economic Method and the International Economics and Philosophy Society. A growing number of conferences and symposia have been devoted to methodological themes, and there have been frequent sessions on economic methodology at the annual meetings of organisations such as the Allied Social Sciences Associations and the History of Economics Society. A growing number of scholars, most of them trained as economists, though a few are trained as philosophers, are engaged in analysing systematically the nature of economics.

Economic methodology is a young subfield with an open future. One purpose of the symposium and of this volume is to coordinate and enhance research activity in this field. Although we have no ambition of channelling research on economic methodology into a single stream, we have been especially impressed with the growing quantity of work that ties methodological inquiry closely to particular problems, theories and practices within economics. This is a departure from the approach one often saw in previous research, which attempted to impose this or that philosophical doctrine about scientific method upon economics. Without denying that the direct application of philosophical systems may sometimes be enlightening, we take it as a sign of maturity among economic methodologists that they can face the details of methodological problems in economics without invoking some single philosophical authority.

We hoped through the symposium and its proceedings to encourage this tendency towards concrete methodological reflection. We thought to do this by inviting proposals for detailed case studies of the underlying structure and presuppositions of particular theories, research practices, or controversies, past or present. Rival philosophical theses could then be compared and challenged by using evidence from the case study. We included economists who are not mainly interested in methodology (but who are interested enough to attend a conference!) to comment on the case studies and to exercise a sort of loose 'control' over the methodological commentary. Our hope was that this approach would promote progress within economic methodology as well as render methodological work more relevant and interesting for non-methodologists.

Late in 1993 and then again in 1994 we solicited proposals for such case studies, and the Programme Committee then winnowed the dozens of exciting ideas down to the six studies of this volume. With ample time for detailed discussion and extensive commentary, those at the symposium and then, later, those reading this volume might, we hoped, be able to achieve a more balanced appreciation of the way in which philosophical and economic considerations are intertwined. Since each of the case studies raises distinct economic and philosophical questions, this volume is, unavoidably, a collection of different arguments, analyses, and subject matters, not a unified treatment of a single subject. Our purpose has been to provide examples of the way in which work in economics builds on work in philosophy and engenders new philosophical conundrums, not to address some one particular problem.

There is, obviously, important common ground among the six case studies, but in accordance with our qualms about premature generalisation and our concern with the details, we would encourage readers to consider each of the six case studies separately. In their conclusion to this volume (chapter 7) our co-editors point to some comparisons, but these fittingly come last. Each of the case studies reveals in a different way how difficult it is to classify issues as 'philosophical' or 'economic'. Each shows ways in which collaboration can be fruitful and how superficial understandings of relevant issues in philosophy or economics can be harmful. Only in the details does work in economic methodology take shape as something more than casual philosophising by economists or superficial application by philosophers.

The subtitle of the volume – 'Crossing Boundaries' – is intended to be ambiguous. We encourage crossing the boundaries between different schools within economics, because such methodological bridging may enhance communication and remove misunderstandings between them; and we encourage at the same time crossing the boundaries between different methodological approaches, believing that detailed evidence helps one to compare rival methodological views. Most importantly, we advocate crossing the boundaries between methodology and economics. In principle it should not be necessary to advocate this, because there should be no clear border to be crossed, but in practice a high wall divides what is called 'methodology' from economic theorising.

The reason why there is no principle boundary dividing economics from economic methodology is that humans form images of their activities. Methodological accounts are such images. Whether explicitly articulated or not, these images shape, guide, and justify practices – in fine arts, business, politics as well as the sciences. Humans are reflective beings. Activities and their images are essentially connected, and any sharp boundary between them is artificial. Every piece of economics involves ineliminable methodological theses. The apparent boundary between methodology and economics is an artifact of intellectual specialisation and division of labour. In advocating crossing the boundaries between methodology and economics, therefore, we aim to overcome problems resulting from excessive intellectual specialisation in academic work. Though crossing the boundaries may change the way that economists think about their activities and carry them out, we are not proposing a revolutionary transformation of economics.

Economics and economic methodology are inseparable, because economics is always shadowed by methodological reflection and because methodology divorced from its object is necessarily empty. Methodologists need to keep in close contact with economics. But these obvious truths do not dissolve the existing institutionalised boundaries between economics and specialised methodological analysis. These institutional barriers still need to be bridged. This symposium and its proceedings aim to bridge them by bringing together methodologists and reflective economic theorists. Our hope is that both parties can learn from one another. The importance of interaction between economists and methodologists is the reason why as much time was devoted to open discussion as to presentation of the papers and discussants' comments (an hour and a half of the three hours allocated to each case study was reserved for open discussion). These discussions were tape recorded, and summaries of them form an important part of this volume.

It would be arrogant to attempt to speak for our distinguished participants, and it would be foolish to summarise imperfectly in this Introduction what they have said so well in their essays. But we would like to say something about the range of methodological issues that arise in the six case studies and about our conception of the subject matter and method of economic methodology.

Each of the six case studies addresses a different area of economics and each raises distinct methodological issues. Maarten Janssen's essay (chapter 1) is concerned with methodological individualism – that is, the philosophical thesis that acceptable explanations in the social sciences must be reducible to explanations in terms of individual human beings. This thesis has been much discussed by both philosophers and economists. Janssen's essay does not, however, retrace familiar steps. Instead he points out that the increasingly common use of game theory in empirical economics poses a problem for the methodological individualist, because it is questionable whether the equilibrium concepts upon which most of game theory depends have an individualistic rationale. His essay thus brings together questions about the empirical applications of game theory, the growing literature concerning the rational justification of playing equilibrium strategies, and traditional philosophical concerns about methodological individualism.

Pierre Salmon's essay (chapter 2) discusses the concept of free riding. The question Salmon sets out to answer has to do with the 'character' of free riding and its use in explanations. He argues that free riding is a mechanism, where 'mechanism' is defined in terms of causal processes and their interactions. Salmon is inspired by recent work in the philosophy of science, which emphasises the gap between the 'messiness' of the phenomena that one observes and the orderly underlying reality that scientific theories claim to identify. In this spirit, he takes free riding to be a 'hidden' or 'underlying' causal mechanism, which may or may not be manifested as actual free riding behaviour, depending on other relevant conditions. This makes traditional ways of testing difficult, but Salmon suggests that this is not a fatal difficulty, because experimentation can provide access to the mechanisms of the economy.

Like Pierre Salmon, Maurice Lagueux in chapter 3 is concerned with conceptual questions related to some traditional issues of collective action, but he approaches these issues by way of conceptual history. Are externalities market failures or merely a symptom of additional 'transactions costs' that inevitably make outcomes worse than they would have been if such costs could be avoided? Just what is an externality? A satisfactory definition is hard to come by, Lagueux argues, because the notion of an externality depends on the notion of a market, and the latter notion is implicit, contested, and fundamental to the whole discipline. Oddities and confusions concerning the notion of an externality thus lead one to conceptual conundrums at the very core of economics.

Michel De Vroey in chapter 4 is also concerned with a complex conceptual issue, whose policy implications are apparently enormous: what is involuntary unemployment and does it exist? As De Vroey emphasises, his question (like Maurice Lagueux's) is highly theoretical, and it turns out to be remarkably slippery. Philosophical and economic questions are intertwined not only in issue about the relations between theory and reality and the limits to equilibrium theorising, but also in the conceptualisation of voluntariness. The methodological questions cannot meaningfully be pried apart from the economic issues.

Thomas Mayer in chapter 5, like De Vroey, is concerned with a lengthy controversy, though the controversy with which he is concerned is focused more immediately on policy. Mayer offers a detailed account of the long dispute concerning whether fixed monetary rules or discretionary monetary policy would better promote prosperity and growth. Philosophers of science have had a great deal to say about controversies between different scientific theories but, as Mayer points out, that work does not immediately enhance our understanding of this controversy concerning a matter of general *policy*. This is not, however, to say that no appraisals are possible, for the inadequacies of the debate are, Mayer argues, palpable. A judicious appraisal must, however, grow out of an appreciation of the details of what is at stake and of the character of the argument.

Although the case study of Hands and Mirowski in chapter 6 is, like the others, intimately involved with the details of economic theory, it is also heavily influenced by general theories of scientific practice. Its inspiration lies more in the sociology than in the philosophy of science, and individual personalities and institutional details play a much larger role in their study than in the other five. Hands and Mirowski are in particular interested in a striking theory of demand formulated by Harold Hotelling. This work has been incorporated into what is now standard economics as an account of the demand by firms for inputs, but Hands and Mirowski challenge us to consider whether Hotelling's theory could not have become the standard general theory of demand. Their essay asks how theories get accepted by real flesh-and-blood economists, who are not perfectly rational and who are not without institutional affiliations and personal loyalties.

Even this brief and cursory summary reveals the enormous diversity among the issues treated in the following case studies. This is reinforced by the vast (and lively) variety of commentaries and critical reflections that were put forward during the sessions around these case studies. What this shows is that methodological reflection has an immense domain. Like Monsieur Jourdain, who has been speaking prose all his life without knowing it, so economists have often been doing methodology without knowing it. It is inevitable that they have been doing methodology, but it is not inevitable that they fail to recognise what they are doing and to unite their concerns with the work of methodologists. Nor is it inevitable that the work of methodologists should be so remote from the specific concerns of theorists. Economists and economic methodologists can together make further progress by recognising what they have been doing and judiciously taking advantage of relevant research by philosophers and sociologists. We hope that the case studies in this volume will convince readers of the range and excitement of methodological reflection concerning economics.

References

Hausman, D.M. (1994) *The Philosophy of Economics*, 2nd edn (Cambridge: Cambridge University Press).

Redman, D. (1988) *Economic Methodology: A Bibliography with Reference to Works in the Philosophy of Science (1860–1988)*, Bibliographies and Indexes in Economies and Economic History, no. 9 (Westport; Conn.: Greenwood Press).

1 Individualism and Equilibrium Coordination in Games[1]

Maarten Janssen
ERASMUS UNIVERSITY, ROTTERDAM, THE NETHERLANDS

1 INTRODUCTION

Game theoretic modelling has become increasingly popular in many branches of economics and other social sciences over the last decades. This development as such is probably not very surprising: the way game theory enables scientists to model social situations is an intuitively natural one. First, agents are perceived to act taking a certain environment as given. The given environment is formally represented in the rules of the game. Second, the actions of all agents taken together produce a collective outcome. Moreover, many of the standard critiques that were levied against the mainstream neoclassical (general equilibrium) model can be encompassed by a game theoretic model. The two elements that characterise the game theoretic approach can be considered as elements of some form of methodological individualism in which, in the terminology of Coleman (1990), the macro-to-micro and the micro-to-macro transition play an important role. Roughly speaking, the macro-to-micro transitions investigate the way existing rules and institutions affect individual behaviour and the micro-to-macro transition studies the way in which individual behaviour 'adds up' to an aggregate (or collective) outcome.

In this chapter I will examine the relation between game theory and methodological individualism (MI) more closely. It will become clear that game theorists themselves discuss the individualistic nature of their field and I will try to interpret that discussion in the light of the methodological one. As MI makes certain claims about the *structure of explanations* in the social sciences (cf. Lukes, 1973), I implicitly assume in this undertaking that game theory has some explanatory ambition. This may need some clarification.[2] Game theory is a technique that does not have any explanatory power as such. However, the technique is employed by economists and other social scientists to arrive at, among other things, explanations of phenomena they are interested in. For example, in the theory of industrial organization game theory is used to explain why firms behave in the way they do (see, e.g., Tirole, 1989). As a technique, game theory imposes certain restrictions on the structure of the explanations in which it is used. The present chapter comments on the question whether the restrictions game theory imposes on explanatory models are in line with the restrictions MI imposes.

The chapter is *not* based on the premise that (game theoretic) explanations in economics *should* conform to methodological individualism. Rather, the idea is that game theorists *themselves* (often implicitly) feel confined to some form of individualism.[3] Given this methodological commitment on the part of the game theorists, this chapter has several aims. First, to argue that the philosophical literature distinguishes between different forms of methodological individualism and that institutions are allowed among the explanatory variables in one form (institutional individualism), but not in another (psychological individualism). Second, to show in some detail that institutions (loosely defined) do play a role as explanatory variables in game theoretic explanations, but that this fact by itself is not an argument to qualify these explanations as non-individualistic.[4] Third, to argue (to the philosophers of science) that a close examination of game theory reveals that the category of institutional individualism is a catch-all and that further philosophical work is required to render the notion more precise.

Roughly speaking, the applied game theorist[5] faces two types of challenges. The first challenge is to argue that the game that is analysed is a fair representation of the real situation: do the actors in reality play a game that is somehow similar to the artificial game that the players in the model are playing? The second challenge is to argue that a certain definite outcome is to be expected in the game that is set up. The first challenge concerns the relation between the game and reality (how to interpret the game) and the second challenge concerns the outcome that is expected within the context of a certain game. As we will see, both challenges are of interest to our concern here. The first challenge for the applied game theorist relates to the interpretation of the rules of the game: are they descriptions of existing institutions, or should they be regarded as mental perceptions of the players? The second challenge relates to the explanation within the context of the game of a collective outcome in terms of the behaviour of individual agents.

Although much of the chapter focuses on theoretical issues, the perspective from which these issues are addressed is that of the above two challenges of the applied game theorist. The applied literature typically 'answers' the second challenge by assuming that the outcome of a game is a Nash equilibrium (or some refinement thereof). By and large, this literature sidesteps the question why in the particular context that is studied a Nash equilibrium might be expected to result. The quest for the (individualistic) foundations of the Nash equilibrium concept have, however, been studied in the theoretical literature. The focus of the theoretical literature is not so much to *explain* certain phenomena, but rather to provide a *justification* of the Nash equilibrium concept. In other words, the theoretical literature is part of a (normative) justification programme and not part of a (descriptive) explanatory programme. Accordingly, when discussing in Sections 3–7 the reasons for assuming that the outcome of a game is a (refinement of the) Nash equilibrium, I shall re-interpret the existing justifications in terms of their usefulness for the explanatory purposes of the applied literature.

The results of the theoretical investigations are largely negative: it turns out to be difficult to regard the Nash equilibrium concept as a consequence of a theory of individual rationality (see, e.g. Bernheim, 1984; Pearce, 1984 and Section 3 below). One of the lessons game theorists have drawn from these negative results is that there is not much hope to justify equilibrium outcomes within the boundaries of the traditional analysis itself. Recently, theorists have looked at ways of broadening the traditional analysis to investigate the issue whether Nash equilibrium outcomes can be justified in these broader games. Sections 4–7 deal with this more recent literature and ask the question whether the justifications for the Nash equilibrium concept that are offered satisfy some form of methodological individualism. Some of the literature that is under consideration in this part of the chapter not only tries to justify a Nash equilibrium as the outcome of a game, but also attempts to select one of the equilibria in case of multiplicity.

The strategy of the chapter is as follows. The notion of methodological individualism will be discussed in Section 2. Instead of providing a definition of the notion I will give a minimum condition that seems to be shared by many adherents of MI. The subsequent five sections (3–7) deal with the second challenge alluded to above, i.e. how to explain that a particular outcome of the invented game will be played. Section 3 will show in some detail how the question of why individual players should choose their part of a particular Nash equilibrium configuration is related to the issue of individualism. Also, the more orthodox justifications for the Nash equilibrium hypothesis are evaluated with respect to their adherence to a form of individualism. Sections 4–7 discuss the alternative approaches that have broadened the traditional analysis. Sections 4 and 5 are devoted to two static approaches to equilibrium selection, while Sections 6 and 7 analyse two dynamic approaches. As these recent contributions may be unknown to some readers, I will provide an elementary example at the beginning of each section to illustrate the main points that are made before going into a more methodological discussion. Section 8 discusses the first challenge to the applied game theorist by commenting on alternative interpretations of the rules of the game and their relation to the real world. Conclusions will be formulated in Section 9. In an Appendix, I provide a brief overview of some basic game theoretic solution concepts that are used in this chapter for those readers who could benefit from a quick refreshment. Other readers may wish to skip the appendix.

2 METHODOLOGICAL INDIVIDUALISM

To my knowledge, a commonly accepted definition of methodological individualism does not exist and it is not the purpose of this chapter to try to develop one. The aim of the chapter is rather to examine the relation between game theoretic explanations of social phenomena and MI. To this end, I will restrict myself in this section to some elements of MI that are relatively uncontroversial and I will make some distinctions between different forms of MI. For a more elaborate discussion the reader is referred to Janssen (1993) and the references mentioned there.

Individual action has an important role in any form of MI. Before proceeding to the core element of MI let us briefly consider two important questions: (i) who are the *individuals* of which MI speaks? and (ii) is there a principle that explains how these individuals *act*? MI does not insist that individual agents be identical to people of flesh and blood (see also Coleman, 1990; Bicchieri, 1993). Households, firms, trade unions and other entities may be regarded as the 'individuals' in so far as the differences in aims and interests of the people that are part of these entities do not seem to be important for the problem at hand. For example, a trade union can be considered an 'individual' entity in an explanation of wage levels based on bargaining power. However, artificial agents (like an 'auctioneer' in markets in which no auctioneer is available) may not be used in individualistic explanations. With respect to the auctioneer, for example, it is either not clear which people are part of the auctioneer, or if one wants to argue that both buyers and sellers are part of the auctioneer, then the differences in interests between buyers and sellers cannot be assumed away. It follows that the type of research question under consideration co-determines what may be regarded as an individual agent.

A second point is that individual *actions* need not necessarily be explained in terms of rationality considerations. For example, boundedly rational behaviour as imitation and rules of thumb can be accommodated in the framework of MI. However, individual action should not be redundant in an explanation in the sense that individual agents are nothing but the carriers of some social custom. Some of the approaches that will be considered below explicitly depart from the rationality hypothesis (see, especially Section 7).

Keeping the above two observations in mind, a minimal (necessary) requirement an explanation has to fulfil to count as individualistic in the sense of MI can then be stated as follows: social groups cannot have distinct aims and interests of their own in explanations of social phenomena (cf. Agassi, 1960). This minimal requirement excludes explanations that are based on impersonal 'forces', such as the Invisible Hand.

The minimal requirement does not mention anything about whether or not non-individualistic entities can play any role in explanations that count as individualistic in the sense of MI; it only asserts that if they play a role they cannot have any aims of their own. Two positions are held with respect to this question. A first position holds that 'natural' conditions, such as the weather or the production technology at a certain point in time, are the only exogenous variables beyond mental states that are allowed. This position is usually called *psychological individualism* (PI).[6] A second position is more liberal. It holds that institutions (loosely defined) that exist at a certain point in time are also legitimate exogenous variables. Following Agassi (1960, 1975), I will call this position *institutional individualism* (II).[7] According to the latter position, the aim of the individualistic programme is 'neither to assume the existence of all coordination nor to explain all of them, but rather to assume the existence of some coordination in order to explain the existence of some other coordination' (Agassi, 1960, p. 263).

When arguing that game theory is in line with the requirements methodological individualism imposes on explanations of social phenomena, Bicchieri (1987, 1992) seems to have PI in mind. She writes that game theory

> tries to explain the endogenous emergence of social structure, how institutions such as markets, prices, committees, voting systems, legal systems or social norms came about. The starting point is never a given institution, but a set of rational individuals, endowed with a given amount of information and a physical description of the situation within which they interact. (Bicchieri, 1992, p. 157)

In the next sections we will have more to say about this characterization of game theory.

So far we have made a few comments on the structure of individualistic explanations. Apart from the structural requirements imposed by MI, PI or II, a few words should be spent on an *empirical* requirement. The comments below are not confined to individualistic explanations, but rather apply to all forms of explanations. The (conventional) empirical requirement is that the explanation be true in the sense that it identifies mechanisms that actually have caused the phenomenon to be explained. As the requirements of MI relate more to the structure of a particular explanation than to its factual status, I will refer the reader to work by Hausman (1992) and Mäki (1994) for a more detailed account of the empirical requirement. What is important for our concerns is that MI also imposes an empirical requirement (whatever the precise content) apart from some structural requirement. For simplicity, this chapter sticks to the empirical requirement formulated above.

In the above comments on different forms of individualism I have tried to give a few statements to which many adherents of MI subscribe. In the next sections we will see that these relatively uncontroversial requirements can illuminate some difficulties game theorists encounter in justifying the assumption of social coordination that is implicitly invoked in justifications of Nash equilibrium.

3 NASH EQUILIBRIUM AND RATIONALIZABILITY

In the appendix to this chapter definitions of the concepts of Nash equilibrium and iterative elimination of dominated strategies (IEDS) are given. To understand how these concepts are related to our investigation into the individualistic nature of game theory let us consider a coordination problem (like the one discussed in Example A.2 in the Appendix). Consider the options *L* and *R* as 'driving on the left (respectively right) side of the road'. Suppose that many people have to make a choice on which side of the road to drive every day. If everybody made the same choice, one could speak of a social convention (see, e.g. Lewis, 1969). The two conventions, driving on the left and driving on the right-hand side, coincide with the two Nash equilibria in pure strategies of the game. Generalizing to all games, a Nash equilibrium can be considered a configuration of choices in which some social coordination is reached: given the choices of others, nobody wants to change their decision. The important question for this chapter then is whether this form of social coordination is simply *assumed* in game theory or whether it can be derived from the behaviour of the individual players.

Before considering different types of orthodox justifications for the Nash equilibrium concept, it is important to consider the rationale for the notion of IEDS first. It is clear that it is part of the rational choice version of MI. But how to conceive of the notion of common knowledge underlying IEDS? It seems to me that naive conceptions of neither PI nor II adequately describe the idea of the common knowledge assumption.[8] This is because the discussion between PI and II has focused on the question whether or not exogenous institutions are allowed in individualistic explanations. The question how to account for interactions between individual agents that constitute the society (model), which are so central to game theory, has been systematically neglected (to my knowledge) in both forms of individualism. The naive conception of PI is too narrow as it asserts that beyond the mental make-up of the individuals (taken in isolation from each other) and natural conditions nothing is allowed as exogenous variable, whereas II allows cultural and institutional variables to play a role in individualistic explanations. The common knowledge of rationality assumption seems to be in between the naive conceptions of PI and II as the mental make-up of *other* individuals is commonly known. Social institutions or cultural variables as such do not play a role. Hence, the idea of common knowledge of rationality is probably closer in spirit to PI than it is to II. If we allow in a more sophisticated version of PI the mental make-up of other players to be part of the mental make-up of individual players, then the common knowledge assumption may be reconciled with PI.

This brings us to a discussion of the more traditional justifications of the Nash equilibrium concept. A Nash equilibrium gives a characterization of a state in which all players have chosen (one of) their best strategies given the strategies adopted by other players. Unlike the definition of a perfectly competitive equilibrium (which uses the concept of market price), the definition of Nash equilibrium only involves the individualistic terms 'strategy' and 'pay-off'. Accordingly, the difficulty with Nash equilibrium does *not* arise in the definition, but instead in the question why individual players are expected to do their part of the equilibrium. In simultaneous move games, players have to decide upon their strategy being ignorant about the strategies chosen by other players. Thus, individual players cannot maximise payoffs given the decisions of other players. Instead, they make a decision that is the most appropriate one given a certain expectation of what others will do. In a Nash equilibrium these expectations coincide with the actual strategies chosen. Roughly speaking, three justifications for the Nash equilibrium hypothesis exist that do not modify the basic elements of the game in any way. This is why we will call these justifications 'orthodox' in contrast with the more recent literature that is discussed in the next four sections. We will first briefly describe the assumptions that are at the core of each of the justifications together with a discussion of these assumptions as it appears in the literature. We will subsequently recast the discussion in the light of what has been written in the previous section.

First, it has been shown (see, e.g. Bernheim, 1986; Tan and Werlang, 1988)[9] that the notion of Nash equilibrium is an inevitable consequence of the assumptions of individual rationality, common knowledge, 'common prior' (the players' beliefs can be derived from a single distribution) and independence (each player believes that the other players act independently of each other). In order to regard this result as a proper (individualistic) foundation for the Nash equilibrium concept the four assumptions should be relatively undisputed. However, there has been some debate about the appropriateness of the assumptions of 'common priors' and 'independence' for a general theory of rational behaviour in games. While arguing in favour of a weaker equilibrium notion, namely that of correlated equilibrium, Aumann (1987) says that a rational player need not conceive of the other players' actions as independent events, because a player may know that two or more other players share a common background (e.g. they went to the same school) so that a player may think that the strategy choices of the other players are correlated. Also, the arguments in favour of the common prior assumption do not seem to be fully convincing. Aumann (1987, pp. 13–14) defends the assumption by arguing that as probabilities are based on information, 'people who have always been fed precisely the same information' should have common priors. However, as has been argued by, Sugden (1991, p. 768), for example, it is often the case that the information that the players have been fed with is mute about the particular game that they play. In all these cases, 'beliefs are underdetermined by evidence'.

A second justification for the Nash equilibrium concept, described in, for example Aumann and Brandenburger (1995) and Brandenburger (1992), is based on two assumptions: (i) individual rationality and (ii) coordinated expectations[10] (all players expect that a certain configuration of strategies results). No assumption about common knowledge is required. A central question with respect to this justification seems to be how individual players come to have coordinated expectations. Jacobsen (1996) critizes Aumann and Brandenburger on this point. He says 'We do *not* think it is legitimate to . . . assume that one player knows what another player thinks. Each player must decide on what to play or expect on an *individual* basis' (p. 75).[11]

From yet another (third) perspective, individual agents should do their part of a particular Nash equilibrium in case the equilibrium is a focal point (Schelling, 1960).[12] A classic example is the question where two foreigners visiting New York City would go in case they have lost each other and they want to meet each other as soon as possible. There is a wide variety of possible alternatives from returning to the spot they were last together, to many tourist places such as the Empire State Building or the 'Met'. Note that each of these alternatives is a Nash equilibrium strategy provided that the other player chooses the same alternative. If for *both* foreigners one and the same place, for example the Empire State Building, stands out for some reason, it is 'rational' (read: reasonable) for each of them to go to that place to meet the other. Of course, for other people there might be other focal points; for still others there might be none. A difficulty for the focal points account of equilibrium coordination is the incorporation into the theory of games. Gilbert (1989, 1990), for example, has argued that there is nothing inherently rational about sticking to the salient option, because it is better not to stick to the salient option if you think that the other player will not do so. We will come back to this point when we discuss focal points in more depth in Section 5.

The above overview of three justifications for the Nash equilibrium concept and their critiques can be recast in methodological terms. In the methodological discussion I will attempt to disentangle two types of issues. The first issue is related to the distinction between II and PI alluded to in Section 2: is it allowed to make assumptions about the *shared background* of players to justify the Nash equilibrium concept? The second issue is related to the factual adequacy of the justification that is provided: is it reasonable in a particular situation to assume the specific form of shared background that is assumed by the justification?

What the three rationales have in common is that they are based on non-individualistic assumptions: common priors, coordinated expectations or a salient option. As these assumptions are not part of the 'natural givens' of a situation it seems to be impossible to regard the justifications as compatible with PI. It seems, however, that at least the first two rationales are compatible with II. In this interpretation the non-individualistic assumptions are considered the (unanalyzed) result of a shared cultural and/or institutional background. Players of the game have certain expectations or priors before they play a game. Players do not question these expectations or priors when playing the game. Because of their common background,[13] expectations are coordinated and priors are common (and independent). A Nash equilibrium results because of this commonality and the hypothesis that players maximise their subjective expected pay-offs. Thus, the first two justifications are in line with Agassi's maxim 'assume some coordination to explain some other form of coordination', and are examples of justifications in line with the structural requirements imposed by II.

The critiques of the first two justifications can then be read in two different ways. Either the critique argues that non-individualistic assumptions are not allowed in an individualistic explanation, i.e. one regards PI as the only sound form of MI, or it argues that in the particular situation the game is supposed to describe it is not realistic to assume the specific form of shared background that is assumed. The quotation from Jacobsen (1996) given above suggests that he criticizes the justifications for not being individualistic in nature on the ground that they do not satisfy the requirements of PI. This suggested interpretation is strengthened by the following quotation from the same paper:

> In a non-cooperative game each player makes up his mind on what to play and expect others to play on a purely *individual* basis. On the other hand, a Nash equilibrium is by definition something *collective,* a collection of strategies with a specific *cross player* property. The problem of justifying Nash equilibrium is the same as explaining how purely individual considerations may lead each player to play or conjecture his part of such a collective plan. (Jacobsen, 1996, p. 68)

In Section 2 I have tried to argue that both PI and II can be considered as part of the general programme of methodological individualism in the social sciences. Hence, I do not see the fact that some assumptions about a common background are made as a ground to dispute the individualistic nature of the first two justifications given above.

Sugden's critique of the common prior assumption suggests that he criticizes the first justification on the ground that it is empirically not convincing to regard the common background of players as specific enough to make them have common priors. A similar critique can be made with respect to the second justification based on coordinated expectations. The point of this critique is that it is not realistic to assume that our cultural background is defined so as to encompass coordinated expectations and/or a common prior.[14] That is why I have proposed to regard them as an *(unanalyzed) result* of, and not an element of, the common background. However, there does not seem to be any analysis showing how coordinated expectations and/or common priors originate from a common cultural or institutional background. To the extent that such an analysis is lacking, the proposed justifications for Nash equilibrium do not fulfil the empirical condition of II.

One way coordinated expectations have been justified is the following. Suppose that apart from defining the game and theorizing about appropriate strategies for individual players, the game theorist also suggests one strategy combination to all players.[15] This suggestion is what is written in 'good' game theory books (and what should be made available to the general public[16]), cf. Sugden (1991, pp. 776–7). The players know that the same strategy combination is proposed to the other players. They therefore check whether any player has an incentive to deviate from the proposed strategy. If the game theorist has proposed a Nash equilibrium each player individually will find out that he does not have an incentive to deviate, i.e. the Nash equilibrium will be played. Against this suggested interpretation, one can argue in line with Section 2 that an impartial game theorist is often not available in situations game theory is supposed to describe. Thus, this suggestion amounts to introducing an artificial agent that is supposed to act in a certain way (namely to propose a Nash equilibrium), which is not allowed in any form of MI.

Let us then briefly turn to the focal point justification of the Nash equilibrium concept. Schelling (1960) has not formalised the notion of focal points or salience. Accordingly, it is not entirely clear what role individual behaviour plays in achieving equilibrium coordination. Mehta et. al. (1994) distinguish between two interpretations of the notion of salience. According to *primary* salience players simply do what first comes to their mind. If, in coordination games with multiple pay-off indistinguishable equilibria, the players share a common culture the same thing comes to the mind of different players and this may explain why they act in the same way. The notion of *secondary* salience is close to Aumann and Brandenburger's justification: each player thinks what the other player will do and optimizes given this expectation. If the players' expectations are coordinated because of their common background, each of them will choose their part of a Nash equilibrium. From the point of view of the discussion in Section 2 one can argue against the notion of primary salience that individuals are nothing but the carriers of a common culture. Accordingly, the individual player is (almost) redundant in explaining equilibrium coordination and, therefore, this interpretation cannot count as individualistic. On the other hand, against the secondary salience argument one can levy a critique similar to the one given above against the justification proposed by Aumann and Brandenburger.

To summarize the discussion of this section: the problem with the above, more traditional, justifications of Nash equilibrium is that they do not provide a fairly realistic description of the common cultural and/or institutional background that, at the same time, leaves enough room for the individual players to co-determine the outcome. Coordinated expectations and a common prior cannot realistically be regarded as elements of the common background and the role the individual player plays in the focal point account seems to be unclear. Based on the above considerations one cannot justify Nash equilibrium on individualistic grounds.

4 STATIC GAMES: I – THE GLOBAL GAMES APPROACH

In the previous section I considered the question whether several 'orthodox' justifications for Nash equilibrium are in line with a minimal set of requirements of MI. In the Introduction I argued that this question was important in the context of the issue whether individualistic explanations of social phenomena can be expressed in a game theoretic language. The 'orthodox' nature of the justifications lies in the fact that the authors tried to justify Nash equilibrium within the standard set-up of a game. In this section and the next three 'non-orthodox' justifications for Nash equilibrium are considered. The first of these non-orthodox approaches I consider is the global games approach initiated by Carlsson and van Damme (1993) and generalised by Morris *et al.* (1995). From the discussion below it will be clear that the global games approach uses the concept of IEDS in a creative way to select among Nash equilibria. Thus, the approach is interesting for the

	L_2	R_2
L_1	X,X	$X,0$
R_1	$0,x$	$1,1$

Figure 1.1

purpose of our chapter because it attempts to keep the influence of cultural and institutional variables to a minimum.

To illustrate the notion of a global game and the procedure that Carlsson and van Damme employ let us look at the following example. Suppose two players play the game that is given in Figure 1.1 in which

$$x \in [x, \bar{x}], \text{ with } x < 0 \text{ and } \bar{x} > 1.$$

For any $x \in (0, 1)$ there are two strict Nash equilibria (like in the game of Example A.2). (R, R) is the Pareto-dominant equilibrium and it is also the risk-dominant equilibrium for $x \in (0, \frac{1}{2})$; (L, L) is the risk-dominant equilibrium for $x \in (\frac{1}{2}, 1)$.[16]

The last important part of the description of the global game is that the players are not completely informed about the pay-off x. In particular, x is supposed to be the realization of a random variable X, which is uniformly distributed over $[X, \bar{x}]$ and each player observes x with some noise: if x is realized each player i observes the realization of a random variable Xi, which is uniformly distributed over $[x - \varepsilon, x + \varepsilon]$. After the players have received their information on x, they choose L or R. All this information is common knowledge among the two players. Thus, the actual game that the players are playing is embedded in a larger (global) game in which there is uncertainty about the pay-offs.

Carlsson and van Damme show that in this framework common knowledge of rationality implies that the players choose the risk-dominant equilibrium, i.e if $x < \frac{1}{2}$ (R, R) will be played and if $x > \frac{1}{2}$ (L, L)

will be played. It goes beyond the scope of the present inquiry to describe the proof of this result in some detail. A good description of the main ideas is provided by Carlsson and van Damme (1993, p. 991–3). What is important for the result is how the uncertainty about the true pay-offs spreads when higher knowledge levels are considered. If player i observes X_i, he believes that the true value of X lies in an interval $[X_i - \epsilon, X_i + \epsilon]$. As players know that the private information they have about the value of x is correlated with the information the other player has, player i knows that the other player believes the true value is in the interval $[X_i - 2\epsilon, X_i + 2\epsilon]$, and so on. At higher levels of knowledge, the uncertainty spreads. At some point in the hierarchy of knowledge, it is important that the players have dominated strategies for x-values smaller than 0 or larger than 1. Individual rationality tells players not to choose a dominated strategy. An infection argument is used that tells players to choose the strategy of the risk dominant equilibrium when rationality and the global game is common knowledge.

How individualistic is the global games approach? In the Introduction we have divided this question into two separate questions: one about the relation between the game and reality and one about the outcome of a specified game. As explained in the introduction, we will deal only with the second question here, leaving the first until Section 8.

The result discussed above is fascinating for the fact that the application of a relatively weak notion as IEDS in a more complex game is able to select a Nash equilibrium in a simple game. Given the rules of the game (which will be discussed in Section 8), it is clear that the outcome of the game is obtained by applying IEDS only. In Section 3 we have argued that IEDS can be regarded as part of PI. Hence, we can conclude that the above justification for (and selection of) Nash equilibrium within the context of a game is in line with the stringent individualistic programme we have distinguished in Section 2.

5 STATIC GAMES: II – RATIONALIZING FOCAL POINTS

In Section 3 we briefly discussed Schelling's work on focal points. It was argued that the role individual behaviour plays in establishing equilibrium coordination is not well articulated in Schelling's work. His work has inspired, however, many game theorists. Recently, some authors have focused on the role of individual rationality in focal point justifications of the Nash equilibrium hypothesis (see, in particular, Bacharach

1991, 1993; Janssen, 1995; Sugden, 1995). Here, we will focus on the direction that was initiated by Bacharach. The following elementary example illustrates the main ideas.

Suppose individuals 1 and 2 are presented with a tray that contains three ball-shaped objects. One of them is green, the other two are red. The two players are sitting in different rooms and cannot communicate. If they pick the same object (indicated by a number inside the objects that is not visible from the outside) both individuals receive a positive pay-off; otherwise they receive nothing. Can the players make a rational choice of which object to point at? Note that the traditional approach would represent this game by a 3×3 matrix similar to Example A.2. Accordingly, there are three pay-off equivalent Nash equilibria and we have seen in Section 3 that the traditional analysis offers no clue as to what players will choose. Intuitively, however, the only sensible choice seems to be to pick the green object.

The two principles that Bacharach (1991) and Janssen (1995) use to arrive at this intuitive solution are the Principle of Insufficient Reason (PIR) and the Principle of Coordination (POC). PIR basically says that a rational choice cannot discriminate between two strategies if they have the same attributes. At a more formal level, the principle is implemented by using the idea that different attributes of different strategies induce a partitioning of the strategy set into cells and that a rational choice treats members of the same cell symmetrically. In this particular example, the colour of the objects divides the strategy set into a cell with one green object and a cell with two red objects. A strategy that respects PIR should give equal probability to the two red objects. On the other hand, POC says that if in the class of strategy combinations that respect PIR there is a *unique* strategy combination that is Pareto-optimal, then individual players should do their part of that strategy combination. In the present example, the class of mixed strategy combinations that respect PIR can be parameterized by $\{(p1, q1, q1), (p2, q2, q2)\}$, with $p1 + 2q1 = 1$ and $p2 + 2q2 = 1$, where $p1$ ($p2$) represents the probability with which individual 1 (2) picks the green object and $q1$ ($q2$) represents the probability with which individual 1 (2) picks one of the red objects. It is easy to see that the unique Pareto-optimal strategy combination that satisfies PIR is $\{(1, 0, 0), (1, 0, 0)\}$. Thus, the combination of the two principles explains the intuitive idea that rational individuals should pick the green object. The example illustrates that by taking the description of strategies into account, it is possible to select among the multiple Nash equilibria of a coordination game.

Two questions are to be answered when this account of focal points is interpreted in view of the discussion in Section 2. First, is the account individualistic in nature? The main point to be clarified in this respect is whether POC and PIR can be considered principles of *individual* rationality or whether they are at odds with MI. In any case, the notion of rationality POC embodies differs considerably from the more common view that rationality is to be interpreted as maximization of subjective utility. Second, what is the role of a common culture in the above account, i.e. *if* the account is individualistic is it to be regarded as part of PI or II?

POC and PIR are not uncontroversial. POC is based on the idea that in common interest games individual players can think of themselves and the other players as members of a team. The best team solution to a problem is to choose a Pareto-optimal strategy combination. Note that every individual player's pay-off is also maximal in the unique Pareto-efficient outcome. In any game each rational player can figure out what the set of Pareto-optimal strategy combinations is. If this set has only one member, all players, *reasoning individually*, know that there is only one way that they can reach this Pareto-optimal strategy combination and that is by doing their part of it. POC was first introduced by Gauthier (1975) and is identical to, or closely related to, the criterion of pay-off dominance (Harsanyi and Selten, 1988) and the hypothesis employed by Crawford and Haller (1990, p. 580) that in (repeated) coordination games 'players play an optimal . . . strategy combination'. There is, however, one important difference with the latter hypothesis. It is that Crawford and Haller apply the Pareto-optimality criterion even to cases in which there is *not* a *unique* Pareto-optimal strategy combination. The difference is important for our concern, because if there are two or more Pareto-optimal strategy combinations each player reasoning individually does not know of which strategy combination to do his part. Crawford and Haller's hypothesis involves a group of players choosing a strategy combination, which is quite different from individual players choosing a strategy. As the group as such does not have the power to choose a strategy combination, Crawford and Haller's hypothesis cannot be accommodated by MI. POC, on the other hand, is less problematic from the point of view a of individual (team member) rationality.[18]

A possible justification for PIR is that rationality is usually associated with 'providing an argument (reason)'. Having a reason to choose strategy $x1$ (and not $x2$) means (i) that on the basis of available information (about pay-offs and labels) players can make an inference that they should play $x1$ and (ii) that there does not exist a similar inference favouring $x2$. Accordingly, there cannot be an argument for either $x1$ or $x2$ if the information players possess is symmetric with respect to $x1$ and $x2$ in the sense that information that would support $x1$ as a choice would also support $x2$. I conclude that PIR can be considered as one of the principles of an (alternative) theory of *individual* rationality.

Let us then briefly consider the second question about the role of a common culture in the above account of focal points. It is clear that the above example is rather contrived: 'real life' coordination problems have many more facets.[19] What is important in the example is that both players consider the situation in a similar way. So, the fact that the shape of the objects is identical can be re-phrased as that in the culture that the two players share differences in shape (or other facets) are not as prominent as differences in colour. The point of this line of research is then that players can use this common cultural background in a rational way. The papers mentioned above pay more attention to the cultural and/or institutional context in which the game is played than other lines of research in game theory.

6 DYNAMIC GAMES: I – RATIONAL 'BAYESIAN' LEARNING[20]

After having discussed two static approaches, this section and the next will discuss two dynamic approaches to the question why individual players would choose their part of a Nash equilibrium configuration. In this section I will concentrate on a Bayesian (or 'rational') learning approach in general and on a sequence of papers by Kalai and Lehrer in particular (see, for instance, Kalai and Lehrer, 1993a, 1993b). I will restrict the discussion of the results Kalai and Lehrer (hereafter K&L) obtain to the two-player coordination game defined in Example A.2.

K&L study repeated games and their concern is with individual players learning the other players' repeated game strategies. At the start of the repeated game, players have prior beliefs over the possible strategies that the opponent plays in the *repeated game*. Given these prior beliefs, each player chooses the repeated game strategy that maximizes their discounted sum of pay-offs. The beliefs are updated using Bayes's rule. Roughly speaking, they show that players will eventually predict the future play of their opponent almost correctly. As players maximize discounted pay-offs, this implies that their strategies will eventually come close to a Nash equilibrium of the repeated game. Formally, the assumption K&L use to obtain this result is that the combination of strategies that is actually played is absolutely continuous with respect to the players' prior beliefs. As the aim of this section is to discuss K&L's approach in the light of the discussion on MI rather than to give a full treatment of their approach as such, I will provide an example in which a stronger condition holds, namely what they call the 'grain of truth' assumption. To illustrate their approach consider the following example.

Suppose player 1's beliefs about player 2 are as follows:

$$P(\text{always } R) = \alpha;\ P(\text{alweays } L) = \tfrac{1}{2} - \alpha\ (0 < \alpha < \tfrac{1}{2});$$

$$P(RLLL\ldots) = \tfrac{1}{3};\ P(RRLL\ldots) = \tfrac{1}{9};\ P(RRRL\ldots) = \tfrac{1}{27} \text{ and so on,}$$

where, for example, $P(RLLL\ldots) = \frac{1}{3}$ is to be read as saying that the prior probability of observing R in the first period and L always after is equal to $\frac{1}{3}$. Suppose, moreover, that player 2 plays always R. The 'grain of truth' assumption says that each player should attach a strictly positive prior probability to the actual strategy that is chosen by the opponent. Observe that the assumption is satisfied in the example considered here. K&L's argument works as follows. After observing R in period 1, player 1 knows that player 2 does not always play L. Bayesian updating requires that the probability mass of $\frac{1}{2} - \alpha$ is distributed proportionally to their weight over the strategies that are possibly played. After observing R in the first two periods, $5/6 - \alpha$ is distributed in this way over the remaining possible strategies. It is clear that for any value of $\alpha > 0$, after sufficiently long time t, player 1 is almost sure that player 2 plays strategy 'always R' and the chance of observing R in period t after having observed a finite number of R's up to time $t - 1$, $P(R_t \backslash R_1 \ldots R_{t-1})$, will be arbitrarily close to one for large t. The optimal response to such a belief is for player 1 to play B in all subsequent (infinite) periods.

To bring out the importance of the 'grain of truth' assumption more clearly, suppose that instead of the above beliefs, player 1's beliefs are (slightly) different:

$$P(\text{always } L) = \tfrac{1}{2};$$

$$P(RLLL\ldots) = \tfrac{1}{3};\ P(RRLL\ldots) = \tfrac{1}{9};\ P(RRRL\ldots) = \tfrac{1}{27}; \text{ and so on}$$

In this case the grain of truth assumption is not satisfied and $P(R_t|R_1$

... $R_{t-1}) = \frac{1}{3}$ for any value of t. Accordingly, at the beginning of every period player 1 thinks (wrongly) that the chance that player 2 plays L in this period is larger than $\frac{1}{2}$ and, consequently, he will play T. Thus, the players will never coordinate given these prior beliefs.

How can the Bayesian learning approach be interpreted in view of the discussion in Section 2? The approach is certainly rationalistic and common knowledge does not play any role. Is this then the ultimate justification for the Nash equilibrium concept that satisfies even the naive form of PI? The critical point in the evaluation seems to be how to interpret the grain of truth assumption that is imposed on the players' priors. One common idea is that priors are subjective and this would be in line with *PI*. However, the second example shows that the priors in K&L's approach cannot just be any subjective priors, because for arbitrary subjective priors their result will not hold.

The grain of truth assumption[21] is a strong condition to impose on the prior beliefs. This is because a positive prior probability can be attached to a countably infinite number of strategies only, whereas there is an uncountable number of strategies from which the true strategy can be chosen. Any countable set of strategies is very small compared to the uncountable strategy set from which the true strategy is chosen. Thus, there is in principle a very large number of priors, each of which assigns a positive probability to a countable number of strategies. From this set of possible priors there is very little reason for individuals to choose a prior of the right sort, i.e. one that assigns strictly positive probability to the true strategy of the opponent.

One can interpret the drastic restriction implied by the grain of truth assumption as saying that priors are of a *conventional nature*. This conventional nature of priors could be defended by arguing that players will not choose 'unusual' strategies and the players 'know' that the other player will not do this, and so on. This means that many of the possible strategies will not be chosen. The point here is that the players should share this 'knowledge', i.e. not only should a player not choose 'unusual' strategies, the other player should also know that he will not do so. An implication of this convention is that certain observations are indicative of particular strategies. Thus, K&L implicitly introduce a conventional aspect in their analysis.

This conclusion is strengthened if one examines the 'grain of truth' assumption also in relation to another famous problem in methodology, namely the Problem of Induction. The main difficulty players face in learning to coordinate is what to infer about future play of the opponent given some observations about past play. In general, there is an uncountable number of hypotheses consistent with a finite number of observations. Players can only hope to make some useful inference about future play if they can argue that one of these hypotheses is more likely to be true than the others. Ultimately, the reason players select one hypothesis and not another rests on some convention (Boland, 1982), be it the language we adopt (Goodman, 1973) or the prior we hold.

Thus, I conclude that despite appearances a common culture or institution does play a role in the rational learning literature. In particular, the restriction that is imposed on the priors individual players have should be interpreted as a convention. Therefore, the way the Nash equilibrium outcome is justified *within* the game is institutional individualistic in nature.

7 DYNAMIC GAMES: II – ADAPTIVE LEARNING AND EVOLUTION

The final approach that I want to discuss is that of evolutionary game theory.[22] We will see that the evolutionary process in economics is often interpreted as one of imitation and adaptive learning. Hence, it is obvious that in this literature agents are assumed to be boundedly rational. As there are many ways in which one can depart from full rationality, there are many different approaches in evolutionary game theory. I have made a somewhat arbitrary selection of recent literature and decided to discuss the concept of evolutionary stable strategies (ESS) and the approach that has been initiated by Kandori *et al.* (1993) and Young (1993).

Maynard Smith (1982) has introduced the notion of ESS in evolutionary game theory. The formal definition of the concept is given in the Appendix. The general idea in evolutionary game theory is that a game is played by individual players who are (randomly) drawn from a large population over and over again.[23] If a population is in an ESS, 'then no mutant strategy could invade the population under the influence of natural selection' (Maynard Smith, 1982, p. 10). Although ESS is a static concept, it implicitly incorporates a dynamic notion of evolution. When the dynamic process is explicated it usually takes the following form. At the end of each period, the average pay-off of each strategy that is played in the population becomes known. In the next period, strategies that have done well are played more frequently than before and other strategies are played less frequently.[24] It is shown that if the evolutionary process converges, it converges to a Nash equilibrium. Moreover, even if the evolutionary process does not converge, strategies that are iteratively strongly dominated will not be played in the long run. This last result gives another justification for the notion of IEDS (cf. Milgrom and Roberts, 1990, 1991).

By means of illustration let us look more closely at the game that is described in Figure 1.1 with $x = \frac{1}{3}$. Suppose that initially 70 per cent of the population plays *L* and 30 per cent plays *R*. Random matching and a large population implies that every player has a 70 per cent chance of meeting an *L* player. Thus, in a large population, the (average) pay-off of *L* players (resp. *R* players) is $\frac{1}{3}$ (resp. 0.3). As the *L* players receive a higher average pay-off, the frequency of *L* players increases and the frequency of *R* players decreases. It is easy to see that the evolutionary process converges to a state in which all the players are playing *L*. Note that the initial configuration of strategies is important in deriving this result: if, initially, more than $\frac{2}{3}$ of the players play *L* the process converges to all the players playing L; if, on the other hand, initially, more than $\frac{1}{3}$ of the players play *R* the process converges to all the players playing *R*. Thus, the outcome of evolution is history contingent according to the ESS approach.

More recently, Kandori *et al.* (1993, hereafter KMR) among others, have shown that under an alternative dynamic process, whatever the initial configuration, the risk-dominant equilibrium will be played in the long run. KMR use a population of students in a student dormitory and their choice of a personal computer as their leading example. For simplicity, let us say (i) that there are two computers, *L* and *R*, from which to choose, (ii) that the students live with nine others in the dormitory, (iii) that they randomly write papers with each other, and (iv) only a few students are able to buy a new computer in any period. The pay-offs are given by Figure 1.1 with $x = \frac{1}{3}$. If the students can replace their computers only occasionally and if there are no new freshmen, it is clear that the initial configuration determines which of the two computers will be driven out (c.f., the result mentioned above holds). KMR introduce freshmen entering the dormitory into their story and they bring their own computers with them. With mutants entering the population of students every year, the dormitory can move from one equilibrium to the other over time. However, more mutants are needed to upset the risk-dominant equilibrium (the equilibrium in which players play *R*) than are needed to upset the other equilibrium. This is easily seen, because the mutants should move the population configuration over the critical point of $\frac{1}{3}$ playing *L* (in between three and four students having computer *L*). From the analysis in KMR it follows that in the ultra-long run the population spends most of the time in the risk-dominant equilibrium if the mutation rate is very small.

How to evaluate these new developments in the context of the discussion in Sections 2 and 3? First of all, it is clear that the ESS approach cannot be part of the programme of PI. This is because apart from individual behaviour and natural conditions, something else (in this case the initial configuration) affects the outcome of the process. If we interpret this historically given configuration as part of the institutional environment, then this approach is in line with the formal structure of II.

At first sight, the results obtained by KMR seem to be completely driven by the behaviour of individual players and mutants. Imitation of successful strategies means that these strategies are played more often. A few observations can be made, however. History-independence only prevails in the (ultra-)long run, whereas dependence on initial conditions plays a role in the 'intermediate run'. This dependence becomes weaker as time passes. More importantly, however, many papers now exists that obtain (somewhat) different results (see, e.g., Anderlini and Ianni, 1996, Binmore and Samuelson, 1994; Goyal and Janssen, 1997). One key assumption turns out to be whether or not the probability with which a player is matched with somebody else in the population is 'location'-dependent. What these alternative assumptions show is that the environment (interaction structure) in which players act is also important for the results that KMR (and the others) obtain. Thus, neither the Young nor the KMR approach can be regarded as part of PI. Instead, it has the formal structure of an II explanation.

8 THE RULES OF THE GAME

So far, we have looked at 'orthodox' and 'non-orthodox' justifications for Nash equilibrium. We have primarily focused on the question whether these justifications are in line with the structural requirements MI imposes on explanations. We have not yet paid much attention to the empirical requirement: how can we justify the rules of the game; or in other words, what is the relation between the artificial world of the game and 'reality'?

At an intuitive level, the idea that there are some rules of the game is quite compelling. One of the reasons may be that when we play parlour games, the rules of the game are indeed written down and fixed for the time the game is played. The number of possible options at each stage is determined by the application of these rules to that particular stage of the game. When a player chooses an action which is not in the feasible set, the other player can legitimately say 'you are not playing the same game'. Another reason why the idea of certain given rules may seem quite compelling is that in many social interactions there are certain rules (embodied in the law or in culture) that constrain our feasible actions or that enable us to engage in certain actions.

The games that we find in economics and/or game theory journals are different, however. The rules of the game in particular instances of the theory of industrial organization, for example, do not reflect some agreed-upon 'rules of the parlour game of competition'. On the other hand, they do not reflect legal and or cultural constraints either. The rules seem to be nothing but the invention of the theorist (who invents the game). Accordingly, it is not at all clear why these invented rules of this invented game should be obeyed by the players of the game (who in many instances do not even seem to be aware of the existence of the theorist who invents the game, let at alone be aware of his/her inventions). For example, the firms whose behaviour game theorists want to model do not seem to be constrained in the same way as the players in the (any?) model: real firms can choose their quantities, prices, quality, advertising campaign, R&D investments, etc. at more or less any moment they want and this is generally not possible in a game model in the industrial organization literature.[25]

The classical interpretation of the rules of the game seems to be that they describe in a rudimentary way the physical events and the institutions in which the players operate. In the previous paragraph I have argued that this is probably not an appropriate interpretation for much of the applied work. In many social interactions players seem to have many more options than are allowed by the strategy sets of any game model. An alternative interpretation, due to Rubinstein (1991), is to consider the rules of the game as rudimentary descriptions of the way players perceive their situation. In this interpretation it does not matter whether agents in the real world have an extremely rich menu from which to choose. What matters is that in the agents' perception there are only a few decision variables, In this case a game with a restricted strategy set may accurately describe the situation. Accordingly, the rules of the game can be considered a player's subjective assessment of a situation rather than an objective one.

Several implications of the two different interpretations of the rules of the game are important enough to be spelled out explicitly. First, most games are supposed to describe the situation of *all* players, instead of the situation of only one player. This indicates that most game theorists implicitly think in terms of the (mistaken) classical interpretation of the rules of the game. When the rules explicate the objective situation in which the players interact, they necessarily need to play the same game. In the alternative interpretation, one and the same situation is described by as many game models as players that are distinguished.[26] In this interpretation one game model suffices only in case of intersubjectivity that all players happen to perceive the situation in the same way. Secondly, if the classic interpretation is taken, PI does not seem to be a feasible interpretation of game theory. The rules of the game are supposed to describe some existing institutions, rules and conventions and these entities are not allowed as exogenous variables in PI. On the other hand, PI seems to be a natural interpretation of game theory if the alternative interpretation is taken.[27] Thirdly, taking a subjective interpretation of the rules of the game has some implications for research in game theory in view of the empirical requirement sketched in Section 2. If we want to explain social phenomena with a subjective interpretation of the rules of the game and require that the explanation be true, then it is necessary to investigate how the agents in social life conceive of their own problem situation.

After these general observations, we briefly reconsider the alternative justifications given in Sections 4–7. In the global games approach by Carlsson and van Damme, each player receives some private information before making a choice and players know that their private information is correlated with the information the other player receives. These rules describe a particular game situation that enables the players to make certain inferences. Despite the ingenuity of the approach, it has to be said that these rules do not seem to describe any feature of existing institutions. Also, it is not clear whether agents in real situations describe their problem situation to themselves in these, rather complicated, terms. Accordingly, it is difficult to see how their approach can answer the question why game theorists are justified in expecting people to play a Nash equilibrium. Future investigations into the way people perceive of their problem situation may, of course, alleviate this criticism.

The consideration of focal points in Section 5 has built the subjective interpretation of the rules of the game explicitly into the model. Objects in coordination games have many attributes that can be considered by the players. Only a few of them come to the mind of individual players. Of the ones that come to mind, a player thinks whether it is likely that they also come to the mind of other players and they choose one of the objects accordingly. If the same attributes come to the mind of different players, they have a high chance of coordinating. The approach has also been tested in an experimental setting and the findings partially corroborated the theoretical results.

In the rational learning approach considered in Section 6, an objective interpretation of the rules of the game is probably the most plausible one. This is because one player updates his beliefs about the other player's repeated game strategy. Bayesian updating makes sense only if there is a fixed known strategy set from which the actual strategy is chosen and if more information becomes available over time which element out of the strategy set is actually chosen. If the rules of the game and, hence the strategy set, is subjective it is difficult to imagine that it is known to the other player. An objective interpretation, on the other hand, is subject to the critique that in many applications of game theory in economics the strategy set of the players in reality does not seem to coincide with the limited set of options players in a game have.

The subjective interpretation of the rules of the game does not seem to be appropriate in the evolutionary game theory literature discussed in Section 7. This is especially true as far as the behaviour of mutants and the nature of the interaction structure is concerned. If we then look at an institutional interpretation of the rules of the game, then it becomes clear that differences in the dynamic processes in the evolutionary game theory approaches are not easily related to the institutions that we are familiar with. These differences are rather driven by the prospect of deriving interesting mathematical results. This, however, seriously limits the justification evolutionary approaches might offer for the Nash equilibrium hypothesis.

9 CONCLUSION

I began these comments on the individualistic nature of game theory with two challenges for the applied game theorist. One challenge is to explain why a certain outcome in an artificial game is expected to result; the other is to interpret the rules of the game. The subsequent analysis dealt mainly with the more theoretical game theory literature that aims at justifying in one way or the other the notion of Nash equilibrium as a solution to a game. I also spent some time discussing alternative interpretations of the rules of the game. It will be clear from the above overview that an explanation why a Nash equilibrium is expected to result in a certain game is not likely to be based on a form of psychological individualism. Almost all existing justifications employ some common background that helps the players to coordinate their strategies on an equilibrium outcome. The only justification we have encountered that has the formal structure of a sophisticated version of PI is the global games approach by Carlsson and van Damme (1993). In the previous section I have argued with respect to this approach, however, that the rules of the game cannot realistically be regarded as descriptions of the situation the individual agents (perceive they) encounter. If it is granted that something other than individual behaviour and natural givens play a role in the other justifications we have considered, then the main question that is left is whether this 'something other' captures some essential aspects of existing institutions in an adequate way. Here, we have raised some doubts: in most cases this 'something other' seems to be more driven by the prospect of deriving interesting mathematical results than by empirical observations.

In the discussion we encountered different assumptions which were classified under the catch-all of 'institutions'. Assumptions like common priors (Section 3), coordinated expectations (Section 3) and the grain of truth (section 6) and assumptions about the prominence of certain attributes (Section 5), the composition of the initial configuration (Section 7) and the details of the interaction structure (Section 7) were classified as non-individualistic, and hence made the explanations part of the programme of II instead of PI. However, the structure of the justifications considered above are very different from each other and these differences cannot be accounted for given the existing terminology of PI and II. The present chapter may be read as an attempt to stimulate philosophers to redefine different versions of MI in the light of developments in the social sciences in general and in game theory in particular.

A last comment should be made to alleviate the critique on the theoretical contributions considered here. By contributing to the justification programme of Nash equilibrium, the papers considered here do not have a well-defined domain of applications. The papers may simply be read as arguing that 'if so and so conditions hold, then the outcome of the game will be a Nash equilibrium'. Theoreticians may argue that it is the job of the applied game theorist to check whether or not the conditions do hold in the particular applications. The applied game theorist, however, rarely considers the question whether it is legitimate to assume that the outcome of the game is a Nash equilibrium. In the applied literature the Nash equilibrium concept is simply imposed without much of an argument.

The world of pure theory and applications seems to be quite far apart. The theoretician provides conditions under which it is justified to regard the Nash equilibrium as the outcome of a game. These conditions are, however, so far from the world of applications that the applied game theorist does not seem to bother about the conditions at all. The relevance of future work in game theory would be much improved if this gap between pure theory and applications were to be filled.

Appendix: An Elementary Introduction to Some Game Theoretic Notions

The most widely employed solution concept in non-cooperative game theory is the Nash equilibrium. A *Nash equilibrium* is a combination of strategies $s = (s_1, \ldots s_n)$, one for each player, such that each player's strategy maximises his own pay-off *given* the strategies of all other players: s is such that $\pi_i(s) > \pi_i(s_i, s_{-i})$ for all admissible s_i, where $\pi_i(s_i, s_{-i})$ is the pay-off to player i given that he plays s_i and all other players play s_{-i}. A refinement of Nash equilibrium is the notion of an evolutionary stable strategy (ESS). The notion is used in Section 7 on evolutionary game theory. The definition is as follows: a strategy combination $s = (s_1, \ldots s_n)$ is an ESS if s is such that (i) $\pi_i(s\ ) > \pi_i(s_i, s_{-i})$ for all admissible s_i or (ii) if $\pi_i(s\ ) = \pi_i(s_i, s_{-i})$, then $\pi_i(s_i, s_{-i}) > \pi_i(s_i, s_{-i})$ for all $s_{-i} \in S_{-i}$.

Apart from the Nash equilibrium notion, the notions of a strongly dominated strategy and iterative elimination of strongly dominated strategies are used in this chapter. A strategy s_i is *strongly dominated* by a strategy s_i if *for all* possible choices of strategies by all other players strategy s_i gives a pay-off that is strictly smaller than the pay-off that i would have obtained under s_i, i.e. $\pi_i(s_i, s_{-i}) < \pi_i(s_i, s_{-i})$ for all $s_{-i} \in S_{-i}$, where S_{-i} is the set of admissible strategies of all players except player i. An important difference between the notion of dominance and the notion of Nash equilibrium is that the first notion compares the pay-offs a player receives when he chooses certain strategies for all strategies the other players may adopt, while the second notion compares only the pay-offs of different strategy choices when the other players adopt their equilibrium strategies.

The notion of *iterative elimination of strongly dominated strategies* (IEDS) can be defined inductively in the following way. A strategy s_i is $Q_{-i}-$ undominated if there does not exist a strategy s_i such that $\pi_i(s_i, s_{-i}) > \pi_i(s_i, s_{-i})$ for all $s_{-i} \in Q_{-i}$. In words, a strategy is undominated on a certain domain (a certain set of strategies Q_{-i} of the other players) if there is no other strategy that is strictly better on that domain. Let $D_i = \{s_i \in S_i | s_i \text{ is } S_{-i}- \text{ undominated}\}$, i.e. D_i is the set of $S_{-i}-$undominated strategies. The set of IEDS for player i, called D_i, can be defined inductively as follows. Suppose that $(D_i^k)_{i=1}^n$ is well defined for some k and let $D_{-i} = X_{j \neq i} D_j$. Then

$$D_i = \{s_i \in D_i | s_i \text{ is } D_{-i}-\text{undominated}\} \text{ and}$$

$$D_i = \{s_i \in S_i | s_i \in D_i \quad \text{for all } k > 1\}$$

The concept of IEDS is a logical consequence of the view that individual players are rational and that this rationality is common knowledge[28] (see, e.g.

	L	M	R
L	2,2	4,1	0,0
M	1,4	3,3	5,2
R	0,0	2,5	4,4

Figure 1.2

Bernheim, 1986; Tan and Werlang, 1988). Intuitively, the argument runs as follows. Rational players will not choose a dominated strategy, i.e. all dominated strategies can be eliminated from the game, i.e. the strategy set can be restricted to D_i. Because of the existing common knowledge, it is known to all players that dominated strategies are not played. Accordingly, players may find additional strategies that are dominated given the knowledge that the other players restrict their choice to strategies that are not dominated in the first round. This implies that there may be more strategies that can be eliminated in the second round, i.e. the strategy set can be restricted to D_i. Subsequent applications of the same argument lead to the conclusion that players choose a strategy that survives the procedure of IEDS: $s_i \in D_i$.

The concepts that are introduced above will be illustrated by means of the following two examples.

Example A.1 A Game to Illustrate the Notion of IEDS

There are two players, called 1 and 2, who have to choose one of the following three strategies: *L*, *M* or *R*. The normal form is given in Figure 1.2. The pay-offs for player 1 and 2 are represented in the lower left and upper right corner, respectively (see Figure 1.2). The game is symmetric. It is easily seen that for both players strategy *M* dominates strategy *R* and *L* and *M* are S_{-i}−undominated. So, $D_i = \{L_i, M_i\}$, $i = 1, 2$.
In a second stage M_i is dominated by L_i: only L_i is D_{-i}−undominated. This means that L_i, $i = 1, 2$, is the unique strategy that survives the iterated elimination of dominated strategy. This is also the unique Nash equilibrium. This is one of the special cases in which the implications of the two notions coincide.[28]

	L	*R*
L	1,1	0,0
R	0,0	1,1

Figure 1.3

Example A.2 A Coordination Game

There are two players, called 1 and 2, who have to choose either *L* or *R*. The normal form is given in Figure 1.3. It is easily seen that none of the strategies is dominated and that there are two Nash equilibria in pure strategies, namely (*L*, *L*) and (*R*, *R*).

Notes

1. A first draft of this chapter was discussed at a FPPE workshop in Helsinki (January 1995). Subsequent versions have benefited from comments by the workshop and conference participants and especially by Sanjeev Goyal, Shaun Hargreaves Heap, Dan Hausman, Uskali Mäki, Philippe Mongin and Jack Vromen.
2. Some authors regard game theory as a language to describe social interaction and observe that, as a language by itself is not explanatory, game theory by itself is not either. For example, Bianchi and Moulin (1991, p. 185) write 'game theory *per se* is no more empirically verifiable than an alleged translation from English into an unspoken language'.
3. A reason for this may (still) be what Brodbeck (1958, p. 6) formulated almost forty years ago: 'to keep the principle of methodological individualism firmly in mind . . . should at least help us to assure that nevermore he [the social scientist] dally with suspect group-minds and impersonal "forces", economic or otherwise'.
4. Note that recently Arrow (1994, p. 1) has argued that 'a close examination of even the most standard economic analysis shows that social categories are in fact used in economic analysis all the time and that they appear to be absolutely necessities of the analysis, not just figures of speech that can be eliminated if need be'. Arrow subsequently argues that this finding goes against methodological individualism. The category of insti-

tutional individualism, as defined below, should make it clear to economists and game theorists that social entities can play an explanatory role without abandoning methodological individualism.

5. I use this terminology to refer to authors who adopt the game theoretic approach in their explanations of economic and other social phenomena.
6. The terminology suggests that this methodological position has close ties to psychology. Despite this appearance, the science of psychology usually does not play any role in explanations that fall under this position.
7. Of course, in some explanations the exogenous institutions are more important than in others. II does not specify the relative 'weights' of the institutions and individual behaviour in an explanation. However it seems natural to require that the role of individual behaviour is not redundant.
8. For an adoptive learning interpretation of IEDS that does not assume common knowledge, see Section 7.
9. Recently De Wolf and Forges (1995) have qualified this result for 2-player games.
10. Instead of coordinated expectations Aumann and Brandenburger use the terminology 'strategy choices of the players are mutual knowledge'.
11. Jacobsen (1996) attempts to give another justification for Nash equilibrium. He is able to show that under the assumption that every individual player formulates exactly one plan (defined as a strategy and belief for *both* players), rational players should choose a strategy that is with some positive probability part of a Nash equilibrium In case there is a unique Nash equilibrium in pure strategies, Jacobsen's result gives a justification for the notion of Nash equilibrium. In other cases, however, his approach does not justify the notion of Nash equilibrium.
12. This interprtation is probably the most appropriate for coordination games and not necessarily for other types of games.
13. The players might not even know they have a common background.
14. Recall that I reinterpret the programme justifying Nash equilibrium in terms of the explanatory purpose of the applied game theory literature.
15. In some novels the author also appears to help the (main) characters to behave as desired.
16. Such a book is Dixit and Nalebuff (1991).
17. The intuition behind the risk-dominance criterion is the following. If a player chooses L his pay-off equals x irrespective of what the other player does. If he chooses R his pay-off is $(1 - p)$, where p is the probability with which the other player plays L. If $x > 1/2$, then it is less risky to choose L in the sense that there is a larger range of beliefs (about what the other player will choose) that supports the choice of L. In particular, all $p > 1 - x$, which is strictly larger than $1/2$, support L.
18. One critique of the above argument, which Shaun Hargreaves Heap mentioned to me in correspondence, is that coordination also follows if some other criteria (e.g. risk-dominance) was followed by all players. In reply to this critique I would say that there is a special connection between individual rationality and POC, which is not shared by other principles that could have been used. It is that POC is the only criterion leading to maximal individual pay-offs if there is a unique Pareto-efficient outcome.
19. This is even true for objects on a tray: they may, for example, differ by

shape size and colour pattern. Experiments conducted by Mehta *et al.* (1994) and Bacharach and Bernasconi (1994) contain more interesting situations and the line of research seems to have the potential of incorporating some essential features of a common culture that we know.

20. This section is partly based on Goyal and Janssen (1996, Section 5).
21. The argument below can be adapted so that it will also apply to the assumption of absolute continuity (see Goyal and Janssen, 1996).
22. For an excellent recent overview of the literature, see Weibull (1995).
23. As has been pointed out by Leonard (1994), Nash had already given a population interpretation of his equilibrium notion (see also Weibull, 1995). This interpretation has, however, for long been neglected.
24. In biological terms, a larger pay-off means more offspring and as the offspring have inherited the genes from their parents, they play the same strategy.
25. Fisher (1989) makes a similar point.
26. It may even be that these different models have a different number of players, as some players do not appear in the perception of other players.
27. Of course conventions and institutions may play a role via the perceptions of the players.
28. A fact *F* is common knowledge if everybody knows *F*, if everybody knows that everybody knows *F*, if everybody knows that everybody knows that everybody knows *F*, and so on.

References

Agassi, J. (1960) 'Methodological Individualism', *British Journal of Sociology* vol. 11, pp. 144–70.

——— (1975) 'Institutional Individualism', *British Journal of Sociology*, vol. 26, pp. 144–55.

Anderlini, L. and A. Ianni (1996) 'Path Dependence and Learning from Neighbours', *Games and Economic Behavior*, vol. 13, pp. 141–78..

Arrow, K. (1994) 'Methodological Individualism and Social Knowledge', *American Economic Review, Papers and Proceedings* vol. 84, pp. 1–9.

Aumann, R. (1985) 'What is Game Theory trying to Accomplish?', in K.J. Arrow and S. Honkapohja (eds), *Frontiers of Economics* (Oxford: Basil Blackwell).

——— (1987) 'Correlated Equilibrium as an Expression of Bayesian Rationality', *Econometrica*, vol. 55, pp. 1–18.

Aumann, R. and A. Brandenburger (1995) 'Epistemic Conditions for Nash Equilibrium', *Econometrica*, vol. 63, pp. 1161–80.

Bacharach, M. (1991) 'Conceptual Strategy Spaces', *Oxford Discussion Paper*.

——— (1993). 'Variable Universe Games', in K. Binmore, A. Kirman and P. Tani (eds), *Frontiers of Game Theory* (Cambridge, MA: MIT Press).

Bacharach, M. and M. Bernasconi (1994) 'An Experimental Study of the Variable Frame Theory of Focal Points', mimeo.

Bernheim, D.B. (1984) 'Rationalizable Strategic Behavior', *Econometrica*, vol. 52, pp. 1007–28.

——— (1986) 'Axiomatic Characterizations of Rational Choice in Strategic Environments', *Scandinavian Journal of Economics*, vol. 88, pp. 473–88.

Bianchi, M. and H. Moulin (1991) 'Strategic Interaction in Economics', in M. Blaug and N. de Marchi (eds), *Appraising Economic Theories* (Aldershot: Edward Elgar).

Bicchieri, C. (1987) 'Rationality and Predictability in Economics', *British Journal for the Philosophy of Science*, vol. 38, pp. 501–13.

——— (1992) 'Reply to Janssen and Rosenberg', in N. de Marchi (ed.), *Post-Popperian Methodology of Economics: Recovering Practice* (Boston: Kluwer).

——— (1993) *Rationality and Coordination* (Cambridge: Cambridge University Press).

Binmore, K. (1988) 'Modelling Rational Players I and II', *Economics and Philosophy*, vol. 3, pp. 179–214; vol. 4, pp. 9–55.

Binmore, K. and L. Samuelson (1994) 'Muddling Through: Noisy Equilibrium Selection', University of Wisconsin-Maddison, mimeo.

Boland, L. (1982) *Foundations of Economic Method* (London: Allen & Unwin).

Brandenburger, A. (1992) 'Knowledge and Equilibrium in Games', *Journal of Economic Perspectives*, vol. 6, pp. 83–101.

Brodbeck, M. (1958) 'Methodological individualisms: definition and reduction', *Philosophy of Science*, vol. 25, pp. 1–22.

Carlsson, H. and E. van Damme (1993) 'Global Games and Equilibrium Selection', *Econometrica*, vol. 61, pp. 989–1018.

Coleman, J. (1990) *Foundations of Social Theory* (Cambridge, MA: Harvard University Press).

Crawford, V. and H. Haller. (1990) 'Learning How to Cooperate: Optimal Play in Repeated Coordination Games', *Econometrica*, vol. 58, pp. 571–95.

De Wolf, O. and F. Forges (1995) 'On Strategic Equilibria and Rational Choice', *CORE Discussion Paper*, 9548.

Dixit, A. and B. Nalebuff (1991) *Thinking Strategically* (New York: W.W. Norton).

Fisher, F. (1989) 'Games Economists Play; A Noncooperative View', *Rand Journal of Economics*, vol. 20, pp. 113–37.

Friedman, D. (1991) 'Evolutionary Games in Economics', *Econometrica*, vol. 59, pp. 637–66.

Gauthier, D. (1975) 'Coordination', *Dialogue*, vol. 14, pp. 195–221.

Gilbert, M. (1989) 'Rationality and Salience', *Philosophical Studies*, vol. 57, pp. 61–77.

——— (1990) 'Rationality, Coordination and Convention', *Synthèse*, vol. 84, pp. 1–21.

Goodman, N. (1973) *Fact, Fiction and Forecast*, 3rd edn (New York: Bobbs-Merrill).

Goyal, S. and M. Janssen (1997) 'Coexistence of Non-exclusive Conventions and Interaction Structure', *Journal of Economic Theory* (forthcoming).

——— (1996) 'Can we Rationally Learn to Coordinate?', *Theory and Decision*, vol. 40, pp. 29–49.

Harsanyi, J. and Selten R. (1988) *A General Theory of Equilibrium Selection in Games* (Cambridge, MA: MIT Press).

Hausman, D. (1992) *The Inexact and Separate Science of Economics* (Cambridge and New York: Cambridge University Press).

Jacobsen, H. (1996) 'On the Foundations of Nash Equilibrium', *Economics and Philosophy*, vol. 12, pp. 67–88.
Janssen, M. (1993) *Microfoundations: A Critical Inquiry* (London: Routledge).
——— (1995) 'Rationalizing Focal Points', *Tinbergen Institute Discussion Papers*, 95–35.
Kalai, E. and E. Lehrer (1993a) 'Rational Learning Leads to Nash Equilibrium', *Econometrica*, vol. 61, pp. 1019–45.
——— (1993b) 'Private-Beliefs Equilibrium', *Econometrica*, vol. 61, pp. 1231–40.
Kandori, M., G. Malaith and R. Rob (1993) 'Learning, Mutation and Long Run Equilibria in Games', *Econometrica*, vol. 61, pp. 29–56.
Kreps, D. (1990) *Game Theory and Economic Modelling* (Oxford: Clarendon Press).
Leonard, R. (1994) 'Reading Nash, Reading Cournot. The Creation and the Stabilisation of the Nash Equilibrium', *Economic Journal*, vol. 104, pp. 492–511.
Lewis, D. (1969) *Conventions* (Cambridge, MA: Harvard University Press).
Lukes, S. (1973) *Individualism* (Oxford: Basil Blackwell).
Mäki, U. (1994) 'Isolation, Idealization and Truth in Economics', in B. Hamminga and N.B. de Marchi (eds), *Idealization VI: Idealization in Economics*, Poznan Studies in the Philosophy of Science, 38 (Amsterdam and Atlanta: Rodopi), pp. 147–68.
Maynard Smith. J. (1982) *Evolution and the Theory of Games* (Cambridge: Cambridge University Press).
Mehta, J., C. Starmer and R. Sugden (1994) 'Focal Points in Pure Coordination Games: An Experimental Investigation', *Theory and Decision*, vol. 36, pp. 163–85.
Milgrom, P. and J. Roberts. (1990) 'Rationalizability, Learning and Equilibrium in Games with Strategic Complements', *Econometrica*, vol. 58, pp. 1255–77.
——— (1991) 'Adaptive and Sophisticated Learning in Normal Form Games', *Games and Economic Behaviour*, vol. 3, pp. 82–100.
Morris, S., R. Rob and H.S. Shin (1995) '*p*-dominance and Belief Potential', *Econometrica*, vol. 63, pp. 145–57.
Pearce D. (1984) 'Rationalizable Strategic Behavior and the Problem of Perfection', *Econometrica*, vol. 52, pp. 1029–50.
Rubinstein, A. (1991) 'Comments on the Interpretation of Game Theory', *Econometrica*, vol. 59, pp. 909–24.
Schelling, T. (1960) *The Strategy of Conflict* (Cambridge, MA: Harvard University Press).
——— (1978) *Micromotives and Macrobehavior* (New York: W.W. Norton).
Sugden, R. (1991) 'Rational Choice: A Survey of Contributions from Economics and Philosophy', *Economic Journal*, vol. 101, pp. 751–86.
——— (1995) 'Towards a Theory of Focal Points', *Economic Journal*, vol. 105, pp. 533–50.
Tan, T. and S. Werlang (1988) 'The Bayesian Foundations of Equilibrium Concepts', *Journal of Economic Theory*, vol. 45, pp. 370–91.
Tirole, J. (1989) *The Theory of Industrial Organization* (Cambridge, MA: MIT Press).

Weibull, J. (1994) 'The "As If" Approach to Game Theory', *European Economic Review*, vol. 38, pp. 868–81.

Weibull, J. (1995) *Evolutionary Game Theory* (Cambridge, MA: MIT Press).

Young, H.P. (1993) 'The Evolution of Conventions', *Econometrica*, vol. 61, pp. 57–84.

Comment

Ariel Rubinstein
TEL AVIV UNIVERSITY, ISRAEL

1 THE CONTRIBUTION OF THE CHAPTER

Chapter 1 includes a clear and knowledgeable assessment of game theoretic ideas and problems. It builds a bridge between the world of game theory and the world of economic methodology. It is quite rare to find a methodological discussion of game theory with so thorough understanding of game theory. Actually, many methodological papers about game theory start (. . . and end) with a discussion of the Prisoner's Dilemma, which is, in my opinion, a non-game theoretical situation. Janssen's chapter, in contrast, does not even mention the Prisoner's Dilemma.

The main question addressed in the chapter concerns the meaning of game theoretical solution concepts: does game theory provide predictions or explanations based on reasoning founded on purely individualistic considerations?

There are two 'trivial answers' to this question. One may argue that the explanation given by a game theoretic model is individualistic in nature since 'the decision unit' in a non-cooperative model, a player, is a single individual; that is, no additional assumption is made about the existence of a 'planner' or 'coordinator'. However, note that a game theoretic model also includes a 'solution concept'; hence, it is in the interpretation of the axioms underlying the solution concept where individualism is questioned. On the other hand, one may think that a game theoretic explanation is not individualistic since, by definition, game theory relates to 'strategic situations', and a strategic situation is one in which a participant explicitly takes into account his thoughts about the other player's actions. In this sense, the Prisoner's Dilemma is hardly within the scope of game theory since when one 'prisoner' makes his considerations, he does not need to reason about the other prisoner's action! If so, game theory does not provide individualistic explanations as one player's prediction of the other player's behaviour typically requires knowledge about that player beyond what is assumed to be common knowledge (that is, a set of alternatives and preferences). Nevertheless, rational behaviour may be, in principle, an outcome of some process in which very little knowledge about the other players is assumed beyond what the model explicitly assumes. For example, in regard to zero-sum situations, we know (due to the maximin theorem) that there is equivalence between the notion of a Nash equilibrium strategy and the notion of a strategy selected by the maximin criterion (i.e. taking the best action possible based on the assumption that the opponent will do the utmost to reduce your pay-off).

By the way, it is not so terribly clear that even decision theory (the study of situations in which a decision maker's action is not based on reasoning about other players) really does provide a pure individualistic explanation of behaviour. Decision theory is built on the notion of a 'consequence'; spelling out a consequence includes some evaluation of other players' behaviours (for example, the attachment of positive value to money reflects on what the decision maker assumes about the way that other people treat money).

In game theory we often classify non-cooperative game theoretical solution concepts into two classes. One includes solution concepts like 'dominating strategy', 'rationalizability' and 'successive elimination of dominated strategies' in regard to normal form games and 'backwards induction' in regard to extensive form games. The other entails concepts such as the 'Nash equilibrium' and its refinements. The first class encompasses solution concepts which relate to the analysis of a game from an individualistic point of view, assumes rationality or even common knowledge of rationality and has some normative claims. The second class includes solution concepts in which, so it seems, an individual's behaviour is based on 'knowledge' of the *behaviour* of the other players. Thus, this classification parallels the distinction between the psychological individualism (PI) and institutional individualism mentioned in the chapter. But is it indeed the case that solution concepts from the first category are 'individualistic' in the sense that they comprise a single player's reflections on a situation? Can a Nash equilibrium strategy also be presented as an outcome of the deliberations of an isolated player sitting in his armchair and planning his play in a game?

This issue has been recognised as central within game theory. The epistemological assumptions at the foundation of game theory have been in the centre of game theoretic activities for a long time. During the last decade, the issue was treated rigorously and in great depth. An excellent discussion of the relevant literature is to be found in Brandenberger (1992). I agree with the author that the issue is also critical for the assessment of an applied game theory programme. If the notion of Nash equilibrium does indeed rely on an additional assumption of knowledge about other players' *actions*, it can be applied only to situations which are 'continuous in time'. Thus, it would be sensible to apply such a concept in regard to the location of two service units which aim to increase their share of the travellers on a highway. However, it would not be sensible to apply it to situations which occur only once, where knowledge of the other players' actions can be only an outcome of a mental assessment based on entering the other players' shoes. Of course, many real-life strategic situations are one-shot events (how many times is a new drug invented or does a candidate run for the presidency?). I also fully agree with the author's criticism of the lack of sufficient thought on the part of most applied game theoreticians about the meaning and suitability of the solution concepts they use. Too often, the concepts are applied mechanically, without enough consideration being given to the applicability of the assumptions.

By incorporating the philosophical discussion of individualism, Janssen's chapter provides an interesting supplement to this literature. He offers a critical assessment of some game theoretical concepts with the aim of pushing the concept of Nash equilibrium as close as possible into the individualistic paradigm.

2 A FEW REMARKS

2.1 The Interpretation of Game Theory

My own opinion is that the best interpretation of 'game theory' is that of a game as a description of the way that the situation is perceived, and a solution concept as a pattern of reasoning about a class of situations. From this point of view, the entire analysis of game theory rests within psychological individualism as the game itself is something which exists only as part of the reasoning process of a player. This is not the place to expand the discussion: for an elaboration of this view see Rubinstein (1991).

2.2 What is a 'Player'?

A 'player' in game theory is an entity who is able to control a certain set of decisions. Game theory is 'invariant' to further details regarding this entity. Thus, although the basic interpretation of a player is of a single individual, we often interpret a player to be a team, and ignore the internal structure of the group. At the other extreme, we allow a single person to appear in a game in the roles of many players, while ignoring the connections between the different selves (for instance, regarding the kinds of messages one self can send to another). Allowing a participant to be split into multiple selves is important when discussing changes in preferences (*à la* Strotz, 1956) or imperfect recall (see Piccione and Rubinstein, 1997).

2.3 Empirical Validity

The fact that a solution concept fits into PI does not mean that it is empirically valid. For example, consider the maximin criterion. Imagine a game in which player 1 has to put a 'treasure' into one of four boxes having the labels *A A B A*. Simultaneously, Player 2 has only one chance to guess the box in which player 1 has to put the treasure. Player 2 wins if and only if his guess is right. The only maximin strategy for each of the players is to equally randomise between the four options. However, experiments have shown a clear tendency for both types of players to choose the second *A* from the left (see Rubinstein *et al.*, 1996). On the basis of these findings, I would not hesitate to recommend to a real 'treasure hunter' to choose the second *A* from the left and not to rely on the game theoretic discussion and to randomise equally between the four boxes.

2.4 The Principle of Coordination

The empirical scope of this principle, discussed in the paper, is far from clear. Consider a situation (see Glazer and Rubinstein, 1995) in which a group of three referees has to decide the fate of a paper. All the referees share the view that a bad paper should be rejected and a good paper should be accepted, and all share the view that each of the referees may reach the wrong conclusion 'with some positive probability'. Assume that the decision mechanism is such that all referees simultaneously make recommendations. The outcome is taken according to the majority of recommendations. In this situation, the Principle of Coordination requires that everybody report his real view. However, other equilibria exist; for example all referees might always recommend a rejection (probably without reading the paper). This is a strong equilibrium inasmuch as each referee may feel that unless there is some chance that his view will be pivotal, he should not waste his time by reading the paper. But this reasonable equilibrium conflicts with the Principle of Optimality, which is Pareto-dominated by another equilibrium.

2.5 Some General Comments on the Methodology of the Methodologists

To Roger Backhouse's list of reasons why we should have methodological discussions of economic theory[1] I wish to add one more. Academic economic research uses public resources and fulfils educational functions. Such activities should be conducted under some kind of monitoring, especially as many economists also make claims daily about real life while basing their arguments on their academic expertise. The only candidates for doing the monitoring are either the economists themselves or philosophers who are well informed about economics.

There is significant benefit to discussions on the concept of 'externality', which reveal the gaps between the way the concept is used in economics and how it is used in natural language. I was impressed by Barrotta's comment on the fallacy made by economists who claim that 'one model is no more than a special case of another model'. On the other hand, I found little interest in the investigation of biographic details of long-dead economic theorists as part of the effort to understand their motives in assessing the meaning of economic models and ideas. I do believe that ideas have an existence independent of their discoverers but, in any case, it would be much more fruitful to conduct such a study within the context of current economic theory. One can find areas of current economics in which the rationale for focusing on a certain model or a particular set of assumptions can be explored in light of external motives. Furthermore, current issues have the advantage that the facts are more easily verified and the 'players' are available for transmitting their own accounts on their motivations.

This conference was unique in its focus on the discussion of a few test cases, and its procedure of having regular economists commenting on the methodological papers. I think that a more radical shift from the conventional conference format would be even more beneficial. It may be even more valuable to start discussions of economic theory with *presentations* of economic theory (good old papers) followed by a methodological discussion.

Note

1. See Chapter 7, Final Discussion, p. 429.

References

Brandenberger, A. (1992) 'Knowledge and Equilibrium in Games', *Journal of Economic Perspectives*, vol. 6, pp. 83–101.

Glazer, J. and A. Rubinstein (1995) 'What Motives Should Guide Referees? On the Design of Mechanisms to Elicit Opinions', mimeo.

Piccione, M. and A. Rubinstein (1997) 'On the Interpretation of Decision Problems with Imperfect Recall', *Games and Economic Behavior*, vol. 30.

Rubinstein, A. (1991) 'Comments on the Interpretation of Game Theory', *Econometrica*, vol. 59, pp. 909–924.

Rubinstein, A., A. Tversky and D. Heller (1996) 'Naive Strategies in Zero-sum Games', forthcoming in W. Guth *et al.* (eds), *Understanding Strategic Interaction – Essays in Honor of Reinhard Selten* (Berlin: Springer-Verlag), pp. 394–402.

Strotz, R.H. (1956) 'Myopia and Inconsistency in Dynamic Utility Maximization', *Review of Economic Studies*, vol. 23, pp. 165–80.

Comment: Individualistic Explanation and Strategic Justification

Philippe Mongin[1]
CNRS AND UNIVERSITÉ DE CERGY-PONTOISE, FRANCE

Maarten Janssen's Chapter 1 aims at clarifying the sense in which game theory (GT) can be said to conform to the requisites of methodological individualism (MI). It takes the view that GT is a technique rather than a theory, but nonetheless imposes specific constraints on the explanations in which it is used. The question then is whether these constraints are compatible with those suggested by the heuristics of MI. As Maarten Janssen stresses, this is a relevant methodological question to ask in relation to Industrial Organization, and those other areas of economics which make use of game-theoretic tools ('applied game theory' in his terminology).

In effect, Janssen's chapter is concerned primarily with a related but different question: does the justification of Nash equilibrium provided by game theorists conform to MI, or does it not? If Janssen had really followed up the initial question he raises, he would have had to scrutinise 'applied' game theoretic models, and decide whether these models are explanatory in a way MI can approve of. What he does instead for most of the chapter is to review those results or arguments in *pure* game theory which address the famous question of whether or not Nash equilibrium results from the independent decisions made by rational players. The two questions are related to the following extent: the game theoretic modelling in Industrial Organization and other economic applications heavily depends on (and indeed often does not go beyond) the use of the Nash equilibrium concept. Economists often take for granted that a phenomenon has been explained once it has been modelled as the Nash equilibrium of some plausible game. This methodological commitment implies that the justification problem, as I shall call it, has a definite bearing on the methodological question initially raised by Janssen. However, it does not exhaust this broader question.

Janssen recognises that when he stresses that in any economic application, not only the chosen equilibrium concept, but also the *modelling of the game* must be appropriate. Unfortunately, he has very little to say about the latter issue. His Section 8 on 'The rules of the game' (p. 22) hardly goes beyond the utterly general point that the rules of the game, as usually defined by game theorists, can receive various interpretations, some of them mostly objective, others mostly subjective. Janssen appears to be sceptical of the relevance of either interpretation to economics, but does not spell out his reasons.

I am thus suggesting that Chapter 1 is not about the topic it was explicitly intended to discuss. One reason why Maarten Janssen has been diverted from his initial question is, I submit, that he is concerned with both justification and explanation, but does not adequately deal with the point that these two concepts have very different epistemological qualities. These distinctive properties are probably well understood, so that the following sketch may be sufficient. Justification is a normative enterprise, whereas explanation is mostly or primarily a factual one. To justify, say, a piece of behaviour is to give reasons for it, in particular by pointing out that it conforms with accepted norms of behaviour. To explain it means to subsume it under laws or regularities, while (on most accounts) uncovering a particular causal chain leading to the explanandum. Now, it has also been argued that reasons can act as causes, and that norms can function as covering laws, so that this distinction is not as clear-cut as it seems. Indeed, economic applications of game theory involve the *explanatory* use of those concepts, such as Nash equilibrium, which game theorists are busy trying to *justify*. The interplay between justification and explanation is typical of empirical applications of rational choice theories. Janssen knows of course that justification and explanation are distinct concepts, and he is also aware of the more delicate point that they are going to interfere with each other in 'applied game theory'. See for instance:

> The focus of the theoretical literature is not so much to *explain* certain phenomena, but rather to provide a *justification* of the Nash equilibrium concept . . . Accordingly, . . . I shall re-interpret the existing justifications in terms of their usefulness for the explanatory purposes of the applied literature. (p. 3, emphasis in the original)

However, despite this excellent start, Janssen never explains how a justificatory argument can be turned into an explanatory one. Worse, he sometimes loses sight of even the basic distinction between the two concepts. Consider the following passage:

> We have not yet paid much attention to the *empirical* requirement: how can we *justify* the rules of the game; or in other words, what is the relation between the artificial world of the game and 'reality' (p. 22, emphasis mine)

The talk of justification, here, creates a false parallel with the earlier discussion of Nash equilibrium, as if the methodological task was to explore *two* justification programmes in succession.

Concerning MI, Janssen argues that it is not restricted to biologically defined individuals. One way or another, the extension of MI to organisations has been defended by Coleman (1990), Boudon (1979), and other major sociologists. The danger of this ecumenical interpretation of MI is that it might turn it into its opposite, i.e. the doctrine of holism that is so repulsive to the individualist. According to Agassi's (1960) authoritative restatement, the demarcation line between the individualist and the holist should be as follows: the former denies that 'collectives' have aims, interests, or stategies *of their own*, whereas the latter is prepared to accept that. Like Janssen, I think that Agassi's criterion is the best available to distinguish between the two positions. How, then, could one apply the apparatus of choice theory to firms, households, companies, or the State, as Boudon and Coleman do in their sociological work, and still claim to be faithful to MI? There must be a proviso to the social scientist's application of choice theoretic methods to collective entities. Janssen formulates it as follows: it is permissible to use these methods only 'in so far as the differences in aims and interests of the people that are part of these entities do not seem to be important for the problem at hand' (p. 4). I have nothing to object to this formulation. The same firm can be modelled as being a strategic actor in various oligopolistic contexts, while it will have to be disaggregated, and its policies viewed as unintended consequences of its employees' strategies, in some other economic contexts. Think of IBM, and the way you would analyse, on the one hand, its conflictual cooperation with Microsoft and on the other, the management's recent drastic decisions to downsize the firm. The suggested proviso creates room to make two different assumptions on the same 'collective', while applying the same methods of analysis – essentially, rational choice theories. Janssen's proviso is in agreement with the best sociologists' practice. The problem I have here is not with its formulation, but its applicability, given the level of abstraction maintained throughout the chapter. Because the author's analysis is nearly exclusively concerned with pure game theory, we do not have any 'problem at hand' to ponder over, as in the IBM or similar examples. Hence, we cannot say whether the game theoretic apparatus is applied in an individualistic or a holistic fashion. Janssen will perhaps object to the empiricism underlying this criticism, and claim that *pure* game theory can be usefully subjected to the proviso. But I do not think that this is a plausible answer. Given its very abstract notions of games, players, and strategies, we have no clue *in game theory itself* to separate between properly individualistic and holistic applications of game theory.

Janssen is faithful to Agassi's conception of MI when he introduces two variants, i.e., psychological individualism (PI) and institutional individualism (II). Essentially, the former does not accept that social phenomena enter the explanatory model as exogenous variables, whereas the latter does accept that. I take it that the exogenous variables of a model play, at least potentially, a *causal* role, and will emphasise this function in the following discussion. Despite Janssen's occasional suggestions to the contrary, it seems to me that the distinction between II and PI is not about whether or not 'collectives' can be seen as acting individuals. This issue has been settled by the proviso just discussed, which I think should apply to *both* forms of MI. What we are inquiring now is whether social phenomena (more generally than collective entities) can legitimately be given a causal role (as opposed to a teleological role). To go back to the previous example, suppose we try to analyse the 'collective decision' made by IBM to shut down factories and reallocate the working force. Can we take the relevant decisions made by the US government as exerting some causal influence on the situation of IBM, despite the fact that the State is another collective entity to be analysed? The distinction between PI and II is about issues of this kind. An institutional individualist would no doubt take the admixture of pro-free trade attitudes and disguised protectionism which has become peculiar to the US administration in the 1980s and 1990s as part of the *data* of his analysis of IBM. He would argue that this is a permissible simplification because this feature has (at least recently) become a relatively stable feature of the company's economic environment, and that it is not likely to be strongly modified by the company's own decisions. The psychological individualist would (although it appears from this example, rather unplausibly) deny that any policy of the US administration may be considered as a *datum*. Allegedly, it would have to be either accounted for in choice theoretic terms, or dropped from the analysis.

This last example already suggests that there is something unsatisfactory with the distinction between II and PI. Let us ponder over the following definition:

> [PI] holds that 'natural' conditions, such as the weather or the production technology at a certain point in time, are the only exogeneous variables . . . that are allowed . . . [II] holds that institutions (loosely defined) that exist at a certain point in time are also legitimate exogenous variables. (p. 5)

To define PI as that doctrine which does not allow social phenomena to be part of the exogeneous variables would make it virtually inapplicable. This much was clear from the sketchy example of IBM and the American government. Except perhaps on Robinson's island the very day when Friday landed on it, endogenous variables will reflect the influence of not only individual actions and natural phenomena, but also of truly social phenomena, in particular institutions. Hence PI must be defined more aptly, or else it will become a purely theoretical standpoint, a straw-man, and in the social scientist's practice, II will coincide with the whole of MI. This is precisely what turns out to be the result of Janssen's chapter. Having found out that all of the constructions he considers in turn (with one curious exception, to be discussed below) fall within the scope of II, he sadly concludes that II is a 'catch-all' category (p. 26). Did we need a survey to discover this conclusion inductively, as it were? Was it not predictable from the author's initial definitions?

I should perhaps make it clear that the criticism just made is not so much directed against Janssen as it is against the methodological literature he is employing. From a casual survey of this literature, it is not at all clear how the line should be drawn between II and PI, so that PI could become a relevant category. Watkins (1952, 1957), who has usefully written on MI, and is actually sometimes described as a psychological individualist, is willing to accept a causal role for social phenomena whenever the latter are themselves *analysable* (rather than actually analysed) in terms of MI. He has usefully stressed the analogy between the individualistic programme in the social sciences and reductionist programmes in physics. Accordingly, let us correct the initial definition and say that PI is that doctrine which *in principle* does not allow social phenomena to be part of the exogenous variables. By which we mean: social phenomena which *in principle* can be reduced will not count as social phenomena; rather they will stand for those individual actions of which they summarise the consequences, given relevant causal variables. A definition of this sort sounds either circular or incomplete (i.e. open to an infinite regression argument), but as Watkins has emphasised, the objection here is perhaps no more serious in the case of MI than those initially raised against scientifically successful reduction programmes such as atomism. I cannot pursue the analysis here, and will simply note that it makes the distinction between II and PI even more elusive than before. How do we know whether or not a social phenomenon is reducible *in principle*? On a crude view of the matter, we can answer this question only if we try to reduce the phenomenon effectively, and either succeed or fail. This test, of course, we cannot, or do not want to, apply. We should be able to discuss reducibility without having to perform the reduction. What might count as a warrant here is a successful *sketch* of a reduction, or some preexisting *theoretical* result to the effect that reduction is indeed possible, or the social scientist's knowledge that reduction has been effectively performed *under similar circumstances*. It is delicate to state criteria, but they are needed. In their absence, the individualist will be naturally inclined to consider every social phenomenon as reducible 'in principle', and this time it is PI, not II, which is likely to become the 'catch-all' category.

There is a further suggestion to consider. By contrasting two kinds of individualism with each other, Agassi presumably meant that institutions – i.e. institutions *properly*, and not institutions 'loosely defined', as Janssen has it – are highly specific social phenomena. They enjoy relative permanence, and often outlive their individual members. They have received formal recognition one way or another. They normally have physical embodiments – the Church has churches, the State has post offices and the Quirinale, and so on. They are 'public' in a quasi-material sense, thus in a way different from conventions, which, Lewis (1969) has argued, can receive a purely mentalistic account. I have no ready-made theory of institutions to provide, but wish to suggest that if we manage to draw the line somewhere between institutions and other recurrent social phenomena, we might be able to give a determinate meaning to Agassi's 'institutional individualism' and thus distinguish it from PI. Interestingly, if we follow this route, we might end up construing II as a more restrictive category than PI. To repeat, the institutional individualist would consent to make the US administration's policies part of the data of the situation faced by IBM. But he would probably not include 'the company's culture' among those data, while the psychological individualist might include it if certain conditions about reduction 'in principle' are met. Janssen sometimes seems to be groping after a specific notion of 'institution'. However, he generally blurs the distinction between institutions, conventions and various other social phenomena. At some point, the fact that players share 'a common culture' (as formalised by common priors or at least mutually absolutely continuous priors) is taken as evidence that II prevails. Quite consistently with this construal, Agassi's defence of II is reformulated as the following very weak requirement: 'assume some coordination to explain some other form of coordination'. It is hardly surprising that the II form of MI proliferates in Janssen's chapter to the point that he feels uneasy about it. He has put himself in this predicament. The distinction between two forms of MI was too shaky to be *imported* from the philosophical literature. In the absence of a satisfactory restatement that the chapter was unable to provide, it was probably better to drop it, and concentrate on the coarser but more usable distinction between MI and holism.

Thus far, I have been critical in two respects: I have suggested that the methodological discussion was preempted by the lack of concrete applications in the chapter, and by its misdirected emphasis on an intractable distinction. But Maarten Janssen's explorations can be read from a different angle. The chapter is instructive when it is viewed as a survey of the 'justification programme' in game theory. The technical sections are pleasantly written and give easy access to valuable material. Janssen makes a start with rationalisability and iterative elimination of dominated strategies, which he explains in detail in the Appendix (p. 28). Perhaps there was more to be said at the general level about these two basic concepts. They rely on computations of cross-beliefs performed by players in isolation from each other. They provide an easy justification of equilibrium play (and no doubt one which has a strong individualistic flavour). However, rationalisability or iterative elimination (which, incidentally, are equivalent to each other only in two-person games) justify *more* than NE, and intuitively justify *too much.* As is well known, in many relevant games (such as 'chicken' or 'the battle of the sexes'), these concepts rationalise every outcome, whereas the NE concept accomplishes an intuitively defensible (but to the game theorist, still insufficient) selection among outcomes. If either rationalisability or iterated elimination is identified with individualism, it will follow that *individualism is not sufficiently restrictive* – a preliminary result which needs emphasising. The drift of the chapter is then to review some more demanding notions than rationalisability or iterated elimination which have been proposed in order to recover no more than the NE concept.

I cannot review the rich game theoretic material of the chapter, and will just single out Janssen's comment on common knowledge. I am willing to agree that common knowledge assumptions sound psychologistic; however, this might turn out to be a deceiving appearance. Perhaps the following example (mentioned in Lismont and Mongin, 1994) will help: an ambulance siren is sounding in my street; not only do I know this fact, and my neighbour knows it, but also I know that he knows it, he knows that I know it, and so on. This daily example illustrates an axiom which is taken for granted in most of the current logical work on common knowledge: intrinsically public knowledge is automatically common knowledge. 'Intrinsically' is a loose term here, to be opposed to the also loose term 'occasionally'. Suppose that a noisy crash has just happened in my street; my neighbour and I know that the crash has happened, which makes it public knowledge; but I might be excused for not knowing that my neighbour knows this fact, because it is just a case of 'occasional' public knowledge. By contrast, a sounding ambulance siren is meant to be heard and recognised by all. The ambulance example was introduced to suggest that common knowledge is sometimes very unproblematic. I am using it again here to suggest that common knowledge assumptions do not necessarily have much *psychologistic* import. They can become both problematic and psychologically loaded when they are used as premises in derivations that are meant to capture the agents' ratiocinations. Suppose that I am planning to fire a gun against someone in my house and I want the detonation to go unnoticed. I could reason as follows: if I, the murderer, fire my pistol at the moment when an ambulance siren is sounding, my neighbour, the detective who is spying on me to prevent me from committing the crime, will know at that moment that I know that he is listening to the siren, and since he is smart, he will immediately suspect that the ambulance was called on purpose. But if I provoke a seemingly accidental noisy crash in the street, these consequences will not necessarily follow, a good thing for me. The conclusion that I know that the detective knows that I know that he will be deafened by the siren was derived from a common knowledge assumption. This somewhat contrived example is meant to illustrate that whatever content and psychological significance common knowledge assumptions have will depend on *how they are put to use*. In some cases, only trivial epistemic implications are exploited; in other cases, this is not so. My fake detective story already involves third-order mutual knowledge, and is probably a borderline case. I wish common knowledge assumptions were assessed relative to the context rather than in the abstract, as is done all too often by commentators of game theory.

Janssen's chapter lays considerable emphasis on the recent work on focal points. This is highly suggestive work, although I am not sure I can see how it fits in a review of solutions to the 'justification' problem. By listing Schelling-type of work just after Aumann-type, Janssen builds a bridge between two fairly different literatures: initially, we were concerned with the problem of refining rationalizability or iterated elimination in order to recover NE; now, we enter a theoretical world in which the NE *concept* is taken for granted, and the problem is how to select one among many NE *outcomes*. To the best of my knowledge (but I might be wrong) salience has been discussed only in the context of selection, not of justification. This means that I find myself slightly uneasy with the comparison made between the Aumannesque rationale for NE and some kind of salience. However, this is a minor reservation since Janssen's discussion of salience and related concepts is in itself very instructive.

At a later point, Janssen discusses the 'principle of coordination'. It states that 'if . . . there is a *unique* strategy combination that is Pareto-optimal, then individual players should do their part of that strategy combination' (emphasis is in the original). Plausible as it sounds, the principle of coordination can be criticized. The following game has two Nash equilibria, one of which only is a Pareto optimum:

$$\begin{array}{cc} & \begin{array}{cc} L & R \end{array} \\ \begin{array}{c} T \\ B \end{array} & \begin{bmatrix} (7,7) & (8,0) \\ (0,8) & (9,9) \end{bmatrix} \end{array}$$

According to the principle of coordination, the two players should choose (*B*, *R*). However, the other Nash equilibrium (*T*, *L*) can be defended on the following grounds: *T* is less risky than *B* for Row, and *L* is less risky than *R* for Column. This intuitive argument can be tightened in terms of the technical concept of risk-dominance. Also, if Row and Column reach a non-binding preplay agreement of playing (*B*, *R*), this preplay agreement might very well not be enforced because of the following reason. By defecting and playing *T* instead of *B*, Row will avoid the 0 pay-off which would result from Column's defection, but he might hope to get 8 (rather than just 7) because it is not impossible that Column will do his part of the agreement. Column can make a similar argument. Naturally, when each player realizes that the other can reproduce his own argument for defection, he is even more inclined to defect! I am using this example, which is attributed to Aumann, in order to suggest that the principle of coordination does not perform completely well. Notice that if the intuitive reasoning presented here does anything at all, it casts a shadow of doubt on the principle in his *selection* device function.

I already said that according to Janssen, the justifications of NE agree with institutional individualism with only one exception. The outlier is the model by Carlsson and van Damme, which is declared to be acceptable by psychological individualism (PI). Even if the chapter is interpreted on its own terms, it is not clear why it deserves a special status. The point that 'IEDS [iterative elimination of dominated strategies] can be regarded as part of PI' is surely wrong, since IEDS plays a pervasive role in game theory, in particular also in models which are said here to conform to II. Perhaps Janssen meant that a model based *only* on IEDS would qualify as a PI model. However, this is another blind alley, because as we reminded the reader, the pure rationalizability or IEDS construction delivers much more than needed. Special restrictions must be added in order to obtain NE, and it is those assumptions to which one should turn in order to decide what kind of individualism underlies the model. Those made by Carlsson and van Damme are ingeniously weak but they amount to endowing the players with a common framework of uncertainty. The technical difference between their assumption and that of consistent prior probabilities in Kalai and Lehrer's article does not seem to justify the difference in the philosophical conclusions that one belongs to PI, while the other belongs to II. Why should the 'conventional' component be stronger in the latter than in the former?

In the course of the discussion, the following general feature of the MI literature has perhaps become apparent: this literature is at such a conceptual distance of game theory that it is not at all easy to apply it to this field. This makes Janssen's attempt bold and meritorious, even it does not fulfil its initial promises. Here is one of the sobering lessons that I have learned from studying the chapter. There is an underlying assumption in the MI literature that I see as a hindrance to a successful application. The writers in the German–Austrian tradition, such as Menger, Popper and Hayek, who are the major contributors to the MI versus holism debate, generally take for granted that the aggregation of individual actions is a mechanical process. Some of these writers emphasize the picture of a regressive method (from macro to micro), others of a progressive method (from micro to macro), but all seem to assume that the micro level can be defined *independently of the macro level.* Given the micro decisions, the macro phenomenon typically results from the unintended consequences of these decisions; the latter are exogenous with respect to the macro phenomenon. This assumption might have been appropriate to the historical and sociological contexts with which the above-mentioned writers were concerned. The fall in value of precious metals in the seventeenth century, or the changing social worth of academic diplomas for the last fifty years, can arguably be explained by models in which individual decisions are made on one side, and social results observed on another side. But game theoretic situations are more recalcitrant. Here, the analogue of the social aggregate is an equilibrium issue of the game, individual decisions are strategy choices, and we know that equilibria and strategy choices should be related to each other internally, not externally. The circularity between the micro and macro levels is in some sense what game theory is about. It is, I submit, an important, quasi-philosophical lesson of the extensive work pursued on NE that one cannot easily disentangle the 'micro' notion of a rational individual strategy from the 'macro' notion of an equilibrium issue of the game. The 'justification programme' has proved most instructive precisely *because* of its failure in accomplishing its initial reduction programme. In its formative years, which go back to the *Methodenstreit* at the end of the nineteenth century, the philosophical writers on MI could not take into account the intriguing circularity exemplified by game theoretic equilibria. Contemporary exponents of this literature in sociology and history are most of the time – no doubt excusably – impervious to this complication. But if methodologists want to connect the work by Agassi, Watkins, Coleman, Boudon and others to the problems of game theory itself, not to mention its economic applications, they should realize that they cannot simply *apply* the former to the latter. The earlier literature should be recast in order to become operative, and this is a non-trivial task.

Note

1. The author is grateful to Roger Backhouse and Dan Hausman for commenting on an earlier draft of this Comment.

References

Agassi, J. (1960) 'Methodological Individualism', *British Journal of Sociology*, vol. 11, pp. 144–70.

Boudon, R. (1979) *La logique du social* (Paris: Hachette).

Carlsson, H. and E. van Damme (1993) 'Global Games and Equilibrium Selection', *Econometrica*, vol. 61, pp. 989–1018.

Coleman, J.S. (1990) *Foundations of Social Theory* (Cambridge, MA: Harvard University Press).

Lewis, D. (1969), *Convention* (Cambridge, MA: Harvard University Press).

Lismont, L. and P. Mongin (1994) 'On the Logic of Common Belief and Common Knowledge', *Theory and Decision*, vol. 37, pp. 75–106.

Watkins, J. (1952) 'Ideal Types and Historical Explanation', *British Journal for the Philosophy of Science*, 3; revised version in H. Feigl and M. Brodbeck (eds), *Readings in the Philosophy of Science* (New York: Appleton-Century-Crofts: 1953), pp. 723–44.

——— (1957) 'Historical Explanation in the Social Sciences', *British Journal for the Philosophy of Science*, vol. 8; reprinted in J. O'Neil (ed.), *Modes of Individualism and Collectivism* (London: Heinemann, 1973), pp. 166–79.

Discussion of Janssen's paper

Daniel Hausman started by discussing Janssen's expansive notion of an individual, as any entity with legal powers. [In the original version of the chapter presented at the conference, Janssen had considered as his 'individuals' any collective entity endowed with decision making powers.] It seems arbitrary to see the law as specifying what counts as an entity and what does not. For example, a particular cartel might or might not have legal powers to set prices, but the notion that it becomes or ceases to be an agent depending on what laws are passed makes the notion of an individual quite superficial.

Wade Hands said that Agassi was not simply trying to include corporations and unions into the explanatory scheme. The problem for Agassi is the notion of an unintended consequence. Popper had the argument that if you have individualism and everything comes out as individuals intend, there is no problem about collective entities. The problem arises when the collective entity does not do what the individuals intended. Hands suggested that Agassi's notion of individualism might sit better with game theory than Janssen's reading of Agassi's notion sits with it. Even the demand curve is an unintended consequence. Hands also remarked that the paper offered a harshly reductionistic reading of individualism. There are softer notions of individualism, such as supervenient individualism.

Janssen replied that there is disagreement over whether supervenience is really individualistic. In addition he argued that supervenience is not the way game theorists think about individualism. Janssen does not want to limit 'individuals' to individual people, because this would end the discussion – all sorts of agents are considered in the applied literature, and many of them are not individuals. Much of the paper does not depend on precisely how agents are defined.

Bennett McCallum found it surprising that the paper suggests that a major objective of game theory is to do a better job than competitive general equilibrium theory in terms of methodological individualism, in the sense of not relying on markets or the concept of an auctioneer. He thought that the main point of game theory is to get away from perfect competition. He also suggested that in deciding what is the appropriate definition of the individual and what kind of knowledge is available, the distinction between short- and long-run issues is very important. A business firm might or might not be an individual, depending on whether one does short- or long-run analysis. This depends on what problems one is trying to solve. **Janssen** said that he agreed with the point about game theory and imperfect competition. However, the criticism that if everyone is a price taker, then there is no one but an invisible auctioneer to set prices, can be rephrased as a methodological argument that such an auctioneer is not allowed by methodological individualism (MI).

Pierluigi Barrotta thought that Janssen's discussion of MI missed an important point. Historically, he suggested, MI tried to explain the rise of new institutions from the action of individuals. Institutions are the unintended consequences of individual action. If this is the core of the individualist's programme, then game theory is inconsistent with its basic heuristic. As an example he cited Bayesian learning. The Bayesian agents' prior probability distributions tend to converge to a unique distribution only if all the agents assign zero probabilities to the same set of events. This is already very troublesome for MI. Even worse than this, one must assume that the space of events is given. If a new kind of event is introduced during the learning process, a new prior distribution has to be introduced. Convergence is interrupted and the process starts again. This rules out the emergence of new institutions.

Janssen, in response to Mongin's claim that the paper is not really about what is purports to be about, said that there is only one 'official' question in his paper: to what extent, in the applied literature, are explanations in line with MI? The Nash equilibrium (NE) assumption is defended in order to answer this question. He responded to Mongin's claim that his definition of MI has little bite by making several points: (a) It is not a definition so much as a minimal requirement for methodological individualism. He observed that not much has been written on methodological individualism. Had he defined it more precisely, it would have been possible for people to object that his definition was not established in the philosophical literature. (b) It has some bite. For example, invisible hand explanations are not allowed, and one of Sugden's possible justifications of NE (that the game theorist suggests a possible outcome to the players) is not allowed.

Janssen suggested that though Agassi might say that institutions have physical embodiment, formal recognition and so on. If he wanted to be specific about institutions, he should have talked not only of psychological individualism and institutional individualism (II), but also of conventional individualism. Given that Agassi does not do this, Janssen interprets him as holding that there is a broad view of individualism and a narrow view, and if something does not fall under the narrow view, it may fall under the broad view. This is how Janssen interprets Mongin's comment that institutional individualism is a catch-all doctrine. He does not think it surprising that most game theory comes under the heading of II, even though some people see it as a form of PI.

Janssen distinguished his principle of coordination from Gauthier's views of constrained rationality by considering a two-person prisoner's dilemma. He pointed out that this game contains three Pareto-optimal outcomes, and so the principle of coordination does not apply.

Janssen was interested in Mongin's suggestion that the MI literature should be left for what it is, but thought this inconsistent with the other suggestion to be more precise in defining MI. He admitted that he had himself struggled with the notion of MI and how to apply it to game theory, and he suggested that one possible conclusion from the paper is that the notion is not suitable for game theory, because in game theory many subtleties that are not part of the MI literature play a role. Another conclusion is that game theory raises issues that people who have discussed MI cannot accommodate. Game theory is a nice test for being more precise about MI. The paper shows that more work needs to be done on the meaning of MI.

Uskali Mäki sought to summarise some of the issues involved.

(1) Janssen's 'minimal requirement' for MI is expressed in terms of actors, which means that explanations that do not involve actors at all (such as functionalist explanations) lie outside MI. They are thus fully consistent with it.
(2) Mäki distinguished five types of agent. (a) Individual human persons. (b) Groups acting dependently, and not independently, of the constituent members, and having the legal power to do so. He saw these two cases as unproblematic. (c) Groups that act in the same way, but do not have the legal power to do so. Organised crime provides examples of such groups. (d) Groups acting independently

of their constituent members and not having the legal power. Such groups do not exist. (e) Groups acting independently and having the legal power to do so. Whereas Janssen suggested that such agents have to be allowed, Mäki suggested that they do not. If such groups have shared beliefs, they act dependent on their constituent members. Mäki then asked whether extending the notion of an agent in this way makes the notion of MI empty. Is anything excluded if we move in this direction?

(3) Janssen also extends the notion of individualism by allowing institutions as exogenous variables as well as agents. This is done using Agassi's notion of II. The problem here appears to be one of infinite regress, for one is allowed to explain institutions in terms of other institutions, and this raises doubts about whether this really is individualism at all. It is a Marshallian time-period-analysis type of approach to the issue of individualism. In the short run one takes institutions as given, but in the long run one explains them.

(4) Putting oneself in another's shoes is at the heart of game theory, therefore game theory is not really individualistic. This adds yet another complication, for it is not about the identity of the agent, but about what beliefs the agent has.

Michael Kaser saw Janssen's paper as helpful in the field of corporate governance in transitional economies. These economies have moved from an organizational form in which principal–agent relations are straightforward – the ministry and the agents in the state enterprise – to one in which there is a diversity of stakeholders (insider and outsider shareholders, investors, the residual power of the State, suppliers and customers) who have no common set of conventions to which they can refer, few legal requirements and highly imperfect markets. How are they to negotiate within the new enterprise to form a coherent game? There is much scope for the II Janssen discusses.

Hausman asked why one should care whether a particular game theoretic model is individualistic or not. He suggested a variety of answers. One might have metaphysical interests: are there such things as games? One might also have a normative interest. Economists think of rationality as applying to individuals, and it is interesting to ask whether it is rational to play a NE strategy. Alternatively, there is Janssen's reason: that whether an explanation conforms to MI or not matters for whether or not it is really an explanation. If MI is not a reasonable constraint on explanations, then Janssen's question loses its interest. If it is considered a constraint, then one can use this to help with the problem of what counts as an individual. One strategy is to require that individuals be real human beings, and if models are not individualistic in this sense, throw them out. Instead, however, one might take the view that there are several different problems. Economists might ask how firms are formed and held together. But they could put that problem aside and suppose the firm is acting as an agent. They could then ask how two firms interact with one another. This would not be a rock-bottom explanation. The issue is what counts as an agent in a particular model. Given this perspective, it might be completely wrong to count as an agent something that has the legal authority to act as an individual. For example, in analysing what is going on within a firm economists might look at divisions of the firm, even though they have no legal authority. The analysis of the role of individuals is going to be heavily context-dependent, but the whole thing is going to depend on how one answers the question about why one should care about whether models conform to individualism.

Janssen responded by noting that in the applied literature, which is now very large, economists using game theory believe that they are providing explanations and that they build their explanations on what they call 'individual behaviour'. It is difficult to be sure, because few of those involved give an explicit account of what they are doing. He is prepared to accept a weak form of MI as a good constraint on explanations: one cannot explain things in terms of vague concepts and groups, but must be clear on the entities that make the decisions.

Nancy Wulwick observed that the paper reminded her of James Buchanan's work on individuals coming to agreements about rules and forming satisfactory contracts.

Mirowski read Janssen's paper largely as exposing a kind of ceremonial individualism that one finds in economics, both in general equilibrium theory and in the discussion of NE. He suggested that the 'Why should we care?' problem arises because the paper does not follow up its strictures. The paper is saying that it is nearly impossible to pretend that the decision procedures being discussed are based on PI, but if this is true, how do we understand what game theorists are doing? Should we understand this entirely as an internalist procedure – a few people talking to each other within economics – or should we understand it in the somewhat larger contextual sense that Janssen argued had to be true even to define common knowledge? Are the economists carrying on a closed, consistent discussion among themselves, or are they hearing voices in the air and reproducing them?

Philip Mirowski noted that philosophers of science had moved through this same pattern at the same time as game theorists. Fifteen years ago it was popular in the philosophy of science to talk about epistemic actors as being Bayesians, and that has petered out. A better discussion of the problems with this can be found in John Earman's book, *Bayes or Bust*, than in any of the writings by Binmore and others on what is wrong with game theory. The newer turn towards thinking of rationality as machine rationality clearly reflects the move to cognitive science in philosophy of science, as an attempt to recast the epistemic actor. Thus the evolutionary considerations in the work of Binmore and Kalai are clearly preceded by movements in cognitive science. Moreover, individual game theorists can be seen as reflecting voices in the air. To understand the Mehta, Starmer and Sugden (1994) paper, and why focal points are so important, it helps to know that Robert Sugden is a radical individualist (*à la* Vienna) so he does not like the neoclassical version of what the individual is, but Judith Mehta is interested in French post-structuralism, and she does not think that it is possible to reduce shared intuitions to simple algorithmic procedures. What Janssen presents as a closed discourse is largely a reflection of different images of what the epistemic actor is.

Instead of trying to decide what an individual is, in a semantic sense, Mirowski suggested a focus on the historical component of game theory. Game theory started as dealing with stylized parlour games, but that did not go very far. From the mid-1940s until it became popular in economics, game theory developed in the RAND corporation and the military. There it was applied, not to individual human beings, but to nations engaging each other in nuclear strategy. The domain of game theory expanded because of where it was developed, not because of conceptions of the individual. The same thing happened again when game theory moved into economics – the idea of the individual has been opened up again. The main use of game theory from the 1960s, at least coming out of RAND, is to programme computers to have automatic strategies, as in the SAGE system, the early-warning system, and so forth. Now it is a machine that is an individual. So why is it surprising that game theorists want to programme automata to play games, and to decide whether Turing machines are an adequate representation of the individual, in order to decide whether NE makes sense? Mirowski is surprised that Janssen and other commentators do not think of the historical dimension as a way of understanding the common knowledge context in which the discussion takes place.

Wulwick cited an example of a company that had a contract to use game theory, based on the Algerian war, to develop material to be used in Vietnam. **Mirowski** said that game theory was used in the early warning system, to programme the computers, because the reaction time is too fast for there to be real-time decisions. He added that the perceptions of game theorists are not the same as what is found in historical records.

McCallum observed that he had been paid a lot of money by various reserve banks as a consultant, but he could not think of any time in which they actually implemented what he suggested. He suggested that all practitioners had in mind when they say that their work is consistent with MI, is that they are trying to avoid fallacies that might arise from pretending that there is some sort of collective entity that doesn't actually exist.

Roger Backhouse suggested that there is a link between Hausman's point about why economists and methodologists should be interested in MI, and the fact there was so much emphasis on equilibrium earlier on. One possible explanation is that when economists are committed to MI they are also committed to seeing the world as a process taking place in time, which is out of equilibrium. He wondered whether, even if we are committed to MI at some deep level, when analysing dynamic processes, they should necessarily be committed to it when constructing equilibrium models. This suggests a link between whether economists are dealing with equilibrium or disequilibrium, and the strength of their commitment to methodological individualism. **Janssen** responded that it is difficult to talk about disequilibrium in game theory, because in game theory, if one brings in movement from disequilibrium to equilibrium, the game theorist would seek to model that movement as an equilibrium in another game.

Uskali Mäki raised the question of how one justifies the depiction of social interaction in terms of game theory. **Janssen** answered this by arguing that there are rules in social reality just as in game theory. **Mäki** replied that this answer evades the question of the existence of games – of the representational power of the metaphor of a game in describing social reality. For one can have rules without games, though not games without rules. **Janssen** observed that games are not complete representations of the situations people are in.

References

Earman, J. (1992) *Bayes or Bust?* (Cambridge, MA: MIT Press).

Mehta, J., C. Starmer and R. Sugden (1994) 'Focal Points in Pure Coordination Games: An Experimental Investigation', *Theory and Decision*, vol. 36, pp. 163–85.

2 Free Riding as Mechanism[1]

Pierre Salmon
UNIVERSITÉ DE BOURGOGNE, FRANCE

1 INTRODUCTION

Free riding illustrates the need to wrestle with ideas which have come up recently in philosophy of science. I am thinking particularly of the growing recognition that some standard views or notions about science, though convincing on paper, are not doing justice to the complexity of the subject matters of most sciences, physics included. The actual world is more 'open' or messy than is still often assumed, and thus it is often the case that science deals with it only indirectly.

In their own very different ways, the books of Roy Bhaskar (1975), Nancy Cartwright (1983, 1989) and Frederick Suppe (1989), among others, reflect this awareness. If there are laws (in some demanding sense, not as simple assertions of impossibility as are most of our laws in economics), most of these laws are to be found or defined at a level of reality which is not that of actual phenomena (see Cartwright, 1983). If properties of models are to be related to properties of real systems by means of theoretical hypotheses, the real systems, again, are not part of the actual world but of a world in which a number of forces are supposed absent (see Suppe, 1989). But the forces, interactions and mechanisms which are identified and studied by science in isolated or closed systems, such as systems created artificially in laboratories, do not cease to operate at the level of the open, actual (non-experimental) world; for the purpose of applications to – and understanding of – this actual world, they must be assumed to operate there also (see Bhaskar, 1975).[2]

There are two reasons to think that these ideas may be particularly relevant in the case of free riding. First, although free riding has different meanings (see, e.g. McMillan, 1979; Sandler, 1992, pp. 16–17; Wolfelsperger, 1995, pp. 56–63; Breton, 1996, pp. 295–6), it is interesting mainly when its interpretation does not place it firmly in the world of manifest phenomena. This requires some explanation. Free riding occurs when some people legally do not pay, or do not pay their share, for some good they draw utility from, but which, whether they pay or not, they cannot be prevented from consuming. The word 'good' refers to anything which has a positive utility, the word 'pay' to anything which has a cost. Technically there are two ways to free ride. A first is when no authority, formal or informal, is endowed with the power to impose taxes or other contributions to users or potential users of the goods, and the goods have the property of non-excludability (goods which have this property include pure public goods and commons). In this situation, free riders need not hide their preferences. Even when known to derive considerable utility from a good, nobody can legally force them to contribute to its provision. The second way is relevant only when people can be made to pay in proportion or in function of the utility they individually derive from a good; then free riding may require negating or understating that utility (and overcoming free riding may require recourse to a preference-eliciting mechanism). In this chapter, I will consider only the first case.

Interpreted literally, as a manifest phenomenon of the actual world, free riding obtains only when there is a 'ride', that is, when the good is actually produced. It refers to the unearned benefit drawn from the good by the free riders. Free riding in this sense hurts our sense of justice but does not raise as serious a problem as it does when its meaning is extended and expresses the fact that the good is not produced or is produced suboptimally. When some people contribute and others free ride (literally), the main problem raised by free riding may be the suboptimality of production rather than the exploitation of the contributors by the free riders.

Even more remarkable is the 'free riding' referred to in the so-called 'strong free riding hypothesis'. That hypothesis is what many authors have in mind when they refer to free riding. It says that the fact that people are not willing to pay for a non-excludable good leads to the good not being produced at all (when the good is discontinuous, it may be sufficient that some people are unwilling to pay for that outcome to obtain). The damage may be particularly important; yet free riding, understood literally, as an actual phenomenon, has disappeared. Since there is no ride, nobody should be said to free ride.[3] This remark applies even more forcefully to some of the other ways in which free riding may vanish. For instance, if it is clear to all that a particular good cannot be produced because too many people would free ride if they were asked to contribute, the matter might not even be raised. Alternatively, people might be compelled to contribute by means of taxation; or there might be other institutional arrangements leading to the same result; or, following Mancur Olson (1965), contributions may be the result of selective incentives. In these examples, although free riding in a non-literal sense or as a non-actual reality may have far-reaching consequences, literally or actually there is none of it.

Altogether, the various cases discussed show that free riding can be interpreted literally or not, as manifest or not, as an outcome or as a cause. They suggest also that the less literal and manifest and the more akin to a cause rather than to an outcome it is, the more important or interesting it is likely to be. This makes it a good object of reflection from the perspective of philosophical ideas which emphasise the non-actual side of reality.

A second reason to consider, perhaps mistakenly, that free riding is a good case is that it has been questioned in a way which is methodologically interesting. The term and whatever it refers to intervene massively in many parts of economics and other social sciences – e.g. in public finance, theory of the State and politics, interest groups, theory of revolutions, economics of trade unions, international relations, altruism or philanthropy, resource conservation and environment, capital markets and theories of the firm, theory of religion – and political philosophy.[4] Todd Sandler even claims that the notion of free riding 'has begun to permeate our everyday language and thought' (1992, p. 12). But, if this 'our' refers to people in general, it is not certain that free riding has been taken in so widely or in depth. Erroneous neglect is pervasive. For example, politicians or journalists do not shy away from advising the members of large groups (currently, in France, doctors) to behave differently if they do not want some collective punishment imposed upon them. In this respect, free riding is akin to comparative advantage: observation of public opinion, confirmed by experience in the class, shows that the idea is both important and counterintuitive.

Given such success in the world of scientific or intellectual endeavours and such upsetting or novelty potential in the world of the public at large, one is inclined to consider free riding as being a major contribution of economic reasoning to social science or to thought *tout court*. But this view is definitely not shared by all commentators. Free riding, as an hypothesis, has been criticised by Brubaker (1975), Johansen (1977), Hirschman (1982) and other well known scholars. The most interesting and powerful critique, however, is the one formulated recently by two political scientists from Yale, Green and Shapiro (1994, 1995), as part of a more general critical examination of the 'applications of rational choice theory in political science'.

One must admit at the outset that Green and Shapiro's arguments seem directed at exactly the right target (polemically speaking). To use Lakatosian language, what they ask for is 'corroborated excess empirical content', or 'attested novel facts'. This is a methodological demand which the programme they are concerned with does not seem particularly able to satisfy. Is it not an obviously legitimate requirement, though? How could an old Popperian like myself not agree with a question formulated as follows: 'Given that any proposed explanation might be wrong, what datum or data should persuade the researcher that this is so?' (1995, p. 266)? And how could I not appreciate the way the two authors formulate their criterion of success or admissibility: 'nonobvious propositions that withstand empirical scrutiny'? When that criterion is applied to free riding and collective action dilemmas, one encounters, they claim, 'arresting propositions that are not sustainable' (e.g. 'that changes in collective incentives have little effect on rates of participation in large groups'), 'sustainable propositions that are not arresting' (e.g. 'that rising selective incentives increases participation in collective action'), seldom applications 'that are at once arresting and sustainable' (1995, p. 236). In their view, 'exceedingly little has been learned' (1994, p. x) from – or 'little empirically supported knowledge has grown' (1994, p. 197) out of – that approach.

With the exception of one paragraph (1994, p. 180), Green and Shapiro are careful not to extend their critique of the applications of the rational choice approach in politics to its applications in economics. That the two authors believe their critique to be applicable to economics transpires clearly, however, in the paragraph just referred to. For example, they note in this paragraph the parallelism between their views and those of Richard Thaler and Alexander Rosenberg. In fact, the economic methodologist they are closer to is Mark Blaug. For these authors, as for Blaug, improved understanding, new insights, re-orientation of the discussion, etc. do not count if not validated empirically, or count only a trifle.[5]

This essay is not devoted to the writings of Green and Shapiro. I quote them because their analyses are very well defended and persuasive, and concern free riding and collective action, which is a subject matter common to both disciplines. But my main reason to start from their position is that it unintentionally illustrates how much and how quickly the philosophical landscape has changed. When responding to the objection that their underlying philosophy is naive, Green and Shapiro (1994, pp. 180–3, 1995, pp. 255–61) deal with the objection as if it were exclusively stemming from the ideas of Kuhn and Lakatos. Inasmuch as the objection is based on the ideas of these authors, Green and Shapiro's response is not inappropriate, I find. But the main challenge to an empiricist position of the kind they adopt is not to be sought nowadays on that side of philosophy (paradigms, tenacity, protected hard core, etc.). It is to be found in the new or renewed awareness, referred to at the beginning of this introduction, that the *actual* world is 'open' or 'messy' and in the methodological consequences of this characteristic which I also referred to.[6]

Insistence on underlying forces, interactions or mechanisms is one of these consequences (it can also be the outcome of different considerations of course). In this chapter, notably as a response to critical arguments such as the ones discussed above, but also as an effect of more intrinsic motivation, I explore the possibility of treating free riding as an underlying or causal mechanism.[7] I have made some effort to overcome my natural reluctance to define and have groped towards the beginning of a definition of mechanisms, in general as well as with special reference to free riding. Section 2 in part reflects this effort. The sections which follow are devoted to comments on two essential aspects of the tentative definition provided in Section 2. In Section 3, I discuss the relationship between real-world mechanisms, constructed models, and hypotheses or conjectures. I try to show that clarifying this relationship may be helpful to interpret some aspects of the literature on free riding. The fact that a mechanism such as free-riding is particularly prone to operate not in isolation but together with other mechanisms is stressed in Section 4, and some of the problems that ensue discussed there and in Section 5. Section 6 consists of brief concluding remarks.

2 TOWARD A DEFINITION OF THE FREE RIDING MECHANISM

What is a mechanism? I am not in the position to provide a general definition of that term. Elster (1989) claims that social science should concentrate on 'explanations by mechanism'. But, as noted by Humphreys (1991), he does not really explain what that means, whilst he illustrations that he gives, in the form of a series of almost independent chapters, are no substitute for such explanation. Stinchcombe (1991) is even less helpful. It is not clear in particular whether he considers mechanisms as theories or as objects of theories. Many economists or social scientists (Blaug as well as Green and Shapiro, incidentally) stress the need to display or spell out 'causal mechanisms' but remain vague about what these mechanisms are.[8]

The account of mechanisms which I have found to be the most precise and interesting so far is the one proposed by my illustrious namesake, Wesley Salmon (1984). According to him, 'causal processes, causal interactions, and causal laws [i.e. laws or regularities which govern causal processes and causal interactions] provide the mechanisms by which the world works; to understand *why* certain things happen, we need to see *how* they are produced by these mechanisms' (p. 132, emphasis in the original). As a non-philosopher, it is particularly difficult for me to gauge the implications of Salmon's views about causal processes and interactions, or more generally about the causal structure of the world (see e.g. Koertge, 1992)). Although I have not found in what I have read an analysis of mechanisms which could replace Salmon's, I do not claim that there is none. Tentatively, thus, I will now use some of his analyses and examples, together with some of the examples provided by Elster, to formulate some rather simple ideas which might serve as ingredients for a more complete or general treatment.

In many cases, it seems, one can say that mechanisms are the sets (I hesitate to use the term 'system' instead of 'set') of causal processes (physical propagation or, in social science, also mental processes) and interactions (notably between processes) which *connect* causes and effects. Thus, a 'switching mechanism' – or perhaps a switching mechanism interacting with an electrical circuit (Salmon, 1984, p. 178) – connects one fact, 'turning a switch', and another fact, 'the light goes on', one being the cause and the other the effect. The chief mechanism of transmission of the plague 'is a flea that bites infected rats and then bites other organisms' (Salmon, 1984, p. 271). Cognitive dissonance reduction is a psychological mechanism which makes people cease desiring what they cannot get, 'as in the story of the fox and the sour grapes'; this mechanism, together with the news that a job has become unavailable, connects the fact that the job was desired and the fact that it is not desired anymore (Elster, 1989, p. 4).

In Elster's formulation here, one fact is the causal antecedent of the other, it has happened previously. But this is not always necessary, it seems. There is no explicit reference to causal antecedents, or things which happened previously, in the case of 'internal causal mechanisms' accounting for the 'nature' of a fact (Salmon, 1984, p. 275) – for instance the internal or underlying causal mechanisms (involving the behaviour of molecules in gases, Avogadro's law, different molecular weights, etc.) which account for the fact that humid air is less dense than dry air (Salmon, 1984, p. 269). In that case, the underlying causal mechanisms 'constitute' the fact or constitute the 'causal structure' of the fact. Would a more general formulation of the sour grapes mechanism (say, simply, that it makes people underestimate the utility of unavailable goods) allow an interpretation along these lines? I do not know whether this would be acceptable. One might want to say that the knowledge of unavailability necessarily precedes on some time scale the underestimation of utility. But, as a more general principle, I think that we must allow that mechanisms also connect social or psychological facts so to say timelessly, in a setting of simple statics.

Where does this lead us to in the case of free riding? By analogy with some of the foregoing examples, I will define the free riding mechanism as being any set of processes and interactions in a group of individuals which, if operating freely and alone, will lead *many* of these individuals to decide, *because* of the non-excludability property of a good, not to contribute to its provision – or, in any case, not an amount at least equal to their marginal valuation of the good – even if the consequence is that the good will not be provided at all. In other words, the free riding mechanism connects a fact to which we give the status of a cause, the non-excludability of a good, with another fact, which we consider as its effect, i.e. many individuals deciding not to contribute to the provision of the good, etc.

Some characteristics of this definition are related to problems which I discussed in the first section about the meaning of free riding. I comment some other characteristics now. First, I use the singular and refer to *the* free riding mechanism. One might prefer to use the plural and refer to several free riding mechanisms (I allude again to that question in the next section).

Second, although in general in this chapter I may be a bit negligent about variations in the meanings of the terms I use, 'free riding' in particular, I feel that the definition proposed here is relatively unambiguous and points rather clearly to a mechanism rather than to an outcome. As an outcome free riding may be unintentional and reflect circumstances such as ignorance, absence, or absent-mindedness. But this is excluded by the way the definition is formulated: people in the group do not merely not contribute (i.e. objectively free ride); they decide not to contribute because – notably – of the non-excludability of the good. Let me note in passing that some so far unmentioned factors are certainly central to this decision. A clear case is the dispositions (psychological and otherwise) of the persons concerned. Whether, in particular in W. Salmon's (1984) framework, these factors should also be called causes, I do not know.

Third, I refer, rather vaguely, to 'many' people. One reason is that I treat the free riding mechanism as an essentially social mechanism (itself involving individual psychological processes of course) rather than as a mainly psychological mechanism as many authors in fact do, I think. That the social character is compelling and should be stressed seems to me to come out particularly clearly from the experimental work and evidence I will refer to later on. Another reason is that, in the real world, this mechanism is most likely to involve stochastic processes. On this point, a relevant analogy is with the mechanism (or mechanisms) of the epidemics of plague as analysed, again, by W. Salmon (1984, pp. 271–3). In the case of both mechanisms, 'many' is implied but not defined precisely, and the causal connection is not with the behaviour or destiny of given persons, except perhaps, implicitly, in the form of propensities ('many' persons also do not contract the plague, but the explanation of the epidemics does not require that we know why).

Fourth, I have attempted to define but not to elucidate the free riding mechanism. This is how it should be, I believe. Even if its methodological aspects are necessarily a concern of this chapter, elucidating the free riding mechanism is a scientific, not a methodological endeavour. As we will see, substantial progress has been made by researchers in the fulfilment of this task. At the same time, the processes and interactions involved in the social mechanism of free riding come out as much more complex and subtle than believed initially.

Two characteristics deserve more extensive comments and will be the objects of the next sections. One concerns the implicit treatment of a mechanism as a part of reality, not as a theory or model; the other the fact, alluded to in the definition, that in the real world the free riding mechanism is likely to operate not in isolation but together with many others.

3 MECHANISMS, MODELS AND HYPOTHESES

Mechanisms are not theories or models. They are first of all part of the real world. I think that this is particularly clear in the analysis of W. Salmon (1984), but is supposed also, often implicitly, in most of the references to causal, generative, hidden, underlying or basic mechanisms that one finds in the literature. How, otherwise, could we say that the mechanism of something is mysterious, unknown, ill-understood, etc.? Now, this does not imply that mechanisms cannot also be included in models. Inspired by the so-called semantic conception of theories (see Giere, 1988; Hausman, 1981a, 1992, Chapter 5; Salmon, 1990), I interpret models as non-linguistic systems constructed to analyse particular aspects of reality.[9] As such, models *can* include anything found in reality and thus can also include mechanisms (though, I must stress, they do not have to).

According to the semantic conception, a model cannot be true or false. But its relationship with some aspects of reality is specified within a hypothesis or, to use Popper's word, a conjecture, and it is this hypothesis or conjecture which is true or false. Within the semantic conception, there are different ways to conceive this hypothesis or conjecture. I have argued in a previous paper (1990) that the semantic conception is mainly interesting or fruitful, for economics at least, when the relationship is not too close, that is, when sufficient distance is left between the model and the aspect of reality it is related to.

The distance is minimal when, as was the case at the beginning of the semantic conception (with Patrick Suppes in particular), the model is used to define a predicate, say *K* (e.g. 'a Keynesian economy') and when the hypothesis consists in pegging the predicate to some part of the real world, asserting that some part of the real world 'is a *K*' (see, e.g. Hausman, 1981a; and, for a critique of this 'exercise in set theory', Giere, 1988, p. 286, n. 7).

The distance is larger in very different ways in the solutions proposed by van Fraassen (1980), Giere (1985) and Suppe (1989) – three major proponents of the semantic conception. Following van Fraassen, hypotheses would consist in specifying certain parts of models (the empirical substructures) 'as candidates for the direct representation of observable phenomena' (1980, p. 64). In the same essay, I have argued that van Fraassen's solution is unhelpful in economics, if only because all economic hypotheses built up as he suggests would immediately be found to be, as he would say, not 'empirically adequate', that is, in Popperian language, refuted. For Giere (e.g., 1985, p. 80), the form of the relation asserted by the hypothesis is as follows: 'The designated real system is *similar* to the proposed model in specified *respects* and to specific *degrees*' (emphasis in the original). Degrees of approximation are eliminated by Suppe (1989) from the formulation of hypothesis but at the price of a reinterpretation of real ('physical') systems as 'characterisations of how the phenomena would have behaved had the idealised conditions been met' (p. 65).

Combining Giere's interpretation of the relationship as 'similitude in certain respects' with Suppe's interpretation of the real-world objects of scientific conjectures as simpler systems than those found in the actual world gives us as large a distance as we may wish between models and 'aspects of reality' – this, in principle, without driving us to be less concerned with truth and testability.

This expression 'aspects of reality' is vague but essentially on purpose. Mechanisms are candidates to become one specification of its content. Mechanisms then are the objects of hypotheses, conjectures or, for that matter, theories;[10] and these hypotheses, conjectures or theories ascribe properties to mechanisms typically (i.e. not necessarily) by asserting some relationship between these mechanisms and models. They (the hypotheses, etc.) are true or false. I avoid the words 'description' and 'representation', because (cf. the Giere's citation of the hypotheses referred to above) it is unclear that real systems such as mechanisms can always be described, or that models necessarily represent. One can, in particular, refer to some properties of a model – or of a mechanism in a model – and assert that the mechanism in the real world has the same properties, or the same properties in certain respects (this implies no isomorphism between the mechanism in the world and, if there is one, the mechanism in the model). To repeat, the assertion is true or false.

The distinction between mechanisms and models is useful to perceive or understand some aspects of the literature on free riding. I will concentrate on two. First, a point made both by Buchanan (1968) and by Olson (1992), is that the analysis of free riding in the context of games with a small number of players, e.g. in a two-person Prisoner's Dilemma, should be used to understand what happens not in situations in which there are two or a few players but in situations in which there is a very large, almost infinite, number of players (e.g. a 'purely' competitive market). As a rule (outside the very peculiar circumstances depicted in the original story), the real-world relationship between any two persons having the pay-offs supposed in the game – i.e. being 'in' a Prisoner's Dilemma with respect to pay-offs – will be completely different (much more complex) than that supposed in the game. In particular (as a consequence) the dismal outcome predicted by the game will typically not obtain. Only when a large number of people are involved is the model of the two-person Prisoner's Dilemma useful as an analogue.[11]

This point deserves some attention because of the common but mistaken practice of defining a real-world situation as a Prisoner's Dilemma – or, for that matter, as a situation of 'chicken', etc. – on the sole basis of the distribution of the pay-offs, as if at least some of the general game theoretic assumptions of non-cooperative games were not essential conditions for the identification of the situation. To use my own framework, the conjecture defended by Buchanan and by Olson as the only one that they (or anybody else should) make when referring to the Prisoner's Dilemma is that some specified properties of the real-world *mechanism* of free-riding in a large group are the same as some specified properties of the two-person Prisoner's Dilemma *model.* One of the properties of the model is that the collective good will not be produced at all. The conjecture can assert that this outcome will be also the outcome of the real-world mechanism – i.e. it can consist of the 'strong free riding hypothesis' referred to earlier – but, if found inadequate (i.e. false), this could easily be attenuated (along the line suggested by Giere, for instance) or dealt with at a later, empirical stage (see below).

A second aspect of the literature on free riding and collective action which the distinction between mechanisms and models may contribute to clarify is the relation between free riding and rationality. As teachers of microeconomics know, the method which consists in deriving the properties of market demand from a rigorous exposition of the so-called 'theory of the consumer', a specification of the optimising rationality model, has many merits but also a serious drawback. It conveys the impression that the properties of market demand are dependent on the fate of that 'theory of the consumer'. Students must be informed that market demand and its properties are not dependent on the supposition that individuals are rational, especially in the form supposed in the 'theory of the consumer'.[12] As illustrated by its treatment in Green and Shapiro, free riding also is too often discussed simply as an *implication* of 'rational choice theory' while it can stand or fall independently of that. An obvious motive not to contribute to the cost of a non-excludable good is what has been called 'greed' in the literature. Another powerful motive identified by the literature is the fear of being a dupe, a 'sucker'. Now, neither greed (or, for that matter, self-interest), nor the fear or reluctance to be a dupe is dependent on rationality. One can be greedy and irrational (inconsistent, etc.) and the fear of being a dupe is even more likely to be pathologically irrational or the product of a non-consequentialist norm.

In other words, perfect, optimising, rationality is not a property to be sought in real-world mechanisms. Its habitat is the world of models. Why is it so used there? On the whole, the hypotheses which refer to models including optimising rationality as a characteristic are, in some sense or for some reason, 'better' than the hypotheses, if any, which refer to models which do not (this statement is itself in part an empirical conjecture). One reason for this superiority is certainly technical. Models incorporating perfect optimising rationality are particularly convenient, neat, versatile, combinable, performing, etc. *as models* to be employed for the formulation of hypotheses or conjectures – the cost involved in assuming in models a perfect rationality which does not exist in the real world not being as important a counterpart to these benefits as it would be if models were interpreted, as they often are, as asserting something about this real world. Anyhow, and this is a second reason, rationality, albeit not of the kind found in the models (much more imperfect, intermittent, etc.) is not altogether absent from the real world. It *is* a tendency or personality trait of human beings – as is probably also self-interestedness. The real-world existence of this double psychological tendency thus contributes to explain, together with technical convenience, that models in which *perfect*-rationality-cum-self-interest is a characteristic are in general performing instruments for the making of conjectures.

In fact, a major *research strategy* of economists is, and has always been, to ask themselves what would happen if humans were perfectly rational and self-interested, and this strategy has been productive, that is, has led to the discovery of interesting mechanisms. Free riding is a mechanism discovered in this way. Although clearly anticipated by Hume and Wicksell, possibly anticipated by Hegel, etc. it would not have been really noticed or would have remained unheeded if there had been no systematic exploration of the consequences of perfectly rational and self-interested behaviour in various specified theoretical contexts (public goods, etc.). In other words, free riding is a product of the rational choice approach as well as of the use of models. But now that it is here, we must not treat it as being necessarily an implication of that approach or a model.[13]

This last point suggests a more general one concerning the dynamic relationship between models and mechanisms. Simplifying outrageously, we can view rationality-cum-self-interest models as leading to the 'discovery' of the free riding mechanism, the elucidation of this mechanism leading in turn to the construction of increasingly sophisticated models (game theoretic models notably), whose use together with empirical work (see below) leads to substantial change in our perception of the mechanism and/or in the discovery of other mechanisms, involving for instance learning or norms, social and moral. Perhaps I should stress at this point that when I used the word 'discovery' in the last sentence – and also in other parts of this chapter – I do not intend by that to deny that there is something artificial or arbitrary in the carving into particular mechanisms of whatever has been discovered.[14] In other words, there are always alternative ways to arrange our discoveries. This applies to the reality we refer to under the name of 'free riding mechanism' as to any other. I do not think, though, that distinguishing between real-world mechanisms and the models which have led to their discovery becomes unimportant as a consequence.

4 FREE RIDING AS A MENTALLY ISOLATED MECHANISM

Free riding, *by nature*, is particularly likely to be a mechanism which, in the actual world, interacts with other mechanisms and forces and thus needs to be referred to and analysed under a 'method of isolation' (Mäki, 1992). Since the need to isolate matters in one's thought and discourse (the method of 'analysis') is not confined to science but pervasive also in ordinary life, I will refer to it simply as 'mental' isolation. Why 'by nature'? Are not – in the actual, non-experimental world – interactions with other influences the fate of most if not all the aspects, forces or mechanisms science deals with, as several contemporary philosophers have stressed – and, before them, Mill (as documented in particular by Hausman, 1981b; Cartwright, 1989)? What is there – in addition, so to say, to this common fate – which is specific to free riding?

Typically, free riding is also a problem to someone (this is in fact the way it is most often referred to – 'the free riding problem'). Solutions are sought to mitigate the problem. Inasmuch as solutions are found, this means that free riding has been combined with other more powerful devices, forces or mechanisms and that as a consequence it is no more an outcome or phenomenon manifest in the actual world, or at least much less manifest than if it had been left to operate freely. But, understanding the institutions, arrangements or other facts which allow the working of these counteractive mechanisms and thus constitute solutions to the free riding problem is difficult or impossible if we do not take into account the free riding mechanism.[15]

The subjects of Leviathan do not free ride but without free riding there would be no need for a Leviathan (to avoid functionalism, we should say that the free riding mechanism explains why individuals accept Leviathan). In similar fashion, there is not much scope for free riding under the arrangements studied by Ostrom (1990) in the context of common-pool resources, but the free riding mechanism is a major cause of these arrangements.[16]

The fact that free riding is a mentally isolated real-world mechanism raises, however, several serious issues. I will consider three – two in this section and the third in Section 5. First, there is the risk of vacuity. In physics, assertions concerning pure or mentally isolated mechanisms are true or false nonetheless. I agree on this point with Suppe (1989) as well as with Mäki (1994). In economics, however, if we put too many things in the category of disturbing forces or factors, there may be the risk that what remains to be said about our isolated mechanism verges on the tautological or the vacuous. I think that it is a merit of the distinction between real-world mechanisms and constructed models and of the relegation of pure rationality to the world of models (both discussed in the preceding section), that they allow for sufficient flesh to be left on the mentally isolated real-world mechanisms. In the case of free riding, as a result of experimentation (discussed below), this is not wishful thinking or a purely programmatic claim. The acid test relevant to this first issue is whether conjectures about a mentally isolated mechanism remain susceptible of being false: as we shall see shortly, the free riding mechanism meets this test.

A different issue, conditional on our answer to the foregoing question, is: How do we know that a conjecture about the free riding mechanism is false? In other words, a second issue is: Assuming that a conjecture is susceptible of being false, is it testable? Now, I think that the answer to this question should take into account the major revolution in method which is currently taking place in some fields of economics, that is, laboratory experimentation. As a consequence of the extension of the use of experimentation in economics, we should now do what has always been done in some other sciences, such as physics, and distinguish sharply between testing conjectures – or more generally acquiring knowledge – about mentally isolated mechanisms, which takes place mainly in laboratories, and analysing the incidence of these mechanisms on phenomena situated in the actual (de-isolated, or messy) world. There are many parts of economics where this distinction may not be really workable as yet, and where as a consequence the two tasks are to a large extent confused, but I think that it is workable in the case of free riding. This allows me to separate the second issue – whether testing conjectures and acquiring knowledge about the mentally isolated real-world free riding mechanism is possible – from a third issue – what can be known about the influence of this mechanism in various actual-world (i.e. mentally de-isolated) settings (the object of next section).

Testing conjectures *about* the free riding mechanism on non-experimental data is fraught with difficulty (as the discussion in and on Green and Shapiro's (1994) book shows particularly clearly).[17]

Admittedly, in one conspicuous case it seems relatively straightforward. This is when the conjecture at stake is that the individuals in the real-world mechanism behave *exactly* as they do in models built up on the double assumption of perfect optimising rationality and narrow self-interest. If the public good is, say, an interest common to the members of a large group, this conjecture entails the prediction that nobody will contribute, that is, that there will be no mobilisation of the group – except if some 'large' members decide to contribute alone (and thus be exploited by the 'small', free riding members), or if there are positive or negative 'selective incentives' of some sort (see Olson, 1965; Hardin, 1982; Taylor, 1987; Sandler, 1992).

I am tempted to side with Green and Shapiro and agree that this particular conjecture about the free riding mechanism is clearly refuted by one salient fact, the *massive* participation of individuals in elections (the public good involved there is one's preferred side winning and/or the expression of support for democracy).

I am less sure about the other observed phenomena that they consider as equally straightforward (demonstrations, militancy, etc.). As noted by a number of authors, if the theoretical prediction is a corner solution (zero participation), all error or noise will be on the same side, which means that the predicted value of the observation (at least when output is a continuous function of inputs) is necessarily positive. At least 50 per cent participation (in a large number of elections involving a large number of persons) is a solid phenomenon which cannot be accounted for in this way. In many other cases, however, this statistical consideration should be kept in mind, especially if it is combined with other difficulties. When some people contribute and many others do not, a decisive variable, the utility of the public good to the non-contributors, is unobservable and thus it is difficult to say whether their non-contribution is due to free riding or simply (loosely speaking) to utility being inferior to cost. Since there are always some selective incentives around (many of them intangible), it is also difficult to say whether those who do contribute would have done so in the absence of these incentives. Testing the implication that the large members are exploited by the small members looked promising at the beginning (in the 1960s) but has become also uncertain in the course of time.

In any case, how important is the refutation of the 'strong free riding' (i.e. 'perfect free riding') hypothesis ? Who ever believed that so extreme an hypothesis could be true (I resist the temptation to write 'literally true')? These rhetorical questions are clearly related to economics being an inexact science, as explained in Hausman (1992). They were raised already, with regard to a similar kind of refutation, by McCloskey, whose amusing formulation I cannot resist paraphrasing as follows: Even if some econometrician told us, on the basis of some data, that the hypothesis of *perfect* free riding is rejected with 95 per cent confidence, the question would be: Why in an *imperfect* world would it matter that *perfect* free riding is rejected (McCloskey, 1985, p. 157; emphasis in the original; the word replaced by 'free riding' is 'arbitrage')? We all know, by introspection or casual observation, that we and others around us sometimes but not always free ride when it is narrowly rational to do so. The strong free riding hypothesis is too strong. The conjectures needed should fall short of so extreme a prediction.

This is why the bulk of empirical work on free riding, now that the possibility has been opened, should and does take place in the laboratory. Free riding has been the object of a great number of experiments (for a very good survey, see Ledyard, 1995). Within a relatively healthy relationship between theoretical and empirical work, many conjectures about free riding have been formed, tested, validated, rejected, etc. The essential point is that we now know a lot about free riding that we did not know some decades ago, and we are learning new aspects of it all the time (this does not mean that we know all there is to know, of course). The mechanism of free riding is becoming progressively less opaque if not as yet nearly elucidated. Thanks to the isolation provided by experimentation, Buchanan's and Olson's already mentioned objections to the use of games such as the Prisoner's Dilemma in the setting of small-group relationships are put in a new perspective: it is possible to arrange experiments in such a way that many of the conditions (not only the pay-offs, but also, for instance, the absence of communication) stipulated in a game are approximated. When this is done, it is not untypical to observe that about half of the participants free ride and half of them do not. This can be considered as a refutation of the strong free riding hypothesis. However, a very important and robust result is that, when the game is repeated, free riding (as a proportion) increases. A possible explanation is that, in the free riding mechanism, the fear or reluctance to be a dupe dominates over greediness. To some extent, this in turn can be tested by proper arrangements (one's contributions made conditional on that of others, etc.). Another possibility is that participants are ignorant and learn. Again, this can be tested and a tentative result is that 'kindness' survives the dissipation of 'confusion' (Andreoni, 1995).

The literature on experiments is so fascinating that one is tempted to linger over their results. The foregoing sample is, I think, sufficient to justify my claim that the free riding mechanism can be isolated mentally without becoming vacuous and that we are learning fast about its content (we are progressively discovering, in the words of Salmon (1984) quoted in Section 2, the 'causal laws' which govern the 'causal processes' and 'causal interactions' making up the mechanism). That the material isolation is imperfect, that some results are unstable, that the particulars of the models on which the conjectures are based distort or reduce the significance of the results are difficulties which should be neither glossed over nor overestimated. Similar complications are found in other disciplines.

5 RE-EXPORTING KNOWLEDGE OF FREE RIDING TO THE ACTUAL WORLD

This third issue raised by the analysis of free riding as a mentally isolated mechanism is in a way the most delicate one. After all, as economists, we are not seeking knowledge about the free riding mechanism independently of the question of how this mechanism influences matters in the actual (de-isolated) world, in interaction or combination with other mechanisms. What are the characteristics of this interaction or combination is a question close to what I will call Mill's problem – i.e. how do tendencies combine? – studied again by contemporary philosophy (see especially Cartwright, 1989). I have nothing particular to contribute to the discussion of this very difficult question. Instead, I would be inclined to argue that for three reasons, or in three ways (all related to the development of experimental economics just discussed), it can be in part evaded.

Let us assume that we have established the existence of and learned a lot about the mechanism of free riding when it is isolated. First, I think (following Bhaskar, 1975) that we are, metaphysically or ontologically, entitled to say, *without additional testing*, that the free riding mechanism also operates, in conjunction with other mechanisms, in the actual world. But, from our knowledge of the mechanism when isolated, we can probably say a little more, without entering into the details of Mill's problem. Free riding will tend to be more important in large groups than in small ones, when the stakes are high rather than a trifle, when people are mutually anonymous rather than known or visible, etc. This should be assumed to carry over to non-experimental settings.[18] Similarly, a general result is that in most experiments, the order of magnitude of free riding, as measured against the optimum, turns out to be somewhere between, say, 30 and 70 per cent and that very often (as already noted) it is close to 50 per cent (see Ledyard, 1995). This kind of knowledge is enough, I submit, to consider as reasonable the unquantified assertion that free riding is also an important force in actual, non-experimental settings. And thus it is also enough, for instance, to contradict a number of claims made by Green and Shapiro. Although they are right to note that measuring the influence or incidence of free riding in the actual world is difficult or uncertain, this does not entail, as they claim or suggest, that the widespread assertion of a very substantial influence or incidence of free riding on group mobilisation, voter participation, production of public goods in general or institutional arrangements is groundless. To use a typically Popperian expression, experiments do provide us with *good reasons* to make that assertion.

My second reason is based on the observation that the situation that we discuss is not very different from those typically encountered in the other sciences. Mechanisms are studied in the laboratory and it is the task of *applied* science or technology (meteorology, etc.) to use the knowledge acquired there to improve the explanation and prediction of the phenomena of the actual world, in an instrumental perspective. Typically, 'low-level' regularities, established, with methods that non-Popperians would call inductive, in close contact and interaction with non-experimental or technological data, are most helpful for the fulfilment of that task. But theoretical knowledge plays a role also. In economics, we are not used to viewing the separation between basic science and applied science in this way. We tend to think that basic science is purely theoretical – that is, unconcerned with empirical testing. I think that experimental economics, where it applies, will bring the discipline closer to the physical science in this respect. Basic research, not directly concerned with the actual world, will be much more related than it is now with the manipulation of data, albeit of a mainly experimental kind. Applied research, i.e. research more directly concerned with actual world problems, will also rely on experiments. The difference between the two kinds of experiments will be related to differences in the problems raised at the two levels. As in physics or biology, we will have to accept that the relationship between the analyses and results of one branch and those of the other will not always be smooth or continuous (as stressed notably by Cartwright, 1983).

The third reason I have to be optimistic about the possibility of eschewing Mill's combination problem is that free riding can enter empirical work on non-experimental data in a more roundabout and less problematic way than the one suggested by this problem. Let me again assume that we have a relatively well corroborated prediction of the kind 'under isolation, and in a wide range of circumstances (repeated interaction, one-shot encounters, small pay-offs, large pay-offs, etc.), free riding will typically range between 30 per cent and 70 per cent of the contributions that would have obtained if there had been no free riding'. This might appear as perfectly useless for the purpose of empirical work on non-experimental data. But it is not: in exactly this form, it can be valuable as a relatively plausible or realistic (but untested) assumption in more encompassing theories or conjectures and it is these theories or conjectures which will be confronted to nonexperimental data.

An example is Iannaccone's analysis of religions and sects (1992). It is sufficient for his purpose that, if nothing was done, some percentage of the membership of a sect would free ride, that is, not participate in all the ceremonies, and this would make these ceremonies less attractive for those who do attend (there are 'positive returns to participatory crowding'); to avoid free riding of that kind, sects implement the 'bizarre behavioural restrictions' for which they are best known (stigma, etc.). A number of empirical predictions are derived from the analysis and tested. In this case, as well as in similar ones, the theory itself makes free riding self-effacing as an actual phenomenon (i.e. free riding is predicted not to be an outcome), but the hypothesis of its existence as a mentally isolated mechanism receives indirect empirical support from the fact that it served as a component of a theory which was itself tested successfully.

Similarly, the mere knowledge that mobilisation of a large group will always be difficult or uncertain is about enough for Olson (1982) to claim that at some point of time some interest groups (i.e. categories) will be organised while others will remain 'latent', and also that, in the course of time, there will be a tendency for an increasing number of groups to be organised. These claims then serve as ingredients or inputs in Olson's theory of growth and the theory itself gets tested (see Mueller, 1983). Whether this theory (or, for that matter, Iannaccone's) is corroborated is largely irrelevant to the methodological point that I am trying to make.

6 CONCLUDING REMARKS

Experimentation has played a large role in my arguments. It is clearly important in the case of free riding and it strengthens the case for mechanisms. I do not claim that either experiments or mechanisms are equally important in all areas of economics. Experimentation is generally interesting, however, also because it introduces a useful complication in the debate between empiricism and its adversaries. It opens the possibility that many hypotheses can be tested empirically, as the empiricists recommend, but only in artificial environments. With regard to the actual, non-experimental, world these hypotheses remain, however, disappointing to the empiricist. They are useful to understand and to explain but not (directly) to predict (they may, though, be useful as ingredients in other, predictive, hypotheses). Seen the other way round, the availability of experimentation means that hypotheses which were considered as untestable, and thus perhaps unscientific, become testable. The whole methodological debate in economics is very much conditioned by the assumption that the discipline is a non-experimental science (and not one benefiting from particularly favourable circumstances like astronomy). That this assumption is becoming less warranted should be taken into account.

Notes

1. I wish to express my gratitude to Alain Wolfelsperger. Some of his detailed and thoughtful observations and suggestions on earlier versions of this chapter have shaped, or have had a profound influence on, several parts of this version; I keep in mind the other suggestions and reflections for future work, perhaps pursued in common. For very helpful comments also, I am grateful to participants in the IEA Conference, especially Roger Backhouse, Nancy Cartwright, Daniel Hausman, Maurice Lagueux, Uskali Mäki, Andrea Salanti and Stefano Zamagni. I am, of course, solely responsible for all the errors and shortcomings which remain or which have emerged in the revisions.
2. My main excuse for venturing amateurishingly into as difficult a subject as contemporary philosophy of science is that keeping away altogether from it might be even more perilous, at least with regard to some of the methodological issues I, as an economist, am concerned with. In addition, I must stress that my objective is limited. I have no desire to interfere in philosophical discussions about, say, causality. As in previous work, my concern is economics, not philosophy, and my main motivation is unabashedly apologetic, based on the conviction that, given the subject matter, the approach characteristic of mainstream economics, although puzzling,

is methodologically correct – or, perhaps more exactly, cannot be shown to be methodologically wrong.

3. Ledyard (1995) and Wolfelsperger (1995) claim that this should prevent us in particular from using the word 'free riding' in the context of the Prisoner's Dilemma. But see n. 16 below.
4. See, e.g. Booth (1985), Grossman and Hart (1980), Hardin (1982), Iannaccone (1992), Keohane (1984), Ostrom (1990), Rawls (1971), Sandler (1992), Sugden (1982), Taylor (1987).
5. Green and Shapiro in particular underestimate the dynamics of argumentation or the heuristic effects of an analysis of collective action such as the one proposed in Olson's book (1965). Before 1965 the presumption was that all groups got organised. The questions were then: Why do not these particular groups succeed in organising themselves? What are the obstacles to their mobilisation? After 1965, the puzzle was: How the devil has this group or category managed to mobilise in spite of the free rider problem? A large literature on rationality and revolution, for instance, is entirely devoted to this problem. Similarly, since the seminal article of Grossman and Hart (1980) a question which has attracted a lot of interest in finance is: Why do takeovers work or even exist, in spite of the rationality of free riding on the part of the small shareholders of the attacked firm? Since I have very much insisted on this aspect of research in previous work (1976, 1994; Mingat *et al.*, 1985), I will not allude to it in the remainder of this chapter.
6. Because Shapiro did in a previous book (1990), I am surprised that Green and Shapiro do not cite at least Bhaskar. The reason may be related to the fact that Bhaskar himself and an economist like Tony Lawson (1994) who uses Bhaskar's philosophy, see themselves, and are seen by others, as supplying arguments against the orthodox or mainstream in general, against neoclassical or mainstream economics in particular. Neither they nor Shapiro are apparently aware that Bhaskar's views about science (as exposed in his first book) can also be used, at least in part, to elucidate the difficult relationship between neoclassical or mainstream economic theory – or more generally the rational choice programme in social science – and empirical data.
7. I have argued elsewhere (e.g. 1994; see also Mingat *et al.*, 1985) that economics has always been based on the presupposition that more or less 'hidden' or deep-seated mechanisms – or interactions, processes, etc. – underlie and explain what we observe in the actual world. Whether we consider Smith, Say, Ricardo, Marx, Marshall or, in this century, Keynes, Franco Modigliani and Robert Lucas, the aim of the analysis is of the same nature: some underlying mechanisms are essential, taking them into consideration will lead to unexpected results, and neglecting them will entail serious mistakes, in both cases at the level of the actual phenomena – which should be of some interest to all (even to those who care only about this level). In addition – this time to the non-instrumentalist subset of the profession only – these mechanisms or interactions are fascinating in themselves, independently of their implications in the actual world. A position such as Green and Shapiro's or Blaug's is not incompatible in principle with the presupposition that mechanisms are essential but it may

be incompatible in practice if the actual world is more messy than they suppose. We must certainly try to test all our hypotheses. At the same time, we must remain free to speculate on possible aspects of the world even when we cannot support empirically these speculations (this justifies the claim that mainstream economics is largely a critical science, as argued in my 1994 paper).

8. E.g.: 'No market test is likely to discriminate between human capital and screening explanations, because the question is not whether schooling explains earnings but rather why it does. It would be difficult to find a better example of the difference between merely predicting a result and explaining it by a convincing causal mechanism' (Blaug, 1980, p. 216).
9. I am not concerned with the structuralist branch of the semantic conception as analysed in Hands (1985). For a particularly clear explication of the non-linguistic character of models in the semantic conception of theories (including what he calls 'theoretical models'), see Giere (1988, Chapter 3).
10. I do not really make distinctions between 'hypothesis', 'conjecture' and 'theory'. But, alternatively, a theory can be interpreted as including the description or specification of a model (or of a population of models) in addition to the assertion of the relationship of this model (or these models) with some part of reality (see Giere, 1988, pp. 84–5). In both cases, a theory, like a conjecture or an hypothesis, is true or false (Giere downplays the importance of that property, but I do not).
11. 'In the original parable', Olson notes, the two prisoners are 'denied communication with one another – and also the possibility of utilising any of the manifold possibilities for making mutually advantageous deals that human ingenuity and social institutions normally supply' (p. x). 'In a sufficiently large or latent group . . . the incentive for strategic interaction – and even the incentive to bargain with other potential beneficiaries of the good – disappears' (p. xv).
12. In turn, the fruitfulness of the partial equilibrium model of demand and supply, focusing on equilibrium, hides the existence in the mind of the economists who use it of a quasi-sociological, unformalised, theory of competitive price adjustments in markets (a theory which is more concerned with processes than with equilibrium). It is largely because of the existence of the latter that there is much confidence in or acceptance of the former. But that they present models in the shadow, so to say, of looser theories is rarely said by contemporary economists. For a development of this argument, see Salmon and Wolfelsperger (1991, pp. 4–6).
13. As a research strategy it can remain fruitful to stick to rationality in spite of apparently contradictory evidence, as has been done, for instance, in the context of agricultural development.
14. A transcendental reality was discovered by Columbus, or some navigators before him, but that it is one America or continent is not transcendental but perfectly human and to a large extent arbitrary.
15. If we gloss over our distinction between mechanisms and models, the same idea is expressed by Peter Ordeshook (1986) as follows:

    Often we might not find prisoners' dilemmas in a specific situation or institution because certain rules or traditions evolve to avoid them. But this absence of dilemmas does not make an understanding of their logic less relevant, because the only way to understand why such rules and traditions persist is to discern the dilemmas that arise without them. (p. 235, emphasis in the original)

16. In the context of a static *model*, especially one in which there is perfect rationality and foresight, a better formulation might be to say that it is the potential for free riding or the fear of free riding which explains, etc. In the real world, however, it is more plausible that free riding will be experienced rather than anticipated and thus more clearly the cause of the institutions which make it disappear (as an outcome). The beggar-my-neighbour policies of the inter-war period, a form of free riding, are a major cause of post-war arrangements such as Bretton Woods or the IMF. Wolfelsperger (1995) considers only models, but if he did not, a similar argument might apply to his objections against the use of the term 'free riding' itself.
17. I do not count as proper tests the retroductive achievements implicit in the understanding (discussed in the text) of the actual institutions and other arrangements whose *raison d'être* is to counter free riding.
18. I put the stress here on features that seem sufficiently robust across experimental settings to be exportable also to the actual, non-experimental world. This is related to what Ferejohn and Satz (1995) write about the universalism which should characterise mechanisms: 'Explanations, as distinguished from descriptions, identify causal mechanisms that are held to apply across all relevantly similar contexts. Causal mechanisms are universalistic in that they can be represented independently of situations in which they are supposed to obtain' (p. 74). For a related discussion, see Cartwright (1994).

References

Andreoni, J. (1995) 'Cooperation in Public-goods Experiments: Kindness or Confusion?', *American Economic Review*, vol. 85, no. 4 (September), pp. 891–904.

Bhaskar, R. (1975) *A Realist Theory of Science*, 2nd edn 1978 (Eastbourne: Harvester Press).

Blaug, M. (1980) *The Methodology of Economics: Or How Economists Explain*, 2nd edn 1992 (Cambridge: Cambridge University Press).

Booth, A.L. (1985) 'The Free Rider Problem and a Social Custom Model of Trade Union Membership', *Quarterly Journal of Economics* (February), pp. 253–61.

Breton, A. (1996) *Competitive Governments: An Economic Theory of Politics and Public Finance* (Cambridge and New York: Cambridge University Press).

Brubaker, E.R. (1975) 'Free Ride, Free Revelation, or Golden Rule?', *Journal of Law and Economics*, vol. 18 (April), pp. 147–61.

Buchanan, J.M. (1968) *The Demand and Supply of Public Goods* (Chicago: Rand–McNally).

Cartwright, N. (1983) *How the Laws of Physics Lie* (Oxford: Oxford University Press).

——— (1989) *Nature's Capacities and their Measurement* (Oxford: Clarendon Press).

——— (1994) 'Mill and Menger: Ideal Elements and Stable Tendencies', in Bert Hamminga and Neil B. De Marchi (eds), *Idealization VI: Idealization in Economics* (Poznan Studies in the Philosophy of the Sciences and the Humanities, vol. 38) (Amsterdam and Atlanta: Rodopi), pp. 171–88.

Elster, J. (1989) *Nuts and Bolts for the Social Sciences* (Cambridge and New York: Cambridge University Press).

Ferejohn, J. and D. Satz (1995) 'Unification, Universalism, and Rational Choice Theory', *Critical Review*, vol. 9 (Winter–Spring), pp. 71–84.

Giere, R.N. (1985) 'Constructive Realism', in Paul M. Churchland and Clifford W. Hooker (eds), *Images of Science* (Chicago: University of Chicago Press), pp. 75–98.

——— (1988) *Explaining Science: A Cognitive Approach* (Chicago: University of Chicago Press).

Green, D.P. and I. Shapiro (1994) *Pathologies of Rational Choice Theory: A Critique of Applications in Political Science* (New Haven and London: Yale University Press).

——— (1995) 'Pathologies Revisited: Reflections on our Critics', *Critical Review*, vol. 9 (Winter–Spring), pp. 235–76.

Grossman, S.J. and O.D. Hart (1980) 'Takeover Bids, the Free-rider Problem, and the Theory of the Corporation', *Bell Journal of Economics*, vol. 11 (Spring), pp. 42–64.

Hands, D.W. (1985) 'The Structuralist View of Economic Theories', *Economics and Philosophy*, vol. 1, no. 2, pp. 303–35.

Hardin, R. (1982) *Collective Action* (Baltimore, MD: Johns Hopkins University Press).

Hausman, D.M. (1981a) *Capital, Profits and Prices: An Essay in the Philosophy of Economics* (New York: Columbia University Press).

——— (1981b) 'John Stuart Mill's Philosophy of Economics', *Philosophy of Science*, 48, pp. 363–85; reprinted in *Essays on Philosophy and Economic Methodology* (Cambridge and New York: Cambridge University Press, 1992), pp. 33–53.

——— (1992) *The Inexact and Separate Science of Economics* (Cambridge and New York: Cambridge University Press).

Hirschman, A.O. (1982) *Shifting Involvements: Private Interest and Public Action* (Princeton: Princeton University Press).

Humphreys, P. (1991) 'Review of John Elster's 'Nuts and Bolts for the Social Sciences', *Philosophy of the Social Sciences*, vol. 21 (March), pp. 114–21.

Iannaccone, L.R. (1992) 'Sacrifice and Stigma: Reducing Free-riding in Cults, Communes, and Other Collectives', *Journal of Political Economy*, vol. 100 (2), pp. 271–91.

Johansen, L. (1977) 'The Theory of Public Goods: Misplaced Emphasis?', *Journal of Public Economics*, vol. 7, pp. 147–52.

Keohane, R.O. (1984) *After Hegemony: Cooperation and Discord in the World Political Economy* (Princeton: Princeton University Press).

Koertge, N. (1992) 'Explanation and its Problems', *The British Journal for the Philosophy of Science*, vol. 43 (1), pp. 85–98.

Lawson, T. (1994) 'A Realist Theory for Economics', in Roger E. Backhouse (ed.), *New Directions in Economic Methodology* (London and New York: Routledge), pp. 257–85.

Ledyard, J.O. (1995) 'Public Goods: A Survey of Experimental Research', in J.H. Kagel and A. Roth (eds), *The Handbook of Experimental Economics* (Princeton: Princeton University Press), pp. 111–94.

McCloskey, D.N. (1985) *The Rhetoric of Economics* (Madison: University of Wisconsin Press); British edn (Brighton: Wheatsheaf Books–Harvester Press, 1986).

McMillan, J. (1979) 'The Free-rider Problem: A Survey', *The Economic Record*, vol. 55 (June), pp. 95–107.

Mäki, U. (1992) 'On the Method of Isolation in Economics', in Craig Dilworth (ed.), *Idealization IV: Intelligibility in Science* (Poznan Studies in the Philosophy of the Sciences and the Humanities, vol. 26) (Amsterdam and Atlanta: Rodopi), pp. 317–51.

——— (1994) 'Isolation, Idealization and Truth in Economics', in B. Hamminga and N.B. De Marchi (eds), *Idealization VI: Idealization in Economics* (Poznan Studies in the Philosophy of the Sciences and the Humanities, vol. 38) (Amsterdam and Atlanta: Rodopi), pp. 147–68.

Mingat, A., P. Salmon and A. Wolfelsperger (1985) *Méthodologie économique* (Paris: Presses Universitaires de France).

Mueller, D.C. (ed.) (1983) *The Political Economy of Growth* (New Haven: Yale University Press).

Olson, M. (1965) *The Logic of Collective Action: Public Goods and the Theory of Groups*, 2nd. edn (1971) (Cambridge, MA: Harvard University Press).

——— (1982) *The Rise and Decline of Nations: Economic Growth, Stagflation, and Social Rigidities* (New Haven: Yale University Press).

——— (1992) 'Foreword' to Sandler (1992), pp. vii–xvi.

Ordeshook, P.C. (1986) *Game Theory and Political Theory: An Introduction* (Cambridge and New York: Cambridge University Press).

Ostrom, E. (1990) *Governing the Commons: The Evolution of Institutions for Collective Action* (Cambridge and New York: Cambridge University Press).

Rawls, J. (1971) *A Theory of Justice* ((Cambridge, MA: Harvard University Press).

Salmon, P. (1976) 'La méthode hypothético-déductive et les raisonnements en termes de "comme si" en économique', *Revue d'Economie Politique*, vol. 86 (September–October), pp. 765–94.

——— (1990) 'La conception sémantique des théories et le contenu empirique de la théorie économique', in *La méthodologie de l'économie théorique et appliquée aujourd'hui* (Paris: Editions Nathan), pp. 102–10.

——— (1994) 'Outrageous Arguments in Economics and Public Choice', *European Journal of Political Economy*, vol. 10 (September), pp. 409–26.

Salmon, P. and A. Wolfelsperger (1991) 'From Competitive Equilibrium to Democratic Equilibrium: Has the Analogy been Fruitful?', *Papers in Political Economy* (Political Economy Research Group, University of Western Ontario, London, Canada), 16 (July).

Salmon, W.C. (1984) *Scientific Explanation and the Causal Structure of the World* (Princeton: Princeton University Press).
Sandler, T. (1992) *Collective Action: Theory and Applications* (Ann Arbor: The University of Michigan Press).
Shapiro, I. (1990) *Political Criticism* (Berkeley: University of California Press).
Stinchcombe, A.L. (1991) 'The Conditions of Fruitfulness of Theorizing about Mechanisms in Social Science', *Philosophy of the Social Sciences*, vol. 21 (September), pp. 367–88.
Sugden, R. (1982) 'On the Economics of Philanthropy', *The Economic Journal*, vol. 92 (June), pp. 341–50.
Suppe, F. (1989) *The Semantic Conception of Theories and Scientific Realism* (Urbana and Chicago: University of Illinois Press).
Taylor, M. (1987) *The Possibility of Cooperation* (Cambridge: Cambridge University Press).
van Fraassen, B.C. (1980) *The Scientific Image* (Oxford: Clarendon Press).
Wolfelsperger, A. (1995) *Economie publique* (Paris: Presses Universitaires de France).

Comment: Free Riders, Altruists and Rationality

Stefano Zamagni
UNIVERSITY OF BOLOGNA, ITALY

1 INTRODUCTION

Pierre Salmon's Chapter 2 is a peculiar one. It blends in a remarkable manner the philosophical and epistemological dimension of economic discourse with its substantive dimension. In a sense, it represents a good example of that relatively new tendency which sees a growing number of scholars of economics and philosophy discussing themes which are of common interest, proposing new lines of research and establishing new grounds for debate. This renewed interest comes after several decades during which the two disciplines, once quite close one to the other, developed separately, isolated one from the other. I read Salmon's chapter as a very interesting contribution to bridging the gap which still remains in many quarters of the profession, or as a good answer to the old question of whether philosophy and economics should proceed independent of each other. I maintain that the best response to that old question is the one furnished by the English historian T.S. Ashton[1] in a debate on the use of alternative methods in historical research: 'It is like discussing whether it is better to move ahead by walking with one foot or the other. People with two feet find it easier to move forward more rapidly with both'.

In view of the above, I find it disquieting that Salmon writes: 'I have no desire to interfere in philosophical discussions about, say, causality. As in previous work, my concern is economics, not philosophy, and my main motivation is unabashedly apologetic, based on the conviction that, given the subject matter, the approach characteristic of mainstream economics, although puzzling, is methodologically correct' (n. 2, p. 81). In this Comment, I intend to show that the case study chosen by Salmon, i.e. free-riding as a mechanism, does not warrant such a separation, so much so that his own prose constitutes a clear evidence of a philosophically oriented economic discourse. I will also take the opportunity to throw some doubts about the methodological correctness of mainstream economics.

2 THE CONCEPT OF FREE RIDING

To begin with, let us remind ourselves how Salmon defines the concept of free riding as a mechanism in the sense of Wesley Salmon: 'I will define the free riding mechanism as being any set of processes and interactions in a group of individuals which, if operating freely and alone, will lead *many* of these individuals to decide, *because* of the non-excludability property of a good, not to contribute to its provision . . . even if the consequence is that the good will not be provided at all' (p. 68). In other words, in free ridership interactions, there is a cooperative outcome yielding high benefits for all and yet it is not achieved or it is not achievable because every individual has the incentive to defect. This seems strange since the resulting mutual defection produces low benefits for all. Whence the attraction of the *n*-person version of the Prisoners' Dilemma, as Olson wrote in 1965. Salmon then passes to characterise free riding in terms of – among other things – two elements: its being a social mechanism rather than a psychological one and the claim according to which it is enough to define free riding and not to elucidate it. Before proceeding to the main point of this comment, let me pause to consider these two elements.

Is mere plurality of agents sufficient for making the mechanism social? I do not think so. The numbers problem is central to many areas of social sciences. In the present context, the relevant question which one should try to answer is: How do numbers affect the likelihood of cooperation? In fact, since free riding is best seen as an impediment to cooperation in the provision of public goods and since cooperation requires – as is well known – trust, one needs to know whether, as the number of agents increases, trust relations become more or less difficult. It is not easy to answer such a question, as the most recent literature on the topic has shown.[2] In any case, it is not enough to count the number of individuals involved in the process; we need a theory or, at least, a theoretical argument. For example, as the number of agents increases, the feasibility of sanctioning defectors diminishes, which creates the possibility of free riding. By the way, this brings me to observe that – contrary to what Salmon seems to believe – the mere existence of an 'authority, formal or informal, . . . endowed with the power to impose taxes or other contributions to users or potential users of the goods' (p. 63) is no guarantee that the free riding is made technically impossible. The power to impose taxes is not the same thing as the power to be able to get taxes paid.

What about Salmon's assertion that 'elucidating the free riding mechanism is a scientific, not a methodological endeavour'? Salmon is content with defining it; he does not want to elucidate the idea of free riding mechanism. However, he indicates possible motives to free ride. It follows that if motives are part of the free riding mechanism and if mechanisms are sets of causal processes, then either one considers motives as causal processes – which is rather difficult to accept – or one has no other alternative but to elucidate the notion of free riding. A specific reason explaining the importance of elucidation is that, as Sen (1989) clarified a formal definition can be extremely precise without being at all a precise representation of the underlying concept to be captured. In fact, if that concept is surrounded by a penumbra of ambiguity, then pretending a precise definition calls for capturing that ambiguity rather than replacing it by some different concept. This is why elucidation is, in these situations, a necessity.

Trying another angle of attack, we know that in many economic situations the agents know quite well how to reach a definite goal. For example, if the target is to attain efficiency, the marginal cost pricing rule is the mechanism adhering to which the target can be achieved. However, as the modern theory of implementation has shown, it is not sufficient to discover or to find out a feasible mechanism; what is necessary is to check whether such a mechanism is also compatible with the 'natural incentives of the participants' (Ledyard, 1987, p. 739) in the process. So, if the goal is the provision of a public good, a Lindahl pricing mechanism would be feasible and successful if individuals followed its rules. But it would not be successful since the mechanism is not incentive-compatible, i.e. since agents would have an incentive to free ride on others provision of that good. However, how do we know that free riding is a 'natural incentive of the participants'? This question brings me to the main point of this Comment. For the time being, I think one can safely conclude that it is not possible to understand free riding as a Salmonian mechanism unless the mechanism is, in one way or another, elucidated.

3 A REAL UNDERLYING MECHANISM

The central idea developed by Pierre Salmon is that if free riding has become so important to economic reasoning – and by extension to social science – it is because it is not a descriptive assumption or a factual prediction. Rather, it is because it is a real underlying mechanism. Salmon carefully distinguishes between real and actual entities. Not everything which is real becomes always actual: a real mechanism can be counterbalanced and even reduced to impotence by other mechanisms or forces. Indeed, Salmon is well aware of the fact that in the actual world, the free riding mechanism can be mitigated or neutralised by selective inducements such as moral sentiments, social norms, coercion and so on. It follows that free riding is often unrealistic in the sense that it is not always the case that it gets actualised; however, it is important since its existence at the deeper level plays a fundamental role in explaining the emergence of these social norms or the flourishing of these moral sentiments or the enforcement of coercive measures. 'But, understanding the institutions, arrangements or other facts which allow the working of these counteractive mechanisms and thus constitute solutions to the free riding problem is difficult or impossible if we do not take into account the free riding mechanism'.

It seems to me that this argument can be accepted only if one is ready to accept, as an ontological assumption, the notion of rationality as maximisation of self-interest. As Sen (1987, 1989) has convincingly shown, mainstream economics has two main and distinct interpretations of its concept of rationality: internal consistency and the maximisation of self-interest, the former being a procedural request without any substantive content as to what is being pursued; the latter being a substantive command to stick only to a particular class of goals – i.e. self-interested ones – without inducing a rigid procedural structure. Now, only if one starts from the premise of self-interested behaviour does it make sense to consider free riding as a 'natural incentive of the participants' to the provision of a public good. For instance, why join a union when, even if you do not join, you will still benefit from any wage increases or reduction of the working day which the union negotiates? A general altruistic concern for the welfare of others may provide a sufficient reason for people not to defect on the cooperative arrangement.

Indeed, it can be proved[3] that when there are sufficient numbers of Kantian agents, the free riding problem is, in many realistic situations, solved. The results stemming from the available experimental evidence – according to which cooperative behaviour tends to be observed more often than it should be on the basis of the standard model of self-interested behaviour – suggest that altruism might be an important motivating factor for agents, at least in certain circumstances. This seems to indicate that the standard paradigm of self-interest may have a self-fulfilling nature: the exposed subjects are brought to perceive self-interest as a *normative* characterisation of rational behaviour and to act accordingly. Thus, rather paradoxically, one could conclude that the takeover of the self-interest paradigm might induce an inefficient social convention in which cooperative deals become harder to enforce than they might otherwise be.

It is certainly true that the idea of linking a richer notion of rational agency with the 'spontaneous' solution of free riding requires a deep breach with the instrumental rationality model of action – which poses some delicate problems. However, this is not incompatible with free riding as a Salmonian mechanism. It follows that the statement: 'the free riding mechanism connects a fact to which we give the status of a cause, the non-excludability of a good, with another fact, which we consider as its effect, i.e. many individuals deciding not to contribute to the provision of the good' (p. 68) is incomplete as a definition of the free riding mechanism. To the non-excludability of a good, it should be added, as a cause, self-interested behaviour. Absent this second fact, the mechanism will not produce its presumed effect.

The above brings me to a general remark. I do believe that the opposition between moral sentiments, such as altruism, and reason is deleterious since it counters a part of ourselves to ourselves, giving to rationality an 'imperative' twist and negating to it the energy generated by moral sentiments. This constitutes a waste of intellectual resources, indeed. It is not efficient to allow that a rigid notion of rationality be let alone to combat a world of sentiments conceived as something negative by itself. Why should economics leave the area of moral sentiments completely to the adversaries of rationality? Since Plato onwards, the idea of sentiments as a support of knowledge has always played an important role in scientific endeavour. Rationality needs motivations and these motivations include self-interest; but, as the etymology reminds us, *inter esse* just means 'to stay in between'. Economics has a lot to gain by using the notion of interest as cement (*inter esse*) between the general rule and the individuals taking part or being part of something.

4 EXISTENCE AND STRUCTURE OF MECHANISMS

One final remark about Salmon's core thesis according to which it is a naive ambition to construct an economic model which is able to generate empirically testable implications because theorising and testability lie on different logical levels. Specifically, Salmon argues that the proper role of models is that of pointing out the existence of *per se* unobservable forces which, although lacking observable proxies, may be needed to justify why certain phenomena are observed. The example of the strong free riding assumption is a good case in point: if there is a generalised incentive to free ride in the production of a public good, none of the public good will be produced; on the other hand, if we do observe that a certain level of the public good is produced and if we notice that such production seems to be connected with the existence of a particular set of social institutions (e.g. institutions that make provision of the public good observable to all and give higher social status to contributors), we can conclude that these institutions are there precisely to prevent the emergence of free riding. In other words, even if free riding as such (in its extreme formulation) is not directly observable, it is a necessary theoretical ingredient to understand what are the observable factors that permit the survival of behaviours which *do not contemplate* free riding.

If this is the case, how can we learn about the existence and structure of mechanisms? In this respect, Salmon points out the potential importance of experimental research – i.e. the observation of causal processes under prepared and controlled conditions. In the case of free riding, for example, experimental research has been able to isolate a series of characteristics of the causal processes which are at work when decision makers face a *pure* problem of public provision under non-excludability – a situation which is seldom if ever met in real situations where such mechanism interacts in a non-identifiable way with a number of other parallel mechanisms. It is *in vitro* knowledge which can be gathered in the laboratory that allows us to recognise and isolate the action of the various mechanisms in actual situations where they interact in a 'messy' way.

The previous considerations do not imply of course that theoretical models *must not* commit to specific interpretations of a causal mechanism; simply, they need not. But then, if we can certainly agree with Salmon when he claims that 'perfect, optimising rationality is not a property to be sought in real-world mechanisms. Its habitat is the world of models' (p. 72) with all the due implications of such a claim, still we cannot refrain from asking, say, how encompassing self-interested optimisation (or any other behavioural paradigm) is as useful a theoretical category (i.e. as a working explanatory parable for a variety of different real-world processes). In other words, the crucial issue raised by Salmon's approach is the following. Speaking of a mechanism without making any commitment on the specific nature of the forces at work (psychological, social, etc.) implies that there are forces of different nature which bring about certain outcomes starting from certain premises in an analogous way; if this were not the case, we could never speak of a 'free rider mechanism' but should rather speak of self-interested behaviour, norm compliance, social conformity, etc. as distinct mechanisms, each leading (if ever) to an idiosyncratic form of free riding, i.e. free riding under own specific conditions and provisions.

In the free riding context, speaking of a mechanism *tout court* means that equivalent examples of free riding behaviour can be obtained under the action of social as well as psychological forces; if processes of a different nature generated different outcomes starting from the same premises then the very notion of a mechanism would lose its usefulness. In principle, Salmon might be right, but he does not seem to provide enough argument and evidence on this crucial point. Coming to his actual argument, it is hardly questionable that one of the main messages of the experimental literature on social dilemma problems such as the standard two-person Prisoner's Dilemma predicts that a share of the experimental population between 30 and 70 per cent is likely to contribute according to cases, but this is clearly not enough to conclude that some all-encompassing mechanism of the sort Salmon has in mind is at work here. To be specific, suppose that a more careful scrutiny of this literature reveals that both under the careful elicitation of social pressure conditions and under the equally careful elicitation of emphatic identification the rate of contribution lies in the above-mentioned range but, in addition, it turns out that in the first case the rate of contribution is *permanently* higher than in the second. Can we conclude that the two situations are different instances of a common mechanism or should we rather qualify our prediction according to the specific nature of the forces shaping individual decisions? If the latter is the case, the 'mental isolation strategy' suggested by Salmon, i.e. tracing the emergence of observable phenomena to the combined action of various basic mechanisms whose properties have been characterised in the artificial experimental environment, loses much of its strength. But then the key to sensible theorising rather goes the other way, i.e. toward a close mapping of the *actual* characteristics of (and in particular a successful identification of the relevant forces at work in) the empirical situation that is being investigated.

One could sum up the previous discussion by saying that the real implication of Salmon's method is that of providing simple one-way causal explanations of observable phenomena like economic institutions by means of mechanisms. The rival thesis that we are suggesting here is that it may be more sensible to assume that the relationship between observables like economic institutions and basically unobservables like individual motivations is a two-way one, that is to say, institutions and individual motivations co-evolve through a complex (typically non-linear) process which is density- and history-dependent, i.e. the actual path of institutional *vis-à-vis* motivational co-evolution depends on a complex series of contextual factors which include the set of initial conditions, i.e. on the initial salience of certain behaviours across the reference population of economic agents. The relevance of free riding as a mechanism for the explanation of an observed set of economic institutions clearly depends on whether free riding has ever been a problem for the actual society under scrutiny, and indeed there are plenty of examples of (mostly small and simple) societies where free riding has never been an issue even in the presence of common pool resources.[4] If this co-evolutionary view is correct, then focusing attention on the one-way explanatory potential of mechanisms is to miss at least one half of the feedback loop that is actually at work with a consequent and serious underestimation of the range of potential alternative outcomes that can be generated by a socioeconomic system starting from given premises.

To conclude, making a case for a 'context-dependent approach to economic theorising' as I have done here does not amount of course to refuting Salmon's thesis but only to pointing out a dialectic alternative. It is consequently constructive and fair to ask for a sharper formulation and corroboration of his thesis to address important and nowadays well recognised issues such as path-dependence and self-referential social evolution.

Notes

1. Quoted from McCloskey (1990, p. 14).
2. See, e.g., Tirole (1996); Lahno (1995); Dasgupta (1988).
3. See Sacco and Zamagni (1996). See also, albeit according to a different perspective, Offerman *et al.* (1996).
4. A most striking result in this respect is that of Parks and Vu (1994) who have found experimentally that individuals coming from highly collectivist cultures (such as the Vietnamese) tend to cooperate substantially more than people coming from individualist cultures and that the former keep on cooperating in spite of the repeated defection of partners, i.e. they seem to interpret the act of cooperating as an end and not only as a means for getting certain pay-offs.

References

Dasgupta P. (1988) 'Trust as a commodity', in D. Gambetta (ed.), *Trust: Making and Breaking Cooperative Relations* (Oxford: Blackwell).

Lahno B. (1995) 'Trust, Reputation and Exit in Exchange Relationships', *Journal of Conflict Resolution*, vol. 39 (September), pp. 495–510.

Ledyard J.O. (1987) 'Incentive Compatibility', in J. Eatwell *et al.* (eds), *The New Palgrave Dictionary of Economics* (London: Macmillan).

McCloskey D. (1990) 'Ancients and Moderns', *Social Science History*, vol. 3 (March), pp. 4–18.

Offerman T., J. Sonnemans and A. Schram (1996) 'Value Orientations, Expectations and Voluntary Contributions in Public Goods', *The Economic Journal*, vol. 106, pp. 817–45.

Olson, M. (1965) *The Logic of Collective Action: Public Goods and the Theory of Groups*, 2nd edn (1971) (Cambridge, MA: Harvard University Press).

Parks C.D. and A.D. Vu (1994) 'Social Dilemmas Behaviour of Individuals from Highly Individualist and Collectivist Cultures', *Journal of Conflict Resolutions*, vol. 38, pp. 708–18.

Sacco P. and S. Zamagni (1996) 'An Evolutionary Dynamic Approach to Altruism', in F. Farina, F. Hahn and S. Vannucci (eds), *Ethics, Rationality and Economic Behaviour* (Oxford: Clarendon Press).

Sen A. (1987) *On Ethics and Economics*, Oxford: Blackwell.

——— (1989) 'Economic Methodology: Heterogeneity and Relevance', *Social Research*, vol. 56, pp. 299–329.

Tirole J. (1996) 'A Theory of Collective Reputations (With Applications to the Persistence of Corruption and to Firm Quality)', *Review of Economic Studies*, vol. 63, pp. 1–22.

Comment: Mechanisms, Models and Free Riders

Uskali Mäki
ERASMUS UNIVERSITY, ROTTERDAM, THE NETHERLANDS

In relation to the richness of its topics and insights, Pierre Salmon's chapter 2 is brief, and therefore not an easy target for commentary. There appear to be four major component claims in the paper that deserve special attention; I will submit brief speculations on each in turn:

(1) Much of economic theorising is about mechanisms defined in terms of causal processes and their interactions
(2) Free riding is a mechanism in this sense
(3) Theorising involves models as non-linguistic entities, along the lines of the semantic conception of theories
(4) Experimentation is beginning to provide access to separate mechanisms which are of relevance to economics, including the free riding mechanism.

This Comment aims at providing two types of service: to suggest refinements of formulation and to raise some open issues. Both are intended as encouragements to proceed further and deeper in the project. The most radical message of this comment suggests a negation of claim (2): free riding *is not* a mechanism.

1 THE METAPHYSICS OF CAUSAL EXPLANATION: MECHANISMS

The first thing to notice about the concept of mechanism is that there is a dramatic disproportionality between its popularity amongst practising scientists, on the one hand, and its philosophical explications, on the other. The concept of mechanism appears to be intuitively appealing in the sciences, economics included. Given this intuitive appeal, and given the philosophical tradition of conceptual analysis as a way of clarifying and justifying scientists' intuitions, one would expect the concept to be well understood. Unfortunately, we do not possess a very good philosophical account of the notion of mechanism. Wesley Salmon's (1984) account is no doubt one of the best available. This is the characterisation that Pierre Salmon adopts in his paper:

> Causal processes, causal interactions, and causal laws provide the mechanisms by which the world works; to understand *why* certain things happen, we need to see *how* they are produced by these mechanisms. (Salmon, 1984, p. 132, emphasis in the original)

Pierre Salmon cites the above summary statement, but does not go into details other than saying that 'mechanisms are the sets . . . of causal processes (physical propagation, or, in social science, also mental processes) and interactions (notably between processes) which *connect* causes and effects' (p. 67, emphasis in the original).

I have myself been fascinated by Wesley Salmon's ideas about causation,[1] but it is obvious that they are not devoid of problems. Some of these problems appear in relation to sciences other than economics, such as physics and biology, but I here focus on economics. There are two important questions that have to be asked: Does economics explain in terms of Salmonian mechanisms? Is free riding a Salmonian mechanism? Pierre Salmon suggests that the correct answer to both is 'yes' (i.e., claims (1) and (2)). My answer to both is 'no', yet I find both questions important and useful. Let us begin with the first question and leave the second for later.

One problem with Wesley Salmon's concept of mechanism is due to its being defined in terms of causal process. The problem is with the narrowness of this notion and its consequent inability to capture some of the popular usages of the term 'mechanism' in scientific practice, including economics. The concept is narrow in that it is defined in terms of a spatiotemporally continuous, self-sustaining causal process, composed of causal production and causal propagation. My current belief is that economists widely – or even mostly – use the term 'mechanism' without implying such an idea of causal process. The uses of the *term* abound in economics: to give a short list of examples, economists talk about the market mechanism, price mechanism, monetary mechanism, wage mechanism, financing mechanism, buffer mechanism, transfer pricing mechanism, payments mechanism, specie flow mechanism, income distribution mechanism, monetary interest rate mechanism, banking mechanism, balance of payments adjustment mechanism, financial mechanism, export mechanism, commercial credit mechanism, income–specie flow mechanism, exchange mechanism, industrial mechanism, governance mechanism, exchange rate mechanism, growth mechanism, economic development mechanism, and transmission mechanisms of different sorts.[2]

My impression is that many[3] of these usages appear in the context of pursuing non-processual equilibrium explanations – rather than causal process explanations. Such equilibrium explanations do not require explicit accounts of continuous causal processes consisting of causal interactions and causal propagations. They are rather concerned to show that for a number of different initial conditions, the same (equilibrium) outcome would have resulted, without tracing the detailed causal processes that actually were involved. Equilibrium explanations provide disjunctions of possible causal scenarios without telling which of the disjuncts is the actual cause.[4] In contrast, Wesley Salmon's model suggests depicting the actual causal trajectory which leads to a given outcome without concerning itself with questions about other non-actual but possible trajectories which would have led to the same type of outcome.

This does not mean that equlibrium explanations do not invoke 'mechanisms', but the point is that such explanations cite 'equilibrium mechanisms' – such as the price mechanism – which are not theorised as Salmonian mechanisms. To be more precise: while many equilibrium explanations given in terms of formal models do not trace causal processes, the non-formal 'stories' attached to such models often do. As we know, there is often a gap between the two: such process stories may be *ad hoc* accounts that cannot be smoothly accommodated by the models. I can think of two ways of articulating the idea. It is the case that economists theorise (or model) mechanisms, but these mechanisms are not Salmonian mechanisms. And it is the case that economists do refer to Salmonian mechanisms at least part of the time when they talk about mechanisms, but they do not theorise them in the sense of formal modelling; they talk about Salmonian mechanisms only 'story-wise'.

Whatever the case, this is what I mean by saying that the Salmonian notion is descriptively narrow (even if one wished to endorse it as defining the normative ideal of explanation): if mechanisms are understood as Salmonian mechanisms, economists do not model mechanisms, or if economists are taken to model mechanisms, they model mechanisms other than Salmonian mechanisms. This has an implication regarding Pierre Salmon's claim that 'economics has always been based on the presupposition that more or less 'hidden' or deep-seated mechanisms – or interactions, processes, etc. – underlie and explain what we observe in the actual world' (n. 7, p. 82). My suspicion is that even if it seems perfectly correct to say that much of economics has been preoccupied with identifying mechanisms and using them for explanations, the bulk of these mechanisms have not been Salmonian mechanisms. The problem is that we don't have a very good understanding of the character of these non-Salmonian mechanisms.

Before addressing the question of whether free riding is a Salmonian mechanism, a different issue involved in Salmon's notion should be mentioned. This is the issue of the role of counterfactuals in the account of mechanisms. Pierre Salmon writes: 'the real systems . . . are not part of the actual world but of a world in which a number of forces are supposed absent' (p. 62). Some qualification is needed here to defend the idea that theories are not about the actual world. First we can replace 'real systems' by 'postulated systems' or 'assumed systems' in the above sentence. We can then suggest that it is one of the characteristics of the postulated system that in this system a number of forces are absent. Such a system is typically not 'part of the actual world' for the simple reason that in the actual world many or all of those forces are not absent. But it is equally important to understand that those forces that are supposed to be present – as well as those supposed to be absent, for that matter – might well be part of the actual world. In other words, if we take 'absence of other forces' to imply 'non-actuality', it is not the non-actuality of forces but rather the non-actuality of absence that amounts to the non-actuality of the postulated system.[5]

2 FREE RIDING AS A MECHANISM

Even if it were the case that economics mostly theorises mechanisms other than Salmonian ones, there are exceptions as I have attempted to demonstrate elsewhere (Mäki, 1992a). Could it be that free riding is such an exception? Could free riding be a Salmonian mechanism? To see this, let us first look at how Pierre Salmon characterises the idea of free riding.

He suggests that in current usage, the term 'free riding' has a variety of referents. It may refer to actual riding (supposing the good has actually been produced). But it often refers to facts which do not involve literal 'riding' at all, for example when the good is not actually produced; according to the 'strong' hypothesis, free riding prevents the production of the good. The upshot is that 'free riding can be interpreted literally or not, as manifest or not, as an outcome or as a cause' (p. 64). Salmon then suggests that

> the less literal and manifest and the more akin to a cause rather than to an outcome it is, the more important or interesting it is likely to be. This makes it a good object of reflection from the perspective of philosophical ideas which emphasise the non- actual side of reality. (p. 64)

Before proceeding further, I would like to suggest refinements to this idea. First, the above seems to suggest that if free riding is not taken to be a manifest phenomenon – such as a type of behavioural episode – this implies that it is not to be regarded as actual. This assumes that actuality consists of something like manifest behaviour or behavioural outcomes. In contrast to this, I am inclined to think that even though free riding were not regarded as a manifest phenomenon, it might still be taken to be actual, namely as an actual mechanism – supposing for the time being that it is a mechanism.[6] Second, it should be evident that 'free riding' is a metaphor when used in the context of economic and social theory. For this reason, one should not accept the claim that 'free riding can be interpreted literally' – literally speaking. Of course, Salmon does not mean to interpret it *literally,* he does not mean to provide a literal interpretation in a literal sense of 'literal interpretation'. His 'literal' interpretation only suggests that there is an actual 'ride' – where 'ride' has to be interpreted metaphorically and where 'actual' refers to manifest behaviour.

Now we are approaching the key issue. Here is Salmon's definition of 'the free riding mechanism': the mechanism consists of

> any set of processes and interactions in a group of individuals which, if operating freely and alone, will lead *many* of these individuals to decide, *because* of the non-excludability property of a good, not to contribute to its provision – or, in any case, not an amount at least equal to their marginal valuation of the good – even if the consequence is that the good will not be provided at all. (p. 68, emphasis in the original)

Given that the notion of mechanism is defined in terms of causal process and interaction, one then has to raise the question concerning the details of the causal processes and interactions that are supposed to be involved in the free riding mechanism. For example, if one adopts Wesley Salmon's (1984) definition, one has to ask questions such as: What is the mechanism 'made of'? Is it a mental or a social mechanism, or does it involve both 'substances'? What are the causal processes involved? What precisely are the interactions? What are the marks that are being propagated through the causal processes?

Such questions are neither answered nor posed in Pierre Salmon's chapter. He appears to think that it is not his task in this chapter to answer them: 'I have attempted to define but not to elucidate the free riding mechanism. This is how it should be, I believe. . . . elucidating the free riding mechanism is a scientific, not a methodological endeavour.' (p. 69). I am inclined to protest. The main claim of the chapter is that free riding is a mechanism. I cannot think of a better – or any other – way to substantiate this claim than to go at least some way towards elucidating the mechanism, whatever the way of elucidation, 'scientific' or 'methodological'. If it were a 'scientific' task to elucidate the mechanism, then Salmon should obviously have to do some 'science' to see whether free riding *is* a mechanism; a chapter like his, devoted to methodological discussion, would not be enough. In contrast, I believe much progress in elucidation can be brought about by way of methodological analysis of existing economic concepts and theories.

My impression is that Pierre Salmon's chapter does not give us any strong grounds for thinking that free riding is a Salmonian mechanism. Let us consider the above questions to see how to look for such grounds. I submit some speculations in pursuit of elucidation with full awareness that they don't take us very far, but I believe they suffice to justify the rejection of Salmon's main claim.

Salmon says basically only two things about the presumed mechanism. One is that it connects a certain cause and a certain effect; the other is that it consists of a set of processes and interactions in a group of individuals. What we would like to learn is what these processes and interactions are like in somewhat more concrete terms.

Salmon's characterisation of the causal connection amounts to saying that

> the free riding mechanism connects a fact to which we give the status of a cause, the non-excludability of a good, with another fact, which we consider as its effect, i.e. many individuals deciding not to contribute to the provision of the good, etc. (p. 68)

So there is a cause, non-excludability, and there is an effect, decision not to contribute, and there is a mechanism connecting the two. I think one refinement would be to say that the decision here is the outcome of a process of decision making. Let us call this outcome simply 'non-contribution'. Another immediate refinement seems to be needed. As cited above, Salmon writes elsewhere that free riding can be thought of 'as an outcome or as a cause' and that 'the more *akin to a cause* rather than to an outcome it is, the more important or interesting it is likely to be' (p. 64, emphasis added). This represents free riding as a cause. But in his characterisation of the causal connection he suggests that free riding is a mechanism connecting a cause and an outcome. Some revision is needed. While it seems appropriate to think of free riding as the behavioural outcome of non-contribution, it will not do to think of it akin to non-excludability, presented as the 'cause' in the key definition above. This problem, of course, is due to the ambiguity of 'cause' – used to designate both the triggering cause of non-excludability and the alleged mechanism of free riding. How then to characterise – elucidate – the mechanism connecting non-excludability and non-contribution?

If free riding is a mechanism, is it a mental or a social mechanism? Now the term 'free rider' appears to refer to a set of individuals, and 'free riding' would seem to refer to what these individuals do due to belonging to this set. Yet, even if referring to individuals, it is obvious that both of these concepts are socially loaded: free riding as behaviour and free ridership necessarily presuppose the contributions of other individuals. In this sense, free ridership is a social role and free riding is social action. But these are not the social connotations Salmon has in mind. He has adopted the idea of 'free riding' as referring to something that precedes such actions by people in such roles, namely an underlying causal mechanism.

Of this mechanism Salmon says that he takes it 'as an essentially social mechanism (itself involving individual psychological processes of course) rather than as a mainly psychological mechanism' (p. 69).[7] He seems to think it is a social mechanism because many individuals are involved: he provides the idea of the mechanism being a social mechanism as a 'reason' for referring to 'many [of these] individuals' being led to decide not to contribute (p. 69). Note that this invokes plurality of individuals differently from what I suggested in the previous paragraph concerning free ridership and free riding behaviour. I said that other individuals *as contributors* are required, and that this constitutes the social aspect of free riding. Salmon seems to say that other – many – individuals *as non-contributors* are involved, and that this makes the mechanism social. But more would be needed, namely some ideas about how these non-contributing individuals are related to one another; mere plurality of individuals is not sufficient for making the mechanism social. What precisely are the social components and social processes of the alleged free riding mechanism?

In any case, the mechanism is obviously supposed to involve major mental components. Salmon does not discuss this question, consistently with his reluctance to elucidate the idea. In one context, he cites what he calls possible *'motives'* not to contribute – namely, 'greed' and 'the fear of being a dupe' (p. 72) – and suggests in another context that they are '*in* the free riding mechanism' and that it is possible that in the mechanism 'the fear or reluctance to be a dupe' dominates over greediness (p. 72). Now this way of speaking suggests that such 'motives' are component parts of the mechanism[8] and that within the mechanism, tensions between the components may occur. According to the Salmonian notion, mechanisms were supposed to be sets of causal processes and causal interactions. On a generous interpretation, one might suggest that one motive dominating over another is a matter of causal interaction. This would require that motives be interpreted as causal processes.

Supposing free riding is a Salmonian mechanism, what precisely are the causal processes involved? Supposing it is a social mechanism with mental components, what are the social and mental processes? Among the latter, one can think of the free rider engaged in a simple process of invoking the capacity to easily recognise non-excludability and immediately deciding not to contribute. Or we can think of the free rider engaged in a complex learning process which will ultimately lead to the recognition of non-excludability and the passive act of non-contribution. These are some of the possible component mental processes. What would be propagated across such processes? The obvious suggestion is: information. Would this exhaust all there is to be propagated?[9] I doubt it. What about the ingredient social processes? The questions are many, and some of them need to be answered to substantiate the idea that free riding is a Salmonian mechanism.

Another interesting question concerning Salmon's definition of the free riding mechanism is this. He says that the mechanism is 'any set of processes and interactions in a group of individuals which . . . will lead *many* of these individuals to decide' (p. 68). This is, of course, in line with experimental results, but we are now interested in the identity of the mechanism. One obvious question concerns the numbers.

Why 'many' rather than all or none or few? Does the idea that many individuals decide not to contribute imply that it is only these individuals who 'participate in' the mechanism and that this decision is made precisely by these individuals? Or is it rather the case that all individuals 'participate in' it, but its impact on manifest behaviour is (in the case of contributors) or is not (in the case of non-contributors) effectively counteracted by some mental mechanisms (those involving, say, altruism and sense of fairness) which do not belong to the free riding mechanism? The only clue we get is when Pierre Salmon explains why his definition refers to 'many' individuals and says – in a non-Salmonian fashion – that this is partly because 'this mechanism is most likely to involve stochastic processes' (p. 69).[10] However, this does not seem to really decide between the two options, it rather serves to hide an issue which is crucial for the elucidation of the possible mechanism.

3 TOWARDS AN ALTERNATIVE ACCOUNT

Let us then try another angle of attack, leading to a rival understanding of the ontology of free riding. The argument begins with a remark on vocabulary. Salmon suggests that free riding itself is a mechanism. Now this appears to be somewhat at odds with the literature on public goods provision and the role of free riding. This literature also explicitly employs the term 'mechanism', but it is mostly taken to refer to something different from what Salmon appears to have in mind. The usage in the literature is in the tradition of 'mechanism design' and here 'mechanism' refers to various institutional arrangements (auction mechanism, voluntary contribution mechanism, marginal cost pricing mechanism, Lindahl mechanism, etc.). Among these arrangements are those that are designed to resolve the 'free rider problem'. Such designed mechanisms are mechanisms of manipulation; their employment is expected to have an impact on free riding behaviour, namely inhibiting it (or enhancing it). These designed institutional arrangements would seem to be some kind of social mechanisms.

Could it be that Salmon refers to a subclass of such institutional arrangements when talking about the free riding mechanism? Could it be that for him, 'Free riding mechanism' = 'Free-riding-enhancing mechanism' (while the other subclass would consist of free-riding-inhibiting mechanisms)? If this were so, then the primary connotation of 'free riding' would be that of a behavioural outcome, namely non-contribution. The claim that those institutional arrangements that enhance free riding as behavioural outcome are free riding mechanisms would be nothing but an implication of terminological convention. The key questions seem to be: Is there a free riding mechanism in addition to free riding-enhancing mechanisms? Are the institutional arrangements used to control or manipulate free riding as behavioural outcome or also to directly manipulate free riding as mechanism?

Salmon is somewhat ambiguous about these questions. What he says seems to imply that there is a distinct free riding mechanism. Without keeping behavioural outcome and mechanism separate, he says, for example: 'The subjects of Leviathan do not free ride (as behavioural outcome) but without free riding (as mechanism) there would be no need for a Leviathan' (p. 74). In a similar vein: 'there is not much scope for free riding (as behavioural outcome) under the arrangements studied by Elinor Ostrom in the context of common-pool resources, but the free riding mechanism is a major cause of these arrangements' (pp. 74–5). The arrangements referred to here are free riding-inhibiting arrangements designed to restrict either free riding as behavioural outcome or the functioning of the free riding mechanism. The free riding mechanism in this context cannot be identical to free riding-enhancing mechanisms. Otherwise it would not make sense to say that 'without free riding there would be no need for a Leviathan' or that 'the free riding mechanism is a major cause of these arrangements'. This seems to imply that 'free riding mechanism' = 'free riding-enhancing mechanism' and that the free riding mechanism exists as distinct from free riding-enhancing mechanisms. On this conclusion I disagree.

Here is an outline of a tentative alternative account of the concept of free riding and the usage of the term 'mechanism' in the literature on free riding. Free riding is best understood as behaviour, in accordance to what our intuition appears to suggest. Free riding is not a mechanism, even though economists talk about mechanisms in this context. There are two kinds of social mechanisms linked to free riding behaviour, namely free riding-inhibiting mechanisms and free riding-enhancing mechanisms, both consisting of institutional arrangements. Economists also invoke a mental mechanism linked to free riding behaviour, namely the mechanism of narrow self-interest seeking subject to constraints. It is the interplay between the social mechanisms and the mental mechanism that generates free riding or lack of it as the behavioural outcome.

The difference between Pierre Salmon's account and the one sketched here can be put as follows, using the elements of non-excludability and non-contribution in Salmon's account. He suggests that there is a free riding mechanism which transforms non-excludability as an input into non-contribution as an output. I suggest that non-excludability is an input to the mechanism of narrow constrained self-interest seeking which, when triggered by free riding-enhancing institutional mechanisms, generates free riding, that is, non-contribution as a behavioural outcome.

The alternative account cites mechanisms, but does not pretend to understand what 'mechanism' means in this context. It is not obvious that free riding-enhancing mechanisms are Salmonian mechanisms. The same applies to the presumed mental mechanisms involved, as theorised by economists. Public economists do talk about mechanisms – what precisely do they mean? No answer will be attempted here.

4 THE ROLE OF MODELS IN DEPICTING MECHANISMS

Pierre Salmon defends both the idea that good theories capture mechanisms and a view of theories which is 'inspired by the so-called semantic conception of theories' (p. 70). On the face of it, it might seem that these two elements in Salmon's view are independent: the semantic view of theories or its modifications are not needed to make sense of the idea that theories capture mechanisms. Yet, it seems that Salmon thinks he has reasons to believe that there is a non-arbitrary link between these two things. The issues involved in this conception of theory are too many and difficult to be discussed here with the thoroughness they deserve.

I am sympathetic with much that Salmon says about the character of theories, even though it seems obvious that he does not spell out a refined account of them. It is easy to share his excitement about Giere's (1988) similarity approach and Suppe's (1989) counterfactual approach, not least because there are affinities with my account of 'the method of isolation' in economics which Salmon also cites favourably. Yet, differences remain, but they cannot be fully explored here. A couple of remarks may suffice.

Salmon says that models are 'non-linguistic systems constructed to analyse particular aspects of reality' (p. 70). He also says that 'a model cannot be true or false' and that 'its relationship with some aspects of reality is specified within a hypothesis ... and it is this hypothesis or conjecture which is true or false' (p. 70).[11]

The usages of the term 'model' are many, also in economics. They imply different ideas about what models are 'made of'. Some models are made of physical matter; they are non-linguistic. Some models are made of mathematical equations or sets of explicitly stated assumptions; this is certainly a popular usage of 'model' in economics, implying that models are linguistic. Some models are mental in that they consist of imagined simple systems; they are conceptual but not linguistic. Something like this last seems to be Salmon's usage.

Thus, in order to make Salmon's ideas more accessible from the point of view of the conventional practices in economics, one might suggest some terminological revision. Instead of just 'models' we might talk about two types of entities: 'theoretical models' on the one hand, and 'model objects' or 'model worlds' or 'imagined systems' on the other. The latter are the simplified and idealised, invented and imagined systems that economists seem to be directly commenting on in their theoretical work. They are the immediate non-linguistic objects of the linguistic models that economists work with. On the other hand, in addition to such imagined model objects, there are the non-invented real objects of the world, much more complex and rich in detail than the simplified objects in the imagined world. Hypotheses then make claims about how model objects are related to respective real objects. In order to make such claims, hypotheses have to provide information about some aspects of the relevant real objects.

I can imagine that a picture of an aspect of theorising along such lines may be in some cases illuminating. Before passing the final verdict, a few questions would need to be answered. What does it mean to say that 'models can include anything found in reality and thus can also include mechanisms' (p. 70)? What does 'include' mean here? If mechanisms are real objects, how can they be 'included' in the imagined systems? Shouldn't one rather say that they are represented by the imagined objects? If so, and given that the imagined systems are regularly expressed in linguistic forms, and further that satisfaction for predicates is akin to truth for sentences, one may wonder whether the difference between the more traditional statement view and the semantic view of theories is that large after all. The crucial question in relation to Salmon's exercise is whether his favoured view of theories is helpful – or more helpful than an alternative statement view based on the idea of theoretical isolation – in understanding the way economists study free riding. No answer will be pursued here.

Two final remarks related to Salmonian mechanisms. First, the semantic view of theories can be criticised for lacking the resources to distinguish lawlike from accidental generalisations. It may have similar difficulties with distinguishing causal processes from pseudo processes – a key distinction in Wesley Salmon's theory – thus making the application of the causal process account of mechanisms to economics incomplete.[12] Second, Suppe (1989), one of the main protagonists of the semantic view, thinks that counterfactual idealisations are an essential component of theories. This is also the view that Pierre Salmon adopts. His definition of the free riding mechanism involves a counterfactual component: 'any set of processes and interactions in a group of individuals which, *if operating freely and alone* . . . (emphasis mine)'. Now this is interesting as Wesley Salmon's (1984) original notion of mechanism was likewise characterised in counterfactual terms. Even more interestingly, Wesley Salmon (1994) has recently modified his notion precisely on this point: he is now trying to do without the counterfactual component. Pierre Salmon's notion is in the spirit of the (1984) rather than that of the (1994) account. My feeling is that he may be better off by sticking to the counterfactual version.

5 EXPERIMENTAL ACCESS TO MECHANISMS

Pierre Salmon indicates considerable optimism regarding experimentation in economics. In particular, he suggests that economists are beginning to have direct experimental access to the free riding mechanism itself. The idea is that, thanks to experimentation, economists can now study free riding directly as a separate mechanism rather than making conjectures about it relying on indirect evidence referring to manifest behaviour in which the influence of other mechanisms is involved. An obvious response to this optimism would be to start listing the uncertainties that accompany experimentation on human subjects. I would rather refrain myself from this and stick to the main issue of free riding as mechanism.

Salmon adopts the distinction between a mechanism – to be identified in isolated experimental conditions – and the manifestation of its functioning mixed with the functioning of other mechanisms – observed in materially non-isolated complex circumstances. He then argues that we can count on it that a mechanism identified in experimental circumstances also acts outside of them. Let us look at part of the first of his three arguments. It seems to conflate free riding as behavioural outcome and as mechanism.

> Free riding [as behavioural outcome] will tend to be more important in large groups than in small ones, when the stakes are high rather than a trifle, when people are mutually anonymous rather than known or visible, etc. This should be assumed to carry over to non-experimental settings. Similarly, a general result is that in most experiments, the order of magnitude of free riding [as behavioural outcome], as measured against the optimum, turns out to be somewhere between, say, 30 and 70 per cent . . . This kind of knowledge is enough, I submit, to consider as reasonable the unquantified assertion that free riding [as mechanism] is also an important force in actual, non-experimental settings. (p. 79)

In the passage, the expression 'free riding' appears three times, the first two denoting behaviour, and the third denoting mechanism. One cannot therefore infer from the premises to the conclusion that free riding is an important mechanism in non-experimental settings. The robustness of free riding as behaviour cannot be directly translated into the robustness of free riding as mechanism.

This passage also creates another puzzle: experiments were supposed to identify the free riding mechanism, but here reference is made to free riding behaviour having been discovered in experiments. This is indeed what experiments seem to be doing. They alternate elements in the environment and the decision mechanism and see what effects this has on free riding as behavioural outcome. Instead of providing access to a pre-existing free riding mechanism, experimentation involves the active construction of mechanisms in order to study their influence on free riding behaviour. The mechanisms set up in the experimental design are found either to enhance or inhibit free riding as behavioural outcome.[13] If these mechanisms are supposed to inhibit or enhance the functioning of some other 'underlying' mechanism, would this 'underlying' mechanism, as invoked in conventional economics, be anything else but narrow self-interested rational choice? If so, what kind of *mechanism* would this be?[14]

Notes

1. For an application of Wesley Salmon's notion of causal process to economics, see Mäki (1992a).
2. This list is based on checking economics book titles in which the word 'mechanism' appears at the library of Erasmus University.

3. To find out precisely how many would take several detailed case studies in methodology.
4. See Sober (1983) for an account of equilibrium explanations, using examples from population genetics. His account puts the emphasis on the stability features of the equilibrium. It may be that not everything that Sober says about his examples would as such apply to standard cases of equilibrium explanations in economics, but I presume the features given in rough outline above in the text are shared by economic explanations.
5. Elsewhere, I have argued for keeping these two ideas separate from one another (see, e.g. Mäki, 1992b). Note that Pierre Salmon's usage of 'actual' seems to lead to the idea that theories are about 'possible aspects of the world' (n. 7, p. 83).
6. Salmon's conflation of being manifest and being actual is reminiscent of Bhaskar's (1978) unfortunate usage of 'actual' – where being actual is defined in terms of being observable. But of course, what is observable does not have to be taken to exhaust the actual world.
7. It is not clear what it means to say that free riding is *mainly* a social mechanism and why Salmon puts it that way.
8. It would be good to have a full list of motives that are supposed to be 'in the free riding mechanism'.
9. Note that Wesley Salmon's (1984) account characterised mechanisms in terms of 'causal processes transmitting 'marks'. The notion of a mark is relatively neutral and permits specifications in terms of, say, energy and information. In his recent work, Wesley Salmon has substituted this idea for the more specific notion of transmission of invariant or conserved quantities (Salmon, 1994).
10. I say this suggestion is 'non-Salmonian' because it does not seem to be consistent with Wesley Salmon's non-probabilistic account of causal processes and mechanisms.
11. Salmon refers to Hausman's (1992) formulation of the idea of models and hypotheses; however, models in Hausman's view do not seem to be 'non-linguistic systems'. For a comment on Hausman's formulations, see Mäki (1996).
12. Note, however, that it is not clear that Wesley Salmon's framework – which does not include a semantic view of theories – has the resources to draw the distinction either.
13. For a very good survey, see Ledyard (1995).
14. This Comment has benefitted from discussions with Jack Vromen.

References

Bhaskar, R. (1978) *A Realist Theory of Science*, 2nd edn (Brighton: Harvester Press).

Giere, R.N. (1988) *Explaining Science: A Cognitive Approach* (Chicago: University of Chicago Press).

Hausman, D. (1992) *The Inexact and Separate Science of Economics* (Cambridge and New York: Cambridge University Press).

Ledyard, J.O. (1995) 'Public Goods: A Survey of Experimental Research', in J.H. Kagel and A. Roth (eds), *The Handbook of Experimental Economics* (Princeton: Princeton University Press), pp. 111–94.

Mäki, U. (1992a) 'The Market as an Isolated Causal Process: A Metaphysical Ground for Realism', in B. Caldwell and S. Boehm (eds), *Austrian Economics: Tensions and New Developments* (Boston: Kluwer), pp. 35–59.

——— (1992b) 'Friedman and Realism', *Research in the History of Economic Thought and Methodology*, vol. 10, 171–95.

——— (1996) 'Two Portraits of Economics', *Journal of Economic Methodology*, vol. 3, pp. 1–38.

Salmon W.C. (1984) *Scientific Explanation and the Causal Structure of the World*, (Princeton: Princeton University Press).

——— (1994) 'Causality without Counterfactuals', *Philosophy of Science*, vol. 61, 297–312.

Sober, E. (1983) 'Equilibrium Explanation', *Philosophical Studies*, vol. 43, pp. 201–10.

Suppe, F. (1989) *The Semantic Conception of Theories and Scientific Realism* (Urbana and Chicago: University of Illinois Press).

Discussion

Pierre Salmon suggested that the two discussants had by-passed his distinction between models and the real world. Zamagni is correct to point to the importance of considerations of rationality in models, but his is a discussion of the real world. Rational choice models are useful to discover phenomena such as free riding, but once one discovers free riding, one has to adopt a wider conception of rationality and consider things like altruism or the fear of being a dupe. These considerations have a role in free riding experiments because people do not want to be seen as free riding or narrowly rational. It has been suggested that the reason why economists free ride but no one else does is that they see themselves as rational in a narrower sense than other people. But none of this is in the world of models: it is a discussion of the real world.

Salmon claimed that Mäki also failed to keep questions about models and questions about reality separate. Mäki argued that the sorts of mechanism Wesley Salmon describes are not important in economics and that most references to mechanisms in economics are to non-processual equilibrium explanations. But Pierre Salmon argued that non-processual equilibrium explanations are in the world of models. If one looked at what economists say about the real world, then one finds something close to what Wesley Salmon calls processes and interactions. For example, in price theory no process that changes prices is specified, but 'behind' the models economists have in mind processes: somebody will raise a price, there will be imitation, there will be some excess supply, and so on. The mechanism is not in the model, but reference to it helps to link the model to reality. In any event he is not committed to Wesley Salmon's view and if philosophers proposed an alternative, he would be prepared to consider it. The literature on experimental economics mentions many processes. Fear of being a dupe is a process. People are in a group, cooperating. They see someone who is not cooperating. They ask why they should cooperate, and so they stop cooperating, and cooperation breaks down. It is a process. Salmon argued that experiments have shown that, on average, people do not follow narrow self-interest. Behaviour is more complicated than that.

Thomas Mayer commented that Douglass North's historical work shows how ideology can get round the problem of free riding, and that in some cases feelings of moral superiority from contributing to a good cause may offset the temptation to free ride. But laboratory experiments provide particularly strong evidence for the existence of free riding, because people act less selfishly when the stakes are low. So if free riding is found in experiments with small stakes, there is good reason to believe that it will exist in the real world where the stakes are higher.

Maurice Lagueux suggested that Salmon had been too precise when he had characterised a mechanism as a link between a cause and its effect, because this only works if there is a very definite and punctual link between cause and effect, such as between a switch and a light. He suggested instead thinking of mechanisms as structural settings, not necessarily institutional arrangements, that permit explanations. Lagueux went on to suggest that Salmon should insist that free riding is a secondary, negative type of mechanism given that people do not necessarily free ride. Free riding explains why economists do not get the result they would otherwise expect, which supports the idea that it is a structural setting.

Daniel Hausman questioned whether one should view different mechanisms interacting in the same way that physical forces interact. The model of forces always acting, as the force of gravity always acts, does not seem the right one to use. Suppose one came across a public good that might be provided, but is not provided. The explanation of why it is not provided might have nothing to do with free riding – perhaps people had simply never thought of it. If they had thought of it then free riding would come into its own. Free riding might thus be cited not to explain what is actually going on, but why what is going on had to be the case. He cited an argument of Philip Pettit's that one might want to explain why a particular outcome is robust and would continue to obtain. Pettit's example was a ball rolling between two rows of nails. If the ball never touches them, the nails have no explanatory value in explaining the ball's motion, but they nonetheless explain why the ball has to roll in a straight line. Free riding might function in the same way – as a mechanism that *would* function were things somewhat different.

Nancy Cartwright focused on different aspects of Salmon's idea of causal processes. A part of Salmon's picture that is more important than any spatio–temporal connection is the fundamental ontology that the world, or the economy, is made up of repeatable, recurring causal processes. She saw this as consistent with Mäki's point that there might be mechanisms that enhance or inhibit the activity. The important point is to discover that there are certain kinds of processes, not simply random correlations. The mark method (putting a mark on the putative cause and getting a mark on the putative effect) is one way of establishing that you have got a recurring, repeatable process. It is because free riding was thought of as a causal process that it was worth trying to study it using experiments.

Philippe Mongin thought that social scientists like Elster used the term mechanism as a second-best notion. Because social scientists realise that they do not have phenomenological laws such as exist in physics, they refer to mechanisms as a second-best.

Michael Kaser commented that the title of his first published article (*Economic Journal*, March 1950) contained the word 'mechanism'. Though he thought that Salmon's point about permanence was very relevant, he wondered whether it might be better to say that it was inherent in the system. It is not one-off. A process or a model can be one-off, but a mechanism cannot be. A mechanism has an input, which may be a signal, a measure or an activity, and it also has an outcome. He suggested that most of the mechanisms listed in the chapter fell within these parameters.

Bennett McCallum turned to Salmon's definition of free riding, which implies that all free riding follows from the non-excludability of goods. If non-excludability is the only thing that leads to free riding, then free riding seems a superfluous concept. But he thought that Salmon did not quite mean this. There are public goods which are non-rivalrous, but are excludable, and he thought Salmon would probably wish to include some of these in his concept. An example is public transportation, where people often take rides at prices that are lower than they would be willing to pay as individuals. Then there is an enormous amount of evidence in favour of free-riding being an important phenomenon, because people rarely pay more than they are charged. **Salmon** responded that there were many such examples of free riding, which could arise for a variety of reasons, but for free riding to exist as a *mechanism* there must be some additional property of the situation. He thought that this was non-excludability or non-rivalry.

Kevin Hoover took up the distinction between free riding as a mechanism and free riding as an outcome. He wondered whether free riding should always be regarded as an outcome, noting with approval Mäki's proposition that free riding involved the interaction of narrow self-interest with additional mechanisms. He thought that Salmon's point that narrow self-interest was experimentally disproved was a disproof of the phenomenon, not of the mechanism. It is not a disproof of gravity that all the things on the table are not hitting the floor, because there are intervening causes. Similarly, narrow self-interest may be an underlying operating mechanism even if other factors counteract it. He thought everything one might want to say about free riding could be cast in terms of the mechanisms mentioned by Mäki or other mechanisms. Free riding seems to be more an outcome than a part of the causal chain. **Salmon** responded that whether one regarded free riding on the one hand or self-interest plus interfering causes on the other as the mechanism was a pragmatic question: Which is most useful?

Andrea Salanti asked about the sense in which experimentation strengthens the case for mechanisms. Can experiments literally prove the existence of mechanisms or do they accomplish something else? He also asked about the meaning of Salmon's comment that as a result of experimentation, hypotheses that had been untestable became testable. **Salmon** responded that experiments only strengthen the case for mechanisms: they do not prove their existence. In arguing for their effect on testability, he had been reacting to the idea of Green and Shapiro that free riding has not been really tested, or if it has been tested it has been refuted. They find the positive tests unconvincing. It is very difficult to know the reasons why people do or do not contribute, and so it is hard to test free riding outside experimental situations.

Pierluigi Barrotta agreed with Salmon's comment that one is entitled to make the metaphysical assumption that free riding operates in the actual world. But he was not clear about how statistics could support such a metaphysical assumption. To apply statistical techniques one needs further assumptions, namely that background noise is not systematically related to the phenomena we are studying. So to use statistics in this contexts begs the question. How can statistics supply us with good reasons to make metaphysical or ontological assertions?

Hausman observed that the case study was extremely valuable for revealing the problems worth the notion of a mechanism. He asked how one would distinguish between the cases where a good was not being provided because of the mechanism, and where it was not being provided for some other reason. Presumably the answer would be that there was a perception on the part of individuals in society that there was this good, that it was non-excludable, and that then for a variety of possible motives people did not contribute. Some may not have contributed because they did not want to be a sucker; others because they were rationally self-interested; others because they were angry at their neighbours and wanted to be spiteful. One might say that there are alternative mechanisms: a not-wanting-to-be-a-sucker mechanism, a self-interest mechanism, a spite mechanism. One might conclude that free riding is an outcome that can be supported by a variety of mechanisms, or one could conclude that because of the robustness (the same phenomenon can arise with a variety of psychological intermediaries) free riding is itself a mechanism. Thinking about this choice helps one understand the possible ambiguities and confusions involved in the notion of a mechanism. **Mongin** saw this as Hoover's earlier point about whether free riding is the outcome, or what precedes the outcome.

Roger Backhouse was attracted by the idea of thinking of free riding as an outcome, not a mechanism. But he then wondered why economists like to think of free riding as a mechanism. There are many other cases (such as adverse selection) where economists also like to talk about mechanisms, so the concept of a mechanism must play a role in the subject. He suggested that the answer to this question lay in Salmon's observation that economists discuss models a lot, yet free riding is a characteristic of the world. Economists like to talk in terms of models, defending them as logical systems. And yet at the same time they want to say something about the real world. There is a contradiction here, for how can an exercise in logic tell us anything about the world? Identifying mechanisms in the models is a way of bridging the gap. It is not that the model is a representation of the world, but somehow that the model captures something that economists believe is happening in the world, and so they want a label for it. They say there is a mechanism of free riding, a mechanism of adverse selection, or whatever. Mechanisms are the way economists think about relating their models to the world. Backhouse also expressed some disappointment that Salmon had not taken up the question, discussed in earlier versions of the chapter, of why free riding has been so influential. His hypothesis that it has been so influential, because it is a mechanism, is worth exploring.

Cartwright took up the question of exportability, either from an experimental set-up, or from a model. You construct a model, which is tightly constrained, and show that a certain result can occur in the model. This is meant to show something even though it is clear that you got it by very careful construction of the model. You talk about robustness to variations in the model, or to variations in experiments. In physics, robustness is over a much wider range. She thought that economists were true to their empiricist convictions and the concepts they exported from their models were fairly operationalisable, which may explain why they do not export very far. Physicists, in contrast, export much more abstract, unoperationalisable concepts, but can export them further away from their original setting. There is a trade-off between these two aspects.

Uskali Mäki returned to his original claim that there were two types of mechanism only – free riding-enhancing mechanisms, and self-interest seeking mechanisms, and that we do not have a good idea of what these are. The task of methodologists is to elucidate the nature of these mechanisms. He asked why economists were not interested in the variety of mental mechanisms that Hausman had mentioned. One reason is that economists seek theoretical unification, as a result of which they are tempted to theorise only one of the various possible mechanisms. **Salmon** suggested that Hoover's and Mäki's solutions to protecting rationality might be interpreted, in a Popperian perspective, as immunising stratagems. People who do not believe in perfect rationality would believe the notion of inhibiting mechanisms was an immunising stratagem to save rationality. To Zamagni, he responded that free riding was also a challenge to collective rationality

Stefano Zamagni suggested that the free riding problem had become so popular in the past few decades because it is nothing but the *n*-person version of the Prisoner's Dilemma. The interest in this problem arises because it is a challenge to the notion of rationality in economics. He also argued that it is right to speak of free riding only where agents are aware of what they are doing. Shirking is, from the point of view of the outcome, the same as free riding, but no one would call it free riding. The difference is that with free riding I try, on purpose, to take advantage of your paying for the public good without paying for it myself. Finally he pointed out that experimental economics cannot take into account the fact that partners in an ongoing social interaction may be chosen strategically. The experimental set-up is prepared by an outsider, not by the agents themselves.

Salmon replied to these three points by noting, first, that free riding is a challenge to collective rationality; that it is legal (shirking is sometimes not); and that some experiments allow people to opt out if their partner is not cooperating and, in any case, that there are many bargaining situations where one cannot choose one's partners.

3 Learning from the Debate on Externalities[1]

Maurice Lagueux
UNIVERSITÉ DE MONTRÉAL, CANADA

According to the opening sentence of Tibor Scitovsky's (1954) paper, 'the concept of external economies is one of the most elusive in economic literature'.[2] Had Scitovsky written his paper forty years later, I am convinced that his opening sentence could have been left unchanged. Indeed, the concept of an 'externality', which was coined in the years following Scitovsky's paper as a more general and more convenient way of referring to the phenomenon I propose to examine here, is still one of the most vaguely defined concepts of economic theory and one which seems to be a source of considerable embarrassment for economists. As late as 1970, after a large number of papers had been published on external economies and externalities and virtually all the definitions which are available today had been provided in one form or another, Kenneth Arrow could still claim that 'nowhere in the literature does there appear to be a clear general definition . . . of "externality"'.[3]

While criticism directed against various aspects of economics is common, it is unusual that it be aimed at an inability to define its basic concepts. However, the concept of an externality seems to be an exception. Three symptoms unambiguously reveal the very peculiar nature of this concept from this point of view. The first symptom is the following: the two authors who have been by far the most widely quoted in the discussion of this concept, Arthur Pigou and Ronald Coase, never used the term 'externality' or even the older expression 'external (dis)economies' except, in the case of Coase, in discussing those who refer to it, and in the case of Pigou, in referring to a phenomenon that is somewhat different from the one which was to influence economists' views on externalities.

The second symptom is the fact that the importance accorded to this phenomenon by the community of economists has fluctuated widely. For a long time, the discussion concerned an important phenomenon (the so-called 'pecuniary externalities') turned out to have been mistakenly identified as a case of genuine externalities. The word then referred to an economic curiosity involving only an apparently very marginal phenomenon. Still later, in the 1950s and 1960s, it became the central theoretical reference of the rapidly growing economics of pollution referring, in this context, to a widespread phenomenon. By this time, it had also become associated with the concept of 'publicness', whose manifestations were pervasive. However, during the 1960s and 1970s, while the number of papers devoted to externalities increased dramatically, many of those who analyzed this phenomenon started to doubt whether it referred to anything very specific, and sometimes argued as if it was possible and preferable to dispense with it altogether.

The third symptom is simply the extreme variety of incompatible meanings attributed to the notion of 'externality' by a number of eminent economists of various intellectual orientation. Indeed, all of the following expressions (or their equivalents) were widely used to characterise externalities: 'lack of appropriate property rights', 'market failure to reach Paretian efficiency', 'interdependencies among consumption or production functions', 'side (or third party, or spillover) effects', 'impossibility of exclusion', 'presence of (wholly or partially) unpriced inputs or of uncompensated services', 'situation leaving room for a free rider (or free loader) effect' and 'situation associated with excessive transaction costs'. Some of these expressions are rather restrictive and others extremely inclusive, but it is clear that they are far from equivalent.[4] Finally, to complicate the matter further, externalities have sometimes been associated in unspecified ways with such phenomena as publicness, jointness of supply and non-convexities, as well as with the so-called 'pecuniary externalities'.

When it comes to explain the peculiarities of the concept of an externality, my hypothesis is that it has always been a 'residual' concept for economists. By this I mean that it is a concept which, rather than characterising a specific phenomenon, is a counter-concept whose function is to designate what is *left aside* by a more basic concept. In the case of the concept of an externality, this more basic concept turns out to be the very concept on which economics is based: the concept of a market. Given that the concept of a market itself is, in some sense, too general and too basic to be defined in a very strict manner, it is hardly surprising that its counter-concept, the concept of an externality, has also remained a kind of floating concept. However, I do not wish to claim that the concept of an externality was *explicitly* characterised and understood as a residual concept in the early stages of its development nor that it has continued to be perceived this way during recent decades.

Consequently, a historical survey of the various ways this concept has been understood and defined seems necessary in the present discussion. More precisely, by following the historical vagaries of the evolution of this concept, my objective is to show that, far from being the well defined technicality that it is usually thought to be, an externality is nothing but a residual entity whose nature and very existence is strictly dependent on the way economists perceive the market of which it is a residual.

Consequently, this chapter will not survey and discuss every important contribution to economics which has been made with the help of the concept of an externality, but only those contributions which have been decisive in determining the very meaning of this concept. Through this discussion, I will try to show how and why the scope of this concept alternately expands and contracts according to whether the prevailing concept of the market was designed in such a way as to require, or not to require, the complementary concept of an externality. Finally, I will show that even with the wide acceptance of the neoliberal concept of an all-embracing market leaving no room for externalities, the concept of an externality has survived with an alternative meaning, though not without introducing some confusion into economic analysis. I will conclude with a few methodological considerations related to the historical vagaries of this concept.

1 THE ORIGIN OF THE CONCEPT AND THE BANISHMENT OF THE PECUNIARY EXTERNALITIES

When it was first coined, apparently by Paul Samuelson in the 1950s,[5] the noun 'externality' filled the long-standing need in economic terminology for a word which would specifically designate the 'external' character of economies and diseconomies which had been involved in a decades-old ongoing debate. As for the expression 'external economies', it had been used, long before, by Alfred Marshall when, in his famous discussion of increasing and decreasing returns, he distinguished 'external economies' realised by a whole industry from 'internal economies' realised by an individual firm.[6] However, the issue was made more complex by Marshall's disciple, Pigou, who analyzed a more general phenomenon which he described in his *Economics of Welfare* as 'divergences between marginal social net product and marginal private net product'.[7] Actually, Pigou referred to cases akin to Marshallian external economies, but he considered them just one type of divergence, and apparently not the most important type. According to Pigou's more general characterisation, divergences occur when 'in some occupations, a part of the product of a unit of resources consists of something, which, instead of coming in the first instance to the person who invests the unit, comes instead, in the first instance (i.e. prior to sale if sales takes place), as a positive or negative item, to other people.[8]

For Pigou, such divergences can be divided into three principal groups identifying these 'other people' as respectively: '(1) the owners of durable instruments of production, of which the investor is a tenant; (2) persons who are not producers of the commodity in which the investor is investing; (3) persons who are producers of this commodity.'[9] As for the first group, it is well known that the improvements (or deteriorations) of rented goods for which a tenant is responsible can be reaped (or supported) by the owner of those goods. However, this phenomenon is of a more juridical than economic nature and, since it is not really typical of what was to be called 'externalities', it will not be discussed further here. It is the second group, the more general one (the 'other people' involved not being limited to those in a specific situation) that was to become representative of what is known as an externality in modern analysis. According to Pigou, divergences of this group emerge when 'one person A, in the course of rendering some service, for which payment is made, to a second person B, incidentally also renders services or disservices to other persons (not producers of like services), of such a sort that payment cannot be exacted from the benefited parties or compensation enforced on behalf of the injured parties'.[10] Of such a phenomenon, Pigou gave a great number of examples which constitute a somewhat heterogeneous but impressive list when one considers that it was published in 1920. Included in this list are uncompensated services or disservices associated with lighthouses, parks, public transport, afforestation, lamps at the front door of houses, smoke from factory chimneys, scientific research, spoiling of houses' environment by neighbouring factories, wearing out of the surface of roads by motor cars, commerce of intoxicants, 'Veblenesque effects' on people's level of satisfaction, purely competitive advertisement, deception in goods presentation, etc.[11] Yet, it was the third group of divergences – involving 'other people' producing the same commodity (in the same industry) – that explicitly referred to the Marshallian notion of decreasing and increasing returns. Pigou devotes his Chapter XI to this phenomenon that is illustrated by various modifications in the market costs incurred by an individual firm when the scale of the whole industry is increased. It was this third type of divergences that was to be at the centre of one of the most memorable debates of the first half of this century: the debate about the 'empty' boxes of increasing and decreasing costs.

This debate was to stretch from the 1920s to the 1940s. Insofar as the question of the nature of externalities is concerned, its principal result was the distinction – made progressively through contributions of Knight (1924), Viner (1931) and Ellis and Fellner (1943) – between pecuniary and technological externalities. This distinction was crucial because it resulted in an exclusion of the so-called 'pecuniary externalities' – which corresponded roughly to Marshallian external economies and to the third type of Pigovian divergences – from the realm of phenomena to be considered under the heading of 'externalities'. Further, as economists came to regard the Pigovian divergences as a source of trouble for economic theory, this distinction amounted to the elimination of this source of trouble, at least insofar as 'pecuniary externalities' – which, by this time, were the only ones that looked worthy of the attention of economists – were concerned. Indeed, if the debate about increasing and decreasing costs, involving internal and external economies and diseconomies, mobilised so many great economists and ignited so many passions, it was because divergences between marginal social net product and marginal private net product implied, according to Pigou, that (without governmental intervention) public welfare could not be maximised by market forces, which were directed only by *private* marginal costs. In this context, one understands how the conclusion that the most significant of the alleged divergences correspond to pure illusions reducible to a pecuniary phenomenon was received as a happy ending by most economists. In this debate, the crucial idea centred around the meaning of an economic rent. It is true that the expansion of an industry – which is out of the control of a firm and, in this sense, 'external' to it – can increase the cost of some factors already employed by the firm and constitute a 'diseconomy' for it. However, as explained by Ellis and Fellner, 'if the expansion of an industry gives a factor a higher per unit remuneration . . . the units already being supplied earn producer's rents . . . and rent is not a cost in social resources'.[12] In such a situation, no extra cost is incurred by society as a whole and there is consequently no reason to diagnose a divergence between marginal social net product and marginal private net product or to recommend government intervention. Thus, it is the market itself which takes care of the so-called 'pecuniary externalities'.

In any case, in this chapter, I am not especially interested in the role of government. I am interested, rather, in the nature of externalities. It is important to see how this debate on increasing and decreasing costs changed the very nature of externalities or, at least, the connotation of the term 'external'. More precisely, when, as a result of the debate, the sphere of significant divergences had been cleared of pecuniary externalities, which were associated with the type of divergence which Pigou said concerned only 'persons engaged in the occupation' (or if one prefers, inside a given industry), economists were left with the second and more general type of divergence associated with the rendering of incidental services or disservices to persons who are in no way engaged in the industry in which those services or disservices are produced. As long as the emphasis was put (as it was with pecuniary externalities pertaining to the Pigovian third group) on economies or diseconomies that were simply *external to the firm*, externalities could not be said to be 'external' to the market. Indeed, while external to the firm, those economies or diseconomies were *internal* to the industry and, since they resulted from a set of transactions in which the firm itself was involved, it would have not made sense to characterise them as external to the market as such. But when we consider situations (those pertaining to the Pigovian second group of divergences) concerning people who do not take part to the transactions going on in the industry, we face a quite different type of divergence.

Let us remember, however, that Pigou never used the term 'external' to refer to divergences while Marshall's use of it did not refer to divergences of *this* type (Pigou's second group). Given this, why characterise the economies or diseconomies associated with these divergences as 'external'? At first glance, it seems to be because they are external to the 'other persons' (or firms) referred to by Pigou as those affected by services or disservices resulting from an activity under the control of a 'Person A'. There is no doubt here that this influence of an economic agent over the welfare of another is the crucial point. However, stigmatising such *interactions* between economic agents would sound rather odd to economists used to manipulating general equilibrium models, were Pigou not to have added 'that payment cannot be exacted from the benefited parties or compensation enforced on behalf of the injured parties'. In such situations, benefited or injured parties are in no way involved in market or non-market moves which affect their welfare. They are simply not players in any market game related to the benefits they enjoy or to the damages they incurred. Typically – think of the case of pollution – these benefits or damages do not come through the market at all. Thus, it would be simply meaningless to pretend that the external economies or diseconomies they experienced are internal to industry or to the market as a whole; rather, they are *external to the market as such.* It was for reasons of this kind that, in contrast to pecuniary externalities, these genuine externalities have been named 'technological externalities'. It is true that this type of externalities was thought to be rather rare by most economists of the time, but since they *conflicted with the normal functioning* of the market, they constituted a challenging theoretical problem for economic theory or, at least, a somewhat troublesome phenomenon. By the end of the debate on increasing and decreasing costs, it became more and more common to regard genuine externalities in this way.

2 THE MEANING OF BEING 'OUTSIDE THE MARKET'

But why would payments not be exacted and compensations not enforced? Why could some services and disservices be transmitted through the market where others could not? What does it mean for services and disservices to be rendered outside of the market? The problem here is that the nature of a market (as a theoretical concept) has never been unequivocally defined by economists, probably because the market is, in a sense, the very horizon of economic analysis. In such a context, it is hardly surprising that the concept of an externality which, as we have seen, represents in some sense what this vague structure leaves out, was itself left undefined. In any case, if one adopts a minimal view according to which a market is a place where goods can be exchanged, and considers that goods have to be appropriable and exchangeable (which is roughly the view advocated by Walras), one would conclude that anything which is scarce and useful but which cannot be exchanged because it cannot be appropriated must be left out of the market and would consequently be considered a source of externalities. Thus, the most natural way to characterise genuine externalities was through the absence of ownership, 'the divorce of scarcity from effective ownership' to use Ellis and Fellner's consecrated formulation.[13] Indeed, in his own definition of 'divergences', Pigou (1962, pp. 174, 183, 214) very nearly suggests that most externalities on actual markets could be eliminated in principle by the establishment of property rights which would cause the resources involved 'to come to the right person'. For his part, Knight (1924, p. 163) based his own argument against Pigou on the proviso of private ownership. Clearly, one cannot count on the market to take care of that which cannot be appropriated.

Now, it was rapidly understood that the crux of the phenomenon was not the fact that some scarce commodities remain unappropriated and possibly unappropriable. Rather, the point is that activities exerted upon these unappropriated commodities affect the welfare of other parties, a phenomenon which was systematically analyzed for the first time by Meade in a famous (1952) paper which is often considered the starting point of the *modern* theory of externalities.[14] Using the example of the interdependence between an apple-grower and a bee-keeper,[15] Meade (1952, p. 67) managed to formalise a concept based on interaction between activities of agents interfering with one another's production function (which also could have been a welfare or a utility function). However, as was underscored by Scitovsky and Bator – and possibly anticipated by Pigou – to be counted as an externality, such interdependence had to be 'direct', in the sense that 'it does not operate through the market mechanism'[16] and in the sense of being 'external to the price system, hence unaccounted for by market valuations'.[17] After all, everything in economics is a matter of interdependence. My utility depends upon the activity of my baker, but as Adam Smith pointed out in a famous passage, it is not by benevolence but by self-interest (and therefore through the market) that he is contributing to it.[18] Thus, while such a situation is a clear case of interdependence, it would be absurd to describe it as a case of an externality because my baker's service is adequately *paid* through the market. If, by contrast, a case of interdependence is described as *external* and as different from what falls under the general rule, it is because 'it does not operate through the market mechanism'. In any case, in the tradition that dominated the 1950s and remained quite important during the 1960s, externalities were thought to be found anywhere the market mechanism failed to internalise – one could almost say to civilise – an interaction going on between economic agents.

In other words, when factors of production are 'unpaid' (like Meade's bees which are unpaid by the apple-grower) or, more generally, when services remain 'uncompensated' or 'unpriced' or 'free', then we must conclude that something is kept external to the market and that, therefore, externalities are present. In a formalised representation of a market, every agent has a utility function (and every firm has a production function) and such functions have various commodities (or factors) as independent variables. But, if some commodities (or factors) are unpaid while being independent variables of a function of the type $x_1 = F\ (l_1, c_1, \ldots;\ x_2,\ l_2, \ldots\ )$, these unpaid commodities (or factors) must be distinguished from those which are paid; therefore, they have to be put at the end of the function, 'to the right of the semicolon'.[19] Thus, in the algebraic representation of externalities typical for this period, the semicolon became the crucial element since its role, in a utility or in a production function, was to separate the standard priced elements (those on the left of the semicolon) from the unpriced elements (those on the right of the semicolon), which are responsible for the externality. According to Mishan, for example, 'the external effects in production may be exhibited by a production function of the form $x = x(a_1, a_m; \tilde{a}_n, \ldots, \tilde{a}_w)$ where x is output, a_1, a_m, the priced inputs, and $\tilde{a}_n, \ldots, \tilde{a}_w$, the unpriced inputs'.[20] In this manner, it was made graphically clear that externalities are nothing but a name for *residual* activities which are left outside the market, 'to the right of the semicolon'.

Now, to understand what it means for an activity to be performed outside a market, we need to know what it means for an activity to be exerted *inside* it. For neoclassical economists, from Walras to Samuelson, a market was characterised by reference to the paradigms of a perfect competition and general equilibrium. On the one hand, a perfectly competitive market requires that many conditions be fulfilled, especially regarding the character of the goods to be exchanged through it (multiplicity of identical, easily appropriable and exchangeable units which are usually also assumed to be perfectly divisible and reproducible). With the market modelled in such a restrictive way, it is not surprising that many activities were considered to be going on outside of it. On the other hand, in a market represented by elegant general equilibrium models, prices of all those goods are strictly determined, given a few fundamental data characterising the situation. In the context of such general equilibrium models, each good has to be *adequately* priced according to the rule of the market. Consequently, 'unpaid', 'uncompensated', 'unpriced' or 'free' goods or services appear clearly to be exchanged *outside* the market. In other words, if, when referring to *a highly demanding modelisation of the price system* such as those implying perfect competition and general equilibrium, one defines 'externalities' as activities external to such a price system, these externalities – which used to be considered rather scarce and looked for only in the bucolic realm of apple-growers and bee-keepers – become necessarily pervasive. These theoretical developments were sufficient to explain how the concept of an externality became associated with a pervasive phenomenon, but to understand its rising practical importance, one has to turn to the sensibility to the problem of pollution which was quickly growing during the 1950s and 1960s. During this period, the concept of an externality was put at the very centre of economic debates about government intervention since it was seen as the natural candidate in explaining why ecological problems remained unsolved by the market.

In a sense, this idea has been generalised to its extreme limit by Francis Bator who associated externalities with the cause of *any form* of 'market failure' to reach a Pareto-efficient solution. For Bator (1958, p. 361), 'the modern formulation of the doctrine of external economies, in terms of direct interaction' is full of merits, but it 'begs the fundamental question' concerning the cause of such externalities. The standard answer to this question in terms of non-appropriability looks quite unsatisfactory to Bator, because if non-appropriability means a simple 'inability of a producer of a good or service physically to exclude users' (p. 361, n. 8) it would be a very poor explanation since '"exclusion" is almost never impossible' (p. 374). Fences, scrambling devices and other gadgets can usually exclude successfully, but such exclusions fail lamentably when the final goal is to produce the Pareto-efficient solution that the market is supposed to. When one resorts to this type of solution, 'there is no price which will efficiently mediate both supply and demand' (p. 362, n. 9). Since the problems associated with externalities are not really solved by exclusion and appropriation, Bator decides to broaden the meaning of 'externality' and to let this word 'denote any situation where some Paretian costs and benefits remain *external to* decentralised cost–revenue calculations in terms of prices' (p. 362). Licensed by this broad definition, Bator and his followers[21] did not hesitate to include as externalities not only 'ownership externalities' (illustrated by Meade's unpaid apple-blossom, by 'shared deposits' of fish, by water and even by 'the training of non-slave labour to skills'), but also 'technical externalities' (illustrated by cases of non-convexities produced either by indivisibility or by 'smooth increasing returns to scale' and even by any structural problems causing monopoly behaviour or misallocation of useful resources), and 'public good externalities' (associated with most kinds of publicness, joint consumption, non-revelation of preferences, etc).[22] Bator's theory illustrates particularly well how, once neoclassical economists of the time had identified the market with a perfectly competitive structure subject to general equilibrium, the externalities, *as the residual left by such a market,* became literally pervasive.

Even without such a comprehensive definition of an externality, one could be tempted to diagnose externalities everywhere the market system fails to arrive at an efficient solution that the adequate pricing of goods and services normally provides. Thus, Mishan proposed the following definition of externalities: 'external effects may be said to arise when relevant effects on production or welfare go *wholly or partially* unpriced' (1965, p. 6, emphasis added). For example, rather than being *excluded* from the consumption of bridge services, individuals would be *charged* for using them. But, what would be an 'adequate' price for a service like that of a bridge which is provided in a situation of increasing return or even in a situation of practically zero marginal cost? Clearly such a service will be 'partially unpriced'. Thus according to Mishan's definition, externalities are also present each time a service, like the service provided by a bridge, is 'positively priced' but not priced 'adequately'. For Mishan, as for Bator, externalities (namely the activities which, in some sense, go on outside the market) are doomed to be pervasive.

I have focused on Bator's and Mishan's approaches because they illustrate the extent to which the idea that externalities are everywhere in the economic system had taken hold by the 1950s and 1960s. Such views were very influential during these decades, even during the 1970s; for example, Heller and Starrett (1976, p. 20) defended a thesis not too different from Bator's, when they concluded that an externality 'can always be associated with the failure of some potential market to operate properly'. In any case, such views illustrate how the concept of an externality tended to be perceived as what I have called a residual concept whose definition was directly dependent on the definition of the market. Once you have precisely characterised the meaning of that which is called a market, you have also determined what is left outside of such a structure, or more exactly, you have characterised the activities which the market does not control and each element of these residual activities will correspond to an externality.

But such a view supposes that something can be left outside a market, which sounded sensible for most neoclassical economists of this period because a market was seen by them as an highly artificial structure. From Walras to Samuelson, *neoclassical* economists had been busily constructing models of ideal markets. Actual markets, they expected, had to be made to conform to such models. When the real world refused to conform to these models, a neoclassical economist of the 1950s or 1960s typically concluded that he or she had to first determine what the situation would be like if a perfectly competitive market prevailed, and then look for a manageable way of attaining the closest approximation of it. Because perfect competition was an omnipresent norm for neoclassical economists, it was normal to diagnose externalities everywhere a gap existed between actual markets and this ideal model.

3 THE NEOLIBERAL APPROACH: 'EXTERNALITIES' OR TRANSACTION COSTS?

Our question now is: 'How has this picture been transformed?' Since I claim that an externality is a residual entity, my answer is, unsurprisingly, that it is transformed when the representation of a market is itself transformed. And indeed, the representation of the market has been radically transformed with the development of neoliberalism during the last decades. If the idea of perfect competition was the paradigm of the market for neoclassical economists from Walras to Samuelson, the idea of 'laissez faire' is the equivalent paradigm for neoliberal economists, whose influence was already decisive at the University of Chicago in the 1950s. According to the neoliberals, a real market has very little to do with the highly artificial structure designed by the neoclassicals. They have little use for the model of the perfectly competitive market, made up of a large number of agents of equal standing and of an indefinite number of standardised goods, all capable of being fully appropriated and easily exchanged without entailing significant transaction costs. For them, the real world does *not* need to be reshaped in the manner of a Walrasian market. For them, actual markets, if not systematically impeded, *are* already capable of providing, not without certain costs of course, a relatively optimal solution to allocational problems. By contrast, the neoclassical market tended to be conceived as a highly artificial and idealised structure whose conditions of realisation were so restrictive that in the actual world a large number of activities (designated as externalities) were going on outside its reach. These externalities were seen as an index of the gap existing between actual markets and this artificial structure. Not being obsessed by the model of a perfectly competitive market, neoliberals could hardly find any meaning in the notion of a 'gap' between actual markets and an ideal market. Consequently, they could hardly acknowledge any real usefulness in the concept of an 'externality'. Since, in other words, activities could no longer be meaningfully characterised as going on outside the market, it was the notion of an externality itself which tended to vanish alongside the development of the neoliberal conception of the market.

But, let us consider further this 'neoliberal' image of the market. It is understood as any place where gains from trade are possible and consequently where negotiations are going on. The agents in such a market need not be of equal standing, like Walrasian agents, but are agents who can hold very different amounts of power and normally make use of the power they have. Moreover, the goods which are transacted do not need to be standardised goods, and if these 'goods' are owned by the above agents, it is not necessarily in conjunction with well defined property rights. From an economic point of view, the crucial point is knowing who possesses the right to use the things which are considered as goods, and not the legal basis of the rights involved. For example, an industrialist operating on the shore of a river, may quite economically dispose of his garbage in the river as long as the law does not prohibit him from doing so. From a pragmatic point of view, and as far as *economic* relations are concerned, his right to use the river in this way is *not fundamentally different* from the right he has to use a commodity he has bought on the market. Similarly, if the law prohibits water pollution for the benefit of those who enjoy swimming in the river, the bathers' right to clean water is not significantly different from more conventional property rights. For economists, and especially for neoliberal economists, this means that in principle such 'rights' can be bought or sold freely on the market. It is true that such atypical commodities are not perfectly exchangeable in the way Walrasian goods are, but various types of transactions and negotiations among those who possess these rights are possible, and, from this point of view, they are similar to the transactions and negotiations that go on between Walrasian traders.

Given that the very presence of any type of trade (or negotiation) resulting in potential gains is enough to characterise a neoliberal market, it is easy to see how there is very little room left for externalities. Actual markets – or, to be more explicit, actual forms of negotiations occurring where gain from trade is possible – fit the paradigmatic model of a market by hypothesis. However, this does not mean that neoliberals consider all the problems which prompted neoclassicals to identify externalities to be nonexistent. Nor does it mean that they consider all those activities which, according to neoclassicals, were carried on outside a market (like the use of a river as a garbage disposal system by an industrialist), as being instead smoothly carried out inside one. Rather, the point was that such activities were seen as a consequence of a particular market situation, namely a situation with prohibitive transaction costs. The main contribution of neoliberal economics to our understanding of the market is probably the consideration and analysis of transaction costs. Indeed, transactions as such are *far from being without costs.* Searching for information, bargaining and decision making, policing, enforcement and monitoring[23] have prices, just as production and transportation have prices. Consequently, it is not always worthwhile to 'buy' the largest possible amount of such things. The consideration of transaction costs does not directly dissolve the concept of an externality, but it suggests that one should characterise the market in such a fashion that the phenomena previously described as externalities appear to be nothing but a consequence of a specific calculation made on the market. Whereas, for the neoclassicals, the scope of the market is limited by the presence of externalities, for the neoliberals, it is the very efficiency of its actual working which is limited by the existence of significant transaction costs.

As is well known, the crucial step in the analysis of such costs was taken by Ronald Coase in his seminal (1960) paper on social costs. Coase's strategy was to underline in a dramatic fashion the role of social costs in a market by carefully analyzing what would happen in their hypothetical absence. And it is this careful analysis which resulted in the famous Coase's theorem. The demonstration of this theorem is straightforward. Given the hypothesis of *zero* transaction costs and rational economic agents, it makes no difference, when it comes to the optimal allocation of resources, whether the rights favour the polluter or those who suffer from the pollution. The same result will prevail in both situations, since both parties will be ultimately led to a unique optimal agreement. For example, in the situation described above, suppose that the benefit from the easy disposal of garbage is greater than the benefit the bathers derive from clean water, but that, beyond a certain amount of pollution, the benefit lost by the bathers becomes larger than the extra benefit the polluter gains by polluting more extensively. If the law is against him, then the polluter will negotiate with the bathers and buy some 'optimal' amount of pollution rights from them. By hypothesis, they will accept compensation up to the point where they would start to suffer more from pollution than they could benefit from the compensation the polluter is ready to offer them. If the law is against the bathers who suffer from the water pollution, then it would be in their own interest to bribe the polluter into reducing the amount of pollution which he creates to the same 'optimal' level as in the previous case and it would be in the interest of the polluter to accept such a bribe and reduce pollution to this optimal level. Naturally, such a conclusion is purely theoretical since, according to Coase himself (1960, p. 15), transaction costs *are* highly significant in such situations. Collecting payments from those who suffer from the pollution and preventing some of them from cheating by not revealing their true preferences would involve, if feasible at all, tremendous costs indeed. However, Coase's intention was not to suggest that the paralyzing effect of such costs could be easily overcome and a smooth market organised but, on the contrary, to suggest that these costs must be accounted for in the normal calculations made on a market.

It is mainly the consequences of Coase's analysis on government policies oriented towards optimality and efficiency that have been extensively analyzed in the literature (produced during the 1960s and 1970s) which discussed externalities in light of Coase's theorem. For most of the authors of these papers, the main question was concerned with finding the appropriate solution to the problem diagnosed in this regard. For them, the essential question was to reevaluate, in this new context, Pigou's scheme of intervention based on taxes and subsidies. Rather than discussing this reevaluation, I would like to concentrate on the consequences of Coase's theorem on the very nature of externalities themselves. Referring no longer, in this context, to activities going on *outside the market*, the concept of an externality indeed looked emptied of its very meaning.

4 A RETURN TO PECUNIARY EXTERNALITIES OR THE VANISHING OF A CONCEPT

In some neoliberal analyses, this last conclusion seems to be verified, in an unexpected way, by the vanishing of the distinction from which, as we have seen, the modern concept of an externality painfully emerged, namely the distinction between genuine technological externalities and the so-called pecuniary externalities. In a paper written in 1964, Harold Demsetz, who was a particularly active defender of Coase's theorem, did not hesitate to discount any difference between these two types of externalities. Like Coase, he consistently avoided the term 'externality', yet the phrase 'side effects' is specifically chosen by him to replace 'external effects' (Demsetz, 1964, p. 11) and he compares these side effects to what he calls 'primary' effects, which are nothing but typical market interrelations or what, in another context, would have been called 'pecuniary effects'. Demsetz claims that 'there exist *no qualitative differences*' between these two types of effects, the only differences being 'those that are implicitly based on quantitative differences in exchange and police cost'[24] or, if one prefers, in transaction costs. To illustrate his point, Demsetz uses the following example. 'Suppose a factory invents a new more efficient furnace which can burn a cheaper grade of coal than can existing furnaces. The burning of cheap coal, we will assume, dirties homes in the neighbourhood (p. 25). No doubt this 'side effect' corresponds to a typical technological externality, but for Demsetz the only important point is that it reduces 'the wealth of nearby homeowners'. However, Demsetz continues, 'if this same factory, by virtue of its new furnace, successfully forces a nearby competing firm out of business, and if the resulting decline in demand for housing reduces the wealth of neighbourhood homeowners, we do not become concerned'. Indeed, this last situation corresponds to a usual market or pecuniary effect. Thus Demsetz raises the question: 'Why the difference in our attitudes toward these two situations which have the same effect on homeowners?' In the case of demand for housing, Demsetz (p. 26) explains, we feel that 'a smoothly operating market' will maximise wealth. If, in contrast, we cannot rely on an existing market in the smoke case, it is because 'the cost of exchanging and policing smoke contracts' (the transaction costs) are too high 'relative to the benefits of marketing smoke'. However, while this circumstance excludes the presence of an actual market, it is fully compatible with the presence of a 'potential market' which, according to Demsetz, 'stands ready'. But, how could any activity be outside the reach of such a potential market? If all the transaction costs are to be accounted by the market, either the smoke level and the values of the houses are actually controlled by the market according to the costs implied or the smoke level is left unreduced and the values of the houses decline accordingly because it is made clear by a *potential* market that controlling the smoke level this way would be prohibitive, given the costs involved including transactions costs. In the first case, there would be, by hypothesis, no externality, and in the second case, if one takes into account the potential role of the potential market, there would be none either.

It was this last conclusion that was to be made explicit and pushed to its extreme limit in a paper published in 1979 by Carl Dahlman. Once transaction costs have been placed on the same footing as the usual production and transportation costs, it seems normal to raise the same question which is raised concerning these familiar costs. Why incur these costs if they are themselves larger than the benefits to be derived from an eventual transaction? After all, you might dream of owning a Ferrari, but if you consider that the (production) costs involved are higher than the benefits expected from owning such a car, you could decide not to realise this dream without concluding that this absence of transaction corresponds to a non Pareto-optimal situation. Dahlman's central idea was to apply such a consideration to transaction costs. According to him, when assessing an optimal situation, it is a mistake to employ a Walrasian model without transaction costs. After all, an ideal world without transaction costs is just as unattainable as an ideal world without production costs.[25] This conclusion seems to make sense, but an odd consequence of it is that, once all transactions costs have been taken into account, *almost any static situation will look optimal.* If no transaction is going on to improve a situation, it is tempting to conclude that it is because the *costs* of an eventual transaction (for example, the cost of organising and monitoring would-be transactors) added to the payment involved in those eventual transactions make it unprofitable. If, for example, our industrialist persists in polluting the river even when the nuisance to bathers is greater than the benefit to the industry of using this polluting technique, it is, in one sense, because the 'transaction' costs (the cost of organising the bathers, of forcing them to reveal their true preferences and of collecting the amount required to convince the industrialist to reduce his operations, etc.) would be so great that, added to the amount of the bribe itself, it *would* exceed the potential benefit to the bathers.

In such conditions, the concept of an 'externality' becomes clearly meaningless. An all-inclusive concept of the market would be capable of absorbing all forms of human interaction, and it is easy to see why. Any potential externality could or could not be eliminated by some type of negotiations involving costs. In the first case, *by hypothesis*, there would no longer be the externality; in the second case, the failure to eliminate the putative externality would be due to *excessive economic (transaction) costs on the potential market*, and thus, strictly speaking, there would be no externality in this case either. Thus, according to such a neoliberal notion of an all-inclusive market, there would be no more reason to identify an externality in this pollution case than in the fact that, because of its high production cost, you refrain from buying the Ferrari you might dream of owning.

Along such lines of argument, one could arrive at the conclusion that any situation whatsoever is optimal since any improvement would be implemented were its costs, including transaction costs, low enough to make it socially profitable. It was just such a conclusion that Mishan anticipated with apprehension when he wrote (1971b) a rather ironic paper entitled 'Pangloss on Pollution'. The reference to Dr Pangloss, the pleasant champion of 'the best of all possible worlds' in Voltaire's *Candide,* was to suggest how the inclusion of transaction costs can dramatically change the analysis of pollution and transform into an optimal situation what was considered as one of the most serious challenges to economists' confidence in the virtues of the market. It might even be possible to push the matter further and suggest that such an argument could optimalise any situation whatsoever. Any dictatorial government, even of a type particularly inimical to liberalism, could be justified by an extension of this neoliberal argument. Dictatorial governments' activities interfere significantly with the consumption functions of their citizens by restricting their individual liberty. However, if the inconvenience suffered by these citizens was really that important, they could bribe the government to reduce its liberty-limiting activities to an optimal amount. If they do not attempt to bribe the government, it is clearly because such transactions would involve costs (information costs, organisation costs, decision making costs and monitoring costs) which would be much higher than the benefits expected. On this ground, it would make sense, according to an extreme – although somewhat inverted – neoliberal point of view, to characterise the situation in this dictatorial country as optimal as it is![26] Naturally, one might object to such an application of the neoliberal theory of the market to a political (as opposed to an economic) situation. However, the *actual* relation between an industrialist and the neighbouring bathers is not a typically economic relation, and consequently, it is not clear that alleged economic and political situations are really as different as first thought. As is well known, a number of prisoners successfully manage to bribe their jailers. And, after all, the application of economic analysis to political situations is, as is also well known, one of the major contributions of neoliberalism. In any case, the goal of this comparison was not to suggest that political and economic situations are equivalent, but to dramatically illustrate that, if pushed to the limit, there is an unexpected consequence to this conceptual change associated with the neoliberal approach: not only the concept of an externality but also its positive counterpart, the concept of a market, might lose their very meanings.

It would be unfair, however, to conclude that Coase, or even Dahlman, are inclined to push their arguments to such a limit. On the contrary, both insist that their views do not prevent appropriate government interventions insofar as the costs of such interventions would be themselves lower than the gains obtained by such interventions and lower than the costs (including transaction costs) involved in reaching a comparable result through the market. In other words, they would recommend government intervention if the costs involved were lower than the costs saved.[27] In any case, concerning the present argument, the point is not that such a neoliberal approach would exclude any type of intervention, but that the scope of such interventions is reduced by the fact that no activities can properly be considered as going on *outside* the market and that consequently no intervention can be justified simply on this ground, without being first submitted to a scarcely feasible measurement of the transaction costs saved by it. The point is that, in such a context, it is apparently no longer meaningful to refer to externalities at all.

5 SURVIVING AS A (USEFUL?) CONCEPT

But if such is the case, how has this concept found its way into so many papers written from a Coasian perspective during the 1960s and 1970s? How was it possible that this concept could have been treated as a useful tool in these papers? To answer this question, it might be helpful to consider another influential paper by James Buchanan and Craig Stubblebine written two years after the publication of Coase's own paper. While their analysis is akin to Coase's, Buchanan and Stubblebine extensively discuss the concept of an externality and even entitle their paper with the single word 'Externality'. The authors gave a definition of an externality which, at first glance, looks quite traditional: 'We define an external effect, *an externality,* to be present when, $u^A = u^A (X_1, X_2, \ldots, X_m, Y_1)$. This states that the utility of an individual, *A*, is dependent upon the "activities", $(X_1, X_2, \ldots, X_m)$, that are exclusively under his own control or authority, but also upon another single activity, Y_1, which is, by definition, under the control of a second individual, *B*, who is presumed to be a member of the same social group.'[28] This definition looks similar to those of Scitovsky and Mishan, which are also based on the idea of interdependence between activities, but is in fact quite different. Buchanan and Stubblebine no longer mention any distinction between 'paid' and 'unpaid' or between 'priced' and 'unpriced' activities. In other words, there is no longer a semicolon in the utility function because there is no longer any distinction between what is inside (paid or priced) and what is outside (unpaid or unpriced) the market. The dropping of the semicolon is not without consequences. Given that my utility is clearly dependent upon the activities my baker performs which are under his control but not under mine, how can one claim that no externalities are involved in our commercial relations without at least implicitly emphasising that I can buy his bread or control his activities to some extent by paying for them, that is, by implicitly contrasting paid activities with the unpaid ones which involve externalities? Clearly, when we remove the semicolon from the definition, it becomes much more difficult to figure out just when an 'absence of control' actually becomes a case of being 'external' to a state of things which presumably would be characterised by 'internal' relations.

In any case, Buchanan and Stubblebine (1962, pp. 371–5) introduced a few new distinctions between various types of externalities and concluded that only what they call 'Pareto-relevant externalities' correspond to the term 'externalities' as it is commonly employed by economists. However, this last remark sounds rather paradoxical if we consider that 'Pareto-relevant externalities' are precisely those which are characterised by the opportunity for 'gains from trade'. Since the opportunity for 'gains from trade' is the typical trait of a neoliberal market, it is implied that the word 'externalities', as usually used by economists, designates what is characterised by the normal working of the market as opposed to designating what is *outside* the market. This illustrates just how far the meaning of the word 'externality' was transformed, and even inverted, when used in the context of a neoliberal view of the market. The paradox, however, is partially dissipated when we consider that Buchanan and Stubblebine (p. 375) maintain that, once a Pareto-equilibrium is reached, 'Pareto-relevant externalities' vanish. Thus, externalities are present when such an equilibrium cannot be reached, mainly when transaction costs are too high and especially when 'costs of organising group decisions . . . will prevent realisation of some "gains from trade"'.[29] In a neoliberal view of the market, situations like those involving our group of bathers, who can hardly organise themselves to exploit the 'gains from trade' which were open to them, can still be characterised as externalities, but these 'externalities' must be defined in such a fashion that they be clearly located *inside* an ubiquitous market. Buchanan and Stubblebine, as well as Coase, place emphasis on the theoretical capacity of the market to internalise any situation of the type previously characterised as an externality. They do this in two stages: (1) such situations are presented as elements of a *potential* market, and (2) potential markets are implicitly treated as extensions or nearly integral parts of *the* market.

But is the word 'externality' an appropriate word to characterise a situation which is almost as internal to the market as situations giving rise to transactions, differing from them only in that potential transactors conclude that these transactions are not worthwhile? Naturally, material situations involved (bathers facing industrialists, farmers facing ranchers or facing smoke emission from trains) are of the same type, and one can understand why economists tend to use the same word to refer to similar material situations. But the word 'externality' refers explicitly to an economic trait (that of being external to something) which is no longer meaningful in this new context. Without doubt this partially explains why Coase (1988, pp. 20–30) himself never used the term 'externality' (p. 27) to expound his thesis and almost always framed it with inverted commas when he reviewed the whole question in a later book. To clarify his discussion of the question, Coase synthesises the usual definition in terms which, like those used by Buchanan and Stubblebine, refer only to interindividual interaction: 'An externality is more usually defined as the effect of one person's decision on someone who is not a party to that decision' (p. 24). This sober definition does not refer to 'direct' or 'unpriced' activities, but it distinguishes between situations in which the person affected by a decision is 'party to that decision' and situations in which that person is not 'party to that decision'. This minimal evocation (being not party to a decision) of what makes the externalities 'external' to the standard working of a market is already too much externalisation for Coase and prompts him to conclude negatively that such a statement is 'representative of the mainstream economic analysis' (p. 24).

It is true that most economists sympathetic to the neoliberal approach have been less reluctant than Coase to use a term so little congenial to their views. Consequently, the term 'externality' has been used extensively after Coase's seminal paper. In any case, the recent literature, which tends to bear as much on externality as on transaction costs, has been devoted to either refining or discussing Coase's approach, applying the resources of game theory to the whole problem, discussing Pigou's tax-subsidy schemes in the context of transaction costs or underscoring the limits of the market solution in the context of pollution or various forms of free riding, etc.[30] However, very little in this relatively recent literature has been devoted to the concept of an externality as such. Consequently, the ambiguity raised by the concept of an externality which is in fact no longer 'external' to anything has not been dissipated.

It seems reasonable to conclude that far from being clarified during its tumultuous history, the meaning of this concept has become increasingly ambiguous. After being perceived more and more as a residual concept associated with the concept of an artificially designed market, the concept of an externality was reduced dramatically as, with the development of neoliberalism, the concept of market expanded to fill the whole place. Having, in the meantime, been associated with the notion of interdependence, it continued to refer to any form of this type of phenomenon. No doubt in order to accommodate the neoliberal conception of the market, the concept of an externality had to be defined vaguely enough to avoid any implicit reference to an outside of the market, which would have restored it to its original meaning and would have, by this very fact, denied the ubiquitous character of the neoliberal market. Alternatively, when this concept has been defined in a more meaningful fashion, it was the very existence of the phenomenon to which it refers that was to be denied in a neoliberal perspective, in such a way that, specifically understood, this phenomenon was treated as a remnant of the old-fashion neoclassical approach that still prevails among those who refer to a highly abstract but perfectly civilised' conception of the market.

* * *

Economists do not seem to be bothered by these ambiguities. When it comes to the policy problems which are most important to them, the proper definition of a residual concept could hardly be determinant, precisely because it is residual. When it comes to deciding whether taxing the polluters, prohibiting pollution or abstaining from any intervention will result in the maximal social product, it seems that economists can arrive at their conclusions without the help of any common satisfactory definition of externalities. Whether we characterise pollution as a market failure or as a situation resulting from excessive transactions costs, it does not seem to affect such results very much indeed. Those referring to market failures would say that transactions do not take place between polluters and pollutees because their relations are external to the (actual) market which breaks down at a given point. Those referring to transaction costs would *also* say that actual transactions do not take place between polluters and pollutees because, while nothing is external to the market, the transaction costs computed on a potential market prohibit these transactions from taking place. Insofar as the only issue at stake – and a large part of the post-Coasian literature on externalities is concerned with similar issues – is an investigation of how a tax on polluters and a banishment of pollution would respectively affect GNP, it is not clear that differences in the way one defines a market (should the market include potential markets or not? should it leave room for externalities or not? . . .) matters very much. With both types of definition of the market and externalities, it is possible in principle to assess the respective effects of the tax and the banishment insofar as it is possible to assess the costs and benefits tentatively associated with each of them. Between both perspectives, the only difference which matters in such computations concerns *what should count as a cost* to be deducted from the benefits, but the answer to such a question does not seem, at first glance, to be *directly* related to the definition of an externality. Saying that a cost should be counted in a cost-benefit analysis is not the same thing as saying that a cost is accounted for by a market. Even if an economist is not inclined to refer to potential markets which are made inoperative by excessive transactions costs, that does not imply that he or she is not sensible to the fact that a prohibition of pollution implies tremendous monitoring costs. But, if such is the situation, why bother with defining a term like 'externality' that we can dispense with without serious trouble? Do we not learn from the long debate on externalities that definitions and methodological considerations do not matter when economic results are involved? I am sure that many economists, including many eminent participants in the debate on externalities, would be inclined to conclude along these lines.

However, from a different point of view, the very fact that economic issues might be independent of the clarification of conceptual issues raises, in itself, a serious question about the meaning of these results of economic analysis. One cannot but be perplexed in considering the fact that the formidable problems that were associated with externalities like pollution, free riding, publicness, etc. have more or less dissolved as economists turned progressively from a Samuelsonian neoclassical approach to a Coasian neoliberal one, from a pure competition to a laissez faire conception of the market.[31] That this formidable challenge to the market was magically dissolved by a wave of the wand which has awakened a multitude of potential markets kept asleep by transaction costs, is in itself an index of a more fundamental issue. Far from implying that such issues are also indifferent to the debate concerning the definition of the market and of externalities, the fact that more typical issues raised by economists are relatively indifferent to this debate raises questions about the very meaning of economists' results.

In fact, what has been saved by the Coasian approach is the *image* of optimality associated with the market. Since Adam Smith's Invisible Hand, the idea of optimality has been more or less closely associated with the notion of the market, even if this idea was formally defined much later. In this context, the concept of an externality was characterised, as we have seen, as the residual of the market. If the market produces optimal results, suboptimal results could be expected outside of its realm. Thus, the distinction between pecuniary and technical externality was received as the definitive annexation by the *actual* market of those situations which were associated with pecuniary externalities: in contrast with those associated with genuine externalities such situations became sheer manifestations of the normal working of the market. But with Demsetz and Dahlman, the market no longer has an outside, since *potential* markets fill the whole space not occupied by actual markets; consequently, the distinction between pecuniary and technological externalities ceased to be a significant one. In such a context, it is the very concept of optimality which starts to be voided of meaning, because no situation whatsoever can fail to be optimal.[32] Actually, the link between market and optimality is ultimately based on the idea that people are not stupid enough to miss taking advantage of an opportunity of gain from trade provided by the market. But suppose that a significant opportunity exists somewhere which is known to all parties but which is not being exploited. Clearly this is because no actual market is organised enough to permit the required trade. It does not help to claim that a potential market exists in principle, because the problem is precisely that it is only in principle that such a potential market exists, which is to say that it has little chance to become an actual market. Markets are nothing but structures which facilitate and make possible trade. Consequently, a market is an actual market (though perhaps not a currently functioning one) or it is not a market at all. If it is practically impossible to create, forget it and acknowledge that we are outside the market! No doubt, the bathers could make an advantageous deal with the polluter, but the problem is that no actual market exists for such a deal to be made. Looking at potential markets and at transaction costs does not help because the transaction costs of creating the potential market are so extreme and so 'unmarketlike' that it sounds reasonable to conclude that acknowledging this fact amounts to saying that no market exists or that markets fail to solve this problem.

Given that the *practical* difference looks so slight between the idea of prohibitive transaction costs and the idea of market failure, it is hardly surprising that conceptual and methodological issues about the definition of externalities seem to be of little importance when it comes to solving an economic problem such as measuring the impact of various policies on national product, but the importance of these methodological issues might reappear after all when it comes to deciding what should count as a cost and consequently what is ultimately the optimal solution. Indeed, the Coasian approach correctly suggests computing all the costs involved in a decision, but it does not say how to draw a demarcation line between various enterprises like organising a multitude of bathers in such a way that (after revealing their true preferences) they act as a single agent to bribe an industrialist, organising an oppressed people to bribe a dictatorial government and induce it to become more liberal, changing the mentality of a whole people on such or such a point, etc. It is true that all these potential activities have tremendous costs, but it is far from clear that this very fact is sufficient for them to be qualified as *market* activities. Above all, it is far from clear that an attempt to force them into the framework of the market will authorise us to apply to such a market the theorems concerning optimality which can be derived from the postulates associated with a typical neoclassical market. If I have attempted to discover the rationale behind the vagaries in the evolution of this concept, it is because I think that it might help in clarifying the meaning of economists' conclusions which are at least implicitly related to optimality, and it is because I suspect that, from this point of view, much can be learned from an analysis of the long and inconclusive debate on externalities.

Notes

1. The author would like to thank Roger Backhouse, Andrea Boitani, Camille Bronsard, Andrew Connochie, Daniel Hausman, Gérald Lafleur, Ejan Mackaay, Robert Nadeau, Michel Rosier, Andrea Salanti, Bruce Toombs and all the participants in the IEA conference for their very useful comments on one or another version of this paper. Thanks also to the SSHRC (Ottawa) and the Fonds FCAR (Quebec) for financial assistance. Some of the views developed in this paper have been previously addressed in French in Lagueux (1990).
2. Scitovsky (1954, p. 143).
3. Arrow (1970, p. 1). Hausman (1992, p. 95) quotes approvingly the same sentence drawn from another paper by Arrow, published in his (1983) *Collected Papers*. About the ambiguity of the concept see also Mishan (1965, pp. 4–5; p. 4, n. 2).
4. In the Appendix of Hausman (1992), Hausman offers a useful sample of various definitions of externalities found in the literature.
5. See Coase (1988, p. 23, n. 35).
6. Marshall (1966, pp. 220, 378).
7. Pigou (1962, pp. 172ff). In fact Pigou had been preceded on this ground by Henry Sidgwick, who in his *Principles of Political Economy* (1887) referred also to a 'divergence between private and public interest' (quoted by Laffont, 1977, p. 14). Incidentally, Pigou referred to another passage of the *Principles* which introduces the famous example of the lighthouse (Pigou, 1962, p. 184).
8. Pigou (1962, p. 174).
9. Pigou (1962, p. 174).
10. Pigou (1962, p. 183).

11. Pigou (1962, pp. 183–203).
12. Ellis and Fellner (1943, p. 247); Frank Knight had previously argued by invoking such a rent in his famous discussion of the traffic example, cf. Knight (1924, pp. 162–3).
13. Ellis and Fellner (1943, p. 262).
14. Meade (1952), is so characterised by Laffont (1977, p. 18).
15. Meade (1952, section IV); in fact he used this example to illustrate only the first of two types of external (dis)economies, but it is with this example that his formal definition has been associated. Incidentally, any less bucolic example of interdependence characterised by subaddictive production functions would have worked just as well.
16. Scitovsky (1954, p. 144).
17. Bator (1958, p. 358).
18. Smith (1937, p. 14).
19. Scitovsky (1954, p. 145).
20. Mishan (1965, p. 6); see also his survey paper for the *Journal of Economic Literature* (Mishan, 1971a, p. 2).
21. Among them the author of such an influential textbook as Ferguson (1969, pp. 461–4).
22. Bator (1958, pp. 363–71).
23. For an enumeration of transaction costs along these lines, see Dahlman (1979, p. 148), quoted approvingly by Coase (1988, p. 6).
24. Demsetz (1964, p. 25, emphasis added).
25. Dahlman (1979, p. 152); see especially n. 17, where he illustrates his point in a somewhat ironic fashion.
26. I have discussed such an example in relation to Coase's theorem and Dahlman's paper in Lagueux (1990, in French).
27. See Calabresi (1968, p. 69); Dahlman (1979, Part IV).
28. Buchanan and Stubblebine (1962, p. 372).
29. Buchanan and Stubblebine (1962, p. 377); see also Turvey, (1963, p. 312).
30. For a few relatively recent examples of interesting theoretical contributions devoted to underscoring, with the help of game theory, the limitations of the Coase theorem as a potential solution to what is sometimes called 'the problem of externalities', see Aivazian and Callen, (1981); Samuelson (1985); Schweizer (1988); Hurwicz (1995); the first of these papers being followed by a rejoinder (Coase, 1981).
31. I have discussed more extensively this distinction between neoclassicism and neoliberalism in Lagueux (1989, in French).
32. For Demsetz situations associated with technological externalities *are not less optimal* than those associated with pecuniary externalities. It is interesting to note that Hausman (1992), who underscores the ethical problem raised by externalities, claims that situations associated with pecuniary externalities *are not less suboptimal ethically* than those associated with technological externalities (pp. 97–8).

References

Aivazian, V.A. and J.L. Callen (1981) 'The Coase Theorem and the Empty Core', *Journal of Law and Economics,* vol. 24, pp. 175–81.

Arrow, K.J. (1970) 'Political and Economic Evaluation of Social Effects and Externalities', in J. Margolis (ed.), *The Analysis of Public Output* (New York: Columbia University Press), pp. 1–30.

Bator, F. (1958) 'The Anatomy of Market Failure', *Quarterly Journal of Economics*, vol. 72, pp. 351–79.

Buchanan, J.M. and W.C. Stubblebine (1962) 'Externality', *Economica*, vol. 29, pp. 371–84.

Calabresi, G. (1968) 'Transaction Costs, Resource Allocation, and Liability Rules: A Comment', *Journal of Law and Economics*, vol. 11, pp. 67–73.

Coase, R.H. (1960) 'The Problem of Social Cost', *Journal of Law and Economics*, vol. 3, pp. 1–44; reprinted: in Coase (1988), 95–156.

——— (1981) 'The Coase Theorem and the Empty Core: A Comment', *Journal of Law and Economics*, vol. 24, pp. 183–7.

——— (1988) *The Firm, the Market and the Law* (Chicago: University of Chicago Press).

Dahlman, C.J. (1979) 'The Problem of Externality', *Journal of Law and Economics,* vol. 22, pp. 141–62.

Demsetz, H. (1964) 'The Exchange and Enforcement of Property Rights', *Journal of Law and Economics,* vol. 7, pp. 11–26.

Ellis H.S. and W. Fellner (1943) 'External Economies and Diseconomies', *American Economic Review*, vol 33, pp. 493–511; reprinted in Stigler and Boulding (1952), pp. 242–63.

Ferguson, C. (1969) *Microeconomics Theory* (Homewood, IL: Irwin).

Hausman. D. (1992) 'When Jack and Jill Make a Deal', *Social Philosophy and Policy,* vol. 9, pp. 95–113.

Heller, W.P. and D.A. Starrett (1976) 'On the Nature of Externalities', in S. Lin, ed., *Theory and Measurement of Economic Externalities* (New York: Academic Press), pp. 9–22.

Hurwicz, L. (1995) 'What is the Coase Theorem?', *Japan and the World Economy,* vol. 7, pp. 49–74.

Knight, F.H. (1924) 'Some Fallacies in the Interpretation of Social Cost', *Quarterly Journal of Economics,* vol. 38, pp. 582–606, reprinted in Stigler and Boulding (1952), pp. 160–79.

Laffont, J.-J. (1977) *Effets externes et théorie économique,* monographie du séminaire d'économétrie, XIII (Paris: Éditions du Centre National de la Recherche Scientifique).

Lagueux, M. (1989) 'Le néo-libéralisme comme programme de recherche et comme idéologie', *Cahiers d'économie politique,* 16–17 (Paris: L'Harmattan), pp. 129–52.

——— (1990) 'Externalités, marché et coûts de transaction', *La méthodologie de l'économie théorique et appliquée aujourd'hui,* Colloque annuel de l'Association française de science économique (Paris: Nathan), pp. 169–79.

Marshall, A. (1966) *Principles of Economics,* 8th edn (London: Macmillan).

Meade, J.E. (1952) 'External Economies and Diseconomies in a Competitive Situation', *Economic Journal,* vol. 62, pp. 54–67.

Mishan, E.J. (1965) 'Reflections on Recent Developments in the concept of External Effects', *Canadian Journal of Economics and Political Science*, vol. 31, pp. 1–34.

——— (1971a) 'The Postwar Literature on Externalities: An Interpretative Essay', *Journal of Economic Literature*, vol. 9, pp. 1–28.

——— (1971b) 'Pangloss on Pollution', *Swedish Journal of Economics*, vol. 73, pp. 113–20.

Pigou, A.C. (1962 [1920]) *Economics of Welfare*, 4th edn (London: Macmillan).

Samuelson, W. (1985) 'A Comment on the Coase Theorem', in A. Roth, (ed.), (1985) *Game-theoretic Models of Bargaining* (Cambridge MA: MIT Press), pp. 321–39.

Schweizer, U. (1988) 'Externalities and the Coase Theorem: Hypothesis or Result?', *Journal of Institutional and Theoretical Economics*, vol. 144, pp. 245–66.

Scitovsky, T. (1954) 'Two Concepts of External Economies', *Journal of Political Economics*, vol. 62, pp. 143–51.

Sidgwick, H. (1887) *Principles of Political Economy* (London: Macmillan).

Smith, A. (1937) *An Inquiry into the Nature and Causes of the Wealth of Nations* (New York: Modern Library).

Stigler, G. and K. Boulding (1952) *Readings in Price Theory*, vol VI, American Economic Association Readings (Chicago: Irwin).

Turvey, R. (1963) 'On Divergences between Social Cost and Private Cost', *Economica*, vol. 10, pp. 309–13.

Viner, J. (1931) 'Cost Curves and Supply Curves', *Zeitschrift für Nationalökonomie*, vol. III, pp. 23–46; reprinted in Stigler and Boulding (1952), pp. 198–232.

Comment: The Growing Role of Externalities in Economic Theory

Andrea Boitani
CATHOLIC UNIVERSITY OF MILAN, ITALY

Maurice Lagueux has done us a service in listing the ambiguities that have plagued the debate on externalities for over half a century and in sorting out some truly misleading definitions of externalities which have been given. However, I suspect I cannot agree with Lagueux's conclusion that the debate on externalities has been inconclusive.

First of all, a good definition of externality is now available (Arrow would probably agree). In a well known textbook, Gravelle and Rees (1981, p. 509) write:

> An externality is said to exist if some of the variables which affect one decision-maker's utility or profit are under the control of another decision maker.

Formally, this definition implies that if agent A has an action $x_A \varepsilon X_A$ (the set of possible actions of A) which enters the pay-off function of another agent B, $\pi_B = f(\ldots x_A))$ in such a way that $\partial\pi_B/\partial x_A \neq 0$ then there is an externality.

I think this definition is a good one, because it is sufficiently abstract to apply independently of any specified institutional setting. Indeed, such a definition is independent of any distribution of property rights and is independent also of any assumption about the nature of competition. Since Pigou externalities have often been defined as those consequences of economic behaviour that a perfectly competitive price system is not able to internalise.

Perfect competition applies in a 'large economy', in which agents can be said to be price takers. In a 'large economy' any *intentional* action by an economic agent affects only his/her welfare, leaving the welfare of any other agent unaffected. Under perfect competition there is no direct interaction among individuals, who are parametrically rational. It should not come as a surprise that – when perfect competition is assumed to be the benchmark of economic theorising – externality is a residual concept. I believe that many of the ambiguities in the debate on externalities come from the fact that the Pigovian economist starts his/her analysis by dealing with a world in which the 'connective tissue' of society is made of (given) prices. It is true, as Lagueux writes, that '[a]fter all, everything in economics is a matter of interdependence'. But, under perfect competition such an interdependence cannot be *used* strategically by economic agents. It is perhaps interesting to notice that the modern notion of perfect competition can be traced back to John Stuart Mill's characterisation of a situation in which 'a person's conduct affects the interests of no person besides himself' (Mill, 1982, p. 142). In such a world 'there should be perfect freedom, legal and social, to do the action and stand the consequence' (Mill, 1982, p.142). That is, in modern terms, in such a world any equilibrium outcome is Pareto-efficient and no government intervention is needed as far as efficiency is concerned (First Theorem of Welfare Economics).

Price taking of course implies that prices are not the outcome of intentional 'actions'. This explains why economists have been so careful in stressing that interdependencies had to be direct, not operating through the price system, to be counted as externalities.[1] What about a Bertrand-like oligopoly model in which prices are the strategic variables, i.e. the price chosen by agent *A* enters the pay-off function of agent *B* (and vice versa)? Should one say that externalities are present in a Cournot-type oligopoly and absent in a Bertrand-type one? I believe this is nonsense. It is a nonsense brought about by the continous reference to a perfectly competitive context, in which prices are not 'set' in a strategic environment but 'taken' as given.

Externality is necessarily a residual and even uncomfortable concept if perfect competition is the canonical context for economic theorising. Outside the realm of perfect competition the notion of externality becomes the cornerstone of both *micro* and *macro* economic analysis and, I would suggest, of political theory as well. After all, political theory, since Hobbes, attempts to design an artificial coordination mechanism – the social contract – that allows 'external effects' to be internalised in such a way that individual incentives are no longer in conflict with the pursuit of shared goals.[2]

One should also stress that externalities become relevant in a Paretian sense only when they are *reciprocal*. That is if $\partial\pi_B/\partial x_A < 0$ but $\partial\pi_A/\partial x_B = 0$ ($x_B \, \varepsilon X_B$, X_B being the set of possible actions of agent *B*) the equilibrium ensuing from individual maximising behaviour cannot be Pareto-improved. In no way the welfare of agent *B* can be improved, while not reducing the welfare of agent *A*. Only *reciprocal externalities* are Pareto-relevant (in the sense of Buchanan and Stubblebine, 1962). And many theorists regard only Pareto-relevant externalities as relevant for political theory. A social contract could never be stipulated between agent *A* and *B* were externalities, not reciprocal, as *A* would not accept a limitation in his/her set of possible actions (identified with his/her Hobbesian natural rights) whenever *B* has no action affecting the welfare of *A*.

In commenting on Buchanan and Stubblebine, Lagueux complains that they drop a crucial 'semicolon' and do not distinguish between 'priced' and 'unpriced' activities. By so doing he proves to be one of the many social thinkers who find it difficult to appreciate fully Coase's path-breaking contribution. Indeed, Lagueux seems more interested in the use that some followers made of Coase than in Coase's profound intuitions.

In The Problem of Social Cost' Coase made it crystal clear that:

> the traditional approach has tended to obscure the nature of the choice that has to be made. The question is commonly thought of as one in which *A* inflicts harm on *B* and what has to be decided is, How should we restrain *A*? But this is wrong. We are dealing with a problem of a reciprocal nature. To avoid the harm to *B* would be to inflict harm on *A*. The real question that has to be decided is, Should *A* be allowed to harm *B* or should *B* be allowed to harm *A*? (Coase, 1960, p. 96).

Coase, of course, ignored game theory. Yet, since Davis and Whinston (1962) it is clear that the existence of reciprocal externalities is equivalent to a strategic decision context and that the inefficiencies due to the presence of externalities are tantamount to the inefficiencies of Nash equilibria[3].

Once this is clear, it should also be clear that Pareto-improvements demand, in one way or another, joint action. To see this, it is useful to return to the two-agents' example and assume there are reciprocal externalities and no property rights. Let us define $S = X \times Y$ as the set of all possible outcomes of the strategic interaction between agents *A* and *B*. $S^{\#} \subset S$ is the set of Nash equilibria, whilst $S^{*} \subset S$ is the set of Pareto-efficient outcomes. Given the presence of reciprocal externalities it may be $S^{\#} \cap S^{*} = \phi$. In order to select a situation $s^{\circ} \varepsilon S$ such that s° Pareto-dominates all $s^{\#} \varepsilon S^{\#}$ and possibly $s^{\circ} \varepsilon S^{*}$, either (i) the two individuals are able to enter some self-enforcing agreement or (ii) they must agree to give rise to some 'institution' which is enabled to select s° or enforce the agreement on s°.

Coase, in his theorem, pointed out that, in the absence of transaction costs, a self-enforcing agreement is always available. As Cheung (1992, p. 53) aptly points out:

> what Coase stated here was something we knew all along, namely the theorem of exchange attributed to Edgeworth and others. But Edgeworth and his contemporaries are caught rushing to the dinner table because the constraints they specified are incomplete'.

Coase specified fully the constraints: the absence of transaction costs. But he did more than that. He tried to let economists understand that 'what we buy and sell are rights to take (or not take), or to prevent or allow others to take, certain actions' (Coase, 1992, p. 74). Once this is realised, the Coase Theorem 'turns into the statement that rights will be acquired by those to whom they are most valuable'. Which implies that, when transactions are costless, there is no need for a well defined set of property rights for the Coase theorem to apply:

> Cheung has even argued that if transaction costs are zero 'the assumption of private property rights can be dropped without in the least negating the Coase Theorem' *and he is no doubt right* (Coase, 1988, pp. 14–15, italics added)[4].

There could not be a more radical departure from the Pigovian tradition, which assumes a *given* institutional context, a *given* and un-marketable set of property rights, besides postulating that there is 'a *prima facie* case for public intervention' whenever there is an externality[5]. Again, it can be seen that the Pigovian tradition is firmly rooted in John Stuart Mill, who maintained that 'as soon as any part of a person's conduct affects prejudicially the interests of others, society has jurisdiction over it' (Mill, 1982, p. 141).

Lagueux correctly points out that 'Coase's intention was not to suggest that the paralysing effect of such [i.e. transaction] costs could be easily overcome and a smooth market organised but, on the contrary, to suggest that these costs must be accounted for in the normal calculations made on a market' (pp. 133–4). Indeed Coase himself (1988, p. 174) writes that:

> the world of zero transaction costs has often been described as a Coasian world. Nothing could be further from the truth. It is the world of modern economic theory, one which I was hoping to persuade economists to leave.

I do not wish to discuss the 'Panglossian' use of Coase made by some of Coase's followers, perhaps against Coase's own intentions[6]. I just want to stress that once Coase's intuitions about the reciprocal nature of externalities are correctly placed within a strategic context, it becomes clear that externalities are more 'primitive' than markets. Whilst there are externalities in an hypothetical state of nature, markets are institutions which require some initial endowment of property rights, and 'for anything approaching perfect competition to exist, an intricate system of rules and regulations would normally be needed' (Coase, 1988, p. 9).

I also wish to briefly argue that reciprocal externalities have become central to many new developments in macroeconomics. It is fair, however, to remark that the explicit interpretation of a macroeconomic phenomenon as an externality was advanced by Baumol (1952), when he discussed the asymmetry in upward and downward flexibility of money wages and prices to explain the inflation trap.

As has been shown by Drazen (1987), Cooper and John (1988), Illing (1993) and John (1995) macro models based on imperfect competition or search that give rise to the Keynesian result of underemployment equilibrium have an underlying structural similarity: both imperfect competition and search models exhibit positive reciprocal externalities (due to demand spillovers, or price competition, or search effort) coupled with strategic complementarity (using the same symbols as above, strategic complementarity exists if $\partial^2\pi_i/\partial x_A \partial x_B > 0$, $i = A, B$)[7].

It is because of the existence of positive reciprocal externalities that one can argue the Pareto-inefficiency of Nash underemployment equilibria in such models. Moreover, when strategic complementarity is sufficiently strong to give rise to multiple equilibria, the existence of positive reciprocal externalities implies that such equilibria are Pareto-rankable. Hence if the economy is stuck in a Pareto-inferior equilibrium there is a *coordination failure*. Attaining a Pareto-efficient equilibrium requires coordinating actions, either by means of 'cheap talk' or by means of credible 'institutions'[8].

It is again because of the existence of reciprocal externalities in imperfectly competitive economies that one can show the existence of an aggregate demand (or macroeconomic) externality in any such equilibrium (Ball, 1987; Blanchard and Kiyotaki, 1987; Ball and Romer, 1991).

A precise definition of a macroeconomic externality is still missing in the literature, but it is possible to give one such definition as soon as one enriches the strategic context used so far. Assume that $\pi_i = f(x_{A},, x_B; \mu)$ is twice continuously differentiable, where is an exogenous parameter. Assume further that the game is symmetric. Let simply x be the common value of action x_i. Then a macroeconomic externality is said to exist if $\left.\frac{\partial \pi_i}{\partial x}\right|_{\bar{\mu}} \neq 0$ for all i. In words a macroeconomic externality exists if, for any given value of the exogenous parameter, a joint variation in the level of all agents' actions has a non-zero effect on the pay-offs of every agent.

Typically, in macroeconomic models the exogenous parameter is the money supply or some other index of aggregate demand, whilst prices and/or wages are the strategic variables. It is easy to show that the presence of macroeconomic externalities in equilibrium entails that a spontaneous reduction of *all* nominal prices and wages will induce higher real aggregate output, employment and welfare, through the well known wealth effect[9]. Hence in an imperfectly competitive macroeconomic equilibrium, given the money supply, nominal prices and wages are too high with respect to social optimum.

It can also be shown that nominal price rigidity is due to the presence of reciprocal externalities and gives rise to a macroeconomic externality of the kind exemplified above. As Ball (1987, p. 615) writes:

> keeping wages and prices rigid has negative externalities, because a rigidity created by one agent hurts the overall performance of the economy and therefore reduces the welfare of other agents.

This means that small costs of reducing rigidities may prevent the attainment of Pareto-superior macroeconomic states as they are not Nash equilibria. Again, due to strategic complementarity, there may be multiple equilibria in price adjustment, giving rise to coordination failures (Ball and Romer, 1991; Andersen, 1994).

It should come as no surprise that Pigovian taxes have been advocated to change the trade-off between the costs of changing prices and the costs of aggregate output fluctuations, that is to cure the macroeconomic externality due to price rigidity (Agell and Dillén, 1994). Whether Pigovian taxes are capable of internalising macroeconomic as well as more conventional microeconomic externalities is still an open question.

However, transaction costs might be too high and property rights too difficult to be defined for an efficient bargained solution to emerge. The problem can be dealt with only by direct comparison of the efficacy and efficiency of different institutional arrangements.

Summing up, the very notion of externality is external to economics as far as the dismal science assumes non-interacting behaviour (i.e. perfect competition) as its *alpha* and *omega*. But as soon as strategic interdependence and game theory come to centre stage, externality can be no longer regarded as a residual concept nor can it be confined to bee-keepers and apple-growers, nor even to polluters and pollutees, as Lagueux seems inclined to do. If game theory is the natural and indispensable structure for understanding any kind of social interaction among human beings – as Elster (1989, chapter 3) convincingly argues – externality becomes a cornerstone concept for social theory at large.

Notes

1. In such a famous textbook as Varian (1978) one may read that there is an externality 'when the actions of one agent affect the enviroment of another agent *other than by affecting prices*' (p. 203, italics added).
2. Of course, there is more than this in political theory. However, the statement in the text is a fair portrait of the contemporary game theoretic literature on the social contract. See Binmore (1994) for a survey and assessment of this literature.
3. It is perhaps interesting to notice that Davis and Whinston (1962, p. 242) stress that 'another result of our approach will be a demonstration that externality problems involve many aspects of duopoly problems'. See also Regan (1972, p. 428) who writes that 'the Coase Theorem is a proposition in the theory of games'.
4. In Boitani and Grillo (1992) it was argued that (1) the Coase theorem can be regarded as a general proposition of efficiency in 'state of nature' where there is no arrangement of property rights, provided that transactions are costless; (2) when transaction costs are positive only incomplete contracts (in the sense of Hart and Holmström, 1987) are available which define an allocation of property rights; (3) such an allocation may well be inefficient insofar as no simultaneous act of exchange is available.
5. See Pigou (1952, p. 331); Samuelson (1947, p. 20; Hahn (1982, pp. 7–8).
6. It has been aptly argued that 'reading Coase's 1960 paper without taking into account the 1937 paper is the premise for the Coasian vulgarisation against which Coase strives in his recent papers aimed at reconstructing his thought. A vulgarisation that presents Coase's arguments [the Coase 'Theorem'] as aimed at prejudicially turning down any normative design, even in the presence of market failures' (Grillo, 1995, p. 16, translation mine).

7. If imperfect competition is of the Cournot-oligopoly variety, there will be negative externalities and strategic substitutability within an industry and positive externalities and strategic complementarities among industries, provided there are demand spillovers across industries. See Boitani (1992), John (1995).
8. Institutions have been defined as 'any shared rule or set of rules which guide individual behaviour by supplementing the conventional "utility" maximising calculations' (Hargreaves Heap, 1994, p. 36). See also Schotter (1981, p. 11) on social institutions and coordination problems. On the general problem of coordination in economic activity see the contributions collected in Friedman (1994).
9. It is obvious that the wealth effect works (or does not work) under perfect as well as under imperfect competition. But one cannot define macroeconomic externalities under perfect competition because there prices are *not* strategic variables, i.e. there is no reciprocal externality in price setting.

References

Agell J. and M. Dillén (1994) 'Macroeconomic Externalities. Are Pigovian Taxes the Answer?', *Journal of Public Economics*, vol. 53, pp. 111–26.

Andersen, T. (1994) *Price Rigidity* (Oxford: Clarendon Press).

Ball, L. (1987), 'Externalities from Contract Length', *American Economic Review*, vol. 77 (4), pp. 615–29.

Ball, L. and D. Romer (1991) 'Sticky Prices as Coordination Failures', *American Economic Review*, vol. 81 (3), pp. 539–52.

Baumol, W.J. (1952) *Welfare Economics and the Theory of the State* (London: Longman Green).

Binmore, K. (1994) *Game Theory and the Social Contract I: Playing Fair* (Cambridge MA: MIT Press).

Blanchard, O.J. and N. Kiyotaki (1987) 'Monopolistic Competition and the Effects of Aggregate Demand', *American Economic Review*, vol. 77 (4), pp. 647–66.

Boitani, A. (1992) 'Post Keynesians versus New Keynesians on imperfect competition and macroeconomic equilibrium', in M. Sebastiani (ed.), *The Notion of Equilibrium in the Keynesian Theory* (London: Macmillan), pp. 223–40.

Boitani, A. and M. Grillo (1992) 'Some Reflections on Externalities, Coase Theorem and the Endogenous Determination of Property Rights', *Metroeconomica*, vol. 43 (3), pp. 309–26.

Buchanan, J.M., and W.C. Stubblebine (1962) 'Externality ', *Economica*, vol. 29 (4), pp. 371–84.

Cheung, S.N. (1992) 'On the New Institutional Economics', in L. Werin and H.Wijkander (eds), *Contract Economics* (Oxford: Blackwell), pp. 48–65.

Coase, R.H. (1960) 'The Problem of Social Cost', *Journal of Law and Economics*, vol. 3, pp. 1–44; reprinted in Coase (1988), pp. 95–156.

——— (1988) *The Firm, the Market and the Law* (Chicago: University of Chicago Press).

——— (1992) 'Comments on Cheung', in L. Werin and H.Wijkander (eds), *Contract Economics* (Oxford: Blackwell), pp. 72–5.

Cooper, R. and A. John (1988) 'Coordinating Coordination Failures in Keynesian Models', *Quarterly Journal of Economics*, vol. 103 (3), pp. 441–63.

Davis, O.A. and A. Whinston (1962) 'Externalities, Welfare and the Theory of Games', *Journal of Political Economy*, vol. 71, pp. 241–62.

Drazen, A. (1987) 'Reciprocal Externality Models of Low Employment', *European Economic Review*, vol. 31, pp. 436–43.

Elster, J. (1989) *Nuts and Bolts for the Social Sciences* (Cambridge: Cambridge University Press).

Friedman, J.W. (ed.) (1994) *Problems of Coordination in Economic Activity* (Boston: Kluwer).

Gravelle, H. and R. Rees (1981) *Microeconomics* (London: Longman).

Grillo, M. (1995) 'Introduzione' to R.H. Coase, *Impresa, Mercato e Diritto* (Bologna: Il Mulino).

Hahn, F.H. (1982) 'Reflections on the Invisible Hand', *Lloyds Bank Review* (April).

Hargreaves Heap, S.P. (1994) 'Institutions and (Short Run) Macroeconomic Performance', *Journal of Economic Surveys*, vol. 8 (1), pp. 35–56.

Hart, O. and B. Holmström (1987) 'The Theory of Contracts', in T. Bewley (ed.), *Advances in Economic Theory* (Cambridge: Cambridge University Press), pp. 71–155.

Illing, G. (1993) 'Search Externalities in Macroeconomic Theory', *Bulletin of Economic Research*, vol. 45 (2), pp. 81–104.

John, A. (1995) 'Macroeconomic Externalities', in H. Dixon, and N. Rankin (eds), *The New Macroeconomics* (Cambridge: Cambridge University Press), pp. 139–70.

Mill, J.S. (1982) *On Liberty* (first published 1859) (London: Penguin).

Pigou, A.C. (1952) *The Economics of Welfare*, 5th edn (London: Macmillan).

Regan, D. (1972) 'The Problem of Social Cost Revisited', *Journal of Law and Economics*, vol. 15, pp. 427–37.

Samuelson, P.A. (1947) *Foundations of Economic Analysis* (Cambridge, MA: Harvard University Press).

Schotter, A. (1981) *The Economic Theory of Social Institutions* (Cambridge: Cambridge University Press).

Varian, H.R. (1978) *Microeconomic Analysis* (New York: W.W. Norton).

Comment: Assessing Human Interactions

Daniel M. Hausman
UNIVERSITY OF WISCONSIN–MADISON, USA

For many years I have been influenced by Maurice Lagueux's work on externalities and I agree with the central thesis of his chapter. If for all pairs of individuals – call them *A* (Adam) and *E* (Eve) – the only way that the actions of *A* bear on *E* and the only way that the actions of *E* bear on *A* are via market relations between Adam and Eve, then there can be no externalities. The notion of an externality is tied to the notion of a market relation. The consequences on *E* of an action of *A*'s are externalities only when they do not come to her via a market interaction with *A*. As the notion of a market relation shifts, so will the notion of an externality. If all interactions are market interactions, then externalities conceived of in this way disappear. Yet the language of externalities persists, and the consequences may be thoroughly confusing. In particular Lagueux wants to argue, I think, that interactions or exchanges that do not occur owing to transactions costs should not always be regarded as market outcomes.

I am, as I said, largely in agreement. What I want to do in this comment is to underscore the ambiguities and difficulties in the definition of an externality and then (rather speculatively) to suggest a notion of a market interaction and use that notion to develop what I take to be Lagueux's critique of the over-extension of the notion of a market. In particular I shall argue that a recognition of transactions costs should not lead one to see all outcomes as market outcomes or to deny that the notion of an externality – as a result 'outside' of markets – has a useful content and role. I shall argue that despite its relevance to questions of efficiency, the notion of an externality is best understood in relationship to claims about the *voluntariness* of market interactions. I shall conclude with some even more speculative comments about the perspective on human relations implicit within economics.

1 DEFINING EXTERNALITIES

Lagueux's chapter exemplifies ambiguities in the notion of an externality even as it attempts to clarify them. What category of thing is an externality? Lagueux says that externalities are 'phenomena', 'characters' of economies and diseconomies, 'activities', 'situations', and 'elements' of residual activities, and he cites Bator's view that externalities are causes of market failures and Coase's remark that a standard view is that externalities are effects of decisions on individuals who are not party to the decisions. Arrow says that externalities 'can be regarded as ordinary commodities' (1983, p. 146), but also that externalities are a subclass of market failures (1983, p. 134). Some of these claims about externalities are mutually consistent, but taken as a whole they reveal remarkable ambivalence. Apparently, there is not even agreement on whether an externality is a situation, an activity, an effect, a cause, or a commodity!

In this brief comment I cannot survey the various uses of the term 'externality'. I think it is reasonable to start by stipulating that externalities are *things* – commodities, services, rights, and so forth – that can be transferred. Externalities *qua* activities are the generation and transfer of these things. Externalities *qua* situations exist when such things are generated and transferred. Though no stipulation will be consistent with everything economists say about externalities, I think it is least awkward and least arbitrary to start with a notion of an externality as an entity – possibly a highly abstract entity – that can be transferred among people.

One way to defend the stipulation that externalities are transferable things is to consider definitions of externalities that conflict with it. Boitani, in his comment in this volume (p. 148), accepts Gravelle and Rees' definition, 'An externality is said to exist if some of the variables which affect one decision-maker's utility or profit are under the control of another decision maker' (1981, p. 509). If one takes this definition literally, virtually every human interaction involves externalities. My choice of words in this Comment affects your utility or profit. Though everything economists would call an externality falls under this definition, too much that economists would not call externalities falls under it too.

The stipulation that externalities are transferrable things provides a necessary condition but not a definition of an externality. Suppose one attempts to define externalities by pursuing Coase's suggestion:

> An externality is any consequence of *A*'s action on *E* (anything transferred from *A* to *E*) that is not transmitted entirely by a market interaction between *A* and *E*.

Call this 'the broad definition'. The broad definition permits both pecuniary and non-pecuniary externalities. Glimpses of my stunning roses are a delightful non-pecuniary externality for my neighbours. Purchases of steel by Ford create an unwanted pecuniary externality for General Motors in the shape of a steel-price increase. Although this consequence is transmitted entirely via market interactions, it is not transmitted by market interactions *between Ford and General Motors*. It is external to any market interactions between them. Notice that externalities are consequences – goods or bads that come to individuals.

According to the broad definition, every non-market interaction between two people – Harriet stepping on Harold's toes, Howard giving Helen directions to Henry's house, or Herman infecting Helga with measles – involves an externality. Obviously, the broad definition is overly broad. Furthermore, economists are not entirely happy with the notion of a pecuniary externality, since the consequences are carried entirely by markets and since pecuniary externalities do not lead to inefficient outcomes. Indeed Lagueux speaks of them as not 'genuine'. (The fact that pecuniary externalities create no inefficiencies does not, of course, mean that they are unimportant. Pecuniary externalities have often shattered people's lives, and as I have argued elsewhere (1992), they raise serious questions concerning distributive justice. But these are not my questions here.)

Many economists have consequently wanted to build inefficiency into the definition of an externality. Abstracting from many details, one might offer the following definition:

> An externality is anything transferred from *A* to *E* that leads to an inefficient outcome.

Call this 'the inefficiency definition'. On the inefficiency definition, pecuniary externalities are not genuine externalities. The inefficiency definition remains overly broad. IRA bombings are not externalities even if they lead to inefficient outcomes. Furthermore, building inefficiency into the definition of an externality implies that efficient pollution involves no externalities. Some economists would be content with this implication, but it severs the connection with older uses of the term 'external' and has awkward consequences. For example, when a firm openly pollutes a stream, the poisoning of the people who live downstream constitutes an externality in this sense only if those poisoned would be willing to pay the firm at least as much as the firm saves from dumping its wastes in the stream.

One gets closer to the notion of an externality that matters to economists by dropping the requirement that externalities involve inefficient outcomes, reinstating the condition that there be a non-market transfer, and adding two new requirements: (a) that externalities arise in the course of market activities and (b) that the consequences of *A*'s actions on *E* are side-effects of what *A* intends and not themselves intended:

> An externality is any consequence for *E* of *A*'s market interactions with others that is not intended and that is not transmitted entirely by market interactions between *A* and *E*.

Call this 'the side-effect definition'. On the side-effect definition, one can talk of both pecuniary and non-pecuniary externalities, though economists are of course free to explain why non-pecuniary externalities are of particular interest. Cases of 'efficient' pollution such as the one sketched above involve externalities, if the poisoning of the people who live downstream was not the objective of the firm. On the side-effect definition, the notion of an externality remains a broad one.

Although many economists have insisted that externalities involve side-effects – that is effects that may be foreseen, but are not intended – the notion of a side-effect fits uneasily into standard decision theory. Preferences for actions derive from preferences over outcomes and beliefs about the outcomes of actions in different states and about the probability of those states. If there is one consequence that is strongly preferred and believed to be sufficiently probable that it greatly boosts the utility of the action chosen, then one might call that consequence the aim or the intended consequence, while all those consequences that boost the utility of the action only a little or lessen its utility can be regarded as side-effects. But the distinction appears shallow and unimportant, and the distinction may break down in cases in which an action is chosen because of many of its consequences. There is thus an excellent case to be made that the notion of a side-effect ought to be expunged from the theoretical perspective of economists. But the distinction between poisoning a stream in the pursuit of profits and poisoning a stream in the pursuit of ethnic cleansing is not one that I've invented, and I am following established usage in regarding only the former as an externality.

2 MARKET INTERACTIONS

Both the broad and side-effect definitions of externalities rely on the notion of a market interaction between two individuals. What is that? Here is my tentative suggestion:

> There is a (bilateral) market interaction between *A* and *E* if and only if (1) *A* voluntarily transfers something to *E* in order to get what she is transferring to him, and *E* voluntarily transfers something to *A* in order to get what he is transferring to her or (2) no transfer takes place because at least one of the parties judges that the transfer does not serve his or her interest.

Consider Adam Smith's memorable remarks, 'It is not from the benevolence of the butcher, the brewer or the baker that we expect our dinner, but from their regard to their own interest. We address ourselves, not to their humanity but to their self-love, and never talk to them of our necessities but of their advantage' (1776, book I, Chapter 5). Smith is pointing to the features of market exchanges that I am emphasising. An exchange takes place or fails to take place because each party judges that the exchange serves or fails to serve his or her own interest.

I do not claim that this definition fits ordinary language perfectly. In ordinary language, we often describe an interaction as a market interaction, when *A* gives something to *E* in order to get what he falsely believes she will give him, whether *A* is misinformed or *E* reneges after *A* does his part. Economists often idealise and assume away ignorance, mistake, and malfeasance, and they are right to distinguish interactions involving such complications from the paradigm cases of market exchanges or non-exchanges. Mistakes raise questions about whether the interaction is voluntary and break the link between market interaction and efficiency. An exchange of shoes between two individuals who are mistaken about each other's shoe size is unlikely to make the parties better off.

Market exchanges are conceived of as exchanges of commodities and services, but given the difficulties in defining commodities and services, it is best to place no limits on what can be exchanged. When *A* and *E* hang out together so that *A* can catch *E*'s measles and *E* can catch *A*'s chicken pox, then one has an unusual market interaction. I shall also count it as a market exchange when *A* gives nothing to *E* in exchange for what she gives him. What distinguishes such a case from one where *E* simply gives a gift to *A* is that the reason why *E* gives *x* to *A* is that doing so benefits *E* and *A* agrees to accept it. When *E* gives *A* the smells of her cabbage cooking and a bowl of the resulting soup that leaves him not preferring a state of affairs without the soup and smell to one with both, one has a market exchange. A transfer between *E* and *A* counts as a market exchange only if the reason why *E* gives *x* to *A* is that doing so is a means to get the *y* that *A* is giving her and similarly for *A*. When this is the case, one can say that the interaction is *mutually instrumental.* A market exchange is an exchange that is fully voluntary and mutually instrumental. *E*'s doing the dishes in exchange for *A*'s accompanying her to the school-board meeting is a market exchange, but their Christmas gift giving to each other is not a market exchange, because it is (let us hope!) not mutually instrumental.

When *E* transfers something to *A* or does something to *A* that is not part of a market exchange, then *A* gets something he did not 'purchase'. He may want what *E* has caused him to have or to experience, or he may not want it. The transfer need not be voluntary on the part of either of the parties (though it might be), and the transfer may make both of the parties worse off. In a market exchange, in contrast, the actions of both parties are voluntary and entirely instrumental. Each chooses exactly what he or she gets from the exchange. Both parties prefer the post-exchange outcome to the pre-exchange state of affairs. When all interactions are market exchanges – when there are no externalities, then, by the light of his or her own preferences, everybody benefits. When some of the exchanges are not market exchanges – that is, when there are externalities – then some people may be made worse off from the exchange.

Economists have argued not only that market exchanges offer Pareto-improvements, but that market outcomes are Pareto-efficient. The second is a much stronger claim. Even if market exchanges are Pareto-improvements, market outcomes will be not be Pareto-efficient if individuals fail to make some Pareto-improving market exchanges. Suppose *A* has *y* and *E* has *x*, what might explain why *A* and *E* do not engage in a market exchange of *x* for *y*? First, and simplest, it might be that one of the parties does not want to exchange: *A* does not prefer *x* to *y* or *E* does not prefer *y* to *x*. Second, even if each prefers what the other has, the exchange between *A* and *E* might be infeasible. It might for example cost too much to transport the goods. In such cases any inefficiency is only apparent: *A* would not prefer to have *x and* to pay the costs to him of making the exchange or *E* would not prefer have *y* and to pay the costs to her of making the exchange. A failure to make an exchange, when individuals prefer not to or when it would be too costly to make an exchange are still market interactions. They are market *non-exchanges*. They are exchanges that are not undertaken because at least one party prefers what he or she has to what he or she will get from the exchange.

Finally, not exchanging might be genuinely inefficient. *A* or *E* may fail to make an advantageous exchange because of ignorance, irrationality, or because of social or legal constraints. In traditional arguments for the efficiency of market outcomes, such problems are assumed away. Notice that on a definition of an externality as 'a situation in which the private economy lacks sufficient incentives to create a potential market in some good and the non-existence of this market results in losses in Pareto efficiency' (Heller and Starrett, 1976, p. 10), non-interactions, including failures to make exchanges, can count as externalities. On the account defended here, in contrast, an externality is a *thing*, a consequence, which is transferred to an individual. It is, I would contend, a virtue of this account that not all market failures involve externalities. When there is an externality there will be a non-market transfer from one agent to another coupled with the absence of some market interaction between them.

3 EXTERNALITIES AS INVOLUNTARY TRANSFERS

According to the side-effect definition, *A* can create an externality for *B* only in the course of a market interaction with someone else, *E*. Suppose that Adam has *x* and Eve has *y* and they exchange. Their exchange creates an externality for a third party, *B*, if and only if:

(1) When *A* and *E* exchange, something is transferred to *B*
(2) That consequence for *B* is not the reason why *A* and *E* carry out their exchange
(3) The consequence for *B* does not come to her via a market exchange between *B* on the one hand and *A* and/or *E* on the other.

Externalities from market exchanges exist because exchanges sometimes have unintended consequences for those who are not party to them, and because the consequences are not always transmitted via a market interaction between the provider and the recipient of the externality. (This formulation suggests mistakenly that if *A* provides an externality to *E*, *E* does not thereby provide an externality to *A*, but it is possible for *A* to provide an externality for *E* at the same time that *E* is providing an externality for *A*.) An explanation for why there is an externality requires (1) an account of why the exchange between *A* and *E* gives rise to consequences for *B*, (2) an account of why none of the parties prevents the transfer of the externality and (3) an account of why the externality is not 'internalised' – of why there is no market exchange between *B* and *A* and/or *E* concerning whatever it is that constitutes the externality. (1) involves technological and market facts involving the circumstances and activities of the parties. (3) involves the same factors as does any explanation for why a market exchange does not occur. One might think that (2), the explanation for why none of the parties prevents the transfer of the externality, is sometimes simply that no one wants to. But then it is questionable whether the transfer of *z* to *B* is not a market exchange after all. So let us assume that the transfer is involuntary for either *B* or *A*: *B* does not want *z* without some compensation, or *A* does not want to give *z* to *B* without some compensation. In so far as the transfer of *z* to *B* is a side-effect, it is in some sense *non*-voluntary: *A* is not making the exchange with *E* in order to transfer *z* to *B*. But it is not necessarily *in*voluntary.

When acts and failures to act are involuntary, the agent lacks knowledge or power. The transfer of *z* from *A* to *B* may be involuntary because of ignorance or because one of the parties lacks the power to prevent the transfer. *A* and *E* may not know that they are transferring *z* or that they are transferring it to *B*, and *B* may not know that she is getting it or who she is getting it from. *A* and *E* may want to prevent *z* from going to anyone or particularly to *B*, but they may be unable to prevent the outcome. *B* may be similarly unable. This inability may result from a lack of rights, unclarities in rights, difficulties in enforcing rights, or costs. The same factors may prevent the exchange from being voluntary, but certain motivations (such as *A* and *E*'s desire to give *B* a gift or to harm her) may also prevent the exchange from being mutually instrumental. Since I've insisted that externalities are unintended, these additional motivational factors are eliminated, and one can conclude that what renders the parties unable to prevent the transfer of the externality is ignorance, absence or unclarity in rights or difficulties in their enforcement or costs, and just the same kinds of factors block the internalisation of the externality. What turns out to be crucial to the existence of externalities is whether unintended consequences are *voluntarily* transmitted and received.

For example, suppose some dioxins in the stream from which *B* gets her drinking water are an externality that *A* transfers to her. Suppose

A knows that he is transferring the dioxins to *B* and prefers to make a market exchange with *E* that has the result that the dioxins are transferred to *B* to not making the market exchange and not transferring the externality to *B*. *A* acts voluntarily, but he does not engage in a market exchange with *B*. Suppose (case (1)) that *B* does not know that *A* is poisoning her water. This ignorance makes her unable to prevent *A*'s actions, and it also explains why she and *A* do not engage in a market exchange. The outcome may still be efficient, though one cannot of course infer that it is from the fact that *B* permits the pollution. This seems a clear case of an externality.

Suppose instead (case (2)) that *B* knows that the dioxins are being transferred to her and that the law does not give her the right to pure drinking water or forbid *A*'s discharges. There remain a variety of ways that she can avoid being poisoned, though she will be worse off whatever she does than she would be without *A*'s activities. She can move away or purchase expensive filters. *B* picks the least bad alternative. This may involve continuing to drink the polluted water, or it may involve incurring some other cost such as purchasing drinking water or bribing *A* to stop polluting.

If *B* is able to bribe *A* to stop discharging the dioxins, the externality will have been internalised. However dubious the outcome might be from the perspective of distributive *justice*, there is no longer any externality. Nothing is transferred from *A* to *B* or from *B* to *A* except via market exchanges, and the result is efficient. Provided that it is possible for *B* to bribe *A* to stop polluting, the same can be said regardless of which alternative she chooses. If there is no externality when *B* pays *A* not to pollute, there is no externality when *B* selects an alternative that is better for her. *A* is then polluting because *B* chooses not to pay him not to, and *B* is accepting the pollution because she prefers to accept it from *A* and to use her money for other purposes. The interaction is voluntary and mutually instrumental.

This argument relies on a controversial notion of 'voluntariness'. On this construal, payments to an extortionist are voluntary. If *A*'s actions leave *B* with a choice of death or penury, one might question how much real choice *B* has in the matter. If, on the other hand, *B* moves into the neighbourhood already knowing about the pollution and happy to pay for bottled water in exchange for the lovely location, then her actions seem fully voluntary. Problems about voluntariness can arise when the actions of one person alter the budget set of another, even when the individual is free to choose within the budget set. An alternative way of thinking about externalities, which I shall not explore here, is to think of them not as unintended non-market consequences on the *outcomes* for others, but as unintended consequences for the *budget sets* of others. The externality has not been internalised if *B* is unable to pay *A* enough to get him to stop polluting and she would have bribed him if she had had the means. Although no efficiency problems arise and she still chooses among the feasible alternatives, *B* cannot be said to enter into a market interaction with *A*, and her actions do not internalise the externality.

4 EXTERNALITIES, FREEDOM, AND TRANSACTIONS COSTS

Markets will not always internalise externalities, particularly when there is ignorance and when the costs and benefits of externalities are spread over so many agents that it is impossible to bring them together to achieve the outcomes they would choose. But is this the right description? When exchanges are not undertaken owing to ignorance, difficulties in organising, limits of power, etc. should these be regarded as cases of *externalities* in which feasible and possibly Pareto-superior exchanges are not made, or should they be regarded as cases where exchanges are not feasible owing to costs and in which, given the costs, no transfers are involuntary? Some of those whom Lagueux calls the 'neoliberals' endorse this last view: there are no externalities. Whenever there is apparently a non-market transfer, all parties have – given the costs of preventing it – chosen to make or accept the transfer. As Lagueux argues, for the neoliberal nothing happens 'outside' the market.

In response to the neo-liberals, Lagueux (p. 143) argues that

> a market is an actual market . . . or it is not a market at all . . . Looking at potential markets and at transaction costs does not help because the transaction costs of creating the potential market are so extreme and so 'unmarketlike' that it sounds reasonable to conclude that acknowledging this fact amounts to saying that no market exists or that markets fail to solve this problem.

Though I agree with the conclusion Lagueux is pointing to, this formulation is obscure. Suppose that transportation costs make it unprofitable to transfer dried cattle manure from the United States to India. There is, let us suppose, no market at all in India for dried American cattle manure. But there is no market failure either. The transportation costs make the exchange uneconomical. In just the same way, neoliberals can argue that the absence of a market in clean sea water off the southern coast of England involves no market failure. The transactions costs make the exchange uneconomical. Non-exchanges reflect the workings of markets just as well as exchanges do, and all outcomes reflect voluntary and mutually instrumental choice.

Lagueux wants to resist this conclusion. As we have just seen, denying that potential markets are actual markets or that markets for clean sea water or American manure exist does not enable one to do so. The neoliberal can concede that these markets do not exist without denying that there are any outcomes that do not reflect voluntary and mutually instrumental choice. How then do 'markets fail to solve this problem'? What (if anything) is wrong with the neoliberal *dissolution* of the problem posed by externalities?

The problem does not lie in treating transactions costs as genuine costs. Suppose I do not like the smell when my neighbour cooks cabbage, and I have legal rights to be undisturbed by such annoyances, but I nevertheless refrain from forcing my neighbour to stop cooking cabbage because of transactions costs. In such a case it seems perfectly plausible to deny that there is any externality. Given the costs, I am better off with the minor annoyance. There is no market in which the externality is internalised, because it is not worthwhile to establish such a market. I have *consented* to the annoyance.

Two key features of externalities need to be kept in the foreground. First, externalities are goods or bads that are transferred to people. Second, one or the other party to the transfer does not voluntarily consent to the transfer or does not voluntarily consent to it without compensation. However deeply concerned economists are with efficiency, I submit that questions about efficiency should not enter into the determination of whether there is an externality. The crucial issue concerns the voluntariness of the transfer. In the case of firms and municipalities polluting the beaches at Brighton, individual bathers have not voluntarily agreed to accept the pollution, if they do not possess the means to stop it. The absence of an Indian market for dried American manure, in contrast, does not involve transferring anything from the United States to India or from India to the United States; and many Indians possess the means to arrange the transport and sale of American manure. They have no wish to do so, since the manure would cost so much, and their not purchasing it, like my living with my neighbour's cooking smells, is consequently voluntary. What distinguishes the cases is not the kind of cost nor whether the outcome is efficient but whether the non-market exchange or the absence of a market exchange is fully voluntary. Even given the extremely broad conception of voluntary actions that I questioned above, externalities do not disappear; and on a more restrictive (and reasonable) conception of which actions are voluntary, the domain of externalities would grow.

5 METHODOLOGICAL AND SPECULATIVE CONCLUSIONS

Let me end with some methodological remarks and some speculations: First, the methodological remarks: the peculiarities of the notion of an externality point to continuing links between economics and philosophy. Although the notion of an externality finds its main applications in welfare economics, it is apparently a part of positive economics. Whether an externality is present is supposed to be a matter of fact and separable from the moral questions of what, if anything, ought to be done about it. Given the connections between externalities and voluntariness that I have emphasised or the connections between externalities and efficiency that Lagueux and others have stressed, it is questionable whether positive and normative can be so neatly separated. And even if the notion of an externality can shake off any normative implications, Lagueux and I have both argued that the notion of an externality gets its meaning in relation to the notion of a market, and the notion of a market is a highly philosophical notion, tied as it is to notions of intention and voluntariness.

Finally to my speculations: I have qualms about the vision of economic life as individual pursuit of private objectives involving by way of interactions between individuals nothing except market exchange. Of course nobody believes that this is the whole of human life, nor does anybody believe that buying and selling are never influenced by anything except the parties' estimates of the gains from trade. But this is the model, the norm, and the divergences in the form of irrationality, externalities, and market failures in general are abnormal, exceptional. This gets things exactly backwards. In the typical case there are complicated interdependencies among individuals that affect third parties in ways they will never know or understand, let alone agree to. When I purchase a box of cereal at the grocery store, one can picture the episode as a bilateral market exchange. I pay my $3 because I prefer to have the box of cereal, and the store lets me have the box of cereal because it prefers my $3. For many purposes, this is a useful picture; and I have no objection to using a variety of conceptualisations for specific purposes. But the notion that this is what economic life basically consists of – apart from peripheral complications such as externalities – is, I suggest, a fundamental mistake. Our purchases at the grocery store help to define our culture, the shape of our environment, the character of our home life and child-rearing, who we will be 10 years from now and who our grandchildren will be half a century from now. Complex *involuntary* interdependency characterises social life. The choices we make are based upon consideration of only a small fraction of their consequences. Cumulatively their intended consequences are insignificant compared with their unintended consequences. The image of markets as rendering individual aims compatible and enabling individuals to achieve their aims efficiently is misleading. In pursuing their individual objectives via markets, people transform themselves and their physical environment in ways they do not intend or imagine. The involuntary interdependencies of human choices should be centre stage. I believe that the problems with conceptualising externalities reflect limitations in the basic picture of economic interactions.

References

Arrow, K. (1983) 'The Organisation of Economic Activity: Issues Pertinent to the Choice of Market versus Nonmarket Allocation', in *Collected Papers, Volume 2: General Equilibrium* (Cambridge, MA: Harvard University Press), pp. 133–55.

Gravelle, H. and R. Rees (1981) *Microeconomics* (London: Longman).

Hausman, D. (1992) 'When Jack and Jill Make a Deal', *Social Philosophy and Policy* vol. 9, pp. 95–113.

Heller, W. and D. Starrett (1976) 'On the Nature of Externalities', in S. Lin (ed.), *Theory and Measurement of Economic Externalities* (New York: Academic Press), pp. 9–22.

Lagueux, M. (1977) 'Learning from the Debate on Externalities', chapter 3 in this volume.

Smith, A. (1776) *An Inquiry into the Nature and Causes of the Wealth of Nations*, reprint (Oxford: Oxford University Press, 1976).

Discussion

Maurice Lagueux expressed qualms about Andrea Boitani's definition. Even the baker's decision to produce more bread could affect one's utility without being under one's control and so would count as an externality in the sense quoted in Boitani's Comment. He also admitted that the examples Boitani gave of uses of the notion of an externality in macroeconomics might demand that he [Lagueux] attenuate his claim that the concept of an externality is vanishing.

In reply to Hausman, Lagueux expressed hesitation about his definition of a market, but noted that Hausman's efforts illustrate the difficulties of defining markets. Boundaries to the notion of a market are nevertheless essential. One should not say that there is a market in prison sentences because of the possibility that a prisoner could bribe a guard. One must clarify the notion that it is possible to create a market and distinguish clearly between markets and merely potential markets.

Pierre Salmon questioned whether externalities should be limited to market economies. He suggested that the extensive pollution in Russia was a side-effect of decisions within particular ministries and might reasonably be regarded as externalities.

Leonid Hurwicz had two comments. The first was that Coase's claim is correct in the absence of transaction costs: whether the polluter is liable or does not make any difference in the real (as distinct from the monetary) sphere – but only if one assumes the absence of income effects. The fact that if one made that assumption one would get the Coase conclusion was noted many years ago by Turvey. However, as Hurwicz had shown in a recent paper, the assumption of no income effects is not only sufficient but also *necessary* for Coase's conclusion to hold. That is very important because it makes his conclusions of much more limited scope than many people believe.

To illustrate this Hurwicz drew two figures: Figure D3.1 – with income effects absent, and Figure D3.2 – with income effects present.

The amount of pollution is measured along the vertical axis, and the amount of income (money) along the horizontal axis, with the income to the first party (the potential polluter) measured from the left and the income to the second (the potential victim) from the right.

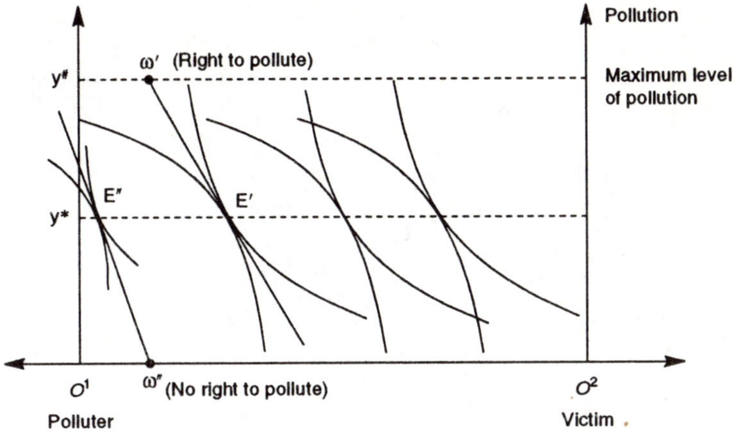

Figure D3.1

The symbol ω′ represents the initial situation ('endowment') if the polluter has the right to pollute (i.e. is not liable for damages), while ω″ represents the initial situation if there is no right to pollute (i.e. the polluter is liable for damages). Regardless of liability, the initial incomes (money holdings) are respectively O^1 ω″ and O^2 ω″ (Figure D3.1).

One can then draw the two parties' indifference curves. Their points of tangency represent Pareto-optima. Competitive equilibria are attained at Pareto-optimal points where the price line is simultaneously tangent to the two parties' indifference curves: *E*′ when there is no liability, *E*″ when the polluter is liable. We see that in the no-income-effects case of Figure D3.1, the equilibrium level of pollution is the same (y^*) regardless of liability rules. This is so because, in the absence of income effects, the contract curve is a horizontal line. But if there is no liability, the polluter gains income (paid by the victim to go down to y^* below the maximum feasible *y*#), while if the polluter is liable he winds up with less than initial income (because he must compensate the victim to be permitted to pollute at level y^*).

The outcome is quite different when income effects are present.

As seen in Figure D3.2, in the presence of income effects the equilibrium level of pollution does depend on the liability situation. If there is no liability, the equilibrium level of pollution is y' (corresponding to the tangency point *E*′ of the price line from ω′) . But when the polluter is liable, the equilibrium pollution level is a lower amount y'' (corresponding to the tangency point *E*″ of the price line from ω″).

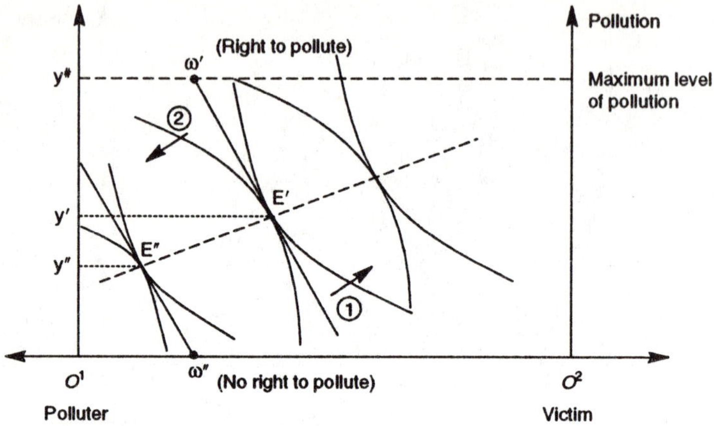

Figure D3.2

This is so because, due to income effects, the contract curve is no longer horizontal. Thus, with income effects in the picture, when there is liability the equilibrium level of pollution is lower than without liability, in accordance with one's intuition.

It is therefore important that when one cites Coase's claim (which Stigler, not Coase, called a theorem) not only transaction costs but also income effects be assumed absent. When Turvey pointed this out, he was talking about firms, which do not have income effects. But one cannot ignore income effects when talking about consumers – nor about firms because the shareholders whose incomes come from profits are, after all, consumers too.

Hurwicz also commented concerning the broad view of Pareto-optimality that takes into account transaction costs. How then is one to avoid Dr Pangloss's system in which we live in 'the best of all possible worlds'? Of course if one takes an extreme deterministic view, there's only one way that causality can go, and then everything that happens is optimal. The question then is why economists should be writing about it. But maybe this is also part of 'the best possible world'. The problem stems from a somewhat excessive use of the term, 'market'. One can describe bribery as a market transaction, but there are different kinds of institutional arrangements in cases where transaction costs really matter. It is excessive to label all arrangements society uses to improve things 'market procedures'.

Daniel Hausman remarked that the distinction between what is intended and what is the side-effect is extremely difficult to draw and virtually impossible to draw within the context of standard decision theory. The distinction between intended consequence and side-effect helps, for example, when thinking about pollution within the former Soviet Union in a non-market context, but it seems superficial.

Bennett McCallum suggested that economics has functioned very well in its treatment of externalities by keeping questions of intent out. Intentions are unobservable, and one does not need to refer to them in this case anyway. Meade's definition seems perfectly adequate: if the level of activity of one agent enters directly into the utility or production functions of another agent, then one has externalities. The definition does not include everything that might be some sort of aberration in a market economy. That is a pretty clear definition of externalities,

Hurwicz returned to the question of the extent to which the notion of externalities is linked to the notion of a market. In economics there are typically two kinds of agents, producers and consumers, and certain variables assumed to be under respective control of those agents. It is important to realise, however, that issues of control are not confined to markets. In the Soviet Union where certainly standard property rights were not fully developed, they had very much the same kind of phenomena, which could be interpreted as externalities. Managers of firms, were (for example) polluting Lake Baikal even though they were not literally owners. If one is clear about which variables are under control of the respective economic agents, then one can define externalities in both market and non-market contexts. An externality is a situation where the outcomes for an agent depend *directly* on variables that are controlled by others.

Lagueux responded that the definition McCallum defended depends on the notion of a *direct* interdependence and there is no way to define what we mean by directness without relying on the notion of a market. Direct dependence is dependence that is not mediated by the market. Most of the interest of the notion of an externality lies precisely in the fact of something being *uncompensated*. How is this to be captured without referring to a market context? If theorists mean that one has no control even over what is done by those with whom one enters into market relations – as one has no control over the baker's decisions – then they have failed to capture the notion of an externality, which needs to be distinguished from a standard market relation. One cannot characterise externalities without defining what is a market.

Uskali Mäki pointed out that the chapters by De Vroey (Chapter 4) and by Lagueux were both devoted to conceptual history, yet the discussion did not address this aspect. One should ask whether these accounts of conceptual evolution reveal a pattern which could be described in more general terms. This is a simple question, but of course hard to answer. It would be interesting to compare the pattern of development in the two conceptual histories. Such a comparison could reveal similarities and differences between the fates of the constituents of economic theories. In this case, it seems that some of the elements of the history are: dependence on other concepts, emergence, disappearance, broadening, narrowing, and so forth. It would be interesting to attempt to identify a general pattern that could be compared with other 'data.'

Lagueux responded that the main element in his history is the dependence of the notion of an externality on the notion of a market and thus the reflection of changes in one notion in developments of the other.

Roger Backhouse pursued Mäki's question by suggesting that when the understanding of the notion of an externality changes, there are at least three possible explanations. One would be that the economists concerned found some conceptual difficulty with the old concept and so developed the new one. A second explanation would be that these economists discovered new examples which could not be captured by the old definition, so one has the interaction of empirical example and old concept. A third explanation might rely on some sort of political 'agenda' creating pressure for a change in concept. These are three possibilities. It would be quite interesting if one of these were to fit case after case of conceptual change in the story. He suspected, however, that the story was pretty messy in some cases. We may find that one explanation was important for Pigou and another for Coase.

Lagueux responded that if he had to chose, probably the third explanation would be the most important, mainly because the fact that externalities are a residual makes changes difficult to explain in the first two ways. It was not as if one found a new sort of externality and as a consequence had to change the definition.

McCallum suggested that it was irrelevant whether the notion of an externality was a residual. One can simply ask instead why the concept of the market changed.

Lagueux replied that changes in the concept of a market have both political sources and sources in dissatisfaction with the character of economics. Friedman, for example, proposed a new approach to economics whose inspiration was partly political and partly based on his concept of economic science. This is then linked to a different conception of the market, and as a result the conception of externalities changes.

Andrea Boitani suggested that any meaningful social situation is one where there is interaction and in which there are externalities from his point of view. Economists attempted to depict the situation where externalities are irrelevant, and they thus invented perfect competition. In perfect competition markets are able to internalise everything. So economists gave a sort of formal picture of J.S. Mill's view of the actions of individuals affecting only themselves – which was not what Mill thought of the market, but of a certain domain of action. Economists then realised that economic life is not that beautiful, that there are social costs. Externalities or social costs are just those things that the market cannot deal with. Not all social interactions can be dealt with by markets. That was the point that Hurwicz made: there are other institutions that deal with problems of social interactions.

Andrea Salanti asked Hausman how a science like economics that focuses on only a few causal factors and is thus separate and inexact could possibly overcome its limited perspective on human interactions.

Hausman replied that it may be useful to focus on a few causal factors and a peculiar model of social exchange whereby what we do intentionally and voluntarily is more important than what we do unintentionally and involuntarily. How useful this is depends on the problem at hand. The difficulties in making sense of the notion of an externality suggest that this is an extremely odd picture of social relations. Hausman also remarked that he thought that Boitani's comment was subversive of standard treatments of externalities. It began by saying in effect: 'here's no problem, we've got this nice definition of externality.' But then it turns out that everything is an externality and there's no place or almost no place left for models which don't have externalities in them – which are most of the models that exist within economics.

Lagueux concluded that Boitani's comment started with one definition, but in introducing Bator's account passed to quite a different and more expansive notion. The comment was subversive in the sense that in passing from one definition to another it illustrated precisely how difficult it was to characterise this concept.

4 Accounting for Involuntary Unemployment in Neoclassical Theory: Some Lessons from Sixty Years of Uphill Struggle[1]

Michel De Vroey
UNIVERSITÉ CATHOLIQUE DE LOUVAIN, BELGIUM

1 INTRODUCTION

During the last few decades, the evolution of economic science has been marked by the decline of standard Keynesian macroeconomics, the upsurge of the new classical school and the subsequent revival of Keynesian theory under the banner of 'New Keynesian Economics'. The objective of the present study is to reflect upon this evolution from a specific angle of attack, by recounting the unfolding of ideas regarding the theoretical acceptability of one particular yet central concept, namely involuntary unemployment. One way of recasting Keynes's programme in his *General Theory* is to state that he aimed to demonstrate the possible existence of involuntary unemployment within a neoclassical framework. Starting from the realisation that, at the time, this concept had no place in neoclassical theory, his aim was to elicit which minimal change in hypotheses could reverse such a state of affairs. Quite sanguinely, Keynes believed that he had carried the day. This was also the prevailing opinion in the years and first decades which followed the publication of the *General Theory*. Now, at the least, this opinion is being questioned. One can ask oneself if Keynes really succeeded in offering a theory of involuntary unemployment or whether such a belief only resulted from some unnoticed semantic sloppiness. Be that as it may, today, many authors believe that Keynesian theory can progress without resorting to the concept of involuntary unemployment, whereas those who still use it do so in a different sense from that in which it was initially used.

The chapter is divided into seven section. Section 2 introduces a series of definitions and distinctions which will prove necessary for subsequent discussions. In Section 3, I present my own reconstruction of the theoretical project Keynes set forth in his *General Theory*. In Section 4, I develop the thesis, which some will find provocative that, despite appearances, the involuntary unemployment result is obtained neither in the *General Theory*, nor in the standard IS–LM models. Section 5 is devoted to Patinkin and Clower's interpretation of involuntary unemployment and to Barro and Grossman's synthesis of their views. In Section 6, I evaluate the anti-Keynesian offensive spearheaded by Friedman and Lucas. In Section 7, I look at the significance of involuntary unemployment in some 'new Keynesian' models. Lastly, I conclude in Section 8 by delving into some broader methodological considerations.

To close this introduction, a few remarks and caveats may be useful.

(a) Although the chapter spans the full period from the publication of the *General Theory* to the present day, it has no pretensions to being exhaustive. On the one hand, its coverage is limited to neoclassical interpretations of Keynes. On the other hand, certain phases in the debate are less well covered than others. The reason is simply that this article is part of a book in progress and that at this point my thinking is more advanced on some issues than on others.[2]
(b) This chapter is mainly concerned with concepts, definitions and other matters of principles, all of which are not particularly fashionable these days. Contrary to the usual practice, whenever semantic issues are encountered, they will be addressed head on rather than being side-stepped.
(c) The chapter's methodology is deliberately retrospective. Its tone is also quite critical, as it is mainly intended to bring to the fore the limitations of the authors discussed. I hasten to add that this tone simply follows from the aim I have ascribed myself rather than from a desire to belittle their works.

2 CONCEPTS AND DEFINITIONS

Before starting my account of how, from Keynes on, economists have come to grips with the involuntary unemployment concept, it is necessary to clarify a series of conceptual matters. The following seven points will be addressed: the definition of involuntary unemployment, semantic pitfalls, the disequilibrium content of involuntary unemployment, the separation of distinct forms of underemployment, the distinction between frictional and involuntary unemployment, other possible definitions of involuntary unemployment and, finally, the meaning of full employment.

2.1 The Reservation Wage Definition of Involuntary Unemployment

Obviously, involuntary unemployment has to do with a lack of participation in the labour market. According to standard microeconomic theory, the fact that an economic agent is not participating has nothing incongruous to it. Simply, it must be the case that the prevailing wage is lower than or equal to his reservation wage. Call this the 'reservation wage principle'. The existence of involuntary unemployment can then be seen as a violation of this principle. It occurs if agents are observed as non-trading, despite the fact that the market wage exceeds their reservation wage.[3] According to the first-order condition of their decision problem – i.e. the equalisation of the marginal rate of substitution between consumption and leisure with the real wage rate – they should be participating yet they are not. Nonetheless trading occurs, rather than an adjustment in the wage rate. At the level of the labour market, involuntary unemployment will manifest itself in the fact that trading occurs on the short side of the market – here demand for labour. In other words, at the real wage/employment mix characterising effective trading, some suppliers are 'off their supply curve' and rationed. This is the meaning in which involuntary unemployment will be interpreted in what follows.

The fact that involuntary unemployment can rather easily be defined in no way guarantees its theoretical acceptability. New classicists could agree that, if a definition of involuntary unemployment were to be given, it would equate with the above without, however, considering this concept as valid.

2.2 Semantic Pitfalls

Discussions about involuntary unemployment are marred by semantic confusions. First, one should draw a distinction between a definition and its possible connotations. In particular, the above definition elicits rather spontaneously the connotation of some infringement on freedom, as it suggests that involuntary unemployment should be understood in the sense of 'forced leisure' as opposed to 'chosen leisure'.

Some agents, it is then asserted, are unable to realise their optimising plans – definitely a feature running counter to economists' basic views about the working of markets.The unemployed through no fault of their own, the view runs, are left aside by the market system and excluded from the opportunity to work. To use a distinction propounded by Dworkin, involuntary unemployment is a matter of 'brute bad luck' rather than of 'option bad luck'.[4] Whether or not this connotation can effectively be attached to the concept is discussed below.

A second semantic problem is that the common-sense and the theoretical meanings of both involuntary unemployment and voluntary unemployment are on a collision course. As far as the *involuntary* unemployment concept is concerned, as will be seen, its integration within economic theory faces formidable obstacles. Yet, in common-sense language, the involuntary nature of unemployment is *grosso modo* taken for granted, to the effect that the adjective looks redundant. As far as the *voluntary* unemployment concept is concerned, when used in the theoretical discourse, it refers to chosen leisure and thus as an optimising refusal to participate in the labour market. The people in point choose (and can afford) to live on unearned income. However, such a choice can be either temporary or long-term. It is a momentary choice in the case of either intertemporal substitution between leisure and work or job-search. Clearly, in the latter case, the chosen leisure terminology is rather unapposite. When it is a matter of long-term choice for leisure, the so-called voluntarily unemployed should be seen as 'rentiers'. Here again, the use of the 'voluntary unemployment' expression is misleading. On the other hand, in common-sense speech, the idea of voluntary unemployment seems perplexing. As presumably people do not like to be in the job-searching position – and hence would not choose it – the affixing of the adjective 'voluntary' to the unemployment term seems odd. It is as if one was talking about being voluntarily ill.

This being stated, the idea of voluntary unemployment can nonetheless receive a common-sense meaning, in one of the following two ways. First, it may refer to a case of shirking. Given the existence of unemployment benefit, people may actually prefer no participation in the labour market yet disguise their true preference and pretend to search for a job in order to enjoy the benefits, if this is the condition for obtaining it. The second occurrence arises when the existence of different stratified labour markets (e.g. according to skill) is taken into account. It then becomes necessary to draw a distinction between the concepts of labour rationing and unemployment. Labour rationing designates a specific market outcome. Unemployment pertains to a typology of active population, where people are classified according to the sort of activities they are engaged in. It applies to those agents whose specific activity is job-searching. Obviously, the two concepts are linked, as labour rationing seems to be a necessary condition for unemployment. Yet it is not a sufficient one. An agent can encounter rationing in his 'normal' market yet get a job in a less skilled market. Or he can be involuntarily rationed in his market and yet be voluntarily unemployed, in that he refuses a job opportunity in a lower market. Hence his classification as voluntarily unemployed (now without any profiteering connotation).[5] With some exceptions, this type of issue is hardly addressed in unemployment models, as attention usually focuses on the operation of only one labour market – a practice which will be taken up here as well. As a result, labour rationing and unemployment become conflated. Yet, to the question of which of these two concepts is the real subject-matter, the answer ought to be 'labour rationing', though the tag reads 'unemployment'!

2.3 In Which Sense is Involuntary Unemployment a Disequilibrium Phenomenon?

Obviously involuntary unemployment can make sense only as a case of disequilibrium yet the point is to see exactly which equilibrium concept is involved. Three distinct issues ought to be tackled.

2.3.1 Equilibrium as End-state or as Process?

Except for the section on Patinkin, my analysis will mainly be concerned with either equilibrium or disequilibrium seen as end-states of adjustment processes.

2.3.2 A Distinction between Individual and Interactive Equilibrium and Disequilibrium

Following on from Patinkin's distinction between individual- and market-experiments (1965, pp. 11–12, pp. 387–92), it will prove useful to draw a distinction between the concepts of 'individual' equilibrium, on the one hand, and 'interactive' equilibrium.

As the terminology indicates, the term 'individual equilibrium' pertains to an individual experiment. It designates the end-result of a given economic agent's optimising decision making process. It expresses itself in individual supply or demand schedules (or excess demand schedules). A further distinction ought be drawn between *determination* and *realisation* of individual equilibrium. Determination refers to the formulation of the equilibrium plan, i.e. the fact that individual agents have succeeded in calculating their equilibrium values with respect to all possible magnitudes of the relevant parameters. Realisation refers to the fact that, at the end of the market process, the agent in question is able to realise one of the trading possibilities comprised in his equilibrium plan. The notion of individual disequilibrium can be understood in contradistinction, as designating the case of an individual who at the end of the market process finds himself in a trading position which does not belong to his equilibrium plan. The problem, however, is that obtaining such an outcome in economic theory as it exists currently is almost impossible. This results from a central yet often neglected institutional hypothesis, namely that markets operate in a centralised or well organised way. They are functioning, it is assumed, on the model of a stock exchange. All participants in the market, the story runs, come together or, at least, are able to communicate within an integrated network. Some device is introduced, either the auctioneer or agents' perfect information, to the effect that trading occurs at market equilibrium magnitude. It ensures that markets come to a close and trading starts only when the plans of all participants have been taken into account and made compatible. This is the reason why one may refrain from considering involuntary unemployment as a case of individual disequilibrium and hence from interpreting it as buttressing some infringement on freedom. As will be seen, those theories which have succeeded in demonstrating involuntary unemployment, according to the reservation wage criterion, can hardly be considered as having renounced individual equilibrium.

The 'interactive equilibrium' concept refers either to a particular market or to the entire economy. It serves the purpose of establishing the positive outcome of the market process whereby individual plans are confronted. To all intents and purpose, my interactive equilibrium concept is what economists have in mind when using the term equilibrium *sans phrase*.[6] Thus, there is interactive equilibrium when the (or some) equilibrium price or price vector obtains.

2.3.3 Two Alternative Concepts of Interactive Equilibrium: Stationary-state or Instantaneous Equilibrium

It should be realised that two alternative concepts of interactive equilibrium exist, namely stationary and instantaneous equilibrium. The first can be traced back to Adam Smith. It was also held by Marshall. The second one originates in Walras' work. In a nutshell[7], stationary equilibrium is based on the idea that there is a hierarchy of equilibrium concepts (and thus of equilibrium price concepts as well), each attached to a distinct time period. In this perspective, an equilibrium arising at the 'lowest' time period (i.e. market-clearing at the market-period) can be a disequilibrium against some higher equilibrium level. Thus, to Marshall a labour market disequilibrium would be a situation where there is labour market-clearing yet arising at a wage/employment mix different from the normal equilibrium magnitude. Such a combination does not arise when the instantaneous equilibrium perspective is adopted. Here, market-clearing is the exclusive meaning attached to the equilibrium concept.

This ambiguity impinges on the definition of unemployment in the following way. Whenever the expression of 'involuntary unemployment equilibrium' is to be found in some writing, it means that the author is reasoning within the Marshallian framework. What he has in mind is a mix of equilibrium and disequilibrium as just evoked – yet the other way round, since it is claimed that a market-period disequilibrium (i.e. lack of market-clearing) is at one and the same time an equilibrium in terms of the 'normal equilibrium' category, to borrow Marshall's terminology. On the contrary, when a instantaneous equilibrium perspective is adopted, properly speaking, the expression of 'involuntary unemployment equilibrium' makes no sense, since in the latter there is only one unique understanding of disequilibrium, namely lack of market-clearing. Here, the right expression should be 'involuntary unemployment disequilibrium'.

2.4 Involuntary Unemployment as a Subcategory of the more Generic Underemployment Category

If the aim of the theoretical work is to generate, as a result, the logical possibility of involuntary unemployment, so defined, the analysis can be done in terms of one unique labour market. It can be also be assumed that markets are well organised, to the effect that adjustment occurs instantaneously and in a costless way. As a result, in this framework, no room is left for a category such as 'frictional unemployment' (more on this below). Nonetheless other related categories ought to be considered.

To bring the point home, let me use the underemployment term to designate any situation where the employment level can be increased

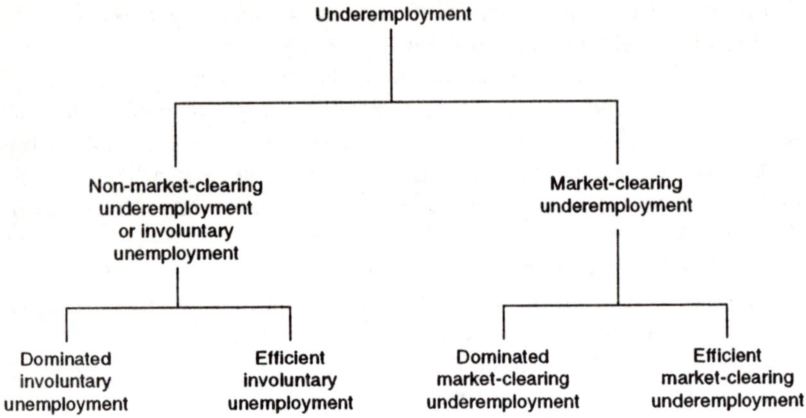

Figure 4.1 Types of underemployment

by some exogenous intervention upon the economy. Its converse can be called 'maximum obtainable employment', i.e. a level at which employment can no longer be increased. This increase should have lasting effects and respect the voluntarity of exchanges. Underemployment can then be seen as a general concept, encompassing distinct subcategories. The tree they form is pictured in Figure 4.1. It results from drawing two successive distinctions, first a distinction between 'non-market-clearing underemployment' and 'market-clearing underemployment', second a further distinction, within each of these two types, aiming at characterising them as either 'dominated' or 'efficient'.

'Non-market-clearing underemployment' is nothing other than involuntary unemployment and I will stick to the latter expression. 'Market-clearing underemployment' refers to a situation where agents are in personal equilibrium – the reservation wage principle is respected – and where the labour market features market clearing. Still, various levels of equilibrium are logically possible. The endogenously prevailing one is amongst them and it happens not to correspond to maximum employment. It is not contested that any gap between effective and maximum employment belongs to the 'voluntary unemployment' category.

Coming to the second distinction, let me first evoke it in reference to market-clearing underemployment. The first of the two subcategories which are separated is called 'dominated market-clearing underemployment'. This terminology is used to signify that, amongst the conceivable employment levels, that which endogenously prevails is not that which allows the most utility to agents. To every agent, it is optimal in the sense that it results from constrained optimising decision making. Nonetheless, a higher utility would be reached if a greater employment level could be obtained, for example, by lifting an externality. The second sub-category, called 'efficient market-clearing underemployment', refers to the case in which, although the effective employment level is submaximum, its increase will not improve agents' utility. As will become clear below, this distinction between dominated and efficient states can be applied to involuntary unemployment as well. Thus, a distinction should be drawn between cases of 'dominated involuntary unemployment' and 'efficient involuntary unemployment.'

Obviously these four forms of underemployment should not be put on the same footing. Only the two 'dominated' forms can lay claim to some 'Keynesian credentials' as, at least in some sense, they refer to market failure states. The same cannot be asserted about the two 'efficient' types. They hardly serve the Keynesian cause. Nonetheless they deserve attention because they have played a significant role in the unfolding of theories.

The opposition between involuntary unemployment and market-clearing underemployment rests on the twin criteria of the breaching of the reservation wage principle and non-market clearance. Yet they also differ on other scores.

(a) The normal context for attempts at generating involuntary unemployment results is that of a unique equilibrium. On the contrary, the market-clearing underemployment result requires multiple equilibria.
(b) The unemployment term (in general and hence also whenever the involuntary adjective is affixed to it) refers to situations where some agents do not participate at all in the labour market. Market-clearing underemployment refers to the situation where all agents who want to participate in the labour market do so. It is just that their participation can be increased through exogenous actions. In other words, whereas involuntary unemployment refers to an unequal distribution of total employment across workers, market-clearing underemployment is a case where it is distributed proportionally. Were the 'unemployment' term to be used at all when the concern is market-clearing underemployment, it should be qualified as 'part-time' unemployment. Thus, only involuntary unemployment accounts for joblessness, properly speaking.

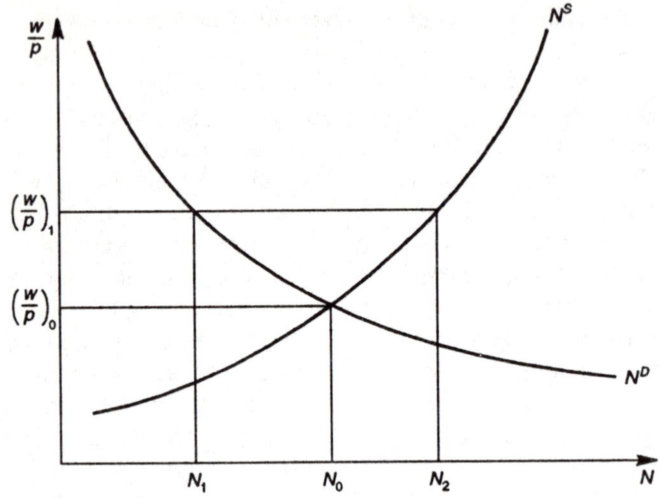

Figure 4.2 The standard labour-rationing graph

(c) Whereas no objection should be levelled against analysing market-clearing underemployment in terms of a representative agent, this is not true for involuntary unemployment. The traditional graphical representation of an involuntary unemployment labour market outcome with short-side trading (cf. Figure 4.2) can be misleading in this respect. Though correct as an aggregate picture, it cannot be interpreted in terms of the representative agent.[8] It can, however, be salvaged if seen as depicting the aggregation of two distinct trading situations. On the one hand, some agents, the employed ones, engage in equilibrium trade – thus, on their supply curves. On the other hand, other agents, the involuntarily unemployed, are both off their supply curves and not transacting at all.

2.5 Frictional or Search Unemployment

In my typology, only one type of unemployment (in the sense of joblessness) is present, namely involuntary unemployment. This raises two issues. The first one is again semantic. What is the rationale, the question may be raised, for the adjective 'involuntary'? It cannot serve to oppose this type of unemployment to any other, except for the misnamed concept of 'voluntary unemployment'. Had the latter always been called 'chosen leisure', the adjective would no longer be necessary. The second and more important question concerns the role of so-called frictional unemployment (or, to give this term a more precise content, search unemployment[9]). Should it be brought into the picture, by stating for example, that, when involuntary unemployment (or any other form of underemployment) arises, it is on top of frictional unemployment? This was Keynes's stance. To me, however, it is not the right way of putting the matter.

I would rather keep involuntary unemployment (as well as the other forms of underemployment analyzed above) and search unemployment separated. The reason is that they are underpinned by alternative assumptions about the organisation of trade. Search unemployment involves a highly decentralised trading set-up. First, markets are seen as functioning continuously, with labour suppliers visiting firms in sequence. In this context, queueing is a normal feature. Second, the unicity of wages is dismissed. Third, trade occurs in a bilateral way. For it to start, no preliminary market-wide equilibrium conditions are required. In this framework, all existing unemployment, however big, should be put under the mantle of search unemployment. Periods of high unemployment are characterised by the fact that search is longer than normal. Thus, there is no need for introducing another category of unemployment. Reference could be made to involuntarity yet in a common-sense meaning. If somebody's offer to work with a firm is refused, his remaining in the pool of the unemployed is, it can be stated, involuntary. If, on the other hand, he refuses a job proposal, his remaining would be voluntary. Yet there would be no involuntary unemployment distinct from frictional unemployment.

Although this is not always made explicit, the underemployment line of research is based on the 'well organised' markets hypothesis. As soon as the latter is adopted, no room is left for the the very phenomenon of search as just depicted.[10]

The pros and cons of the underemployment or search approaches are not discussed here. My contention is simply that they constitute distinct lines of research which should not be mingled. Be it only implicitly, Keynes choose to reason in terms of well organised markets and his disciples followed suit. Hence little attention will be paid to frictional unemployment in the sequel.

2.6 Other Definitions of Involuntary Unemployment

The reservation wage definition of involuntary unemployment adopted in this chapter is the most accepted one. It has also firm roots in the

General Theory. Nonetheless, other definitions can be found in the literature, most of which, it turns out, can be associated with one of the forms of underemployment distinguished above. First, the term 'involuntary unemployment' is sometimes used to designate dominated market-clearing underemployment. Involuntarity can then be understood, in a somewhat looser way, as referring to some impotence or powerlessness. The means of endogenously reaching some welfare-dominating higher level of employment are, it is argued, lacking. This line can be traced back to Haavelmo (1950). It is to be found, for example, in Howitt (1985). A second alternative strand consists of defining involuntary unemployment as any lack of maximum employment. This viewpoint has been defended by Darity and Horn (1983) and Meltzer (1988).[11] Finally, as will be seen, authors such as Lindbeck and Snower (1988) defend still a different definition, where envy is considered the basic criterion for involuntarity.

Of course, terminology, in itself, is of minor importance, as soon as the different possible meanings are disentangled. Yet whatever terminology is used, it remains that all these definitions should not be put on the same footing. They hardly serve Keynes's project in the same way, if at all. The challenge their integration in economic theory raises also differs significantly.

2.7 Full Employment: The Descriptive and Theoretical Meanings

Hitherto, no reference has been made to the concept of full employment. Theoretical discussions, it might be argued, would probably gain from dispensing with it. Yet, for the purpose of this chapter, it cannot be left aside, since it has been abundantly used in the literature. The problem about full employment is that it can be understood either as a statistical category, belonging to a descriptive discourse about the 'real world', or as a theoretical concept, pertaining to the economic theory fictitious parable.[12] As soon as these two interpretations become mingled, semantic muddle cannot but result.

When reasoning at the descriptive level, full employment is identified with the maximum employment attainable. It is assumed that duration of work and the size of active population are given. Full employment is then seen as the minimum feasible rate of unemployment, supposedly an objective exogenous magnitude. In this context, it seems obvious that any progress towards full employment improves social welfare, as it amounts to bringing the unemployed (implicitly thought of as involuntarily unemployed) back into work.

When reasoning in theoretical terms, the matter is different, as 'full employment' and 'maximum employment' can no longer be considered as selfsame. In the theoretical scenario, one reflects on the problem of choice of a representative agent who envisages participating in the labour market. In the basic model, leisure is the choice variable, working-time following on automatically. His maximum employment level – as calculated on a certain basis, for example a daily one, assuming the annual number of days of work to be fixed – is then his time endowment *less* the number of hours considered indispensable to his physical reproduction. It refers to a physical limit rather than a normative quantity, as in the descriptive account. As far as the meaning of full employment is concerned, it refers to all the points belonging to the supply of labour curve, as Patinkin underlined long ago.[13] In other words, it designates the amount of waged work which turns out to be optimal for the representative agent, as a function of the size of the real wage. As such it cannot be assimilated to the maximum attainable employment level, except in the case in which the economic agent wishes to consume no leisure. In this theoretical context, assuming a standard (i.e. monotonically increasing) supply of labour curve, no increase in employment is conceivable without a parallel increase in the real wage. It would run counter to the voluntarity of exchange and decrease the agent's utility. Note, however, that, to compound the matter, there is one occurrence where such an increase would be possible, namely if involuntary unemployment, with its accompanying off the supply curve trading, existed. Hence the view that, if any increase in employment proves possible without change in the real wage, this can be interpreted as the indication of the prior existence of involuntary unemployment.

The difference between the descriptive and theoretical meanings of full employment is that in the former it is put in contradistinction with underemployment in general, whereas in the latter it is opposed to involuntary unemployment, as a specific form of underemployment. Clearly, for the purpose of this chapter, it is necessary to stick to the theoretical interpretation. It then follows that the underemployment categories other than involuntary unemployment all feature full employment, in the theoretical sense. Put differently, market-clearing underemployment cases refer to situations characterised by multiple full employment points.

3 KEYNES'S PROGRAMME: A RECONSTRUCTION

The *General Theory* is a complex book, mixing different objectives more or less explicitly. This makes a reconstruction necessary though, most likely, none of the possible ways of doing it can hope to gain unanimity. My own standpoint in this respect is that Keynes's programme in the *General Theory* can be recast as composed of four elements, namely three objectives and one requirement.[14] First of all, there is the objective of demonstrating the logical existence of involuntary unemployment, after this concept has been given rigorous definition. A second objective is to put forward involuntary unemployment as manifesting a 'system failure' rather than as just a labour market flaw. The third objective is to justify demand stimulation as its proper remedial policy. The requirement is that these objectives should be achieved jointly and in full respect of the methodological canons of neoclassical theory (which Keynes dubbed classical theory).

3.1 Involuntary Unemployment

Keynes was not the inventor of involuntary unemployment – surprisingly enough, Pigou used this concept without qualm – yet, for better or for worse, he brought it to prominence.[15] His contribution is to have located the precise point in economic theory where it could be anchored, namely in what he called the 'second postulate' of the classical theory of employment.[16] To all intents and purpose, the conception of involuntary unemployment brought about in chapter two of the *General Theory* coincides with the 'breaching the reservation wage principle' definition of involuntary unemployment given above. As an aside, it can be noted, following Leijonhufvud (1968, p. 94), that Keynes' formal definition of involuntary unemployment is best interpreted as a test for its existence, rather than as a definition, properly speaking.[17] Against my above typology of forms of underemployment, it is clear that Keynes aimed at making a point about involuntary unemployment rather than market-clearing underemployment. Note also that Keynes' introduction of involuntary unemployment in the *General Theory* can be interpreted as an attempt at turning upside down the Marshallian approach on this matter. As seen above, in a Marshallian perspective, no objection would be levelled against a case where the labour market would jointly feature market-day equilibrium and normal disequilibrium. Keynes, however, wanted the inverse result: a situation of lack of market-clearing, i.e. market-period disequilibrium, which could qualify as a normal equilibrium.

3.2 A System Failure

One of Keynes's basic insights was that involuntary unemployment results from some flaw in the workings of the market economy. Its existence must temper, if not upset, the optimistic interpretation of this system put forward by economists since Adam Smith. In other words, Keynes's interest in involuntary unemployment followed from the presumption that it expressed some system failure. In particular, he wanted to link it with a deficiency in aggregate demand for output as a whole, itself associated with some leakage from the productive towards the financial sector.[18]

The claim that involuntary unemployment follows from some system failure affects the type of analysis which should result. The common explanation in the time of Keynes was that unemployment was the result of wage levels being too high. Such an explanation, it must be underlined, is part of a Marshallian analysis in which one market, here the labour market, is considered in isolation from the rest of the economy. Keynes wished, it can be argued, to escape this framework and to find an explanation of labour rationing outside the labour market.[19] Even though he could not have put it in these terms, what he actually was striving for was to move the analysis of unemployment from a partial to a general equilibrium framework.[20]

3.3 Justifying a Demand-stimulation Policy

Keynes believed that the flaw in the economic system that his analysis was to bring to the fore could be remedied. Even though, here, as well he was rather evasive, it can at least be thought that the interpretation which quickly became popular, that the appropriate remedy was state-induced demand stimulation, fits well with the *General Theory*'s central message. If this view is accepted, it turns out that Keynes wanted to produce a theoretical model resulting in this precise policy conclusion. In other words, to him, there was no point in having a theory concluding that lowering wages is necessary to combat involuntary unemployment.

* * *

Given the time in which Keynes was writing, it is understandable that no basic methodological objections were levelled against his overall project. The theoretical scenario to which it lent had a strong ring of relevance to the economic situation of the time. The fact that unemployment was massive was seen as an indication of its involuntarity. So were the views that some system failure was present and that it could be cured by state intervention. Thus, the direct empirical relevance of Keynes's analysis allowed a cover-up of its conceptual ambiguities. The latter were to arise only much later on. Yet, with the benefit of hindsight, it can safely be stated that Keynes's programme was more daunting than he himself would have thought.

4 INVOLUNTARY UNEMPLOYMENT IN THE *GENERAL THEORY* AND IN THE FIRST GENERATION OF KEYNESIAN MODELS: THE MISSING PIECE[21]

Keynes believed that he had succeeded in demonstrating involuntary unemployment in the *General Theory* and generations of readers followed suit. In this section of the chapter, I contend that this is wrong. The impression that Keynes rose to the challenge of making involuntary unemployment acceptable within neoclassical theory follows only from conceptual confusions. My aim here is to bring them to the fore.

Leaving aside Keynes's misleading use of the term postulate to designate what is in fact a first-order condition and thus a result drawn from earlier premises,[22] the explanation lies, I suggest, in the relationship of equivalence established by Keynes between the concepts of involuntary unemployment and effective demand deficiency – in my opinion, a central yet hardly underlined theme of the *General Theory*.[23] Involuntary unemployment has been defined above. As regards effective demand deficiency, its existence is assessed through an experiment of the style 'the proof is in eating the pudding'. It exists, it is stated, if an exogenous increase in aggregate demand has an employment instead of a wage effect. In contrast, if the level of employment cannot be augmented, full employment is said to prevail. Against my above typology, demand deficiency can be seen as similar to underemployment, it being further added that the means by which underemployment can be resorbed ought to be demand expansion.

The 'claim of equivalence' states that involuntary unemployment and effective demand deficiency constitute the same occurrence, approached from two distinct angles. They are two sides of the same coin. Assume the claim is valid. Then, as soon as demand deficiency is demonstrated, involuntary unemployment can be taken as demonstrated as well (and vice versa). This may explain why the involuntary unemployment concept, which in the first chapter of the *General Theory* receives pride of place, progressively loses its importance. If it barely intervenes in the remainder of the book, it is simply, one might argue, that the onus of the proof has been shifted to the equivalent concept of effective demand-deficiency.

In De Vroey (1997a), it is argued that no other foundation for involuntary unemployment than the procedure of taking demand deficiency as a proxy for it is to be found in the *General Theory*. Hence Keynes' justification of involuntary unemployment hinges entirely on the claim of equivalence. Its robustness is thus crucial. It is invalidated as soon as it proves possible to demonstrate cases of involuntary unemployment unaccompanied by a deficiency in effective demand or the inverse. Now this is exactly what the unfolding of Keynesian theory reveals. As will be seen below, in those models which have succeeded in demonstrating involuntary unemployment, demand deficiency is conspicuous by its absence whereas, on the contrary, models which get a demand deficiency result are not based on involuntary unemployment. With hindsight, it is clear that the claim of equivalence is untenable.

As far as Keynes was concerned, he was unaware of the role this claim played in his construction. Small wonder then that he did not think it through and did not realise what it involved. In terms of my typology of forms of underemployment, he implicitly assumed that the market-clearing underemployment category was empty or, in other words, that involuntary unemployment was the only possible form of underemployment. In effect, he affirmed that involuntary unemployment could be defined either by the violation of the reservation wage principle or by the absence of full employment (1936, p. 26). This assertion is right if full employment is taken in its theoretical sense but not if it is taken in its broader descriptive sense; and, clearly, a shift occurred from the former to the latter.

Hence the claim that Keynes was able to demonstrate involuntary unemployment indirectly, through the proxy of demand deficiency, cannot be vindicated. Accepting that the *General Theory* may well have made a breakthrough about demand deficiency, this is insufficient to conclude that involuntary unemployment has been obtained as well. To this end, one must be able to assess that the type of underemployment which has been brought about is involuntary unemployment rather than other forms of underemployment. Therefore, it would in turn be necessary to have a precise account of the state which the labour market is in. Unfortunately, on this point, the *General Theory*'s reader is left hungry.

It is thanks to Modigliani (1944) that the gap was filled, in a manner which was to become standard in the IS–LM literature. The labour market is here characterised as featuring a particular labour supply curve. It takes the form of an inverse *L*, with employment on the abscissa, a shape which is supposed to capture sociological factors that affect labour supply.[24] Figure 4.3 illustrates this. Full employment is defined as maximum employment, i.e. the level of employment from which stimulation only has a wage effect (supposing that the second segment is vertical). It thus corresponds to the kink in the supply curve. When the demand for labour crosses the supply on the horizontal part, underemployment is present, on a magnitude equal to the distance between the kink and the intersection (*AB* in Figure 4.3(a)). An exogenous increase in the demand for labour can absorb it, assuming additionally that productive capacity is available. The snag is to know how this underemployment should be qualified. In the literature, the step of calling it involuntary unemployment has often been made. Were this stance admissible, then Keynes's claim about involuntary unemployment would be vindicated.

Still, this conclusion cannot resist serious critical reflection, and it is surprising that this point has been so little underlined. The question should be raised of what type of preferences underlie this special supply of labour curve. The answer to this question is simple yet it has a devastating implication: the preferences of the representative agent depicted by such a curve exhibit a perfect substitution between consumption and leisure. His indifference 'curves' are in fact linear (cf. the Figure 4.3(b)). Corner solutions will prevail, except when the real wage is equal to the absolute value of the slope of his indifference lines. This is exactly what happens at the wage magnitude corresponding to the horizontal section of the supply curve. At this wage, all levels of employment are indifferent for him. Hence, if employment can be increased without increase in wage, this has no effect upon utility. What is wrongly called involuntary unemployment is in fact nothing other than efficient market-clearing underemployment.

How is it that such a defect could have passed unseen, with only few exceptions?[25] The reason, it seems to me, is the intrusion of the descriptive account of full employment into the theoretical discourse. Seen against the background of my previous discussion, the labour supply curve *à la* Modigliani hides a twofold pitfall. First, it is true that with such a labour supply the maximum level of employment belongs to the set of full employment points (in the theoretical sense). Yet, it does not welfare-dominate the other submaximum full-employment points. Thus, it deserves no prominence. Obviously, in IS–LM models with a

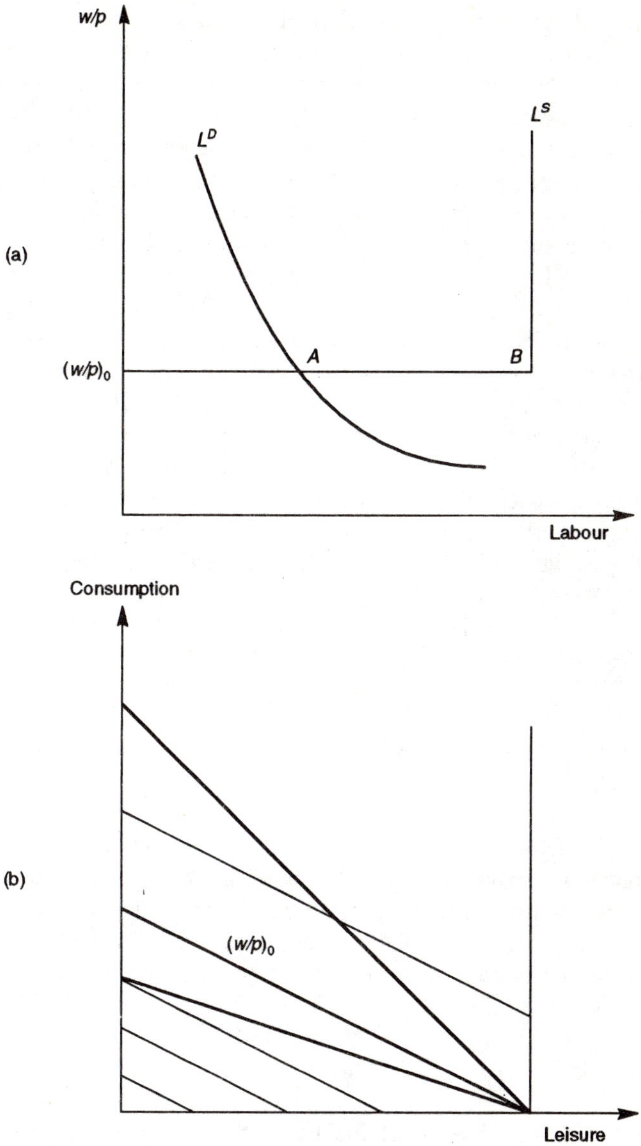

Figure 4.3 The inverse-*L* supply of labour and its choice theoretical foundation

Modigliani labour market, this principle is hardly respected. On the contrary, it is erroneously taken for granted that more employment is always better. Thereby, a proposition which may be valid concerning the descriptive account, is unjustifiably carried over to the theoretical discourse. In the second place while, as seen, a growth in employment at the same wage level is inconceivable at full employment (in the theoretical sense) when the labour supply curve is standard, it is conceivable with a supply curve *à la* Modigliani. Hence the risk of falling into another pitfall, consisting of transposing the 'proof of the pudding' argument, from the standard supply of labour case, where it is valid, to the inverse-*L* supply of labour case, where it is not.

In retrospect, it then turns out that 'old' Keynesian views are seriously wanting. Whereas their authors claimed to have succeeded in demonstrating labour market rationing, as soon as their semantic sloppiness is perceived, this claim proves vacuous. The only type of underemployment whose existence these 'old' Keynesians were able to demonstrate, efficient market-clearing underemployment, is uninteresting. Oddly enough, this flaw has hardly been denounced, with the ironic result that, even nowadays, these models continue to be either criticised or defended on the false assumption that they have obtained a rationing result.[26]

5 INVOLUNTARY UNEMPLOYMENT IN OTHER KEYNESIAN WRITINGS

Although the IS–LM models with a labour market *à la* Modigliani constituted the standard account of Keynesian theory, alternative interpretations were also proposed. Prominent amongst them were Patinkin's and Clower's conceptions. Their standpoints were further synthesised by Barro and Grossman, who paved the way for the so-called French disequilibrium school.[27]

5.1 Patinkin

In Chapters XIII and XIV of his book *Money, Interest, and Prices* (1965), Patinkin explicitly raised the issue of the possibility of integrating involuntary unemployment in economic theory. Of course, he was better equipped than Keynes to grasp its whereabouts. On the one hand, he realised that the corpus within which such an integration had to take place was general equilibrium theory. On the other hand, he was perfectly cognisant of the characteristics of this theory. Notably, he realised that, as long as the analysis was confined to the domain of the existence of equilibrium, involuntary unemployment was doomed to be unacceptable. Nonetheless, there remained, he perceived, still one way open for grounding involuntary unemployment, namely to consider it as arising during the formation of equilibrium process. Hence his basic claim that involuntary unemployment can exist only as a disequilibrium phenomenon, arising in between positions of equilibrium. In this perspective, the disequilibrium notion should be understood as referring to the adjustment process through which the general equilibrium result is obtained, rather than to some end-state of the economy, as above. The occurrence of involuntary unemployment then hinges on the assumption that the price mechanism operates slowly. Any existence it may have is transitory, since market forces will progressively eliminate it. Clearly, this is a significant retreat from Keynes's own standpoint, at least if one thinks, as I do, that Keynes wished to demonstrate the phenomenon of involuntary unemployment as an end-state equilibrium concept.

The problem with Patinkin's conception is that, whereas he wants to put his analysis under the mantle of Walrasian general equilibrium theory, his insight that disequilibrium trade is an effective reality lies on a collision course with this theory's conception of price formation. According to the latter, at each point in time at which trade occurs, the equilibrium prices are supposed to be formed instantaneously or in logical time. Therefore, disequilibrium states have only a virtual existence. They are eliminated before becoming effective. No room is left for the occurrence of the false trading phenomena which Patinkin wanted to bring to the fore.

Actually, Patinkin is aware of the difficulty and his theory can be seen as an attempt at getting away with the standard conceptualisation of price formation. Yet he is unable to give a rigorous account of how an economy might function out of equilibrium. Anticipating further work on stability theory, he proposes some non-tâtonnement process, where trading at false prices is allowed to take place (without, of course, referring to the non-tâtonnement concept). As a starting point, he assumes that some exogenous increase in the demand for bonds occurs, resulting in a decrease in the demand for commodities. Inventories of commodities pile up, to the point that firms decide to restrain their demand for labour. To use later terminology, they shift from notional to effective demand for labour. Involuntary unemployment then ensues, as the rationing arising in the goods market spills over into the labour market. Patinkin is aware that if prices were formed in the standard way, this could not occur.[28] Unfortunately, his story about how the economy behaves in disequilibrium and how disequilibrium gets eventually reabsorbed is wanting. Its basic flaw is its presumption that, after a shock, the economy will go back to the same equilibrium which prevailed beforehand. This result, which is just stated but not demonstrated, cannot be accepted. First, the mere fact of the initial shock should lead to a new equilibrium situation (in terms of both quantities and prices). Second, the acceptance of disequilibrium trading should induce a further shift in the equilibrium position, due to income effects. Thus, Patinkin offers us just a story. It may well have a realistic flavour yet he is unable to transform it into a model. In the light of the subsequent development of stability theory (or rather the lack thereof), this failure is rather unsurprising.

The drawback of Patinkin's programme, it turns out, goes beyond the issue of involuntary unemployment itself. It follows from the fact that, to date, its prerequisite, i.e. a general equilibrium theory of disequilibrium behaviour of agents and disequilibrium states of the economy, is still lacking.[29] Were such a general theory existing, the analysis of involuntary unemployment could be derived as a particular case. Thus, Patinkin's interpretation falls within a line of research which, *a priori*, looks consistent yet which, for technical reasons, has failed to be implemented.

5.2 Clower

Clower's celebrated article 'The Keynesian Counterrevolution: A Theoretical Appraisal' (1965) can be read in two different ways. Looking at the model it contains, one finds a scenario close to that of Patinkin, a case of rationing in a market which has a spill-over effect on another market. Only this time the rationing arises in the labour market and spreads to the goods market. Moreover, Clower addresses the issue of the possibility of involuntary unemployment at equilibrium, rather than as existing only during the price formation process, as in Patinkin's analysis.

But Clower's article also contains another thread of reasoning, surfacing when it is read in the light of Leijonhufvud's interpretation (1968) and of Clower and Leijonhuvfud's joint later work (1975). In this light, it appears that Clower wished to emphasise price signalling problems and, beyond the latter, the possibility of coordination failure in a decentralised economy – in particular, the phenomenon of self-fulfilling predictions locking the economy into inefficient states. With hindsight, it has turned out that such issues have now been tackled with a fair degree of success yet in reference to the dominated market-clearing underemployment concept and thus in a multiple equilibria context. Yet Clower was, in a sense, more ambitious as his target was involuntary unemployment. He and Leijonhufvud also perceived that, to this end, the tâtonnement hypothesis needed to be radically discarded, since its adoption amounted to assuming away coordination failures. An alternative trade technology needed to be devised, which would better take into account the main characteristics of real-world decentralised economies. Such is the theoretical project to which Clower was led and which, jointly with Leijonhufvud, he started working on.

The problem with Clower's diagnosis is less to ask if it is right – many, including me, think so – but to know whether it can be made operational in some rigorous model. It is here, it was quickly realised, that the shoe pinches. In effect, it proved highly difficult for Clower and Leijonhufvud to push their views beyond the blueprint stage. To date, the scenario of a decentralised economy with money as a social link, in which the auctioneer is substituted by private merchants and in which multiple disequilibria could be the norm, has hardly been transformed into a full-fledged theory.

5.3 Disequilibria *à la* Barro and Grossman

Patinkin and Clower's insights have been synthesised in the works of Barro and Grossman (1971, 1976).[30] Taking a model of general equilibrium in which prices are formed in the institutional framework of tâtonnement, they suppose that, for some unexplained reason, the process of price formation is blocked before its normal end. It is as if the auctioneer had cried out a first price vector, but that afterwards nothing else occurred, with the result that prices were stuck at this initial vector. Most plausibly, they will be 'false prices' yet, by chance, it could be the case that the equilibrium price vector has been hit at once. Different configurations for the economy can be distinguished as functions of the type of price vector obtained. They can be contrasted according to the prevailing market situation (that is the identification of the short side of the market), on the one hand and, on the other, the policy which could correct the observed distortion (that is, which would provoke the type of price change which the auctioneer would have put in place had his role not been thwarted). Barro and Grossman show that nine configurations are possible, amongst which are the situations analysed in the Clower and Patinkin models (Barro and Grossman, 1976, p. 87). One of these is called 'Keynesian unemployment' as it fits well with Keynes's objective, as stated above: it corresponds to Keynes's definition of involuntary unemployment and it requires exogenous demand stimulation for goods and services as its remedy. Barro and Grossman's model obviously belongs to the general equilibrium approach. It thus seems that the Keynesian project is, at last, realised.

Unfortunately, a basic criticism can be levelled against this model, namely that the conception of a blocked tâtonnement is ad hoc and runs counter to the spirit of the tâtonnement hypothesis. A good formulation of this stricture is to be found in a passage of Lucas's *Models of the Business Cycle*. In this passage, Lucas starts by voicing his reservations regarding the possibility of producing a phenomenon such as unemployment in a framework based on tâtonnement. Yet, if this framework is adopted, he goes on to observe, the least one might do is to be true to its spirit. Why recur to the theoretical artefact of the auctioneer, if it is only to arbitrarily prevent him from doing the very job for which he was created?[31] Actually, Barro and Grossman were amongst the first to admit to this criticism. The odd result ensued that many economists started to tread in their footsteps, while they, themselves, had already disowned their model.

6 THE ANTI-KEYNESIAN OFFENSIVE

Evidently, the decline of Keynesian theory after the end of the 1970s was hardly the result of a frontal attack on the concept of involuntary unemployment. It rather followed from a broader offensive, put under way by Friedman's criticism of the Phillips curve during his presidential address at the American Economic Association (1968) and carried through by Lucas.

The Friedman address is a short text which, on examination, can be judged as confused. Still, it marked a decisive point in the evolution of ideas. Whereas, on first reading, the criticism he advances seems to be modest and of limited scope – the conciliatory tone he adopts is not unrelated to this impression – in fact, it is devastating. Friedman would certainly have made a formidable lawyer, particularly because of his gift of appearing to embrace the point of view of his opponents in order to ultimately draw opposing conclusions.[32] His stroke of genius is to have realised, more or less wittingly, that the Phillips curve, deemed to be a cornerstone of Keynesian theory, could actually be used as a weapon against it, as much from the conceptual point of view as in terms of policy implications.

The concept of equilibrium used by Friedman is Marshallian. A distinction is thus drawn between a short- and a long-term equilibrium. The unique natural rate of employment is understood as a long-term magnitude, the quantity counterpart of the real long-term equilibrium wage. Note that, in this context, a situation of labour market disequilibrium is characterised only by the fact that the wage and unemployment levels are different from their natural levels, and not by the existence of involuntary unemployment or labour market rationing, contrary to what Tobin might have thought (see n. 32).

In itself, the concept of the natural rate of unemployment could have been accepted by Keynes. Its introduction would signify simply that the category of frictional unemployment, which he thought could be put aside, was still taken into account. His theoretical objective then would have to be reformulated as that of demonstrating the existence of an unemployment rate higher than the natural rate, the excess unemployment being of a different nature and eliciting no feedback.

Friedman hypothesises at the beginning of his argument that the (unique) natural rate of unemployment is already realised. In fact, as soon as this hypothesis is made, the issue is sealed and Friedman's conclusion becomes compelling. The level of employment corresponding to the natural rate of unemployment is full employment less frictional unemployment. If the latter category is left aside, Friedman's argument appears to consist of affirming that, if full unemployment is realised, demand stimulation policies would have no lasting effects. In other words, it is declared that *overemployment* cannot persist. But who would be opposed to such a thesis? To undertake demand stimulation when full employment prevails is absurd, since all defects that such a policy might correct are conspicuous by their absence. The success of Keynesian policy should only be assessed in the context in which it has some raison d'être.[33]

Seen in this way, the reasoning of Friedman seems pretty trivial. Why then did it hit so hard, profoundly damaging Keynesian theory as existing at the time? I, for one, would explain this by the conceptual weakness of the latter theory. Keynesians were in a bad position because they had no alternative model to offer, where a really Keynesian result was obtained. That is, a model where the prior existing level of unemployment would be higher than the natural rate and where the effect of demand stimulation would be lasting. In brief, a model featuring some dominated underemployment – if not involuntary unemployment, at least dominated market-clearing underemployment.

Without referring directly to Keynes, Friedman also takes up the argument by which the latter justifies the concept of involuntary unemployment in the *General Theory*. As stated above, Keynes's formal definition of this concept can be seen as a test of its existence. Assume a situation where the money wage is fixed yet the general price level increases, as the result of a monetary expansion. If it then happens that employment increases, it can be inferred, Keynes argues, that involuntary unemployment was previously present. In effect, if before the intervention, labour supply and demand were matching, the falling real wage would have led to a contraction of labour supply and the observed increase in employment would not have been possible. The very existence of some increase in employment is, in other words, interpreted as manifesting a return towards the full employment equilibrium, from some initial situation of rationing. It is this interpretation which the argument of Friedman is able to upset. According to him, such a growth is possible only because workers suffer from money illusion. Contrary to Keynes, Friedman does not interpret the increase in employment as testifying to the correction of a disequilibrium. Rather, he sees it as the manifestation of a fresh disequilibrium, grafted on a previous equilibrium state and occasioned by an unwarranted monetary expansion.

To conclude with Friedman, two methodological remarks can be made. First, the preceding observation is somewhat frustrating. The point is not that Friedman is right over Keynes (or the opposite) but rather that the discussion suggests that this sort of question might never be settled. The second remark is that Friedman's contribution may serve as negative benchmark for further Keynesian developments. If Keynesian theory is to be associated with a vindication of demand policy, only models disproving Friedman's result, that the increase in employment following on demand activation is only provisional and at the cost of increasing inflation, could deserve the Keynesian label.

Lucas took Friedman's argument one decisive step further, by formalising it more rigorously and relieving it of its lack of rationality content, namely workers' money illusion. His demonstration of a trade-off between employment and inflation, as fully an equilibrium phenomenon, is definitely a great intellectual achievement. It amounts to enlarging the scope of the theory of value, since the business cycle is now part of its purview, whereas earlier it was believed that these were irreconcilable subject-matters. According to Lucas, his result dismisses what he considers as Keynes's project. In his eyes, Keynes wanted to construct a theory of the business cycle but believed that this could not be done without abandoning the equilibrium framework, at least concerning the labour market.[34] The very fact that his own theory is able to do the task without such a renunciation, indicates, he claims, that Keynes had thrown in the towel too early, with a devastating effect on the development of economic theory.

Concerning the involuntary unemployment concept, Lucas's attitude is one of flat dismissal. To him, the concept is simply meaningless. Two arguments are given in favour of this view. First, the unemployed, he claims, could always find some job at once yet are often wise to refuse the first opportunity arising. Hence unemployment is voluntary. Second, in whatever frustrating outcome – and thus also in unemployment – there is always an involuntary and a voluntary element.[35] The first of these arguments pertains to the distinction between labour rationing and unemployment evoked in part I above. In De Vroey (1995a), I have sorted out the conditions of its validity. The second claim will be briefly taken up (and partially endorsed) in the conclusion of this chapter.

Lucas's tremendous influence on the general evolution of economic theory has trickled down on the view taken about the relevance of the involuntary unemployment concept. Whereas, before, it was used without qualm, now scepticism is prevailing. Many Keynesian economists believe that it is unnecessary to the Keynesian cause. Those who continue to use it have grown defensive and tend to take refuge in arguing that semantic discussions are useless.[36]

7 INVOLUNTARY UNEMPLOYMENT IN NEW KEYNESIAN ECONOMICS

Evidently, the new classical attack on Keynesian economics did not put an end to the debate. On the contrary, by a standard dialectical effect, it stirred up a revival of Keynesian thought, known as 'new Keynesian economics'. Actually, the label 'post-new Classical Keynesianism' could do as well, to emphasise how much, for better or for worse, the members of this school are marching to the beat of the new classical drums. Without any qualm, they agree to wage the battle on the field imposed by new classicists. Like them, they reason only in terms of existence of equilibrium and take the micro-foundation requirement as the *sine qua non* of any admissible theoretical proposition. Moreover, the name 'new Keynesian school' is somewhat deceptive, since it actually includes a diverse group of theories. Efficiency wage, of which there are several versions, insider–outsider, coordination failure, imperfectly competitive general equilibrium and 'menu cost' models are its major components. In the present chapter, discussion of these will be rather brief. I will first examine the case of implicit contract theory, less because it was a sustainable advance for the Keynesian cause, than because it initiated a restricted interpretation of the involuntary unemployment concept which is now the most used. After this, I will take three of the above mentioned models, namely efficiency wage, insider–outsider and perfectly competitive coordination models, and examine the extent to which they succeeded in implementing Keynes's project.

7.1 Implicit Contract Theory

The theory of implicit contracts[37] probably represents the first attempt at a Keynesian retort to Lucas, accepting his way of putting issues, in particular the micro-foundations requirement. As I see it, the route taken is to change the equilibrium concept by driving a wedge between the concepts of individual equilibrium and market-clearing. The first of them is considered fundamental and intangible, but not the second. The aim is then to invalidate the existence of market equilibrium in the very name of the individual equilibrium, that is, to make market rationing appear as a result of optimising behaviour. In this way, Lucas would be beaten on his home turf. 'Oh, you want optimising behaviour' one would say, 'then you'll get it and it will lead to a Keynesian result!'

As is well known, Azariadis's argument does not stand up to a closer scrutiny. The main criticism levelled against his model is that its results depend on particular hypotheses, such as the indivisibility of labour time and the exclusion of the possibility that firms can pay indemnities to workers without work. But even if these flaws were absent, the question ought to be raised of whether Azariadis's result fits with Keynes's objective. It is true that it abides by Keynes's definition of involuntary unemployment, since it features a violation of the reservation wage principle. Certain agents are without work, even though at the prevailing wage they wish to be employed. To have got this result with robust micro-foundations is a feat. Yet the involuntary unemployment Azariadis derives is efficient. Paradoxically enough, in terms of agents' utility, involuntary unemployment dominates full employment! Hence the need for the efficient involuntary unemployment subcategory in my typology of forms of underemployment. At bottom, the central feature that Keynes wished to associate with involuntary unemployment, that it illustrates some basic inefficiency, is conspicuous by its absence. As Bryant (1978) notes, the letter of Keynes's project may be saved yet its spirit is sacrificed.

Concerning employment theory, the main legacy of Azariadis's model is a more restricted interpretation of involuntary unemployment, wherein the only substantial content associated with it is the frustration idea. The involuntarily unemployed are envious of their employed colleagues. In Azariadis's terms (1987, p. 734), 'the employed workers receive a wage in excess of unemployment insurance, and are therefore to be envied by laid-off colleagues – a situation that many economists would call "involuntary unemployment"'. On the other hand, the connotation that involuntary unemployment buttresses a restriction on freedom and that the unemployed are not responsible for their fate, is now openly discarded.[38] In as far as Azariadis's restricted interpretation has been taken up in other, more robust, models of involuntary unemployment, it is useful pondering upon it.

Keynes, it may be surmised, saw involuntary unemployment as an unchosen result. Clearly, this makes its insertion within neoclassical theory problematic – in short how can one conceive of obtaining an unchosen result from the premise that people are free choosers? Implicit contract theory resolves the dilemma in an ingenious manner, thanks to the inclusion of uncertainty and the lottery device. In a simplified version of the theory, the representative agent must choose between two lotteries. It is assumed that there are just two possible states of the world. One lottery leads to having work with certainty at a given wage, whatever the prevailing state of the world. The other results in a higher wage if the state of the world is favourable. Yet, if it is not so, the agent receives neither employment nor pay. Azariadis demonstrates that under certain conditions it is optimising to prefer the second lottery over the first. In doing this, if the state of the world is unfavourable, some agents will find themselves out of work, thereby testifying to involuntary unemployment. One may effectively say that they are 'voluntarily in an unchosen situation'. The term 'voluntarily' refers to the fact that theirs is a free, rational and optimising choice, i.e. accepting the lottery, for which they feel fully responsible. The term 'unchosen' now signifies 'undesired', i.e. the fact that the result obtained is not the one that they had wished for. In terms of Dworkin's distinction, evoked above, the price to be paid for making the involuntary unemployment concept acceptable within neoclassical theory is the replacement of its initial 'brute bad luck' connotation by that of 'option bad luck', quite a significant change.

This feature impinges on the assessment to be made about models based on Azariadis's restricted interpretation of involuntary unemployment. It is true that, formally, a result is obtained where the breaching of the reservation wage principle effectively occurs. Some people are not working and yet the wage rate paid to those who are working exceeds their reservation wage . The point, however, is to see whether the case at hand qualifies as an individual disequilibrium. Whereas the spontaneous answer would be affirmative, upon reflection, it turns out that this is wrong. No link should be established between the breaching of the reservation wage principle and individual disequilibrium. On the contrary, the breaching testifies to a state of individual equilibrium, whereas its absence would mean the converse! In still other terms, whereas to Keynes, breaching the reservation wage, individual disequilibrium and lack of market-clearing were three aspects of the same reality, here, one of them – individual disequilibrium – is dropped and is replaced by its opposite – individual equilibrium. Clearly, such a shift is far from benign. On the other hand, this twist, it may be asserted, is the price to be paid for demonstrating involuntary unemployment, in its reservation wage definition.

7.2 Involuntary Unemployment in Efficiency Wage Models

My attention here is restricted to Shapiro and Stiglitz's seminal 'shirking' model (Shapiro and Stiglitz, 1984). These authors use the involuntary unemployment concept in the same sense as Azariadis. However, their result, though often criticised, is deemed to be more robust. Thus, about fifty years after the publication of the *General Theory*, the challenge of demonstrating a result of involuntary unemployment, according to Keynes's definition, has finally been met.

Concerning Shapiro and Stiglitz's understanding of involuntary unemployment, it is clear that they see frustration as its core element. Yet, do they also reject the exclusion or infringement of freedom connotation? This is more difficult to assess because they hardly elaborate on the whereabouts of workers' allocation across the employed and the unemployed status, except for stating that it occurs through a lottery. The subtext of their model is, in a sense, Marxian, which allows for Bowles's recasting (1985). It may be interpreted as stating that firms hold the power, unilaterally decide to fix the wage according to the efficiency wage principle and impose the lottery to the workers who cannot help. Yet such an account does not fit in the neoclassical framework, where market relationships are considered as democratic and devoid of coercion. Thus, a more congruent story would have it that the firm and its pool of workers together reach the conclusion that a lottery may be the most efficient allocative procedure, to the effect that workers should be seen as participating freely into it. If this line is taken, the observations made above apply here as well.

Anyhow, Shapiro and Stiglitz's result cannot be considered as realising Keynes's project in its entirety, since the system failure and justification for demand stimulation objectives are not fulfilled. To see how efficiency wage theory departs from Keynes's insights, the following points are worth considering. First, it marks a return to a partial equilibrium perspective. Second, the default that it reveals has more to do with Hobbesian human nature than with the specifics of a decentralised economy. In this type of model, it can be remarked, involuntary unemployment is less a problem than the solution to a problem, namely shirking and moral hazard. Hence it might be an evil but then it is a necessary one, to the effect that it would prove to be a case of efficient involuntary unemployment.[39] Third, even if it is accepted that Shapiro and Stiglitz's result opens some space for state intervention, the latter can hardly be seen as Keynesian.[40] Fourth, their theory amounts to bringing about a supplementary ingredient to the natural rate of unemployment. On the contrary, to serve Keynes's project, it would be necessary to get unemployment in excess of the natural rate. Thus, their theory does not permit challenging Friedman's argument.

To conclude, the emergence of efficiency wage theory brings about a rather ironic conclusion. When, at last, Keynes's aim of demonstrating involuntary unemployment is achieved, it turns out that this realisation hardly serves the purpose which motivated Keynes in launching this concept! But then, some would question, is it still worth the effort to work towards the goal of demonstrating involuntary unemployment?[41]

7.3 Insider–Outsider Theory

Lindbeck and Snower's insider–outsider model is another well-known contemporary theory which is worth considering here.[42] In Lindbeck (1993, pp. 47–8), involuntary unemployment is defined in the following way:

> At prevailing current wages and future expected wages, some workers are unsuccessful in finding jobs because, at no fault of their

own, they face a more limited choice set between work and leisure than employed workers, even if the wage demands of the former are adjusted for productivity differences, including unavoidable (production-related) resource costs in connection with hiring and firing of workers.

Three comments are in order. First of all, as acknowledged by Lindbeck and Snower, their definition is different from the reservation wage definition. For the non-hired outsiders, the wage at which it would be worth for the firm hiring them is below their reservation wage. Thus, the reservation wage principle is not breached. Second, the exact meaning of their 'more limited choice set' term is somewhat cryptic. This occurrence arises, they state, as soon as some threshold is passed. Whereas they call it the 'involuntary unemployment constraint', I will name it the 'envy threshold', because this is really what it is all about. Its underlying principle is that outsiders do not feel discriminated against by and envious of insiders as long as the difference between insiders' wage and their own reservation wage does not exceed the objective difference in cost between the two types of employment incurred by the firm. When, on the contrary, the wage differential is higher, the envy threshold is passed and involuntary unemployment is stated to exist.[43] Frustration, it then turns out, is a central component of their conception of involuntary unemployment. Third, contrary to what was the case above, their definition takes up the exclusion or infringement on freedom connotation. Their involuntarily unemployed are in no way responsible for their fate.

All this looks quite plausible. It may well be true that the reservation wage criterion is dropped but this, it may be argued, is countervailed by the fact that, at last, the exclusion connotation is taken up. Unfortunately, Lindbeck and Snower's definition comprises a basic yet unnoticed flaw. When it is brought to the fore, the conclusion ought to be drawn that their theory does not serve the purpose they assign it. Let me make my point in reference to their 'hiring-firing' model.[44]

In this model, it is assumed that hiring costs (designated as HI) are 'production-related' (i.e. they refer to objective differences in the costs of employment between insiders and entrants), whereas firing costs (designated as F) are 'rent-related' (i.e. they follow from insiders' ability to capture a rent). As stated, the envy threshold ought to be established whilst shelving rent-related costs yet considering production-related ones. Thus, entrants accept a wage differential of HI. In reference to Figure 4.4, the 'envy threshold' ($\tilde{w}_I$) is $\tilde{w}_I = R + HI$, where R is the reservation wage (the same for insiders and outsiders). Envy arises

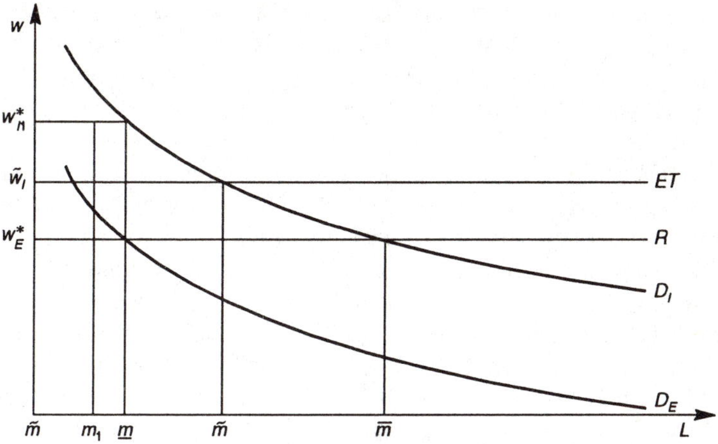

Figure 4.4 Wage-setting, employment and the envy threshold in Lindbeck and Snower's hiring-firing model

as soon as $w_I^* > \tilde{w}_I$, where w_I^* is the insiders' optimal wage. Whether or not the threshold will be passed, depends on the relative size of the incumbent work force. It will be so as soon as $m < \tilde{m}$, where m is the actual incumbent work force and $\tilde{m}$ is the incumbent work force size which will prompt insiders to fix w_I^* at the $\tilde{w}_I$ level. On the contrary, if $m \geqslant \tilde{m}$, the outsiders have no reason to envy the insiders. According to Lindbeck and Snower's definition, they ought to be considered as voluntarily unemployed.

Look now at what Lindbeck and Snower call the 'hiring scenario'. It refers to a case where the number of incumbents is small with respect to demand, i.e. in terms of Figure 4.4, where $\underline{m} > m$. In this scenario, insiders will set the wage at the maximum they can obtain without being replaced by outsiders (i.e. it will be equal to the reservation wage plus total turnover costs:

$w_I^* = R + HI + F$), to the effect that the envy threshold is always passed. It will be optimising behaviour for the firm to hire $(\underline{m} - m)$ outsiders at their reservation wage.

The oddity of Lindbeck and Snower's criterion for involuntary unemployment, i.e. the passing of the envy threshold, now surfaces. It follows from their definitional stance that the entrants ought to be considered as belonging to the 'involuntary unemployment' category. At the limit, it may be imagined that all outsiders become entrants (if $N_E = \underline{m} - m$, where N_E is the total number of outsiders), to the effect that full employment and involuntary unemployment would coexist. Thus, when their definition is accepted, the set of the involuntarily unemployed people may be larger than that of the unemployed! Put differently, unemployment is not a necessary condition for involuntary unemployment. A sufficient condition is that insiders are able to fix the wage above a certain threshold, stirring up outsiders' envy. Hence employment status is not decisive for classifying somebody as belonging to the involuntary unemployment category.

Underlying this awkward classification, we have an interesting case of a subtle and only half-acknowledged shift in theoretical explanandum. Whereas Lindbeck and Snower's initial intention must certainly have been to study unemployment, they have ended up by tackling a different subject-matter, namely the issue of the conditions under which members of an unprivileged group will effectively become jealous of those of a privileged group. In their model, this never hinges on the employment status. A sharp contrast then emerges between the use of the involuntary unemployment concept in efficiency wage and insider–outsider models (besides the difference in definition). Whereas, in the former, frustration is the result of unemployment – to the effect that they disappear concomitantly – in the latter theory, it becomes an autonomous feature, liable to exists on its own, i.e. without unemployment. This is why Lindbeck and Snower's view recalls Lewis Carroll's Cheshire Cat. We may have the grin (frustration) without the cat (unemployment)![44]

7.4 Coordination Failure Models

Finally, I briefly turn to another type of new Keynesian theory, that of perfectly competitive models of coordination failures.[46] In these, the concept of involuntary unemployment, according to Keynes' definition, is renounced, even though certain authors do continue to use the term. The reservation wage principle is not violated and the labour market clears. Strikingly enough, the counterpart of the abandonment of the objective of involuntary unemployment is an advancement of the two other objectives. In these models, multiple equilibria arise as the result of externalities and transactions costs, each equilibrium being associated with different levels of social welfare. When the underemployment equilibrium obtained endogeneously is dominated by other equilibria, a demand stimulation policy causes a superior equilibrium to emerge. The concept of underemployment put to work in these theories is thus that of dominated underemployment equilibrium. This is the sort of model which could be put to use in order to retort to the Friedman–Lucas viewpoint.

8 CONCLUDING REMARKS

To conclude, I would like to make some general observations of a methodological nature. Though some of the points they bring up would ideally solicit an article on their own, they are dealt with here only in a sweeping way. Still this is better, I think, than leaving them undiscussed.

(1) To the question of whether Keynesian theory has succeeded in implementing Keynes's programme, as set out above, the answer is, at best lukewarm affirmative, if not negative. Many results which appeared to have been achieved were revealed to be weak and based on some semantic confusion. This criticism applies particularly to the *General Theory*, as well as to IS–LM models. Decades after the appearance of Keynes's book, his overall theoretical project has not yet been implemented.[47] This negative judgement must, however, be tempered by two factors. The first one is the realisation that Keynes's programme amounts to an uphill struggle. As long as economic theory posits issues in the way it does, the odds are stacked against generating rationing results. The second factor is that, despite this drawback, serious progress has nonetheless been made, as the above account testifies. Eventually, the concept of involuntary unemployment has, in some way, been made admissible in neoclassical theory. Moreover, it may be argued that now some implementation of Keynes's programme is within closer reach than before.[48]

(2) The unfolding of the debate has illustrated that attempts at elucidating the unemployment puzzle face a basic dilemma as to which of two possible research tracks to prioritise, either the specificity of the employment relationship or economic interdependence, i.e. the presumption that any labour market results from flaws arising elsewhere in the economy. Both of them should be considered as important. Yet handling them together seems a formidable task. To note just one aspect, the first of them is better dealt with in a partial equilibrium framework, whereas the second one requires a general equilibrium set-up.

(3) Unemployment theory is a field in which much headway has been made during the last decade or two. Yet it should be noted that its

linchpin has been conceptual rather than empirical. Whenever existing models have been discarded or new ones have imposed themselves, it occurred mainly on conceptual rather than empirical grounds. This is obvious, for example, for what concerns the dismissal of fix-price theory or implicit contract theory. The discussion about the validity of efficiency wage theory also bears witness to this. Likewise, I would argue that Friedman's criticism of the Phillips curve was as much conceptual as empirical. Noticeably, the effective theoretical practice to be found in the literature surveyed here is on a collision course with the explicit empiricist methodological stance taken by most participants in the debate.

(4) The dilemma faced by many Keynesian economists is that they are convinced that in the real world something exists which deserves to be qualified as involuntary unemployment – and bearing the connotations mentioned above, in particular the unemployed's non-responsibility.[49] Yet at one and the same time, they are compelled to admit to the difficulty of introducing this concept into neoclassical language. This uncomfortable position could perhaps be somewhat alleviated by accepting that a dividing line ought to be traced between propositions pertaining to the theoretical scenario, on the one hand, and those which pertain to the real-world, on the other. The above unfavourable assessment, it could then be stated, concerns only theoretical admissibility. Drawing conclusions from it concerning real-world existence would be a mistake. Likewise, the fact that one may put forward solid arguments as to such an existence would not be a sufficient condition to give it theoretical legitimacy. Unfortunately, this principle of a separation between two levels of discourse is accepted and hence respected neither by Keynesians nor by new classicists. Examples in the Keynesian literature are the passage from a statistical to a theoretical definition of full employment or the justification of price rigidity within tâtonnement by the fact of their real-world stickiness. However, new classicists are equally wanting on this front, as they never hesitate to transpose to the real world conclusions which are valid only in the special construct of the theoretical parable.

(5) It may be worth pondering on the meaning of voluntarity in general. At stake is a larger philosophical issue, pertaining to nothing less than the subject-matter of freedom. Ought individuals, the underlying question runs, to be considered as responsible for their present condition? Whenever this question receives a straightforward 'yes' answer, it means that the 'option luck' perspective is

exclusively adopted. The rejection of any involuntary outcome ensues automatically. All consequences of actions ought to be seen as voluntary. Think, for example, of a thief caught after a robbery and sent to jail. According to the strong acceptation of voluntarity, he is behind prison bars voluntarily. Before committing the robbery, he knew the odds of being caught. Likewise, a heavy smoker who ends up with lung cancer, ought to be qualified as 'voluntarily ill'. This 'full responsibility' view has a polar image wherein, on the contrary, individuals are seen as socially determined, in particular because of their class. This is the way in which classical economists, such as Smith and Marx, used to depict wage-earners. The latter were seen as participating in the labour market not by choice but because it was their only alternative to starvation. If their entering into the employment relationship was already considered as involuntary – in the sense that, had their choice set contained any positive alternative, they would certainly have taken it – then, their unemployment, which amounts to their falling into starvation, should *a fortiori* be considered as involuntary.

These remarks are undoubtedly too schematic, but they may have the merit of showing that the two extreme positions are wanting. One can make neither the hypothesis that the agents are entirely responsible for their fate – since to underline just one point, at what age would one fix the first responsible choice, out of which all subsequent ones would stem? – nor that they are not at all. However, no conclusion should be drawn from this as to the irrelevance of the involuntary unemployment category. The latter may still make sense in as far as it is accepted that some 'responsibility boundary' can be drawn. Placing this limit at a high (low) level, would mean that one veers towards (away from) the full responsibility viewpoint. By studying the occupational trajectory of individual unemployed people and by knowing the configuration of their choice sets, it should be possible in principle to assess whether or not an individual could be qualified as involuntarily unemployed. To put some flesh on this, think of the following case. A highly skilled person, around his 50s, has lost his job because the firm where he used to work went bankrupt. Assume moreover that the branch he was working in is declining. Whereas his age is a handicap to getting a lower-skill job, he lacks the means to become self-employed. Suppose also that the emigration solution is precluded. Then, against the background of the labour rationing/unemployment distinction, this person can be described as experiencing both labour rationing and unemployment. The question at hand is whether his unemployment qualifies for the involuntary prefix. The answer to this question hinges on where to put the responsibility boundary. At the age of 40, this person could have anticipated the frailty of the firm employing him and quit it immediately, in which case he would have found a job. Placing the responsibility boundary at a high pitch amounts to judging that it was in his reach to make such a judgement and his responsibility to draw consequences. Hence the conclusion that he should be considered as voluntarily unemployed. On the contrary, placing the boundary lower amounts to considering that expecting people to be able make such judgements and decisions amounts to overtaxing their rationality. Hence he should be classified as involuntarily unemployed. Noticeably, in such a framework, nobody could be '100 per cent involuntarily unemployed', because some responsibility is always involved. It should come as no surprise that the proportion of the involuntarily unemployed within the pool of the unemployed would be higher in a context of depression. Therefore, the association made by Keynes between involuntary and mass unemployment is quite plausible.

(6) Lucas is then wrong when stating that, even in principle, it is impossible to classify people in terms of the voluntary/involuntary divide (see n. 35). Yet, the making of this sort of assessment will probably be of little use to economic theory.[50] On the other hand, Lucas seems right when stating that all unemployment situations buttress a mix of voluntarity and involuntarity. This statement, it turns out, matches up with the above reflection. Nevertheless, he should be criticised on other grounds, namely for his failure to see that his statement bites as much at his own conception of economic theory as at that of Keynesians. If it is accepted that the assertion 'Mr *X* is 100 per cent involuntarily unemployed' is too extreme, the opposite assertion, that his unemployment is 100 per cent voluntarily, is just as wanting. Now the problem is that this is precisely the viewpoint on which neoclassical theory is based. Therefore, it is fully vulnerable to the very criticism which Lucas addressed to the Keynesians.

(7) Finally, the question should be raised of whether the abandonment of the involuntary unemployment concept, in its reservation wage definition, would be so dramatic. Not necessarily so, is my answer. First of all, in as far as the principle of a separation between the two levels of discourse is accepted, this theoretical abandon-

ment should have no impact on assessments made about reality. Second, the reason for its dismissal should be taken into account. The hypothesis of an extremely strong rationality, as existing in neoclassical theory – and its corollary, an extremely strong viewpoint about freedom – is defensible, in particular on the grounds of tractability and lack of better alternatives. But then there is nothing to boast about its adoption. If involuntary unemployment is deemed to be theoretically unacceptable only on such grounds, there is no reason to make a fuss over its dismissal. Third, the issue is less that an involuntary unemployment result cannot be obtained (since it has) than to judge whether it is the best track to tread. In other words, it might be the case that this objective reveals itself as an obstacle to setting up models liable to vindicate Keynes's other and perhaps even more basic insights. It can actually be surmised that, to him, the concept of involuntary unemployment was instrumental in the realisation of a larger cause, namely the denunciation of a system failure and the vindication of state intervention in the economy. If this concept has been an object of controversy, it is mainly, I would conjecture, because it was a metaphor for another problem, that is of the general judgement to be made on the efficiency of a competitive market system, and of the opportunities for state intervention in it. Wanting to defend the involuntary unemployment concept then amounts to taking up a sceptical stance about the virtues of laissez-faire, and to defending the view that outside interference in the market can be beneficial. Similarly, the opposition to involuntary unemployment would then stem from the fact that one supports full laissez-faire. This is the real issue in the dispute. But this debate does not necessarily need the involuntary unemployment concept.

Notes

1. This research has been supported by a grant 'Action de Recherches Concertées', no. 93/98–162 of the Ministry of Scientific Research of the Belgian French Speaking Community. Comments by C. Arnsperger, R. Backhouse, P. Berten, P. Bridel, J. Cartelier, F. Donzelli, J. Drèze, D. Hausman, K. Hoover, A. Leijonhufvud, U. Mäki, M. Messori, F. Ranchetti, H.-M. Trautwein and C. Wampach are gratefully acknowledged. An earlier version of this chapter was published in the *Revue économique*.
2. To wit, perfect competition coordination models will just be touched on,

whereas imperfect competition general equilibrium models will not even be mentioned. Another conspicuous absentee is Hicks.

3. The reservation wage is the highest value of the real wage such that the demand for leisure is equal to the total time endowment of the agent concerned.
4. 'Option luck is a matter of how a deliberate and calculated gamble turns out – whether someone gains or loses through accepting an isolated risk he or she should have anticipated and might have declined. Brute luck is a matter of how risks fall out that are not in that sense deliberate gambles. If I buy a stock on the exchange that rises, then my option luck is good. If I am hit by a falling meteorite whose course could not have been predicted, then my bad luck is brute' (1981, p. 293).
5. This matter is further pursued in De Vroey (1995a).
6. This practice will also be taken up below. Whenever the equilibrium term is used alone, it will have the interactive meaning.
7. For a more detailed analysis, cf. De Vroey (1997c).
8. The latter, facing an off his supply schedule trading proposition, as depicted in the graph in Figure 4.2, should refuse to do any trade under such terms and veto the opening of trade. To see this, recall first that only the points on the curves express agents' individual equilibrium plans. Let it moreover be accepted that markets work in a centralised and democratic way. By this I mean that every agent has a right, in realising his equilibrium plan, to demand that prices be changed and to postpone the opening of trading in the meanwhile. In other words, a market serves the purpose of making all individual plans compatible. Any agent participating in it can expect this outcome to be effective. Hence his right to oppose any other outcome. Against this background, it is clear that an agent will never trade a positive amount of labour off his supply curve. The following analogy may help to bring the point home. Imagine someone who is due to receive a certain amount of money, as the result of a well specified and indisputable contract. Now, at the date of payment he is told that, for spurious reasons, he will receive only half of the amount due. Some might argue that he should accept the deal, because half the amount gives a higher utility than nothing. Yet it is more plausible to assume that this person, feeling that his rights have been encroached on, will prefer to block the whole process (in order for example to start a judicial action) rather than receiving the smaller amount. The same applies to a participant in market trading, seeing his right in individual equilibrium denied.
9. Cf. Okun (1981, Chapter II) and Pissarides (1990).
10. An author such as Diamond (1984) has introduced some elements of search in a tâtonnement context but then this is quite different from the search models on which, for example, Okun's reasoning is based.
11. As stated by Meltzer 'Involuntary unemployment is the difference between the point at which the supply curve of labour becomes vertical and any equilibrium position at a lower level of employment' (1988, p. 166).
12. The 'descriptive discourse' terminology is, I admit, somewhat vague. It refers to views which may be found in newspapers articles and political speeches. These insights can be and to some extent have been transformed

into a theoretical construct. Yet, it then turns out that the latter belongs to the search rather than the underemployment perspective.

13. 'As long as workers are on their "supply curve" – that is, as long as they succeed in selling all the labour they want at the prevailing real wage rate – a state of full employment will be said to exist in the economy. . . . It also follows that the bench mark of full employment is not an absolute constant, but something which itself varies with every change in the real wage rate or in the subjective or objective determinants of the labour supply curve" (1965, pp. 314–15).
14. It is vindicated in De Vroey (1997a).
15. On the origins of the term 'involuntary unemployment', see Corry (1996, p. 12).
16. 'The utility of the wage when a given volume of labour is employed is equal to the marginal disutility of that amount of employment' (1936, p. 5). In modern terminology, the real wage is equal to the rate of substitution between consumption goods and leisure.
17. 'My definition is therefore as follows: Men are involuntarily unemployed if, in the event of a small rise in the price of wage-goods relatively to the money-wage, both the aggregate supply of labour willing to work for the current money-wage and the aggregate demand for it at that wage would be greater than the existing volume of employment' (1936, p. 15).
18. In Leijonhufvud's terms: 'Keynes was concerned with a *systemic* problem that could be defined neither in terms of individual decision situations nor in terms of interactions between buyers and sellers in a single market. His "involuntary" unemployment is the result of *effective demand failures*' (Leijonhufvud, 1983, pp. 195–6). See also Coddington (1983, p. 27) and Kregel (1987, p. 135).
19. As Meltzer puts it, 'the problem is manifested in the labour market, but it does not arise in the labour market' (1988, p. 197).
20. Cf. Patinkin (1987, pp. 27, 35), Weintraub (1979, p. 39).
21. This section draws on De Vroey (1997a).
22. Keynes bluntly asserted that the proposition to be removed in order to introduce involuntary unemployment was a postulate. This is wrong. The equality between the consumption/leisure marginal rate of substitution and the real wage rate stems from deeper choice theoretical premises, as Leontief aptly emphasised long ago (1947, pp. 233–4). Keynes effectively ignored this and proceeded as if he was simply replacing a postulate by another one.
23. What Keynes called 'effective demand' was soon to be understood as meaning aggregate demand. Textual evidence about the argumentation put forward in the following paragraphs is to be found in De Vroey (1997a).
24. Whereas in Modigliani's article the argument was put in terms of a rigid money wage, it soon became recast in terms of real wage rigidity. Noteworthy, both formulations run counter to Keynes's initial intention. Ironically enough, one of Keynes's indictments against Pigou was that he assumed an inverse-*L* supply of labour (Keynes, 1973, p. 54; see also Collard, 1981, pp. 122–32). On the other hand, it should be granted that, if the first generation of Keynesian economists fell back on such an assump-

tion, it is because no alternative ways for bringing together Keynes's insights seemed available.

25. For example, Patinkin (1965, p. 342); Stiglitz (1992, p. 73).
26. A further consequence of this state of affairs is worth mentioning. One of the distinct contributions of new classicists, besides rational expectations, it is often stated, is their market-clearing result. Yet such a proposition makes sense only if it were true that before non-market clearance result had prevailed, which is false. With the exception of the short-lived fix-price model episode, economic theory, from Smith to Keynes (if my above criticism is accepted), through Marshall and Walras, has always pertained to markets where demand and supply were matching (cf. De Vroey, 1997c). Thus, new classicists have hardly invented market-clearing. They have only brought to the fore a theoretical practice which was already present but only unwittingly.
27. In the sequel, I will not be concerned with this school and will limit myself to comments on the views of the above-mentioned founding fathers.
28. Patinkin's account of the standard mechanism is misleading. He states that, under the standard adjustment assumption, the economy would 'quickly return to a full employment position at a lower level of wages, prices, and interest' (1965, p. 318). This statement is ambiguous in two respects. On the one hand, Patinkin asserts that the problem he wants to emphasise will not arise if adjustment forces proceed quickly. Casting the issue in this way is misleading, though. In a Walrasian economy the formation of prices should be considered as taking place instantaneously. 'Instantaneous' and 'quick' are not the same thing. On the other hand, this statement is mute about quantities. In fact, the latter will change as well.
29. Cf. Fisher (1983).
30. To work out this synthesis, Barro and Grossman had to do violence to both Patinkin and Clower's ideas. They abandoned Patinkin's governing idea, according to which involuntary unemployment could exist only during the process of price formation, to substitute this by an existence of equilibrium analysis. In the same way Clower could consider that his main hunch was betrayed in their synthesis, since Barro and Grossman still take tâtonnement as their organisation of trade assumption. Let me add that this 'betrayal' can be justified by the intractability of Clower and Patinkin's initial insights.
31. 'The fix-price model cannot help us get past the limits of the Walrasian scenario, on which the equilibrium models rest because it, too, accepts the Walrasian abstraction from any kind of continuing relationship between buyers and sellers, or between firms and employees. What we mean, in ordinary usage, by 'unemployment' is exactly disruptions in, or difficulties in forming, employer–employee relationships. Simply hamstringing the auctioneer in a Walrasian framework that assigns no role at all to such a relationship is not going to give us the understanding we want. If we are serious about obtaining a theory of unemployment, we want a theory about unemployed people, not unemployed 'hours of labour service'; about people who look for jobs, hold them, lose them, people with all the attendant feelings that go along with these events. Walras' powerfully simple scenario, at least with the most obvious choice of 'commod-

ity space', cannot give us this, with cleared markets or without them' (1987, pp. 52–3). See also Mankiw (1990, p. 1665).

32. The following passage from a recent article by Tobin testifies to the confusion which has prevailed as to the exact content of Friedman's views: 'Until I re-read Friedman's Presidential Address in order to write this chapter, I had the impression that Friedman accepted a Keynesian non-market clearing explanation of unemployment in excess of the natural rate' (1995, p. 40).
33. Hahn (1982) and Modigliani in an interview with Feiwel (1989, p. 570) are amongst the few Keynesian authors to have underlined this point. In Hahn's terms: 'It is puzzling to find it [the short-run Lucasian Phillips curve] put forward as a discovery that a higher inflation rate will not increase the full-employment level of employment: Keynes and the Keynesians would not have claimed otherwise. . . . In fact, the world that they [the Lucasians] describe quite plainly needs no macro-policy. Keynesians were concerned with the problem of pushing the economy to its natural rate, not beyond it. If the economy is already there, we can all go home' (1982, pp. 74–5).
34. I, for one, would rather argue that Keynes was aiming at developing a static involuntary unemployment theory.
35. 'Nor is there any evident reason why one would *want* to draw this distinction [between involuntary unemployment and voluntary unemployment: MDV]. Certainly the more one thinks about the decision problem facing individual workers and firms the less sense this distinction makes. The worker who loses a good job in prosperous times does not *volunteer* to be in this situation: he has suffered a capital loss. Similarly, the firm which loses an experienced employee in depressed times suffers an undesired capital loss. Nevertheless the unemployed worker at any time can always find *some* job at once, and a firm can always fill a vacancy instantaneously. That neither typically does so *by choice* is not difficult to understand given the quality of the jobs and the employees which are easiest to find. Thus there is an involuntary element in all unemployment in the sense that one chooses bad luck over good; there is also a voluntary element in all unemployment, in the sense that however miserable one's current work options, one can always choose to accept them . . . Involuntary unemployment is not a fact or a phenomenon which it is the task of theorists to explain . . . Is it the task of modern theoretical economics to 'explain' the theoretical constructs of our predecessors, whether or not they have proved fruitful? . . . It does not appear possible, even in principle, to classify individual unemployed people as either voluntary or involuntarily unemployed depending on the characteristics of the decision problem they face. One cannot, even conceptually, arrive at a usable definition of full employment as a state in which no involuntary unemployment exists' (1978; reprinted in Lucas, 1981, pp. 242–3).
36. The following excerpt from Stiglitz's *Journal of Economic Literature* survey illustrate this: 'Critics might say at this juncture, "Aha, so unemployment is really voluntary". We think little is gained from a semantic debate over whether unemployment is, in this sense, voluntary or involuntary' (Stiglitz, 1987, p. 35).

37. The three founding articles are Azariadis (1975), Baily (1974), and Gordon (1974). Here I will refer only to the first of these authors.
38. As stated by Hahn and Solow: 'Involuntary unemployment has nothing to do with any metaphysical conundrum about "free will"'(Hahn, 1983, p. 225). 'The key point here is that the notion of "involuntary unemployment" is not metaphysical or psychological; it has little or nothing to do with free will' (Solow, 1986, p. S 33).
39. This is an idea which Phelps toyed with in his textbook, *Political Economy*: 'There is no doubt, then, that this involuntary unemployment is bad. It is an unfortunate side effect, or third-party effect, that the employers in trying to guard against the shirking and quitting of their own employees *inflict on others* – the workers whom they would otherwise have employed in addition. The result is a failure of labour markets to achieve ideal efficiency. But what as a practical matter can be done about it? What can be done to shrink the pool of involuntarily unemployed workers – the pool that young would-be workers must swim in until fished out by an employer – without making employed workers (who may have swum in that pool) and owners of firms (who may have once been unemployed also) worse off? There is not necessarily much or anything that can be done that would work and not harm anyone. Some things are regrettable but are not genuine *problems*, because they have no solutions!' (Phelps, 1985, p. 421). Whenever this interpretation is accepted, involuntary unemployment ought to be considered as efficient. Since then, Phelps's ideas have, however, evolved.
40. Certain efficiency wage authors, as Bowles and Gintis (1988), find nothing to object to in such an observation. Effectively, for them, this theory need not be used to achieve Keynes' project, in which they do not believe, but rather serves the purpose of justifying the idea that an alternative governance structure of firms would be more efficient.
41. Kolm is one of those who would respond negatively to the question: 'But above all, the theory of efficiency wages by itself leads to the exact opposite conclusions of the one it wishes to demonstrate *in fine*. The original intention was to find a base from which to counter the "new classical" assertion that "the government should not intervene (with Keynesian policies) because the labour market is in competitive equilibrium and is thus Pareto-efficient". The "efficiency wage" does yield a labour market in disequilibrium and "involuntary unemployment". But the situation it describes is Pareto-efficient since it corresponds to an unconstrained profit-maximisation in the labour market by the firms choosing both employment and wages. This theory does not justify therefore government intervention to improve the efficiency of the economy' (1990, p. 230).
42. Their main articles have been collected in Lindbeck and Snower (1988). See also Lindbeck (1993).
43. In Lindbeck and Snower's terms: 'Whenever the differential between the insider wage and the outsider's reservation wage exceeds the insider–outsider productivity differential, we classify the unemployment as "involuntary", in the sense that outsiders face a more limited choice (in terms of labour services offered and remuneration received) than that of the insiders' (1988, p. 63).

44. A more extended analysis is given in De Vroey (1995b), where Lindbeck and Snower's harassment–cooperation model is also considered.
45. Lindbeck and Snower are aware of this oddity, which they coin as 'job discrimination' (1988, p. 107). Yet, they fail to draw its implications, namely that even when unemployment and frustration arise together, the former cannot be seen as the cause of the latter.
46. Cf. Cooper and John (1988); Diamond (1982); Howitt (1985); Bryant (1983); Heller (1986).
47. This judgement, made here with respect to Keynes's 'pragmatic' or neoclassical project merits, in my eyes, to be extended to his 'radical' project, which was not considered in this chapter. Despite many attempts, all promising at the start, heterodox Keynesian theories never really took off, or quickly fell flat.
48. The next step to be taken is to construct models which synthesise the factors producing involuntary unemployment and those which lead to a multiplicity of natural rates of unemployment. Cf., for example, Blanchard and Summers (1986); McDonald (1990); Phelps (1994).
49. As once stated by Solow, 'I believe that what looks like involuntary unemployment is involuntary unemployment' (1980, p. 3).
50. It is nonetheless surprising that economists have devoted so little attention to existing sociological or psychological studies of the unemployed. An exception in this respect is Clark and Oswald (1994).

References

Azariadis, C. (1975) 'Implicit Contracts and Underemployment Equilibria', *Journal of Political Economy*, vol. 83, pp. 1183–2002.

——— (1987) 'Implicit Contracts', in *The New Palgrave. A Dictionary of Economics*, vol. 2, ed. M. Milgate, P. Newman, J. Eatwell (London: Macmillan), pp. 733–36.

Baily, M. (1974), 'Wages and Employment under Uncertain Demand', *Review of Economic Studies*, vol. 41, pp. 37–50.

Barro, R. and H. Grossman (1971) 'A General Disequilibrium Model of Income and Employment', *American Economic Review*, vol. 61, pp. 82–93.

——— (1976) *Money, Employment and Inflation* (Cambridge: Cambridge University Press).

Blanchard, O. and L. Summers (1986) 'Hysteresis and the European Unemployment Problem', *NBER Macroeconomics Annual*, pp. 15–77.

Bowles S. (1985), 'The Production Process in a Competitive Economy: Walrasian, Neo-Hobbesian and Marxian Models', *American Economic Review*, vol. 75, pp. 16–36.

Bowles, S. and H. Gintis (1988), 'Contested Exchange, Political Economy and Modern Economic Theory', *American Economic Review*, vol. 78, pp. 145–50.

Bryant, J. (1978) 'An Annotation of "Implicit Contracts and Underemployment Equilibria"', *Journal of Political Economy*, vol. 86, pp. 1159–60.

——— (1983) 'A Simple Rational Expectations Keynesian-Type Model', *Quarterly Journal of Economics*, vol. 98, pp. 525–8.

Clark, A. E. and A. J. Oswald (1994) 'Unhappiness and Unemployment', *Economic Journal*, vol. 104, pp. 548–659.

Clower, R. (1965) 'The Keynesian Counterrevolution: A Theoretical Appraisal', in F. Hahn and F. Brechling (eds), *The Theory of Interest Rates* (London: Macmillan; reprinted in D. Walker (ed.) (1984), pp. 34–58.

Clower, R. and A. Leijonhufvud (1975) 'The Coordination of Economic Activities : A Keynesian Perspective', *American Economic Review*, vol. 65, pp. 182–8.

Coddington, A. (1983) *Keynesian Economics. The Search for First Principles* (London: Allen & Unwin).

Collard, D. (1981), 'A.C. Pigou, 1877–1959', in D.P. O'Brien and J. Presley (eds), *Pioneers of Modern Economics in Britain* (London: Macmillan), pp. 36–71.

Cooper, R. and A. John (1988) 'Coordination Failures in Keynesian Models', *Quarterly Journal of Economics*, vol. 103, pp. 441–63.

Corry, B. (ed.) (1996) *Unemployment and the Economists* (Edward Elgar).

Darity, W. and B. Horn (1983) 'Involuntary Unemployment Reconsidered', *Southern Economic Journal*, vol. 49, pp. 717–33.

De Vroey, M. (1995a) 'From Chicago Welding to California Grapepicking or Does Labour Market Rationing Entail (Involuntary) Unemployment?', mimeo.

——— (1995b) 'Professor Lindbeck and Snower's Cheshire Cat Definition of Involuntary Unemployment', *IRES Discussion Paper*, 9506, Université Catholique de Louvain.

——— (1997a) 'Involuntary Unemployment: The Missing Piece in Keynes' General Theory', *European Journal of the History of Economic Thought*, vol. 4 (2), pp. 258–83.

——— (1997b) 'Keynes, Keynesian Programmes and the Unemployment Decision Tree', in P. Fontaine and A. Jolink (eds) *Historical Perspectives on Macroeconomics: 60 Years After the General Theory* (London: Routledge) forthcoming.

(1997c) 'Equilibrium and Disequilibrium in Economic Theory. A Confrontation of the Classical, Marshallian and Walrasian Conceptions' (mimeo).

Diamond, P. (1982) 'Aggregate Demand Management in Search Equilibrium', *Journal of Political Economy*, vol. 90, pp. 881–94.

——— (1984) *A Search-Equilibrium Approach to the Micro-Foundations of Macroeconomics* (Cambridge MA: MIT Press).

Dworkin, R. (1981) 'What is Equality? Part 2: Equality of Resources', *Philosophy and Public Affairs*, vol. 10, pp. 283–345.

Feiwel, G. R. (1989) 'Testimony II: An Interview. Franco Modigliani', in George R. Feiwel (ed.), *The Economics of Imperfect Competition and Employment. Joan Robinson and Beyond* (London: Macmillan), pp. 569–81.

Fisher, F. M. (1983) *Disequilibrium Foundations of Equilibrium Economics* (Cambridge: Cambridge University Press).

Friedman, M. (1968) 'The Role of Monetary Policy', *American Economic Review*, vol. 58, pp. 1–17.

Gordon, D. F. (1974) 'A Neoclassical Theory of Keynesian Unemployment', *Economic Inquiry*, vol. 12, pp. 431–49.

Haavelmo, T. (1950) 'The Notion of Involuntary Economic Decisions', *Econometrica*, vol. 18 (1), pp. 1–8.

Hahn, F. (1982) *Money and Inflation* (Oxford: Basil Blackwell).

——— (1983) 'Comment on Axel Leijonhufvud's "Keynesianism, Monetarism and Rational Expectation": Some Reflections and Conjectures', in R. Frydman and E. Phelps (eds), *Individual Forecasting and Aggregate Outcomes, Rational Expectations Explained* (Cambridge: Cambridge University Press), pp. 223–30.

Heller, W.P. (1986) 'Coordination Failures under Complete Markets with Applications to Effective Demand', in W. Heller, R. Starr and D. Starret (eds), *Equilibrium Analysis: Essays in Honor of Kenneth J. Arrow*, vol. II (Cambridge: Cambridge University Press), pp. 155–75.

Howitt, P. (1985) 'Transactions Costs and the Theory of Unemployment', *American Economic Review*, vol. 75, pp. 88–100.

Keynes, J.M. (1936) *The General Theory of Employment, Interest, and Money* (London: Macmillan).

——— (1973) *Collected Writings*, vol. XIV, D. Moggridge (ed.) (London: MacMillan).

Kolm, S.-C. (1990) 'Employment and Fiscal Policy with a Realistic View of the Role of Wages', in P. Champsaur, M. Deleau *et al.* (eds), *Essays in Honour of Edmond Malinvaud*, vol. 2, *Macroeconomics* (Cambridge MA: MIT Press), pp. 226–81.

Kregel, J.A. (1987) 'The Effective Demand Approach to Employment and Inflation Analysis', *Journal of Post Keynesian Economics*, vol. 10 (1), pp. 133–45.

Leijonhufvud, A. (1968) *On Keynesian Economics and the Economics of Keynes: A Study of Monetary Theory* (Oxford: Oxford University Press).

——— (1983) 'What Would Keynes have Thought of Rational Expectations?', in D. Worswick and J. Trevithick (eds), *Keynes and the Modern World* (Cambridge: Cambridge University Press), pp. 179–203.

Leontief, W. (1947) 'Postulates: Keynes' *General Theory* and the Classicist', in S. Harris (ed.), *The New Economics, Keynes' Influence on Theory and Public Policy* (New York: A.A. Knopf), pp. 232–42.

Lindbeck, A. (1993) *Unemployment and Macroeconomics*, (Cambridge, MA: MIT Press).

Lindbeck, A. and D. Snower (1988) *The Insider–Outsider Theory of Employment and Unemployment* (Cambridge, MA: MIT Press).

Lucas, R.E. Jr. (1978) 'Unemployment Policy', *American Economic Review*, reprinted in R. Lucas, *Studies in Business Cycle Theory* (Cambridge, MA: MIT Press, 1981), pp. 240–7.

——— (1981) *Studies in Business Cycle Theory* (Cambridge, MA: MIT Press), 1981, pp. 240–7.

——— (1987) *Models of the Business Cycle*, Basil Blackwell: Oxford.

McDonald, I. (1990) *Inflation and Unemployment. Microeconomics with a Range of Disequilibria* (Oxford: Basil Blackwell).

Mankiw, G. (1990) 'A Quick Refresher Course in Macroeconomics', *Journal of Economic Literature*, vol. 28, pp. 1645–60.

Meltzer, A. (1988) *Keynes's Monetary Theory. A Different Interpretation* (Cambridge: Cambridge University Press).

Modigliani, F. (1944) 'Liquidity Preference and the Theory of Interest and Money', *Econometrica*, vol. 12 (1), pp. 45–88.

Okun, A. (1981) *Prices and Quantities. A Macroeconomic Analysis* (Oxford: Basil Blackwell).

Patinkin, D. (1965) *Money, Interest and Prices*, 2nd edn (New York: Harper & Row).

——— (1987) 'Keynes, John Maynard', vol. 3, *The New Palgrave. A Dictionary of Economics* (London: Macmillan), pp. 19–41.

Phelps, E. (1985) *Political Economy* (New York: W.W. Norton).

——— (1994) *Structural Slumps: The Modern Equilibrium Theory of Unemployment, Interest, and Assets* (Cambridge MA: Harvard University Press).

Pissarides, C. (1990) *Equilibrium Unemployment Theory* (Oxford: Basil Blackwell).

Shapiro, C. and J. Stiglitz (1984) 'Equilibrium Unemployment as a Worker Discipline Device', *American Economic Review*, vol. 74, pp. 433–44.

Solow, R. (1980) 'On Theories of Unemployment', *American Economic Review*, vol. 70, pp. 1–11.

——— (1986) 'Unemployment: Getting the Question Right', *Economica*, vol. 47, Supplement, pp. 23–34.

Stiglitz, J. (1987) 'The Cause and Consequences of the Dependence of Quality on Prices', *Journal of Economic Literature*, vol. 25, pp. 1–48.

——— (1992) 'Methodological Issues and the New Keynesian Economics', in A. Vercelli and N. Dimitri (eds), *Macroeconomics. A Survey of Research Strategies* (Oxford: Oxford University Press), pp. 38–85.

Tobin, J. (1995) 'The Natural Rate as New Classical Macroeconomics', in R. Cross (ed.), *The Natural Rate of Unemployment. Reflections on 25 Years of the Hypothesis* (Cambridge: Cambridge University Press), pp. 32–42.

Weintraub, E.R. (1979) *Microfoundations. The Compatibility of Microeconomics and Macroeconomics* (Cambridge: Cambridge University Press).

Walker D. (ed.) (1984) *Money and Markets. Essays by Robert Clower* (Cambridge: Cambridge University Press).

Comment: Involuntary Unemployment One More Time

Axel Leijonhufvud
UNIVERSITY OF TRENTO, ITALY

In the *General Theory*, Keynes fashioned a theoretical concept to which he assigned the name 'involuntary unemployment'. As De Vroey's chronicle and semantic clarifications make clear, we have had trouble – almost nothing *but* trouble with the concept ever since.

We might agree, I think, that Keynes's choice of name for the concept was unfortunate. For two reasons. First, the term really does not give much of a clue to Keynes's original concept (with the consequence, if I may say so, that it was neither used nor discussed for some thirty years). Second, everybody or almost everybody feels that 'involuntary unemployment' has a common-sense meaning that is perfectly obvious and needs only a little sharpening to become a rigorous theoretical concept. So, everybody or almost everybody who mentions the term at all proceeds in effect to dictate what they think the concept should mean – or, often, what they *feel* the concept should mean. Thus, Robert Lucas invents *his* concept of 'involuntary unemployment' only to turn on his own creation and denounce it as inoperational and meaningless while, on the other side, Frank Hahn defines *his* notion of what it should mean and proceeds to declare it of great importance to macroeconomic theory and policy.

'The Question', the Red Queen told Alice, 'is who is to be Master – that's all!' In a democratic society, everyone is his own master. So, everyone is free to have his own meaning of 'involuntary unemployment', I suppose, although communication in such a Tower of Babble tends to be somewhat unproductive.[1] The meanings attached to the term by various people have multiplied as is amply demonstrated by DeVroey's considerable effort to bring some semantic order to it all. Sorting through all of this, classifying, rejecting and accepting, and so on, does not seem a promising task unless we know what we want –

and what we want it for. And if we do know what we want it for, there is probably a more direct route that can be taken.

I choose, instead, to make another attempt at stating what Keynes's concept was. We can then consider whether it is useful enough so that we will want to keep a place for it in our theoretical armoury – under some name or other.

1 MARSHALLIAN OR WALRASIAN NEOCLASSICISM?

Keynes' price theory was Marshallian, not Walrasian. It is of some importance to be clear on this because the 'microfoundations requirement' (as De Vroey calls it) imposed by the New Classicals is utterly Walrasian and methodologically anti-Marshallian. To accept it on the terms dictated, as the various 'post-new Classical Keynesians'[2] do, concedes more than half the battle.

De Vroey mentions that Marshall's market day equilibrium was a disequilibrium when judged by the condition of his short-run equilibrium, etc. and that Keynes interchanged the two. This, if I'm not mistaken, is Keynes's 'reversal' of Marshall's ranking of the price and output adjustment speeds that I discussed 30 years ago (Leijonhufvud, 1967, 1968). I was not quite correct then, as Hershel Grossman pointed out, and De Vroey is not quite right now. The correct statement is that, in Keynes' theory, wages adjust less rapidly than output rates and that prices adjust either as fast or faster than output rates.

The more important point concerns the distinction between Walrasian equilibrium and the Marshallian equilibria (market-day, short-run, or long-run). The Walrasian concept requires the mutual *consistency* of all plans. In contrast, the Marshallian short-run equilibrium (for example) requires the *constancy* of output rates, i.e. that at some point in time, *t*, the rate of change of industry output is zero. De Vroey regards Keynes as having had the aim 'to demonstrate the possible existence of involuntary unemployment within a neoclassical framework'.[3] But we have to distinguish which neoclassical tradition we are talking about. Keynes's persistent unemployment state obviously could not possibly be any kind of Walrasian equilibrium. But coming from an entirely Marshallian background, and staying within that tradition, he was entitled to use the equilibrium terminology.

Marshall's agents are adaptive. They are not *ex ante* optimisers. At any one point in time, most of them will be 'in motion' – moving on some gradient towards higher utility or profit. When Marshall's competitive industry is in short-run equilibrium, his representative firm is at rest, its supply price equal to the market price. This equilibrium condition for the representative firm is best interpreted *ex post*: it is at rest when the marginal cost *incurred* equals the price *realised* in the market. This conception of competitive equilibrium does not entail that the firm faces a 'perfectly elastic' demand curve *ex ante* and it requires none of the familiar conditions for 'perfect competition', such as strict homogeneity of product, a continuum of insignificant agents on both sides of the market, or centralised price formation (with 'false trading' prohibited). Marshall did not contribute to the development of the concept of 'perfect competition' and Keynes had no use for the concept of 'imperfect competition'.

The Marshall–Keynes market does not have an exogenous agency setting a unique price at which one side or the other is 'rationed'. The market process is not a *tâtonnement* with the auctioneer prevented from doing his job. The assumption that the 'short side dominates' market interaction is not generally valid. Marshallian firms can make output mistakes. When they have produced more than the equilibrium output, they find themselves on the 'long side' of both the output and the labour input markets. 'Rationing' is not in general a useful description of 'not getting what one wants' in a market, not even when the disappointed expectations were thought to have been realistic.

One more Marshallian note. His consumers did, of course, base their demands on *realised* income, not on planned sales of labour. To Keynes, Clower's 'dual decision' hypothesis was the natural way to think about household behaviour.

2 KEYNES ON THE CLASSICS

In general, discussions about 'involuntary unemployment' obey no rules, but I would like to propose a rule for discussions of Keynes's concept of it. That rule would be that, to be at least provisionally acceptable, a proposed interpretation of the Keynesian concept should, first, clearly exclude every form of unemployment that Keynes explicitly calls 'voluntary' and, in addition, make *coherent* sense of the *General Theory*, Chapter 2 and the Appendix to Chapter 19. In Chapter 2, Keynes (1) rejects the 'Second Classical Postulate' that 'the utility of the wage . . . is equal to the marginal disutility of employment', (2) criticises Classical theory for admitting 'no such thing as involuntary unemployment in the strict sense', and (3) declares Say's Law invalid. In the Appendix to Chapter 19, he goes on and on criticising Pigou for dealing with the labour market as if labour were bartered for wage goods so that the price formed in that market would be the real and not just the money wage.

To Keynes, the 'Second Postulate' does not define the usual Walrasian labour supply schedule (and particularly not a static or stationary one). It should be understood, instead, in Marshallian terms as a locus of potential equilibria at which the market process *might* come to rest depending upon demand conditions:

> Disutility must here be understood to cover *every kind of reason* which might lead a man *or body of men* to withhold their labour rather than accept a wage . . .

'Every kind of reason' includes 'frictional' unemployment as well as unemployment 'due to intermittent demand'.[4] In addition, to 'voluntary' unemployment of these kinds, the following catalogue[5] should also be understood as *built into the supply-schedule* which Keynes was referring to:

> unemployment due to *the refusal or inability* of a unit of labour, as a result
> (1) of legislation
> (2) or social practices
> (3) or of combination for collective bargaining
> (4) or of slow response to change
> (5) or of mere human obstinacy (sic!)
> to accept a reward corresponding to the value of the product attributable to its marginal productivity.

I think we can take it that minimum wage laws are excluded by (1), implicit contracts and efficiency wages[6] by (2), insider–outsider theory by (2) and (3), Patinkin-type unemployment by (4), . . . and so on. Moreover, Keynes's catalogue makes clear that De Vroey's 'breaching of the reservation wage principle', while it may be a necessary, cannot possibly be considered a sufficient condition for the presence of 'involuntary unemployment' in the sense of Keynes.

So much for what 'involuntary unemployment' *isn't*. But what *is* it?

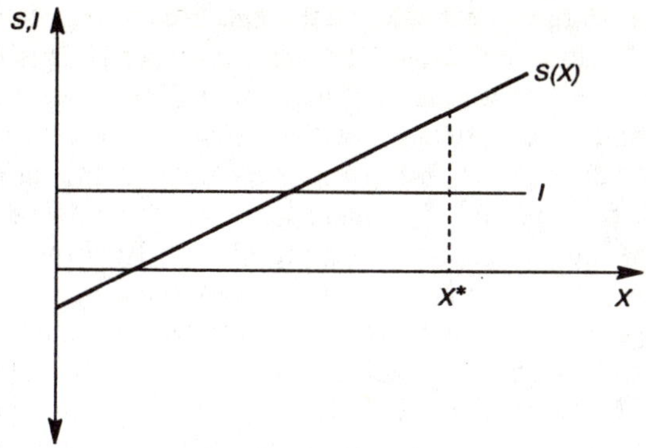

Figure D4.1

3 WHEN SAVING EXCEEDS INVESTMENT

A long, long time ago, the teaching of 'Keynesian economics' began with a simple diagram like Figure D4.1.

Does anyone remember? If X^* is 'full employment output', and $S(X^*) > I$, it used to be said, we had an aggregate demand deficiency at full employment. Patinkin in his various writings on Keynes insisted that the distinguishing characteristic of Keynes's theory was that the system would respond to such a demand deficiency by output rather than price level adjustment. Such, indeed, used to be Lesson 1 in Macroeconomics 1.

Figure D4.1 asserts something else as well (and I would fault Patinkin and others for not attaching equal significance to it), namely, that *the rate of interest fails to coordinate saving and investment.* When saving exceeds investment at the natural rate of unemployment, the market rate of interest must also exceed the natural rate of interest. Intertemporal prices are wrong. Saving in itself does not constitute an effective demand for future consumption goods. And of all prices in Keynes's theory, the (long-term) real rate of interest is the slowest adjusting: 'it may fluctuate *for decades* about a level which is chronically too high' (*General Theory*, p. 204, emphasis added).[7]

In his discussion of the 'anti-Keynesian offensive', De Vroey attributes the 'decline of Keynesian theory' (quite accurately, in my opinion) to the 'offensive, put under way by Friedman's criticism of the Phillips curve . . . and carried through by Lucas.' But De Vroey is understandably puzzled: 'the reasoning of Friedman seems pretty trivial. Why then did it hit so hard, profoundly damaging Keynesian theory as existing at that time?' Good question. The answer is perfectly simple.

Friedman assumes that employment will differ from that associated with the natural rate of unemployment only as long as the money wage rate has not yet adjusted fully to past changes in the money stock. As a general proposition, this is *false*. Money wage adjustments will make employment converge on its general equilibrium value *only if* intertemporal relative prices are right, otherwise not. Friedman's so-called Keynesian opponents were 'devastated' because they had not learned their Lesson 1 properly. Back in the 1950s, they would all have flunked Macroeconomics 1. And Lucas's 'post-new Classical Keynesian' opponents were practically falling all over themselves in their eagerness to obey all the neo-Walrasian ground rules, amongst which one apparently finds the proposition that rational expectations and efficient markets guarantee that the system is always in intertemporal equilibrium.[8] [As those Japanese bankers used to say: 'You cannot go wrong in real estate.']

> As a corollary of [Say's law] it has been supposed that any individual act of abstaining from consumption necessarily leads to, and amounts to the same thing as, causing the labour and commodities thus released from supplying consumption to be invested in the production of capital wealth. (*General Theory*, pp. 104–5)

Well, from Friedman onwards this corollary 'has been supposed' all over again! But to understand the state of the labour market that Keynes associates with involuntary unemployment, this Old-and-New Classical supposition has to be abandoned – for Keynes' analysis of unemployment presupposes the characteristic $S(X^*) > I$ intertemporal effective demand failure. Were this *not* the case, downward adjustment of money wages *would* work to restore unemployment to its 'voluntary' level – just as in Friedman.

4 BARGAINING FOR REAL WAGES AND FOR MONEY WAGES

Keynes's long list of what involuntary unemployment isn't is meant to make clear that 'neither individually nor collectively do the transactors of the system . . . "refuse to cooperate"'.[9] His definition of what it *is* goes as follows:

> Men are involuntarily unemployed if, in the event of a small rise in the price of wage-goods relatively to the money-wage, both the aggregate supply of labour willing to work for the current money wage and the aggregate demand for it at that wage would be greater than the existing volume of employment.

For labour, the 'test' is whether they will accept a small cut in real wages in order to find work. But it has a bit of modern signal-extraction in it: a rise in consumption goods prices is understood to lower the wage in all jobs equally, whereas a cut in one's money wage is likely to mean that higher paying jobs may exist on some other 'island'. At a given point in time, therefore, the elasticity of labour supply with respect to the money wage is much higher than with respect to the real wage. De Vroey's 'reservation wage principle' does not make this distinction between variations in the nominator and denominator of w/p. Is this omission of any importance?

To the interpretation of what Keynes was about: Yes. As already mentioned, his critique of Pigou focused altogether on the inadmissibility (as Keynes saw it) of dealing with the labour market 'as if' work was bartered directly for wage goods.

The significance of this, if it was not clear before, was made clear by the evidence found at Tilton after the death of Lydia Keynes. Volume XXIX of Keynes' *Collected Writings* (Keynes, 1979) containing the manuscripts belatedly discovered at Tilton, includes a couple of drafts of introductions to the *General Theory*. One surmises that Keynes discarded them because they were getting excessively lengthy with no end in sight. But they do spell out at length some arguments that appear only in desperate, and hence cryptic, abbrevation in the *General Theory*.

In these drafts, Keynes contrasts two types of economic systems. In a hypothetical 'Cooperative Economy', he assumes, labour is basically bartered for the goods produced by the cooperative. The bargain is for real wages in the sense of wages in kind. Thus, the offer of labour constitutes *ipso facto* an effective demand for wage-goods (*op. cit.*, pp. 76ff.) Various forms of 'voluntary' unemployment can occur in this system: some managers may be unwilling to pay a worker his full marginal product, some workers may ask for more than their marginal product, some will spend time searching for the cooperative at which their marginal product is the highest – and, not to forget, the possibility of unspecified forms of 'human obstinacy'! But *'involuntary unemployment' is impossible* in the Cooperative Economy.

In Keynes's 'Entrepreneur Economy', the entrepreneur who hires labour cannot be certain that labour's marginal product will sell. The wage bargain is for money. The entrepreneur economy has the Clowerian transactions structure: Labour buys money and money buys goods but labour does not buy goods (Clower, 1967). The offer to work is *not* an effective demand for wage goods. When competition in depressed output markets will cause prices to fall *pari passu* with money wage concessions, labour cannot offer employers a deal that will make them expand. The potential for 'involuntary unemployment' inheres in the possibility of this type of effective demand failure.[10]

5 IS THE KEYNESIAN CONCEPT OF ANY USE?

Keynes's involuntary unemployment, it turns out, is not a concept that will do much to satisfy all those economists who have been trying to concoct some unemployment concept that the New Classicals would have to accept and which would imply the desirability of active stabilisation policy. Keynes's is the kind of unemployment that should be curable by 'pump-priming', albeit that in the wake of some major financial disaster the pump may have to be primed for some time before system liquidity is restored to normal.

In more 'average' business cycles, there may be some involuntary unemployment on the margin of employment fluctuations. But significant consumption multiplier effects (which would have their counterpart in involuntary unemployment) should emerge only when unemployment benefits and household financial buffer stocks are more or less exhausted.[11] The effect on the demand for consumer goods is not as insignificant as the permanent income hypothesis would suggest, however. Transitory income variations may not affect the flow-rate of household consumption much in 'utility' terms; but the changes in liquidity with which they are associated can still have significant effects on the timing of consumer durables purchases.

My conclusion is that these Keynesian concepts are of considerable theoretical significance – even if the theory in question is less pure and rigorous than the neo-Walrasian code would demand. Empirically, they are of major significance only in the context of major financial disasters. The long-lasting double-digit unemployment of several European countries today, for example, is not to be cured by Keynesian pump-priming.

6 CONCLUSION

In conclusion, a reflection on 'the theoretical project to which Clower was led' (De Vroey, p. 199) and the riddle of how to make it 'operational in some rigorous model'.

Clower's 'Keynesian Counter-revolution' was extremely effective in the way that it put the Keynesian and Walrasian traditions on a collision course. The paper made it clear, in a flash, that as formulated at that time, they were inconsistent – so something needed to be done.

What many of us thought needed to be done was to put Keynesian economics on 'microeconomic foundations'. In the early going, most economists interested in this realised that this would require some considerable modifications in neo-Walrasian general equilibrium theory: some form of non-tâtonnement dynamics allowing 'false trading', some less 'ad hoc' way of bringing money into the structure and, of course, some way to allow for the possibility of effective demand failures. One thought it might be doable. It was not obvious at the time that resolving the inconsistencies in this manner was an ill-conceived and basically hopeless project. And, in the early going, no one was as yet thinking of eliminating the inconsistencies by sticking with an entirely *unmodified* neo-Walrasian construction and simply jettisoning whatever macroeconomics wouldn't fit, as became the Lucasian solution.

The chimera of 'micro-foundations' was the belief that grounding all propositions in someone's optimising behaviour would, without further ado, produce a macroeconomics at the same time rigorous and useful. But optimal choice forces (Walrasian) equilibrium forces (Walrasian) intertemporal equilibrium. So, optimal choice theory without market clearing was tried and produced fix-price general equilibrium models and (transitorily) imperfect competition general equilibrium models. Not 'rational' enough. Choice theory with 'temporary equilibrium' market clearing, following Lindahl and Hicks from the 1930s, could produce macroeconomically interesting dynamics. Not intertemporarily rational enough. Etcetera. So, you end up with Rational Expectations plus market clearing and models isomorphic with Arrow–Debreu. Since stochastically complete knowledge is assumed, these show no genuine adaptation, no learning, no evolution.[12]

In Keynes's theory, the on-going mutual adaptation of agents in a money-using system can under certain conditions produce effective demand failures; these cause the adaptive market processes to go off course and produce the *unintended outcome* of social interaction that Keynes termed 'involuntary unemployment.' I thoroughly agree with Lucas when he states:

> It does not appear possible, even in principle, to classify *individual* unemployed people as either voluntarily or involuntarily unemployed *depending on the characteristics of the decision problem they face.* (Quoted by De Vroey, p. 219, italics mine)

Indeed, this unintended outcome of social interaction cannot possibly be characterised as a feature or property of a fully rational, optimising choice of a single individual. It is a silly endeavour to insist on trying, by hook or crook, to produce some sort of 'involuntary unemployment' which could be called 'Keynesian' and which would at the same time obey all the strictures of the neo-Walrasian code.

De Vroey's title refers to 'Sixty Years of Uphill Struggle'. I have already given my opinion on the first thirty (p. 225). The last thirty years seem to this observer to have been *downhill* almost all the way. So much of the literature which De Vroey optimistically sees as showing some progress, I see as silly beyond all expectation[13] and unscholarly beyond all endurance.

Notes

1. I recall arousing Frank Hahn's considerable ire by calling the discussion of the term 'unproductive' and begging off from participating. Cf. his 'Comment' in (Frydman and Phelps, 1983).
2. This phrase is also De Vroey's. I think it is well put.
3. To me this 'aim' sounds a bit too much like the ambition of some young academic hoping to make tenure at MIT or Chicago. Keynes, surely, was trying to figure out *why on earth* the industrialised world was not snapping back from mass unemployment as the economic theory of his day (and now again ours) suggested that it should – and what, therefore, was wrong with that theory.
4. Here I am simply paraphrasing my (1968, pp. 92 ff).
5. Which is italicised and turned into a numbered list for present purposes but without change in Keynes's wording.
6. I totally disagree with De Vroey's opinion (p. 206) that 'about fifty years after the publication of the *General Theory*, the challenge of demonstrating a result of involuntary unemployment, according to Keynes's definition, has finally been met [by the Shapiro and Stiglitz efficiency wage model]'. The work of Shapiro and Stiglitz bears no relationship whatsoever either to Keynes's concept of 'involuntary unemployment' or to any broader 'aim' on Keynes's theoretical or economic–political agenda.
7. Spoken like an eminent post-Victorian! It is not a doctrine one would seek to revive today. We are more likely to have problems of intertemporal coordination arising from movements in the real rate of interest that are *too large*.

8. Once Lucasian signal-extraction problems have been resolved and attendant labour-leisure substitution errors corrected.
9. Leijonhufvud (1968, p. 93). I do not find anything that needs changing in my discussion of involuntary unemployment on pp. 91–109. There is one thing to add, namely, the evidence from Vol. XXIX of Keynes's *Collected Writings* referred to below.
10. I have had to reassert my 1968 interpretation of Keynes on this matter before. Cf. my (1988).
11. My (1973) was an attempt to put the practical importance of the Keynesian type of coordination failure into reasonable perspective.
12. But they do have multiple equilibria. Thus, the latest, possibly last, hope: as long as we have indeterminacy, how can you be absolutely *sure* that a genuinely interesting macromodel cannot be produced in strict obedience to the neo-Walrasian code?
13. . . . rational or otherwise.

References

Clower, R.W. (1967) 'A Reconsideration of the Microfoundations of Monetary Theory', *Western Economic Journal*, vol. 6 (4), pp. 1–8.

Frydman, R. and E.S. Phelps (eds) (1983) *Individual Forecasting and Aggregate Outcomes: 'Rational Expectations' Examined* (New York: Cambridge University Press).

Keynes, J.M. (1936) *The General Theory of Employment, Interest and Money* (London: Macmillan).

——— (1979) *The Collected Writings, Volume XXIX: The General Theory and After: A Supplement* (Cambridge: Macmillan and Cambridge University Press).

Leijonhufvud, A. (1967) 'Keynes and the Keynesians: A Suggested Interpretation', *American Economic Review*, vol. 57 (2), pp. 401–10.

——— (1968) *On Keynesian Economics and the Economics of Keynes: A Study in Monetary Theory* (Oxford and New York: Oxford University Press).

——— (1973) 'Effective Demand Failures', *Swedish Economic Journal*, vol. 75 (3), pp. 27–48; reprinted in Leijonhufvud, *Information and Coordination* (New York: Oxford University Press, 1981).

——— (1988) 'Did Keynes Mean Anything? Rejoinder to Yeager', *The Cato Journal*, vol. 8 (1), pp. 209–17.

Comment: Keynes, Marshall and Involuntary Unemployment

Kevin D. Hoover
UNIVERSITY OF CALIFORNIA, DAVIS, USA

In his highly interesting chapter Michel De Vroey contrasts a realm of theory in which the economist resides and a realm of description in which the economic actor (consumer, worker, policy maker) resides and argues that the two realms should be kept distinct. De Vroey presents the history of unemployment theory after Keynes's *General Theory* as a working out of Keynes's own programme of reconciling involuntary unemployment with neoclassical theory. This exercise belongs to the theoretical realm. In this case De Vroey's distinction is misleading. Keynes belongs to a Marshallian tradition in which, as a matter of methodological principle, the realms of theory and description are constantly conflated. Similarly, Marshall conflates methodological and economic analysis. Marshall (and Keynes), because of the tendency to blur the boundaries, appeal to the philosophical pragmatist, such as I count myself, who regards the distinction between theory and practice as artificial, albeit in many cases useful. To understand the methodological issues raised in De Vroey's paper, it is important to restore Keynes to his Marshallian context. We proceed pragmatically, mixing economic and methodological considerations.

1 KEYNES AND THE NEOCLASSICAL PROGRAMME

A capsule summary of De Vroey's history of the concept of involuntary unemployment runs something like this. In the face of the joblessness of the 1930s Keynes defined *involuntary unemployment* somewhat indirectly to be the situation in which workers were rationed in the labour market: in Keynes's language the real wage exceeded the marginal disutility of labour so that the number of workers seeking employment exceeded the number that firms were willing to hire at the current wage (in De Vroey's language, involuntary unemployment is a breach of the *reservation-wage principle*). Keynes then attempted to demonstrate that, in such circumstances, increases in aggregate demand would raise output and lower involuntary unemployment, so that the ability of an increase in aggregate demand to raise output could itself be regarded as defining the existence of involuntary unemployment. Keynes claims that defining involuntary unemployment as rationing and defining it as a positive elasticity of output to aggregate demand are equivalent. De Vroey regards Keynes as muddled on this point, and unable to sustain the claimed equivalence. There is then a gap in the heart of Keynesian unemployment theory.

The history of unemployment theory after Keynes can be regarded as attempts to fill this gap in various ways. Every development that sought to remain true to a Keynesian inspiration – and not all did – sought a model of the macroeconomy in which something could be interpreted as the theoretical analogue of mass measured unemployment, in which such unemployment was suboptimal, and in which demand policy could have some remedial effect. What De Vroey ably demonstrates is that most of the claimed theoretical successes abandoned the fundamental criterion for Keynesian involuntary unemployment. De Vroey correctly observes that this is first and foremost a rationing notion. The history of unemployment theory after Keynes is a history of equivocation: most of the theoretical models abandoned the notion of rationing, substituting notions of deviations from some technically or economically defined maximum output (e.g. the supply side of Modigliani's 1944 IS–LM model) or notions of Pareto-suboptimal equilibria (e.g. models of coordination failures); or, in cases in which rationing was clearly present (e.g. efficiency-wage models or in implicit-contract models), introduced it in a form in which it was not socially suboptimal or remediable by policy.

The equivocations and the lack of clarity in De Vroey's view begin with Keynes himself and arise from three related confusions. First, the distinction between 'voluntary' and 'involuntary' is a philosophically fraught one. Failure clearly to understand it can misdirect theoretical ambitions. Second, theory and description operate on different planes and must not be confused. Third, the phenomenon of underemployment should really be classified according to two two-way distinctions: between *market-clearing* and *non-market-clearing* (i.e. rationed) unemployment on the one hand, and *efficient* (i.e. socially optimal) and *dominated* (i.e. socially suboptimal) unemployment on the other. Only dominated, rationed unemployment should be regarded as involuntary unemployment in the sense required in Chapter 2 of *The General Theory*. Yet, unemployment theory – from Chapter 3 of *The General Theory* on – has really captured one of the other three possibilities.

2 AN ALTERNATIVE READING OF KEYNES

De Vroey, I believe, does an admirable job of sorting out the different strands of unemployment theory after Keynes. I do not believe, however, that he draws the right methodological lessons from his history. In large part, this is because he understands Keynes differently than I think he should. I must, therefore, explain how I believe Keynes ought to be understood.

In my view, Keynes's primary definition and the definition from which he never wavers is that a worker is involuntarily unemployed when his marginal disutility of labour (or as we might say, *post* Hicks and Allen, his marginal rate of substitution between goods and leisure) is less than the real wage. Keynes (1936, p. 18 *et passim*) is explicit in applying this criterion, even though he formally defines involuntary unemployment according the 'test' of what happens when the price of wage goods rises in the face of fixed money wages. Keynes is also clear about the connection between this definition of involuntary unemployment and the definition based on the elasticity of output: increases in aggregate demand raise output only when firms are able to find workers at a real wage that is profitable. If, as demand rises, prices rise faster (or fall slower) than wages, then real wages fall and it is profitable for firms to increase employment and output. Workers are willing to work at lower real wages because even a somewhat lower real wage exceeds the marginal disutility of their labour. But, at the point at which the real wage equals the marginal disutility of labour, workers will not supply more labour, and firms cannot increase output further. This is Keynes's definition of the point of economically full employment. It is grounded in the behaviour of firms and workers and bears no direct relationship to any notions such as 'maximum obtainable employment'. Rather it is the maximum employment consistent with optimisation on the part of firms and workers.

There is then not the slightest mystery or ambiguity in the manner in which Keynes connects his two definitions. Still, his account of the labour market is not fully satisfactory. The difficulty is just that it would appear to be a profit-increasing strategy for firms to reduce the money wage they pay to the reservation wage (given the price level) for the amount of labour they wish to hire. Keynes argues that firms will not do so, but he never provides a completely satisfactory account of why not. Some of his arguments in Chapter 2 and especially in Chapter 19 are dynamic, general equilibrium arguments that stress the effect of systemic wage cuts on aggregate demand. He appears to believe as well that there are static arguments for the failure of money wages to move smartly to clear markets. Keynes (1937, p. 210) was himself dissatisfied with his account in Chapter 2. I have argued elsewhere (Hoover, 1995) that Keynes's argument is best understood as one that appeals to the sort of considerations that we now recognise as the efficiency-wage hypothesis: the need to motivate workers, to gain their cooperation, to avoid subtle or blatant disruptions of production. De Vroey is of course correct that the typical modern efficiency-wage model will not help with Keynes's argument because it renders involuntary unemployment socially efficient and, because it generates *real* not nominal wage stickiness beyond the power of aggregate demand policies to mitigate. Keynes, however, stresses the importance of wage relativities. Wage relativities are a property of money wages, and concern for them may make firms reluctant to reduce *nominal* wages irrespective of real wages. Aggregate demand policies can now be effective because increases in prices reduce real wages without upsetting relativities. Chapter 2 is confusingly written. Keynes never makes this argument in as straightforward a way as I have just done. He does say many things about the workings of the labour market, all of which can be understood as consistent on the basis of such an interpretation.

3 INVOLUNTARY UNEMPLOYMENT AND MARSHALLIAN METHODOLOGY

I believe that De Vroey is precisely right to describe the history of research into involuntary unemployment after Keynes as an attempt to find a place for involuntary unemployment within a *neoclassical* framework that also addressed Keynes's desire for a systemic account in which aggregate demand policies were effective. This effort is cogently documented in De Vroey's chapter. The effort is largely theoretical and is reflected in a sequence of strongly idealised models: models that are Walrasian (or, perhaps more accurately, Debreuvian), and that often feature but one good, one labour market, and a representative agent. The mappings between these models and real world data are stylised and imprecise.

De Vroey's account of the development of the notion of involuntary unemployment is not just a description of its history, it is also advocacy: De Vroey himself seems to endorse the neoclassical programme as the way that economics should move forward toward greater understanding of unemployment. For example, he advocates the stylisation involved in concentrating on a single labour market playing by strict Walrasian rules (pp. 181–4), while finding it a telling criticism of Barro and Grossman's fixed-price model that they slip the Walrasian traces and play by a modified set of rules (pp. 199–200).[1]

Beyond the apparent personal endorsement, De Vroey enlists Keynes himself as the founder of the programme, so that he writes as if contemporary unemployment theory were simply attempts to finish what Keynes had started but not brought to a satisfactory close. According to De Vroey, Keynes operated under the requirement that a successful model 'should be achieved jointly and in full respect of the methodological canons of neoclassical theory (which Keynes dubbed as classical theory)' (p. 190). Later he refers to neoclassical unemployment theory as having made progress on 'Keynes's programme' and to the hope that 'some implementation of Keynes's programme is within closer reach than before' (p. 211).

De Vroey, I believe, has got this wrong. Keynes should not be regarded as the founder of a neoclassical programme in unemployment research; and, although much contemporary work does aim to capture Keynesian insights in the sense of developing models in which unemployment is undesirable and remediable by demand policies, it has hardly followed a Keynesian methodology.

It is of course quite true that Keynes wanted to persuade his fellow economists, many of whom, Pigou explicitly among them, he regarded as 'classicals'. His strategy was one of minimising the innovations to classical theory. This is why, for instance, he did not challenge the first classical postulate – i.e. that the real wage is equal to the marginal product of labour. Yes, he wished to pick his battlefield to his best advantage; yet to believe that he did not seek real battle would be gravely to misunderstand his purpose.

Keynes's early critics did not misunderstand him. As De Vroey (p. 190) correctly observes Keynes did not invent the concept of involuntary unemployment: it can already be found in Pigou. But as Peter Clarke (1988, p. 279 *et passim*) makes clear, Keynes offered a *perfectionist* account of involuntary unemployment. For Pigou and the classics, involuntary unemployment was the result of a spanner in the economic works: the actions of unions, of government, or even of the bloody-mindedness of workers. But these were all potentially, at least, remediable features of the economic system. This is an *imperfectionist* account: one could conceive of an idealised free market economy in which all markets cleared and no involuntary unemployment could occur and to which, but for the presence of these imperfections, the actual economy approximates. Keynes, on the other hand, wanted to claim that, even in a perfected economy, the possibility of involuntary unemployment would always be present. His early critics were well aware of his aim. The thesis of Viner (1936) and Leontief (1936), among others, was that Keynes was wrong: only imperfections could explain involuntary unemployment.[2]

Keynes opposed his theory to the 'classics', by which he meant the English economists in the line from Ricardo through Mill, Edgeworth and Marshall to Pigou. This tradition overlaps at its later end with what is now commonly meant by the 'neoclassicals', but it is not as De Vroey implies coextensive with it. Keynes (1936, p. 3, n. 2) indeed was well aware that he was stretching a point to regard the whole line as a unified tradition. Pigou bears the brunt of Keynes's rhetoric, although Pigou should be regarded as the flowering of the plant, the root of which is Marshall. On the analysis of involuntary unemployment Keynes opposed Marshall (and Pigou) as De Vroey (p. 190) observes. Yet De Vroey fails to notice how much Keynes remains a Marshallian economist. Keynes attacked Pigou; and Pigou was heir to Marshall; yet Keynes too was Marshall's intellectual child – a rebellious son perhaps, but by no means a bastard.

The heart of the difference between Keynes and Marshall is this: for Marshall during the market period, the labour market, like other markets, clears; for Keynes workers are rationed.[3] De Vroey (p. 191) correctly observes that Keynes sought a general equilibrium analysis: the economics of the determination of output as a whole is the economics of the system, not of a particular market. De Vroey implies that Keynes stands in contrast to Marshall's 'partial equilibrium' analysis. Again, I believe that De Vroey has missed the methodological point. Like Friedman, I believe that it is wrong to regard Marshall as an advocate of partial equilibrium analysis.[4] Marshall recognised that the economic system was an interacting whole. He sought methods to account for that fact in a pragmatic way, summarising the elements less central to the problem at hand. Thus, income is a summary measure in demand analysis for the systemic effects of the complete vector of relative prices in the economy.[5]

The distinction between partial and general equilibrium is anachronistic.

Neither Keynes nor Marshall draws it, because it is only against the backdrop of the Walrasian model that one would want to draw it. Keynes may in a broad sense advocate general equilibrium, but he is not a Walrasian in any sense: Walras is hardly mentioned in all of Keynes' economic writings, the Walrasian vision of general equilibrium not at all. Keynes's argument for a theory of output as a whole, of which his unemployment theory was a key element, did not call for a rejection of the Marshallian conception of the economy – certainly not in favour of a Walrasian one – but for the recognition that Marshall and the classics had made a mistake in their theorising that allowed them to believe that one could provide the theory for the economy as whole simply by aggregating the behaviour of the rational individual. Methodologically, Keynes remained a Marshallian.

Keynes was a Marshallian in Friedman's sense: an economist who viewed economics as 'an engine for the discovery of concrete truth' and 'substantive hypotheses, based on factual evidence about the manner and actions of causes ' (Friedman, 1949, p. 490). Friedman contrasts the Marshallian to the Walrasian, who sees economics as the development of formal theories to be judged by their generality and mathematical elegance, but not by their success at describing causal mechanisms in the real world. The unemployment theories that De Vroey describes, even the ones that are 'partial equilibrium' theories, and the methodology that informs his paper are Walrasian in the relevant sense.

In contrast, Keynes's methodology is Marshall's. Marshall combined a narrow vision of the proper realm of economics ('action . . . connected with the attainment and with the use of material requisites of well-being', 1920, p. 1) with a broad vision of individual and social action. For Marshall, economic considerations were points of attraction for economic behaviour, but did not necessarily dominate that behaviour. The economic realm was not comprehensive. Marshall's attitude is well illustrated in this description of how an economist should analyse the contribution of labour costs to supply price:

> In all these calculations he would not concern himself specially to inquire how far mankind are under the exclusive influence of selfish or self-regarding motives. He might be aware that anger and vanity, jealousy and offended dignity are still almost as common causes of strikes and lockouts, as the desire for pecuniary gain: but that would not enter into his calculations. (1920, pp. 365–6)

On the one hand, Marshall recognises that non-economic factors may sometimes dominate; on the other hand, *qua* economist he is concerned with the economic factors exclusively. Keynes in Chapter 2 of *The General Theory* remains close to this sensibility. Labour, he believes, might resist a reduction of money-wages but not of real wages, and he hopes to explain this consistent with economic logic. 'But, whether logical or illogical, experience shows that this is how labour in fact behaves' (p. 9).

Marshall throughout his *Principles* and Keynes throughout his *General Theory* hold richly detailed views of the economy in the background. For both the urge to develop economic logic never warrants pushing into the background ubiquitous facts of economic experience Both note, for example, that labour is heterogeneous and imperfectly mobile, so that the theory of unemployment cannot be legitimately grounded in the analysis of a single labour market (see *inter alia*, Marshall, 1920, Book VI, Chapter I, Sections vi, vii, *passim*; Keynes, 1936, Chapter 2, Section 3). And, similarly, for both, the desideratum of economic analysis is not the behaviour of the individual, even though economic decisions are made by individuals, but of the market or the economy as a whole (e.g., Marshall, 1920, p. 25 *et passim*). This, along with the heterogeneity of labour and therefore the inherent ambiguity of 'the going wage', probably explains why Keynes chose to define involuntary unemployment, as De Vroey notes, using a market test, rather than by direct reference to the violation of the reservation-wage principle.

In a Marshallian light it is easy to see the distance between Keynes's own analysis of unemployment and the neoclassical programme that followed. De Vroey draws a distinction between the realm of theory and the realm of description (e.g. p. 212) and chides economists who confuse the two. This is not a distinction that would have appealed to Marshall. Marshall wanted to join economics more closely to the world, even to the point of deferring to the language of businessmen:

> A true sense of proportion requires us not to burden our work with the incessant enumeration of details of secondary importance, of which no account is taken in customary discourse, and which cannot even be described without offending against popular convention. (1920, p. 78, cf. pp. 51–2)

Economics for Marshall was the perfection of common sense. On the one hand,

> A man is likely to be a better economist if he trusts his common sense, and practical instincts, than if he professes to study the theory of value and is resolved to find it easy. (1920, p. 368)

On the other hand

> the apparent simplicity of popular phrases veils a real complexity, and it is the duty of science to bring out that latent complexity; to face it; and to reduce it as far as possible; so that in later stages we may handle firmly difficulties that could not be grasped with a good grip by the vague thought and language of ordinary life. (1920, p. 129)

Book I, Chapters III and IV of the *Principles* discuss the interplay of theory and description, how the facts motivate theorising and how theories illuminate the facts. For Marshall, there are no separate realms.

Both Keynes and Marshall would, I imagine, value De Vroey's detailed four-way classification of underemployment as bringing out the latent complexity inherent in the labour market and clarifying the structure of different models. On the other hand, they would surely deplore the attempt to drive a wedge between those models and the world. In any case, De Vroey, I think, is on thin ice in insisting that the world's notion of full employment is, at the descriptive level, 'the maximum employment attainable' (p. 188). The man in the street knows full well that the level of employment at the peak of a boom is not as high as employment can go: the young, the old, the infirm could work and those working could work longer. He may benefit from Marshall's or Keynes's perfection of his common-sense categories, but even without tuition he knows that the idea of full employment involves personal and social norms. Indeed, from talking to undergraduates, I am convinced that common sense does not suppose, as De Vroey (p. 188) writes, that 'the minimum feasible rate of unemployment [is] supposedly an objective exogenous magnitude'. On the contrary, the economist is typically hard-pressed to convince common sense that the minimum level of unemployment is not just a malleable, social choice.

What Keynes believed economics could teach common sense was surely nothing to do with metaphysics. Keynes showed no interest, writing as an economist, in the semantic questions that exercise Lucas, De Vroey, Stiglitz and others concerning the degree of voluntariness of any particular failure to be employed. It is enough for his purposes that, in a state of higher demand and lower real wages, large numbers of workers would regard themselves as better off. The issue of voluntariness arises for Keynes only in the context of denying that workers have the power to obtain this more favourable situation by their own direct action. This is the question of why the money wage does not fall smartly to clear the market. Lucas's focus on the partial voluntariness of all employment decisions evades the true question, because the true question is, how do firms behave in the face of a surfeit of qualified workers? and not, how do workers set their reservation wages? De Vroey rightly deplores Lucas's claim that Keynes' definition of involuntary unemployment involves conceptual confusion, but he himself focuses on a metaphysical question that Keynes, as an economist and follower of Marshall, has no reason to engage in this context.

Keynes need not regard such questions as uninteresting or unimportant, for he shares Marshall's broad vision of human possibilities, but he is free to regard them as uneconomic, because he also shares Marshall's narrow vision of the scope of economics. In Book I, Chapter II of the *Principles*, Marshall describes a hierarchy of human ends and motives. Economics deals with the lowest order of those ends – not just those that are material but, more specifically, those that can be measured in money. Although these ends are important, albeit not the most important, it is more significant for Marshall that they provide the most constant and regular motives for human action, and thus the ones most amenable to scientific analysis. Other ends condition human action. They cannot be forgotten by the economist, who must 'deal with man as he is: not with an abstract or "economic" man; but a man of flesh and blood' (1920, p. 27).

Once Marshall recognises the hierarchy of ends and their incommensurability (the money metric is tricky to apply at the best of times), he absolves the economist of the necessity of assuming continuous optimisation. Unlike neoclassical theory in which utility maximisation is sometimes defined to be tautological, utility maximisation for Marshall can at best represent the attraction point of tendencies that might be overridden by higher-order considerations or by ignorance or chance.

In De Vroey's history, neoclassical unemployment theory is in the thrall of a modelling imperative: find some way to generate involuntary unemployment consistent with optimisation on the part of all agents. As a follower of Marshall, Keynes was not similarly enthralled. Keynes would not have appreciated De Vroey's admonitions not to mingle separate lines of research (p. 187), to play either by precise Walrasian or Marshallian rules but not both (pp. 182–3), or to limit the use of an analytical device because it does not accord with the presupposition that markets are centralised and democratic (p. 216, n. 8). The apotheosis of the modelling imperative is the new classical representative-agent model. These models call to mind the psychologists' wheeze: a neurotic is someone who builds castles in the air; a psychotic lives in them. A disciple of Keynes can afford to be a bit neurotic and work on formal idealised models in the hope that they will shed light on real problems; but, since to follow Keynes is, methodologically, to follow Marshall, they will also realise that the only reason to study 'economic man' is to better understand men of flesh and blood.

Notes

1. He stigmatises Barro and Grossman's concept of 'blocked tâtonnement' as ad hoc, but it is unclear why Walras' original concept of tâtonnement, especially given Walras' own discussion and justification of it, should be regarded as anything but ad hoc: a convenient theoretical device to help theory avoid the need to model pricing mechanisms in the real world.
2. The grounds on which these authors challenge Keynes undermines De Vroey's (p. 177) claim that the success of Keynes's account of involuntary unemployment was not challenged in the first years and decades after *The General Theory.*
3. De Vroey (p. 201) quite rightly points out how very Marshallian Friedman's analysis of short-run unemployment is.
4. Friedman (1949, 1955); Hoover (1988, Chapter 9, Section 2); Colander (1996) draws special attention to Note 21 of the 'Mathematical Appendix' to Marshall's *Principles*.
5. Surprisingly Walras (1954, pp. 307–8) also agrees, especially in respect of dynamic problems, that some prices are more central than others.

References

Clarke, P. (1988) *The Keynesian Revolution in the Making, 1924–1936* (Oxford: Clarendon Press).

Colander, D. (1996) 'Marshallian General Equilibrium Analysis', in D. Colander (ed.), *Beyond Microfoundations: Post Walrasian Macroeconomics* (Cambridge: Cambridge University Press).

Friedman, M. (1949) 'The Marshallian Demand Curve,' *Journal of Political Economy*, vol. 37, no. (6), pp. 463–95.

——— (1955) 'Leon Walras and His Economic System', *American Economic Review* vol. 45, no. (5), pp. 900–9.

Hoover, K.D. (1988) *The New Classical Macroeconomics: A Sceptical Inquiry* (Oxford: Blackwell).

——— (1995) 'Relative Wages, Rationality, and Involuntary Unemployment in Keynes's Labor Market', *History of Political Economy*, vol. 27, no. (4), pp. 654–85.

Keynes, J.M. (1936) *The General Theory of Employment, Interest and Money* (London: Macmillan).

——— (1937) 'The General Theory of Employment', *Quarterly Journal of Economics*, vol. 52, no. (1), pp. 209–23.

Leontief, W. (1936) 'The Fundamental Assumption of Mr. Keynes's Monetary Theory of Unemployment', *Quarterly Journal of Economics*, vol. 51, no. (1), pp. 192–7.

Marshall, A. (1920) *Principles of Economics*, 8th edn (London: Macmillan).

Modigliani, F. (1944) 'Liquidity Preference and the Theory of Interest and Money', *Econometrica*, vol. 12, no. (1), pp. 44–88.

Viner, J. (1936) 'Mr. Keynes and the Causes of Unemployment', *Quarterly Journal of Economics*, vol. 51, no. (4), pp. 147–67.

Walras, L. (1954) *Elements of Pure Economics*, trans. William Jaffé (Philadelphia: Orion Editions); 1984 reprint of 1954 edn (London: George Allen & Unwin).

Discussion

Michel De Vroey expressed his agreement with his two discussants, explaining how the distinction between stationary and instantaneous equilibrium, which he learned from Franco Donzelli, had dominated his recent work. Keynes was a Marshallian economist, but he wanted to generalise the Marshallian framework – to do general equilibrium analysis. In doing this Keynes faced a series of obstacles, and Keynesian economics came to be torn between Marshall and Walras. The first models, such as IS–LM, were a mixture of Marshall and Walras, after which there was a shift to Walras, as a result of which Keynesians were cornered, for there is no room for Keynesian themes in Walrasian theory. Keynesians thus faced the series of obstacles that De Vroey sought to document in his chapter. It was in response to these obstacles that they retreated into the methodology implicit in efficiency wage theory.

Bennett McCallum offered two comments. The first was that he thought the chapter misleading in that it did not pay enough attention to phenomena that are temporary, but long-lasting enough to be of importance. This caused De Vroey mistakenly to conclude that unemployment was voluntary for Friedman, but involuntary for Barro and Grossman. Barro and Grossman's analysis, McCallum contended, was nothing other than a fully articulated version of what Friedman must have had in mind. The second was that Hoover and Leijonhufvud were right in saying that Keynes must be read in the light of Marshall, but from that perspective they were too sympathetic to Keynes: the *General Theory* was just a theoretical failure, indeed virtually a fraud. Marshall, Pigou, Lavington and everyone recognised that unemployment could exist temporarily, so the true component of Keynes's message was that we should pay more attention to temporary phenomena. But to say that would not have attracted any attention, so he tried to develop an argument that unemployment would not be eliminated over time by market mechanisms. In doing this he claimed to play by rules with which any Walrasian would be happy – to play by the same rules as Lucas would play by. Any reader of Patinkin's (1976) book can see how many logical errors there were in the *General Theory*. This was sorted out by Hicks, Modigliani and Patinkin, with useful additions by Clower, Leijonhufvud and Barro and Grossman. McCallum added that, in saying this, he was not claiming that Keynes was aware that his argument was a fraud: he just did not care. He was too busy with other things to care about theoretical niceties, and as a result published the book as a mess.

Axel Leijonhufvud responded that McCallum was wrong all the way through, both in mixing Friedman with Barro and Grossman, or in mixing Keynes or Clower with them. Barro and Grossman have a Walrasian auctioneer who is allowed to call one price, but is then prevented from doing his job, resulting in fixed-price rationing models that have nothing to do with Friedman and nothing to do with Keynes at all. On the point about the *General Theory* being a fraud, Leijonhufvud argued that in the *Treatise on Money* you have a theory that is very similar to Pigou and Lavington (though it is more Wicksellian). That theory is classical theory with frictions. There are two steps from there to the *General Theory*. One is that Keynes realised that if the initial effect of deflation is on output (the reversal of the adjustment speed ranking) then all pressure for a fall in the interest rate disappears. The other is that Keynes realised that the unemployed have no effective demand for consumer goods, so the upward pressure on consumer goods prices which should also stimulate employment was missing too. There is nothing fraudulent about this, and it is not playing by Lucas' rules. It is foolish to interpret Keynes by Lucas' rules. Most of the errors Patinkin finds are errors of interpretation, not logical errors in Marshallian theory. **McCallum**'s response was to argue that Keynes was simply wrong in claiming that price and wage changes would not affect employment in the long run.

Thomas Mayer argued that the classical economists treated unemployment as due to special factors, whereas Keynes sought to bring it into the mainstream of classical theory. Mayer agreed with McCallum that Keynes was impatient about theoretical niceties, but unlike McCallum he thought that he was right to do so. He had what he thought to be a major breakthrough – the income approach, relating spending to income, and he had a reason not to spend time working out all the details: there was a major depression going on. He thus concentrated on getting what he saw as the major things right, being sloppy over details that he thought unimportant. As for not providing a formal definition of involuntary unemployment, this was a brilliant rhetorical trick: it was obvious that there were unemployed people who were prepared to work at the prevailing money wage, so his opponents were forced to acknowledge that it existed. They could not claim that because he could not define it, it did not exist.

Kevin Hoover, citing Clarke (1988), suggested that, contrary to appearances, it was the *Treatise on Money*, not the *General Theory*, that was the more topical book. Whereas the background to the former was Keynes's involvement in the Macmillan Committee and worrying about the problem of unemployment, the latter was a more detached book, where Keynes sought to work things out more carefully.

Philippe Mongin liked the idea of bringing Dworkin's distinction between 'option bad luck' and 'brute bad luck' into the discussion, but commented that it was difficult to incorporate it within formal decision theory. It is hard to distinguish between someone who fails to insure against a natural disaster and someone who goes to a casino to play: the distinction between risks that are experienced and risks that are taken. This matters because the distinction is a natural one to make, and psychologists have shown that attitudes towards risk are different in the two situations. The difficulty economists have in making sense of involuntary unemployment might be due to a defect in the underlying decision theoretic framework that they are using.

Leonid Hurwicz suggested paying attention to the earliest attempts to formalise Keynes, in particular those of Hicks and Lange. De Vroey was right in emphasising that it was essential for Keynes to explain why unemployment could not be cured by cutting wages – in the 1930s wholesale wage cuts had failed. One explanation was extrapolations: that if wages were cut, employers would expect them to be cut further and would not increase employment. There is a crucial difference here between extrapolative and rational expectations, for the former opens up the possibility of getting a sort of Nash equilibrium, where entrepreneurs do not hire because they do not expect to be able to sell the output, and this behaviour causes their expectations to be realised. This is not a Walrasian equilibrium. Hurwicz also cast doubt on the adequacy of the preference theory that is used in most economic modelling. The type of phenomenon that he had in mind was that people will not voluntarily fasten seat belts when they drive, but they would vote in favour of a law requiring everyone to do so. If you ask them whether they prefer to have seat belts fastened, the answer is that at one level they do, but at another level they do not. There is a social aspect to preferences, that has to be taken into account in explaining attitudes to accepting lower-paid jobs. **Hoover** pointed out that relative wage arguments appear in Chapter 2 of the *General Theory* and that Keynes made exactly the same point concerning extrapolative expectations in Chapter 19.

De Vroey argued that it was wrong to see Friedman and Barro and Grossman as working in the same line of research. In the Walrasian tradition adjustment is instantaneous, so it makes no sense to speak of slow adjustment. In contrast, in the Marshallian tradition, adjustment takes place over time. He placed Barro and Grossman in the former tradition. In contrast, **McCallum** made the point that Barro and Grossman have a chapter in their book where they describe such adjustment. Most of the time they analyse equilibrium given wages and prices, but they also propose an adjustment mechanism for nominal wages and prices, operating in real time. They are just like Friedman, even having adaptive expectations. **De Vroey** disagreed, claiming that such arguments mixed two equilibrium concepts. In response, **McCallum** argued that this was simply an argument what words were used to describe various equilibrium concepts. Problems could be avoided by avoiding such terminology, simply discussing what things are being conditioned upon in discussing our equilibrium concepts. Why should we care what words – Walrasian, Marshallian – are being used? **De Vroey**, in contrast, considered that reluctance to discuss the wording was the cause of confusion.

Maarten Janssen drew attention to a paper by Roberts (1987) that gave an equilibrium explanation of involuntary unemployment in terms of Nash equilibrium.

Nancy Cartwright broadened the discussion to raise the question of whether we can have, or actually have, a theory which covers all economic factors. This is currently unfashionable in the literature on methodology, where people are now talking about piecemeal models and piecemeal methodologies. There was a lot of impetus against the Enlightenment ideal that there is a general theory. She was interested in the sociology of economics, for the main theories in economics still seek to provide a general theory. Why, she asked, did economists not think it necessary to defend the approach of seeking a general theory? **Hoover** saw Marshallian methodology as consistent with a piecemeal approach. Thus he could not accept De Vroey's criticism of McCallum and of Barro and Grossman for mixing Walrasian and Marshallian approaches. It is all right to violate what seem like conceptual distinctions if there is a good, pragmatic reason for doing so. Thus why should Marshallian considerations not be brought into what is basically a Marshallian approach?

De Vroey replied by drawing a distinction between theory and meta-theory. Marshall's meta-theory was that he wished to deal with flesh-and-blood people, yet his theoretical practice was different: his corn market was an abstract construction, not a realistic account of how markets worked. There is an antagonism between his theoretical practice and his meta-theory. **Roger Backhouse** could not accept this characterisation of Marshall. If one looked at Marshall's algebra, there was a difference between his theory and his meta-theory. But the algebra is not Marshall's theory: the theory is messy. When Samuelson (1967) referred to Marshall's seeking to have his cake and eat it, he was referring to Marshall's construction of his theory, not to his methodology. Samuelson looked at Marshall's theory and said he found it inconsistent and incoherent. This is Marshall trying to be realistic, putting his methodology into practice, as with his idea of the representative firm. Relevant to this context is Marshall's characterisation of long-run equilibrium: in the long run there is change going on, but it is so slow that it can be ignored. Keynes is doing the same thing when he says that deflation could raise employment via a real balance effect, but this is quantitatively insignificant. So he is looking at a Marshallian type of long-run equilibrium, which is not really a long run according to modern criteria, according to which if there is an effect there it must be taken into account. The result is a theory that is messy by modern standards. Thus Backhouse thought that, even if there were problems with Marshall's theory, he was at least being consistent with his methodology.

Andrea Boitani argued that post-Lucasian macroeconomics had gone in a direction that was neither Marshallian nor Walrasian. Using new tools, many insights of Keynes and others can be made precise. This is not following Lucas, but just trying to make things comprehensible to other people. Roberts' model is a good example. There are many other models based on game theory which depict involuntary unemployment as arising from coordination failure. Perfect competition has to be abandoned. **McCallum** thought that the objections De Vroey listed to various models in Section 7 of his chapter would also apply to these more recent models. In such models there would be no response to monetary expansion: the models do not generate what De Vroey would consider Keynesian unemployment.

Leijonhufvud argued that mixing Marshall and Walras made a mish-mash of theory. The simplest example would be ways in which their respective supply and demand diagrams were constructed. In Marshall, quantity is the independent variable, and demand (or supply) price the dependent variable. Today we draw Walrasian behaviour schedules in Marshall's space. A Marshallian supply-price schedule, for example, is not the result of an optimising conceptual experiment. A point on his market supply curve is to be understood as a point attractor of a collective, adaptive, error-learning process. Marshall's comparative statics depended on the implicit assumption that these market adjustment processes always converged on this simplest kind of attractor. This was a leap of faith for which he did not (and could not) have any mathematical guarantee – which might explain his reservations about the use of mathematical methods in economics.

De Vroey argued that the clue to understanding what economists are doing is to realise that they are, more or less unwittingly, engaged in a political-philosophy discussion. This stems from Adam Smith's discussion of the viability or superiority of a decentralised economy over other types of economic organisation. Economists draw on facts about the economy to make points about the ideal organisation of society. The real world is there at the beginning, as an inspiration, and at the end, as the reality that people wish to transform into what they believe is an ideal organisation of society. They do this in an elaborate language. Problems arise because there are many languages and many syntaxes.

References

Clarke, P. (1988) *The Keynesian Revolution in the Making* (Oxford: Clarendon Press).

Patinkin, D. (1976) *Keynes's Monetary Thought: A Study of Its Development* (Durham, NC: Duke University Press).

Roberts, J. (1987) 'An Equilibrium Model with Involuntary Unemployment at Flexible, Competitive Prices and Wages', *American Economic Review*, 77, pp. 856–74.

Samuelson, P.A. (1967) 'The Monopolistic Competition Revolution', in R.E. Kuene (ed.), *Monopolistic Competition Theory: Studies in Impact* (New York).

5 Monetarists and Keynesians on Central Banking: A Case Study of a Flawed Debate

Thomas Mayer*
UNIVERSITY OF CALIFORNIA, DAVIS, USA

1 INTRODUCTION

The study of economics is justified more by the practical uses of economics than by its aesthetic value. Economists therefore feel obligated to offer policy advice on various issues on which they do not have compelling evidence. That is to the good. But they are tempted in these cases to lay claim to more knowledge and certainty than is warranted, in part because consumers of economics, that is policy makers and students, want unequivocal answers. Moreover, their rivals, e.g. journalists and politicians are not at all reluctant to overstate the value of their wares. But exaggerating the degree of confidence that one's conclusions warrant can lead to a degradation of the debate as schools form that pay insufficient attention to what others are saying, and as battle lines are sharply drawn.

I will argue that this is what has happened in the debate about whether central banks should undertake stabilisation policy or have the money stock grow at a fixed rate. I do not claim that the participants *intentionally* overstate their cases. They believe in what they say. But their motivation is not the issue. What matters is the outcome, an unwarranted claim to knowledge that has inhibited understanding, in part by posing a false dichotomy. The methodological obstacle to resolving the debate has not been some subtle issue, such as economists not knowing their Popper, or adhering to an outdated philosophy of science, but a failure to stay within the bounds of rational conversation. It would be interesting to see if a similar tendency shows up in the natural sciences when they deal with issues of environmental policy.

The two sides to the debate are the monetarists, led by Milton Friedman, Karl Brunner and Allan Meltzer who advocate that the money supply should grow at a fixed, or at least a stable rate, and those who advocate countercyclical monetary policy. I will, rather loosely refer to the latter as 'Keynesians'.[1] I deal only with the question whether discretionary countercyclical policy (henceforth just called countercyclical monetary policy) is feasible, and not with the entire issue of monetarism versus Keynesian theory. It is quite possible that Keynesian theory is superior to the quantity theory; for example, that fiscal policy has a powerful effect on GDP, and accounts for as large proportion of the GDP variance as do changes in the money supply, and yet effective countercyclical policy cannot succeed because of lags, forecast errors and principal–agent problems. Conversely, there is nothing in the quantity theory that denies the efficacy of countercyclical monetary policy. This chapter therefore deals only with part of the Keynesian–monetarist debate. I also do not take up the subsequent debate between Keynesians and the New Classicals, since that involves quite different issues.

I start in 1947 when Milton Friedman published his critique of Abba Lerner's recommendations for stabilisation policy, and essentially end forty years later, with just a brief look at some subsequent literature. Although the debate has continued beyond 1987, it has been substantially influenced by some new factors: the breakdown in the stability of velocity in the early 1980s, the widespread acceptance of time-inconsistency as a major problem for monetary policy, and the consequent emphasis on feedback rules.

I start by discussing the nature of the issue and the background in which it arose before turning to the monetarist case. One part of this case is that since monetary policy operates with long and variable lags, and since the forecasting ability of central banks is limited, effective countercyclical policy is not feasible. This requires looking at the length and variability of the lag, and at the Keynesians'[1] response that control theory shows that such a policy is feasible after all. I then turn to the other part of the monetarists' case, that even if effective stabilisation policy were technically feasible, central banks would be unlikely to carry out such a policy. While monetarists have offered considerable, but not conclusive historical evidence on this issue, Keynesians have largely brushed it aside with disdain. Subsequently I discuss the Keynesian criticisms of a fixed monetary growth-rate rule, and then turn to empirical tests, and to some recent developments that have changed this debate. Since this debate is hardly a model of what McCloskey (1985) calls 'good conversation', I then ask what went wrong. Sections 9 and

10 deal with the relation of this debate to some doctrines of philosophy of science, and suggest some reasons why the debate was not more productive.

2 WHAT IS THE QUESTION?

The issue is often formulated as 'rules versus authorities', that is as a discretionary monetary policy versus a stable growth-rate rule for some monetary aggregate. Such a broad formulation is dubious. One should distinguish between at least three regimes, that is rules governing policy actions. One is a *strict* rule, that requires the central bank to generate a specific growth rate for a particular monetary aggregate, come what may. The second, a *moderate rule,* allows the central bank to change the monetary growth rate in response to supply shocks, or to perceived secular changes in velocity and in potential real growth, but not for the sake of undertaking countercyclical policy. The third is our current system of discretionary policy in which the central bank is free to vary the monetary growth rate for any purpose. Within these three regimes different variants are possible. For example, a central bank may be permitted to undertake countercyclical policy only in response to severe cycles, or else decisions to respond to perceived secular changes in velocity and to supply shocks may require approval by the legislature. While Friedman (1960) has advocated the strict version of the monetary rule, Brunner (1984) has advocated a carefully circumscribed moderate version.

These three regimes should not be confounded. Evidence against the strict rule is not necessarily evidence against the moderate rule. For example it would have been a disaster had the Fed adopted a strict monetary rule in 1980, because of the subsequent sharp fall in the trend of velocity. But that does not mean that the moderate rule, with its prohibition of countercyclical policy would have been bad. Similarly, evidence that the central bank does not possess the information required for effective countercyclical policy does not suffice to establish the case for a strict monetary growth-rate rule.

Furthermore, suppose there is strong empirical evidence that discretionary monetary policy has led to a better outcome than a strict monetary rule would have done. This does not suffice to make the case for countercyclical monetary policy, because the superiority of discretionary policy could be due entirely to its accommodation of secular changes in velocity. Conversely, if a monetary rule shows a better outcome, a policy of responding only to secular and not to cyclical changes in velocity might be better still.

In the vehemence of the debate such considerations have often been ignored. Monetarists have frequently written as though convincing evidence that central banks lack the information and the resolve needed for effective countercyclical policy suffices to establish the case for a stable monetary growth-rate rule, while Keynesians have often argued as though the existence of secular changes in velocity and the occurrence of supply shocks provides a compelling case for countercyclical policy.

3 BACKGROUND

It is certainly not surprising that by, say, 1946 countercyclical stabilisation policy had become a central tenet of mainstream economics . Although this was hardly a new contribution of the *General* Theory (see Keynes, 1924), the *General Theory* had provided such policy with a much more coherent theoretical justification, and the Great Depression had appeared to give it a practical justification.

Lerner's *The Economics of Control* (1944) provides a paradigm of the 'new economics'.[2] Monetary policy, having been freed from the constraint of the gold standard and the irrational constraints of 'orthodox finance' can now be used entirely for domestic goals, with international equilibrium being treated with benign neglect. Countercyclical fiscal policy no longer needs a special justification now that Keynes has decisively refuted the so-called 'Treasury View' that government deficits crowd out private expenditures dollar for dollar, and that Lerner has shown that an internally held government debt is harmless.

Lerner could therefore set out the following welfare maximising rules for macro policy: If aggregate demand is insufficient, lower taxes, raise government expenditures, or lower interest rates. If aggregate demand is excessive do the opposite. The appropriate choice between these three tools depends on microeconomic considerations, that is on the marginal social products of consumption, government expenditures and investment.[3] To finance its deficits the government should either print money or, if it wants interest rates to rise, borrow. It all seemed very simple, except for the task of inducing politicians and the general public to abandon their irrational prejudice. Macro-policy has finally reached the age of enlightenment in which reason rather than tradition and prejudice governs. Indeed, it is likely that much of the enthusiasm for the Keynesian revolution resulted from its seeming ability to make economists extraordinarily useful. In the 1960s there was much debate about whether the business cycle still existed, or had been eliminated by modern macroeconomic policy.

Lerner was a theorist with little, if any, interest in institutions.[4] He saw his role as setting out abstract economic principles, with the problems of implementation left to administrators. While other economists, particularly the institutionalists, held a less pure view of economics, it is still true that by modern standards mainstream macroeconomics at that time showed little concern with the problems that arose in implementing their policy recommendations. For example, in the 1960s many US economists wanted to make fiscal policy more flexible by having Congress grant the President the power to adjust tax rates as economic conditions change. They could not understand why politicians scoffed at this 'logical' step. Similarly, until the late 1950s almost nothing had been published on the lags of monetary policy.

It would be going too far to say that most macroeconomists were unconcerned with *all* practical details. For example, they were willing to specify by *how much* interest rates should be changed. But they did not feel compelled to work through all the steps required to translate their general policy prescriptions into coherent advice in a world in which policy makers have imperfect information and serious principal–agent problems exist. At the time that did not seem an interesting set of problems.

This deficiency of mainstream macroeconomics soon came under attack. In his review article of Lerner's *Economics of Control,* Friedman (1947) mounted a powerful methodological critique by arguing that Lerner purported to give practical advice, when he actually did little more than tell the government that it should behave intelligently. To Friedman the question of whether Lerner's policy recommendations can be effectively implemented is not something that an economist should ignore.

> To make . . . [his recommendations for countercyclical policy into] a prescription to 'produce full employment', Lerner must tell us how to know when there is 'insufficient total demand', whether this insufficiency is a temporary deficiency in the process of being corrected or the beginning of an increasing deficiency . . . He must tell us how to know what medicine to use when a diagnosis has been made, how large a dose to give, and how long we may expect it to take for the medicine to be effective. The casual reader of Lerner's book – *or, for that matter, of the majority of works on the control of the business cycle* – might suppose that these are simple questions. . . .

> [T]hey are anything but simple. . . . An easy answer to these difficulties is to say that . . . errors in these actions are unimportant since they can be corrected quickly. . . . This answer is, of course, too easy. It conflicts with the hard fact that neither government action nor the effect of that action is instantaneous . . . Unfortunately, it is likely that the time lags are a substantial fraction of the duration of the cyclical movements . . . By the time an error is recognised and corrective action taken, the damage may be done, and the corrective action may itself turn into a further error. This prescription of Lerner's . . . thus turns into an exhortation to do the right thing with no advice how to know what is the right thing to do. (Friedman, 1947, pp. 413–15, emphasis added)

I have quoted this passage at length because about thirty years before Keynesian theory lost its hegemony, it summarizes so well one of the two basic monetarist challenges to Keynesian macro-policy.[5]

4 LAGS AND FORECAST ERRORS

Friedman returned to the question whether governments know enough to conduct an effective stabilisation policy in his 'The Effects of a Full-Employment Policy on Economic Stabilization: A Formal Analysis', originally published in French in 1951 and reprinted in his *Essays in Positive Economics* (1953).[6] In it he poses the following questions: 'Under what conditions will counter-cyclical action succeed in its objective of reducing instability? Under what conditions will it actually increase instability? How does its effectiveness depend on the magnitude of action?' (Friedman 1953, p. 117). Thus Friedman goes much further than others towards posing the practical questions that have to be answered for stabilisation policy to be effective. Yet he is almost apologetic for the abstraction of his analysis, writing:

> The present note considers these questions on a highly formal level. Its purpose is primarily to make clear that they are important and relevant questions; secondarily, to indicate in general terms the considerations on which an answer in any particular case depends. (1953, p. 117)

Specifically Friedman interprets stabilisation in a statistical framework as the minimisation of the standard deviation of income. The variance of income if stabilisation policy is undertaken is $\sigma_x^2 + \sigma_y^2 + 2R\sigma_x\sigma_y$ where σ_x^2 the variance of income in the absence of stabilisation policy, σ_y^2 is the size of the stabilisation policy (measured by the change in income that it generates), and R is the correlation coefficient of σ_x^2 and σ_y^2 that is the measure of how well timed the stabilisation policy is. The optimal size of the stabilisation policy equals $-R\sigma_x$, and the policy will be destabilising if $\sigma_y/\sigma_x > -R$. This implies that it is far from obvious that the central bank can succeed in significantly reducing the magnitude of fluctuations. If it adopts a strong policy it may well be destabilising, while a modest and cautious policy means that it cannot do much good. It is by no means unreasonable to expect even an only moderately ambitious central bank to destabilise income. Assume, for example, that the central bank tries to offset, say one-third of the standard deviation of income. It surely does not know with any accuracy by how much it has to change interest rates or the growth rate of reserves to set $\sigma_y/\sigma_x = 1/3$. And suppose it does change income by just this amount, its policy will be destabilising if the change in income is badly timed, so that $R < -0.7$. But to time the policy better than that the central bank has to predict with sufficient accuracy the behaviour of income in the absence of the policy, that is σ_x, as well as the distributed lag in the effect of its policy.

Does the central bank possess the required knowledge? Friedman does not provide any estimates of the relevant parameters, and hence cannot answer this question. Indeed, given the available data, there is no way in which he could have estimated them. But what he does show is that in the absence of supporting empirical evidence one cannot dismiss out of hand the likelihood that a substantial stabilisation policy will destabilise income. In other words, Friedman did not *refute* the Keynesian belief in the effectiveness of stabilisation policy, but he did show that this belief rested on an unsupported assumption, and he conjectured that this assumption is invalid.

The severity of this problem was even greater at the time Friedman wrote his paper than it is now. The Fed did not make any explicit forecasts of GDP; indeed until well into the post-war period the Fed's staff was *forbidden* to make any forecast, and staff members could be fired for making one. To be sure, policy-makers had to make implicit forecasts, but presumably they did so primarily by projecting current conditions and trends into the future. Since at that time the Fed believed that monetary policy affects income with only a very short lag, this was not entirely unreasonable. But the Fed had no evidence that the lag of monetary policy was short, and apparently had not even studied this matter. Moreover, there is no reason to think that the Fed, or anyone else around the time, knew with any degree of accuracy by how much a given change in the interest rate or in the money supply would change GDP.

Let us imagine that one were writing a rational reconstruction of a debate on discretionary monetary policy that obeyed the basic rules on which just about all methodologists – except the Austrians – are in agreement. Economists would then have reacted in one of three ways. One is to follow up on Friedman's analysis by seeing, when data on Fed forecasts became available, if the empirical estimates of σ_y^2/σ_x^2 and R support Friedman's conjecture that a stabilisation policy of significant size cannot succeed. The second is to present an alternative framework that allows one to test this conjecture. The third is to admit that we do not know whether countercyclical monetary policy can be a significant stabilizer. But that is not what happened.

Advocates of countercyclical stabilisation policy essentially ignored both Friedman's review of Lerner and his 1953 paper. Although most of Friedman's papers are cited massively, his review article of Lerner's book is cited only six times in the *Social Science Citation Index (SSCI)*, and none of these citations refer to Friedman's criticism of Lerner's stabilisation policy. The sum-of-variances paper has been occasionally cited, but with one exception the citations I found are not critical. Most are hat-tipping citations that merely mention the paper, or cite it approvingly, or else use it rather than criticise it. The one exception is a paper (Orr, 1960) pointing out that Friedman's framework applies only to a policy of stabilizing GDP around a given trend, and not to a policy that tries to reduce a persistent gap between actual and potential GDP. Yet for much of the post-war period the emphasis was as much, if not more, on the latter than on the former. But Friedman made it clear that he was considering only countercyclical policy.[7]

Since it is foolhardy to claim that a certain a certain paper has been cited critically only once, I will not do so. But I can say that *if* another explicit criticism of Friedman's sum-of-variances paper was published it was an outlier that did not play a meaningful role in the debate.[8] And it is most unlikely that there is much of a literature that responded to Friedman's paper without citing it. On the other side of the debate Friedman himself did not often refer to this paper, perhaps because it presents only a possibility argument.

The neglect of these two papers cannot be due to economists not being aware of them. Friedman's review article appeared in the *Journal of Political Economy*, hardly an obscure source, while his 'Formal

Analysis' essay appeared in a book that had high visibility, since it contains his much-cited essay on the methodology of positive economics. Indeed, rightly or wrongly, William White (1961, p. 142) referred to it as 'well-known', and as 'one of the most important sources of this skepticism about anticyclical measures.' And the failure to respond to Friedman can hardly be attributed to a tendency to ignore the work of a young, unknown scholar, since by that time Friedman was already a leading economist who had won the AEA's John Bates Clark medal in 1951.

A cynic might attribute it to the reluctance of the (at the time) mostly liberal economics profession to pay attention to papers written by a member of the Chicago school. But this explanation will not do. Friedman's other writings have garnered a vast number of citations. Moreover, Friedman was not the only one who contended that stabilisation policy might very easily be destabilising. Four years later A.W. Phillips (1957), who formulated the economic stabilisation problem in a control-theory setting, concluded that:

> [I]f the lags in the real economic system are at all similar to those we have used in the models it is unlikely that the period needed to restore any desired equilibrium conditions after an economy has experienced a severe disturbance could be much less than two years, even assuming that the regulating authorities use the policy which is most appropriate to the real system of relationships existing in the economy. *As these relationships are not known quantitatively, it is unlikely that the policy applied will be the most appropriate one, it may well cause cyclical fluctuations rather than eliminate them.* (Phillips 1957, p. 276, emphasis added)

Subsequently, William Baumol (1961), also using control theory analysed the effects of stabilisation policy, both with and without lags, in the setting of a multiplier–accelerator model. He described his results as: 'somewhat frightening. Plausible and reasonable contracyclical policies turn out to be capable of increasing the explosiveness and frequency of economic fluctuations. In fact, none of the possibilities examined proved to be entirely harmless in these respects' (Baumol, 1961, p. 24).

Karl Brunner (1980), too, presented his own variant of the infeasibility argument. He pointed out that long and variable lags are not the basic issue. Instead, the basic issue is whether the central bank possesses enough information about the future course of GDP and about the effects of its policy. But Brunner did not present as elegant a formulation of the problem as Friedman had done.

These papers had little if any effect on the prevailing consensus, as shown, for example, by the treatment of stabilisation policy in elementary textbooks. One possibility is that they were not considered a major challenge, because although they established the possibility that countercyclical policy is destabilising they did not provide any empirical evidence to support their conjecture that such policy actually is destabilising. This possible explanation needs detailed discussion.

4.1 Empirical Implementation

In Friedman's formulation the parameters that determine whether macropolicy is stabilising are the size of policy-induced variance in GDP relative to the initial variance, and the correlation of these two variances. Assuming that the central bank is single-mindedly devoted to stabilisation policy (an issue discussed below), this correlation depends on the accuracy with which it can forecast GDP and also predict the effects of its policy.

One determinant of the ability to forecast GDP is the horizon of the forecast, and this is what the discussion focused on. Obviously, if the lag in the effect of monetary policy were a decade, then stabilisation would be a hopeless task, while if it were a week, then a central bank that is well informed about current GDP should be an effective stabiliser. Not only would its estimate of the deviation of GDP from its target be accurate, but if it made a mistake in estimating this deviation, or in estimating the effect of its policy on GDP, it could readily reverse its policy.

Friedman and Schwartz (Friedman, 1958, 1961; Friedman and Schwartz,1963a) estimated the lag of monetary policy, and hence the forecast horizon, by comparing the turning points in the growth rate of money with business cycle turning points. They found what at the time were considered long lags: for peacetime cycles a lag of sixteen months at peaks and twelve months at troughs (Friedman, 1961). Using instead of the turning points in the growth rate of money, the dates at which persistent changes in the money growth rate occurred, the lag is shorter, five months at peaks and four months at troughs. All of these are measures only of the 'outside lag', that is the lag between the change in the growth rate of the money supply and cyclical turning points, thus excluding the lag between the time a change in monetary policy is needed and the time at which the Fed changes the money supply.[9]

Many other estimates made around the same time, or shortly thereafter, using various methods reached roughly similar results. So did a number of subsequent studies that measured the lag in monetary policy by seeing for how long an increase in the quantity of money lowers the interest rate.[10] Although a few studies of the lag found it to be much shorter than Friedman and Schwartz's estimate, this was not so for most.

However, Friedman and Schwartz's estimate of the lag was challenged by John Culbertson (1960) and by John Kareken and Robert Solow (1963). Although Kareken and Solow claimed that their results show a shorter lag than Friedman's, this is not so.[11] Culbertson's conceptual criticism is more telling and led to a debate with Friedman (Culbertson, 1961; Friedman, 1961) in which the main issues were Friedman and Schwartz's comparison of the turning points in the *rate of change* of money with turning points in (essentially) the *level* of business activity, and also the direction of causality between money and income.

This debate was superseded by the deeper criticism of William Brainard and James Tobin (1968) and Tobin (1970) which is embedded in their basic challenge to Friedman's inference of a causal relation from the timing of changes in money and in income. Brainard and Tobin simulated a small econometric model that exhibited cases in which peaks in endogenous variables lead peaks in exogenous variables. Tobin then demonstrated this result for two theoretical models, one Keynesian and one monetarist.[12]

The controversy about Friedman's measurement of the lag sounds dated because nowadays the standard procedure for estimating the lag is to use an econometric model to simulate the effect of a change in monetary policy. These simulations usually exhibit lags that are longer than those estimated by Friedman and Schwartz (see Table 5.1). This is not surprising since in such essentially Keynesian models usually much of the effect of monetary policy on expenditures comes through the long-term interest rate, and that rate is treated as adjusting only slowly to changes in the instruments controlled by the central bank.

Suppose the econometric models are correct in showing a long lag. Does that prevent stabilisation policy from succeeding?[13] The answer is not obvious, and raises four questions. First, what is the relation between the length of the lag and the central bank's forecast errors? Second, how does the length of the lag affect the feasibility of offsetting prior errors? Third, can the central bank estimate the length of the lag with sufficient precision? Fourth, does the lag vary substantially from case to case, so that knowledge of the *average* lag does not suffice?

At first glance it may seem obvious that the longer the lag, and hence the forecast horizon, the less accurate is the forecast. But that is not necessarily so for less extreme cases than the ones previously mentioned. The variable that the central bank has to forecast is not the percentage change in GDP that occurs, say five quarters from now, but what the gap between actual and desired GDP will be then. And the more quarters there are between the current quarter and the quarter being forecast, the greater is the chance that the errors made in estimates for the intervening quarters will cancel out. It is therefore not surprising that, as Stephen McNees (1988, p. 22) found, although forecast errors do tend to decline as the forecast period is reduced, at first: 'the improvement is quite gradual and summary error measures are virtually constant as the forecast horizon decreases. We know little more today about what will happen in a given quarter a year from now than we do about a quarter two years from now.'

Another, and probably more serious problem that a long lag creates relates to the reversibility of the effects of monetary policy. Assume that only 10 per cent of the effect on GDP occurs in the first quarter, and 50 per cent occurs in the fourth quarter. Suppose now that the central bank realizes that it has made a mistake and wants to reverse within the next quarter the effect of a restrictive policy that it adopted three quarters ago. It could, in principle, do so by initiating an expansionary policy that is five times as strong as the previous restrictive policy. Subsequently, it would then have to adopt an even stronger restrictive policy to offset the effects of the strong expansionary policy in later quarters. But no central bank is likely to do that. It is often uncertain about what its policy should be, and that makes it reluctant to undertake strong policies that might turn out to be wrong, if only because it has to be concerned about its reputation. Moreover, large policy shifts generate wide swings in interest rates, and central banks favour interest rate stability. There is even some danger of instrument instability, that is an explosive increase in the variability of instrument settings, though that is not as likely a possibility as may appear at first glance (see Holbrook, 1972).

An additional problem is that the central bank does not have a reliable estimate of the length of the lag. It is therefore uncertain about what future GDP gap it should aim at. And even if the central bank knew which model's estimate of the lag is correct, it would still face the problem that these models estimate only the mean lag. A central bank deciding what to do at a particular time needs to know, not the mean lag, but what the lag will be in this particular instance. There is no reason to assume that the variance of lags is small enough for the mean lag to be a reliable guide for specific policy decisions.

When Friedman and Schwartz (1963b) measured the lag of monetary policy by comparing turning points in the growth rate of money and cyclical turning points they found the lag to be highly variable. But, as already discussed, such a comparison of turning points is not easy to interpret (see also Mayer, 1967). Better evidence on the variance of the lag comes from two papers that use variable-coefficient techniques. Cargill and Meyer (1978) estimated for the 1950s and 1960s the impact of monetary policy in the St Louis model and also in a small Keynesian model, allowing the coefficients to vary over time. They found that both the length and the shape of the distributed lag of monetary policy varied significantly, depending upon when the policy was inaugurated. They argued that this provides one more reason to avoid 'overly zealous' stabilisation policies, though they left open the possibility that the differences in lags might be predictable. J.E. Tanner (1979) considered this possibility in a paper using a simplified version of the St Louis model. He found that the lag was substantially longer in the 1960s than in the 1950s, and that the length of lag strongly depends on the type of policy (with a restrictive policy having a longer lag than an expansionary policy). It also depends on the stage of the business cycle; in a recession policy is impotent for at least eight quarters. Moreover, the lag is longer for a tight policy than for a restrictive policy.

These findings suggest that the estimate of the distributed lag that an econometric model provides, i.e. the mean lag for its sample period, is not sufficient for effective policy-making. Admittedly, neither study is beyond criticism. Both use the St Louis model, which has been strongly criticized (most effectively by Modigliani and Ando, 1976), and has performed very badly in recent years. To be sure, Cargill and Meyer also use a small Keynesian model. But that treats the money supply as an exogenous policy variable, even though the Fed largely accommodates changes in the demand for money, so that this model *may* suffer from serious OLS bias. But if we reject the results of these two papers we have to admit that we do not know the variability of the lag at all, and that it could be substantial.[14]

One might therefore expect that the Cargill and Meyer and Tanner papers played a significant role in the debate about discretionary monetary policy. But they did not. Although the SSCI lists several citations for both papers, these citations are all in contexts other than the feasibility of discretionary policy.

It is not clear just how much of a problem the variability of the lags creates. Haskel Benishay (1971), using a control theory model in which the central bank estimates income by an autoregressive function, obtained the counterintuitive result that the more variable the lag, the greater is the optimal stabilisation policy. However, using another control theory model, also employing an autoregressive forecast of income, J. Phillip Cooper and Stanley Fischer (1972a) obtained the more intuitive opposite result. In another paper (Cooper and Fischer 1972b) they showed that in a certain type of model it is the variability of the lag, and not its length that reduces the feasible degree of stabilisation.

All in all, it is far from obvious whether the long lags shown by econometric models, and the variability of the lags shown by Cargill and Meyer and by Tanner prevent an effective countercyclical policy altogether, or just reduce its effectiveness. To answer that question one would have to know, not just the length and variability of the lag, but also how well the central bank can both forecast GNP, and predict by how much its policy actions change GDP. These questions attracted little, if any, attention. One must therefore conclude that the empirical literature just discussed, while important for other purposes, does not answer Friedman's challenge.[15] Instead another approach was tried.

4.2 Applying Control Theory

In the second half of the 1960s and in the early 1970s as econometric models matured, a subliterature developed that used control theory to derive stabilisation rules from these models. The results now obtained differed sharply from Baumol's earlier ones. A number of studies showed that if a particular econometric model, e.g. the Wharton model is valid, then feedback rules derived from control theory are superior to constant monetary growth (see for instance, Cornwall, 1965; Lovell and Prescott 1968; Cooper and Fischer 1974; Cooper 1974; Friedman 1975). Moreover, Craine, Havenner and Berry (1978), applying the Fed's FMP model to a short period, 1973–III to 1975–II, found that the policy the Fed had actually followed in that period was 'slightly better', than a stable monetary growth-rate policy which, in turn, performed better than the Cooper–Fischer and Bronfenbrenner (1961a and b) feedback rules. Finally, there seemed to be evidence that countercyclical policy can succeed.

But there were three problems. First, the results were model-specific, as well as time-specific. Brunner (1980, p. 53) argued that: 'There is substantial evidence that the optimal control settings are not robust with respect to variations over the spectrum of models'. Indeed, all

Table 5.1 Dynamic multipliers: nominal GDP/unborrowed reserves or money stock

Quarter of change	*BEA*	*DRI-74*	*St Louis FRB*	*MPS*	*Wharton Mark III**	*H–C annual*	*Wharton annual*	*Liu–Hwa monthly*
1	0.0	0.3	1.2	0.4	1.3	N.A.	N.A.	0.0
4	0.2	4.3	5.3	3.6	4.1	1.5	1.8	1.5
8	0.5	8.8	5.1	11.4	6.8	1.3	7.6	7.4
12	0.8	7.9	5.1	17.4	8.2	0.9	16.1	14.0
16	0.9	4.9	5.1	24.7	8.0	0.1	25.8	N.A.

Notes:
* Standard Anticipation Model.
The policies and conditions for the simulations of the various models are not exactly the same, but are similar.

Codes for Models
BEA: Bureau of Economic Analysis, US Department of Commerce
DRI: Data Resources Inc.
St Louis FRB: Federal Reserve Bank of St Louis model
MPS: Board of Governors model (MIT–Pennsylvania–Social Science Research Council)
Wharton: Wharton Associates
H–C: Hickman–Coen model (Stanford University)
Lui-Hwa: Luis–Hwa model (Cornell University)

Source: Fromm and Klein (1976, p. 25).

the models may lack sufficient accuracy (see Brunner, 1983b). Not until 1988, when Bennett McCallum applied feedback rules to a wider variety of models, was the problem of model specificity ameliorated to some extent, though only with respect to feedback rules, and not with respect to discretionary counter-cyclical policy.

Second, even if for every plausible econometric model control theory were to show that within this model countercyclical policy could succeed, that would not suffice. Different models dictate different policy actions, not only because their GDP predictions differ, but also because, as Table 5.1 shows, their predictions of the impact of a given policy action differ substantially.[16] For example, to offset a shortfall of GDP four quarters from now, the BEA model shown in this table implies a required open market purchase about twenty times as large as does the DRI model. So, control theory models do not provide central banks with an adequate operating guide.

Third, there is that sturdy standby of sceptics, the Lucas critique. It seems likely that the temporary demise that these feedback models experienced in the late 1970s was due to the Lucas critique.

5 THE POLITICAL ECONOMY OF MONETARY POLICY

The discussion reviewed so far has treated the central bank as a perfectly obedient agent of a principal with only one argument in its utility function, economic stabilisation. It also assumed that the central bank acts in a technically competent manner, using modern economic theory instead of discredited doctrines. In doing so, it ignored an important part of the monetarists' case against countercyclical policy. When Milton Friedman described the issues about stabilisation policy on which he disagreed with Franco Modigliani, one of them was:

> the assumption that if in fact you adopt a policy of accommodation [that is offsetting fluctuations in aggregate demand], Franco Modigliani will be twisting the dials. I have increasingly . . . become impressed with the need for a positive science of politics, of political science. All of us . . . have tended to follow the attitude: Well, now, what we need to do is to figure out the right thing. If only we can tell them what the right thing to do is, then there is no reason why able, well-meaning, well-intentioned people should not carry out those ideas. But we then discover over and over again, that well-intentioned, able people have passed laws, or have established institutions – and lo and behold, they don't work the way able, well-intentioned people expected or believed they would work. And it isn't an accident that that happens . . . once you adopt a policy of accommodating to changes [in aggregate demand] there will be all sorts of changes that . . . [Modigliani] and I know should not be accommodated, with respect to which there will be enormous pressure to accommodate . . . *I have increasingly moved to the position that the real argument for a steady rate of monetary growth is at least as much political as it is economic.* (Modigliani and Friedman, 1977, pp. 17–18, emphasis added)[17]

Similarly, Karl Brunner (1981b, p. 37) wrote that it is wrong to assume that: 'a monetary authority will naturally pursue the optimal social benefit achievable with cleverly designed stabilization policies . . . They will have incentives to trade off degrees of achievable stabilization for political and personal benefits of various kinds' (see also Brunner, 1983a).

5.1 The Record of Monetary Policy[18]

One way to see whether the Fed actually gives priority to its stabilisation goal, and pursues this goal in a technically competent manner, is to look at the historical record. Thus Friedman (Friedman and Heller, 1969, p. 77) wrote: 'The reason I believe you would do better with a fixed [monetary] rule . . . is because I have examined U.S. experience with discretionary monetary policy.'

Friedman and Schwartz (1963a) provided massive evidence on the pro-cyclical nature of Fed policy during the 1930s (see also Wicker, 1966).[19] But one might respond that the Fed has learned from this experience. It now has the high employment goal first mandated by the 1946 Employment Act, and is not likely to repeat the mistakes it made in the 1930s. Friedman and Schwartz end their story in 1960, and in their discussion of the 1950s they do point out that the Fed has moved away from its prior adherence to the real-bills doctrine towards emphasizing the growth rate of the money stock. With the money stock then growing at a stable rate Friedman and Schwartz did not have much criticism of the Fed for its policy in the 1950s. Indeed, Friedman (1960, p. 22) wrote: 'Except for the sharp price rise in 1950–51, our monetary experience since 1948 has been admirable by previous standards.'[20] To be sure, he did claim that even in the 1950s the actual record of monetary policy is inferior to that which a stable growth rate rule would have provided (Friedman, 1960, pp. 93–4). But, as he himself pointed out, he had analysed the record only in a casual way (Friedman, 1960, p. 97). Thus he did not make explicit allowance for the lag of monetary policy.

Subsequent to the period discussed by Friedman, the Fed generated, or at least accommodated, an inflation that between 1965 and 1982 almost tripled the GDP deflator. To be sure, one might argue that this was not the Fed's fault, that this policy was largely imposed on it by the intellectual and political currents of the time. But for the purpose of evaluating countercyclical policy it does not matter whether the Fed was the source or merely the conduit of mistaken policies. A somewhat more plausible defence of the Fed is that much of this inflation resulted from a policy of accommodating supply shocks. Had these shocks not been accommodated they would have generated massive unemployment, so that the Fed was right in permitting high inflation.

Although Brunner and Meltzer devoted less attention to monetary history than did Friedman they, too, have criticized the Fed's record, pointing out that in the post-war period the growth rate of money has been pro-cyclical (Brunner and Meltzer, 1983a, p. 97). But a pro-cyclical monetary growth rate is not necessarily inappropriate. One reason is that, given the lag of monetary policy it is *possible* that the monetary growth rate should rise faster during expansions than during recessions. Another is that since early in a recession GDP is still above its trend-adjusted mean, while early in the expansion it is below its trend-adjusted mean, effective stabilisation does not mean raising GDP throughout the recession and lowering it throughout the expansion (see Argy, 1979).

Looking at the record of US monetary policy therefore provides perhaps some evidence, but certainly not compelling evidence that countercyclical policy cannot succeed. Learning takes place. Fed policy during the last few years is a great improvement over previous policy. To make a strong case against countercyclical policy requires showing that there are systemic factors that inhibit effective policy making by central banks.

5.2 The Monetarist View of Central Bank Behaviour

What factors could prevent central banks from being as effective stabilisers as their ability to forecast allows them to be? One possibility is that they are not free to determine their own policies. A second is that they tend to adopt policies that serve their own interests. Third, their policies may be suboptimal due to cognitive failures, such as the ones that organisation theorists have discussed, e.g. groupthink. Finally, even otherwise efficient policies can have bad effects due to a coordination problem between the central bank and the public.[21] Monetarists have raised all of these issues.

Friedman (1960, 1968) has argued that central banks are not free agents and that in case of serious conflicts with government policy, the government gets its way. Brunner (1981a, p. 69), too, sees the central bank as placing the interests of its masters ahead of its stabilisation task: 'stabilization policies rank comparatively low among the interests of the clientele [of central banks] compared to the potential gains to be expected from allocative arrangements frequently pursued under the guise of monetary policy.' Brunner (1983) suggests that such a wish to accommodate their clients explains why central banks prefer to target interest rates.

Here are some concerns raised by other monetarists. David Meiselman (1986) found evidence of a political business cycle after 1960. David Fand (1986) cited specific instances in which the Fed had succumbed to political influence. More generally, Robert Weintraub (1978) argued that presidents get the monetary policy they want. He showed that major changes in monetary policy were associated with the election of a president who had different views than his predecessor on monetary policy. Moreover, whenever a president with sharply different views on monetary policy was elected, monetary policy changed. Although these conclusions are not fully supported by events subsequent to Weintraub's paper his examples still make an impressive case.[22]

Robert Hetzel (1986) argues that a significant function of monetary policy is to redistribute income by controlling interest rates in accordance with the wishes of politically powerful groups. He does not claim that the Fed necessarily does so frequently, but only that at least at times it does. To maintain its freedom to respond to such pressures the Fed is unwilling to set monetary targets it will adhere to. Hetzel argues that there is therefore a flaw in the basic Keynesian case for stabilisation policy. This case is that due to long-term contracts the private sector is slow to adjust to changes in aggregate demand, while the public sector can respond quickly. But, says Hetzel (1986), the importance that the political system attaches to the distributional consequences of monetary policy eliminates much of the seeming flexibility of monetary policy.

William Poole (1986) looks beyond the influence of politicians and argues that the public's pressure distorts monetary policy. It concentrates on the currently pressing problem: in recessions it demands expansionary policies, and in periods of high inflation contractionary policies. Because of the lag in monetary policy such pressures push the Fed towards destabilising policies. (See also Lombra, 1988.)

Many monetarists reject a popular solution to the problem of political pressures, giving central banks much greater independence. They argue central banks would then have even more freedom to follow their self-interest, and that this is incompatible with effective stabilisation policy.

To show that the Fed follows its own interests Friedman (1982, 1986) gives several examples of Fed behaviour that he believes can best be explained that way. One is its reluctance to adopt serious monetary targets in place of money market conditions targets. Friedman attributes this to monetary targets providing greater accountability, and thus reducing the central bank's autonomy. Another is the reluctance to adopt a fixed monetary growth-rate rule, something that would greatly reduce the importance and status of Fed policy-makers. The third is the Fed's inflationary bias, which Friedman (1982), following Mark Toma, attributes to the Fed's gain from seigniorage. The fourth is the Fed's concern about keeping member banks from leaving the Federal Reserve System, because having many member banks enhances its prestige, importance and lobbying clout.[23] Still another example is the Fed's open market churning, that is, its undertaking a great volume of open market operations that are soon reversed. Friedman attributes this to the Fed's wish to be seen as important. An additional example is the delay in releasing the Federal Open Market Committee's Directive on open market operations. He argued that by thus keeping financial markets in the dark the Fed enjoys a sense of importance, and also creates well paid, private-sector job opportunities as Fed watchers for its staff.[24] Friedman places much emphasis on the central bank not having a bottom line, so that the public cannot readily evaluate its performance.

Moreover, both Brunner (1980) and Friedman (1986) raise a basic question. Why assume that, although agents in the private sector are driven by self-interest, in the public sector agents do not try to maximise their own welfare, but conscientiously do their principal's bidding?

As Brunner (1984) pointed out, the heterogeneity of the central bank's principals and the ambiguity of their interests provide a central bank with the opportunity to attend to its own interests. Examples of self-interested policies that Brunner (1983b) cited are the Fed's preference for complex instruments, its concern about retaining member banks, and its attempt to curb dissent within its own ranks. William Poole (1986) has argued that Fed officials are convinced that the Fed's independence is essential. To protect this independence they may therefore sometimes adopt policies that they know are not appropriate for stabilising GDP.

Despite the usual reluctance of mainstream economists to consider irrational behaviour, monetarists devote substantial attention to the Fed's cognitive errors. In their *Monetary History* Friedman and Schwartz (1963b) discuss in much detail the damage done by the Fed's adherence to the discredited real-bills doctrine. This stubborn adherence results perhaps from a defect that Friedman (1986, p. 188) attributes to a central bank: that 'an independent central bank will almost inevitably give undue emphasis to the point of view of bankers', which, he believes, induces it to confuse money and credit. Moreover, central banks are myopic. 'If each case is considered on its merits, the wrong decision is likely to be made in a large fraction of the cases because decision-makers are examining only a limited area and are not taking into account the cumulative consequences of the policy as a whole' (Friedman, 1968, p. 192). Beyond this, the absence of a bottom line makes it hard for a central bank to learn from experience, and thus fosters bureaucratic inertia. Examples of such inertia are adherence to the real bills doctrine, interest rate pegging after the Second World War, and the system of lagged reserve requirements.[25]

Brunner and Meltzer, like Friedman, pay much attention to the Fed's cognitive errors. In 1964 they published a pathbreaking evaluation of the Fed's thinking and procedures (Brunner and Meltzer, 1964a and 1964b). They found utter confusion. The Fed had no clear idea about the process leading from its open market operations to GDP (that is why Brunner and Meltzer developed the targets and indicator approach). It suffered from 'money market myopia', thus greatly underemphasizing the effects of its policy on the rest of the economy, and was often confused about whether its policy was expansionary or restrictive. For example, it described its policy in 1960 as expansionary, even though it reduced money and bank credit. Brunner and Meltzer built a strong case for believing that the Fed's strategy was so flawed by technical errors, that countercyclical policy was at least as likely to destabilise as stabilise GDP. I have the impression that many monetary economists, who previously had assumed that the Fed was professionally competent, were shocked by what Brunner and Meltzer had found. It is quite possible that even the Fed itself was shocked, because shortly thereafter it strengthened its research staff, and its economic analysis became more professional (Brunner and Meltzer, 1983, p. 60). In addition, more professional economists, some with strong academic reputations, were appointed to the Board of Governors and to Reserve Bank presidencies.

But according to Brunner (1983b) these are largely superficial changes. Although the Fed may now use the jargon and techniques of economic analysis, it does not take economic analysis seriously. To do so would be risky for it since economic analysis 'injects a subtle constraint on the future range of possible actions', and thus poses a danger to the welfare of the Fed's bureaucracy (Brunner, 1983, p. 104). The Fed therefore prefers an eclectic position that provides it with a greater range for tailoring its explanation to any conclusion it wants to reach. Brunner argues that it is not alone in this, citing the Bank of England, the Bundesbank, the Belgian National Bank and the Banque de France as other examples. Hence, although the Fed's staff uses econometric models, the results shown by these models are frequently disregarded (Brunner, 1980, 1984; see also Lombra and Moran, 1980). In addition, the Fed ignores criticism of its policy by academic economists (Brunner, 1983b).

Another monetarist, and former president of the St Louis Federal Reserve Bank, Lawrence Roos, discusses the cognitive-errors problem with the insight of someone who has served on the Federal Open Market Committee (FOMC):

> Never once in my participation in meetings of the Federal Open Market Committee (FOMC) do I recall any discussion of long range goals of economic growth or desired price levels. It was like trying to construct a house without agreeing upon an architectural design. . . . [T]he Federal Reserve is supposed to solve all sorts of problems, including inflation, unemployment, lagging real output growth, high interest rates, balance of payments disequilibrium, volatile exchange rates, depressed stock prices, a sagging housing industry, and the world debt crisis . . . Imposing such a laundry list . . . on the Fed reflects a total lack of understanding what the Federal Reserve is able or not to do. This kind of thinking hampers the workings of the FOMC . . . I recall no consensus on long-range goals nor do I recall serious efforts to set policy on any other than the shortest time horizons . . . I have always had the feeling that the discussion was 'Where do you think the economy will be a year or two in the future, and how can we best set targets so that we won't have egg on our face if this doesn't come about?'. (Roos, 1986, pp. 772–5)

In their study of FOMC behaviour in the early 1970s Raymond Lombra and Michael Moran (1980, p. 43) conclude that: 'without the guidance or discipline offered by an analytic model and formal targets for nonfinancial variables, the formulation of monetary policy often seemed to be a seat-of-the-pants operation'. In commenting on their paper James Pierce (1980, p. 84), a former senior FOMC economist (and *not* a monetarist), reports that:

> if the formation of monetary policy is to be understood and reformed, much more work needs to be done in developing an understanding of the group dynamics that produce the kind of FOMC performance described by Lombra and Moran. The members of the FOMC are basically intelligent people, and many have training in economics. They all have access to staff and outside advice. Yet when they get together we get policy by 'the seat-of-the-pants'.

Elsewhere, Lombra (1988) points out the difficulty that the FOMC faces in taking timely action, such as raising interest rates when unemployment is still high. Given the fragility of their forecasts, it is understandable that policy-makers are afraid to become restrictive at such times. My own studies of the Fed's thinking during the 1973–75 recession and its analysis of Regulation Q (Mayer, 1990b, Chapters 6, 7) support such critical evaluations.

Finally, countercyclical policy creates coordination problems. Thus Friedman (1960) objects to the Fed's frequently unpredictable changes in its policy, presumably because they make it hard for the public to coordinate its actions, such as price setting, with the Fed's policy. Brunner (1983b), too, objects to the Fed's exacerbation of uncertainty. Moreover, Cukierman and Meltzer (1986) argue that central banks have an incentive to create uncertainty. The greater the uncertainty, the longer is the effectiveness of some policies, such as raising output by adopting a more expansionary policy. And keeping one's actions shrouded in mystery is also a good defence against criticism. Brunner (1983b) also refers in this connection to time-inconsistency.

5.3 Evaluation

These monetarist arguments obviously lack rigorous development, and some of them seem more like interesting issues for further research than carefully worked out conclusions.[26] It may seem that this is inevitable since neither the theory nor the empirical evidence required for a more convincing treatment is available. But this is not quite correct. Much work has been done outside the monetarist debate, and even outside of economics that monetarists could have cited.

There is an extensive literature on the existence of political business cycles (for surveys see Beck, 1990, 1991; Woolley, 1994). Reasonable people might take either side on this issue.[27] But the possibility that political business cycles exist is surely not something that should be ignored when discussing the limitations that political pressures place on countercyclical monetary policy. Yet few monetarists have taken it up.[28] Moreover, public choice economists, such as Thomas Havrilesky (1993), have generated an extensive literature on the Fed acting in its self-interest.[29] Monetarists have not made much use of it, though Friedman (1986) does praise it.

There is much less literature, other than in the writings of monetarists themselves, on cognitive errors in monetary policy-making. But there exists a large literature on the role of cognitive errors in other types of economic behaviour, and that may perhaps be relevant for monetary policy.[30] Finally, monetarists have paid some, but only limited attention to the one coordination problem of monetary policy that has received great attention, time-inconsistency.[31]

It is *possible* that many or even most monetarists believe that political business cycles do not occur, are sceptical of much of the public choice literature on monetary policy and of the evidence on cognitive errors, and do not think that time-inconsistency is a serious problem. They may be right. So perhaps they should not be blamed for not making greater use of the literature on these topics. But where does this leave us? Consider, for example, the hypothesis that Fed policy makers are motivated by self-interest. At times that will induce them to act in ways contrary to the public interest. But, as Albert Hirschman once remarked, policy makers have an incentive to engage in obituary-enhancing behaviour. By and large, that means engaging in socially desirable behaviour. Unnecessary secrecy may enhance the prestige of Fed governors, but so does the avoidance of recessions and inflation. The reach of the invisible hand is not confined to the private sector.

Moreover, it may well be true that the Fed is subject to political pressures, attends to its own interests and makes cognitive errors. There is no doubt that such factors can degrade the quality of discretionary monetary policy. But by how much? Do they just reduce the feasible degree of stabilisation to a small extent, or do they cause discretionary policy to be destabilising? Monetarists claim the latter, but their evidence seems also consistent with the former.[32] Here, as in the case of lags and forecast errors, they have raised a serious *challenge* to a fundamental assumption of the Keynesian position, but that is all.

5.4 The Keynesian Response on Central Bank Behaviour

The Keynesian response (if that word is appropriate) to this challenge has been either to ignore it, or to dismiss it with disdain.[33] This is illustrated by a Keynesian argument that was popular prior to the discovery of time-inconsistency. As Stanley Fischer (1990, p. 1157), following Buiter (1981), tells us:

> At the formal level, Friedman's analysis suffers from the logical weakness that discretion seems to dominate rules: if a particular rule would stabilize the economy, then discretionary policy-makers could always behave that way – and retain the flexibility to change the rule as needed.

This argument completely ignores a substantial part of the monetarist case, even though Fischer does add in a footnote: 'However, Friedman did confront the issue of why a formal rule might be preferable to a discretionary policy, making an analogy to the Bill of Rights.'[34] Friedman in a debate with Modigliani stated that his case for a rule is based : 'at least as much' on political considerations as on lags and forecast errors. (Modigliani and Friedman, 1977, p. 18) and has written vastly more on these political considerations than merely referring to the Bill of Rights. Yet the footnote cited above is the only mention of Friedman's political argument in Fischer's survey of 'Rules versus Discretion in Monetary Policy'. To be sure, Fischer devotes much space to the time-inconsistency argument for a monetary rule, but that hardly explains why he ignores Friedman's analysis. This analysis is by the nature of its subject-matter not rigorous, but it has much more empirical support than does the time-inconsistency theory of monetary policy. Indeed, why that theory has become so popular, despite its lack of empirical substance (see Mayer, 1993, pp. 87–92), is a topic that deserves a separate paper (see also McCallum, 1995).[35] A prime suspect is the self-interest of economists who need a role for their game theory tools.

Perhaps a reason why many economists may brush aside the monetarists' interpretation of Fed behaviour is that those of us who are acquainted with Fed policy makers know them to be able and dedicated public servants, not people who would consciously put their own interests above those of the public. I suspect that such personal knowledge can be highly persuasive. But it can be misleading. Friedman concludes his criticism of specific Fed policies as follows:

> [L]et me emphasize that I am not saying that people in the [Federal Reserve] system deliberately pursue these measures for these reasons. Not at all. As economists, we treat a business enterprise as if it were solving a large number of complex simultaneous equations . . . We justify that procedure by saying that if we analyze them *as if* they are rationally and knowingly pursuing the maximization of profit, we'll get a good approximation of their behavior . . . I am trying to analyze the forces at work, not to describe the detailed motivation or personal behavior of the people involved. All of us know that what's good for us is good for the country. (Friedman, 1982, p. 116, emphasis in original)

One need not view Fed policy makers as incompetent or selfish to allow for the possibility that their policies are far less efficient than our knowledge of economics makes possible. For example, even selfless people often have an exaggerated view of the importance of their organisation. Hence, one would expect even the most dedicated Fed officials to overvalue the benefits of the Fed's autonomy, and hence to adopt policies that enhance its political power, and to excessively avoid policies that subject it to politically potent attacks (cf. Kane, 1990; Pierce, 1990; Willett and Keen, 1990). Moreover, central bank officials, like all of us, are tempted to avoid the feeling of regret that comes from realizing that we have made a mistake, and hence may be slow to abandon mistaken policies. They are also likely to be excessively influenced by the views of their colleagues (see Klein, 1994; Mayer, 1990a).[36] Consequently, it is not sufficient to say, as Modigliani (Modigliani and Friedman, 1977, p. 21) does, that: 'I have personally no reason to believe that the United States government . . . is not able to attract able people who are interested in common welfare and can do a good job.'

5.5 Ideology and Value Judgements

Keynesians sometimes dismiss the monetarist case for stable monetary growth as politically and ideologically grounded. Thus Tobin (1976, p. 336) contends that:

> Distinctively monetarist policy recommendations stem less from theoretical or even empirical findings than from distinctive value judgements. The preferences revealed persistently in those recommendations are for minimizing the public sector and for paying a high cost in unemployment to stabilize prices.

Similarly, Modigliani tells us that the dispute between monetarists and Keynesians on the need for stabilisation policy is attributable not only to differences in empirical estimates, but 'to no less a degree to differences in *social philosophy and attitudes*' (Modigliani, 1986, p. 7, emphasis in original).[37] Presumably Tobin and Modigliani intend to imply that the monetarists' evidence on stabilisation policy should therefore not be taken all that seriously.

It is hard to know what to make of this. Friedman (1960, p. 85) in his discussion of a monetary rule does refer to his general preference for the rule of law over the rule of men, but does so only very briefly. Almost all of Friedman's discussion of the political aspects of a monetary rule deals with positive and not normative considerations.

A cynical interpretation of Tobin's and Modigliani's reference to value-judgements is that this is a rhetorical argument (in the derogatory sense of the term) running something like this: 'We Keynesians are concerned about the welfare of ordinary people, and empathize with the poor. So we advocate policies that will reduce unemployment. Those who disagree with us do so because they are less concerned with the misery of the unemployed. We appeal to the reader, who no doubt shares our value judgement, to support our position.' But there is no warrant for such a cynical interpretation.

Another reading is that, as discussed below, Modigliani and Tobin simply do not understand how monetarists can disagree with their positive judgements. So, they think that the difference in policy recommendations must be due to a difference in value judgements. And there *is* a big ideological distance between Friedman, Brunner and Meltzer on the one hand, and Modigliani and Tobin on the other.

6 OBJECTIONS TO A MONETARY GROWTH-RATE RULE

Instead of meeting the monetarists' challenge to their assumption about central bank behaviour directly, Keynesians have followed the principle that the best defence is offence by showing that a monetary growth-rate rate rule would not work well.[38]

One problem with a growth-rate rule is the difficulty of finding a measurable counterpart to the theoretical term 'money'. Is it M1, M2, or Mwhat? As Tobin (1965) has remarked, Friedman admits that he does not know what money is, but he wants whatever it is to grow at a fixed rate. Monetarists respond that it does not matter all that much whether one picks M1, M2 or M3, since their growth rates are highly correlated. But, even in the period 1959–82 the correlation was far from close. Subsequently, the correlation between the growth rates of M1 and M2, as well as the correlation of the growth rates of M1 and M3 disappears. Only the growth rates of M2 and M3 are highly correlated.[39] Moreover, the current measures of M1, M2 and M3 are not the only possible measures of money, and some other measure may be the appropriate one.

Keynesians therefore have here a good argument against a stable monetary growth-rate rule. But it is not a valid argument for countercyclical policy. The central bank could acknowledge that it does not have an operational definition of money, and hence shift occasionally (but not frequently) in an *ad hoc* fashion between various measures of money. Or it could use an interest rate or the growth rate of credit as its target variable, without in either case attempting countercyclical policy.

The other problem with a monetary growth-rate rule is the familiar one that whichever measure of money is chosen, its velocity is likely to be unstable, if not now, then sooner or later. When in the early 1980s the velocity of M1 became erratic, monetarists pointed to the stable velocity of M2. But in the early 1990s that velocity, too, became unstable. Adding shares in mutual bond funds to M2 helped for a time, but not for long.

But here, too, one needs to distinguish between a strict monetary growth-rate rule, and the moderate rule of abstaining from countercyclical policy, while adjusting monetary growth for longer-run changes in velocity. The two key questions are again whether the central bank can predict both cyclical changes in velocity and the effect of its policy actions with sufficient accuracy, and whether it can be trusted with the power to adjust the monetary growth rate counter-cyclically. These questions are not answered by pointing to substantial fluctuations in velocity. Secular changes in velocity and the appropriate measure of money are only weak arguments for countercyclical policy.[40]

7 EMPIRICAL TESTS

Since the historical record does not provide the opportunity for a good direct test of a monetary growth-rate rule, relatively few empirical tests have been undertaken. Bronfenbrenner (1961a, 1961b) calculated the growth rate of money that is optimal for price stability on the assumption that velocity is unaffected by the policy followed. He then compared this optimal growth rate of money to (a) the actual growth rate that occurred under Fed discretion, (b) two versions of a stable monetary growth-rate rule and (c) an adaptive rule that made the monetary growth rate a function of the prior year's or quarter's increase in the labour force, labour productivity and change in velocity. Bronfenbrenner's results with quarterly data (though not those with yearly data) favoured the adaptive rule.

Modigliani (1964), criticized Bronfenbrenner's assumptions that velocity is unaffected by the growth rate of money, and that money affects income without a significant lag (see also Argy, 1971). However, Modigliani assumed that the effect of money on income occurred within half a year, an assumption that is both critical to his results and open to question (see Attiyeh, 1966; Mayer, 1967). Moreover, Attiyeh (1966) pointed out that Modigliani ignored the lagged effects of monetary policy, as well as Okun's law. On the other hand, in a subsequent paper designed to deal with these problems, McPheters and Redman (1975) found that discretionary policy was on the whole superior to a fixed monetary growth-rate rule, or to a rule that put limits on the monetary growth rate.

It may therefore seem that Modigliani's test, as further developed by McPheters and Redman, provides the rationale that Keynesians relied on in rejecting the monetarist challenge. But that would be pseudo-history. Although Modigliani's paper has received a respectable number of citations, these citations are not ones that use it to justify stabilisation policy, but deal with other issues.

Victor Argy (1979) in a somewhat similar study of seven countries took residuals from a stable growth trend of money and, using an econometric estimate of the lag, calculated their impact on industrial production. On the whole, his results showed that departures of money growth from its trend destabilised industrial production. In another test for eight countries he looked at the effect of money growth on velocity, and again found discretionary policy to be destabilising. However, both tests require the strong assumption that money is exogenous, as well as the acceptance of Argy's estimate of the lag. Argy attributed the poor performance of discretionary policy to political pressures on central banks, and to their focus on goals other than stabilisation.[41]

Another test is to see whether GDP grew at a stabler rate in those periods in which the monetary growth rate was fairly stable. Modigliani (1986) found that in two post-war periods when the US money supply was growing at a relatively stable rate, GDP was highly unstable, though in a third period of relatively stable monetary growth, GDP was also growing at a stable rate. From this Modigliani (1986, p. 37) concluded that stable money growth is neither a necessary nor a sufficient condition for economic stability. There are two problems with this conclusion. First, there is the question whether one should look at periods when the growth rate of money was stable, or as Friedman (Modigliani and Friedman, 1977) maintains, at periods when the growth rate of money was changing at a stable rate.[42] Second, given the Fed's tendency to accommodate changes in the demand for money, one would expect money growth to be more erratic at times when GDP growth is more erratic.

In a somewhat similar test Starleaf and Floyd (1972) compared the relative stability of monetary growth rates and GDP in thirteen countries. They showed that countries with a stabler money growth rate also had stabler GDP growth. However, it is not clear whether the unstable money growth caused unstable GDP growth, or the converse.

Using an (apparently independently developed) framework similar to Friedman's (1953) Robert Fix and Charles Sivesind (1978) looked at the correlation between changes in velocity and changes in the monetary growth rate in a sample of countries. They compared the actual changes in money growth to the changes that would have been appropriate, given the correlation between changes in velocity and money. They found substantial variation among countries; in particular the US experience was not representative. Their results generally support discretionary policy. However, they had to make the strong assumption that the observed changes in velocity are independent of changes in the monetary growth rate.

Another test of countercyclical monetary and fiscal policy jointly is to compare the stability of the US economy in the post-war period, when stabilisation policy was used, with its stability before 1929 (see, for instance, Modigliani, 1977; Heller in Friedman and Heller, 1969). Such a test is not persuasive because the post-war economy differs from the pre-1929 economy also in many other ways. Thus, Keynesians should expect greater stability because of the greater relative size of the public sector and the prevalence of automatic stabilizers, while monetarists should expect greater stability because of the avoidance of the massive bank failures that frequently accompanied major recessions.[43]

All in all, these empirical tests do not provide monetarists with the evidence they need to make strong claims, nor do they provide Keynesian with a justification for rejecting the monetarist position.

8 RECENT DEVELOPMENTS

In recent years this debate has been swept up in the controversy about new classical theory. New classical economists have reached the same policy conclusion as hard-core monetarists, but have done so because they believe that markets clear rapidly, not because they believe that central banks respond inefficiently. Two other developments have also changed the debate. One is the importance that many economists now attribute to the danger of time-inconsistency. The other is the erratic behaviour of velocity. These two developments have lead to a focus on a compromise position; the use of feedback rules.[44] Feedback rules are accepted by some monetarists, such as Meltzer (1987), but not by others, such as Friedman. They represent an obvious adaptation of monetarism to the brute fact that velocity is no longer stable. This compromise is compatible with monetarists' distrust of central banks, and with their belief that we lack the knowledge required for effective countercyclical policy. At the same time, feedback rules also have some appeal for others because by constraining central banks they avoid the time-inconsistency problem.

That does not mean, of course, that the debate is over. Presumably many, perhaps most Keynesians prefer an entirely discretionary monetary policy. Thus two leading Keynesians, Benjamin Friedman (1988) and Modigliani (1988), have questioned the case for feedback rules. All the same, there now exists a coherent compromise position.

9 WHAT WENT WRONG?

The three failures that occurred in the debate can now be summarized. First, a false dichotomy was posed. Instead of asking whether a fixed growth-rate rule is preferable to all types of discretionary monetary policy, two distinct questions should have been posed, one about the validity of the hard monetarist position that prohibits all discretionary policy, and the other about the validity of the moderate position of eschewing just countercyclical policy.

The second failure was that many monetarists overstated their case, in part, by treating evidence for their moderate position as though it were evidence for their hard position. They also treated a possibility argument – or perhaps one should say a plausibility argument – about lags and forecast errors as though it were much more conclusive than it actually is. Similarly, they did not develop their political argument against discretionary monetary policy sufficiently. They did present a serious challenge to the naive view of the central bank as a good and wise *deus ex machina*, but then jumped to the conclusion that it behaves more like Frankenstein. Their evidence that various factors inhibit rational and socially efficient central bank behaviour fails to show that these factors prevent discretionary monetary policy from doing good on average. And their historical evidence if interpreted as more than merely a suggestive argument, is open to the objection that learning takes place.

The third failing in the debate is that the Keynesians did not take sufficiently seriously the evidence presented by their opponents. They ignored Friedman's fundamental contribution of treating the stabilisation problem as one of minimising the sum of two variances. They also brushed aside the monetarists' scepticism about the motivation of central banks, despite the evidence that the monetarists and public choice economists had provided for it. To be sure, by writing as though a fixed monetary growth-rate rule was the only alternative to a countercyclical policy, monetarists made it tempting for Keynesians to criticise such a rule instead of addressing the serious questions about the status of their basic assumptions. But Keynesians should have resisted the temptation.

I believe it was Lord Russell who said that a half-truth is a good enough stick to beat a dogma with. If so, the overstatements of the monetarists may deserve some understanding. But they surely did not contribute to the smooth advance of knowledge. All in all, both sides claimed to possess knowledge they did not have.

10 RELATION TO THE PHILOSOPHY OF SCIENCE

In evaluating this debate I have not made use of various approaches in the philosophy of science because they deal with more sophisticated issues than the ones that have hobbled this debate. But it is useful to see if the way the debate has proceeded has any implications for the relation of philosophy of science to economics.

My evaluation supports falsificationism, albeit in an indirect way. A major criticism of falsificationism is that it is prescriptive and not a good description of what scientists actually do. But this is a problem only when considering sciences that are successful enough for the philosopher-critic to have little to contribute. The debate about the monetary growth-rate rule has not been so successful. Regardless of the epistemological status of falsificationism, a whiff of falsificationism would have improved this debate. While neither of the rival hypotheses could have been compellingly falsified, more empirical testing would have been useful. Moreover, a Popperian mind set, particularly if it were what Boland (1994) calls the Socratic version of Popperianism, would have made economists on both sides more aware of the precariousness of their positions. In particular, it might have induced Keynesians to ask whether their assumptions about the central banks' information set and motives are valid. It might also have induced monetarists to realise that much of their case consists of only possibility arguments. To be sure, such a development would not have required falsificationism, but emphasis on falsificationism would have made it more likely. In academia it may take a steam-shovel to do what could be done just as well with a spade.

A Kuhnian interpretation of the debate would have little to contribute.

To be sure, on the issue of central bank behaviour there seems to be something that resembles a Kuhnian incomprehension of the other side's position, but the resemblance is far from close. Both sides agree on what the question is, and would look at essentially the same strong evidence if it were available. The difference is that monetarists judge central bank misbehaviour to be a major and unavoidable problem, while Keynesians judge it to be a minor and remediable problem, and both sides are puzzled by the other side's judgement. As Bennett McCallum in his comments rightly points out, monetarists look at the Fed's past behaviour, while Keynesians look at what an enlightened Fed could do in the future. But that is not quite a Kuhnian chasm. With sufficient effort the protagonists could have understood each other. And in principle, evidence on the Fed's capacity to change could resolve the issue. On the issue of lags and forecast errors there is no sign of paradigmic differences. Suppose, for example, that a new econometric model could predict GDP extremely accurately. Then, it is likely that many monetarists would concede that the Fed now has the skills needed for effective countercyclical policy. Conversely, if forecasts were to deteriorate substantially in the future, at least some Keynesians would shift in a monetarist direction. Both sides look at much the same evidence, albeit through different glasses.

Lakatosian methodology fits at most only slightly better. If one formulates the debate in Lakatosian terms one would say that for Keynesians the hard-core propositions are that central bankers are capable and dedicated to their stabilisation task, and that they can forecast with sufficient accuracy.[45] Disputes about such issues as the length of the lag, and the reason the Fed targets money market conditions, or its ability to control money growth are disputes in the protective belt. But such a Lakatosian formulation is not insightful. The words are right, but the music is out of tune. The debate about protective-belt propositions seems stunted. Supposedly hard-core propositions are attacked or defended directly. The problem is that if the Lakatosian concept of research programmes fits anything, it is more likely to be the entire monetarist and Keynesian programmes or, better still, neoclassical economics as a whole, rather than just positions on a stable monetary growth-rate rule.

To some extent the debate seems to fit the Hegelian schema, with the Keynesian thesis and the monetarist antithesis giving rise to the synthesis of feedback rules. But it is far from obvious that feedback rules are widely enough accepted, and that they will survive the ongoing dispute long enough to be considered a synthesis.

Quite apart from the philosophies of science just discussed, as a description of prevailing practice this debate provides some support for a moderate constructionist view, closer to what Mäki (1992) calls the ethnographic version than to the Edinburgh version. That adherents to the dominant paradigm ignored the questions monetarists raised shows how in this case knowledge was socially constructed, in the sense that it was considered acceptable to ignore relevant information. It is likely that the disposition to ignore the monetarist challenge had something to do with the tendency of many major US economics departments to employ no, or almost no, Chicago graduates. The monetarist challenge is therefore something that one might read about, but does not have to face on a day-to-day basis. The way academic networks are constructed may affect the way economics is constructed.

To be sure, one might respond that it is not knowledge *per se*, but only the 'knowledge' of a particular group that is here socially constructed; that when one group of scientists ignores important evidence, another group will bring this evidence into the open. This did happen here. But was it inevitable? Suppose that Friedman had become, say, a statistician instead of an economist, that Karl Brunner had not received the fellowship that allowed him to come to the Cowles Commission at Chicago, and that Allan Meltzer had therefore not studied with him. Would there have been a thriving monetarist school to challenge the implicit Keynesian assumptions? One can respond that the arguments made by these monetarists were out there waiting to be discovered, if not by them, then by others (cf. Mäki, 1992). Self-interest impels economists to search for undervalued arguments. But if they had been discovered and advocated by economists less gifted than the three just mentioned, and in particular if these others had lacked the persuasive skills of Friedman, would many people now know about them? Eventually the monetarist challenge would probably have to come into its own, but eventually is a long time.

11 WHY DID THIS DEBATE GO SO BADLY?

One can only speculate about the reasons why the debate was so inefficient. The first failure, asking too broad a question, is probably related to the vehemence of the general monetarist debate. Mussa (1994, pp. 138–9) refers to it as 'fundamentally a religious controversy, intrinsically related to the age-old dispute over free will versus predestination'. Pierce (1995, pp. 33, 30) also calls the overall monetarist–

Keynesian debate 'largely a religious debate', and refers to 'a singular unwillingness for the proponents on either side to listen to the propositions of the other'.

In turn, the vehemence of the debate may be due to some extent to ideological factors, that is, to the Chicago school sharply disagreeing with other economists on so many issues, and with Friedman being so strongly identified with pronounced free market views. Is this combination of monetarism and a strong belief in free markets just accidental, as Tobin (1981) suggests? Surely, one can believe that the lag of monetary policy is long and variable, and that our ability to forecast GDP and to predict the effect of monetary policy is limited, without opposing the welfare state. One can also accept the monetarist argument about political pressures on central banks and about their inefficiencies and self-interested behaviour, and yet subscribe to a left-leaning political philosophy. That is true in principle. But those who consider the government benevolent and efficient enough to remedy various market failures are likely to believe that it can also remedy that great market failure, unemployment. Similarly, those who question the ability and benevolence of the government in general, are not likely to see the central bank as able and benevolent. Much of the dogmatism shown in this debate may therefore be ascribed to its political nature, thus illustrating the difficulty of doing 'scientific' work on a politically-charged topic.

Apart from the vehemence of the debate, professional rivalries may also have made the leaders on both sides disinclined to look for a compromise that would have separated the hard monetarist position from the moderate one. Moreover, neither side had all that much of an incentive to look for such a compromise. Keynesians, being in the majority, lacked an incentive since if the debate focused on the moderate monetarist position, there was at least some danger that they would lose their majority status. A fixed monetary growth rate, come what may, is a much more inviting target than is a policy of eschewing countercyclical policy. And until velocity became highly unstable in the early 1980s, monetarists may have lacked the incentive to strengthen their case against countercyclical policy at the expense of weakening their case against changing the monetary growth rate in response to secular changes in velocity. They may have been afraid that if the central bank is allowed any discretion at all it will surreptitiously follow countercyclical policies.

The second lapse from good practice, the monetarists' overstatement of their case, is not all that an unusual a lapse, and not only in economics. In his *Treatise on Probability* Keynes (1921, p. 427) tells us: 'In writing a book of this kind the author must, if he is to put his point of view clearly, pretend sometimes to a little more conviction than he feels. He must give his own argument a chance, so to speak, not be too ready to depress its vitality with a wet cloud of doubt.' It should not be difficult to find examples of overstatements even in the most respectable sciences. All the same, the fewer the better, and monetarists certainly deserve to be criticised for their overstatements.

The third lapse, the Keynesians' disregard of the monetarists' evidence, is probably due, in considerable part, to the politicisation of the debate. Another likely reason is that the monetarists challenged not some technical issue in Keynesian theory, but something in which Keynesians take great pride, the ability to reduce unemployment, and thus prevent much misery. It is also likely that the Keynesian reaction is due to a fundamental metaphysical belief seemingly shared by many Keynesians: that with sufficient goodwill and intelligence it *must* be possible to reduce human suffering.[46]

Another possible reason is that, as already discussed, many Keynesians may not have taken the monetarists' suspicions of the Fed seriously. The public choice view of government, which monetarists generally adhere to, and the public interest view, which many Keynesians adhere to, are different 'visions'. As David Colander (1994a, 1994b) has stressed, economists are reluctant to confront differences in vision.

Colander (1994a, 1994b) also discusses the useful distinction between the science of economics and the art of economics, the latter adding to economic hypotheses certain hypotheses from other fields, such as politics or public administration, that are needed to make policy recommendations. Economists feel uneasy about discussing the art of economics because they cannot do so with the degree of rigour to which they pretend. So they concentrate their discussion on the science part of the argument. But this is often of little general interest, and most economists do want to deal with matters of widespread interest. To avoid this dilemma they act as though the strength of an argument is as strong as its *strongest* link, and hence as though only the science of economics matters (see Mayer, 1993). Hence, they are tempted to disregard the art statements of those they disagree with as though they were mere asides. But that means sweeping problematic assumptions under the rug, and pretending to more knowledge than one possesses.

That may also explain why neither side made much, if any, use of the political science literature dealing with the Fed and with bureaucratic behaviour in general. This sort of parochialism is common in economics (see Hausman, 1992). An alternative explanation is that this literature does not provide enough strongly confirmed propositions. But if political science propositions are a necessary part of the argument, then that is less of a justification for ignoring what is available in the political science literature than for expressing one's conclusions with humility.

The profession's great emphasis on the application of sophisticated techniques probably also played a part. Central bank behaviour is an issue that is best studied by looking at specific events using tools more akin to those of the historian than those of the mathematician. Few economists are willing to do that type of work.

Still another likely reason why Keynesians did not attend adequately to the monetarist challenge may be the way monetarists presented their argument. Had they presented it explicitly as a challenge to Keynesians to bring into the open and to justify their implicit assumptions about the central banks' ability to predict and about its motivation, the debate might have been more productive. Instead, by putting their argument in terms of the desirability of a monetary rule, they presented Keynesians with a much easier target than having to discuss their own assumptions. It is much easier to criticise Friedman's rule (see Lerner, 1962; Goldfeld, 1982; Tobin, 1983) than to justify the Keynesian assumptions.

Finally, both monetarists and Keynesians claimed more knowledge than they possessed because they were addressing not only a professional audience, but also policy makers and the politically aware public. Friedman's main statement of his position (Friedman, 1960) originated in series of lectures he gave to a general audience, while Keynesians advocated their position in many popular magazines and in congressional testimony. Such audiences are used to overstatements and indeed would not be moved by arguments that start with: 'we cannot be certain, but it seems likely to me that . . .'. Policy debates foster overstatements; economists who say 'on the one hand, . . . but on the other hand', are not popular.[47]

12 IN CONCLUSION

All in all, economists cannot feel proud of the debate about the monetary growth-rate rule. But before placing an order for sackcloth and ashes one should consider three things. First, it is precisely this type of topic that is likely to generate an unsatisfactory debate, in part because of its high art component, and in part because it engages political sympathies so strongly. The difficulty of bringing empirical evidence to bear must also have contributed to the low quality of the debate. Other aspects of the overall monetarist debate, such as the debate about the behaviour of velocity, or about the St Louis model, are much closer to meeting the standards of good conversation. It might be useful to see to what extent other debates that engage political attitudes, such as the debate between the 'two Cambridges', and the debate about the appropriate level of unemployment benefits, fail to measure up to reasonable standards.

Secondly, as Feyerabend has taught us, even in the physical sciences debates do not always conform to idealised notions of 'science'.[48] It would be interesting to see if in the natural sciences those debates that challenge basic presuppositions are conducted all that much better than the debate reviewed here. A study of controversies in fields such as medicine might also indicate whether it is common for debates that question the ability to do good to be particularly vehement.

Thirdly, despite all the roadblocks the discussion has advanced our knowledge. The avoidance of countercyclical policy is no longer identified with a fixed monetary growth-rate rule. Moreover, I suspect, though I cannot document it, that more economists now pay serious attention to the monetarists' concerns about lags and forecast errors and to the possibility of socially perverse behaviour of central banks than was true in 1986, the end of the period I am discussing (see Blinder, 1987). At the same time, it is likely that many monetarists have abandoned a fixed growth-rate rule, and like Meltzer now support feedback rules. Admittedly, the hard fact of velocity no longer being stable may have been more influential in this than the sweet voice of reason. Given the importance of the questions being asked, such progress does represent a respectable rate of return on the resources that were expended in this debate. But the same results could have been achieved at a substantially lower cost; economists were operating far from the production frontier.

Notes

* I am indebted for helpful comments to Roger Backhouse, Daniel Hausman, Uskali Mäki, Michael Kaser, Sherman Shapiro and my two discussants. Bennett McCallum's comments at the Conference induced me to replace 'failed' with 'flawed' in the subtitle.

1. Purely for convenience I will use the term 'monetarists' to denote those who for the reasons given by Friedman and by Brunner and Meltzer reject

the use of counter-cyclical policy. They should actually be called 'strong monetarists', since one can be a monetarist without going that far. (See Friedman, 1983) Similarly, one can accept the essence of the *General Theory*, while opposing counter-cyclical policy. But the use of the term 'Keynesian' for advocacy of counter-cyclical monetary policy can be defended by reference to Keynes's *A Tract on Monetary Reform* (1924).

2. In 1984 Scitovsky called it 'the generally accepted framework within which many, perhaps most, economists think and argue about fiscal and monetary policy' (Scitovsky, 1984, p. 1561).
3. Lerner's book deals mainly with microeconomics, and sets out the optimisation rules for economic efficiency applicable to both capitalist and socialist economies.
4. Indeed, a main theme of his *Economics of Control* was that the issue of capitalism versus socialism was of little relevance, that one can specify optimality rules, e.g. setting marginal social benefits equal to marginal social costs, that are the same for capitalist and socialist economies.
5. Previously Friedman (1942) had already argued that we know very little about the quantitative relationships in our economy.
6. Five years earlier in a long footnote in his review article of Lerner's book Friedman (1947, pp. 414–15) had already stated the basic insight of this paper. The term 'formal' in Friedman's title should, of course, be read in the context of the time, nowadays this paper would not be considered 'formal'.
7. There is, however, at least one paper that seems to criticise Friedman's conclusion without citing his paper. Buiter (1981) showed that a closed-loop system, that is a system in which policy responds to the state of the economy, is superior to an open-loop system. This is formally correct if, as Buiter assumes, the authorities respond correctly. His results can readily be obtained within Friedman's framework. As long as R is negative there is some stabilisation policy, however weak, that reduces the variance of income. Hence, in a formal sense, Friedman's scepticism with respect to any countercyclical policy however small cannot be justified on the basis of lags and forecast errors alone. But this does not have much practical significance. If R though negative is very small in absolute terms, then even an ideal countercyclical policy would reduce fluctuations ony slightly. For example, suppose that $R = -0.2$. Then, on the strong assumption that the central bank estimates correctly the effect of its policy actions on GDP it could eliminate only 4 per cent of the GDP variance. But since it is uncertain about the effect of its policy it should aim at less than 4 per cent, say 2 per cent. Since even that modest goal is worth achieving it may seem that Buiter has refuted Friedman. But Friedman did not claim that due to lags and forecast errors stabilisation policy cannot reduce GDP fluctuation at all. He only claimed that lags and forecast errors severely limit the feasible extent of stabilisation even if central banks single-mindely pursue a stabilisation goal, and then went on to argue that they do not behave that way.
8. I have two grounds for saying this. First, over the years I have followed this literature closely, and do not recollect such a paper. Second, I undertook an admittedly not exhaustive (but certainly exhausting) search of the

SSCI for the years 1955–74 when the paper, being new, is most likely to have evoked a critical response. I did not cover subsequent years because of the labour involved in tracking down references to this paper. The SSCI index lists a vast number of references to Friedman's *Essays in Positive Economics*, but only a small proportion of these relate to this particular essay.

9. Friedman and Meiselman (1963) also measured the lag by running lagged correlations between money and income. These suggest a three–four quarter lag. But Friedman and Meiselman's analysis is problematic, see Modigliani and Ando (1965) and DePrano and Mayer (1965).
10. For a survey of the earlier studies see (Mayer, 1967). For an example of an approach that subsequently became widespread see Cagan and Gandolfi (1969). Hammond (1996) provides a thorough discussion of the debate on Friedman's lag estimate.
11. Kareken and Solow estimate lags for various types of expenditures, but do not combine them into an overall lag. When one does so, one obtains a lag that is not shorter than Friedman's, see Mayer (1967). In general, the Kareken–Solow paper appears to be somewhat incomplete, which might perhaps be explained by having been written under a deadline.
12. Part of Friedman's (1970) reply to Tobin is that his conclusion that money is causal is based much more on historical evidence drawn from specific instances than on the sequence of turning points. Indeed, he has referred to the turning point evidence as: 'by no means decisive' (Friedman, 1961, p. 449). But that weakens the case for inferring the length of the lag from a comparison of turning points.
13. In a paper which for some reason did not make the impact on the debate that it deserves, Donald Tucker (1966) pointed out that the relevant lag is not measured correctly by the length of time it takes a dollar of new money to raise GDP. Suppose that it takes a long time for firms to increase investment when interest rates fall. If so, to equilibrate the money market interest rates have to fall further than they would do otherwise, thus stimulating additional investment early in the period and reducing the weighted mean lag. This makes the story much more complicated, with the timing of the effect of monetary policy now depending on lags in the money demand function as well as on lags in the expenditure functions. However, Tucker's argument applies only if the central bank sets a certain growth in the money supply (which is what monetarists recommend) and not if it sets the interest rate.
14. At certain times considerably more of the effect of monetary policy may occur in sectors which have a relatively short lag, such as consumption expenditures and residential construction, than at other times.
15. The only attempt during the period discussed to assess Friedman's challenge directly is, as far as I know, a paper (Mayer, 1958) which deals primarily with the length of the lag, but does plug some numbers into the sum-of-variances equation as more or less an afterthought. It suggests that a small degree of cyclical fluctuation is feasible. Subsequent to the period discussed here I made a more elaborate attempt to implement Friedman's analysis empirically (Mayer, 1990b, Chapter 5), but that attempt has met with a quite negative reaction.

16. Table 5.1 comes from a model comparison undertaken in the mid-1970s. More recent model comparisons also show substantial differences in the impact multipliers (see Mayer, 1990b, p. 102).
17. For a similar statement a few years later, see Friedman (1983).
18. Because of my unfortunate ignorance about the history of central banking in other countries, I confine the discussion to the United States.
19. Peter Temin's defence of the Fed does not seem convincing; see Mayer (1978).
20. However, twelve years later, in discussing a longer period, 1952 to October 1979, Friedman (1982) argued that the Fed began to pay increasing lip service to a monetary aggregates target, but that this did not change its procedures.
21. These four categories do not, of course, present distinct divisions in the sense that a particular characteristic of central bank behaviour can fall into only one of them.
22. In 1979 a sharp change in monetary policy occurred without a change in presidents. And the same was true of 1982. A political scientist, not identified with monetarism, John Woolley (1984, p. 111), reaches the more moderate verdict that 'Rather than conclude that presidents generally get the monetary policy they want, it would be more accurate to say that only infrequently are presidents extremely unhappy with the monetary policy they get'.
23. State-chartered banks have a choice whether to be member banks.
24. In 1994 the Fed greatly reduced this uncertainty by releasing at each Federal Open Market Committee meeting its target for the federal funds rate.
25. Shortly after Friedman wrote this, the reserve requirement system was changed.
26. Thus Levin and Meulendyke (1982) show that Friedman's criticism of the Fed's open market churning is flawed.
27. One reason why it is so difficult to test the political business cycle hypothesis is that, at least for the United States with its four-year electoral cycle, there are so few observations. Secondly, it is not clear whether the statement 'there are political business cycles' is intended to mean that they occur at all presidential elections, at many of these elections, or that there has been at least one political business cycle in the post-war period. Carter's bid for a second term provides evidence against the first proposition, while Nixon's successful pressure on the Fed in 1972 (see Woolley, 1995) provides evidence for the third proposition. In countries with a parliamentary system there is an additional problem: elections are sometimes endogenous with respect to economic conditions.
28. For an exception see Meiselman (1986). That monetarists pay little attention to political business cycles is not likely to be due to the rational expectations criticism of conventional political business cycle theory since Friedman is hardly a strong supporter of rational expectations. Moreover, the rational expectations case against political business cycles is weak (see Mayer, 1993).
29. Much, but not all, of it is reprinted in Toma and Toma (1987).
30. Useful sources are Thaler (1991, 1993). For an interesting application of such analysis to decision making in another area of public policy, foreign

policy, see Vertzberger (1990). For an attempt to apply cognitive dissonance theory to monetary policy, see Mayer (1990a, Chapter 16).

31. Time-inconsistency refers to a situation in which a policy that is rational at one time is no longer rational at a later time. For example, it may be rational to tell a child it will be punished if it does a certain thing. But after it does so, punishment will not undo its action.
32. I say they 'may' rather than they 'do', because all an opponent of stabilisation policy has to show is that the effect of these problems when combined *with the effects of lags and forecast errors* make stabilisation policy counterproductive.
33. There may, of course, be some Keynesians who have taken the monetarists' argument seriously; I do not claim to have read the entire literature. But if so, their position is unusual and out of the Keynesian mainstream.
34. As Bronfenbrenner (1966, p. 174) put it: 'The optimal discretionary authority (call him Superman) will always outperform any rule limiting his discretion . . . Making a case against Superman is like making a case against Santa Claus. The first question is, 'Does he exist?'
35. As Fischer (1990, p. 1173n.) points out: 'Even aside from Switzerland and Germany, it is clear from history that inflationary bias is only a sometime thing.' Michael Mussa (1994, p. 139n.), in discussing the US inflation of the late 1960s and 1970s, points out that 'there is little factual support' for the hypothesis that the Fed generated this inflation to deceive the public' (see also Mayer, 1993, pp. 63–6).
36. Furthermore, policy makers may well have an exaggerated idea of their own abilities, and hence adopt policies that are too risky. They have become policy makers because they have been successful in the past. Part of their success was due to luck, part due to ability. It is only natural to underestimate the role of luck and overestimate the role of ability in one's success.
37. Modigliani appears to define 'value judgments' very broadly to include what conventionally would be called 'prejudice' or 'presuppositions' (see Modigliani and Friedman, 1977, p. 10).
38. Goldfeld (1982) provides a useful summary of some of the arguments.
39. For the period 1959–60 to 1981–2 the adjusted R^2s between the annual growth rates of M1 and M2, M1 and M3 and M2 and M3 are 0.30, 0.46 and 0.61 respectively. For the 1982–3 to 1993–4 period they are 0.02, 0.00 and 0.85. These R^2 come from regressions unadjusted for serial correlation, despite some of the Durbin–Watson statistics being very low, because they are not intended to search for causality, or even for a good forecast, but merely to show how different a policy of stable M1 growth would be from a policy of, say, stable M2 growth.
40. Weak, but not entirely groundless. Since the central bank cannot tell right away whether a change in velocity is cyclical or secular, if it refrains from responding to what it thinks are only cyclical changes it will tend to be late in responding to secular changes.
41. In an earlier study using seventeen countries Argy (1971)had obtained inconclusive results, but as Argy points out, his procedure biases the results against the monetary growth-rate rule.
42. Friedman's argument is that recessions occur when money is growing at a slower rate than the public expects, and that the public forms its expecta-

tions regressively. Tobin (1983, p. 508) also argues that from 1950 until 1973, a 'remarkably stable' period the Fed was 'vague, responsive and active'. But it was so also in the subsequent less successful period.

43. In addition, as the debate originated by Christina Romer (1983) has shown, the difference in stability is not as great as was believed in the 1970s.
44. Feedback rules are rules which set out how policy will respond to specific developments.
45. It may seem strange to call a hypothesis about the behaviour of central bankers a hard-core proposition. But the importance of Keynes's own faith in the goodwill and ability of an intellectual governing class formed an important part of his political views (see Buchanan and Wagner, 1977, pp. 78–81). In the United States some eminent Keynesians seem to take a somewhat similar position.
46. See Mayer (1994). The flavour of such an attitude is conveyed by the following statement of Modigliani 'Nonmonetarists accept what I regard to be the fundamental practical message of *The General Theory*: that a private enterprise economy . . . *needs* to be stabilised, *can* be stabilised, and therefore *should* be stabilized' (Modigliani, 1977, p. 1, emphasis in original).
47. There is the story of a businessman who told a friend that he plans to hire a one-armed economist because he is tired of hearing his current economist say 'on the one hand . . ., but on the other'. His friend said, 'yes, but before you hire such an economist ask him how he came to lose his other arm'.
48. Thus Feyerabend (1995, p. 64) reports: 'An iron curtain formed by a firm belief in the excellence of Maxwell's equations, and so on and so forth, protected physics from Ehrenhaft – an iron curtain of precisely the same kind as had protected Galileo's opponents'.

References

Adams, F.G. and L. Klein (1990) 'Performance of Econometric Models of the United States', in Lawrence Klein (ed.), *Comparative Performance of U.S. Econometric Models* (New York: Oxford University Press).

Argy, V. (1971) 'Rules, Discretion in Monetary Management and Short-Term Stability', *Journal of Money, Credit and Banking*, vol. 3 (February), pp. 102–22.

——— (1979) 'Monetary Stabilization and the Stabilization of Output in Selected Industrial Countries', *Banca Nazionale del Lavoro, Quarterly Review*, no. 129 (June), pp. 155–66.

Attiyeh, R. (1966) 'Rules versus Discretion: A Comment', *Journal of Political Economy*, vol. 73, pp. 170–2.

Baumol, W. (1961) 'Pitfalls in Contracyclical Policies: Some Tools and Results', *Review of Economics and Statistics*, vol. 43 (February), pp. 21–6.

Beck, N. (1990) 'Political Monetary Cycles', in Thomas Mayer (ed.), *The Political Economy of American Monetary Policy* (New York: Cambridge University Press).

——— (1991) 'The Fed and Political Business Cycles', *Contemporary Policy Issues*, vol. 9 (April), pp. 1–14.

Benishay, H. (1971) 'A Framework for the Evaluation of Short-term Fiscal and Monetary Policy', *Journal of Money, Credit and Banking*, vol. 4 (November), pp. 779–810.

Blinder, A. (1987) 'The Rules-versus-Discretion Debate in the Light of Recent Experience', *Weltwirtschaftliches Archiv*, vol. 73, no. 3, pp. 399–413.

Boland, L. (1994) 'Scientific Thinking Without Scientific Method', in R. Backhouse, *New Directions in Economic Methodology* (London: Routledge), pp. 154–72.

Brainard, W. and J. Tobin (1968) 'Pitfalls in Financial Model Building', *American Economic Review*, vol. 58 (May), pp. 99–122.

Bronfenbrenner, M. (1961a) 'Statistical Tests of Rival Monetary Rules', *Journal of Political Economy*, vol. 69 (February), pp. 1–14.

——— (1961b) 'Statistical Tests of Rival Monetary Rules: Quarterly Data Supplement', *Journal of Political Economy*, vol. 69 (December), pp. 621–5.

——— (1966) 'Monetary Rules: A New Look', *Journal of Law and Economics*, vol. 8 (October), pp. 173–94.

Brunner, K. (1980) 'The Control of Monetary Aggregates', in Federal Reserve Bank of Boston, *Controlling Monetary Aggregates III* (Boston: Federal Reserve Bank of Boston).

——— (1981a) 'Policymaking, Accountability and the Social Responsibility of the Fed', in Shadow Open Market Committee, *Policy Statement and Position Papers, March 15–16, 1981* (Rochester: Graduate School of Management, University of Rochester).

——— (1981b) 'The Case Against Monetary Activism', *Lloyds Bank Review*, vol. 39 (Spring), pp. 20–39.

——— (1983a) 'Has Monetarism Failed?', *The Cato Journal*, vol. 3, pp. 23–62.

——— (1983b) 'The Pragmatic Intellectual Tradition of Monetary Policymaking and the International Monetary Order', *Schriften des Vereins für Socialpolitik, Gesellschaft für Wirtschaft und Sozialwissenschaften*, vol. 138 (January), pp. 97–142.

——— (1984) 'Monetary Policy and the Monetary Order', *Aussenwirtschaft*, no. 3, pp. 187–206.

Brunner, K. and A. Meltzer (1964a) *Some General Features of the Federal Reserve Approach to Policy*, US Congress, House, Committee on Banking and Currency, Subcommittee on Domestic Finance, 88th Congress, 2nd session.

——— (1964b) *The Federal Reserve's Attachment to the Free Reserves Concept*, US Congress, House, Committee on Banking and Currency, Subcommittee on Domestic Finance, 88th Congress, 2nd session.

——— (1983) 'Strategies and Tactics for Monetary Control', *Carnegie–Rochester Conference Series on Public Policy*, vol. 18 (Spring), pp. 59–104.

——— (1989) *Monetary Economics* (Oxford: Basil Blackwell).

Brunner, K., *et al.* (1985) *Monetary Policy and Monetary Policy Regimes* (Rochester: Graduate School of Management, University of Rochester).

Buchanan, J. and R. Wagner (1977) *Democracy in Deficit* (New York: Academic Press).

Buiter, W. (1981) 'The Superiority of Contingent Rules over Fixed Rules in

Models with Rational Expectations', *Economic Journal*, vol. 91 (September), pp. 647–71.

Cagan, P. and A. Gandolfi (1969) 'The Lag in Monetary Policy as Implied by the Time Pattern of Monetary Effects on Interest Rates', *American Economic Review*, vol. 59 (May), pp. 277–84.

Cargill, T. and J. Meyer (1978) 'The Time Varying Response of Income to Changes in Monetary and Fiscal Policy', *Review of Economics and Statistics*, vol. 60 (February), pp. 1–7.

Colander, D. (1994a) 'Vision, Judgment, and Disagreement Among Economists', *Journal of Economic Methodology*, vol. 1 (June), pp. 33–42.

——— (1994b) 'The Art of Economics by the Numbers', in R. Backhouse, *New Directions in Economic Methodology* (London, Routledge), pp. 35–49.

Cooper, J.P. (1974) *Development of the Monetary Sector, Prediction and Policy Analysis in the FRB–MIT–Penn Model* (Lexington: Lexington Books).

Cooper, J.P. and S. Fischer (1972a) 'Simulations of Monetary Rules in the FRB–MIT–Penn Model', *Journal of Money, Credit and Banking*, vol. 4 (May), pp. 384–96.

——— (1972b) 'Stabilization Policy and Lags: Summary and Extension', *Annals of Social and Economic Measurement*, vol. 1 (October), pp. 407–18.

——— (1974) 'Monetary and Fiscal Policy in a Fully Stochastic St. Louis Econometric Model', *Journal of Money, Credit and Banking*, vol. 6 (February), pp. 1–22.

Cornwall, J. (1965) 'The Structure of Fiscal Models', *Quarterly Journal of Economics*, vol. 79 (November), pp. 608-22.

Craine, R., A. Havenner and J. Berry (1978) 'Fixed Rules vs. Activism in the Conduct of Monetary Policy', *American Economic Review*, vol. 68 (December), pp. 769–83.

Culbertson, J. (1960) 'Friedman on the Lag in the Effect of Monetary Policy', *Journal of Political Economy*, vol. 68 (December), pp. 617–21.

——— (1961) 'The Lag in the Effect of Monetary Policy: Reply', *Journal of Political Economy*, vol. 69 (October), pp. 467–77.

Cukierman, A. and A. Meltzer (1986) 'A Positive Theory of Discretionary Policy, the Cost of Democratic Government and the Benefits of a Constitution', *Economic Inquiry*, vol. 24 (July), pp. 367–89.

DePrano, M. and T. Mayer (1965) 'Tests of the Relative Importance of Autonomous Expenditures and Money', *American Economic Review*, vol. 55 (September), pp. 729–52.

Fand, D. (1986) 'Comment', *The Cato Journal*, vol. 6, Fall, pp. 581–6.

Feyerabend Paul K. (1995) *Killing Time* (Chicago: University of Chicago Press).

Fischer, S. (1990) 'Rules Versus Discretion in Monetary Policy', in B. Friedman and F. Hahn (eds) *Handbook of Monetary Economics*, vol. 2 (Amsterdam: North-Holland).

Fischer, S. and J. Cooper (1973) 'Stabilization Policy and Lags', *Journal of Political Economy*, vol. 81 (July–August), pp. 847–77.

Fix, R. and C. Sivesind (1978) 'An Assessment of the Income Stabilization Impact of Monetary Policy in Twelve Industrialized Countries', *Journal of Money, Credit and Banking*, vol. 10 (November), pp. 476–90.

Friedman, B.M. (1975) *Economic Stabilization Policy: Methods in Optimization* (Amsterdam: North-Holland).

——— (1988) 'Conducting Monetary Policy by Controlling Currency Plus Noise: A Comment', *Carnegie–Rochester Conference Series on Public Policy*, vol. 29 (Autumn), pp. 205–12.

Friedman, M. (1942) 'Discussion of the Inflationary Gap', *American Economic Review*, vol. 32 (June), pp. 308–14.

——— (1947) 'Lerner on the Economics of Control', *Journal of Political Economy*, vol. 55 (September), pp. 405–16.

——— (1953) *Essays in Positive Economics* (Chicago, University of Chicago Press).

——— (1958) 'The Supply of Money and Changes in Prices and Output', in US Congress, Joint Economic Committee, *The Relationship of Prices to Economic Stability and Growth: Compendium* (Washington, DC: Government Printing Office).

——— (1960) *A Program For Monetary Stability* (New York: Fordham University Press).

——— (1961) 'The Lag in the Effect of Monetary Policy', *Journal of Political Economy*, vol. 69 (October), pp. 447–66.

——— (1968) *Dollars and Deficits* (Englewood Cliffs, NJ: Prentice-Hall).

——— (1970) 'Money and Income: Post Hoc Ergo Propter Hoc?: Comment', *Quarterly Journal of Economics*, vol. 84 (May), pp. 318–27.

——— (1982) 'Monetary Policy, Theory and Practice', *Journal of Money, Credit and Banking*, vol. 14 (February), pp. 1–19.

——— (1983) 'Monetarism in Theory and Practice', *Monetary and Economic Studies*, vol. 1 (October), pp. 1–14.

——— (1986) 'Economists and Economic Policy', *Economic Inquiry*, vol. 24 (January), pp. 1–10.

Friedman, M. and W. Heller (1969) *Monetary vs. Fiscal Policy* (New York: W.W. Norton).

Friedman, M. and D. Meiselman (1963) 'The Relative Stability of Monetary Velocity and the Investment Multiplier in the United States, 1897–1958', in Commission on Money and Credit, *Stabilization Policies* (Englewood Cliffs, NJ: Prentice-Hall).

Friedman, M. and A. Schwartz (1963a) 'Money and Business Cycles', *Review of Economics and Statistics*, vol. 45 (February), *Supplement*, pp. 32–64.

——— (1963b) *A Monetary History of the United States, 1867–1960* (Princeton: Princeton University Press).

Fromm, G. and L. Klein (1976) 'The NBER/NSF Model Comparison Seminar: An Analysis of Results', *Annals of Economic and Social Measurement*, vol. 5 (Winter), pp. 1–28.

Goldfeld, S. (1982) 'Rules, Discretion and Reality', *American Economic Review*, vol. 72 (May), pp. 361–6.

Gordon, R. (1970) *Milton Friedman's Monetary Framework* (Chicago: University of Chicago Press).

Hammond, D. (1996) *Theory and Measurement* (New York: Cambridge University Press).

Hausman, D. (1992) *The Inexact and Separate Science of Economics* (Cambridge and New York: Cambridge University Press).

Havrilesky, T. (1993) *The Pressures on American Monetary Policy* (Boston: Kluwer Academic Publishers).

Hetzel, R. (1986) 'A Congressional Mandate for Monetary Policy', *The Cato Journal*, vol. 5 (Winter), pp. 797–820.
Holbrook, R. (1972) 'Optimal Economic Policy and the Problem of Instrument Instability', *American Economic Review*, vol. 62 (March), pp. 57–65.
Kane, E. (1990) 'Bureaucratic Self-Interest as an Obstacle to Monetary Reform', in T. Mayer (ed.), *The Political Economy of American Monetary Policy* (New York: Cambridge University Press).
Kareken, J. and R. Solow (1963) 'Lags in Fiscal and Monetary Policy', in Commission on Money and Credit, *Stabilization Policies* (Englewood Cliffs, NJ: Prentice-Hall), pp. 1–163.
Keynes, J.M. (1921) *A Treatise on Probability* (London: Macmillan).
——— (1924) *A Tract on Monetary Reform* (London, Macmillan).
——— (1936) *The General Theory of Employment, Interest and Money* (London: Macmillan).
Klein, D. (1994) 'If Government is So Villainous, How Come Government Officials Don't Seem Like Villains?', *Economics and Philosophy*, vol. 10 (April), pp. 91–106.
Lerner, A. (1944) *The Economics of Control* (New York: Macmillan).
——— (1962) 'Review of *A Program for Monetary Stability*', *Journal of the American Statistical Association*, vol. 57 (March), pp. 211–20.
Levin, F. and A. Meulendyke (1982) 'Monetary Policy: Theory and Practice, Comment', *Journal of Money, Credit and Banking*, vol. 14 (November), pp. 399–403.
Lombra, R. (1988) 'Monetary Policy: The Rhetoric vs. the Record', in T. Willett (ed.), *Political Business Cycles* (Durham, NC: Duke University Press).
Lombra, R. and N. Karamouzis (1990) 'A Positive Analysis of the Policy-Making Process at the Federal Reserve', in T. Mayer (ed.), *The Political Economy of American Monetary Policy* (New York: Cambridge University Press), pp. 181–96.
Lombra, R. and M. Moran (1980) 'Policy Advice and Policymaking at the Federal Reserve', in *Carnegie–Rochester Conference Series on Public Policy*, vol. 13 (Autumn), pp. 9–68.
Lovell, M. and E. Prescott (1968) 'Money, Multiplier-Accelerator Interaction, and the Business Cycle', *Southern Economic Journal*, vol. 35 (July), pp. 60–72.
Mäki, U. (1992) 'Social Conditioning of Economics', in N. de Marchi (ed.), *Post-Popperian Methodology in Economic: Recovering Practice* (Boston: Kluwer Academic Publishers).
Mayer, T. (1958) 'The Inflexibility of Monetary Policy', *Review of Economics and Statistics*, vol. 40 (November), pp. 358–74.
——— (1967) 'The Lag in the Effect of Monetary Policy', *Western Economic Journal* (*Economic Inquiry*), vol. 5 (September), pp. 324–42.
——— (1978) 'Money and the Great Depression: A Critique of Professor Temin's Thesis', *Explorations in Economic History*, vol. 15 (April), pp. 125–45.
——— (1990a) 'Minimizing Regret: Cognitive Dissonance as an Explanation of FOMC Behavior', in T. Mayer (ed.), *The Political Economy of American Monetary Policy* (New York: Cambridge University Press).
——— (1990b) *Monetarism and Macroeconomic Policy* (Aldershot: Edward Elgar).
——— (1993) *Truth versus Precision in Economics* (Aldershot: Edward Elgar).

——— (1994) 'Why is There So much Disagreement Among Economists?', *Journal of Economic Methodology*, vol. 1 (June), pp. 1–14.

——— (1995) *Doing Economic Research* (Aldershot, Edward Elgar).

McCallum, B. (1988) 'Robustness Properties of a Rule for Monetary Policy', *Carnegie–Rochester Conference Series on Public Policy*, vol. 29 (Autumn), pp. 173–204.

——— (1995) 'Two Fallacies Concerning Central Bank Independence', *NBER Working Paper*, 5075 (Cambridge, MA: NBER).

McCloskey, D. (1985) *The Rhetoric of Economics* (Madison: University of Wisconsin Press).

McNees, S. (1988) 'How Accurate are Economic Forecasts?', Federal Reserve Bank of Boston, *New England Economic Review* (July–August), pp. 15–36.

McPheters, L. and M. Redman (1975) 'Rule, Semirule and Discretion during Two Decades of Monetary Policy', *Quarterly Review of Economics and Business*, vol. 15 (Spring), pp. 53–64.

Meiselman, D. (1986) 'Is there a Political Monetary Cycle?', *The Cato Journal*, vol. 6, Fall, pp. 563–79.

Meltzer, A. (1987) 'Limits of Short-Run Stabilization Policy', *Economic Inquiry*, vol. 25 (January), pp. 1–14.

Modigliani, F. (1964) 'Some Empirical Test of Monetary Management and Rules versus Discretion', *Journal of Political Economy*, vol. 72 (June), pp. 211–36.

——— (1977) 'The Monetarist Controversy or Should We Forsake Stabilization Policy?', *American Economic Review*, vol. 67 (March), pp. 1–19.

——— (1986) *The Debate over Stabilization Policy* (Cambridge: Cambridge University Press).

——— (1988) 'The Monetarist Controversy Revisited', *Contemporary Policy Issues*, vol. 6 (October), pp. 3–18.

Modigliani, F. and A. Ando (1965) 'The Relative Stability of Monetary Velocity and the Investment Multiplier', *American Economic Review*, vol. 55 (September), pp. 693–728.

——— (1976) 'Impacts of Fiscal Actions on Aggregate Income and the Monetarist Controversy: Theory and Evidence', in J. Stein (ed.), *Monetarism* (Amsterdam, North-Holland).

Modigliani, F. and M. Friedman (1977) 'The Monetarist Controversy', Federal Reserve Bank of San Francisco, *Economic Review* (Spring), pp. 5–26.

Mussa, M. (1994) 'Monetary Policy', in M. Feldstein (ed.), *American Economic Policy in the 1980s* (Chicago: University of Chicago Press).

Orr, L. (1960) 'A Note on the Inflexibility of Monetary Policy', *Review of Economics and Statistics*, vol. 42 (August), 329–31.

Phillips, A.W. (1957) 'Stabilization Policy and the Time Forms of Lagged Responses', *Economic Journal*, vol. 67 (June), pp. 265–77.

Pierce, J. (1980) 'Comments on the Lombra–Moran Paper', *Carnegie–Rochester Conference Series on Public Policy*, vol. 13 (Autumn), pp. 79–86.

——— (1990) 'The Federal Reserve as a Political Power', in T. Mayer (ed.), *The Political Economy of American Monetary Policy* (New York: Cambridge University Press).

——— (1995) 'Monetarism: the Good, the Bad and the Ugly', in K. Hoover and S. Sheffrin, *Monetarism and the Methodology of Economics: Essays in Honor of Thomas Mayer* (Aldershot: Edward Elgar).

Poole, W. (1986) 'Monetary Control and the Political Business Cycle', *The Cato Journal*, vol. 5 (Winter), pp. 685–700.

Romer, C. (1983) 'Is the Stabilization of the Postwar Economy a Figment of the Data?', *American Economic Review*, vol. 76 (June), pp. 314–34.

Roos, L. (1986) 'Inherent Conflicts of U.S. Monetary Policymaking', *The Cato Journal*, vol. 5 (Winter), pp. 771–6.

Scitovsky, T. (1984) 'Lerner's Contribution to Economics', *Journal of Economic Literature*, vol. 22 (December), pp. 1547–71.

Starleaf, D. and R. Floyd (1972) 'Some Evidence with Respect to the Efficacy of Friedman's Monetary Policy Proposals', *Journal of Money, Credit and Banking*, vol. 4 (August), pp. 713–22.

Tanner, J.E. (1979) 'Are the Lags in the Effects of Monetary Policy Variable?', *Journal of Monetary Economics*, vol. 5 (January), pp. 105–21.

Temin, P. (1976) *Did Monetary Forces Cause the Great Depression?* (New York: W.W. Norton).

Thaler, R. (1991) *Quasi Rational Economics* (New York: Russell Sage).

——— (1993) *Advances in Behavioral Finance* (New York: Russell Sage).

Tobin, J. (1965) 'The Monetary Interpretation of History', *American Economic Review*, vol. 55 (June), pp. 464–85.

——— (1970) 'Money and Income: Post Hoc, Ergo Propter Hoc?', *Quarterly Journal of Economics*, vol. 84 (May), pp. 301–17.

——— (1973) 'Monetary Policy: Rules Targets and Shocks', *Journal of Money, Credit and Banking*, vol. 15 (November), pp. 506–18.

——— (1976) 'Reply: Is Friedman a Monetarist?', in J. Stein, *Monetarism* (Amsterdam, North-Holland), pp. 332–6.

——— (1981) 'The Monetarist Counter-Revolution Today – An Appraisal', *Economic Journal*, vol. 91 (March), pp. 29–42.

——— (1983) 'Monetary Policy: Rules, Targets and Shocks', *Journal of Money, Credit and Banking*, vol. 15 (November), pp. 506–18.

Toma, E. and M. Toma (1987) *Central Bankers, Bureaucratic Incentives and Monetary Policy* (Boston: Kluwer Academic Publishers).

Tucker, D. (1966) 'Dynamic Income Adjustment to Money-supply Changes', *American Economic Review*, vol. 56 (June), pp. 433–49.

Vertzberger, Y. (1990) *The World in Their Minds* (Stanford: Stanford University Press).

Weintraub, R. (1978) 'Congressional Supervision of Monetary Policy', *Journal of Monetary Economics*, vol. 4 (April), pp. 341–63.

White, W. (1961) 'The Flexibility of Anticyclical Monetary Policy', *Review of Economics and Statistics*, vol. 43 (May), pp. 142–7.

Wicker, E. (1966) *Federal Reserve Monetary Policy, 1917–33* (New York: Random House).

Willett, T. and E. Keen (1990) 'Studying the Fed: Towards a Broader Public Choice Perspective', in T. Mayer (ed.), *The Political Economy of American Monetary Policy* (New York: Cambridge University Press).

Woolley, J. (1984) *Monetary Politics* (New York: Cambridge University Press).

——— (1994) 'The Politics of Monetary Policy: A Critical Review', *International Journal of Politics*, vol. 14 (January–March), pp. 57–85.

——— (1995) 'Nixon, Burns, 1972, and Independence in Practice', unpublished manuscript.

Comment: Mayer's Version of the Monetarist vs Keynesian Debate

Bennett T. McCallum
CARNEGIE MELLON UNIVERSITY AND NATIONAL BUREAU OF ECONOMIC RESEARCH, USA

Thomas Mayer's chapter (1996) is a rich and knowledgeable contribution on a topic that has been of great interest to many economists.[1] It is a long chapter, in which many arguments, assertions, and evaluations are put forth. Of these, I find myself in substantial agreement with a very large fraction and in enthusiastic agreement with several.[2] Nevertheless, I do have some non-trivial reservations about aspects of Mayer's discussion, so most of what follows will be devoted to an explanation of these differences. Briefly put, I think that Mayer is somewhat too negative in his characterisation of the debate as one that 'went wrong' and ultimately 'failed'.[3] Also, I think that he is wrong to limit his coverage, both temporally and substantively, and especially to downplay the paradigmatic differences between Keynesians and monetarists. In addition, I am slightly critical of his decision to single out this particular disagreement[4] between Keynesians and monetarists – there were several – as best representing a 'failed' debate. In the following paragraphs I will elaborate on these points.

First, let me argue that Mayer significantly overstates the extent to which the constant money-growth rule debate was a scientific failure, an example of a poor 'conversation'. In this regard it is important to recognise – as Mayer does in passing – that today the mainstream position among macroeconomists actually does represent a compromise that is quite close to the one that Mayer evidently regards as reasonable in light of existing theory and evidence, namely, one favouring a 'moderate' monetary policy rule that involves adjustment of money growth rates to changing conditions. That the profession came to such a position seems itself an indication that the debate was not an outright failure. More generally, however, I would contend that leaders on both sides of the debate were taking positions during the 1960s and 1970s that were not unreasonable, given their beliefs about what constitutes good scientific practice in macroeconomics.[5] To develop this argument will take a bit of discussion.

A crucial portion of Mayer's account of the debate involves Friedman's 'formal analysis' of the effects of activist stabilisation policy as developed in Friedman (1953) and outlined on pp. 259–61 of Mayer's chapter. In his original exposition, Friedman concentrates on the decomposition

$$Z(t) = X(t) + Y(t) \tag{1}$$

where $Z(t)$ represents actual income (nominal or real) in period t and $X(t)$ is the value that would prevail in the absence of any (maintained) countercyclical policy. Both these variables – and also $Y(t)$, which is defined by (1) as the component of income that is due to the ongoing existence of stabilisation policy – are appropriately thought of as measured relative to growing trends (Friedman, 1953, p. 122).[6]

Then Friedman's analysis is based on the variances[7] σ_x^2, σ_z^2, σ_y^2 and the correlation $r = \sigma_{xy}/\sigma_x \sigma_y$ (where σ_{xy}^2 is the covariance of X and Y). The crucial point is that Friedman treats all of these moments as time-invariant features of the stationary multivariate stochastic process that generates X and Y values. Then to affect σ_z^2, the policy maker is depicted by Friedman as selecting an appropriate (or perhaps inappropriate) value of σ_y^2. Depending upon the prevailing values of r and σ_x^2, the choice of σ_y^2 could either increase or decrease σ_z^2 in relation to σ_x^2.

But to an analyst working within the framework of a (presumably well specified) dynamic econometric model, the foregoing analysis appears quite inadequate. For in most such models there will be various exogenous and/or predetermined variables that will affect the *conditional* moments (means, variances, and covariances) of the components $X(t)$, $Y(t)$ and $Z(t)$. Consequently, to these analysts the specification of desirable stabilisation policy behaviour will involve period-by-period reactions that depend upon prevailing values of predetermined and exogenous variables. And from this perspective, Friedman's *unconditional* moments are simply not adequately enlightening.[8] Instead of considering such moments, the proper way to proceed would be to determine whether, within the context of a dynamic econometric model, feasible countercyclical policy responses could be useful. Thus the cited studies by Modigliani (1964), Cooper and Fischer (1972), Friedman (1975), McPheters and Redman (1975), Craine, Havenner and Berry

(1978), and others represented a rebuttal to Friedman's formal analysis that could be considered decisive by a researcher who viewed macroeconomic stabilisation issues from the perspective of estimated econometric models. And, in the years before publication of Lucas' (1976) 'critique' paper, this would include the majority of leading macroeconomics specialists.[9]

One (fatally) weak link in the Keynesian position is, of course, the presumption that the analyst has at hand a well specified and accurately estimated econometric model. Today, decades of experience have taught the profession that the acquisition of such a model is, at best, an extremely difficult task and recognition that such would be the case formed a significant part of the monetarist position, especially as presented by Brunner (1980) and Brunner and Meltzer (1983). But during the 1960s and 1970s it was perhaps not unreasonable to believe that specifying and estimating such a model was a straightforward technical task that would be achieved within a few years' time.

In light of the foregoing, it is interesting that, as indicated by Mayers, Friedman himself placed more emphasis on his political economy arguments (regarding central bank motivations) than on his 'formal analysis'. But in that case we must consider how to evaluate the Keynesians' propensity to ignore or 'dismiss . . . with disdain' (p. 277) the political economy arguments of Friedman and also Brunner and Meltzer. Here again we have a difference in the two sides' positions that is fundamentally paradigmatic. In particular, the Keynesians' overriding concern is with *normative* analysis of monetary policy behaviour, whereas this part of the monetarists' position was basically *positive* in nature. But one can see how the latter would fail to be compelling to a Keynesian, who might think that it makes no sense to argue that monetary policy *should not* be designed to be countercyclical because in the past it *had not* been conducted in that manner. An economist's principal job, after all, is to design better policies than have existed in the past.[10]

Thus the Keynesian position was not, I have argued, unreasonable given prevailing views about the scope and nature of economics. At the same time, the monetarist position regarding monetary policy makes perfectly good sense – in spite of the excessive nature of some claims, rightly noted by Mayer – if it is interpreted as prescribing not central bank behaviour, but rather institutional settings for the central bank to be placed in. Thus it seems that today one can sensibly view the Keynesian analysis to have been concerned with a central bank's way of conducting monetary policy, and the monetarist analysis to have been about an appropriate institutional setting for a central bank. From this perspective, both lines of analysis could have been valid and useful even if the participants in the debate were stressing disagreements and hurling insults at each other.

The foregoing paragraphs have already indicated some ways in which the Keynesians and monetarists of the 1960s and 1970s had substantial paradigmatic differences, with the former approaching monetary policy design through the medium of estimated econometric models and the latter strongly rejecting such an approach. Since the econometric model paradigm was at the time predominant in the macroeconomics profession, no special justification for the Keynesians' practice is needed to support my contention of the reasonableness of the two sides' positions. As for the monetarists, Friedman's methodological objection to 'Walrasian' as contrasted with 'Marshallian' analysis, mentioned in Friedman (1953, pp. 89–92; 1972, p. 920), clearly carries over into empirical studies as a preference for single-equation or non-time series studies over many-equation quarterly econometric models. For his part, Karl Brunner devoted much effort to the formal philosophy of science and, on the basis of two conferences that he organised, edited a book of papers on econometric modelling that were in large part critical of the standard practices of the time (Brunner, 1972). For these reasons, I am uncomfortable with Mayer's suggestion that paradigmatic differences were not of major importance in the debate.

Let me now turn to Mayer's decision not to 'take up the subsequent debate between the Keynesians and the New Classicals' and also his decision to limit the time frame to 1947–87. These two limitations are of course related, since the new classical school became progressively larger and more influential during the 1980s.[11] But the problem is this: as Brunner and Meltzer came to embrace the rational expectations (RE) hypothesis, and as Robert Lucas, John Taylor and myself came to think of ourselves as very close relatives of the monetarists,[12] the distinction between monetarist and new classical positions became quite unclear. Thus to limit the analysis as Mayer has done is to lose sight of ways in which the debate did in fact successfully proceed along rational and constructive lines.[13] Also, the development of the dynamic-inconsistency line of argument, in the work of Kydland and Prescott (1977) and Barro and Gordon (1983), drastically altered the terms of the discussion – and did so before 1987. In particular, these papers emphasised that the distinction between activist and non-activist policies is different from the distinction between rules and discretion, at least given their now-standard definition of the latter.[14] Mayer's discussion suffers to an extent, I believe, from a failure to be clear about this distinction.

On the other hand, one could criticise Mayer for not actually observing his own chosen limitations. Thus in a few places he mentions issues that actually pertain to the Keynesian versus new classical debate, rather than to the one that he means to be concerned with. For example, on p. 292 he says that Buiter (1981) seems to criticise Friedman's conclusion without citing his paper. But Buiter's argument was directed at the policy ineffectiveness proposition that played a major role in early new classical/RE analysis. A second place is in Mayer's reference (p. 268) to the Lucas critique. In addition, his own time-span limitation is violated extensively in the discussion.

In addition, although not in direct criticism of Mayer, I would like to mention an aspect of the Keynesian–monetarist debate, that in my opinion has reflected a truly drastic communication failure. This is the belief, voiced by numerous Keynesians and other anti-monetarists, that monetarist conclusions rely upon a presumption that in practice central banks typically behave in ways that render money-stock growth rates *exogenous*.[15] Since in fact most central banks use operating procedures that involve interest rate instruments, and even more generally since activist responses to inflation rates, unemployment rates, exchange rates, and other aggregative variables are a central feature of actual behaviour, such a presumption would clearly be counterfactual and thus invalidate monetarist conclusions. But of course Friedman, Brunner and Meltzer have never contended that typical central bank behaviour does *in fact* feature exogenous money growth rates. On the contrary, these writers have frequently been critical of actual central banks precisely because of their responses (in terms of money growth rates) to cyclical conditions.[16] Since the belief in question is so clearly counterfactual, the fact that it has been held by anti-monetarists is a compelling indication that these individuals were not reading monetarist writings with any degree of thoroughness. Nevertheless, it must be admitted that Friedman and Schwartz (1963, pp. 686–95), for example, have written passages that if taken in isolation and read hurriedly could conceivably lead critics to the belief that money growth exogeneity was a presumption of monetarist analysis of the historical record.

In conclusion, I would like to add that, although several of my comments above are more sympathetic to the Keynesian side of the debate, it is my judgement that on most of the basic disputes – the presence or absence of a long-run trade-off between inflation and unemployment, for example, or the efficacy of monetary versus fiscal policy actions for stabilisation purposes – the monetarist position has (rightly) won out. Indeed, today's mainstream macroeconomists who call themselves Keynesians, and conduct intellectual battles with proponents of the real-business cycle school, mostly subscribe to views that are much closer to 1970s monetarism than 1970s Keynesianism.

Notes

1. In particular, it has been of active interest to me since 1963, when I began my training in economics at the Ph D level. Prior to that, I had read the challenge to activist orthodoxy in Friedman's *Capitalism and Freedom* (1962, pp. 53–5), which struck me as outrageous but fascinating. Mayer himself has, of course, discussed the debate extensively (e.g. in Mayer, 1978).
2. For example, his conjecture that 'the vehemence of the debate may be due to some extent to . . . the Chicago school sharply disagreeing with other economists on so many issues, and . . . Friedman being so strongly identified with pronounced free market views' and that 'the profession's great emphasis on the application of sophisticated techniques probably also played a part' in inhibiting communications.
3. At the time of the conference, the chapter's subtitle was 'A Study of a Failed Debate'.
4. That is, the disagreement over the desirability of a constant money-growth rule. In McCallum (1981), I argued that it would be more valuable to consider disagreements over more fundamental beliefs about the economy that led monetarists and Keynesians to reach different conclusions regarding the desirability of such a rule.
5. This statement should not be interpreted as an assertion that it is crucial for the success of a debate for the initial participants to come to an agreement. I view the scientific process as a communal effort, in which it is not necessary (for example) for one individual to both develop a hypothesis and also conduct tests (i.e. possible falsifications) of it.
6. It might be even better to think of them as measured relative to some 'natural rate' path of (real) income.
7. These are unconditional variances of the variates generated by a multivariate stochastic process that is assumed to be stationary, and thus to have the same unconditional moments for each t (although the conditional moments will in general be different from period to period as the conditioning values of predetermined variables differ).
8. It is also possible that these analysts reasoned that r would not be structural – i.e. policy invariant. Such would certainly be the judgement of most economists today.
9. The discussion of these last two paragraphs implies, moreover, that the evaluation of average (unconditional) lengths of policy-effect 'lags' is not the crucial consideration.

10. Today, of course, the design of better institutions is widely regarded as a more appropriate job description.
11. Mayer does not define what he means by 'new classical'. Clearly the term implies adoption of rational expectations, but whether a belief in complete price flexibility is also required is unclear. For the purposes at hand, I think this issue is not critical.
12. What, for that matter, differentiates Stanley Fischer from monetarists?
13. Indeed, one might with some justification caricature Mayer's argument as one that halts coverage of the debate just before it is resolved, and then criticises it for not producing a resolution!
14. That this definition is not entirely clear is argued in McCallum (1994). It is my view, incidentally, that Mayer's three-way distinction among strict rules, moderate rules and discretion is not satisfactory. One reason is that discretion is not clearly spelled out; another is that the notion of changing the money growth rate 'in response to supply shocks, or to perceived secular changes in velocity [or] in potential real growth, but not for the sake of undertaking countercyclical policy' is ambiguous since such shocks will have cyclical effects.
15. Exogenous, that is, to other principal macroeconomic variables. Technically, for x to be exogenous to y, it must be statistically independent of current and past values of the latter.
16. See, for example, Friedman (1960, pp. 40–3); Brunner and Meltzer (1983).

References

Barro, R.J. and D.B. Gordon (1983) 'A Positive Theory of Monetary Policy in a Natural-Rate Model', *Journal of Political Economy*, vol. 91, 589–610.

Brunner, K. (1980) 'The Control of Monetary Aggregates,' in *Controlling Monetary Aggregates III* (Boston: Federal Reserve Bank of Boston).

——— (1992) *Problems and Issues Current Econometric Practice* (Columbus, OH: Ohio State University Press).

Brunner, K. and A.H. Meltzer (1964) *The Federal Reserve's Attachment to the Free Reserves Concept*, US Congress, House Committee on Banking and Currency, Subcommittee on Domestic Finance, 88th Congress, 2nd session.

——— (1983) 'Strategies and Tactics for Monetary Control', *Carnegie–Rochester Conference Series on Public Policy*, 18 (Spring), 59–104.

Buiter, W. (1981) 'The Superiority of Contingent Rules over Fixed Rules in Models with Rational Expectations', *Economic Journal*, vol. 91 (September), 647–71.

Cooper, J.P. and S. Fischer (1972) 'Simulations of Monetary Rules in the FRB–MIT–Penn Model', *Journal of Money, Credit, and Banking*, vol. 4 (May), 384–96.

Craine, R., A.Havenner and J. Berry (1978) 'Fixed Rules vs. Activism in the Conduct of Monetary Policy', *American Economic Review*, vol. 68 (December), 769–83.

Friedman, B.M. (1975) *Economic Stabilization Policy: Methods in Optimization* (Amsterdam: North-Holland).

Friedman, M. (1953) *Essays in Positive Economics* (Chicago: University of Chicago Press).

——— (1960) *A Program for Monetary Stability* (New York: Fordham University Press).

——— (1962) *Capitalism and Freedom* (Chicago: University of Chicago Press).

——— (1972) 'Comments on the Critics', *Journal of Political Economy*, vol. 80, 906–50.

Friedman, M. and A.J. Schwartz (1963) *A Monetary History of the United States, 1867–1960* (Princeton: Princeton University Press).

Kydland, F.E., and E.C. Prescott (1977) 'Rules Rather than Discretion: The Inconsistency of Optimal Plans', *Journal of Political Economy*, 85, 473–90.

Lucas, R.E., Jr (1976) 'Econometric Policy Evaluation: A Critique', *Carnegie–Rochester Conference Series on Public Policy*, vol. 1, 19–46.

Mayer, T. (1978) *The Structure of Monetarism* (New York: W.W. Norton).

——— (1996) 'Monetarists and Keynesians on Central Banking: A Study of a Failed Debate', Working Paper; now Chapter 5 in this volume.

McCallum, B.T. (1981) 'Monetarist Principles and the Money Stock Growth Rule', *American Economic Review Papers and Proceedings*, vol. 71, 134–8.

——— (1994) 'Discretion versus Policy Rules in Practice: Two Critical Points: A Comment', *Carnegie–Rochester Conference Series on Public Policy*, 39, 215–20.

McPheters, L. and M. Redman (1975) 'Rule, Semirule, and Discretion during Two Decades of Monetary Policy', *Quarterly Review of Economics and Business*, vol. 15 (Spring), 53–64.

Meltzer, A.H. (1984) 'Overview', *Price Stability and Public Policy*, Federal Reserve Bank of Kansas City.

Modigliani, F. (1964) 'Some Empirical Tests of Monetary Management and Rules versus Discretion', *Journal of Political Economy*, vol. 72 (June), 211–36.

Comment: Technical Task Uncertainty in Economics

Nancy J. Wulwick
BINGHAMTON UNIVERSITY, USA

The modern philosophy of science typically has concerned the conflict between the received view of science associated with logical positivism and the criticism of the received view, the *Weltanschauungen* analyses of Kuhn and Feyerabend, among others (Suppe, 1977, pp. 6, 125). Science, according to the received view, is a unified, rigorous deductive system precisely tested against independently given quantified, empirical observations. The critics have held that real world science has contradicted positivist prescriptions for science. For the critics who seek merely to describe what scientists do, 'anything goes'. Thomas Mayer (1993, 1995), an applied economist, has turned the argument between the received view and its critics virtually on its head; to his mind, economists have shown good sense in neglecting the overly ambitious positivist prescriptions. But, Mayer cautions, the neglect of bad prescriptions does not imply that economists need no methodological rules at all.

Mayer, a self-described 'reflective positivist', sees economics ultimately as a field that solves practical, empirical problems in the public policy arena. Thus, the empirical economic scientist requires both the ingenuity of the dentist treating unique maladies and the general analytic abilities of the theoretical physicist. In Mayer's vision, the economist like the statistician should have a good feel for data and sound intuition rooted in common sense. The experiences of Mayer and his 'exemplar', Milton Friedman, as monetary economists have confirmed their Marshallian outlook on economic method (Mayer, 1993, dedication, p. 5). After all, monetary theory, as Hicks perceived, 'belongs to monetary history, in a way that economic theory does not always belong to economic history. Indeed, it does so in two ways. . . . [A] large part of the best work on Money is topical . . . [M]oney itself has been evolving' (1967, pp. 156–7). So, in the Marshallian image, simple statistical modelling, abduction (the meshing of short chains of deductive reasoning with practical insights), and explanations of every aspect of economic life (however mundane or grand) have marked Mayer's approach to economics.

Mayer's chapter is an historical case study of applied monetary economics. The essay studies the debates between academic economists during 1947–87 about central bank intervention in the real world economy. The debates focused on alternative kinds of intervention, including the discretionary contracyclical policy proposed by Keynesian economists and the steady money-growth rate rule proposed by monetarist economists. Mayer, in studying the historical debates, raises important issues for philosophers of science. What, Mayer asks, did economists really know about the effects of central bank intervention? What evidence did the economists present? Did they have good reasons to support their positions? The chapter shows that economists with contrasting policy preferences exaggerated their claims to knowledge about the effects of intervention. The debate deepened 'battle lines' that rational discourse would have diminished. Economists narrowed the range of feasible policy alternatives, neglected to answer key empirical questions raised by the opposition, and groundlessly read into what empirical results they did reach definite confirmation of their partisan positions.

Mayer's case study suggests the presence of four constraints on the commitment to knowledge of Keynesians and monetarists.

(1) *Audience*: Monetary policy in drawing lay audiences with particular interests exposes economic discourse to external, or non-scientific influences.
(2) *Ideology*: Keynesians' gut reaction to economic problems was that there must be something economists can do to improve the real economy. Monetarists reckoned that nothing economists could do would make the real world better.
(3) *Institutional carriers*: University graduate programmes transmitted the dispute about monetary policy to future faculty members.
(4) *Technical task uncertainty*: Empirical research failed to modify views of the disputants partly because each party arrived at conflicting empirical conclusions. That researchers used distinctive research techniques to do similar tasks permitted the generation of conflicting output.

Generally, as sociologist R. Whitley remarked, in disciplines such as applied economics in which technical task uncertainty is common:

> the use of technical procedures will be highly tacit, personal, and fluid. It will not be very obvious when particular methods should be used . . . [R]esults are difficult to compare systematically . . . [T]ask outcomes are non-standard and subject to various interpretations and descriptions . . . [S]olutions to problems will vary considerably across work-places, and so too will the ways in which problems are understood so that standardized, stable formulations are improbable. (Whitley, 1984, pp. 121, 125; Mäki, 1992, pp. 85–9)

Technical task uncertainty appears to be more common in applied economics than in medicine, another applied science dealing with human society (Whitley, 1984, p. 124). The consensus within the medical community about the main lines of approach to dealing with newly diagnosed epidemics of polio and, more recently, human immunodeficiency virus, is remarkable. Yet, the medical community experiences a high degree of technical task uncertainty when faced with diagnosing the effects of human-produced toxins.

Contact with toxins invokes symptoms that appear with long and variable lags. Consider the herbicide Agent Orange, made with the toxin dioxin, that the US military used in the Vietnam war (Tesh, 1990, pp. 131–53; Evans, 1993, pp. 197–8). Did the prolonged exposure to Agent Orange cause the subsequent chronic illnesses and fatal cancers of the veterans, and the strange defects of their offspring? Scientists at the Centers for Disease Control (CDC) and the American Medical Association (AMA) shared the belief of the chemical companies, the Defense Department, and the Veterans' Administration that the exposure of veterans to Agent Orange was harmless. Yet an editorial in the *Journal of the American Medical Association* supported the claims of veterans' organisations and public interest groups that wartime exposure to the herbicide was hazardous. (I personally know a normally sceptical doctor who had a colleague who died of the cancer lymphoma 20 years after his exposure to Agent Orange in Vietnam. My friend strongly believes Agent Orange caused his colleague's death.)

The conflicting evidence about the effect of Agent Orange presented by scientists at Congressional hearings and court proceedings rested partly on conflicting ideas about rules of evidence: The absence of 'proof' – or precise knowledge of how contacts with Agent Orange lead to diseases – weighed against the veterans. Different kinds of evidence – statistical correlations between exposure and incidence of disease, laboratory experiments on various animals, mutagen tests, and so on – often yielded conflicting results. Thus, assessing the effects of

Agent Orange involved a classic case of technical task uncertainty.[1]

I suggest that technical task uncertainty arose in the case of Agent Orange for two main reasons, a real-world medical and a social reason. Toxins, unlike viruses, are not traceable in systems diseased after long and variable lags. And medical output that confirmed the hypothetical causal link between the toxin and illness gelled with certain social values and fiscal commitments. It is easy to imagine that researchers' gut reactions about the effect on veterans of the military's use of Agent Orange induced the researchers to use methods yielding answers to support their beliefs.

I see an analogy between the technical task uncertainty in the Agent Orange story and Mayer's economic study. The complicated path by which money affects the real economy permitted technical uncertainty to arise. And monetarists and Keynesians unintentionally exploited the uncertainty about econometric techniques to demarcate political positions.

Econometrics in the United States was politicised early on (Epstein, 1987, pp. 60–70, 99–140, 225–28). The goal of the Cowles Commission for Research in Economics during the 1940s was to make econometrics, as the coalescence of general equilibrium theory and statistics, the basis for 'social engineering' (Epstein, 1987, p. 61). A few theoretical econometricians 'promoted good workmanship, not 'isms'.[2] The theoretical econometricians during the next three decades admonished colleagues who offered unrefined output to policy-makers. While the theorists focused on how to construct and evaluate models, the applied econometricians, captured by the 'spirit' of the grand enterprise, rushed into estimation (Fromm and Klein, 1972, pp. 53–4). Competing models proliferated. What economic hypotheses were being estimated often remained opaque since practitioners poorly understood the statistical underpinnings of the models (Basmann, 1972, pp. 15–53).

Difficult problems of interpreting econometric estimates arose in the case of models with lagged dependent variables.[3] It is always the case that the test statistics from which the observed level of statistical significance are computed have theoretical distributions derived deductively from definite assumptions. One of those assumptions is that the predetermined variables are fixed. That assumption does not hold in the presence of lagged dependent variables. Then the distributions of the estimated coefficients and the test statistics differ from the classical case and are unknown in non-trivial cases. Only a thorough investigation of a model and its parameter values can show whether the levels of significance calculated on the basis of the classical assumption are robust. Econometric statisticians knew about the problem. Had the econometricians engaged in the Keynesian–monetarist dispute acknowledged the uncertainty about the robustness of the estimates of their models and sought help from statisticians, it is likely that the arguments about the lag lengths would have been less heated and more fruitful.

Notes

1. The government eventually set up a fund for certain claims.
2. R.L. Basmann used the quoted words in conversation with the author (18 June 1996).
3. Basmann and Wulwick (1992, 162–3); a conversation between Basmann and Wulwick (7 September 1996).

References

Basmann, R.L. (1972) 'The Brookings Quarterly Econometrics Model: Science or Number Mysticism?', in K. Brunner *Problems and Issues in Current Econometrics Practice* (Columbus: Ohio State University).

Basmann, R.L. and N.J. Wulwick (1992) 'Reflections on the History of Econometrics', *Methodus*, vol. 4, no. 1, 154–65.

Epstein, R.J. (1987) *A History of Econometrics* (Oxford: North-Holland).

Evans, A.S. (1993) *Causation and Disease: A Chronological Journey* (London: Plenum Medical Books).

Fromm, G. and L. Klein (1972) 'The Brookings Econometrics Model: A Rational Perspective', in K. Brunner, *Problems and Issues in Current Econometrics Practice* (Columbus: Ohio State University).

Hicks, J. (1967), 'Monetary Theory and History: An Attempt at Perspective', in J. Hicks, *Critical Essays in Monetary Theory* (London: Oxford University Press).

Mäki, U. (1992) 'Social Conditioning in Economics', in N. de Marchi, *Post-Popperian Methodology of Economics: Recovering Practice* (London: Kluwer Academic).

Mayer, T. (1993) *Truth versus Precision in Economics* (Aldershot: Edward Elgar).

——— (1995) *Doing Economic Research* (Aldershot: Edward Elgar).

——— (1997) 'Monetarists and Keynesians on Central Banking: A Study of A Flawed Debate', Chapter 5 in this volume.

Suppe, F. (1977) *The Structure of Scientific Theories* (London: University of Illinois Press).

Tesh, S.N. (1990) *Hidden Arguments: Political Ideology and Disease Prevention Policy* (London: Rutgers University Press).

Whitley, R. (1984) *The Intellectual and Social Organization of the Sciences* (Oxford: Oxford University Press).

Discussion

Thomas Mayer opened his response to McCallum by conceding that the debate did get somewhere, but he asserted that it got there extremely slowly and inefficiently. In response to McCallum's claim that the Keynesians could use an econometric model, he pointed out that it was not just a matter of someone having the right model, but of knowing which model was the correct one. Though choosing the wrong model would probably not have made much difference in forecasting GNP, the impact multipliers are very different in different models, which means that the assumption that the Fed is using the correct model is a very strong assumption. Furthermore, if the issue really was models, it should have been addressed more sharply in the discussion than it was.

Mayer said that McCallum was correct to argue that Keynesians talked about what central banks *ought* to do, whilst monetarists talked about what they *had done*. These were, however, related, for monetarists drew the conclusion that if central banks had done wrong things in the past, they could be expected to do wrong things in the future. The question of how monetarists regarded the exogeneity of the money stock is, Mayer argued, a tricky one. In looking at specific episodes they treat money as exogenous, but at the same time they criticise the Fed for making money endogenous.

Mayer agreed with many of Wulwick's comments, especially concerning why the debate lasted so long. Economists, in talking to the public, had an incentive to be dogmatic. He agreed that technical task uncertainty contributed to the difficulty in resolving the debate, but he considered that there was another factor – an underlying philosophical, or metaphysical, issue. Many Keynesians believe that there *must* be a way to ameliorate problems, whereas the conservative view is that we may not be able to make things better.

Kevin Hoover took up Wulwick's Agent Orange example, wondering why there was such a positive policy response to the veterans, when the epidemiological evidence was so weak. A major reason is a loss function that strongly favours the veterans. This raises the question of what sort of loss function one wants to use when there is considerable ignorance, which tied in to Mayer's point about ignorance of the models. Part of the debate involved what goes into the loss function, and the nature of the asymetries in the loss function. The public demanding action against unemployment is a statement about a very asymmetrical loss function: unemployment must be eliminated even if the costs are high. To this point **Mayer** responded that there was a problem of time-inconsistency in the public's attitude. They might attach great weight to unemployment now, but if inflation rose their weights would change. In addition, if there is no long-run trade off between inflation and unemployment, we have no loss function to worry about.

Daniel Hausman suggested that Mayer gave the impression that methodological considerations had very little purchase on this debate because the inadequacies of the debate were so elementary – the fallacy of false dichotomy; not paying attention to evidence and arguments of the other side. He argued that there was a great deal of methodological interest in this controversy if we see it as a policy controversy raising the issue, actively discussed by philosophers, of how one should design policy in the face of massive uncertainty. One response is to rely on our best guess, but is this adequate? Friedman, for example, might have said: 'Our best guess about the effects of intervention is very uncertain, so let's choose the option that keeps government small.' Or Modigliani might say: 'Even though its a wild guess, we can't tell the unemployed that we can't do anything.'

Philippe Mongin pointed out that if we assume a quadratic social welfare function, the variance of the instruments can influence social welfare in a straightforward way. Then we have a simple model in which the more uncertainty monetary policy generates, the worse it is, supporting some sort of a fixed rule. The point here is that we have a model of the relationship between objectives and policy conclusions. This raises the question of the degree to which the objective function of the central bank, or society as a whole, was made explicit during the debate.

Bennett McCallum thought this result about variability of the instrument was first developed by Bill Brainard, a participant on the Keynesian side of this debate. McCallum took this as evidence that people were trying to pursue reasonable science in this debate, for the result that instrument variability might lower welfare was derived by someone interested in promoting active stabilisation policy. **Hoover** responded that this was a narrow technical point, requiring that one first establish the model over which one is optimising, that does not address Mayer's more radical point about uncertainty concerning the model. **McCallum**

agreed, noting that much of his own work had been concerned with finding an activist policy rule that is robust to model specification. But it took time to find out that there were such big differences between models. As far back as 1970 there was a big conference organised by the Fed and the SSRC (responsible for the Brookings model) aimed at answering just this kind of question. The conference volume contained not only the results of different econometric models, but had one of Lucas' first papers on his critique of Keynesian economics. This is testimony that the profession was taking seriously the charges against it.

Michel De Vroey was sceptical about Mayer's conclusion that something went wrong with the debate, considering that it rested on an idealised, almost naive, view of scientific activity. The debate illustrates business as usual, with economists engaged in argument and persuasion about laissez faire and state intervention in a decentralised economy. People start with a commitment (whether from reading Friedman or Marx) and seek to build that insight into a structured language. He found it quite normal for people to be committed in that way. Their arguments have to be interpreted as political philosophy, a function of the history of economic thought being to highlight such commitments. In view of this, De Vroey was puzzled by the gap between this and the positivistic, naturalistic interpretation that economists place on their work even when (like Friedman) they have strong *a priori* commitments. He believed that progress in economic theory took the form of arguments becoming more structured, doubting that there was any narrowing of the range of disagreement. Because disagreement stems from basic presuppositions, it will not be narrowed by empirical work. **Mayer** did not agree with this, believing that people did change their minds. He also made the point that focusing on debates inevitably exaggerates the extent of disagreement among economists.

McCallum responded that though he was inspired by *Capitalism and Freedom*, he found the book's arguments utterly outrageous and preposterous, and he wanted to set such people straight. As time went on, his views changed.

Uskali Mäki asked whether the question Mayer was addressing was whether economists could have done better relative to some ideal standard, or better subject to the constraints that they faced. He noted that Wulwick had listed some of these constraints: audience; ideological differences; academic institutions; technical uncertainty in empirical research. To this he added limitations in the cognitive capacity of individual researchers. It is simply not possible that economists are familiar with all relevant theories. Also, to have a preconceived idea of the constitution of society may be a constraint imposed by such limitations. He argued that we should pay close attention to constraints such as these, and to the extent to which they are inescapable, take on board lessons from other fields such as cognitive science, or the politics, sociology and economics of science.

Pierluigi Barrotta supported Mayer's claim that the episode had little to do with philosophy of science – with concepts such as paradigms, *Weltanschauungen*, research programmes and so on. Keynesians and monetarists agreed on the basic model. The controversy concerned simply the psychology and sociology of the situation, having nothing to do with the logic of controversy. **McCallum** responded that though they agreed on the IS–LM portion of the model, they disagreed on the rest of the model. It would thus be wrong to say that they agreed on theory. More important, it turned out, as was shown by Sargent and Lucas, that the way in which one viewed econometric tests of the model depended on whether expectations were viewed as rational or as fixed-lag expectations. Attempts to conduct empirical tests of the part of the system on which there was substantive disagreement between monetarists and Keynesians led to tremendous theoretical and empirical developments in macroeconomics. **Mayer** commented that he had trouble distinguishing between theoretical and empirical disagreements. If theory means 'grand theory' there were no theoretical disagreements, but at a lower level there were. **Hoover** found the claim that empirical differences over the slopes of IS and LM curves separate monetarists and Keynesians interesting because even though it was not correct, as both Friedman and Tobin recognised, it persisted because it got built into textbooks. This happened through looking for common ground, and through looking for pedagogical simplicity. He found it very puzzling that though there is a real dispute, it is not where the textbooks are located.

Maarten Janssen suggested that a possible lesson from the debate was that scientific disputes are carried out very differently when important policy issues are involved. He suggested looking at debates in the natural sciences where policy issues were involved, such as over nurture versus nature. It is possible to have progress on details, but not resolve the fundamental dispute. In response, **Mayer** pointed to the example of Continental Drift, which had been settled.

Roger Backhouse drew attention to the close links between the debates discussed in Mayer's and De Vroey's chapters (Chapters 5 and 4). The background to both debates is very dramatic changes in the way macroeconomics has been conceptualized: changes in econometric practices and in theoretical models. In view of this he suggested that perhaps we ought to be looking for parallels between the two debates.

Mongin asked about the empirical relevance of the Lucas critique. **Hoover** replied that Neil Ericsson had concluded that the Lucas critique was conceptually right, but irrelevant in practice. He pointed out that models could fail either because they are mis-specified, or for Lucas-type reasons, and it is hard to decide between these two possibilities. **McCallum** observed that the Lucas critique is really returning to the Cowles Commission view that only structural models can be used for policy making. Lucas's work had such an impact because he argued that Keynesian models of the time could not plausibly be regarded as structural. McCallum went on to argue that Ericsson looked in the wrong place, for Lucas-type problems are most likely to occur where expectations are important – in relationships between real and nominal variables, such as the Phillips curve. He also argued that there was substantial empirical evidence that the Lucas critique was important here. **Backhouse** conjectured that McCallum's answer to this question was typical of answers that macroeconomists would give in the sense that he adduced three studies, none of which is in themselves decisive, mainly because the data do not correspond sufficiently closely to the theoretical counterparts they are being used to describe, but which when taken together make a case that is considered persuasive.

Hausman asked how much attention should be paid to such evidence. **Mayer** responded that if one looked at the minutes of the Federal Open Market Committee and saw the type of evidence that they used, it would be clear that even this evidence, inadequate as it is, would be better.

McCallum drew attention to the importance of the distinction, made by Kydland and Prescott and later Barro and Gordon, between (a) activist versus non-activist rules, and (b) rules versus discretion. Realising that these were two different distinctions had an tremendous effect on the way the debate developed, and represented a type of progress. This grew directly out of rational expectations work and, through Lucas, is a direct descendent of Friedman's interests. Central Banks have a private motive not to officially adopt a monetary rule, because to do so is to turn yourself into a formula. If you do this, there is no reason for you to get your picture on the cover of *Time* magazine. Nevertheless, the Federal Reserve and the Bank of England have done a lot of work on policy rules, such as building up on the policy rule that I proposed, and the Board of Governors is now very interested in the rule proposed by John Taylor. There's much more concordance between the way policy people and academics talk about these issues than there was twenty years ago. This, he claimed, was progress.

Nancy Wulwick agreed that disputes lead to progress, and with Mayer's point that the way in which economists compete is a dialectical process. She claimed, however, that the disputes remained, taking another ground.

6 Harold Hotelling and the Neoclassical Dream

D. Wade Hands and Philip E. Mirowski[1]
UNIVERSITY OF PUGET SOUND, USA, AND
UNIVERSITY OF NOTRE DAME, USA

> There is no path, there is no path at all,
> Unless perhaps where abstract things have gone
> And precepts rise and meta-physics fall,
> And principles abandoned stumble on.
> No path, but as it were a river in spate
> Where drowning forms, down-swept, gesticulate.
> (Malcolm Lowry)

1 DOWN TO THE FIELD OF DREAMS IN OUR TIME MACHINE

There is a daydream that many intellectual historians seem to share, indulging in it at the slightest provocation. In this dream, they climb into a time machine and are transported back to the classical origins of their discipline or doctrine. The time machine apparently has no difficulties in locating this *omphalos*, since it merely has to retrace (in reverse) the single lineage which stretches in a straight line from Now to Then.

We would like to invite the reader into our own version of an intellectual time machine. In particular we would like to transport the reader back to the time when the 'theory of demand' was little more than the suggestion that a stable relationship existed between the price of a good and the quantity of the good that would be sold. But we caution our fellow-travellers in this virtual dreamtime that they may be in for a rather bumpy ride, primarily because the destination lacks determinate coordinates. By this we mean that our trip will be quite different from the trip provided by those such as Creedy (1992) or Stigler (1965) who would whisk us back three centuries to a single point of origin like the 'King–Davenant Law' or something of the sort. Rather, we will set the controls for a more unsettled time, a time when there was little agreement about 'demand' being anything other than a phenomenal regularity in price–quantity space, and yet at the same time it was widely recognized that such a mere phenomenal relationship was simply not good enough; this regularity needed desperately to be explained, and there existed a wide variety of possible explanations.

But while our destination is a tumultuous time, we will not be able to consider all of the different individuals who contributed to the intellectual fervour. We will restrict ourselves to the class of economists who would acknowledge that they operated within the same rough doctrinal school or foundational orientation: an orientation that we will, for want of a better term, call 'neoclassical'. Those accepting the neoclassical orientation generally agreed that: market demand curves were (in some sense) the sum of individual demand curves; the 'agents' behind the individual demand curves would be maximising a well-defined objective function (amenable to the differential calculus); and prices would be taken as parameters (and not choice variables) for the relevant agents. So, for instance, although some contemporary American Institutionalists like Frederick Mills were also equally absorbed by the empirical implications of price–quantity interactions, we shall omit him from our itinerary. Hence, the place where we should like to transport the reader is to the time just before the neoclassical orthodoxy (or what some modern textbooks – Mas-Collel, Whinston and Green, 1995, for instance – call 'classical consumer theory') coalesced around the apparatus of income and substitution effects, Slutsky symmetry conditions, parametric prices and the tools of simultaneous equation econometrics. Our destination thus lies somewhere between Alfred Marshall and the Cowles Commission.

But why should the reader join us in our little outing? Well, for one thing, we promise a much different trip than what has previously been available in the literature. The conventional straight line from Marshall to Slutsky to Hicks–Allen to Samuelson neglects most of what we think is the interesting and relevant part of the story. A wide range of important actors and their interactions (both at the time and in retrospect) are often neglected in the conventional straight line story; while our focus will be on Henry Schultz and Harold Hotelling, the list could easily be expanded to include Henry Ludwell Moore, Edwin Bidwell Wilson, Sewall Wright, Nicholas Georgescu-Roegen, Charles Roos, Jacob Marschak, Griffith Evans, Milton Friedman, Holbrook Working and a host of others. Also, we shall restrict ourselves to events in the United

States, partly for convenience, although also partly upon principle: national context and culture seem to matter for the story we wish to tell.

Yet the more tangible the destination, the less some readers will be willing to come along for the ride. 'Why Schultz and Hotelling?', they might ask. 'How could these relatively minor figures really matter to the development of modern demand theory?' Therein lies our tale. One of our major themes is that even within the arbitrarily narrow parameters we have just set, there is not, nor has there ever been, a single discrete neoclassical demand theory, and that this may have something to do with its demonstrable power. Our story is one of negotiation and relative stabilisation, not one of refutation or a single crucial test.

We will focus our attention on one of demand theory's 'hopeful failures'. By 'hopeful failures', we mean programmes or approaches that seemed to provide solutions to a number of the discipline's recognised problems, and yet did not survive intact into the later stages of the field's development. Such hopeful failures do not get much attention in the conventional linear histories of science. According to most of these conventional histories, science exhibits consistent and systematic progress; those views that are rejected by the scientific community are, for the most part, rejected for the right reasons and hopeful failures are interesting only to the extent that they were proven wrong. Social and contextual factors might be used to explain why such failures were retained as long as they were, but the reason for their failure resides in the nature of world and not in any of the contingencies of the social context. Such histories are often tied to a particular normative philosophy of science – there exists a proper (and relatively simple) 'scientific method' that constitutes the 'right reasons' – and that method is manifest in the history of successful science. Such histories are fundamentally evaluative and the historian's argument for why a particular view gets evaluated as it does is the same as the winner's argument for why they are winners; the values of the winners are deployed in the evaluation of the losers.[2] While there do exist histories of economic thought by figures such as Leo Rogin, Wesley Clair Mitchell and Keith Tribe, that seek to transcend this asymmetry between success and failure, we would argue that for various reasons they do not adequately engage the history of neoclassical demand theory, the topic of our present concern.

Recent more contextual and sociologically-inspired studies in the history of science are more likely to treat successes and failures in a more symmetric way, and are thus less likely to take such a dismissive stance toward rejected knowledge. For example, in *Leviathan and the Air Pump* (1985), Steve Shapin and Simon Schaffer examine the 1660s controversy in natural philosophy between Thomas Hobbes and Robert Boyle. Hobbes was clearly the loser in this debate, and as a result his work was written out of the history of science by the late eighteenth century (despite his status and prestige in other areas of philosophy). Unlike the standard history of this episode, the narrative provided by Shapin and Schaffer does not evaluate Hobbes's position from the winner's perspective. Their story treats accepted knowledge (Boyle) and rejected knowledge (Hobbes) symmetrically and attempts to understand the various forces that were influential in determining which adjective came to be attached to which knowledge claim. Such stories may involve the traditional philosophical idiom of 'empirical facts' and 'epistemic virtues', but they do so in a substantially more solicitous and nuanced way than these terms are used in conventional histories.

This chapter considers a bit of rejected knowledge, a hopeful failure, from the history of early twentieth-century demand theory; we shall maintain that it is a mistake to neglect this incident or to uncritically regard it as minor. The rejected knowledge we shall highlight is the theory of demand presented in Harold Hotelling's paper on 'Edgeworth's Taxation Paradox' in the *Journal of Political Economy* in 1932 (Hotelling, 1932a). We will examine this paper in detail, and demonstrate that it solves quite a number of the discipline's perceived problems – problems from the 1930s as well as problems associated with the Arrow–Debreu general equilibrium model in the 1950s and 1960s – and then offer a contextually situated discussion of why Hotelling's model nonetheless did not survive intact into the body of accepted knowledge of neoclassical economics.

We feel impelled to insert at least three *caveats* before we climb into our time machine and embark upon our tale. First, we would like to make it clear that we do *not* seek to argue that Harold Hotelling was 'right' and Eugene Slutsky was 'wrong' about the proper elaboration of neoclassical demand theory. Our narrative is certainly not a story about what 'should' or 'should not' have emerged from this tumultuous period; it is not an attempt to revive, or even show an injustice was done to, Hotelling's theory of demand. Such a normative project would violate our own historiographical principles by subverting our stated intention to treat winners and losers in a more symmetric way.

Second, this account cannot stand alone as a self-sufficient chapter of the history of neoclassical demand theory. We are painfully aware of what it would take to adequately demonstrate the existence of many neoclassical demand theories in all their detail and historical splendour. After all, it is our position that the conventional boxes in which the story has previously been retailed – say, the 'history of econometric ideas' (Morgan, 1990; Christ, 1985; Epstein, 1987); the 'history of empirical studies of consumer behaviour' (Stigler, 1965); 'the development of utility theory' (any history of economics textbook); 'the discovery of the law of demand' (Creedy, 1992); the history of methodological doctrines (Blaug, 1992; De Marchi and Blaug, 1991) and yes, even 'the history of energy physics' (Mirowski, 1989) – are a big part of the problem. One can only tell the symmetrical story of rejected knowledge which we propose by violating those categories, and bursting asunder all those neatly stacked boxes on the storage shelf of economic knowledge. But that, in turn, would require a thorough rewriting of the received history of neoclassical economics: one in which we are already engaged (Mirowski, 1989, 1990, 1994; Hands, 1984, 1994), and one which when completed will stretch from Francis Edgeworth and Henry Ludwell Moore through to the construction of the Chicago school and the Arrow–Debreu stabilisation (Weintraub, 1991; Weintraub and Mirowski, 1994). Yet even while admitting those perhaps vaulting ambitions, it does seem to both of us that the Hotelling–Schultz encounter is one of those pivotal events around which the entire structure of neoclassical demand theory pirouetted, wobbled, but then miraculously recovered its balance. For Henry Schultz was an avowed disciple of Moore at Columbia, who himself had earlier clashed precipitously with Edgeworth over the very issue of the viability of empirical demand estimation, and while Schultz was on the faculty at the University of Chicago one of his most illustrious undergraduate students was Paul Samuelson; he also mentored Milton Friedman and encountered George Stigler. Harold Hotelling's contribution, on the other hand, was prompted by Edgeworth's paradoxical paper on taxation: and while teaching mathematical economics and statistics at Columbia, Milton Friedman was one of his students. Many of the major streams of neoclassical thought about the nature of demand converged with alacrity upon these two men, and out of their struggle with these issues was conceived the three major skeins of 1960s American neoclassical orthodoxy: the MIT revealed preference doctrine, the Chicago Marshallian variant, and the Cowles general equilibrium approach. It is a great story, and there is no way we can tell it all here.

Thirdly, and equally humbling, is the fact that we do not feel we can draw any simple methodological rules out of our present narrative – unlike, say Green and Moss (1994) or Chapter 6 of Blaug (1992) –

basically because we believe that no simple set of methodological rules can adequately account for the fact that one variant was chosen and stabilised, eventually coming to dominate another; our story is no more a meta-lesson for philosophers than it is a parable for economists. This is a thesis we can only hope to illustrate with the story here, postponing for a later venue the extended argument. While it should be clear that we are favourably inclined toward Science Studies and the Sociology of Scientific Knowledge (SSK) – perspectives that characterise science as a complex product of interests, communities, unanticipated consequences and cultural formations – it should also be clear that we are not rigidly committed to any one particular programme or approach within these general frameworks. What happened in economics was as much the product of the Great Depression and the Second World War or contemporary upheavals in physics as it was of perspicacious far-sighted theorists and empiricists subjecting their ideas to stringent tests; nothing less in the way of narrative accounts will do, as we will attempt to illustrate. Nevertheless, the absence of any clean 'scientific method' does not imply that randomness, whimsy or bald power plays were the predominant order of the day.

The remainder of this chapter is organised along the following lines. Section 2 provides a relatively abstract statement of Hotelling's proposed solution to the problem of grounding empirical demand theory in a coherent foundational theory of individual maximisation. We have dubbed this solution 'Hotelling's Dream', not only because it would serve his own specific purposes, but also because it would address some issues associated with a later version of the neoclassical programme, as well as conform to one of its major heuristics (identified in Section 3). Section 4 demonstrates in a telegraphed manner just how Hotelling's version of demand theory would have addressed some of the stated concerns of neoclassical economists, if it had only survived intact. Section 5 is intended to buttress the preceding account by providing a thickly textured history of the actual Schultz–Hotelling encounter, based upon both published and archival sources. Precisely because of the increased texture, the story becomes appreciably more complex in this section than in our preceding outlines. Section 6 of the chapter provides a brief sketch of what happened to neoclassical demand theory after the 1930s – when much of Hotelling's Dream was abandoned and the rest was downgraded to Hotelling's Lemma – and after both our protagonists had abandoned the field. Some major figures, such as Paul Samuelson, play an influential role in these developments; but historical accident and social context are also important factors. We conclude in Section 7 by offering some partial explanations for this phenomenon, and drawing a few cautionary consequences for the field of economic methodology.

2 HOTELLING'S DREAM

The original motivation for Hotelling's (1932a) paper was the so-called 'Edgeworth taxation paradox': the rather counterintuitive argument that a tax imposed on one good may actually lower the price of that good as well as the price of certain related goods. Edgeworth first published the result in Italian in 1897, but it was accessible to Hotelling in Edgeworth's *Papers Relating to Political Economy* (1925, I, 132, 143ff, II, 401). Edgeworth's original example was based on a profit maximising monopoly railway supplying two classes of passenger rail service. Hotelling's 1932 paper employed an early example of the optimisation-based differential comparative statics that subsequently became standard in post-*Foundations* (Samuelson, 1947) economic analysis, and demonstrated that in the case of interrelated commodities it was possible for a tax on one good to cause a reduction in the prices of both goods, even when they were sold under conditions of 'free' competition. Edgeworth's result did not depend on monopoly, Hotelling insisted, but rather was an implication of the interrelatedness of commodity demands.

Hotelling's characterisation of demand in this paper was quite different from the consumer choice characterisation that is now standard in microeconomics textbooks; the modern view descended more directly from Fisher (1892), Pareto (1927), and Slutsky (1915) than Hotelling. While the standard textbook version was also present, and perhaps even dominant, during the 1930s – particularly after Hicks and Allen (1934) – the word 'dominant' should be used rather gingerly. The entire programme of what is now called neoclassical microeconomics was still quite inchoate during the 1930s and that instability would continue for the next thirty years or so; 'dominant view' in this context means only that it was the characterisation of consumer choice that seemed to be most accepted by the specific coterie of economists who were concerned with the theoretical grounding of demand curves under conditions of interdependent multicommodity utility maximisation.

Before turning our attention to Hotelling's approach, it may be useful for comparison purposes to quickly review the 'standard' textbook approach to demand theory. In the standard n-good consumer choice problem the consumer maximises utility subject to a budget constraint. The utility function $U(x)$ is a real valued function of the quantities of the n goods given by the vector $x = (x_1, x_2, \ldots, x_n)$. The budget constraint simply says that the money value of the goods purchased at the price vector $p = (p_1, p_2, \ldots, p_n)$ must be equal to the available money income M. The standard consumer choice problem can thus be written as,

$$\max\ U(x)$$

$$\text{subject to: } \sum_{i=1}^{n} p_i x_i = M$$

where the utility function has sufficient structure to satisfy the second-order conditions for this constrained optimisation problem (it is strictly quasi-concave).

The $n + 1$ first-order conditions for this problem are given by,

$$\partial U/\partial x_i - \lambda p_i = 0 \quad \text{for all } i = 1, 2, \ldots, n$$

$$\text{and } M - \sum_{i=1}^{n} p_i x_i$$

where λ is the Lagrangian multiplier. Solving these $n + 1$ first-order conditions determines the n demand functions $x(p, M)$ and the optimal value of the Lagrange multiplier $\lambda(p, M)$.

Unlike this standard model of constrained consumer choice, the demand functions in Hotelling's 1932 paper were derived from the unconstrained maximisation problem of an 'entrepreneur', someone who purchases goods in order to resell them. By focusing on 'entrepreneurial' demand Hotelling was 'restricting attention to those cases in which money is spent, as the saying is, to make money' (1932a, p. 592).

Hotelling started with the sales or total revenue function of the entrepreneur. This function is given by,

$$U(x) = U(x_1, x_2, \ldots, x_n) \tag{1}$$

where $x = (x_1, x_2, \ldots, x_n)$ is the quantity vector of the n commodities. With $U(x)$ as total revenue, the entrepreneur's objective function of net revenue (or profit) is given by,

$$U(x) - \sum_{i=1}^{n} p_i x_i \tag{2}$$

where $p = (p_1, p_2, \ldots, p_n)$ is the vector of commodity prices.[3]

The first-order conditions for this (unconstrained) maximisation of the objective function in (2) are given by,

$$\partial U/\partial x_i = p_i \quad \text{for all } i=1, 2, \ldots, n \tag{3}$$

These n first-order conditions can be solved for the n (inverse) demand functions:

$$p_i(x) = p_i(x_1, x_2, \ldots, x_n) \quad \text{for all } i=1, 2, \ldots, n \tag{4}$$

Hotelling assumed these could be inverted to yield the demand functions,

$$x_i(p) = x_i(p_1, p_2, \ldots, p_n) \quad \text{for all } i=1, 2, \ldots, n \tag{5}$$

Differentiation of the first order conditions in (3) gives,

$$\partial^2 U/\partial x_i \partial x_j = \partial p_i/\partial x_j = \partial p_j/\partial x_i = \partial^2 U/\partial x_j \partial x_i \quad \text{for all } i \text{ and } j, \tag{6}$$

which implies that the (inverse) demand functions satisfy the following reciprocity (symmetry) conditions,

$$\partial p_i/\partial x_j = \partial p_j/\partial x_i \quad \text{for all } i \neq j \tag{7}$$

Hotelling calls these symmetry conditions the 'integrability conditions' (1932a, p. 591) for entrepreneurial demand functions. These conditions are much stronger[4] than the (Slutsky) symmetry conditions for the standard consumer choice problem.[5] The symmetry (or immediate integrability) conditions in (7) are written for the inverse demand functions $p_i(x)$, but since $[Jp] = [Jx]^{-1}$ these conditions also imply the symmetry of the demand functions $x_i(p)$.[6] Thus the conditions,

$$\partial x_i/\partial p_j = \partial x_j/\partial p_i \quad \text{for all } i \neq j \tag{8}$$

also hold for Hotelling's demand functions. The particular way the choice problem is specified guarantees the symmetry of both the inverse and regular demand functions.

The symmetry conditions in (8) imply that a potential function exists for the vector field defined by the demand functions $x_i(p)$.[7] Hotelling calls this potential function the 'price potential':

> Just as we have a utility (or profit) function U of the quantities consumed whose derivatives are the prices, there is, dually, a function of the prices whose derivatives are the quantities consumed. The existence of such a function, which heretofore does not seem to have been noticed, is assured by (7). On the basis of physical analogies we may call this the 'price potential'. (1932a, p. 594)

In this paper as well in later work Hotelling used the symmetry conditions (7) and (8) for exercises in welfare economics (or more properly, for exercises in the kind of economic analysis that eventually came to be called welfare economics). As Hotelling says in his 1938 paper:

> In the paper on 'Edgeworth's Taxation Paradox' . . . I have shown that there is a good reason to expect these integrability conditions to be satisfied, at least to a close approximation, in an extensive class of cases. If they are satisfied, the surpluses arising from different persons, may be added to give a meaningful measure of social value. (1938a, p. 247)

If we focus exclusively on the demand side of the market (thus neglecting producer's surplus) then Hotelling's social welfare argument can be interpreted in the following way. When the symmetry condition (7) holds, the (inverse) demand functions $p_i(x)$ define an exact differential. This means that the Welfare line integral (W), defined by,

$$W = \sum_{i=1}^{n} \int p_i(x)dx_i \tag{9}$$

is independent of path (it has the same value for any two endpoints regardless of the path that is taken between those two endpoints).[8] In addition, if the path is a closed curve – if it begins and ends at the same point – then the value of the welfare integral is zero; the demand functions $p(x)$ generate a 'conservative' vector field. The welfare measure W is the natural general equilibrium extension of Marshall's notion of total social benefit: the concept of total social benefit that forms the basis of consumer's surplus calculations. Consumer's surplus and the related concept of dead weight loss continues to be the theoretical mainstay for most applied welfare economics and cost-benefit analysis;[9] Hotelling's demand functions guarantee that such measures are appropriate tools for the evaluation of social utility in the multiple (and interrelated) market context.

Despite his repeated reference to 'entrepreneurial' demand, Hotelling clearly believed that his model captured a wide class of empirically interesting demand curves. He says for example :

> Not only entrepreneurs, but also purchasers of goods for their own consumption, tend to proceed according to the same principle. To be sure, the buyer may not have in mind a quantity so definite as net profit to maximize, and may behave in an irregular and inconsistent manner. But so far as he weighs in a consistent manner the relative utilities of various goods, considering whether one prospective purchase is 'a better bargain' than another, it is clear that there is a function u of the quantities purchased which he is trying to make a maximum. (Hotelling, 1932a, p. 591)

He mentions the (now) standard budget constrained model (pp. 592–3) but speaks as if it were (at least empirically) the special case. He suggests that the only difference between the two views is the 'atypical' (p. 593) case of a Giffen good such as the 'rising demand curve for bread sometimes supposed to occur' (p. 593). He also made similar arguments about the empirical relevance of entrepreneurial demand in unpublished correspondence with Henry Schultz (as we shall discover below in Section 5), and it is also clear from the earlier discussion that he continued to insist on the empirical relevancy of his model in his later (1938a) work on welfare economics.

Schultz read an early version of Hotelling's paper and pointed out that Hotelling's symmetry conditions (7) could be derived from the standard consumer choice problem if the (Marshallian) assumption is added that the marginal utility of money (λ) is constant with respect to (independent of) prices. To see this, recall that solving the first-order conditions for the standard consumer choice problem generates not only the demand functions $x(p, M)$, or the inverse functions $p(x, M)$, but it also the optimal value of the Lagrange multiplier λ: which in general will also be a function of the parameters (p and M, or x and M). Now suppose that the Lagrange multiplier λ is a constant (not a function of the parameters of the problem).[10] In this case differentiation of the above first-order conditions with respect to some arbitrary x_j gives,

$$\partial^2 U/\partial x_i \partial x_j = \lambda \partial p_i/\partial x_j \quad \text{for all } i \text{ since } p_i \partial\lambda/\partial x_j = 0$$

and this in turn generates the symmetry conditions in (7) in exactly the same way that they were generated by the equalities in (6).

Since many contemporary readers will agree with Schultz that Hotelling's model is a 'special case' of the standard problem with the additional assumption of the constancy of the marginal utility of money (or the assumption of 'homothetic preferences' which has the same implication) it is useful to give some attention to this claim. First of all, the Hotelling model is most certainly not a special case in the sense that if one starts with a utility function that exhibits the constancy of the marginal utility of money (or homothetic preferences) and then uses that same utility function as the total revenue function in Hotelling's problem, the exact same demand functions will be produced in both cases. While the reader can prove this to themselves with a simple two variable case,[11] it should be obvious since the standard problem, even under the assumption of the constancy of the marginal utility of money or homothetic preferences, will always produce (at least some) demand functions with money income (M) as an argument, while the Hotelling demands will be functions of prices alone. Second, the homogeneity properties of the two types of demand functions are not the same, and the two problems have different second-order conditions. The differences in the second-order conditions imply that many utility functions satisfying these two special conditions could never be the objective function for Hotelling's problem: much less one that produces the exact same demands. Finally, while both problems generate a potential function, it is not the same potential function (the difference amounts to the difference between 'integrability' and 'immediate integrability'[12]). These are simply two different problems and adding the assumption of the constancy of the marginal utility of money or homothenticity does not make one a special case of the other. All that can be said is that adding one of these restrictions to the standard consumer choice problem produces demand functions that have symmetric cross-partial derivatives: a property that also holds for Hotelling demands. We argue later that one of Schultz's epistemic priors was an 'operationalist' perspective; this may have contributed to his rather narrow focus on what he believed to be the most operational implications of the two models: the symmetry conditions (8) for the Hotelling model and the Slutsky conditions for the consumer choice problem. Since the constancy of the marginal utility of money converted the latter into the former, the two models had the same operational implications along the single dimension that Schultz considered relevant, and thus they were for him, equivalent. This is certainly not the same as being a 'special case' in any more general way.[13]

While we have focused on the one particular aspect of Hotelling's paper that did not become part of standard neoclassical theory – his demand functions – it is important to note that the paper has generally been quite influential and that many of its other theoretical innovations have been integrated into mainstream neoclassical theory. For example, when the symmetry conditions in (8) are applied to the factor demand functions of a perfectly competitive firm, they become 'Hotelling's Lemma', a result that is enshrined in the production chapter of almost every modern textbook. Hotelling's paper also played a prominent role in Samuelson's discussion of 'maximum principles' in his Nobel Lecture (1971); out of the myriad of applications of maximum principles in economics that Samuelson might have chosen to discuss, he opted for precisely those offered in Hotelling's 1932 paper.[14] Finally, as suggested above, Hotelling's papers had an important impact on applied welfare economics and cost-benefit analysis. An example of this impact is provided by John Chipman when he cites 'the authority and influence of Hotelling' (1982, p. 55) as one of the main reasons why Samuelson's work did not have a greater influence on cost-benefit analysis.

3 BACK TO THE FUTURE, WITH ALARM CLOCK, PART 1

By the 1960s, most of the economists involved in the Arrow–Debreu programme seemed to have reached a consensus regarding the programme's basic structure, approach, and theoretical concerns. Of course not all aspects of the programme were of equal interest to every participant, nor was the programme's theoretical focus entirely isolated from the other interests of those involved in general equilibrium research. The theoretical concerns of this community, like those of any scientific community, were deeply intertwined with the other interests – practical, personal, pragmatic, political, cognitive, etc. – of the programme's participants as well as the wider social context in which the programme was embedded.

Despite this interdependency and diversity, it seems possible to isolate a few of the characteristic theoretical concerns of the Arrow–Debreu approach to neoclassical theory. After the introduction of some useful symbolism in the next paragraph, we will isolate and specify five such theoretical concerns. In addition to these relatively agreed-upon concerns we will also specify what we consider to be one of the programme's governing heuristics. Since we will eventually argue that neoclassical economics is not a single framework, but rather three overlapping but separable programmes, the decision to focus exclusively on the Arrow–Debreu variant may seem a bit arbitrary. There are a number of reasons for our choice. First, general equilibrium theory is the version of neoclassical economics that is most transparent in its display of Hotelling's potential benefits. Second, it is the version of neoclassicism considered to be the most highbrow of them all, and continues to play an important role in the graduate training of professional economists. Third, the programme has available canonical texts such as Debreu (1959) and Arrow and Hahn (1971). And finally, space considerations simply preclude the consideration of the other two cognates (although Section 6 contains some suggestions about how it might go).

Since most of the theoretical discourse regarding the Arrow–Debreu general equilibrium model has taken place within the context of a relatively formalised mathematical structure, introducing some of that structure seems to be useful in characterising the theoretical concerns of the Walrasian programme. The easiest way to proceed is to specify one particular generic version of the Arrow–Debreu model and then to use that version as a general framework for introducing both the programme's goals in this section, and also returning to Hotelling (1932a) in the following section. Of course the model we will present is just one particular version of a very general class of models; not every general equilibrium model of the period had exactly this structure or employed this particular symbolism. Since we are primarily concerned with demand theory, we will neglect production and focus exclusively on a pure exchange economy. We will also restrict ourselves to a differential version of the model; in addition to its mathematical convenience, this will also make the connection to the neoclassical economics of the 1930s as clear as possible.[15]

Let the economy have H individual traders indexed by $h = 1, 2, \ldots, H$ and $n + 1$ goods with unit of account prices given by $p = (p_1, p_2, \ldots, p_{n+1})$ with $p_i > 0$ for all $i=1, 2, \ldots, n + 1$. Each individual h has an endowment vector ω^h and maximises a strictly quasi-concave utility function subject to the income constraint $M^h = \Sigma p_i \omega_i^h$.

The demand for good i by individual h is given by the function $x_i^h(p)$. The aggregate excess demand for good i at price vector p will be given by $Z_i(p)$ where,[16]

$$Z_i(p) = X_i(p) - \omega_i = \sum_{h=i}^{H} x^h{}_i(p) - \sum_{h=i}^{H} \omega_i^h$$

The most common assumptions on the aggregate excess demand function $Z(p) = [Z_1(p), Z_2(p), \ldots, Z_{n+1}(p)]$ were Walras's Law (W) and zero degree homogeneity (H) at all prices. Thus,

$$\sum_{i=1}^{n+1} p_i Z_i(p) = 0 \tag{W}$$

$$Z_i(\lambda p) = Z_i(p) \quad \text{for all } i \text{ and } \lambda > 0 \tag{H}$$

The aggregate excess demand function $Z(p) = [Z_1(p), Z_2(p), \ldots, Z_{n+1}(p)]$ with restrictions (W) and (H) became the core theoretical concept for the Arrow–Debreu Walrasian general equilibrium model. There were many special cases with additional structure, but this remained the basic model. Under (H) prices can be normalised. One common way to normalise prices was to let good $n + 1$ be the numeraire; this means that $p_{n+1} = 1$ and the prices of the n other goods are given as relative prices in terms of good $n + 1$. We will continue to use the same symbolism (p) for normalised or non-normalised prices.

We can now proceed to identify five theoretical concerns of Arrow–Debreu programme, as well as what we consider a governing heuristic. The first three should be uncontroversial; they are clearly identified by the programme's participants and/or the authors of the canonical texts. The next two issues on our list may be slightly more controversial, but we doubt they will raise much of a fuss. These two concerns were also clearly identified in the canonical texts; what makes them slightly different from the first three is that there was less agreement about what it would take to successfully address these theoretical concerns.[17] Our heuristic, by contrast, is not one that has been uniformly identified or much discussed by the authors of the canonical texts or by subsequent commentators, although one can find it in the margins of many of their texts, as we shall demonstrate. This heuristic connects the Arrow–Debreu programme with the neoclassicism of the late nineteenth century via the argument presented in Mirowski (1989).

(i) The first issue is *existence*: the question of whether the Arrow–Debreu model has an equilibrium price vector. Informally it answers the question: Does there exist a price vector p^* that simultaneously clears all markets? A bit more formally (while still restricting ourselves to strictly positive prices) the existence question is whether the equilibrium price set defined by

$$E = \{p^* \mid Z_i(p^*) = 0 \quad \text{and } p_i^* > 0 \text{ for all } i\}$$

is non-empty

(ii) The second theoretical issue is *uniqueness*. Is the equilibrium price vector p^* unique (i.e. does there exist only one such vector)?

Since excess demand functions are homogeneous of degree zero (H), if any non-normalised price vector p^* is an equilibrium price vector, then λp^* is also an equilibrium price vector for all $\lambda > 0$. When prices are normalised then uniqueness literally means uniqueness, i.e. the set E contains only one element.

(iii) The third issue is the *stability* of the equilibrium price vector. The intuition behind the concept of stability is that when the system is not in equilibrium, prices should adjust on the basis of the 'law of supply and demand' (Gale, 1955); prices should increase when the quantity demanded is greater than the quantity supplied, and prices should decrease when the quantity supplied is greater than the quantity demanded. There are a number of different ways to formalise the idea of a price adjustment process based on the 'law of supply and demand', but the standard approach has been the so-called Walrasian tâtonnement adjustment mechanism. The simplest version of this mechanism is given by the following system of ordinary differential equations:

$$dp_i/dt = Z_i[p(t)] \quad \text{for all } i \tag{T}$$

Following Samuelson (1941, 1942a, and 1944), the equilibrium price vector p^* is said to be *locally stable* if the price path $p(t)$ generated by the system of differential equations (T) converges to p^* for any initial price vector within some positive ε of p^*. Thus p^* is locally stable if,

$$\lim_{t \to \infty} p(t) = p^* \text{ for all } p \text{ within some } \varepsilon \text{ neighbourhood of } p^*$$

Alternatively, the equilibrium price vector p^* is *globally stable* if the price path $p(t)$ generated by (T) converges to p^* for any initial price vector. Early contributions to the literature on the global stability were Arrow and Hurwicz (1958) and Arrow, Block, and Hurwicz (1959); the most influential survey of the early stability literature was Negishi (1962).[18]

(iv) The fourth theoretical issue is *general equilibrium comparative statics by means of the 'Correspondence Principle'*. In his 1942 stability paper Samuelson coined the term the 'Correspondence Principle' for the relationship between the dynamic stability (in his case, local stability) of an economic model and the comparative statics properties of the model. During the 1960s and 1970s a number of attempts were made to apply the correspondence principle to the Walrasian general equilibrium model. The class of results that were desired would have shown that determinate comparative statics were always implied by the stability of a general equilibrium system. Unlike the cases of existence, uniqueness and stability, there was far less professional agreement about what exactly would be a reasonable thing to expect from the successful application of the correspondence principle. Signs of all possible comparative statics results? Some signs? Own effects but not cross-effects? Signs for specific special cases?

(v) The fifth theoretical issue concerns *welfare economics*: welfare economics in the sense that many economists were searching for an economic theory that would provide the ability to pass normative judgement upon various policy proposals and evaluate the desirability of various possible configurations of economic institutions. Demonstrating that a competitive market economy is 'optimal' or 'efficient' (or the related project of showing why it might not be optimal or efficient) had clearly been a long-standing concern for general equilibrium theory (and neoclassical economics more generally). But the question of how precisely this should be done – that is, what exactly should be the proper approach to questions of optimality and efficiency – is a topic where there has been much less consensus. If one takes a very weak optimality notion like Pareto optimality, then one can prove some general theorems about the desirability of competitive institutional arrangements. On the other hand, if one takes a stronger notion of optimality, say one involving the gain or loss in consumer's or producer's surplus, then one may be able to make more specific policy recommendations. Neoclassical economists have traditionally sought welfare results, but there has been some ambiguity regarding the exact form those results should take.

In addition to these five goals we would also like to consider one of the guiding heuristics of Walrasian general equilibrium theory (and all of neoclassical economics). This guiding heuristic is clearly not one that the programme's participants have openly acknowledged (or one they would uniformly agree to if it were pointed out to them); it is the accommodation of the energy metaphor found in classical physics. In Mirowski (1989) and related work, one of the authors of this paper has mounted a systematic and sustained argument regarding one, and perhaps the most important, of the intellectual origins of and guiding heuristics for what eventually became neoclassical economics. It is the appropriation by various economists of the mathematics and structure of the energy concept from mid-nineteenth century physics. The 'marginalist revolution' can be understood as little more than the replacement of 'energy' in the mathematical framework of energy physics with the 'utility' of neoclassical economics. This appropriation of the energy metaphor not only shaped neoclassicism from the very beginning, it has continued to play an active role in what is and is not accepted as legitimate neoclassical theorising ever since. We hereby claim that accommodating the original energy metaphor was an important theme, or implicit guiding principle, of neoclassical theorising in the 1930s and 1940s as well as later general equilibrium theory.

We will call the project of successfully addressing all five of these theoretical concerns plus satisfaction of the physics heuristic *The Neoclassical Dream*. This is not to suggest that these six things were the only things that interested the programme's participants – indeed, the reason we are engaged in writing a history as opposed to a 'rational reconstruction' is because there clearly were other concerns – and it is most certainly not to say that 'theoretical' issues (these or others) were the only factors that determined the kind of theoretical discourse the profession ultimately produced. There existed simultaneously concerns and interests of other types, as well as various constraints and impediments, at work in the determination of the various theoretical strategies that ultimately came to dominate the discourse of general equilibrium theorists. But in recounting the interests which appear to govern a scientific community at a given historical nexus, one must start somewhere. In the weighting of goals and interests we find ourselves in much the same predicament as were the actors themselves: by merely bringing objectives to light we are attempting to enroll allies, block opponents and redirect the existing research programme. Constitution of interests and evaluation of findings interact and change through time, depending upon the locations of the protagonists (Pickering, 1995a); this is one of the primary reasons why a serious historiography cannot presume an unchanging entity like 'neoclassical price theory'.

We will demonstrate in the next section that a general equilibrium theory based on the rejected knowledge of Hotelling's demand functions would have fulfilled the Neoclassical Dream by following Hotelling's heuristic. The remaining sections of the chapter will carefully examine the history of American neoclassical economics in the 1930s–1940s in order to address the question of why it was, given its potential fecundity, that Hotelling's approach did not become the standard view of demand. But before turning to these issues, let us briefly set the coordinates of our time machine for a quick trip back to the present, in order to check just how well the programme that managed to become the mainstream view – namely, Arrow–Debreu general equilibrium theory – succeeded in achieving these five goals.

Our time machine lands us truly at an impasse: the short answer is that the standard theory did not succeed very well at all. Out of the five concerns, only the first, existence, has an unequivocally satisfactory solution. The main existence result of Arrow and Debreu (1954) has stood the test of time and continues to be accepted as a definitive answer to the existence question; this one issue has been successfully addressed. Unfortunately this is not the case for the other four issues. Uniqueness is not a general result; it holds in a number of restrictive special cases, like all goods being gross substitutes or when the aggregate excess demand Jacobian has a dominant diagonal, but there are no general results. As Ingrao and Israel say in their history of general equilibrium theory: 'It is quite clear that uniqueness theorems can only be obtained on assumptions so restrictive as to appear unacceptable' (1990, p. 360). Similar things can be said about stability, where the results are 'unquestionably negative' (1990, p. 361). The counterexamples in the papers by Gale (1965) and Scarf (1960) initiated a flood of similar counterexamples, and more recently the Sonnenschein–Mantel–Debreu (SMD) results on aggregate excess demand functions have made it even easier to produce examples of Walrasian economies that lack stability.[19] Stability, like uniqueness, is only available for a few, quite restrictive, special cases and the desired general results have not been achieved. So too with the Correspondence Principle, which Arrow and Hahn declared 'isn't' (1971, p. 321). The absence of adequate stability results certainly infected the comparative statics that general equilibrium theorists were trying to derive from them.[20] Finally there is the issue of welfare economics. There has been some limited success on this fifth issue; the first and second fundamental theorems of welfare economics relating the set of Pareto-optimal allocations to the competitive equilibrium (or equilibria) are important results that are displayed prominently in every modern microeconomics textbook. It is also true that 'applied' neoclassical economists regularly use cost-benefit analysis to evaluate the economic feasibility of various projects and microeconomic policy changes. The problem is that there is no clear and systematic linkage between the criterion used in these 'applied' welfare evaluations and the first and second fundamental theorems of abstract theory. While there has undoubtedly been some success in the area of welfare economics, even here things are not entirely as the profession would like.

The 'failure' of the physics heuristic is perhaps the most ironic of all, because it was less a matter of a yawning gap between desire and realisation than it was one of failed renunciation. In the 1940s, representatives of the programme such as Gerard Debreu and Tjalling Koopmans suggested that the importation of new mathematical tools and techniques had effectively liberated neoclassicism from its earlier acknowledged dependence upon physical metaphors, freeing it to explore the pure economic logic of the Walrasian system.[21] Our narrative suggests a different reading: the Cowles programme of Arrow, Debreu, Koopmans and others did indeed set out to explore one possible logical framework which diverged in certain specific ways from the physics framework, the heuristic which stood much closer to Hotelling's model, and which they had rejected. But in the process of exploring the logic of their own preferred variant, they eventually discovered that it was disappointing: as noted above, they only got one-fifth of what they wanted, and worse, Cowles lost faith in its own programme of structural econometric estimation. Now, if the Hotelling–physics version had been more successful in crucial respects than their own innovations, then one implication is: their very attempt to free themselves from their origins in the energy metaphor was responsible for the frustration of their other objectives. It was in this curiously inverted sense that the heuristic of the imitation of energy physics failed.

4 THE DREAM FULFILLED, IF ONLY VIRTUALLY

In this section we will show how a general equilibrium model with Hotelling's demand functions would fulfil the Neoclassical Dream. Before addressing each of the individual concerns it is useful to derive a few mathematical results for an economy with Hotelling's demands.

Recall the first-order conditions for the entrepreneurial demands from (3) above,

$$\partial U/\partial x_i = p_i \quad \text{for all } i = 1, 2, \ldots, n$$

The second-order conditions for this (unconstrained) maximisation problem require the Hessian matrix $[HU]$ with representative element $U_{ij} = \partial^2 U/\partial x_i \partial x_j$ to be negative definite. This implies that the matrix has principal minors that alternate in sign starting negatively (i.e. each ith-order principal minor has sign $[-1]^i$). Such matrices are often called N–P matrices.

But notice from the first-order conditions in (3) that the Hessian matrix of U is the Jacobian matrix of the inverse demand functions $p(x)$. We thus have the following result,

$$\partial U/\partial x_i = p_i \quad \text{for all } i \Rightarrow \partial^2 U/\partial x_i \partial x_j = \partial p_i/\partial x_j$$
$$\text{for all } i, j \Rightarrow [HU] = [Jp]$$

which means that $[Jp]$ is also negative definite.

Since the Jacobian of the demand functions $x(p)$ is the inverse of the Jacobian of the inverse demand functions $p(x)$, i.e. since $[Jp] = [Jx]^{-1}$, and since a matrix is negative definite if its inverse is negative definite, we have that $[Jx]$ is also a negative definite matrix (and an *N–P* matrix).

Thus we have that any individual who solves the Hotelling choice problem (2) generates a demand function with a negative definite Jacobian matrix. Since this negative definiteness is preserved under aggregation, the aggregate excess demand Jacobian will be negative definite for a pure exchange economy composed exclusively of traders who solve Hotelling's choice problem (2). If we call a pure exchange economy where the demands of all individuals are generated from Hotelling's choice problem a *Hotelling Economy*, then the above results can be summarised in the following way,

$$[JZ] \text{ is negative definite for a Hotelling Economy} \tag{10}$$

Armed with this result let us return to the neoclassical dream.

Very little needs to be said about the first goal of *existence*. The standard existence results for the Walrasian model should carry over to the Hotelling Economy in a relatively straightforward way.[22]

It is easy to demonstrate that the Hotelling Economy satisfies the second goal; it has a *unique equilibrium*. Most of the uniqueness results for general equilibrium models involve an application of the Gale and Nikaidô (1965) theorem on the global univalence of mappings. Applied to the case of a Walrasian general equilibrium model it requires the aggregate excess supply Jacobian matrix $[-JZ]$ to be a *P*-matrix (have all positive principal minors).[23] We know from (10) that $[JZ]$ is negative definite for a Hotelling Economy, which means that $[JZ]$ it is an *N–P* matrix, but if $[JZ]$ is an *N–P* matrix, then $[-JZ]$ is a *P*-matrix and the equilibrium is unique.[24]

The *global stability* of the Hotelling Economy follows immediately as well. Arrow and Hurwicz (1958, p. 536) prove that if the aggregate excess demand Jacobian matrix is negative definite then the system exhibits global stability of the (unique) general equilibrium price vector p^*.[25] From (10) a Hotelling economy has such negative definiteness.[26]

There are some *comparative statics* results available for a Hotelling economy. Since the excess demand Jacobian of a Hotelling economy is an *N–P* matrix the following result holds: 'if there is a shift in tastes away from the numeraire commodity to commodity *i*, all other excess demand functions being unchanged, the equilibrium value of the *i*th price increases' (Quirk and Saposnik, 1968, p. 210). This is certainly not a very strong result, but given the general paucity of such comparative statics information, it represents a significant step beyond what is available for the standard (even stable) Walrasian model.

The implications of a Hotelling Economy for *welfare economics* are much stronger. As demonstrated in the next section, Hotelling's overarching motivation was the construction of the rigorous foundation for a welfare economics. His symmetry condition (7) guarantees that the welfare line integral defined in (9) measures social welfare. In a world composed exclusively of Hotelling demand functions the concepts of consumer's surplus and dead weight loss that are commonly used in 'applied' economics, would be entirely appropriate as measures of social utility from the viewpoint of formal general equilibrium theory. If Hotelling's symmetry condition is added to the standard consumer choice problem – if we start not with Hotelling's problem, but with the standard problem and add the additional restriction of the symmetry condition (8) – the result is a model with 'homothetic preferences.'[27] As Chipman states, 'Thus, within the context of the neoclassical theory of consumer behavior, Hotelling's "integrability conditions" are equivalent to the assumption that preferences are homothetic' (1982, p. 56).

Finally, it is quite clear that the Hotelling system completes the metaphor of utility as potential energy much more cleanly and much more obviously than the standard approach to neoclassical demand theory. In the standard theory the translation of energy into utility is there but it is submerged, hidden in the Slutsky symmetry condition; the translation is not hidden, nor is it denied in Hotelling. In presenting the case for the role of the energy metaphor in neoclassical economics Mirowski (1989) argued that the complete translation of energy into utility would require money and utility to be 'ontologically identical'; while this result followed from the mathematics (prices constitute a conservative vector field) it created a tension since one of the (other) scientific cornerstones of neoclassicism was to ground the economy in a 'natural' principle beyond money.

First notice that in the Hotelling system prices clearly constitute a conservative vector field; this is an immediate result of the symmetry condition (7). It is also the case that 'given a scalar field of utility . . . the price vector field may be deduced from it' (Mirowski, 1989, p. 223). In fact, since the derivatives (gradient) defines a scalar field, the first-order condition, $\partial U/\partial x_i = p_i$ for all i, not only says that prices can be deduced from such a field, it says that prices are identical to the field.

Also notice that in the Hotelling Economy, in contrast to the standard neoclassical model, the 'ontological identity' of money and utility is not repressed; it is entirely explicit. Recall that in Hotelling's objective function: total revenue (utility) and income ($\Sigma p_i x_i$) are literally added together. Since the symmetry conditions imply that prices $p(x)$ form a conservative vector field, the Hotelling model is quite literally a case where money and utility are effectively ontologically identical, because they may be extensively added together and conserved in the process. Hotelling wanted economics to become a science on a par with physics, and what that meant for him was postulation of certain crucial invariants patterned upon similar invariants in physics. These invariants, in turn, would serve to underwrite a legitimate economic empiricism, as well as to promote a situation where political interventions in the system would exhibit certain predictable regularities. That which has been repressed, or at least hidden, in much of neoclassical economics in the interim is worn proudly on the face of the Hotelling model. It clearly fulfills the neoclassical theory dream.

5 HENRY AND HAROLD: THE DETAILS

If possible, let us now reactivate once more our time machine in order to escape all these bloodless ideas clashing noiselessly in hyperspace, and return to a dreamtime where a few devoted flesh-and-blood people worked long and hard over their Monroe calculators to elevate economics to a plane where sensible ideas with clear foundations could be used to guide activity in the world. It is a place where a lone economist of middling reputation and modest means could set out upon a European grand tour and personally consult every economist of moment to his intellectual project.[28] It was a fabled time where, even though the community of mathematical economics was small and dispersed, one committed researcher could seek out another with whom he shared so much common ground that they would spontaneously write letters to each other every couple of days for weeks at a stretch about the thorny technical and philosophical issues which absorbed their professional lives.[29] Yet it was also a decade when unemployment was so rampant that it mocked the pretensions to expertise of each and every economist, and incubated ideologies so virulent that belief in rational choice seemed more a leap of faith than any religious commitment.

What was it that drew Henry Schultz, Polish immigrant, and Harold Hotelling, West Coast mathematician, together? Clearly their primary concern was neoclassical price theory, but dominating even that theme was their shared appreciation for an understanding of science which overrode their substantial differences. Both passionately believed that science was transparently mathematical, that it was firmly based upon the collection and statistical processing of empirical data, and that physics was the embodiment of the success of the scientific method. Hotelling, as we shall see shortly, had a very advanced grasp of physical theory, whereas Schultz's appreciation tended more towards the philosophical. In economics, they both adopted as first principles the idea that demand functions, i.e. some sort of price–quantity function, really did exist out there in the world: it was an objective relationship, and all other economic relationships were derivative from it. However, unlike the British Marshallians, they also subscribed to the basic creed that demand functions were obviously interdependent, functionally linked together by rational adjustments to other prices, incomes, as well as various accidents; therefore any simplistic phenomenological price–quantity plot was bound to be misleading. What was sorely needed was a general theory of the constitution of the demand function, the laws behind the law, as it were, in order to sort out the character and extent of the interdependencies; further, only a mathematical theory would do the job. Both turned to the same authors, essentially Walras, Pareto and Edgeworth, to provide the mathematical framework needed to sort through the interdependencies. Yet this set of commitments did not exhaust their common interests. Both started out in the 1920s engaged in extremely pragmatic tasks, estimating demand functions for agricultural staples, in response to the dire problems besetting the American farm community in that decade. Their interest in theory was never predominantly for its own sake, but rather was subordinate to having something convincing to say concerning tariffs, crop subsidies, production quotas, and the like. This background allowed for much greater prior commitment over the relevance and quality of the data than might generally obtain between two such mathematically inclined economists. More unusually, they also shared a very *avant garde* appreciation for the potential applicability of Fisherian statistical hypothesis testing. Thus, well prior to the crusade of Cowles econometrics, they had glimpsed the potential symbiosis of linear regression analysis and neoclassical demand theory; Schultz (but not Hotelling) was one of the very first to carry out a large-scale empirical inquiry informed by both traditions.[30] The extent of their agreement on a wide range of intellectual issues is all the more impressive when one considers that political orientation was not numbered among their shared enthusiasms. Hotelling was a fairly consistent advocate of market socialism throughout his career, whereas Schultz tended to veil his conservative politics behind a stance of technocratic neutrality. Less harmoniously, there was one more experience that they ultimately shared: both were deeply frustrated at the end of the 1930s with the way their joint project had panned out.

Much of this may sound so trivial to the reader that he or she may be wondering why it is even necessary to cover this ground. Are not the prognostications of this duo just another obvious moment in the long sequence of anticipations of modern neoclassical demand theory? Are not these just minor variations upon a common theme? No, they are not. Our point is precisely that in America in the 1930s there was no single 'theory of demand', no widely shared set of commitments which embodied a consensus neoclassical view of the relationship between the price of a good and the quantity of that good that would be sold. The closest thing to what passed for orthodoxy was Marshallian demand theory, which in practice simply denied the importance of interdependencies, worked in terms of separable utility functions, generally appealed to a putatively constant marginal utility of money, and up to that point had encouraged no systematic quantitative empirical research. The two main inspirations of the Schultz–Hotelling inquiry were anti-Marshallian in this specific sense, though historians of economics have not paid much attention to this variation in early neoclassicism. For instance, Henry Ludwell Moore was contemptuous of the Marshallian inability to confront real data; but he also came to believe that Walras and Pareto could not provide the requisite theoretical underpinnings for the demand curves which he never doubted were out there in the real world (Mirowski, 1990). Francis Edgeworth, on the other hand, represented the polar opposite position; he was unshakable in his belief in the palpable reality of individual utility maximisation, but thought the direct implication of the theory was that Marshallian demand curves did not, in general, exist (Mirowski, 1994). Thus circa 1930 it was not clear that there was any specific doctrine that qualified one as a neoclassical economist in good standing: demand curves did/did not exist; demand curves were primary/derived phenomena; individual utility maximisation did/did not exist; mathematical expression was essential/inessential to the theory; demand functions were separable/interdependent; demand theory was restricted to competitive situations or not. . . . the list goes on and on.

So what was it like to establish oneself as an economist amidst such confusion? No one seemed particularly paralyzed: they just presumed that everyone else was working on the same rough research project, unless acrimonious controversy convinced them otherwise. If there had been a cavernous split within American economics at this particular juncture, it would have been between the Institutionalists and the Marshallians, although even that divide could be easily overstated.[31]

Hotelling also did not seem to hold his Institutionalist colleagues at Columbia in high regard. As he wrote in 1962, 'I actually did teach economics there, but it was economics so mathematical that no member of the distinguished economics faculty there could understand it' (quoted in Darnell, 1990, p. 3). Nonetheless, there is a big difference between the pragmatic intellectual tolerance which characterised the working economist *in media res*, and the historian's attempt to homogenise everyone into a smoothly progressive narrative after the fact. In the thick of things it is never clear whether some disagreement over 'integrability' or the 'identification problem' will become central to one's identity as a neoclassical economist, since one's standing in the profession is a function of a wide range of considerations, some of which cannot be readily mapped into abstract doctrinal issues. Only well after the fact does one find a protagonist haplessly pigeonholed into categories and schools that determined his fate, if only in retrospect. Yet it must be stressed that the essence of being a neoclassical economist was exceptionally evanescent in the 1920s and 1930s, and that even restricting ourselves arbitrarily to what became known later as 'microeconomics', very little could have been taken for granted. The division of labour between theorists, empiricists and builders of econometric instruments which imposes so much doctrinal uniformity in the modern world had not yet taken hold before the Second World War.

Henry Schultz's induction into economic theory came at Columbia University under the tutelage of Henry Ludwell Moore, Wesley Clair Mitchell and Edwin Seligman. After a stint in the US Army in the First World War, he attended classes at the LSE and Galton Laboratory, where he learned statistics from Arthur Bowley and Karl Pearson. Upon returning to Columbia to pursue his doctorate, he served as statistical expert in an array of governmental agencies, from the Census Bureau to the Department of Labor. His 1925 thesis, written under Moore, the 'Statistical Law of Demand as Illustrated by the Demand for Sugar', was first published in the *Journal of Political Economy* in 1925, and then expanded into a book-length treatise (1928). Upon the strength of his work on demand, he was appointed to a position in the Economics Department at the University of Chicago in 1926, where he remained until his death in a car accident near San Diego on 26 November 1938. He devoted his entire professional life in his Chicago period to the creation and nurture of his own 'laboratory' for the collation of data and the graphing and hand calculation of the least-squares estimates of demand functions for various commodities; it was the innovation of Big Science in economics along the lines pioneered by Mitchell at Columbia. The results of this massive effort were compiled in his book *The Theory and Measurement of Demand* (1938), which appeared just after his untimely death. As Hotelling reported in his obituary, 'He had left Chicago for a semester to teach at UCLA while making a fresh start after the task that had absorbed him for so long. He jestingly remarked after the completion of the book that it was a good time to die' (1939, p. 98).

Since Schultz came to demand estimation somewhat ahead of Hotelling, it will be useful to try and characterise his early orientation towards the project. In both style and substance he openly proclaimed himself a protégé of Moore. In style, he was a master of the relevant literatures in many European languages, as well as maintaining a fair sophistication in mathematical tastes, at least relative to the economic orthodoxy of the day. He also followed Moore in his adherence to Pearsonian statistics and Pearsonian philosophy of science. In substance, he imitated his master in the use of link relatives and trend ratios to pre-process the data and allow for imponderable causes before fitting demand curves. However, quite early on he began to express some reservations about Moore's understanding of the 'law of demand'. Whereas Moore, having had his work disparaged by both Marshall and Edgeworth and therefore relatively unwilling to resort to constrained utility maximisation to buttress his findings (Mirowski, 1990), resisted most attempts to provide a theoretical grounding for the stability of his curves, Schultz seemed more insistent upon the provision of some underlying rationale for the 'laws' of which he was in pursuit. This tendency to look for the laws beneath the laws already shows up in a letter to Moore from December 1924.[32] There he queries Moore as to whether the demand curve derived from the method of link relatives is a static or dynamic law, and what effect the method has on the interpretation of the estimated elasticity of demand. Moore himself did provide an answer, but one which did not make reference either to utility or to the micro-interdependence of markets (Moore, 1925; 1926). What is striking about Schultz is that he continued to protest his allegiance to Moore's programme till his dying day, but in actual fact started moving towards the Walrasian model and away from Moore as early as 1928.

It may seem incongruous today to think of Walrasian general equilibrium as providing a superior operational framework for empirical microeconomics, but it is important to realise that in the 1920s one had to make some such move in order to extricate one's self from the perceived Marshallian paralysis. Here was how Schultz characterised the horns of the dilemma (note that he uses 'neo-classical' to mean Marshallian):

> To derive the ordinary (neo-classical) demand curve as a special case of the general demand function of the mathematical school... is to effect an improvement over the neo-classical approach. The neo-classical economists simply *ignored* the other variables, without troubling themselves first to introduce them into their demand equation and then to assign them constant values... Though the theoretical advantages of the Walras–Pareto over the neo-classical type of demand function are quite apparent, it may be asked whether its very generality renders it useless for practical purposes... How can we deal with such complicated functions in any practical problem? The answer is that, although *in theory* it is necessary to deal with the demand function in all its complexity in order to show that the price problem is soluble, *in practice* only a small advantage is gained by considering more than the first few highly associated variables. Which are the most highly associated variables cannot be answered *a priori*. (Schultz, 1928, pp. 26–7)

If one could summarise the increasing separation between Moore and Schultz over the demand side of the 'law', it was that Moore believed that this pragmatic choice of demand variables 'external' to own-price and quantity would not gain much in the way of effective guidance from the Walras–Pareto tradition, if only because it's 'generality' was empirically intractable on the one hand, and yet hobbled on the other by a litany of patently unrealistic assumptions (perfect competition, static equilibria, no account of nature of disturbances, etc.) (Moore, 1929, p. 53). Schultz, on the contrary, increasingly came to regard Moore's own principles of selection and his various 'corrections' to the data as arbitrary, perhaps even to the extent of vitiating his claim to find stable demand elasticities, and therefore sought what he hoped would be a more scientific grounding in Walrasian general equilibrium.

There was nothing acrimonious about this difference of opinion between the two men: indeed, their letters reveal a friendly discussion of the issues; the publications of each honour the other with laudatory citations throughout the mid-to late-1920s as they struggle with this conundrum; we have found no evidence that Schultz ever objected to Moore's marked Nietzschean philosophical relativism. Yet the ongoing conversation was abruptly cut short when Moore suffered something akin to a nervous breakdown in November 1927.[33] His illness forced him to retire from Columbia University in April 1929, just prior to the publication of his *Synthetic Economics*; he never published anything further up to his death in 1958 (Mirowski, 1990, p. 604). After an extensive search for an empiricist of commensurate reputation, Moore was replaced at Columbia by none other than: Harold Hotelling.

The paths of Hotelling and Schultz had already crossed prior to this point.[34] One of the distinguishing characteristics of Hotelling *vis-à-vis* Schultz was just how very little background and familiarity he had with economics (Darnell, 1990, p. 3). Hotelling had earned a degree in journalism at the University of Washington in 1919, but after some disappointment with that career, rejoined the University to study mathematics in 1920. He wrote his Master's Thesis on 'A Mathematical Theory of Migration' in 1921, and it was at this time apparently, that he conceived the guiding principle of his subsequent work:

> The combination of science and political economy led to the thought of applying methods proven so useful in the exact sciences to discover new truth in economics and political science . . . Ideas of flow and diffusion in mathematical physics looked as if they might have applications to human migration and to the flow of commodities.[35]

From there he obtained a scholarship to study mathematics at Princeton, writing his PhD on topology under Oswald Veblen in 1924. He claimed in retrospect, 'In going to Princeton I had intended to study mathematical economics and statistics; actually I found there was no one there who knew anything about either subject. I therefore studied the topology, differential geometry, analysis, mathematical physics and astrophysics that Princeton then offered, and all of these have to some extent contributed to my later work' (ibid.). In this he was fortunate, since Princeton was then in the forefront of upgrading American physics into the world-class status it would enjoy in the 1940s. Jobs for pure mathematicians were scarce, so Hotelling accepted a position at the recently-created Stanford Food Research Institute (SRI) as a mathematical and statistical consultant in 1924. One of his duties at SRI was to aid in the estimation of demand and supply functions for wheat and other crops; it was this, and his close cooperation with Stanford colleague Holbrook Working, that turned Hotelling's attention to problems of demand theory and estimation.

In 1927 Hotelling was appointed to a full-time position in the Stanford mathematics department, where he remained until his recruitment by the Columbia Economics department in 1931. His publications in the Stanford period reveal an ongoing interest in economic questions, but are scattered over subjects somewhat distant from pure Walrasian demand theory: the entire corpus consists of a 1925 paper applying Hamiltonians to the problem of optimal depreciation, the 1929 paper on the spatial distribution of oligopolists, and the 1931 paper on exhaustible resources. What one can glean from these early efforts is Hotelling's clear admiration for Cournot and Edgeworth as economic theorists. His writing on demand theory is essentially bounded by the 1932 article on Edgeworth's taxation paradox – the centrepiece of our current narrative – and some responses to critics in 1939; though publishing more than 40 further papers in the next two decades, there were no more substantial contributions to economic theory or empirical economics in their number. The coincidence of this lapse into silence with Schultz's death is striking, although Hotelling's work for the Statistical Research Group during the Second World War and his move to the University of North Carolina in 1946 should also be taken into account. Hotelling's withdrawal from demand theory has not been the subject of any commentary on the part of previous historians; we shall defer our consideration of this incident till the next section of this paper.

Hotelling himself tells us in the 1932 paper that his concerns about demand theory dated back 'several years' in discussions with Holbrook Working; it appears he had also been discussing them with Henry Schultz, as a subset of a larger conversation about the future of statistical theory.[36] Schultz was the editor of the Edgeworth paradox paper for the *JPE*, and his attempts to come to grips with the implications of the Hotelling Economy for his own massive project of estimation of demand curves sparked an extensive correspondence on these and related issues. We shall here weave a commentary upon the published text of Hotelling (1932a) with some discussion of the correspondence, since the latter influenced the final shape of the former.

And what a curious shape it is! From the title and the introduction, one might anticipate a straightforward explication of the conditions in orthodox price theory under which one would encounter the Edgeworth phenomenon of a tax on sellers reducing equilibrium prices; but we are warned right off that, 'For a random case, the purely deductive reasoning now available fails to tell us definitively whether it is more probable that a tax will increase or decrease the price paid by buyers' (p. 583). Hotelling sketches the reasons for this impotence of the mathematical theory in the broadest possible terms, but in fact he misrepresents the contents of the Pandora's Box which Edgeworth had pried into. For starters, Edgeworth produced his counterintuitive numerical example in order to undermine the whole idea of a stable demand curve, but Hotelling recasts the problem set by Edgeworth as one of finding out the conditions under which interdependent demand curves could rule out the appearance of the 'paradox'. Furthermore, to ask the question presumes the existence of a stable consensus on neoclassical price theory to serve as a point of departure, which we have argued did not then exist outside of Cambridge, UK. To top it off, the theory should then indicate a small number of parameters to be estimated, whose magnitudes would dictate the empirical appearance or absence of the paradox; but Hotelling must have known that situation was remote, since there was no reigning agreement as to the correct estimation of parameters – Schultz being one of the world's authorities on the attendant practical problems. Despite all this, Hotelling chose to portray the main impediment to an understanding of the Edgeworth paradox as a theoretical comprehension of interdependent demand functions, or as he put it, 'It is easy to fall into the error of supposing that demand functions for several commodities need satisfy no condition except the decrease of demand for each commodity when its price increases' (p. 582). Schultz, as the referee on Hotelling's paper, probably recognised a soulmate in the bearer of such cautionary tidings.

Following hard upon the insistence that the solution to the paradox must be theoretical, Hotelling's paper traverses the most amazing set of 'digressions', as he calls them; with one exception, most are ignored in subsequent citations of this paper. Section 4 proposes to derive the general form of the demand and supply curves of a single isolated commodity from the cumulative normal distribution function; but in fact it is an extreme special case for the milk market, with the derivation of the supply curve dependent upon some very specific spatial assumptions about production, and then some rather brazen hand-waving to construct the demand curve in a symmetrical fashion. The most noteworthy aspect of this section is that the curves are not derived from the constrained maximisation of utility, a fact then ignored in the next section on 'Demand and Supply Functions for Several Commodities'. This section contains the 'Hotelling Economy' which we have outlined above; it is also the section to which Schultz raised objections in the correspondence. In his letter of 14 July 1932, he asked how one should interpret the sum of prices times quantities in the system, as well as the meaning of Hotelling's insistence that the integrating factor λ would only come into play in the presence of an 'absolute limitation' of money expenditures. Hotelling's response that, 'Perhaps my tendency to neglect λ is due to the feeling which I have more strongly than Walras, Pareto or Fisher, that the bulk of buying and selling is done under circumstances in which the marginal utility of money does not play a very important part' was not entirely satisfying, since it could easily be confused with the standard position of the Marshallians.[37] Schultz subsequently opted to regard this line of defence of the 'price potential' model as an assertion of the special case of a constant marginal utility of money (as did Samuelson later), but that was not a faithful rendering of Hotelling's intentions. It is unlikely that Hotelling had in mind a particular thesis regarding the marginal utility of money and then wrote down his equation $U(x) - \Sigma px$ in order to give it expression; rather, he wanted to arrive at a price potential model analogous to that found in mechanics, and saw that this was how it could be done. The pay-off was a much sleeker and simpler version of neoclassical theory, one which 'excludes both supply curves which slope downward and demand curves which slope upward in the neighborhood of the solution ... These results hold not only for each seller but for the aggregate of sellers, analogously in the case of demand' (p. 597). This interpretation is borne out by the remainder of the 1932 paper.

The Section 6 of the (1932) paper develops a measure of elasticity of demand for competing versus complementary goods, patterned upon the formula for the classical correlation coefficient. Here again we observe Hotelling straining to construct a quasi-probabilistic foundation for demand theory, acknowledging 'those subtle analogies of economics with the theory of probability to which Edgeworth was so fond of alluding' (p. 599).[38] But more significantly, the symmetry of partial derivatives (our equation (8) above) which he dubs 'the integrability conditions' are elevated to the status of the core empirical content of his revised theory of demand. 'The difference of two symmetrically placed coefficients could be taken as a measure of the degree of inconsistency in buyer's judgments, or of the rigidity of an absolute limit on their money expenditures' (p. 598). The comparison of 'irrationality' with the existence of a strict budget constraint telegraphs Hotelling's unflattering view of what later became the orthodox mode of framing the maximisation problem. Section 7 on 'Taxation Under Free Competition' makes use of the Hotelling Economy model to extend the Edgeworth paradox to conditions of free competition, so as to argue that the phenomenon has nothing intrinsically to do with monopoly. Instead, the Hotelling Economy permits one to specify the general conditions under which the paradox will be observed, namely, whenever the commodities taxed compete in consumption and in production, with the proviso that one conforms to his own proposed definition of 'competing commodities'. In this section, Hotelling also suggests some of the social implications of the theory by indicating that certain forms of taxation and tariffs might have positive welfare effects in a Hotelling Economy. Section 8 reintroduces monopoly, in order to suggest 'cases of competition may exist which are as much as one pleases like monopoly' (p. 608); the unstated implication being that government intervention need not be predicated upon divergence from perfect competition.

The (1932) paper was daring in its ambitions, its structure and its politics. Starting with a 'counterintuitive' numerical example, it proceeded to propose a revision of demand theory which preserved some of the neoclassical idiom ('utility', 'maximisation', 'elasticity' and so forth) which gave 'laws' of supply and demand that everyone could understand; it also managed to endorse government intervention in the market on individualist welfare grounds; and if the sceptic still demanded a coherent rationale for the strange-looking equation $U(x) - \Sigma px$, they would be told that it could account for all existing 'anomalies' in demand theory without recourse to Giffen goods and perverse income effects. But best of all, this was real science in his view, because it displayed the sweet consistency one found in physics, and promised to put an end to endless metaphysical strife. As Hotelling wrote in the same year:

> To the doubts whether utility is objective, the reply may be made that demand and supply functions are objective things, and that if utility is defined as an integral or other functional of these func-

> tions, it too is objective. In this sense, utility has the same legitimacy as a physical concept such as work or potential, which is the line integral of force, provided certain integrability conditions are satisfied. The weaknesses of discussions of utility which start on a psychological basis are those of treatments of force which start from muscular exertions. (1932b, p. 452)

This was music to Schultz's ears; after all, he was the man who exhorted his students to read Percy Bridgman's operationalist opus *The Logic of Modern Physics* (1927) in their classes at Chicago. Although Hotelling probably did not know it, his model was also a recapitulation of the set of images from energetics which had prompted the 'Marginalist Revolution' in the first place (Mirowski, 1989).

From their correspondence, we can see that Schultz immediately set his laboratory to work calculating the demand functions and estimating the partial derivatives to test for the symmetry condition of the Hotelling Economy, as well as the quasi-correlation coefficient to measure complementarity. The letter of 22 September 1932 bore bad news: the symmetry or 'integrability' conditions had frequently failed to hold, and worse, sometimes the signs differed, so the complementarity coefficient would give conflicting results when the order of calculation was inverted.[39]

The ensuing correspondence is a wonderful illustration of the ways in which scientists scramble to react when things go awry and empirical results apparently bear bad tidings. Philosophers from Popper to Kitcher fail to adequately capture this sense of impending chaos and how scientists of good will struggle to keep it from getting out of hand. The pragmatic routine is to keep the news under wraps until a very small community of researchers decides how to approach, interpret and report the news. In the case of Schultz and Hotelling, the injunction to pause and reconstruct the meaning of their activities was especially imperative, given that their shared credo had been to insist that demand theory was meaningless in the absence of an acknowledgement of the pervasive interdependence of the economy. This sword proved two-edged, because when simple stories of the nature of that interdependence were impugned, as they were in this instance, then a mantra that 'everything depends upon everything else' was a prescription for all hell breaking loose. Because everything they believed in was now potentially up for grabs, it was necessary to restrict the discussion to the principals in the interests of reimposing a little order. Here is where the impressive range of prior sympathies between Schultz and Hotelling was crucial: they could more readily jointly assess possible escape routes precisely because they could take so much agreement for granted.

One could always resort to the standard moves for neutralising the test, and Schultz immediately put these on the table: 'An easy way to explain these exceptions is, of course, to assume that the economic behavior of farmers is not always rational – which may be a true assumption. I prefer, however, one of both of the following hypotheses: (1) the data are inaccurate and/or inadequate; (2) the equations do not contain relevant factors which ought to be taken into account' [HHC, Box 1: 10/31/1932]. However, neither Schultz nor Hotelling was satisfied with such rebuttals and both sought to try and turn the contrary evidence into more elaborate or (even better) new explanation. To that end, at various junctures of their correspondence they tried out all of the following options on each other:

(a) Attempt to link the lack of confirmation to the categories of 'completing versus competing' commodities (we would now say 'complements versus substitutes'). This directly follows up on the 1932 Hotelling paper.
(b) Locate the problem in the functional forms of the demand equations.
(c) Schultz noticed that the residuals of the individual equations were correlated, and wondered if this might signal some flaw in the estimation procedure. In retrospect, some might view this as an anticipation of the Haavelmo simultaneous equations critique.
(d) Perhaps there are other, more intuitive restrictions on the individual demand elasticities (such as their relative magnitudes) which should have been taken into account.
(e) In the Hotelling economy individual demands were supposed to aggregate up to market demands with no problem, but perhaps there was something about aggregation that spoiled the results after all.
(f) There may be macroeconomic problems, such as monetary and price level fluctuations, which supervened upon the outcomes. Schultz had attempted to correct for this by calculating 'real' prices. (This was, after all, the Great Depression!)
(g) One less appealing possibility was to give up on the Hotelling Economy and move instead to a model where utility was maximised subject to an independently given budget constraint, as in Walras and Pareto. But then, what would it mean for income or budget to be 'constant' in a regime where prices and expenditures were frequently changing? [HHC, Box 1: 1/29/33]

(h) Perhaps the Hotelling symmetry conditions couldn't be tested unless the demands for all relevant commodities were included. But this way lay empirical perdition.
(i) The meaning of 'integrability' was still contentious, even in physics, so perhaps it could be redefined and reinterpreted.
(j) So perhaps one should not try and test the conditions, but simply *impose them a priori* upon the demand estimations. The benefit would be that the extra information would render estimation more efficient and make individual demand curves simpler. This was the approach that was taken by most of those who followed Schultz in the field of empirical demand estimation.[40]

One lesson which might be drawn from this discussion is that under conditions of controlled criticism, scientists will sometimes range widely over a broad spectrum of various conjectural responses to bad news, that this may be a function of the extent to which they can control negotiations, and that a history of events which restricted itself to 'theory' or 'empiricism' or disciplinary boundaries or 'rational reconstructions' might (or more likely would) misconstrue where most of the action is located. Here Schultz and Hotelling ran the gamut: from rejecting the data to rejecting the legitimacy of least squares estimators, from tinkering with functional forms to locating the problem in their individualist grounding, from depending upon mathematical formalism to appealing to intuitions, and from simply imposing the theory *a priori* to scrapping it in favour of an unsavoury (for Hotelling) alternative. Of course, leanings toward one or the other response correlated with prior interests: Hotelling leaned towards theoretical elaboration of the Hotelling Economy, though he might entertain innovation in the theory of statistical estimation; Schultz would be the only one to maintain control of the actual empirical process, and was persistently on the lookout for auxiliary hypotheses in that domain. We can readily imagine a different combination of priors in a counterfactual third party to the negotiations who, say, did not share the commitment to agricultural demand functions that Schultz and Hotelling took as gospel, deeply mistrusted most statistical estimation procedures, and wanted to repress the physics metaphor more actively by denying the importance of integrability conditions – say, someone like Paul Samuelson.

By February of the next year, Schultz had more or less provisionally settled upon his version of events; after clearing it with Hotelling, it was published as (1933c). Earlier in the year, Schultz had revisited a problem that had worried him since his student days with Moore, namely, whether it was better to estimate demand curves using a time trend in the equation, or reprocessing the data into trend ratios or link relatives (1933a). Now he presented this paper as his first foray into the problem of interdependent demands for 'related goods', although this also had bothered him for almost a decade. While in many respects the paper is just a summary report of the correspondence with Hotelling, it is interesting to see how he distances himself from the Hotelling Economy, even while using it to structure his empirical programme. He begins by deriving what he calls the 'integrability condition' from a model with a fixed budget, but with the further specification of a constant marginal utility of money. He then acknowledges,

> The conditions . . . were first deduced by Professor Harold Hotelling, who followed a different procedure . . . by analogy from mechanics, [where he] made use of the notion of 'price potential,' whose partial derivatives are the quantities of the various commodities. I prefer, however, to adopt as my point of departure the fundamental classical definitions of related and independent commodities in terms of utility functions. (1933c, p. 481)

This may well be the first time someone had referred to the combination of generalised utility function and independent budget constraint as 'classical', something we now commonly observe in neoclassical theory textbooks. After describing Hotelling's pseudo-correlation measure of complementarity, he rejects that as well (p. 484). Finally, he reports his regression equations for barley, corn, hay and oats. The major interest in the estimated coefficients is their possible conformity to the 'integrability conditions', which are reported in his Table VII (p. 500). The news, as we know, was not good: of the six pairs of comparisons, two had opposite signs, three more were not significantly different from zero, and the barley–hay relation suggested that the commodity demands were independent, so that integrability conditions were unnecessary. The long final section of the paper is taken up with a list of auxiliary hypotheses which are intended to explain away what is plainly presented as a disconfirming result. It is of interest to note that at no time in the text does Schultz entertain the notion that it is the underlying neoclassical theory – that is, the constrained maximisation of an independently given utility function – which should be rejected; this stands in contrast to the correspondence, where he admits this should be entertained 'only as a last resort' [HHC, Box 1: 2/2/33]. Instead, he presents seven options in the paper, only to repudiate most of them: (1) the order of consumption is relevant; (2) the marginal utility of money is not constant; (3) the demand curve is shifting about through time; (4) some related goods were left out of the estimation procedure; (5) the demand curves for separate commodities actually refer to different populations of consumers; (6) data quality is poor; (7) something about the estimation procedure cannot account for the fact that elasticities turn out to have different magnitudes when one inverts the demand curves and regresses price on quantities rather than vice versa.

This is of course a good example of what philosophers of science would call the Duhem–Quine (or underdetermination) problem; rather than reject the theory, the negative implications of contrary evidence are aimed at the auxiliary hypotheses in the original test system. Schultz's response to this problem – a problem that is often called the problem of 'where to aim the arrow of *modus tollens*' – seemed to be not to actually aim the arrow at all, but rather to fire a shotgun blast quite blindly into the set of auxiliary hypotheses.

Although Schultz's report would hardly seem encouraging for Hotelling's project, the two men remained in close contact, still worrying away at the meaning and implications of integrability. There was a personal visit in June, and a brace of letters in July, and another visit in August as Schultz prepared to embark upon his year-long tour of Europe. This persistence is all the more remarkable given that political differences also threatened to flare up.[41] Schultz's travels were salutary from the vantage point of learning what others were doing about the foundations of demand theory and problems of statistical estimation of interdependent functions,[42] but it did tend to put the damper on the correspondence and the empirical work, as Schultz lost almost the entire staff of his laboratory during his absence. Hotelling took advantage of the hiatus, however, to compose his own response to Schultz's research report, which appeared as 'Demand Functions with Limited Budgets' (1935). This is the next critical juncture in the history of neoclassical demand theory, since up to this point neither Schultz nor Hotelling was aware of Slutsky's 1915 paper, and it is at this nexus that a third character, Milton Friedman, makes a critical appearance.

Hotelling (1935) is a curious paper, and one ignored by just about everyone. It indicates on page one that it is intended as an extension of the 1932 paper, but also that it takes off from Schultz (1933c). One striking thing about it is how Hotelling dismisses the negative empirical findings.[43] But that is just a prelude, for the paper is unremittingly theoretical; indeed, lacking even the spare level of 'economic content' found in the preceding paper of 1932. The paper reads as if Hotelling decided that he would present his Hotelling Economy at a higher plane of rigour, and then produce a parallel model of constrained maximisation of utility subject to independent budget constraint (a model Schultz had prematurely called 'classical') at the same level of rigour; the object would appear to be to compare the two and demonstrate the palpable superiority of Hotelling's version. But things didn't quite work out as planned: the integrability conditions for the 'classical' model were a mess as he conceived them, and the only restrictions which could be derived from them for demand functions were some inequality constraints (equation 5.1, p. 76) which could not even be aggregated up with any dependability to market level demands. The paper ends there quite abruptly, perhaps because the implications of the exercise remained unclear even to the author.

Given subsequent developments in the history of neoclassical demand theory, we think one of the great ironies of this narrative is that the first mention of the Slutsky equations among our protagonists was by Milton Friedman.[44] Friedman was the other major link between Schultz and Hotelling. Beginning as a graduate student under Schultz at Chicago, he worked with Hotelling in 1933–4, only then to return to Chicago in the fall of 1934 to re-establish Schultz's statistical laboratory upon his return from Europe (Schultz, 1938, p. xi). Schultz himself did not seem to be clear exactly when he 'discovered' the 1915 Slutsky paper, hinting at one place (1938, p. 38n.) that he knew about it in 1933, and in another (1938, p. 620) in 1934; but it is most likely it was brought to his attention during his European tour. However, there is no question about when Hotelling was informed of its relevance. We reproduce most of the body of a letter from Friedman to Hotelling, written from Chicago, dated 6 March 1935:

> I have been reading your article in the last issue of Econometrica and was interested in applying your condition (3.9) to those pairs of commodities studied by Schultz in his inter-relations paper, which did not satisfy the original integrability conditions. In each case condition (3.9) is satisfied. You may be interested to know that Slutsky in his paper in *Giornale degli Economisti* for 1915 developed valid integrability conditions under the assumption that income is fixed. He proceeded by getting expressions for the derivatives of the quantities with respect to income as well as to price. The basic he result he obtains is (translated into your symbols):

$$\frac{\partial q_j}{\partial p_i} = \lambda \frac{M_{ij}}{M} - q_i \frac{\partial q_j}{\partial m},$$

where M is the determinant of the φ_{ij}'s bordered by the p's. Since M is symmetrical, M_{ij} is equal to M_{ji} and we can write the integrability condition:

$$\frac{\partial q_j}{\partial p_i} + q_i \frac{\partial q_j}{\partial m} = \frac{\partial q_i}{\partial p_j} + q_j \frac{\partial q_i}{\partial m}.$$

This condition reduces to the simple one, of course, when the marginal utility of money is kept constant. This paper by Slutsky is really most remarkable. He clearly recognises the difficulty presented by the non-measurability of utility and indeed presents a proof that it is impossible to obtain the second derivatives of the utility function from empirical data. His paper contains practically everything that is in the Hicks–Allen paper recently published and much more besides.

One thing that has been bothering me is the question of the conditions under which the Slutsky integrability condition will hold for the aggregate demand if it holds for the individual demand curves. [HHC, Box 1, Friedman to Hotelling]

Schultz, at least, thought this was the equation of his dreams, the long-sought clarification of the general theory of interdependence of demands. After a long hiatus, he wrote Hotelling on 6 May 1935:

> I had intended to write to you about my discovery of Slutsky's paper . . . but Milton Friedman anticipated me. The paper is remarkable for completing Pareto's work on demand and supply and for giving the Hicks–Allen results in a simpler and more understandable form. The discovery of this paper necessitated my rewriting a section of the first chapter of my forthcoming book which I thought had reached its final stage some three years ago. Believing that you would be interested in my summary of the Pareto–Slutsky results, I am enclosing my revised chapter as well as a translation of Slutsky's paper. [HHC, Box 1: 5/6/35]

Hotelling's response of 17 May to this letter is revealing; it is also the last bit of correspondence between the two we have been able to find on the topic. He provides comments on what would become Chapter 1 of (Schultz, 1938) and he also reasserts the relevance of the inequalities derived in his 1935 paper, which, by the way, never gets cited in the final text of Schultz's book *The Theory and Measurement of Demand*. Then comes the crucial paragraph on Slutsky:

> Slutsky's paper is a valuable find. You have performed a useful service by discovering it. I wish that I had known of it and of the work of W. E. Johnson and of Hicks and Allen in order to refer to them in my Econometrica article. Fortunately for me, all these writers narrowly missed finding my main result, the inequality (3.10). They also missed the integrability condition (1.5) on demand functions. But to my surprise I find that Slutsky discovered some relations which I did not. These include particularly his equations involving variation of demand with respect to income (i.e. the partial derivatives of quantities with respect to income), and the cyclic relation in the middle of p. 24 of the manuscript, which is the dual of my relation (1.5) in that prices are interchanged with quantities. This latter relation is of much interest, inasmuch as it implies the existence of a *price potential*, a function of the prices whose derivatives are proportional to the quantities. A complete duality between prices and quantities is thus established. In view of this, I suspect the later sections of my recent article might be rewritten and improved. [HHC, Box 1: 5/17/35]

So there we have it: forgotten precursors are unearthed, the scales fall from everyone's eyes, all players converge upon an interpretation of events we recognise in retrospect as our own orthodoxy, empirical puzzles are clarified, testing and criticism finally lead to the truth. But wait – not so fast. Even in the above passage, there remains a note of discord: Hotelling is still asserting the primacy of a price potential, even in the Slutsky model. But we have argued in previous sections of this paper this is precisely what one must relinquish when one moves from the Hotelling Economy to the Arrow–Debreu model. Did Hotelling in fact repudiate his own prior model? Or was it repudiated for him by someone else?

The next development in the sequence of events was Schultz's (1935) *JPE* paper, written with the assistance of Milton Friedman. The objectives of the article were to promulgate the Slutsky conditions as the culmination of the Paretian tradition in price theory, linking changes in income to those in price and demand; but also to provide a comparative 'test' of the Slutsky conditions *vis-à-vis* the earlier Hotelling integrability conditions. It is clear from the text of this article that Schultz believed that here was the potential explanation for the poor showing of his earlier empirical foray; he now asserted 'they rest[ed] on weak foundations' (p. 457), so now the Hotelling conditions should only be treated as a special case. Of course, 'generality' is in the eye of the beholder – and as Schultz himself had admitted in the previous decade, too much generality might not have a salutary effect on a useful theory – so he proposed to drive the point home by an empirical comparison of the Hotelling and Slutsky symmetry conditions in newly-estimated demand curves for beef, pork and mutton in the United States during the period 1922–33.

Yet once more, things did not turn out as anticipated. Many of the standard errors were too large, and in the case of pork versus mutton, the estimated partials had opposite signs. Worst of all, the Slutsky 'correction' didn't seem to correct much of anything from the viewpoint of the theory. Schultz's prognosis was restrained: 'the two conditions are satisfied only approximately, the more general Slutsky condition, which is free from the assumption of the measurability of utility and the constancy of the final utility of money, yielding approximately the same results as the simple Hotelling condition' (p. 477). It seems possible to date the suppression of the Hotelling Economy on purely conceptual grounds from this point. The ironies of this impasse were apparently not savoured by the duo. Hotelling, who all along had restricted his search for a more scientific demand theory to theoretical considerations, had found their empirical consequences largely intractable; whereas Schultz, the champion of an empirical operationalism, found himself downplaying empirical results in the interest of theoretical generality as he perceived it. One reasonable interpretation of Schultz's results would have been that Slutsky was not an empirical improvement upon the Hotelling Economy; and worse, all this concern over the interdependent character of demand was going nowhere, since none of the restrictions derived from those formally-derived quantitative considerations were apparently supported by the empirical estimations. These were pointedly not the interpretations broached in Schultz's conclusions, who opted instead to conclude that 'so apparently simple a concept as independent consumptions turns out to be a complex and elusive notion' (p. 481).

How about Hotelling? Did he renounce his Neoclassical Dream? Not by a long shot. Because the correspondence ceases here, we must depend upon the last published statements he made on price theory, namely a short popular piece (1936), his 1937 Presidential Address to the Econometric Society (1938a), and his review of Schultz's final book (1938b). A summary synthesis of his position in the late 1930s would need to incorporate all of the following points (although it would be possible to dispute Hotelling's weighting of their relative importance): first, demand curves are still treated as the primary economic phenomenon. Second, the interconnectedness of demands is treated as a fact, and by implication, the Walras–Pareto tradition is the right way to try and get at the nature of the phenomenon. Third, Hotelling showed no inclination to challenge Schultz's findings by actually going out and estimating some demand functions himself, although he continued to insist that the integration of theoretical and empirical studies was the hallmark of successful science. Thus, the dispute would be prosecuted on the theoretical plane, if at all. To our knowledge, he mentioned the poor showing of Schultz's tests only once, avoiding any admission that they may have impugned his own model (1939, p. 100). Fourth, henceforward he would always cite Slutsky as an interesting elaboration of the question of the symmetries of multiple demand functions, without actually endorsing it one way or the other as the sole correct approach. Fifth, he continued to cite his own symmetry conditions as valid, at one point writing, 'I have shown that there is good reason to expect these integrability conditions to be satisfied, at least to a close approximation, in an extensive class of cases' (1938a, p. 247). Sixth, he continued to advocate an approach to welfare economics that required demand curves to satisfy his (not Slutsky's) symmetry conditions; he followed the previous quote on integrability conditions with: 'If they are satisfied, the surpluses arising from different commodities, and also the surpluses belonging to different persons, may be added to give a meaningful measure of social value' (1938a, p. 247). And finally, directly related to his welfare economics and perhaps of overriding significance, he proceeded to make use of the interdependence of demands in neoclassical theory in order to prosecute his own political agenda and to propose his own analysis of the causes of the Great Depression.

The upshot is that Harold Hotelling never firmly repudiated his own Dream model in favour of the Slutsky formulation, because there was no good reason to do so. Neither version produced a superior empirical fit to the data; and the Slutsky formula was less attractive theoretically for certain purposes, which appeared to be the primary consideration for Hotelling. There was no question of his ever capitulating to Schultz's interpretation that it was to be downgraded to a minor special case of a constant marginal utility of money in the 'true' fixed income model with the Slutsky symmetry conditions. The two models remained for Hotelling, if not for Schultz, rival interpretations of how interconnected demands might mesh.

Perhaps it is no accident that at the point at which Hotelling decided to become more insistent about the political content of the theory he favoured, the pipeline to Chicago and the correspondence were both shut off. Hotelling continued to provide employment opportunities for Chicago products such as Milton Friedman and George Stigler during the war, in the Statistical Research Group at Columbia (Stigler, 1988, p. 61), but the bloom seemed to be off the rose, and their later works such as Friedman and Wallis's (1942) paper on indifference curves and his paper on the income tax (1952) were intended as reprimands of Hotelling's programme. What Hotelling did in his last economics papers was use both the Slutsky version of neoclassical theory and his own Hotelling Economy to argue that government intervention at the micro level was eminently justified by these theories. Sometimes he might use the Slutsky version, as when he argued for the superiority of an income tax over excise taxes; but just as frequently he would use the Hotelling Economy in order to point to a 'meaningful measure of social value' to make welfare arguments. His policy prescriptions, never entirely spelled out, seemed to imply a kind of quasi-nationalisation of production which would 'put into effect a system of sales at marginal cost, with overhead paid out of taxes on incomes, inheritances, and the site values of land, [then] there would exist a possible system of compensations and collections such that everyone would be better off than before' (1938a, pp. 257–8).

It is here that reactions to the Great Depression and general economic conditions have a looming presence in understanding subsequent attitudes and responses to the appropriate elaboration and development of neoclassical price theory. In a Hotelling Economy, incomes are not broken out as a separate invariant term but conflated with utility in one over-arching conservation principle: therefore, Hotelling did not believe that aggregate shortfalls of income/expenditure were the root cause of the Depression; rather it had to do with the impact of technological development upon the number of industries facing falling marginal costs (1938a). Hence, for Hotelling, the solution involved microeconomic manipulation of the price system by the government under the guidance of his Dream-based welfare economics. In contrast, Schultz felt that existing theory said nothing about the causes of the Depression. This was acknowledged by Hotelling in his eulogy for Schultz: 'His results do not, for example, offer an explanation of business cycles. He was aware of this, and preferred to study static theory, rather than joining the great procession into monetary and business-cycle theory' (1939, p. 99). But there was nothing sacrosanct about this interpretation of the Slutsky version of price theory, either. Since income was broken out as a separate magnitude in the Slutsky equation, one could equally maintain that Slutsky-based demand functions were the ideal scientific microfoundations for an income-driven Keynesian macroeconomics, an interpretation which gained two different sets of adherents in Cambridge, MA and at the Cowles Commission. These schools simply opted to ignore the warnings of Hotelling and Schultz that the Slutsky version did not seem to have nice properties under aggregation. And then there were those who wanted to repudiate all of the above because of their not-so-hidden socialist tendencies, to suppress the interactive income terms, and return to a 'Marshallian' mode of theorising in the sense that Schultz had disparagingly used the term in 1928. This position, of course, is exemplified by Frank Knight, Milton Friedman and the Chicago School from the late 1940s onwards.

A common narrative in the literature of economic methodology is a saga where mathematical savants take various imprecise intuitions in applied sciences, render their implications more clear and transparent in the idiom of formalised theory, and then pass them on to statistical specialists in empirical work, who test the mettle of the tradition with quantifiable decision rules. At first glance, the collaboration of Schultz and Hotelling would seem a prime historical candidate exemplifying this 'method' (Christ, 1985; Morgan, 1990; Mosak, 1987) but our story should raise doubts about the validity of such a tale. Schultz, of course, always made ceremonious appeal to this construal of his project: 'The equations summarising the interrelations in question constitute a category of laws which is comparatively rare in the social sciences: they specify *quantitatively definite relations* which must exist between the variables – if the theory is true' (1938, p. 646, emphasis in original). Yet, as we have seen, nothing was ever quite so clean as this image of bold precise conjecture and definitive attempted refutation. What happened instead was some polite sparring over the conceptual legitimacy and exact implications of the mathematical restatement of the theory which were never completely reconciled, and some statistical exercises which were delphic, at best, in their endorsement of any versions of the theory being entertained. Worse, this was the best that the duo could produce after extensive pre-publication negotiations over any number of auxiliary hypotheses, negotiations carried out under the most favourable circumstances one could ever hope for: out of the limelight, between two fundamentally friendly parties, sharing a commitment to essentially the same research programne. When all was said and done, the only excuse that Schultz could come up with after labouring so mightily to bring forth such meagre results was to appeal to a view of science which, if broached in the 1990s, would be referred to with disdain as 'social constructivist':

> The foregoing summary strongly suggests that the success of a new method or idea depends on the social and intellectual milieu in which it is launched. At best, statistical research is difficult, expensive, time-consuming, and not so productive of doctoral dissertations as is historical or literary research. A student may spend several years in an effort to determine the factors affecting the demand for or the supply of a commodity and have little to show for his work, while the same time and effort spent on antiquarian research would almost certainly have yielded material for one or more publications. Unless, therefore, conditions are exceptionally favorable to statistical research in economics, it will fail to take root and proliferate. (1938, p. 660)

Although this is not the way the subsequent history is usually presented (with mathematical neoclassical economists and econometricians fighting a brave uphill battle against all the formidable social forces arrayed against them) because we are favourably inclined towards SSK, we shall entertain it briefly. Although it is certainly true that the risks of Big Science are palpably greater than the cottage handicraft science of days of yore, it is not at all obvious that the reason something like Schultz's vision of price theory eventually came to dominate economic orthodoxy was technological progress in empirical economics leading to a fall in the costs of computation and data compilation, to the point where they were comparable to what he calls 'antiquarian research'. The best way to telegraph this point is to temporarily cast our gaze forward to subsequent 'tests' of the Slutsky symmetry relations in the period after Schultz and up to the present.

Let us ask a potentially embarrassing question: if the Slutsky relations did not pan out so nicely for Schultz in the 1930s, when did they finally become empirically respectable, so the doctrine could occupy its contemporary price of place enshrined in modern textbooks? The answer is that it never happened. You would not glean this from most textbooks; instead, one has to look for this admission in some of the explicitly methodological writings of econometricians (Gilbert, 1991; Keuzenkamp 1994; Keuzenkamp and Barten, 1995) or the few comprehensive surveys of 'consumer behaviour' (Deaton and Muellbauer, 1980). (One might also observe that the economists admitting this are almost exclusively Europeans, whereas the active stabilisation of neoclassical price theory was primarily an American phenomenon, as described in the next section.) It seems that, even in the face of the infinite number of compromising considerations which bedevil estimation of a system of demand equations, the Slutsky symmetry conditions and the related condition of zero degree homogeneity in prices are persistently rejected in statistical tests.[45] The relative silence which greets this unmistakably disappointing outcome is deafening; but more to the point, the excuses which are tendered a half-century after Schultz, after massive investments of time and effort about which he could only dream, show very few signs of improved imagination or innovation:

> We do not believe that, at this stage, it is necessary to abandon the axioms of choice in the face of the results of this chapter. Ultimately, of course, given sufficiently convincing evidence, we should be prepared to do so. But, for reasons given in this last section, it is clear that there are many more obvious misspecifications that should be corrected first. (Deaton and Muellbauer, 1980, p. 82)

We would like to signal to methodologists that our narrative of the development of neoclassical demand theory is making progressively less reference to notions of hypothesis testing and rigorously formulated theory as we move forward in time. That was certainly the case for Hotelling and Schultz, at any rate. Hotelling, as we have observed, essentially dropped out of the neoclassical theory community by 1943. There is some evidence that he did so out of disappointment in the direction that the economics profession had taken. In a 1959 letter to Carl Shoup, he wrote:

> I have had the impression that few people ever read my 1932 paper and it is good to know that you, at least, think it worth taking seriously. Each of my two articles in the *Journal of Political Economy*, the 1931 article on mineral economics and the 1932 to which you allude, represented about a quarter of my time for several years and it is a pleasure to know that the work was not in vain. (Quoted in Darnell, 1990, p. 23)

As for the other member of our duo, there are some indications that Schultz was not held in high esteem by his colleagues towards the end of his tenure at Chicago (Stigler, 1988, pp. 25–7; Reder, 1982; Houthakker, 1983, p. 60, n. 7; Friedman in Hammond, 1993, p. 222). Frank Knight's contempt for Schultz was openly expressed; and what is of greater moment for our narrative, there is some indication that Schultz's favoured student may have begun to turn on him: 'Two of the students not favourably impressed by Schultz were Friedman and Stigler' (Reder, 1982, p. 4). This hostility is apparently the origin of numerous slurs cast upon Schultz's mathematical abilities in the secondary literature (Reder, 1982, p. 4; Stigler, 1988), which seems to be overstated. Even Samuelson engages in this disparagement, while revealing that one of the primary inputs to the *Foundations* was his own attempt to provide a resolution to the impasse precipitated by Schultz. 'Already in 1936, on a trip back to Chicago, I had unsuccessfully tried to interest Henry Schultz in Jacobian conditions for rigorous aggregation (functional dependencies of separability). Also, I spent countless hours pursuing testable regularities that aggregate demand data must theoretically obey' (Samuelson, 1986, p. 223). This rush to press an indictment of crippling mathematical deficiencies against the man who brought the issue of the scientific pretensions of neoclassical theory to a head would seem, at least to an historian, itself to require some serious explanation. While Schultz clearly treats Hotelling as the superior mathematician in their correspondence, Hotelling treats him in return with unhesitant respect as an equal.

Schultz, as already mentioned, died in a car crash in November 1938; but his *The Theory and Measurement of Demand* was a sad anticlimax for those who had closely followed his earlier publications. The book was largely a reprint of the two articles discussed above (1933c and 1935), with a few more estimated demand curves to augment the empirical report; but the conclusions were basically the same. 'Most of the terms of the calculated conditions agree in sign but differ in absolute value, while the others differ also with respect to sign. Furthermore, the standard errors of the statistical parameters are so large that no conclusion about the integrability conditions of the *true*, underlying demand functions has a large degree of probability' (1938, p. 600). Thus the neoclassical price theorist at the end of the 1930s was confronted with a book that insisted upon the 'integrability conditions' of Slutsky as the core empirical content of that theory, but simultaneously reported that said content was either wrong, or so inaccessible to state-of-the-art empirical techniques of the time such that very little could be said one way or the other about the theory.

But something of the encounter with Hotelling had rubbed off, and it had to do with the reasons why one had to keep hammering away at the integrability conditions, even though results to date had been so very disappointing. In the Hotelling Economy, as we argued earlier, the price potential is modelled upon a system of potential forces in mechanics; and Hotelling's 'symmetry conditions' were the analogue to the law of the conservation of energy. Schultz understood that he was trying to extend the analogy to the Slutsky symmetries, but that the programme had yet to settle upon the definitive invariants.

> The third principle [in physics] is that of the conservation of energy and is the most important of all . . . But what equations of motion and what laws of conservation of comparable scope do we have in economics? To ask the question is to answer it. There are none that have the definiteness and universal applicability of the corresponding physical laws. Our economic laws of change are simply empirical extrapolations of the present situation . . . True we can write down equations which are analogous to the laws of conservation . . . we can think of the total utility function – if it exists – as corresponding to the energy potential whose partial derivatives measure the forces which guide the movements of the individual. But, unfortunately, we know neither the values nor the forms of the required functions. (1938, p. 57)

Incongruously, herein lie the origins of how such an unpropitious set of events and circumstances could become within two decades the basis for the core doctrine of a growing, thriving, self-confident school of economic analysis. Two mathematical theories of price were proposed, closely related by their heuristic inspiration drawn from the king of the sciences, physics. They differed by what seemed at first a minor variation: the treatment of income in the optimisation problem. Both protagonists recognised that the choice of theoretical variant had something to do with the postulation of conservation principles within their respective constructions of the economy, but there they rested in a state of suspended animation, stymied by the lack of any transcendental criterion with which to convince the other of a demonstrable superiority. Notions of conceptual generality, empirical success, political efficacy, logical necessity, mathematical tractability, sociological efficacy – nothing would do the job right; no argument could decisively trump the others. Neither Schultz nor Hotelling could overcome the obstacle, and thus they were removed by Chance or withdrew by Choice from the arena.

It is our thesis that *this impasse marked the defining moment of the postwar American neoclassical orthodoxy*, one whose significance was buried by the subsequent contest between at least three distinct schools to transcend the impasse between the 'price potential' model and the Slutsky symmetry interpretation. Most of the major players of the three schools were present at the creation, and two of them – Milton Friedman and Paul Samuelson – played supporting roles in the Hotelling–Schultz dialogue. The stinging truth we can see in retrospect, and documented as such in prior sections of this chapter, is that the Hotelling Economy could have given neoclassical economics what it wanted, if only they had not gotten so hung up on the interpretation of what they considered to be the 'correct' budget constraint. Why was this particular treatment of the budget constraint the itch that absolutely had to be scratched, when neoclassicals of all schools were willing to overlook numerous other bizarre, counterintuitive and outlandish aspects of their models? Discussion of this question deserves an entire chapter, one which we beg the reader's indulgence to postpone till a future date and setting. For now, we merely wish to indicate how the treatment of the 'income effect' in demand theory is the key to the splitting of the American neoclassical orthodoxy into the three distinct schools of the post-Second World War period.

6 DEMAND DEMENDED; OR, THE DREAM DEFILED

We offer one last invitation to step into the time machine, now to be transported to the travails of a nation at war. War disrupted the careers of most of the protagonists of the next chapter of our saga; but it did more than that. First, it provided a five-year hiatus right at the point where the death of Schultz and the failure of the Schultz–Hotelling project had helped raise the question: 'Whither mathematical economics?' There is some evidence that the crisis was not merely localised around these two individuals: for instance, a case can be made that the Cowles Commission was floundering in the years 1937–8, and perhaps through 1942.[46] The Chicago Economics Department was also in trouble in the early 1940s (Reder, 1982, pp. 5–6). Although it seems almost crass to mention such a trivial consideration in the midst of a major worldwide conflagration, the war did provide breathing space to take time out and reconsider the possible options for a future neoclassical theory. But, second, the war had a more profound impact upon the next generation of social scientists in terms of the way that they understood 'science'. While some were recruited to government jobs strictly for their economic expertise, the individuals we are most concerned with were thrown together with physical scientists in some entirely novel situations. Often because of their mathematical expertise they were engaged in research that might normally be the province of engineers or meteorologists or physical statisticians alongside physicists who were also temporarily engaged in 'applied' work; sometimes this new form of collaboration gave rise to a new hybrid called 'operations research'.[47] The importance of this phenomenon for our present narrative is that it fostered the enhanced importation of newer notions of science into the economics profession, as well as blurring the conceptual boundaries between persons and things. Given some of the subsequent programmatic statements of the principals, it is all too easy to overlook the fact that in the heat of battle each school brandishing a different reaction to the problems of income effects in neoclassical price theory made explicit reference to how they thought analogous problems were handled in physics, as we shall indicate below.

As our time machine whizzes past bombs bursting in air, it may be prudent to suggest how our narrative of events might differ from more conventional versions. The first, and most obvious, is that where many historians see unity of purpose and concepts, we see diversity. At any particular juncture, for rhetorical or tactical purposes, protagonist 1 could assert that he was discussing the same entity as protagonist 2, but there is no rule of thumb that protagonist 2's acquiescence was a prerequisite for the discipline to maintain its integrity. The second difference is that many methodologists write as though some protagonist first adopts a methodological stance or set of principles, and only after that fashions a theory or empirical exercise to conform with those epistemological beliefs. While there certainly are cases where epistemic priors have an influence on the local practices of a particular researcher (Schultz's operationalism being a case in point) the influence is nowhere near as significant or as unidirectional as often claimed. Indeed, we suspect that much of the methodological warfare, backpedalling and inconsistency of Friedman, Samuelson and others is as much an artifact of their initial commitments in the arena of price theory as it is of their philosophical 'influences'. In other words, we think it as likely that research schools coalesce around certain doctrinal theses – say, the treatment of the budget constraint and the Slutsky symmetry conditions – as around some abstract methodological ukase about 'testing' or 'rationality' or 'science'. Third, we find that our narrative inverts a whole range of conventional wisdom about how economics ended up the way it did. For example, in our view, it was Keynesian doctrine which acted in a critical way to determine the shape of neoclassical microeconomics in America, rather than (initially) the other way round. Or, again, it was neoclassical price theory which shaped the initial orthodox configuration of econometrics, especially in its treatment of error terms, rather than the other way round. Or, once more, Chicago did not reject the Slutsky-tinted version of general equilibrium theory in the 1940s because they were somehow lagging in appreciation for its cogency, perhaps due to a deficit in mathematical sophistication; they rejected it after being responsible for its introduction into the American context. Things are indeed not what they often seem.

As we have repeatedly intimated in this text, we believe there were three major reactions to the breakdown of the Schultz–Hotelling programme, each characterised primarily by its approach to the budget constraint and the treatment of the 'integrability' or symmetry conditions, precisely because that is where our duo had located the problem. There were, of course, yet other options; but we will make no attempt to deal with them here.[48] There was also a further development which muddied the waters and obscured the sharp outlines of these three schools, namely, von Neumann's axiomatisation of 'expected utility theory' which raised the stakes of the challenge as to the appropriate location of stochastic considerations within the theory of consumer choice. Again, we must beg the reader's indulgence for not dealing with this issue here, even though it is of utmost importance for a comprehensive history of postwar neoclassical price theory. Instead, the reader should understand we are only dealing with purely deterministic consumer choice theory, in artificial isolation from all considerations of production, uncertainty, knowledge, strategic behaviour as in game theory, questions of less than perfect competition, and the like.

With those caveats, let us briefly fly over the three main schools precipitating out on the American landscape in the immediate post-war period: the Cowles Commission approach, which incorporates Arrow–Debreu general equilibrium theory as a later development; the Chicago approach of Frank Knight and Milton Friedman; and the approach of Paul Samuelson, which became regnant at MIT. Each of these three schools could be compared along a number of different dimensions, such as their conception of methodological individualism, their politics, their favoured mathematical formalism, their vision of empiricism, and so on; but we wish to make the strong assertion that many of their earmarks or traits can be readily organised and rendered comprehensible through their characteristic treatment of the symmetry conditions and budget constraint in neoclassical price theory. While it would take prodigious documentation and a fair amount of explication to elevate such seemingly obscure doctrines to pride of place in the topography of neoclassical economics, we opt here to simply point in the directions of the history which needs to be written. We will start with the Cowles view of neoclassicism.

The origins of the Cowles school can be traced to the appointment of Jacob Marschak as Research Director in 1943, and can be divided into two periods which more or less correspond to the directorships of Marschak (1943–8) and Tjalling Koopmans (1948–54). In the first subperiod, Cowles was engaged in the development of structural estimation econometrics, a story which has been told in a number of different places.[49] Because Marschak has not received the attention lavished by historians upon the other Cowles luminaries, it is not widely recognised that he took as one of his immediate research tasks the clearing up of the débâcle left by Schultz: namely, estimation of restrictions upon demand equations dictated by the Slutsky version of neoclassical theory. Marschak had already made one pass at the problem of conceptualising the budget constraint in his (1939); upon arrival at Cowles he published his (1943), which was an attempt to test price homogeneity and the Slutsky symmetry for the demand for meat. As we are now growing accustomed, things did not turn out favourably for this version of neoclassical price theory.[50] Marschak's response was to push research into two directions: into Keynesian theory, which he believed sanctioned the possibility of price level changes having real effects, and into Haavelmo's insight that there might be something fundamentally biased about statistical techniques constructed to estimate single equations in a situation where the appropriate specification involved simultaneous systems of equations.

Thus Cowles embarked upon the econometrics programme for which it is most fondly remembered. The original impetus for the fascination with identification problems, Neyman–Pearson hypothesis testing, simultaneous equations estimation bias, and the rest was the *a priori* conviction of the interdependence of all economic phenomena through the Walrasian–Slutsky lens, again a tribute to Schultz. Marschak had a good sense of who might share this prior orientation, and from his experience in New York recruited Haavelmo, Koopmans, Lawrence Klein and Kenneth Arrow, among others. And yet, in the words of one historian of the field, 'Econometrics started to become a secondary interest of the Cowles staff as the 1940s ended' (Epstein, 1987, p. 110). This decline in econometric focus occurred for a number of different reasons; the primary one being not that it had worked, but rather, in the judgement of many members of the Cowles staff, it had failed its original promise. The new-fangled simultaneous estimation techniques rarely gave coefficient estimates much different from simpler OLS techniques; and worse, the track record of predictions from the models was fairly abysmal. For all of Koopmans' attacks on the bumbling research devoid of theory at the NBER, actual quantitative restrictions implied by neoclassical price theory rarely held in the empirical exercises undertaken at Cowles. And in addition, the Cowles staff had to put up with Milton Friedman's attendance at their seminars, training his formidable debating skills and withering scepticism upon their enthusiasms for Keynes, structural econometrics, and Walrasian price theory.[51]

The second subperiod of Cowles neoclassicism began with Koopmans' accession to the research directorship, but is best exemplified by the work on general equilibrium theory by Kenneth Arrow and Gerard Debreu (Weintraub and Mirowski, 1994). Since we have already run through this model above, perhaps we can simply point to the ways in which the treatment of the budget constraint helped constitute the school. The hallmark of this school is an admission that neoclassical price theory may have been prompted by physical analogies in the past, but that the modern task was to extract the 'abstract structure' of Walrasian system and subject it to the most rigorous axiomatic scrutiny; in this way they managed an acknowledgment that the imposition of the budget constraint had caused the model to diverge from the Hotelling Economy. This abstract structure took the postulate of an independently fixed budget constraint for the individual agent as inviolate, and then sought to elaborate the logical consequences for a system of completely interdependent demand functions. However, the Slutsky symmetry conditions were obscured by the choice to rephrase the data of 'preferences' in more abstract set theoretic terms, eschewing any reliance upon the differential calculus. This, in turn, had substantial implications for the way that a 'dynamics' of price adjustment would need to be conceptualised (Weintraub, 1991; Hands, 1994). Nevertheless, one can discern the skeleton of the Slutsky conditions buried within the system, as we have explained above. Unfortunately, axiomatic elaboration also eventually led to the conclusion that the system placed no effective restrictions upon excess demand functions, thus subverting the original impetus for the research programme.[52]

It would round out a much more ambitious narrative to note how much of Hotelling's Dream is still sustained in Arrow's conception of this programme. Although to our knowledge he only promoted the actual model in one paper (Arrow and Hurwicz, 1962), Hotelling's protégé has kept alive in spirit many of his original motives.[53] For instance, like Hotelling, Arrow has never accepted that the fundamental justification of the neoclassical programme could be grounded in empiricism *per se*. 'But then the question arises . . . After all, why bother with theory? Go out and estimate your demand functions . . . The reason we do rely on theory is because we feel that these empirical estimates are not very good' (Arrow in Feiwel, 1987, p. 205). Note that in Arrow's words 'theory' becomes conflated with one variant of neoclassical theory, while statistical endeavour is relegated to a definite subordinate role. In another vein, Arrow has for much of his career promoted a politics of market intervention very similar in style to that of Hotelling. Further, Arrow has tended to express the 'relevance' of abstract general equilibrium theory through an attempt to construct and prosecute a 'new welfare economics'; the divergence from Hotelling comes from the fact that his treatment of the budget constraint blocks access to Hotelling's simpler welfare theory where value is interpersonally comparable.

Before leaving Cowles, it may help cement our case that there exist three substantially distinct schools of neoclassicism to observe that Arrow has differentiated himself from our other protagonists. While one of the most courteous and open-minded of economists of his generation, he has been known on occasion to venture a minor rebuke to Samuelson and Chicago. For instance, 'Samuelson has been less systematic than Walras or Hicks in his pursuit of GET' (in Feiwel, 1987, p. 204). Or, in a defence of general equilibrium theory,

> [I]t allows you to keep in mind a sense of what the economy is all about. As far as I can see, nobody within the neoclassical tradition can deny the validity of GET. For example, no matter how much the Chicago school tends to stress the methodological advantages of the partial equilibrium approach, they cannot deny that what they are talking about is embedded in a GE world. Their only defense is that by limiting their scope they can do more practical things. (in Feiwel, 1987, p. 201)

But let us move to Chicago, the second main school of neoclassicism, and decide whether the sources of difference are as simple as a mere preference for partial over general equilibrium exercises. While the school sports many luminaries, we shall restrict ourselves here to three texts which outlined the explicit response to Schultz: Friedman and Wallis (1942), Knight (1944) and Friedman (1949).[54] The secondary literature on Friedman has grown to enormous proportions; and some of it we have found quite helpful (e.g. Hirsch and De Marchi, 1990; Reder, 1982); but it would seem that even the most useful misses important facts in Friedman's career, namely, that he began by writing up part of Schultz's *Theory and Measurement* book, spent some time with Hotelling, and then spent the next decade or more criticising, repudiating and perhaps even obscuring their entire project. Thus the private ironies must have been bittersweet when E.B. Wilson wrote Friedman in November 1946 asking for 'a list of half a dozen books in economics which you think thoroughly good'. Friedman replied in December:

> Another book I am somewhat uncertain about is Henry Schultz, *The Theory and Measurement of Demand.* It is an exceedingly careful and systematic attempt to put empirical content into a pre-existing theory. I have excluded it because there seems to me no reverse influence of the empirical work on the theoretical structure. Schultz took the theory as fixed and given, and tried to measure what he thought were essential functions in the theory. He imposed extremely high standards of care and thoroughness in the measurement process – but he nowhere attempted what seems to me to be the fundamentally important task of reformulating the theory so it would really generalise the observable data; he always tried to wrench the data into a pre-existing theoretical scheme, no matter how much of a wrench was required. (in Stigler, 1994, p. 1200)

If you look at this as if it were an abstract epistemological manifesto, it looks puzzling, confused, inconsistent, or worse (Hirsch and De Marchi, 1990, Chapter 1). But that is because Friedman without Schultz and Hotelling is like Hamlet without Rosencrantz and Guildenstern. In effect, Friedman's reaction to Schultz's impasse was to first repudiate the attempt to extract laws of utility from price data (Friedman and Wallis, 1942); next, extricate price theory from any binding commitment to the Slutsky relations (Knight, 1944), and as the *pièce de résistance,* deny the practical importance of income effects for demand theory. Now, this definitely was not the same move as suppressing the independent budget constraint, as Hotelling had done. Rather, Friedman packaged his programme as returning to Marshall – but not the actual historical personage of Alfred Marshall – no, the return was to the 'Marshallians' that Schultz had declared as his sworn enemies. These were the folks who could ignore interdependent utility and demand functions, lay down tear gas whenever they wanted to make some 'long-run' arguments, reaching for their immunising stratagems in a 'classical' theory of money, and cluck their tongues with steely disapproval whenever someone wanted to raise some fine points about mathematical inference. This was all done in the name of a neoclassical economics that 'works'. Income effects were not denied outright; they were just treated as uninteresting second-order effects whose general influence were inherently unknowable.

Was this bland nostalgia for simpler days of yore? While it certainly was 'conservative,' it was also substantially much more than that. For example, Knight (1944) provides an extensive critique of the physics metaphor which underpins the Walrasian system: 'There is no direct analogy with equilibrium between objects stationary in a field of force. The true physical analogy would require an elaborate construction hardly undertaken so far in the literature' (p. 309). But there was also a subtle economic point, namely, there had been no good reason given for presuming that income could remain fixed during a virtual movement along a demand curve: 'the negative price elasticity of demand for a good cannot be dissociated from declining positive income elasticity, all prices being constant and with the consumer free to add new items' (p. 297). In Knight's mind this mistaken notion that one could separate out income effects was the first step down the primrose path to Keynesianism: 'the general point of view and habit of mind reflected in the Hicks–Slutsky analysis has wide ramifications in recent literature and has led to utter confusion in the whole body of economic thought. We refer, of course, to the huge corpus of discussion beginning with Keynes's *General Theory*' (p. 300, n. 10). Knight and his students read what they considered to be misunderstandings about income to actually be surreptitious statements about the nature of money, which reinforced their convictions about the validity of classical monetary theory. And when the Keynesians weren't trying to turn income effects into a kind of macroeconomics, then they were concocting some sort of illegitimate welfare arguments out of a price theory supposedly free of personal biases (Friedman, 1952).

The upshot of all these objections became clearer through the subsequent work of Milton Friedman. The main prescription was to stop searching for the 'real laws' underneath the demand curves; rather, one should learn to manipulate the few theoretical entities that you could generally trust. This did not imply jettisoning utility theory *tout court*. Knight may have maintained that you could not legitimately derive a demand curve from a set of indifference curves (1944, p. 301); but Friedman took the line that there were too many different demand curves that might be deduced from the constrained maximisation of utility, and that most of them were empirically inaccessible (1962, Chapter 2). But when push came to shove, demand functions were real, or as Knight (1944, p. 310) put it, 'undoubtedly the most solidly real of all the functional relations dealt with in economic theory'. This unswerving commitment to demand functions superimposed upon an acknowledgment of the essential impossibility of grounding them in anything remotely more 'fundamental' or lawlike patterned upon physical analogies, combined with the tenuous residual commitment to neoclassical utility theory, explains Friedman's infamous methodological pronouncements on the unimportance of assumptions, the salience of predictions, and statements like, 'The purpose of ceteris paribus is methodological not substantive. One really is not asking what will or will not remain constant but rather what principle will be used to select provisionally the things that are assumed to remain constant' (1962, p. 23).

This brand of Marshallianism was an anathema to someone who had observed it up close and firsthand, and agreed with Schultz's fundamental suspicions about it: Paul Samuelson. But Samuelson also seemed to have a residual appreciation for the Chicago scepticism about the vaunted generality of the Walrasian general equilibrium (1947, p. 8), combined with an enthusiasm for the rhetoric operationalism of Schultz. Mix this together with a scepticism about statistical demand curves reminiscent of Arrow, and an avid enthusiasm for Keynes, and it would seem we would have very little left in the way of microeconomics to work with. Yet the originality of Samuelson was to combine these disparate elements and innovate a middle ground between the full general equilibrium of Cowles and the pragmatic Marshallianism of Chicago, namely, the theory of 'revealed preference'.

The twists and turns in the purported goals of 'revealed preference theory' from the 1930s to the 1950s have been effectively documented by Wong (1978), so we need not recapitulate them here; rather, we need only add that augmenting his account with the Schultz–Hotelling discussion connects his narrative to the larger history of neoclassical price theory. Samuelson initially set out to liberate demand functions from any dependence upon utility theory, by positing a few simple axioms concerning consumer behaviour 'up front' which could (purportedly) be validated either by introspection or by direct observation of realised price–quantity pairs. This move is in direct contrast to Schultz, where one instead pursued the empirical implications of the theory at 'the back end' of the process, namely, comparisons restrictions upon statistical estimates of the elasticities of the demand curves. Samuelson thus shifted the entire focus of where 'the empirical' was to enter into the theory of demand; if preferences were operationally 'revealed' then the empirical was already in at the start of the theoretical exercise and thus there wasn't any reason to 'test' empirical implications as Schultz had attempted to do. Samuelson could claim operationalist purity – as Schultz had done before him – but without all of the messy consequences of actually confronting demand theory with the empirical data. This, of course, is one of the reasons that Samuelson would loudly trumpet the irrelevance of the integrability conditions throughout this period (injecting more than a little surplus confusion into discussions of the relative importance of the Slutsky conditions ever since). Samuelson seemed to believe that he had effectively liberated demand theory from both the problems of statistical testing and the metaphor of physical force fields, and that he had done so in a way that followed the example of modern physics, a field that he believed to be coldly operationalist and behaviourist in its approach.

As Wong explains, this entire pretence of a rival theory of demand fell apart when Houthakker demonstrated in 1950 that the full content of demand theory required a 'strong axiom of revealed preference' which, *mirabile dictu*, was a restatement of the despised integrability conditions. Although modern textbooks tend to omit this fact, Samuelson himself was forced to concede 'in principle there is nothing to choose between the formulations' (Wong, 1978, p. 111); and therefore Samuelson had pioneered a *cul de sac* rather than an escape route from Schultz, the defective physics metaphor, the unsavoury consequences of income effects, Slutsky integrability conditions, and everything they entailed. But by this time, Samuelson had instituted an entire MIT style and school which had come to dominate a broad swathe of American graduate education, not to mention many economics journals, which one might call 'mid-range theory'. Aspects of this style included the neoclassical Keynesian 'synthesis,' government interventionist politics combined with scepticism regarding welfare economics (particularly welfare economics of the Hotelling sort[55]), frequent resort to representative agent models while maintaining a veneer of multimarket interdependence,[56] a coolness towards econometric innovation,[57] a distance maintained from Bourbakist abstraction, the finessing of dynamics with the 'correspondence principle,' and so on and so on.

7 CALIFORNIA DREAMIN'

One thing about dreams: they rarely conform to the rules of narrative, with a clear-cut beginning, middle and end. Our story has no definitive end, because we and our fellow economists are still stuck in the middle of it. This is where the methodologist frequently gets dissatisfied and wants to rewrite the ending, like one of those bad 1950s movies where everyone either gets married or goes to jail in the last 5 minutes. They wanted to get demand curves out of Walrasian general equilibrium? Well, the axiomatic method and the Sonnenschein–Mantel–Debreu (SMD) results show they cannot, so hooray for mathematics and good-bye neoclassicism (e.g. Ingrao and Israel, 1990). Or: who cares about Walrasian general equilibrium now that economists have seen the strategic light of game theory and changed the subject? (cf. Rizvi, 1994). Or: if only those earlier generations had seen that effective empiricism is really about the construction and 'calibration' of small-scale 'empirical general equilibrium' models, and not fruitless estimation of demand systems, then we need not have wasted all this effort on a grand detour! Or . . .

Or what is it that neoclassical economists really believe in? At one time the answer would have been 'The Law of Demand'. One objective of this history is to demonstrate that that particular response really will not wash: not for the present, and not for the past. The reason Hotelling and Schultz set out upon their dialogue was a dissatisfaction with 'phenomenological' demand curves and a desire to find the 'laws' beneath or behind the Law of Demand. There were other collateral motivations as well, but mostly their concerns came down to specifying the symmetry conditions, the 'invariant' of value theory from which one could build up various practical observable results. This quest for the lawlike entity 'behind' the prices and quantities is actually an old search, one familiar to historians of economics. Some neoclassicals may deny they have any need for a theory of value, that they are agnostic, but we can see now that is just one more variant reaction to Hotelling's and Schultz's conundrum.

If this evocation of the language of value theory has a musty smell of long-forgotten controversies wafting about it, the musk of metaphysical cobwebs that positivists and operationalists had thought they had brushed away long ago, then so be it. For our narrative has another lesson for economic methodologists that we have not given much prominence in this narrative. It is our expectation that once the story of twentieth-century demand theory is fully written, then it should become much less possible to continue to berate Marxian economists for becoming stranded on the shoals of the 'transformation problem', For what, after all, is the relevant difference between the Marxian search for the true principles of value which lay 'behind' the phenomenal price and quantity data, and the quest for the true underpinnings of the curves of demand and supply initiated by Hotelling and Schultz?

Notes

1. We would like to thank Kenneth Arrow, Roger Backhouse, Randall Bausor, Nancy Cartwright, Annie Cot, Ross Emmett, Duncan Foley, Daniel Hammond, Daniel Hausman, Kevin Hoover, Leonid Hurwicz, Uskali Mäki, Mary Morgan, Andrea Salanti, Roy Weintraub and Nancy Wulwick for helpful comments on earlier versions of this chapter.
2. 'Here we see the germ of a standard historiographic strategy for . . . handling rejected knowledge in general. We have a dismissal, the rudiments of a causal explanation of the rejected knowledge (which implicitly acts to justify the dismissal), and an asymmetrical handling of rejected and accepted knowledge. First, it is established that the rejected knowledge is not knowledge at all, but error. This the historian accomplishes by taking the side of accepted knowledge and using the victorious party's causal explanation of their adversaries' position as the historian's own. Since the victors have thus disposed of error, so the historian's dismissal is justified' (Shapin and Schaffer, 1985, p. 11).
3. In general we will not adhere to the symbolism used in the papers we discuss. For example Hotelling used q, not x, for the quantities of commodities. In this case though, it should be noted that Hotelling did use U for total revenue; not TR, but U. While Hotelling talks about $U(x)$ as 'sales' (1932a, p. 590) he also seems to suggest that it could be utility; for example he says 'we have a utility (or profit) function u of the quantities consumed' (1932a, p. 594).
4. Empirically these conditions imply that a change in the quantity of apples purchased will have the same impact on what the buyer is willing to pay for oranges, as a change in the quantity of oranges purchased will have on what the buyer is willing to pay for apples: the same in both direction and magnitude.

   Mathematically these conditions imply that the differential form,

   $$\sum_{i=1}^{n} p_i(x)dx_i$$

   is immediately integrable. We follow Afriat (1980) in making the distinction between an 'integrable' differential form – one where an integrating factor exists – and an immediately differential form' – one where the integrating factor is 1.
5. If $x(p, M)$ is the n-dimensional demand function (standard problem) then the Slutsky equation is given by:

$$\frac{\partial x_i}{\partial p_j} = S_{ij} - x_j \frac{\partial x_i}{\partial M} \qquad \text{(S)}$$

where the Slutsky terms (S_{ij}) are symmetric so: $S_{ij} = S_{ji}$ for all $i \neq j$.

6. Throughout the chapter we will use the symbol $[Jf]$ for the Jacobian matrix of a function $f{:}R^n \rightarrow R^n$ with representative element $[\partial f_i/\partial x_j]$, and the symbol $[Hf]$ for the Hessian matrix of a function $f{:}R^n \rightarrow R$ with representative element $[\partial^2 f/\partial x_i \partial x_j]$.
7. The conditions in (8) imply that there exists a function $F(p)$ such that $x(p) = \nabla F$ (i.e. $x_i(p) = \partial F/\partial x_i$ for all i). The function F is called the potential function for the vector field x.
8. Here, as elsewhere in this paper, we focus exclusively on demand theory and neglect the supply side of the story. Hotelling's actual welfare measure was,

$$W = \sum_{i=1}^{n} \int [p_i(x) - s_i(x)]dx_i$$

where $s_i(x)$ is the supply price of good i at the quantity vector x (marginal cost of good i).

9. See Harberger (1971), or the discussion of 'Hotelling–Harberger' welfare measures in any cost-benefit textbook (Zerbe and Dively, 1994, pp. 480–4, for instance). The necessity of neglecting income effects in consumers' surplus-based welfare economics in emphasised in Chapter 10 of Mas-Colell, Whinston and Green (1995).
10. As Samuelson (1942b) demonstrated, it is not possible for $\lambda(p, M)$, or $\lambda(x, M)$, to be independent of all the parameters in the problem, but it is possible to have $\partial\lambda/\partial p_i = 0$ for all i [or $\partial\lambda/\partial x_i = 0$ for all i]. The relationship between Hotelling's integrability conditions and the standard Slutsky conditions are discussed in Pfouts (1995).
11. Try $U(x_1, x_2) = x_1 x_2$, which is homothetic.
12. See n. 5.
13. Samuelson (1950, p. 357, n. 3) offers a special case of the standard problem that generates demand functions that have basically the same properties as the demands generated by Hotelling's problem. It is the case of quasilinear (or money metric) preferences where the utility function has the form, $U(x) = x_1 + V(x_2, x_3, \ldots, x_n)$, and good 1 is chosen as numeraire. Even here the cases are not identical. Technically the quasilinear case in n dimensions produces the same demand functions for goods $x_2, \ldots, x_n$ as the Hotelling problem in n-1 dimensions with $V(x_2, x_3, \ldots, x_n)$ as the objective function. It produces the same demands only in the sense that there exists a Hotelling problem of one less dimension that produces the same demand functions for all non-numeraire goods. It is not at all clear which should be considered the special case, the problem with a constraint and an additional choice variable, or the problem with no constraint and fewer choice variables. Again, they are different problems with some of the same implications.
14. 'One of the pleasing things about science is that we do all climb towards the heavens on the shoulders of our predecessors. Economics, like phys-

ics has its heroes, and the letter 'H' that I used in my mathematical equations was not there to honour Sir William Hamilton, but rather Harold Hotelling' (Samuelson, 1971, p. 7).

15. This means that the Arrow–Debreu model we will be considering will look more like Arrow and Hahn (1971) or Quirk and Saposnik (1968), than Debreu (1959).
16. In general we will use lower case letters for individual demand (x) and excess demand (z), and upper case letters for aggregate (market) demand (X) and excess demand (Z). The symbol $x(p)$ was used for the special case of the individual Hotelling demand in the previous section to distinguish it from the standard neoclassical demand function $x^h(p)$ in this section.
17. Arrow and Hahn (1971) clearly documents the importance of these five concerns. Chapters 2 and 5 of Arrow and Hahn are dedicated to the first issue on our list. Their Chapter 9 focuses exclusively on the second, while Chapters 11 and 12 are dedicated to the third. Finally, their Chapter 10 focuses on our fourth concern, and Chapter 4 is dedicated to our fifth. The importance of these issues is equally apparent in other texts of the period, for example Quirk and Saposnik (1968) or Takayama (1974). It is also quite clear from the only history of modern general equilibrium theory, Ingrao and Israel (1990), where the last three chapters of their book are dedicated respectively to our first, second and third issues.
18. Weintraub (1991) gives a detailed and context-sensitive history of the literature on the stability of general equilibrium.
19. The Gale and Scarf counterexamples are discussed in Hands (1984). The SMD results are contained in Debreu (1974), Mantel (1977), McFadden *et al.* (1974), and Sonnenschein (1972, 1973). Shafer and Sonnenschein (1982) provide a survey and some of the implications are discussed in Kirman (1992).
20. 'In my view, the correspondence principle was always a nonstarter. It was motivated by the right reasons and it was in some sense natural, but it never had a chance of bearing much fruit for the simple reason that economic theory when the principle was first stated, just as now, has no accepted propositions on disequilibrium dynamics and thus no necessary stability conditions of equilibrium. Less important, it is also true that if our ad hoc dynamic adjustment model is of any order higher than two, the necessary conditions for (local) stability are not powerful enough to deliver the desired comparative statics predictions' (Hahn, 1983, p. 35).
21. For instance, in his extremely influential *Three Essays*, Koopmans noted that, 'A utility function of a consumer looks quite similar to a potential function in the theory of gravitation' (1957, p. 176), but this is deemed irrelevant since with the advent of formalist axiomatization, 'the absence of any natural meaning of mathematical symbols, other than the meaning given to them by postulate or definition, prevents the associations clining to words from intruding upon the reasoning process' (1957, pp. 172–3). Likewise, Debreu has admitted that, 'theoretical physics had been an inaccessible ideal towards which economic theory sometimes strove . . . The benefits of that special relationship were large for both fields; but physics did not completely surrender to the embrace of mathematics and to its inherent compulsion towards logical rigor . . . in these directions,

economic theory could not follow the role model offered by physical theory' (1991, p. 1). The claim that this Bourbakist movement had cut itself loose from its physical moorings is critically examined in Weintraub and Mirowski (1994).

22. One potential problem stems from the fact that Hotelling demands are not homogeneous of degree zero (H). A possible solution might be to 'price' utility (at say $r > 0$) making the Hotelling objective function,

$$rU(x) - \sum_{i=1}^{n} p_i x_i$$

This objective function has appeared in the 'life cycle' literature on labour supply and commodity demands and generates demand functions that are homogeneous of degree zero in the $n + 1$ prices $(r, p_1, p_2, \ldots p_n)$. This objective function is called the 'consumer's profit function' and it shows 'the maximum profit attainable from selling utility (to him or herself) at a price r, subject to the technology of utility production, i.e., the utility function, and the prices of the inputs' (Browning, Deaton and Irish, 1985, p. 508). An alternative approach to proving existence for the Hotelling economy would be to exploit the existence results for 'compensated equilibria' in Walrasian systems (Arrow and Hahn, 1971, Chapter 5; Honkapohja, 1987; Fuchs-Seliger, 1993).

23. See Arrow and Hahn (1971, pp. 208–11).
24. See Theorem 13, p. 235 of Arrow and Hahn (1971).
25. The argument is basically as follows. The equilibrium price vector p^* is globally stable if there exists a real valued *Liapunov function* $V(p)$ with the following three properties:

$$\text{(i) } V[p(t)] > 0 \quad \text{for all } p \notin E$$

$$\text{(ii) } dV[p(t)]/dt < 0 \quad \text{for all } p \notin E$$

$$\text{(iii) } dV(p^*)/dt = 0$$

Let the following function be a candidate Liapunov function,

$$V[p(t)] = \frac{1}{2}\sum_{i=1}^{n} Z_i^2(p)$$

Given (T), the time derivative of V is given by,

$$\frac{V[p(t)]}{dt} = \sum_{i=1}^{n}\sum_{j=1}^{n} Z_i(p)\frac{\partial Z_i}{\partial p_j} Z_j(p) = Z^T JZ(p)Z$$

where Z is the aggregate excess demand vector. This function satisfies (by construction conditions (i) and (iii) of the definition of a Liapunov function. If the Jacobian $JZ(p)$ is negative definite then $dV/dt < 0$ for all $p \notin E$ and condition (ii) is met as well. Thus, if the aggregate excess demand Jacobian is negative definite everywhere, then the system exhibits global stability.

26. This result has been anticipated in a number of ways by a number of

different authors. An early case is Court (1941) where it was proven that if demand functions (and supply functions in a production model) were based of Hotelling's 'entrepreneurial' maximisation, then the general equilibrium would exhibit Hicksian perfect stability (local stability as characterised by Hicks, 1939).

Another case is Samuelson's discussion of 'the stability of a stationary position which is also a maximum' (1942a, pp. 17–18; 1947, pp. 301–2). This Samuelson case is discussed in detail by Weintraub (1991) and Hands (1994).

Varian (1982, pp. 103–6) proves the result directly (although without reference to Hotelling); first he proves stability for a gradient system, which a Hotelling Economy clearly is, and then he considers a particular special case of an economy where the utility function of all traders is linear in money. Varian's example of utility being linear in money is the same utility function that Samuelson used to generate Hotelling's demands as a special case of standard demand theory (see n. 8). The paper by Keenan (1985) draws heavily on Varian's result. The Arrow and Hurwicz (1962) paper in the Hotelling *Festschrift* volume (Pfouts, 1962) also exploits the fact that Hotelling demands generate a gradient system.

27. The Slutsky equation and the symmetry condition (8) together imply that,

$$\left(\frac{M}{x_i^h}\right)\frac{\partial x_i^h}{\partial M} = \left(\frac{M}{x_j^h}\right)\frac{\partial x_j^h}{\partial M}$$

i.e. all goods have the same income elasticity. But if all goods have the same income elasticity for a consumer who satisfies the standard budget constraint, then the income elasticities must all be unity. This implies that preferences are homothetic.

28. Here we refer to the diary kept by Henry Schultz of his European trip from 26 August 1933 to 12 August 1934, a copy of which can be found in the archives of the Cowles Foundation, Yale University. Quotation from a typed transcript of this handwritten diary in the Cowles archives will hereafter be cited as [HSDY, date: page no.].

29. This refers to the extensive correspondence between Schultz and Hotelling about the issues covered in this chapter stretching from 1932 until Schultz's death in November 1938. This correspondence can be found in the Harold Hotelling papers, Special Collections, Columbia University Library. Citations to letters from this archive will be indicated by [HHC, Box: date].

30. Indeed, (Keuzenkamp and Barten, 1995, p. 108) trace their brief history of the origins of the 'testing' of neoclassical price theory from Schultz's books.

31. Nevertheless, that is the way that Schultz and Hotelling saw the line-up of the contestants. One can speculate that one of the reasons that Schultz was hired at Chicago was his disaffection from the Institutionalists he had encountered at his alma mater. As he wrote in his (1928, p. 95):

> Some economists, among whom are to be included not a few members of the institutionalist school, have, unfortunately, gotten the impression that any attempt to derive a law of demand needs to be based on no

better a psychology than that of James Mill. A few of them even go so far as to deny the very existence of a law of demand. What these economists overlook, is the existence of a law of demand is an objective fact, quite independent of one's psychological preconceptions.

32. Schultz to Henry Ludwell Moore, 19 December 1924. Henry Ludwell Moore Papers, Special Collections, Columbia University Library.
33. Moore to Henry Schultz, 23 April 1928, Moore Papers, Box 3, Special Collections, Columbia University.
34. Schultz had already commented upon some work of Working and Hotelling on statistical estimation of trends in (1929). The biographical information on Hotelling in the subsequent section is taken from (Darnell, 1990; Arrow, 1987; Smith, 1978; Pfouts and Leadbetter, 1979).
35. Excerpt from an unpublished typescript by Hotelling entitled 'Western Hotelling and Allied Families on Epic of Migration', in the Hotelling papers. This excerpt is quoted in Darnell (1990, p. 4).
36. See, for instance, the letter from Schultz dated 11 May 1932: 'It is good to learn that you have become interested in factor analysis. Several years ago I spent lots of time on it myself . . . but when Spearman, Wilson and Kelley got tangled up in the psychological–mathematical aspects of the problem, I thought it advisable to step out. I am working, on and off, on another aspect of psycho-physics about which I would like to talk to you' [HHC, Box 1].
37. Hotelling to Schultz, 16 July 1932 [HHC, Box 1]. These letters also initiate an inquiry into the impact of inverting a demand function and estimating quantity as a function of prices rather than the inverse. This query led to Hotelling's duality results.
38. This practice of Edgeworth of trying to justify utilitarianism on the ground of analogies with the theory of probability is discussed in the Introduction to Mirowski (1994). What is fascinating about both Edgeworth and Hotelling is their combination of familiarity with formal probability theory and their reluctance to build it into the foundations of price theory. They both finesse the issue by evoking formalisms that 'look like' ones found in existing probability theory. Hotelling resembles Edgeworth in that probability can be epistemic for the empirical scientist (hence their work in statistics), but somehow not for the economic actor. One could speculate this may have had something to do with their own prior commitment to the existence of economic laws.
39. Henry Schultz to Harold Hotelling, 22 September 1932 [HHC: Box 1]. The letter of 31 October 1932 reiterated the results in great detail. However, it also reports that: 'I have been asked by two of the younger men of our Department to give them an explanatory talk on your paper . . . It is attracting the attention of the few really serious and competent students.'
40. For example after discussing various attempts to test the Slutsky conditions Phlips (1974, p. 55) says: 'Given that the demand equations have to be specified in some way, a valid testing against unrestricted data is probably impossible. We therefore think that, if we want measurement to be meaningful, we must *impose* the general restrictions whatever the results of the sort of test just referred to' (emphasis in original).

41. See the letter of 3 August 1933:

> Your stock in Chicago has gone up by leaps and bounds. As you probably know, we do not think much of the so-called economists and statisticians who are connected with the NIRA administration. We have very good reason to believe they are economic ignoramuses, and that, well-meaning as they are, their work is likely to lead to another crash . . . When my colleagues would 'kid' me about the statisticians and economists who are prominent in the councils of the NIRA, my effective reply was: Are they *economists*? Are they *statisticians*? But when the news appeared that you and Roos were going to join their staff, I had no effective reply. Your letter, however, shows me that you are still the clear thinker you have always been, that you are not being taken in by shibboleths, and that your heart is in the right place. I am impatient to show your letter to Frank Knight as soon as he gets through with his class in the next few minutes.

Schultz's equivocal results were testing the patience of his auditors in the atmosphere of Chicago in the 1930s. The nature of the dissatisfaction is revealed in the following note by an anonymous student to Homer Jones, in the Frank H. Knight Papers, Regenstein Library, University of Chicago, Box 45, Folder 2. From the first sentence, its date appears to be late 1933:

> Have you seen the Schultz article in the Oct. *JPE*? F.H. just sent me a copy. What are we to do about such things? Just ignore them? There is no one here who has the slightest inkling of what it is all about. Furthermore they do not care. I appreciate the fundamental inadequacy of the old graphical and arithmetical [sic] presentation, but since all theoretical economics so illy fits facts, is there any use of going deeper into the subtleties? Does F.H. feel that this complicated mathematical treatment would be of vital importance in the allocation and coordination of resources in a rational socialist state? Since liberalism is dead and competition and the market become more and more myth, will not the Chicago School of Automatic Economics (CSAE) be forced to turn its attention to the social economic dictatorship?

42. Schultz's diaries provide a salutary window into his thinking just after the first round of intense negotiations with Hotelling. They reveal. for instance, that Schultz was not that enamoured with the Hicks–Allen approach, which he discussed with them personally. It also would disabuse the tendency of modern historians to dismiss Schultz as some sort of prematurely obsolete thinker. See, for instance, the accusation (in Morgan, 1990, p. 156) that Schultz's work 'was already outdated in some respects by 1938' in that it ignored Tinbergen and Frisch's approach to identification (p. 188); or the complaint in (Hendry and Morgan, 1995, p. 29) that 'Schultz was not, as far as one can see, a natural statistician like Yule, and found it difficult to see how data behave'. The fact that such indictments lose their sting when situated in context is mooted by diary entries such as the following:

> Frisch has a wonderful command of technique and almost inexhaustible energy. Would that he had better statistical and economic judgment! . . . The work in dynamic economics is proceeding at a rapid pace. The papers by Tinbergen, Frisch and Kalecki are notable achievements. There is need, however, for a better synthesis of newer procedures with those of Walras and Pareto. I should like to see individual demand and supply functions introduced in the equations. [HSDY, Oct. 2, p. 6]

It would seem data only 'behave' when one knows the rules of their conduct *a priori*.

43. 'Schultz's results as a whole seem to confirm the applicability to these commodities of the integrability conditions. It must be remembered that even though a single discrepancy may be judged significant when it exceeds double its standard error, still, among six, it is quite probable that one will fall beyond this limit' (Hotelling, 1935, pp. 66–7, n. 1).
44. The relationship of Milton Friedman's profound about-face with regard to the centrality of the Slutsky relations and the goal of the empirical recovery of utility functions to the rise of the 'Chicago School' will be discussed in the next section. We believe that an understanding of this incident sheds light on his promotion of a 'Marshallian' over a 'Walrasian' approach to neoclassical theory (Hirsch and De Marchi, 1990, Chapter 1), as well as help in decoding his confusing essay on the methodology of positive economics.

45. [As methodologists] 'we have to be able to explain why the rejection of additivity [of utility] was accepted by the profession while the rejection of symmetry and homogeneity, implied by the same studies, were apparently ignored. Equally we need to explain why Blundell et al (1989) were prepared to ignore the rejection of symmetry on their micro dataset but at the same time were concerned to reject rank two specifications of the income terms' (Gilbert, 1991, p. 151).

    We have looked at different models, each embodying different approximations, and these have been fitted to different data sets from several countries, but *the same conclusions have repeatedly emerged. Demand functions fitted to aggregate time series data are not homogeneous and probably not symmetric* . . . But these models produce a conflict with the theory. The restrictions of homogeneity and symmetry, basic to the assumptions of a linear budget constraint and the axioms of choice, *are consistently rejected by the data* (Deaton and Muellbauer, 1980, pp. 78, 80, our emphasis).

46. The evidence comes from Christ (1952, pp. 17–18). In January 1937, Charles Roos resigned as Research Director to move to the private sector, from which he never returned to academia. Harold Davis took his place for eight months, but then he, too, decamped to the Northwestern mathematics department. Neither individual was especially favourably inclined towards Walrasian neoclassical theory. Ragnar Frisch, Jacob Marshak and Theodore Yntema were recruited as replacements, but all declined to move to Colorado

Springs. The upshot was that Cowles was bereft of a research director for two long years. In the absence of strong leadership, the unit threatened to devolve into another stock market research organization, still the primary interest of its benefactor. The situation was permanently resolved by the death of Alfred Cowles's father in January 1939, requiring him to move to Chicago. Cowles and his attorney Laird Bell, a trustee of the University of Chicago, negotiated with Robert Hutchins to move the unit to Chicago in September 1939. Christ (1952, p. 20) paints the move as constituting a conscious replacement for Schultz at Chicago, but the circumstances belie this interpretation. Elements of the Economics Department were hostile to endowing Cowles with University status. Yntema, who was in the Business School, was named Research Director, but seems to have been on leave during much of his brief tenure from 1939–42.

47. There is a growing consensus in the science studies community that something rather dramatic happened to the social sciences in America in the Second World War; partly it has to do with such 'external' considerations as being ushered into the era of Big Science and governmental funding, but many have argued it extends to the very content of the social sciences, which became much more patterned upon specific aspects of physics and the other natural sciences. See, for instance, (Pickering, 1995a; 1995b; Heims, 1991; Mirowski, 1992; Leonard, 1995; Fortun and Schweber, 1993). It may be that the history of modern neoclassical price theory would be much more closely linked to broader cultural trends if it were situated in this new understanding of 'cyborg science'.

    The wartime activities of the postwar neoclassicals have yet to receive any attention. For instance:

    - Arrow worked at the Weather Division at the US Air Force.
    - Friedman and Stigler, along with Wald and some early game theorists worked for the Statistical Research Group at Columbia under Hotelling.
    - Samuelson worked at the MIT Radiation Lab, the same unit which housed Philip Morse's Operations Research unit.
    - 'By 1942, something like half the staff at Cowles Commission had been drawn into work directly or indirectly connected with the war effort' (Christ 1952, p. 23).
    - 'Kenneth Arrow's two Nobel-status contributions to economics were financed by the Office of Naval Research and the RAND Corporation' (Samuelson, 1986, p. 867).

48. Griffith Evans, Nicholas Georgescu-Roegen, the Cassel version of disavowing utility altogether in favour of demand functions – to name just a few.
49. For the econometrics see Christ (1952, 1994); Epstein (1987); Hendry and Morgan (1995); or Morgan (1990); for the change in regime see Weintraub and Mirowski (1994).
50. Keuzenkamp and Barten (1995) identify this as the first attempt to statistically test the zero degree homogeneity condition of demand theory. This paper also illustrates our contention that philosophy takes its cue from price theory as much as vice versa. Apparently, Karl Popper claimed that this paper by Marschak inspired his own 'zero method' (Popper, 1961, p. 141).

51. 'By 1944, a fairly intense struggle was underway between Knight and his former students on one side, and the Cowles Commission and its adherents on the other . . . It continued for almost 10 years' (Reder, 1982, p. 10).
52. See n. 19.
53. Arrow has dedicated his *Collected Papers* to Hotelling in ringing terms: 'who encouraged my entrance into the field of economics, bolstered my limited self-confidence, and set the example of human concern combined with analytical rigor that I have always attempted to follow' (1983, p. i).
54. We are obviously limiting ourselves to elements of what might be called first and second generation Chicago, and neglecting entirely the messy issue of the third generation of Lucas *et al.*
55. 'In closing I should like to state my personal opinion that nothing said here in the field of consumer's behavior affects in anyway or touches upon at any point the problem of welfare economics, except in the sense of revealing the confusion in the traditional theory of these distinct subjects' (Samuelson, 1938, p. 71).
56. It is interesting to note that one place where Samuelson might have significant overlap with the Arrow–Debreu programme is on the topic of the use of the Weak Axiom of Revealed Preference in Walrasian systems (initiated by Wald, 1951), and yet Samuelson is quite critical of this application. The Weak Axiom applied to aggregate (as opposed to individual) excess demand produces a model which behaves 'exactly as if the market consisted of a single rational consumer' (Dorfman, Samuelson and Solow, 1958, p. 375, n. 2); in other words it behaves like a Hotelling Economy.
57. 'Some of the skepticisms of Knight and Jacob Viner concerning the empirical statistical studies that their colleagues Paul Douglas and Henry Schultz were attempting, I readily admit, were well taken' (Samuelson, 1986, p. 792).

References

Afriat, S.N. (1980) *Demand Functions and the Slutsky Matrix* (Princeton, NJ: Princeton University Press).

Arrow, K.J. (1983) *Collected Papers, Vol. I* (Cambridge, MA: Harvard University Press).

——— (1987) 'Harold Hotelling', in J. Eatwell, M. Milgate and P. Newman (eds), *The New Palgrave* (London: Macmillan), pp. 670–1.

Arrow, K.J. and G. Debreu (1954) 'Existence of an Equilibrium for a Competitive Economy', *Econometrica,* vol. 22, pp. 265–90.

Arrow, K.J. and F.H. Hahn (1971) *General Competitive Analysis* (San Francisco: Holden-Day).

Arrow, K.J. and L. Hurwicz (1958) 'On the Stability of the Competitive Equilibrium I', *Econometrica,* vol. 26, pp. 522–52.

——— (1962) 'Decentralization and Computation in Resource Allocation', in R. Pfouts (ed.), *Essays in Economics and Econometrics: A Volume in Honor of Harold Hotelling* (Chapel Hill: University of North Carolina Press), pp. 34–104.

Arrow, K.J., H.D. Block and L. Hurwicz (1959), 'On the Stability of the Competitive Equilibrium II', *Econometrica*, vol. 27, pp. 82–109.
Blaug, M. (1992) *The Methodology of Economics*, 2nd edn (Cambridge: Cambridge University Press).
Blundell, R.W., P. Pashardes and G. Weber (1989) 'What Do We Learn About Consumer Demand Patters From Micro-Data?', paper given to IFS–LBS conference on 'Aggregation in Economic Modelling' (October).
Bridgman, P.W. (1927) *The Logic of Modern Physics* (New York: Macmillan).
Browning, M., A. Deaton and M. Irish (1985) 'A Profitable Approach to Labor Supply and Commodity Demands Over the Life-Cycle', *Econometrica*, vol. 53, pp. 503–43.
Chipman, J.S. (1982) 'Samuelson and Consumption Theory', Chapter 2 in G.R. Feiwel (ed.), *Samuelson and Neoclassical Economics* (Boston: Kluwer Nijhoff), pp. 31–71.
Christ, C. (1952) 'History of the Cowles Commission, 1932–52', in *Economic Theory and Measurement: A Twenty Year Research Report, 1932–1952* (Chicago: Cowles Commission), pp. 3–65.
——— (1985) 'Early Progress in Estimating Quantitative Economic Relationships in America', *American Economic Review*, vol. 75, pp. 39– 52.
——— (1994) 'The Cowles Commission's Contributions to Econometrics at Chicago, 1939–1955', *Journal of Economic Literature*, vol. 32, pp. 30–59.
Court, L.M. (1941) 'Invariable Classical Stability of Entrepreneurial Demand and Supply Functions', *Quarterly Journal of Economics*, vol. 56, pp. 134–45.
Creedy, J. (1992) *Demand and Exchange in Economic Analysis* (Aldershot: Edward Elgar).
Darnell, A. (ed.) (1990) *The Collected Economics Articles of Harold Hotelling* (New York: Springer Verlag).
De Marchi, N. and M. Blaug (eds) (1991) *Appraising Economic Theories* (Aldershot: Edward Elgar).
Deaton, A. and J. Muellbauer (1980) *Economics and Consumer Behavior* (Cambridge: Cambridge University Press).
Debreu, G. (1959) *Theory of Value: an Axiomatic Analysis of Economic Equilibrium* (New Haven: Yale University Press).
——— (1974) 'Excess Demand Functions', *Journal of Mathematical Economics*, vol. 1, pp. 15–23.
——— (1991) 'The Mathematization of Economic Theory', *American Economic Review*, vol. 81, pp. 1–7.
Dorfman, R., P.A. Samuelson and R. Solow (1958) *Linear Programming and Economic Analysis* (New York: McGraw-Hill).
Edgeworth, F. Y. (1925) *Papers Relating to Political Economy*, 3 vols (London: Macmillan).
Epstein, R. (1987) *A History of Econometrics* (Amsterdam: North-Holland).
Feiwel, G. (ed.) (1987) *Arrow and the Ascent of Modern Economic Theory* (New York: New York University Press).
Fisher, I. (1892) *Mathematical Investigations in the Theory of Value and Prices* (New Haven: Yale University Press).
Fortun, M. and S. Schweber (1993) 'Scientists and the Legacy of WWII: The Case of Operations Research', *Social Studies of Science*, vol. 23, pp. 595–642.
Friedman, M. (1949) 'The Marshallian Demand Curve', *Journal of Political Economy*, vol. 57, pp. 463–95.

——— (1952) 'The Welfare Effects of an Income Tax and an Excise Tax', *Journal of Political Economy,* vol. 60, pp. 25–33.

——— (1962) *Price Theory: A Provisional Text* (Chicago: Aldine).

Friedman, M. and A. Wallis (1942) 'The Empirical Derivation of Indifference Functions', in O. Lange, F. McIntyre and T.O. Yntema (eds), *Studies in Mathematical Economics and Econometrics: In Memory of Henry Schultz* (Chicago: University of Chicago Press), pp. 775–89.

Fuchs-Seliger, S. (1993) 'A Reformulation of the Theory of Demand by Compensated Demand Functions', *Journal of Economics*, vol. 57, pp. 279– 93.

Gale, D. (1955) 'The Law of Supply and Demand', *Mathematica Scandinavica,* vol. 3, pp. 155–69.

——— (1965) 'A Note on Global Instability of Competitive Equilibrium', *Naval Research Logistics Quarterly,* vol. 10, pp. 80–7.

Gale, D. and H. Nikaidô (1965) 'The Jacobian Matrix and the Global Univalence of Mappings', *Mathematische Annalen,* vol. 159, pp. 81–93.

Gilbert, C. (1991) 'Do Economists Test Theories?', in N. De Marchi and M. Blaug (eds), *Appraising Economic Theories* (Aldershot: Edward Elgar), pp. 137–68.

Green, E. and K. Moss (1994) 'The Reorientation of Neoclassical Consumer Theory', in T. Horowitz and A. Janis (eds), *Scientific Failure* (Lanham, MD: Rowman & Littlefield).

Hahn, F. H. (1983) 'On General Equilibrium and Stability', in E.C. Brown and R.M. Solow (eds), *Paul Samuelson and Modern Economics* (New York: McGraw-Hill), pp. 31–55.

Hammond, J.D. (1993) 'An interview with Milton Friedman on methodology', in B.J. Caldwell (ed.) *The Philosophy and Methodology of Economics* (Cheltenham and Lyme, NH: Edward Elgar) pp. 216–38.

Hands, D.W. (1984) 'The Role of Crucial Counterexamples in the Growth of Economic Knowledge: Two Case Studies in the Recent History of Economic Thought', *History of Political Economy*, vol. 16, pp. 59–67; reprinted with revisions in Chapter 2 of Hands, 1993.

——— (1993) *Testing, Rationality and Progress* (Lanham, MD: Rowman & Littlefield).

——— (1994) 'Restabilizing Dynamics: Construction and Constraint in the History of Walrasian Stability Theory', *Economics and Philosophy*, vol. 10, pp. 243–83.

Harberger, A.C. (1971) 'Three Basic Postulates for Applied Welfare Economics: An Interpretive Essay', *Journal of Economic Literature,* vol. 9, pp. 785–97.

Heims, S. (1991) *The Cybernetics Group* (Cambridge, MA: MIT Press).

Henderson, J. and R. Quandt (1971) *Microeconomic Theory*, 2nd edn (New York: McGraw-Hill).

Hendry, D. and M. Morgan (eds) (1995) *Foundations of Econometric Analysis* (Cambridge: Cambridge University Press).

Hicks, J.R. (1939) *Value and Capital* (Oxford: Oxford University Press).

Hicks, J.R. and R.G.D. Allen (1934) 'A Reconsideration of the Theory of Value, Parts I and II', *Economica*, NS, vol. 14, pp. 52–76, pp. 196–219.

Hirsch, A. and N. De Marchi (1990) *Milton Friedman: Economics in Theory and Practice* (Ann Arbor: University of Michigan Press).

Honkapohja, S. (1987) 'On the Continuity of Compensated Demand', *International Economic Review*, vol. 28, pp. 545–57.

Hotelling, H. (1921) 'A Mathematical Theory of Migration', Master's Thesis, Department of Mathematics, University of Washington.

——— (1928) 'Review of *Mathematical Researches into the Mathematical Principles of the Theory of Wealth* by A. Cournot', *American Mathematical Monthly*, vol. 35, pp. 439–40.

——— (1932a) 'Edgeworth's Taxation Paradox and the Nature of Demand and Supply Functions', *Journal of Political Economy*, vol. 40, pp. 577–616.

——— (1932b) 'Review of *New Methods of Measuring Marginal Utility* by Ragnar Frisch', *Journal of the American Statistical Association*, vol. 27, pp. 451–2.

——— (1935) 'Demand Functions with Limited Budgets', *Econometrica*, vol. 3, pp. 66–78.

——— (1936) 'Curtailing Production is Anti-social', *Columbia Alumni News*, vol. 28; reprinted in Darnell (1990).

——— (1938a) 'The General Welfare in Relation to Problems of Taxation and of Railway and Utility Rates', *Econometrica*, vol. 6, pp. 242–69.

——— (1938b) 'Review of *The Theory and Measurement of Demand* by Henry Schultz', *Journal of the American Statistical Association*, vol. 33, pp. 744–7.

——— (1939) 'The Work of Henry Schultz', *Econometrica*, vol. 7, pp. 97–103.

Houthakker, H. (1983) 'On Consumption Theory', in E. Brown and R. Solow (eds), *Paul Samuelson and Modern Economic Theory* (New York: McGraw-Hill), pp. 57–68.

Hurwicz, L. (1971) 'On the Problem of Integrability of Demand Functions', in J.S. Chipman, L. Hurwicz, M.K. Richter and H.F. Sonnenschein (eds), *Preferences, Utility and Demand* (New York: Harcourt Brace Jovanovich), pp. 174–214.

Ingrao, B. and G. Israel (1990) *The Invisible Hand: Economic Equilibrium in the History of Science* (Cambridge, MA: MIT Press).

Keenan, D. (1985) 'Global Stability for Homothetic Preferences in a Distribution Economy', *Economics Letters*, vol. 18, pp. 101–4.

Keuzenkamp, H. (1994) 'What if an Idealization is Problematic? The Case of the Homogeneity Condition in Consumer Demand', in B. Hamminga and N. De Marchi (eds), *Idealization VI: Idealization in Economics* (Amsterdam: Rodopi), pp. 243–54.

Keuzenkamp, H. and A. Barten (1995) 'Rejection without Falsification: On the History of Testing the Homogeneity Condition', *Journal of Econometrics*, vol. 87, pp. 103–27.

Kirman, A.P. (1992) 'Whom or What Does the Representative Individual Represent?', *Journal of Economic Perspectives*, vol. 6, pp. 117–36.

Knight, F. (1944) 'Realism and Relevance in the Theory of Demand', *Journal of Political Economy*, vol. 52, pp. 289–318.

Koopmans, T. (1957) *Three Essays on the State of Economic Science* (New York: McGraw-Hill).

Lange, O., F. McIntyre and T. Yntema (eds) (1942) *Studies in Mathematical Economics and Econometrics: In Memory of Henry Schultz* (Chicago: University of Chicago Press).

Leonard, R. (1995) 'From Parlor Games to Social Science: von Neumann, Morgenstern, and the Creation of Game Theory 1928–1944', *Journal of Economic Literature*, vol. 33, pp. 730–61.

Mantel, R.R. (1977) 'Implications of Microeconomic Theory for Community Excess Demand Functions', in M.D. Intriligator (ed.), *Frontiers of Quantitative Economics IIIA* (Amsterdam: North-Holland), pp. 111–26.

Marschak, J. (1939) 'Personal and Collective Budget Functions', *Review of Economics and Statistics*, vol. 21, pp. 161–70.

——— (1943) 'Money Illusion and Demand Analysis', *Review of Economics and Statistics*, vol. 24, pp. 40–8.

Mas-Colell, A., M. Whinston and J. Green (1995) *Microeconomic Theory* (New York: Oxford University Press).

McFadden, D., A. Mas-Colell, R. Mantel and M. K. Richter (1974) 'A Characterization of Community Excess Demand Functions', *Journal of Economic Theory*, vol. 9, pp. 361–74.

Mirowski, P. (1989) *More Heat Than Light: Economics as Social Physics: Physics as Nature's Economics* (Cambridge: Cambridge University Press).

——— (1990) 'Problems in the Paternity of Econometrics: Henry Ludwell Moore', *History of Political Economy*, 22, 587–609.

——— (1992) 'More bleat than bite: responses to Barnes, Cohen, Hands and Wise', *Philosophy of the Social Sciences*, vol. 22, pp. 131–41.

Mirowski, P. (ed.) (1994) *Edgeworth on Chance, Economic Hazard and Statistics* (Savage, MD: Rowman & Littlefield).

Moore, H.L. (1925) 'A Moving Equilibrium of Demand and Supply', *Quarterly Journal of Economics*, vol. 39, pp. 357–71.

——— (1926) 'The Partial Elasticity of Demand', *Quarterly Journal of Economics*, vol. 40, pp. 393–401.

——— (1929) *Synthetic Economics* (New York: Macmillan).

Morgan, M. (1990) *A History of Econometric Ideas* (Cambridge: Cambridge University Press).

Mosak, J. (1987) 'Henry Schultz', in J. Eatwell, M. Milgate and P. Newman (eds), *The New Palgrave* (London: Macmillan), pp. 261–2.

Negishi, T. (1962) 'The Stability of a Competitive Economy: A Survey Article', *Econometrica*, vol. 30, pp. 635–69.

Pareto, V. (1927) *Manual of Political Economy*, trans. A. Schwier (New York: Augustus M. Kelley, 1971).

Pfouts, R. (1995) 'Integrability and Aggregation in the Theory of Demand', *Atlantic Economic Journal*, vol. 23, pp. 176–88.

Pfouts, R. (ed.) (1962) *Essays in Economics and Econometrics: A Volume in Honor of Harold Hotelling* (Chapel Hill: University of North Carolina Press).

Pfouts, R. and M. Leadbetter (1979) 'Harold Hotelling', *International Encyclopedia of the Social Sciences*, vol. 18, pp. 325–8.

Phlips, L. (1974) *Applied Consumption Analysis* (Amsterdam: North-Holland).

Pickering, A. (1995a) *The Mangle of Practice* (Chicago: University of Chicago Press).

——— (1995b) 'Cyborg History and the WWII Regime', *Perspectives on Science*, vol. 3, pp. 1–45.

Popper, K.R. (1961) *The Poverty of Historicism* (New York: Harper).

Quirk, J. and R. Saposnik (1968) *Introduction to General Equilibrium Theory and Welfare Economics* (New York: McGraw-Hill).

Reder, M. (1982) 'Chicago Economics: Permanence and Change', *Journal of Economic Literature,* vol. 20, pp. 1–38.
Rizvi, S.A.T. (1994) 'Game Theory to the Rescue?', *Contributions to Political Economy,* vol. 13, pp. 1–28.
Ross, D. (1991) *The Origins of American Social Science* (Cambridge: Cambridge University Press).
Samuelson, P.A. (1938) 'A Note on the Pure Theory of Consumer's Behaviour', *Economica,* vol. 5, pp. 61–71.
——— (1941) 'The Stability of Equilibrium: Comparative Statics and Dynamics', *Econometrica,* vol. 9, pp. 97–120.
——— (1942a) 'The Stability of Equilibrium: Linear and Nonlinear Systems', *Econometrica,* vol. 10, pp. 1–25.
——— (1942b) 'Constancy of the Marginal Utility of Income', in O. Lange, F. McIntyre, and T.O. Yntema (eds), *Studies in Mathematical Economics and Econometrics: In Memory of Henry Schultz* (Chicago: University of Chicago Press), pp. 75–91.
——— (1944) 'The Relation Between Hicksian Stability and True Dynamic Stability', *Econometrica,* vol. 12, pp. 256–7.
——— (1947) (1st edn) *Foundations of Economic Analysis* (Cambridge, MA: Harvard University Press).
——— (1950) 'The Problem of Integrability in Utility Theory', *Economica,* vol. 17, pp. 355–85.
——— (1966a) *The Collected Scientific Papers of Paul A. Samuelson, Vol. I,* J. Stiglitz (ed.) (Cambridge, MA: MIT Press).
——— (1966b) *The Collected Scientific Papers of Paul A. Samuelson, Vol. II,* J. Stiglitz (ed.) (Cambridge, MA: MIT Press).
——— (1971) 'Maximum Principles in Analytical Economics', *Les Prix Nobel in 1970* (Stockholm: The Nobel Foundation); reprinted in *Collected Scientific Papers of Paul A. Samuelson, Vol. III,* J. Stiglitz (ed.) (Cambridge, MA: MIT Press).
——— (1986) *Collected Scientific Papers of Paul A. Samuelson, Vol. V,* J. Stiglitz (ed.) (Cambridge, MA: MIT Press).
Scarf, H. (1960) 'Some Examples of Global Instability of the Competitive Equilibrium', *International Economic Review,* vol. 1, pp. 147–72.
Schultz, H. (1928) *Statistical Laws of Demand and Supply, with Special Application to Sugar* (Chicago: University of Chicago Press).
——— (1929) 'Discussion of Working and Hotelling', *Proceedings of the American Statistical Association,* vol. 24, p. 86.
——— (1933a) 'A Comparison of Elasticities of Demand Obtained by Different Methods', *Econometrica,* vol. 1, pp. 274–302.
——— (1933b) 'Frisch on the Measurement of Marginal Utility', *Journal of Political Economy,* vol. 41, pp. 95–116.
——— (1933c) 'Interrelations of Demand', *Journal of Political Economy,* vol. 41, pp. 468–512.
——— (1935) 'Interrelations of Demand, Price, and Income', *Journal of Political Economy,* vol. 43, pp. 433–81.
——— (1938) *The Theory and Measurement of Demand* (Chicago: University of Chicago Press).
Shafer, W. and H. Sonnenschein (1982) 'Market Excess Demand Functions',

in K.J. Arrow and M.D. Intriligator (eds), *Handbook of Mathematical Economics, Vol. II* (Amsterdam: North-Holland), pp. 671– 93.

Shapin, S. and S. Schaffer (1985) *Leviathan and the Air-Pump: Hobbes, Boyle, and the Experimental Life* (Princeton, NJ: Princeton University Press).

Slutsky, E.E. (1915) 'Sulla teoria del bilancio del consumatore', *Giornale degli Economisti*, vol. 51, pp. 1–26, trans. in G. Stigler and K.E. Boulding (eds), *Readings in Price Theory* (Homewood, IL: Richard D. Irwin, 1952), pp. 27–56.

Smith, W.L. (1978) 'Harold Hotelling, 1895–1973', *Annals of Statistics*, vol. 6, pp. 1173–83.

Sonnenschein, H. (1972) 'Market Excess Demand Functions', *Econometrica*, vol. 40, pp. 549–63.

——— (1973) 'Do Walras' Identity and Continuity Characterize the Class of Community Excess Demand Functions?', *Journal of Economic Theory*, vol. 6, pp. 345–54.

Stigler, G. (1952) *The Theory of Price* (rev. edn) (New York: Macmillan).

——— (1965) *Essays in the History of Economics* (Chicago: University of Chicago Press).

——— (1988) *Memoirs of an Unregulated Economist* (New York: Basic Books).

——— (1994) 'Some Correspondence between Milton Friedman and Edwin B. Wilson; Nov–Dec. 1946', *Journal of Economic Literature*, vol. 32, pp. 1197–1203.

Takayama, A. (1974) *Mathematical Economics* (Hinsdale, IL: The Dryden Press).

Varian, H.R. (1982) 'Dynamical Systems with Applications to Economics', in K.J. Arrow and M.D. Intriligator (eds), *Handbook of Mathematical Economics, Vol. I* (Amsterdam: North-Holland), pp. 93–110.

Wald, A. (1951) 'On Some Systems of Equations of Mathematical Economics', *Econometrica*, vol. 19, pp. 368–403.

Weintraub, E. R. (1991) *Stabilizing Dynamics: Constructing Economic Knowledge* (Cambridge: Cambridge University Press).

Weintraub, E.R. and P. Mirowski (1994) 'The Pure and the Applied: Bourbakism Comes to Mathematical Economics', *Science in Context*, vol. 7, pp. 245–72.

Wilson, E. B. (1912) 'Mathematical Economics: Review of *Manuel d'Economie politique* by V. Pareto', *Bulletin of the American Mathematical Society*, vol. 18, pp. 462–74.

Wong, S. (1978) *The Foundations of Paul Samuelson's Revealed Preference Theory* (London: Routledge & Kegan Paul).

Yonay, Y. (1994) 'When Black Boxes Clash: Competing Ideas of What Science is in Economics, 1924–39', *Social Studies of Science*, vol. 24, pp. 39–80.

Zerbe, R.O. Jr. and D.D. Dively (1994) *Benefit-Cost Analysis: In Theory and Practice* (New York: Harper Collins).

Comment

Leonid Hurwicz[1]
UNIVERSITY OF MINNESOTA, USA

The Hands and Mirowski (hereafter H/M) chapter is an impressive piece of work and a monument of erudition. Unfortunately, I can agree neither with its main points, nor with most of its numerous *obiter dicta*. Since in a brief comment one could not possibly do justice to the wealth of claims and ideas found in this chapter, I shall try to focus on what seems to be its central thesis. Silence on other issues should not be interpreted as concurrence. I regret having to be negative concerning a prodigious research effort, but I feel that in a matter of such importance for the history of economic thought we owe to future generations of scholars, as well as to the 'giants upon whose shoulders we stand', nothing less than complete candour and absence of ambiguity.

What I see as the central H/M claim is that the objectives[2] they impute to the neoclassicists[3] could have been attained if these neoclassicists had not 'rejected'[4] – especially in the post–Second World War period – Hotelling's (1932) model of demand in which budget limitations are absent.

1 ELEMENTS IN THE H–M CLAIM

There are *three elements* implicit in this H/M claim. I shall briefly state each and then indicate why I cannot accept it. Detailed argument will follow.

First element: the H/M interpretation of what they call 'Hotelling's dream', attributes to him the intention of constructing a theory of consumer demand free of budget constraints. But in fact Hotelling had two models of demand formation. His model of consumer demand did take budget limitations into account. The one without budget limitations referred to the demand of a profit maximising enterprise but was not intended to apply to consumer choice.

Second element: H/M claim that the prevailing theory of consumer choice, based on the postulate of satisfaction maximisation subject to budget limitations, constitutes a post-Second World War 'rejection'[5] of the alleged Hotelling 'dream'. The alleged rejection is blamed on the neoclassicists.

But the budget constraint had already been an integral component of consumer choice theory in the nineteenth century and had certainly been standard by the 1930s. The models of the 1950s (the neoclassicists' in particular) picked up where their predecessors left off. Hotelling's unlimited budgets model was not even under consideration for consumer choice theory, and hence there was no opportunity for rejection, hence no rejection, of Hotelling's unlimited budgets model as a basis for consumer demand theory. Since there was no rejection, no one is guilty of it. But, of course, it is true that modern consumer choice theory does not use Hotelling's theory of the firm to explain consumer behaviour.

Third element: H/M impute to the neoclassicists (mainly Arrow, Debreu, and Samuelson) a programme containing a set of five objectives (Section 3, especially pp. 336–8). These are listed as existence, uniqueness and stability of competitive equilibria; comparative statics, and welfare economics, and are referred to (p. 339) as the 'neoclassical dream'. A sixth issue is the 'physics heuristic'. (The problem of aggregation, discussed elsewhere, seems to have status akin to that of the five goals.) According to H/M the prevailing approach, based on budget-limited consumer demand, has failed in attaining these objectives, while eliminating the budget limitation postulate (and thus following Hotelling's alleged 'dream') would have led to success. The latter claim is argued in Section 4, entitled 'The Dream Fulfilled, if Only Virtually'. The failure of the 'neoclassical dream' is argued in Sections 5 and 6.

The five topics listed by H/M are indeed among the major concerns of economic theory, have been since at least the nineteenth century, and many were intensively studied in the 1930s. To illustrate:

- *Welfare economics* concern dates back at least[6] to the first half of the nineteenth century (Dupuit), then Walras, Marshall, Pareto; and Hicks in the late 1930s and early 1940s
- *Existence* was Walras' major concern in the nineteenth century (by the counting of equations; this was long before Brouwer's fixed point theorem); it was Wald's and Schlesinger's (among others) concern in the 1930s
- Walras and Marshall were concerned with *stability*; Hicks devoted a great deal of attention to stability issues in his *Value and Capital*, although none of them used a formal dynamic (differential or difference equations) model

- Walras and Marshall produced examples of *multiple equilibria*, Wald had a result on *uniqueness*
- The classic problem of tax incidence is an example of *comparative statics*.

Third element reconsidered (the alleged neoclassical objectives): To think of the study of these topics as initiated by post-Second World War neoclassicists would certainly do violence to well known facts of history of economics. But in speaking of the 'neoclassical dream', H/M seems to attribute to neoclassicists not merely a desire to study these issues, but also the desire to prove that the neoclassical model implies specific answers to these problems, in particular that, given the neoclassical model of perfect competition, equilibrium must exist, be unique and stable. Thus inability to supply such proofs would be evidence of failure.

There was no need for a 'neoclassical dream' to stimulate concern about such issues as stability or multiplicity of equilibria. As soon as the concept of equilibrium occupied the centre stage, as was certainly the case by the time of Walras, the question of stability was a natural one to arise.

No one familiar with Walras, Marshall, and the literature of the 1930s would have tried in the 1950s to prove either universal uniqueness of equilibria or the absence of unstable ones, since examples of locally unstable equilibria, due to Walras and Marshall, were already known.[7] On the other hand, the Walras and Marshall examples of *local* instability of particular equilibria did not contradict the possibility of '*global* stability of the system'.[8] While in the late 1950s various classes of economies were shown to possess global system stability, the examples of the 1960s proved that global instability was also a possibility.

By contrast, as pointed out in H/M (pp. 342–3), it follows from a result in Arrow–Hurwicz (1958) that stability would be guaranteed if one assumed that the Hessian of the profit function with respect to quantities sold is negative definite (a sufficient, but not a necessary, condition for profit maximisation).

But I doubt that the 'classics' of the nineteenth- and early twentieth-century period would have abandoned the idea of consumer budget limitations just because so doing might get rid of inconvenient phenomena such as instability or absence of uniqueness of equilibria.

As for the problem of *existence* of equilibrium, it was long clear that in order to guarantee existence some restrictions (e.g. convexity, continuity) would have to be imposed on the characteristics of consumers and producers. The great accomplishment of Wald, Arrow, Debreu and others has been to find a variety of (sufficient) conditions that would indeed guarantee existence. Their 'general equilibrium' models have both consumers and producers, thus agents with, as well as those without, budget limitations.

The existence problem is of crucial importance for *comparative statics* analysis since the latter, by definition, involves comparisons of equilibria. In the absence of information as to existence, attempts at such analysis may easily result in fallacies. On the other hand, when existence proof is available, we are free of internal inconsistencies.

The issue of *aggregation* has, I believe, special status because of its relationship to econometric research. Since much econometric research (and this, I believe, includes the studies of Henry Schultz) uses data aggregated over certain populations or collections of firms, there arises the question as to which properties known to hold for individual agents carry over to aggregates. One reason why this issue is important is that identifiability assumptions used (and needed) by econometricians are often derived from theoretical (or introspective) considerations applicable to *individual* economic agents.

That aggregates do not inherit all of the individual properties has been known for a long time. For instance (as shown by Arrow and Hurwicz, 1958), under certain frequently made assumptions, isolated multiple equilibria can only arise for aggregated excess demand curves (i.e. when there are two or more agents). But it is only more recently that it has been shown (by Sonnenschein, Debreu, Mantel, Richter and others) how little is implied for aggregate demand functions by the restrictions of the neoclassical model if no additional conditions such as similarity of preferences or distribution of wealth are introduced.

This fact may indeed have surprised or disappointed some researchers. It shows that neoclassical general equilibrium theory is by itself inadequate for aggregate prediction purposes, and more specifically that additional information concerning the distribution of various characteristics among economic agents (consumers, firms) is needed. Interesting steps in this direction have indeed been taken, in particular by W. Hildenbrand, M. Jerison, and others, investigating – both theoretically and empirically – the hypothesis called 'the law of market demand'. This law, governing aggregate behaviour, can be derived from two types of hypotheses: those on individual behaviour and on the frequency distribution of characteristics. The derivation is based on the Slutsky decomposition of individual consumer (household) behaviour into substitution and income effects, thus recognising the budgetary constraints. The two hypotheses are: negative *average* substitution effect and positive *average* income effect. Clearly, these hypotheses embody certain distributional features. But, in my opinion, without such features one cannot hope to obtain a theory of aggregate behaviour. These features are grafted onto the standard – but distributionally enriched – neoclassical theory of consumer behaviour.

My conclusion: the H/M concept of a neoclassical dream is based on an illusion.

First element reconsidered (Hotelling's alleged dream): Let us look at the evidence. Hotelling published two famous papers on the subject of demand functions: 'Edgeworth's Taxation Paradox and the Nature of Demand and Supply Functions' (1932), and 'Demand Functions with Limited Budgets' (1935). In the (1932) paper Hotelling considers two models, (*A*) without and (*B*) with budget limitations respectively, but primarily the former (*A*).

Let there be n commodities, and denote respectively by q_i and p_i the quantity and price of the ith commodity purchased. We shall also use vector notation and write $q = (q_1, \ldots, q_n)$ and $p = (p_1, \ldots, p_n)$. The symbol $p.n$ denotes the sum of the cross-products, i.e.

$$p.q = p_1q_1 + p_2q_2 + \ldots + p_nq_n \quad [1]$$

As reported in H/M, model (*A*) postulates the *unconstrained maximization* with respect to the quantities $q_1, \ldots, q_n$ (with prices treated as given) of the function we shall denote by $\phi(q)$, and given by

$$\phi(q) = u(q_1, \ldots, q_n) - p_1q_1 - p_2q_2 - \ldots - p_nq_n$$

i.e. more briefly,

$$\phi(q) = u(q) - p.q \quad [2]$$

The 'dream problem' is how to interpret the functions $u(.)$ and $\phi(.)$ and to see what type of economic agent is involved in this maximisation.

Assuming the differentiabiility of the function $u(.)$, the first-order necessary conditions yield Hotelling's equation system

$$\partial u/\partial q_i = p_i, \; i = 1, \ldots, n \quad [3]$$

For the solution vector q^* of this system to be a (local) maximiser of $\phi(q)$, it is sufficient that a certain set of strict inequalities also be satisfied. q^* is a function of the prices. Under these conditions, q^* is a function of the price vector, $q^* = F(p)$ in Hotelling's (1). F represents the direct demand functions. The inequalities make F invertible so that (1) can be solved for prices as functions of quantities, $p = f(q)$ in Hotelling's (2); thus f represents what we call the *indirect* demand functions. (Hotelling notes that it is legitimate to consider prices as functions of quantities, even though the buyers are assumed to consider the prices as fixed!)

Implicit differentiation of (3), together with some algebraic manipulation yields the famous system of (*indirect demand slope*) *symmetry conditions*

$$\partial f^i/\partial q_j = \partial f^j/\partial q_i \tag{4}$$

for all pairs (i,j) ranging between 1 and n inclusive. This corresponds to Hotelling's (4), although with a slight change of notation. Hotelling refers to these as integrability conditions, which they are, but I use the more explicit term above because other integrability conditions are also in the picture.

The question of interpretation is whether this model represents the behaviour of a household (consumer) or of a firm. H/M opts for the former. So let us see what Hotelling says. He introduces the problem by saying: 'Consider first an *entrepreneur*. . . . he succeeds in making *sales amounting, in money, to* $u = u(q_1, \ldots, q_n)$. Since he spends $p_1q_1 + p_2q_2 + \ldots + p_nq_n$, his *net profit* will be $u - p_1q_1 - p_2q_2 - \ldots - p_nq_n$' (I have italicised the terms that point to what I think is a natural interpretation).

It is difficult to think of this terminology as referring to anything but that of a firm whose total revenue as a function of the quantity sold vector is $u(q)$, the total cost is given by $p.q$, and the difference – to use Hotelling's own expression – is its net profit. It is true that this formulation in the (1932) paper is followed by a remark that suggests the applicability of model (A) not only to entrepreneurs but also to 'purchasers of goods for their own consumption'.

But right after this remark Hotelling presents the classical formulation of consumer behaviour, that of maximising utility subject to a budget limitation, i.e. model (B). In his formulation this limitation is expressed by the requirement that 'the total expenditure $p.q$ must have constant value' in which case the previously obtained condition (3) is replaced by

$$\partial u/\partial q_i = \lambda p_i \tag{3'}$$

where now $u(.)$ is explicitly referred to as the utility function and λ is 'the marginal utility of money'. In that case the integrability requirement becomes Hotelling's (4′), of which the above symmetry condition (4) is a special case.

Algebraically, the first-order conditions (3) for model (*A*) are a special case of the first-order conditions for model (*B*) when the marginal utility of money happens to equal one. This is noted by Hotelling (although not quite in these words) who makes two comments of considerable interest for the interpretation at issue. First, he observes that what we call model (*A*) has the property – as he puts it – of 'obviating the factor λ by restricting attention to those *cases in which money is spent, as the saying is, to make money*' (again, my italics). Hotelling uses as illustrations purchases such as a salesman's haircuts and trousers-pressing 'in order to increase his sales', as well as 'a good deal of food, clothing and entertainment which are consumed, at least in part, with a view to making more money'. This seems to indicate that even though model (*A*) may be appropriate for some personal expenditures on consumer goods, these expenditures are in the nature of inputs for a profit making activity.

Second, since the equilibrium and integrability conditions of model (*A*) constitute a special case of model (*B*), Hotelling says: 'For the purpose of the present paper we prefer to consider functions satisfying the stricter conditions (3). If cases of Edgeworth phenomenon can be found for them, such cases belong *a fortiori* to the wider class also.' Thus, *in the context of the Edgeworth taxation paradox*, even if model (*A*) from some point of view lacks full generality, as long as (*A*) is not ruled out among special cases of model (*B*), it is legitimate to construct paradoxical examples of taxation phenomena within the more restrictive framework of model (*A*). (In this connection, it is of interest to consider the two special preference cases, homothetic and parallel, discussed below.) And, after all, this paper was devoted to a taxation paradox!

But again there is a subsequent remark. In the course of a comparison of the two models, Hotelling says 'Apart from rentiers, most buyers even in their personal transactions, resemble our hypothetical stockholders [who impose a budget limitation: LH] less than the more common stockholder, who is far better pleased if the net profit $u - p.q$ (where u represents gross receipts and $p.q$ expenses) is a maximum than if $p.q$ is restricted by some other consideration' (I use the inner product notation where Hotelling uses summations of cross-products). This might be interpreted as going beyond the salesman type of example, although the meaning is far from clear. Fortunately, whatever Hotelling's thinking on this point might have been when writing the (1932) paper, the matter was I feel completely clarified in the 1935 paper 'Demand functions with limited budgets' in favour of interpreting the (*A*) model as pertaining to a firm, with the (*B*) model as appropriate for consumer choice.

The (1935) paper begins with the summary of relations characterising model (*A*), including the symmetry equations, now written as

$$p_{ij} = p_{ji} \tag{1.3}$$

where $p_{ij} =: \partial f^i / \partial q_j$, followed by the second-order strict inequalities (formula (1.4)). Hotelling then says that these inequalities

> which generalise the condition that a demand curve shall decline, have been deduced on the assumption that the buyers are entrepreneurs, or others adjusting their purchases for maximum profit, in such a way that their purchases could be increased without effective limit if they should lead to sufficiently increased profits. Similar conditions were deduced for supply functions. In case a buyer's budget is limited, it was pointed out that his demand functions will not, in general, satisfy the conditions (1.3), but will satisfy

$$p_i(p_{jk} - p_{kj}) + p_j(p_{ki} - p_{ik}) + p_k(p_{ij} - p_{ji}) = 0. \tag{1.5}$$

The last equation is, of course, the same as the integrability condition for model (*B*) represented by (4′) in the (1932) paper.

Speaking of the (limited budget – model (*B*)) conclusions, Hotelling then makes the following comment:

> The [limited budget type (*B*) model: LH] results obtained are applicable not only to the purchases of individuals, where we are dealing with commodities for actual consumption, and forming a substantial part or all of their expenditures, but likewise to departments of corporations or governments, which often have their budgets fixed in advance, with little opportunity for variation on account of price changes within a budget period.

It seems to me significant that while this remark points to the applicability of the limited budgets model beyond the standard consumer choice problem, there are no remarks in the (1935) paper suggesting that the (*A*) model, with budget limitations absent, is applicable except where Hotelling explicitly assumes a profit maximising entrepreneur.

These views are significantly reinforced by the contents of the letter

Kenneth Arrow wrote to me after reading the H/M chapter. I would have preferred to have it attached in extenso as an Appendix to this note, but excerpts will have to suffice (letter dated 21 August 1996, with a copy simultaneously sent to Professor Mirowski).

Arrow writes

> I am a bit of a witness. I took Hotelling's course in mathematical economics in Fall 1940. (This is not just memory; at Adrian Darnell's request, I looked through my papers and found my course notes about four or five years ago. Unfortunately, I don't at the moment know where they are.) I do not recall the slightest hint that the 1932 model was appropriate for consumer behavior. It was the theory of the firm, as the 1935 paper was the theory of the household. When I read Hicks's *Value and Capital* or Samuelson's papers in *Econometrica* about that time, I was not conscious of any difference of viewpoint . . . I see no evidence in the papers that he was unaware of the difference or that he thought that the unconstrained case was an adequate basis for consumer theory. The one hint to the contrary is the third paragraph of section 5 of the 1932 paper. But later in the same section he shows that he already understood perfectly the difference between the two cases and that the constrained case is the appropriate one.[9]

This testimony and my preceding analysis lead me to conclude that the H/M interpretation of Hotelling is contrary to the evidence. The 'Hotelling dream' hypothesis is based on an illusion.

2 LIMITED-BUDGET CONSUMERS WITH PREFERENCES SATISFYING THE HOTELLING SYMMETRY CONDITIONS

While my own reading of Hotelling convinces me that the model (*A*) was clearly intended as a theory of the firm rather than consumer choice, the Hotelling symmetry conditions themselves ((4) in 1932), are of independent interest for certain special cases of consumer choice theory based on utility[10] maximisation *subject to a budget constraint*.

It is easy to find (indirect) demand functions derived from budget-constrained maximisation that violate the Hotelling symmetry conditions. But, as already noted by Samuelson (1942, p. 81, n. 6 in the volume of studies in memory of Henry Schultz), and subsequently analyzed in depth by Chipman and Moore (1976, pp. 106–8), there are utility functions whose (budget-constrained!) indirect demand functions satisfy Hotelling's symmetry condition (1932, (4)).

There are two cases of interest: (1) homothetic preferences and (2) 'parallel' preferences. It was the homothetic ('expenditure proportionality') case that was first noted by Samuelson in (1942). The case of parallel preferences ('constant marginal utility of income') was discussed by Samuelson in (1950, p. 357, n. 3). Both cases are discussed by H/M but some additional exposition may not be superfluous.

(1) *Homothetic preferences*: A person's preferences are said to be homothetic if, for every positive number k, 'bundle x is preferred to bundle y' implies and is implied by 'bundle x^* is preferred to bundle y^*' where $x^* = kx$ and $y^* = ky$ (see Chipman, 1974). When preferences are continuous and monotone increasing, homothetic preferences are representable by linearly homogeneous utility functions (see Katzner, 1970, esp. pp. 23–5 and 76–8). Under standard assumptions (see Chipman, 1974) it is shown that demand is proportional to income and, when the demand functions are differentiable, that for each commodity j, its elasticity of demand with respect to income e_j equals unity, i.e. $e_j =: (M/h^j)\,(\partial h^j/\partial M) = 1$; here income is denoted by M and $h^j(p,M)$ is the (direct) demand for the jth good, with p denoting the price vector. (This relation is referred to as the unitary elasticity of demand property.) Conversely, integrating the unitary elasticity equation one deduces that the demand is proportional to income, hence (Chipman, 1974, Theorem 2, and Chipman and Moore, 1976) homothetic.

Thus to show that Hotelling's symmetry property implies homotheticity, it is sufficient to show that it implies unitary elasticity of demand with respect to income. I am not aware of this having been shown explicitly in the literature, most likely because it was considered obvious. Here is a sketch of the argument. We assume that preferences have a differentiable utility representation. Hence the Slutsky symmetry (integrability) conditions hold. These can be written as

$$s_{ij} = s_{ji} \tag{*}$$

where $s_{ij} = : \partial h^i/\partial p_j + x_j.\ \partial h^i/\partial M$ and $x_j = h^j(p,M)$. By hypothesis, Hotelling's symmetry conditions hold, i.e. (by inversion)

$$\partial h^i/\partial p_j = \partial h^j/\partial p_i. \tag{**}$$

Using (**) in (*), we conclude that

$$x_j \, \partial h^i/\partial M = x_i \partial h^j/\partial M$$

or, equivalently, that

$(1/x_i)\partial h^i/\partial M = (1/x_j)\partial h^j/\partial M$ for all i and j holds as an identity.

Let us denote the common value of all $(1/x_i)\partial h^i/\partial M$ by $f(p, M)$, so that

$$\partial h^i/\partial M = x_i.f(p, M) \qquad (+)$$

By differentiating the budget equation $p.x = M$, we obtain the relation

$$\Sigma p_i \, \partial h^i/\partial M = 1 \qquad (++)$$

By (+), this becomes

$$\Sigma p_i x_i \, f(p, M) = 1$$

or

$$f(p, M) \, \Sigma \, p_i x_i = 1$$

Since, by definition, the summation in the last expression equals income M, the equation tells us that $M.f(p,M) = 1$, hence

$$f(p, M) = 1/M \qquad (+++)$$

But since, for all i, we have $(1/x_i)\partial h^i/\partial M = f(p, M)$, it follows from (+++) that

$$(1/x_i)\partial h^i/\partial M = 1/M$$

which is equivalent to

$$(M/x_i)\partial h^i/\partial M = 1$$

or $e_i = 1$, which is the unitary elasticity property.

As indicated above, from this we can conclude that the preferences are homothetic, thus confirming the findings of Samuelson (1942) as well as Chipman and Moore (1976, esp. pp. 106–8 and 116).

(2) *'Parallel' preferences*: These are representable by quasi-linear utility functions that can be written as $u(x, y) = x + f(y)$ where x is a scalar (money) and y is a vector of *(non-money)* commodities. If y is one-dimensional, and in the (x, y)-plane x is the abscissa, the indifference curves are 'parallel' horizontal translates of each other (with some complications near the boundaries). When the valuation function $f(y)$ is differentiable, at an interior point (x^*, y^*) the first-order condition for the jth commodity (component of the vector y) is

$$\partial f / \partial y_j = p_j \ (\#)$$

hence independent of 'money' x, and the coefficient λ in Hotelling's (3′) equals 1, hence is constant, i.e. the 'marginal utility of money' is constant. The above equation (#) defines the jth price as a function of the ys, hence represents the indirect demand function for the jth non-money good. When the valuation function $f(y)$ is twice differentiable , the cross-derivatives are equal, and hence the Hotelling symmetry condition ((4) in 1932, (1.3) in 1935) is satisfied for any pair of *non-money* commodities. This is the gist of Samuelson's (1950) observation. The italicization distinguishes the parallel preferences case situation from the homothetic case where the symmetry condition holds for all pairs of goods *without an exception for 'money'*.

Second element (the alleged rejection by the neoclassical consumer choice theory of Hotelling's (unlimited budget) demand functions in favor of the budget constrained model) *reconsidered.*

I disagree with this claim for the following reasons: (a) the use of the budget-constrained model of consumer choice originated not later than with the nineteenth-century marginalists (Jevons, Walras, Fisher), was implicit in Marshall, and was taken for granted in the 1930s; (b) Hicks in 1939 observed that the absence of the income effect distinguished production (firm) theory from consumer choice theory; (c) based both on careful reading of the relevant passages of Hotelling's (1932) and (1935) papers, as well as on Kenneth Arrow's testimony, I am convinced that the main 1932 model ((1)–(6)) was intended to be a model of the firm, while the (1935) model, as well as the alternative (1932) model ((3′)–(4′)) were intended to be models of consumer choice.[11]

Since Hotelling's model (*A*) was not intended or understood to be appropriate for consumer choice theory, it was not under consideration for this purpose, hence not 'rejected'. The developments of the post-Second World War period in this area are a natural continuation of what had been the standard approach already for the nineteenth-century classics.

H/M are, of course, not unaware of the nineteenth-century origins of the model in which the consumer maximises utility subject to the budget constraint, with the important consequence that in equilibrium marginal utilities are proportional[12] (but not in general equal) to prices. Indeed, on p. 328, they refer to such models in Fisher (1892),[13] Pareto (1927), and Slutsky (1915), a formulation developed in the Hicks and Allen (1934) papers, in Hicks's (1938) *Value and Capital*, and Samuelson's *Foundations* (whose preface to the first edition is dated 1945).

Significantly, the budget-constrained model (here called model *B*), in addition to being formulated (although as a digression) in Hotelling's (1932) paper, is also the main subject of Hotelling's (1935) paper entitled 'Demand Functions with Limited Budgets'.

Indeed, H/M say: 'While the standard textbook version[14] was also present, and perhaps even dominant, during the 1930s – particularly after Hicks and Allen (1934) – the word "dominant" should be used rather gingerly'. (p. 328). What follows in H/M is the justification for this warning:

> The entire programme of what is now called neoclassical microeconomics was still quite inchoate during the 1930s and that instability would continue for the next thirty years or so; 'dominant view' in this context means only that it was the characterisation of consumer choice that seemed to be most accepted by the specific coterie of economists who were concerned with the theoretical grounding of demand curves under conditions of interdependent multicommodity utility maximisation. (p. 328).

Consumer behaviour theory based on utility maximisation subject to budget constraint was indeed standard from the 1870s on, and what H/M call a 'coterie' included Jevons, Walras, Fisher, Pareto, Marshall (1890, comments on the Giffen phenomenon), as well as Antonelli (1886), Johnson (1913) and Slutsky. Can all of them be credited with prescience in 'rejecting the knowledge of Hotelling's demand functions', decades ahead of the publication of the (1932) 'Edgeworth's Taxation Paradox'?

It is interesting that H/M first speaks of the dominance of the standard (budget constrained) model during the 1930s and all the way back to the 1870s, but then retreats and asks that 'the word "dominant" be treated rather gingerly'. Is it because this set of founders of modern economic theory in most of its many flavours constituted some kind of a clique? Is it because of the H/M, pp. 323–4, (I believe, regrettable) decision 'to restrict ourselves to events in the United States' and (among the H/M citations) only Irving Fisher qualified?[15]

Actually the budget-constrained model was routinely used by theorists for a long period preceding the 1940s and 1950s. On the other hand, M/H itself asserts that 'The entire programme of what is now called neoclassical economics was still quite inchoate during the 1930s' (That is, of course, assuming that there was such a programme.)

What in fact the sequence of events suggests is that by the time neoclassical economics arrived on the scene, the budget-constrained model of consumer behaviour was the natural one to be used, hardly an innovation or controversial.

Finally, may I be permitted to include my own observation concerning the 1930s? My first exposure to the budget-constrained model (and most then 'modern' economic theory) was at the London School of Economics during the 1938/9 academic year, mostly from the lectures of R.G.D. Allen and from reading *Value and Capital,* which had just then been published. As students, we considered as innovative Hicks's stress on invariance with respect to monotone transformations of the utility functions (as in the definition of complementarity), his analysis of stability and multiperiod processes, and a number of other features, but not the use of the budget constraints. The latter seemed self-evident, perhaps the most realistic assumption of economic theory! I do not recall either of Hotelling's papers on demand theory being cited, much less 'rejected'. (In *Value and Capital,* Hicks did refer to Hotelling's (1938) *Econometrica* welfare economics paper.)

It is interesting to note that, in analysing technical complementarities for firms, Hicks (1939, p. 90) observes:

> 'in the case of production, we do not have anything similar to the income effects which gave us so much trouble in utility theory'.

This is precisely the distinction that separates Hotelling's main[16] (1932) model (with budget constraint absent) from the 'limited budget' model of (1935). (The (1935) Hotelling paper was presented in June 1934; it has no reference to Hicks and Allen (1934) nor to Slutsky.)

Allen's *Mathematical Analysis for Economists* (1938, p. 60), refers to Hotelling's (1932) paper but only in a problem dealing specifically with Edgeworth's taxation paradox. Allen (1936) has no references to Hotelling.[17]

In the light of the totality of evidence, my conclusion is: there was no 'rejection'.

Notes

1. In writing this comment I have benefited from conversations with Kenneth Arrow, John Chipman and Paul Samuelson, but, of course, the responsibility for its contents remains mine. In addition, Kenneth Arrow wrote me a letter (from which I quote below) commenting on certain points in the Hands/Mirowski paper, and also sent me a copy of his letter to Professor Mirowski with corrections to an earlier version of the chapter. It is my understanding that most of these corrections have been incorporated in the final version of the chapter except the statement that Arrow had worked for the Statistical Research Group at Columbia, which in fact is incorrect since in fact he did not.

   In the interest of full disclosure, let me warn the reader that I am guilty of close and continued contacts with many of the neoclassicists discussed in the H–M paper. I was once Samuelson's research assistant; Kenneth Arrow and I have been co-authors of a number of papers; I was a member of the Cowles Commission in its Chicago period.
2. Variously called goals, concerns, programmes, and dreams.
3. I am following the H/M designation of Arrow, Debreu and Samuelson as 'neoclassicists', without endorsing it as totally appropriate or doing justice to their range of contributions.
4. See H/M, p. 325, referring to Hotelling's model as 'a bit of rejected knowledge'.
5. Or worse, a defilement! Section 6 has the heading 'Demand Demended; or the Dream Defiled'. But it may be that this heading refers to the sad fate that H/M believe befell what they call the 'neoclassical dream.'
6. Or perhaps to Adam Smith's 'invisible hand'.
7. Admittedly, the early examples were graphic and somewhat intuitive, and they mostly dealt with the two-commodity case. Arrow and Hurwicz (1958) provided an analytical example of multiplicity (and hence local instability of one equilibrium point) for the two goods, two traders case. (I do not know whether an earlier analytical example of multiple equilibria exists in the literature.)
8. A *system* is said to be *globally stable* if it is the case that there is convergence to some equilibrium from any initial position. A system can be globally stable even though some equilibria are locally unstable, and that is what happens in the Walras, Marshall, and Arrow–Hurwicz (1958) examples. The latter paper showed that, under certain assumptions, global stability would prevail when there were only two goods or only one agent, or

under gross substitution. The Scarf (1960) example showed that global instability may occur when there are three goods and three traders. Gale (1965) provided another example of global instability with three goods but only two agents; significantly, the instability was due to the Giffen paradox (hence the presence of an income effect). The results due to Sonnenschein and others (see McFadden *et al.*, 1974) show that global instability is not a rare phenomenon in multiagent (more than one) multicommodity (three or more) models.

9. I have confined my discussion to issues raised by H/M that relate to the history of ideas as distinct from the scientific merits of basing consumer theory on budget–unconstrained utility maximisation. On p. 325 (emphasis in the original), H/M say:

> We do *not* seek to argue that Harold Hotelling was 'right' and Eugene Slutsky was 'wrong' . . . [it] is . . . not a story about what 'should' or 'should not' have emerged from this tumultuous period; it is not an attempt to revive, or even to show an injustice was done to, Hotelling's theory of demand. Such a normative project would violate our own historiographical principles by subverting our stated intention to treat winners and losers in a more symmetric way.

In his letter, on the other hand, Arrow did take a position on the merits of the idea, attributed (incorrectly in Arrow's view as well as mine) to Hotelling by H/M, that consumer choice theory should ignore the budget constraint. Arrow writes: 'There are, of course, obvious objections to using the unconstrained case to analyze consumer demand. After all, the budget constraint is such a patent fact that it is a clear falsification'.)

10. Here and elsewhere in this note, I am speaking of utility maximisation in order to conform to the Hotelling formulation. More recent models typically speak of preferences without necessarily referring to utility representations.

11. In each case, Hotelling also discussed less standard cases. For instance, in the (1935) (limited budget) paper (Darnell, 1990, p. 126) he says:

> The [limited budget model CLH] results obtained are applicable not only to the purchases of individuals, where we are dealing with commodities for actual consumption, and forming a substantial part or all of their expenditures, but likewise to departments of corporations or governments, which often have their budgets fixed in advance, with little opportunity for variation on account of price changes within a budget period.

12. Hotelling makes this point in the (1932) paper, (3'), where the proportionality coefficient λ is referred to as the 'marginal utility of money'. Hotelling comments: 'This proportionality of prices to marginal utilities is familiar.' He goes on to say that 'For the purposes of the present paper we prefer to consider functions satisfying the stricter conditions (3). If cases of Edgeworth's phenomenon can be found for them, such cases belong *a fortiori* to the wider class also.' His motivation will be discussed below.

13. Fisher, in turn, refers to Jevons (1871).
14. 'The standard textbook version' is the version of maximisation subject to budget constraint.
15. On p. 346, H/M makes the point that

> in America in the 1930s there was no single 'theory of demand,' no widely shared set of commitments which embodied a consensus neoclassical view of the relationship between the price of a good and the quantity of that good that would be sold. The closest thing to what passed for orthodoxy was Marshallian demand theory, which in practice simply denied the importance of interdependencies, worked in terms of separable utility functions, generally appealed to a putatively constant marginal utility of money, and up to that point had encouraged no systematic quantitative empirical research.

If this statement is historically correct, and I have not had a chance to explore this issue, it points all the more to the importance of taking seriously into account the European developments with regard to the theory of demand. Also, references to the constancy of the marginal utility of money only make sense in a budget-constrained framework.
16. 'Main' – because of references to the limited budget model already present in the (1932) paper (see n. 10 above).
17. In n. 3, p. 120, Allen (1936) says:

> Since the present article went to press, Professor Henry Schultz has published a long article on 'Interrelations of Demand, Price and Income' . . . (*Journal of Political Economy*, August 1935) in which he gives essentials of Slutsky's work. It appears that Schultz discovered Slutsky's *Giornale* article rather earlier than, but quite independently of, Hicks and myself.

Also on p. 120, referring to the (1934) Hicks and Allen 'A Reconsideration . . .' article, Allen says:

> In the article, much use was made of the ideas of the mathematical work of Johnson [citing Johnson's 1913 *Economic Journal* paper], but we thought that some of the results attained, as apart from the method of approach, were entirely original. More recently, however, our attention has been drawn to an important article by Professor Slutsky . . . published as long ago as 1915. It is now clear that many of our results were first given explicitly by Slutsky.

Schultz (1935), while citing and discussing Slutsky (1915) and Hicks and Allen (1934), and placing much emphasis on the role of income, seems to have no references to Hotelling (1935). Of course, the two papers were published essentially at the same time.

References

Allen, R.G.D. (1936) 'Professor Slutsky's Theory of Consumers' Choice', *Review of Economic Studies*, vol. 3, pp. 120–9.

——— (1938) *Mathematical Analysis for Economists*, Macmillan, London.

Antonelli, G.B. (1886) (original publ.) *Sulla Teoria Matematica della Economia Politica*, Capitolo Primo, Concetto di Utilita, Pisa, Tipografia del Folchetto, trans. J.S. Chipman and A.P. Kirman in J.S. Chipman, L. Hurwicz, M.K. Richter, and H. Sonnenschein, (eds), *Preferences, Utility, and Demand* (New York: Harcourt, Brace, Jovanovich, 1971).

Arrow, K.J. and L. Hurwicz (1958) 'On the Stability of Competitive Equilibrium, I', *Econometrica*, vol. 26, pp. 522–552.

Chipman, J.S. (1974) 'Homothetic Preferences and Aggregation', *Journal of Economic Theory*, vol. 8, pp. 26–38.

——— (1982) 'Samuelson and Consumption Theory', Chapter 2 in G.R. Feiwel (ed.), *Samuelson and Neoclassical Economics* (Boston: Kluwer Nijhoff).

Chipman, J.S. and J.C. Moore (1976) 'The Scope of Arguments of Consumer's Surplus', in A.M. Tang, F.M. Westfield, and J.S. Worley (eds), *Evolution, Welfare, and Time in Economics, Essays in Honor of Nicholas Georgescu-Roegen* (Lexington: Lexington Books, D.C. Heath and Co.), pp. 69–123.

Darnell, A. (ed.) (1990) *The Collected Economics Articles of Harold Hotelling* (New York: Springer Verlag).

Fisher, I (1892) (original publication), *Mathematical Investigation in the Theory of Value and Price*, reprints of Economic Classics (New York: Augustus M. Kelley, 1965).

Gale, D. (1965) 'A Note on Global Instability of Competitive Equilibrium', *Naval Research Logistics Quarterly*, vol. 10, pp. 80–87.

Hicks, J.R. (1939), *Value and Capital* (Oxford: Oxford University Press).

Hicks, J.R. and R.G.D. Allen (1934), 'A Reconsideration of the Theory of Value, Parts I and II', *Economica*, NS, vol. 14, pp. 52–76, 196–219.

Hildenbrand, W. (1994), *Market Demand: Theory and Empirical Evidence* (Princeton: Princeton University Press).

Hotelling, H. (1932) 'Edgeworth's Taxation Paradox and the Nature of Demand and Supply Functions', vol. 40, pp. 577–616.

——— (1935) 'Demand Functions with Limited Budgets', *Econometrica*, vol. 3, pp. 66–78

——— (1938) 'The General Welfare in Relation to Problem of Taxation and of Railway and Utility Rates', *Econometrica*, vol. 6, pp. 242–69.

Jerison, M. (1984) 'Aggregation and Pairwise Aggregation of Demand when the Distribution of Income is Fixed', *Journal of Economic Theory*, vol. 33, pp. 1–31.

Jevons, W.S. (1871) (first edn.) *The Theory of Political Economy*, fifth edn., reprint (New York: Augustus M. Kelley and Millman Inc. 1957).

Johnson, W.E. (1913) 'Pure Theory of Utility Curves', *Economic Journal*, vol. 23, pp. 483–513.

Katzner, D. (1970) *Static Demand Theory* (London: Macmillan).

Marshall, A. (1890) *Principles of Economics*, Vol I (London: Macmillan).

McFadden, D., A. Mas-Colell, R. Mantel and M.K. Richter (1974) 'A Characterization of Community Excess Demand Functions', *Journal of Economic Theory*, vol. 9, pp. 361–74.

Pareto, V. (1906) (original edn), *Manuale di Economia Politica, con una Introduzione alla Scienza Soziale* (Milan: Società Editrice Libraria).

Samuelson, P.A. (1942) 'Constancy of the Marginal Utility of Income', in O. Lange, F. McIntyre and T.O. Yntema (eds), *Studies in Mathematical Economics and Econometrics: In Memory of Henry Schultz* (Chicago: University of Chicago Press), pp. 75–91.

——— (1947) *Foundations of Economic Analysis*, 1st edn (Cambridge, MA: Harvard University Press).

——— (1950) 'The Problem of Integrability in Utility Theory', *Economica*, vol. 17, pp. 355–85.

Scarf, H. (1960) 'Some Examples of Global Instability of Competitive Equilibrium', *International Economic Review*, vol. 1, pp. 147–72.

Schultz, H. (1935) 'Interrelations of Demand, Price, and Income', *Journal of Political Economy* vol. 43, pp. 433–81.

Slutsky, E.E. (1915) 'Sulla teoria del bilancio del consumatore', *Giornale degli Economisti*, series 3, 51, 1–26; English trans. by O. Ragusain, *Readings in Price Theory*, ed. K. Boulding and G. Stigler (1952), vol. 4 (Homewood, IL: Irwin, pp. 27–56.

Sonnenschein, H. (1973) 'Do Walras' Identity and Continuity Characterise the Class of Community Excess Demand Functions'?, in McFadden *et al.* (1974) pp. 345–54.

Walras, L. (1874) (first (French) edn.), *Elements of Pure Economics*, trans. William Jaffé (1954) (Homewood, IL: Irwin).

Comment

Nancy Cartwright
LONDON SCHOOL OF ECONOMICS, UK

'Harold Hotelling and the Neoclassical Dream' is like a modern food processor that comes with separate attachments for separate jobs. There is one paper proper, comprising sections 2 through 5. Then there is an Introduction that affirms the symmetry thesis that rejection and acceptance of scientific claims and techniques require the same kind of explanation. Then there is a sketch, in sections 6 and 7, of a second paper, or rather a sketch of a set of conclusions that a second paper could aim to establish. I will not comment on this second still-to-be-written paper. The entire package is an odd piece to offer for case studies in the methodology of economics since, even with attachments, it is clearly not designed to serve that purpose, and no advice is offered for how to use it to do the job. The Introduction could have been turned to this purpose; but instead of addressing general issues about the methods for practising economics it talks about methods for writing histories of economics.

The central piece is a study of two papers of Harold Hotelling. It discusses how the results of these papers solved a number of important problems in the theory of demand, how Hotelling and Henry Schultz together tried to understand them in the face of Schultz's empirical disconfirmations and of the news about Slutsky's related results, and how their views in the end diverged, with various remarks about the subsequent attitude towards Hotelling among Chicago economists. The piece has two aims: to demonstrate that [Hotelling's approach] solves quite a number of the discipline's perceived problems – problems from the 1930s as well as problems associated with the Arrow–Debreu general equilibrium model in the 1950s and 1960s – and then to offer a contextually situated discussion of why Hotelling's model nonetheless did not survive intact into the body of accepted knowledge of neoclassical economies. In fact Hands and Mirowski believe that Hotelling's approach solved the six problems they select as of central concern *better* than the 'programme that managed to become the mainstream view'. It is clear the 'nonetheless' in their statement of aims matters, for the question that spurs their second aim is 'why it was, *given its potential fecundity*, that Hotelling's approach did not become the standard view of demand' (p. 339, emphasis mine). I shall confine myself to one comment: the chapter still needs a great deal of additional material to support its aims, so it is a pity the extra space and effort has been spent in attachments to do other jobs rather than the details of evidence and argument that could fulfil the aims set out.

I begin with a brief defence of the symmetry principle, which Hands and Mirowski advocate. The acceptance of certain theories or explanatory strategies, the use of particular techniques, the building of instruments, the gathering and processing of data and the testing of hypotheses are all human actions and they are, like all human actions, to be explained by a combination of desires, beliefs and intentions. Hands and Mirowski are opposed to what they call 'linear histories', which assume that 'views that are rejected by the scientific community are, for the most part, rejected for the right reasons, and . . . the reason for their failure resides in the nature of the world and not in any of the contingencies of the social context' (p. 324). This is a very strong historical thesis and surely they are right to question it. But more to the point of the symmetry thesis is an obvious corollary of the fact that scientific decisions are human actions: even when we are motivated to accept a theory for good reasons or on account of the evidence, the facts do not cause us to accept the decision directly, in the way that gravity may directly cause us to topple over. Rather the facts and reasons must be mediated both by our beliefs about what the facts and reasons are and also by our beliefs that these constitute a good reason for accepting the theory; and of course we may ask in turn how these beliefs are formed and what affects them. But if our reactions are not mediated by these kinds of beliefs, they are not rational after all, no matter how good the reasons and evidence we confront might be.

This is just why Hands and Mirowski need to provide thicker detail in their own 'contextually situated discussion' of Hotelling's model. We are offered six problems that are supposed to be of central concern for demand theory, and a series of proofs that Hotelling's model solves these at least as well and often better than 'the programme that managed to become the mainstream view – the Arrow–Debreu general equilibrium theory'. Then we are invited to be puzzled about how then the Arrow–Debreu general equilibrium theory did manage to become mainstream.

But the details are missing for establishing a proper historical case and the dates are all wrong. Hands and Mirowski themselves admit the incompleteness of their case on both fronts, the first when they choose as 'the easiest way to proceed' to present 'one particular generic version of the Arrow–Debreu model' (p. 335), and the second when they describe the set of six problems as 'problems from the 1930s as well as problems associated with the Arrow–Debreu general equilibrium model *in the 1950s and 1960s*' (p. 325, emphasis added). For it to be a puzzle why Hotelling's model was not accepted, the problems it solved better had to be recognised as more central problems than those solved by the alternative (and recognised by whomever it is that is claimed to have been in the business of keeping Hotelling's model from becoming mainstream) and Hotelling's superiority at solving them should have been clear as well.[1] The works offered by Hands and Mirowski begin only 24 years after the second Hotelling paper. In the text the only references for the centrality of the problems are Debreu (1959) and Arrow and Hahn (1971) with Quirk and Saposnik (1968) and Takayama (1974) cited in footnotes; and the evidence for the success of Hotelling at these tasks is entirely in references in footnotes: Court (1941), Samuelson (1942), Varian (1982), Keenan (1985) and Arrow and Hurwicz (1962).

In fact the discussion at the time, on Hands and Mirowski's account, was about the alternative offered by the Slutsky symmetry conditions; and almost nothing is reported about the six problems in Hands and Mirowski's account of this discussion, with the exception of the last – the hunt for an economic analogue of potential. Nor do we yet have a detailed account of the reactions of those who rejected Hotelling and of their own views of the problems most in need of solution. The remarks about the connection of Knight, Friedman, Stigler and others with Hotelling and with Schultz and their attitudes towards each of them suggest that there may be a story to be told. But it is not yet there. What we do have is a nice account of the mutual interaction of Hotelling and Schultz and an argument that Hotelling himself clung to his own version over Slutsky's, and for good reasons. We do not have laid out the response of others to these reasons nor any connections these reasons might have been understood by the protagonists to have to the six problems fixed upon by Hands and Mirowski. No doubt most economists reading these papers will have their own views about what the reasons should have been and what the connections are. But, as Hands and Mirowski stress, current views about what the 'right' connections are do not provide a good enough basis for determining how the historical actors saw things.

With their story of Hotelling and Schultz, Hands and Mirowski fill in a piece of this history. But their account of the superiority of

Hotelling's model that sets the historical puzzle about its failure to be accepted is still only a promissory note towards a history, a promissory note that they may well be able to fulfil – or may not. It is on this account hard to reconcile the arguments they provide up to now with Hands and Mirowski's description of what their aims are. They wish to write a history of a piece of rejected knowledge and of how it came to be rejected. But the arguments they give in the paper are appropriate to support not the historical thesis but a thesis they emphatically deny as their own – 'that Harold Hotelling was "right" and Eugene Slutsky was "wrong"'.

With respect to the methodology – the intended focus of this volume – the remarks about Schultz and Hotelling that Hands and Mirowski make in Section 5 seem exemplary of the obvious but important rule of enquiry: when something goes wrong look hard and look everywhere you can for why. The case also illustrates the natural tendency of economics in the face of empirical disconfirmation of all alternatives to retain the ones that fare well on other criteria and that have some immediate possibility for development.

But what are these other criteria and how do they interact? Notoriously, despite the highly mathematised formulation of its hypotheses and models, economics is not very good at precise prediction. Yet hypotheses are keenly contested and getting it right is thought to matter both for understanding and for projections into the future. Standard methodologies have little to offer as either an account or as a recommendation of how decisions among competing alternatives are arrived at since all at base look to direct empirical confirmation (even if some, like that of Lakatos, are more liberal than others about when the confirmation comes and how complete it must be). The case of Hotelling and Schultz looks to be a very good example for trying to figure out in detail exactly how in a specific instance various considerations combined to support different degrees of confidence in different alternatives and to look for general lessons that might be drawn.

Note

1. Unless the puzzle is 'Why were they unable to see that Hotelling solved these problems better?', which equally makes presuppositions that need detailed historical support.

References

Arrow, K.J. and F. Hahn (1971) *General Competitive Analysis* (San Francisco: Holden-Day).

Arrow, K.J. and L. Hurwicz (1962) 'Decentralization and Computation in Resource Allocation', in R. Pfouts (ed.), *Essays in Economics and Econometrics: A Volume in Honor of Harold Hotelling* (Chapel Hill: University of North Carolina Press), pp. 34–104.

Court, L.M. (1941) 'Invariable Classical Stability of Entrepreneurial Demand and Supply Functions', *Quarterly Journal of Economics*, vol. 56, pp. 134–45.

Debreu, G. (1959) *Theory of Value: An Axiomatic Analysis of Economic Equilibrium* (New Haven: Yale University Press).

Keenan, D. (1988) 'Global Stability for Homothetic Preferences in a Distribution Economy', *Economic Letters*, vol. 18, pp. 101–4.

Quirk, J. and R. Saposnik (1968) *Introduction to General Equilibrium Theory and Welfare Economics* (New York: McGraw-Hill).

Samuelson, P.A. (1942) 'Constancy of the Marginal Utility of Income' in O. Lange, F. McIntyre and T.O. Yntema (eds.) *Studies in Mathematical Economies and Econometrics: In Memory of Henry Schultz* (Chicago: University of Chicago Press), pp. 75–91.

Takayama, A. (1974) *Mathematical Economics* (Hinsdale, IL: The Dryden Press).

Varian H.R. (1982) 'Dynamics and Systems with Applications to Economics', in K.J. Arrow and M.D. Intriligator (eds), *Handbook of Mathematical Economies, Vol. I* (Amsterdam: North-Holland).

Discussion

Wade Hands began by agreeing with Nancy Cartwright's comment that there is always diversity in history, but he questioned whether most economists would agree: history in economics is simplistic and whiggish. Even if the approach in the chapter may not seem radical to historians, it challenges the way economists think about the history of their subject. Hands denied that he and Mirowski were insisting that theirs was the single right way to do history, and he agreed that they had not fully succeeded in doing the sort of history they would like to do. He pointed out, however, that the project was not yet complete and, in any event that it was too large to encompass in a chapter.

Passing on to more detailed issues, Hands noted that if one takes standard demand theory and adds the constancy of the marginal utility of money with respect to prices, then one gets the symmetry condition. Schultz was interested in testing this condition, and so he regarded Hotelling's theory as a special case. In Schultz's view, the only thing interesting about the theory is its operational consequences.

His and Mirowski's point is that this is not the only reading of Hotelling. They are considering a period when there was little agreement as to what was the right way to do demand theory, and they are concerned with what the individuals concerned thought. There are other implications of the Hotelling model which modern economists might find silly, but which were very important to Hotelling. In the correspondence with Schultz he did not want his theory to be downgraded to a special case, because he wanted those implications for other reasons.

Hands then responded to Hurwicz's remarks. He conceded that one needs evidence to determine whether the goals of contemporary theory are as he and Mirowski said, but the objectives may be implicit in actual theoretical activities. Hands and Mirowski did not mean that people in 1959 thought about uniqueness and stability explicitly as goals.

Leonid Hurwicz questioned how these could even implicitly have been goals. If theorists posed questions about uniqueness and stability and answered that there are multiple equilibria or that they are not stable, why infer that there was even an implicit goal of demonstrating uniqueness or stability?

Hands continued by arguing that the central issue in interpreting Hotelling's work is whether he is offering only a theory of factor demands. If one picks up a standard textbook today – indeed if one picks up Hands's own text – and you look up Hotelling's Lemma, you find that it has something to do with factor demand functions and integrability conditions. That's the place where the Hotelling model has settled in contemporary theory. But this does not mean that this is all that Hotelling had in mind. He had a general view of where demand comes from and a general vision of how one can characterise demand functions. The current way of reading the past is not the only possible reading.

Philip Mirowski remarked that this work is distinct from both standard history and philosophy of economics, and both historians and philosophers are critical of it. He insists on the relevance of history, because he lives in a profession that has historical horizons of about five to seven years. He and Hands are demonstrating that a different kind of history can be conceived in this situation, that's all. Why is that so threatening?

Bennett McCallum argued that there is one important goal of the Arrow–Debreu general equilibrium programme that Hands and Mirowski do not discuss. That goal is to write down a general equilibrium model. Hotelling's model is a model of firm demand. But actually firms do not just float around in mid-air; they are owned by individuals who receive an income generated by the firms and who use that income to purchase consumption goods. At this point one is right back in the standard framework that is familiar from undergraduate textbooks. Hotelling's description of demand functions as consumers' demand functions disappears, because they simply were not. One cannot write down a general equilibrium model with such demand functions.

Nancy Cartwright remarked that Mirowski and Hands are talking about Hotelling's work and his understanding of it, not 'Hotelling's model'. It may be that we do not know what Hotelling thought, but this is not the sort of thing that is impossible to know. When McCallum says that the theory disappears for just the reason we know, that is an historical claim and just as vulnerable as Mirowski's and Hands's claims.

Hurwicz agreed on the need for documentary evidence, and argued that he could provide some that was brief but convincing. In the following quotation, it is very difficult to interpret Hotelling's u functions as anything except ordinary revenue functions. He made a mistake denoting it by u, but it's a revenue function, not a utility function. Hotelling writes

> Consider first an entrepreneur. By using quantities $q_1, \ldots, q_n$ of the several commodities . . ., he succeeds in making sales amounting, in money, to $u = u(q_1, \ldots, q_n)$. Since he spends $p_1q_1 + p_2q_2 + \ldots + p_nq_n$, his net profit will be $u - p_1q_1 - p_2q_2 - \ldots - p_nq_n$. (1932, p. 590)

Hurwicz questioned why one would interpret u as anything other than revenue.

Mirowski responded that the passage Hurwicz cited was rewritten after Shultz asked Hotelling why he wrote the text of the (1932) paper. In the letters Schultz and Hotelling continue to talk about the general theory of consumption. Hotelling encouraged Shultz to test whether the demand functions he fitted corresponded to what Hotelling's theory, interpreted as a theory of consumer demand, would predict. This provides some some evidence for Hands and Mirowski's interpretation. Furthermore, when Schultz and Hotelling learned of the Slutsky relation, they both viewed it in their discussions as a competing hypothesis. This is the reason why Hands and Mirowski take Hotelling as offering a general theory of demand.

Pierluigi Barrotta noted that Hands and Mirowski's paper is not faithful to the 'strong programmeme' in the sociology of knowledge, which they purport to follow. The strong programme insists that one should explain historical changes in terms of non-epistemic factors, such as social negotiation, class struggle or contingent interest. Shapin and Schaffer, for example, try to explain the controversy between Hobbes and Boyle by referring to the different ways Boyle and Hobbes try to preserve social harmony or unity. Hands and Mirowski's paper, in contrast refers again and again to epistemic factors. For example, it says that Samuelson was moved to put forward revealed preference theory, because he wanted to make economic theory empirically testable.

Barrotta also expressed scepticism about claims that one model is a special case of another. Usually economists have in mind the possibility of a syntactic derivation. While necessary, such a derivation is not sufficient, because the semantics of the supposed special case must also be captured.

Nancy Wulwick agreed that demand theory was still wide open in 1940, and she wondered whether Hands and Mirowski's focus excludes some of the important streams. For instance she was surprised when she saw in the translation of Pareto's work and in the rendering of that work by W.E. Johnson in the (1913) *Economic Journal* that they both presented the possibility that you could have a system of n demand curves with $n - 1$ of them positively sloped. Wulwick wonder why such an option is excluded by Hands and Mirowski's story. Is it because because there are no energetic metaphors alive in such a system?

Mirowski argued that the separation of consumer theory and production theory was not nearly as important for Hoteling and Schultz as it is for economists today. Other considerations – as documented in the chapter – influenced them more. For example, Hotelling thought that the solution to the Great Depression would be to intervene in microeconomic markets. In order to do that, one needed a very clear welfare economics. If one accepted the Slutsky interpretation of demand theory, it would be much harder to make clear welfare statements. Notice also that Hotelling and Schultz were both concerned specifically with agricultural commodities. They did not really care whether demand for wheat was a final demand or some kind of intermediate demand.

There is a large-scale negotiation going on here concerning the right way to prosecute an empirical mathematical programme. A myriad of considerations enter, and there is no one right answer for either of these people. One fascinating feature is that Hotelling and Schultz were able to join in sketching their mathematical programme despite sharp disagreements about politics. Shultz really does not like interventionism and Hotelling is a market socialist. With the increasing division of intellectual labour that one finds now, people do not really get down and negotiate on all these levels as to what is acceptable and what is not. Instead one has pronouncements about what is true and what is not and what everyone knows. Economists are in a different world now than they were then.

McCallum remarked that even if Hotelling and Schultz did not care about the distinction between firm demands and consumer demands, economists who were working on the Arrow–Debreu general equilibrium programme in the 1950s did. It is then no mystery why they did not consider Hotelling's theory as a contending theory of demand. There is a role for sociological, historical and contextual analysis when something silly or illogical survives. But when an illogical argument disappears and a more logical argument supersedes it, it is a waste of time using sociological arguments to explain why. The problem for sociological analysis here is why Hotelling and Schultz continue to talk about these functions as consumer demand functions in their correspondence with each other, when they know better.

Uskali Mäki commented that the history of economic methodology is full of simplistic importations from philosophy of science, but that now the field is going beyond this stage. Hands and Mirowski's programmatic description of their approach is a similarly simplistic importation – this time of ideas from social theories of science critical of a naive vision of nature simply speaking the truth to scientists. But economists all admit that many elements in their theories are not true (though perhaps there are important truths in them despite the many minor falsehoods). So some adjustment would be needed to avoid misleadingly simplistic accounts. Clarification about the rejection of 'normative' approaches is needed, too. Is not an approach that proscribes questions about truth and falsehood itself normative?

Hands and Mirowski said that their approach is symmetrical and that a symmetrical approach somehow excludes a consideration of truth and falsity: both true beliefs and false beliefs have to be explained in social terms. This is in contrast to what McCallum said. Mäki would part company with McCallum by suggesting that both true and false beliefs can be and have to be explained in social terms. But he would also part company with Hands and Mirowski, because true and false claims may have different social explanations, in part because of their truth or falsity. Maybe the attainment of truth might be dependent on some favourable social organisation of academic work, whereas an explanation of error might refer to some unfavourable social arrangements. The history of any science or theory has to be written as a social history but it is a more complex history than Hands and Mirowski take it to be, and questions of truth and progress remain live issues in the context of such a social history.

Cartwright agreed with Mäki and emphasised the point that if one is in the business of explaining beliefs, then one has got to explain the ones that are warranted by the evidence as well as the ones that are not warranted by the evidence. In both cases, one needs an explanation of how we came to have these beliefs, symmetrically, of course. It may well be the case that we've got our institutions in this particular society well arranged, so the fact that the evidence warrants the belief is often in science a part of the explanation of why the belief is held. But that itself is an historical thesis in need of defence.

Hurwicz agreed with Mirowski that Hotelling was concerned about the welfare implications of demand theory, but he views that as an additional point. The basic conclusion was that the price charged by a firm should be proportional to marginal cost. Again the focus was on the firm. It is of some interest that in the (1942) volume published in memory of Henry Schultz, there was a paper by Samuelson about the various meanings and implications of the constancy of the marginal utility of money or income. In particular Samuelson had a little footnote in which (without referring to Hotelling by name) he raises the question of the conditions under which one could have Hotelling's symmetry condition in a demand theory containing a budget constraint. Symmetry in the form of $\partial p_i/\partial q_j = \partial p_j/\partial q_i$ is equivalent to homotheticity. The implication goes both ways. What is interesting in the context of Hands and Mirowski's chapter is why theorists do not make such a simplifying assumption about demand in order to permit aggregation. Hurwicz also registered a qualm about whether a realistic history was possible that looked only at people writing in America.

Hands remarked that the economists' reactions to the chapter – that he and Mirowski are doing bad undergraduate economics, and 'any idiot knows better' than to confuse Hotelling's theory with demand theory – were entirely predictable. The complaints that he and Mirowski are not living up to their own dictates (or rather the caricature of their approach that Hands used to motivate it) are predictable too, as are the complaints that they are not orthodox sociologists of science.

It is like trying to walk in the middle of the road without being slammed by cars coming both ways. Practising economists, serious philosophers of science, and those who insist on a more sociological approach will all be tempted to slam his and Mirowski's work. He and Mirowski are trying to get people to communicate who do not usually talk to one another and to get them to think in different ways. When Hands first read Hotelling, his reaction was, 'his is just silly, it's just about factor demands, there's nothing interesting going on here'. It has taken seven years of trying to stop thinking this way to appreciate this history.

Mirowski added that he is surprised that everybody is so complaisant about contemporary demand theory and the research programme that took us to it. Cartwright is correct to say that there are several papers within his and Hands's piece. One paper at the front attempted to attract attention by saying that there are some things that Hotelling's model gives you that contemporary theory does not. This part is abstract and it is not history. Then there is a middle part concerned with what Hotelling says, with the discussion between him and Schulz about their goals, their own understanding and their disappointments. Then there was a treatment of how demand theory was consolidated. In Hands and Mirowski's view, no one has made a good case concerning how all these things got settled.

7 Final Discussion

Andrea Salanti introduced the final discussion with two general points. The first concerns the style of the discussion: when people interested in economic methodology meet 'pure' economists, the common ground tends to become economics *tout court*, rather than economic methodology. On the one hand this is a good news because it shows that economic methodologists know their economics. On the other hand, this raises the problem of what one can expect from 'case studies in economic methodology'. If one wanted to be provocative, one might describe the content of the conference instead as 'case studies in recent history of economics.' The discussion about what happened submerged attempts to discuss how and why it happened.

The second point was already raised in Salanti's paper in the 1989 special issue of *Ricerche Economiche*, to which other people attending this conference also contributed. Its title was 'Recent Work in Economic Methodology: Much Ado about What?' and it reflected upon the implications of the growing consensus among economic methodologists that they should pay more attention to what economists do than to what economists preach about methodology. Coupled with this consensus there has been a growing scepticism about searching in the philosophy of science for a ready-to-use prescriptive methodology. The essay then goes on to ask what one may hope to learn about the methodology of economics when focusing on what economists do in particular cases. The same question can be asked about this conference. Does it provide lessons of general validity about the epistemological status of the discipline?

Roger Backhouse pointed out that to pursue Salanti's questions, one needs to consider in more detail what the role of methodology is. He pointed out that methodological analysis can play at least the following roles:

(1) *Explicating concepts*: Economists frequently use concepts (such as competition, rationality, equilibrium, or even the firm) that turn out on close examination to be more problematic than they appear. Philosophical analysis of such concepts involves raising questions

that might not otherwise be asked, possibly leading to new ways of thinking about the theories in which the concepts are embodied.

(2) *Explicating methodology*: Methodological principles underlie all inquiries, but these principles are frequently not made explicit; and the formulations that result when economists attempt to make them explicit are not always reliable. There is a need for methodological analysis to make methodology explicit and to understand it.

(3) *Explaining the methodological choices of economists*: The intellectual values underlying economists' work have changed over time, sometimes dramatically, with enormous consequences for the content of the resulting economic theories. It is important to understand how and why economists made the choices they did.

(4) *Exploring the extent to which economists achieve either their stated aims or other aims which they might be expected to achieve*: This role is contentious, for it brings up the question of appraisal and casts the methodologist in the uncomfortable role of judge.

(5) *Understanding what economics is about*: There are many definitions of economics, ranging from Marshall's (mankind in the ordinary business of life) to Robbins' (the allocation of scarce resources between competing ends). Though such definitions are common, they are inadequate. Methodology may help to provide better understanding of what economics is about, either through suggesting generalisations about the subject or through making clear where and why such generalisations fail, perhaps due to the heterogeneity of the subject. Two recent examples are Rosenberg's (1992) attempt to argue that much of economics makes sense only if it is seen as a branch of political philosophy, and Hausman's (1992) claim that economists are seeking to create a discipline that is separate from other disciplines such as psychology or sociology.

Though many economists would see the provision of answers to such questions as either a luxury, or a waste of time that could otherwise be spent pursuing substantive economic inquiries, answering such questions is important. For example, explicating concepts would be unnecessary if all that was necessary to settle a dispute was to agree on a model and work out its implications. But a problem arises because models need to be interpreted – the symbols appearing in the model have to be given meanings, and these meanings can frequently be established only by careful analysis of a type that should be regarded as methodological. Explicating methodology and the related task of understanding economists' methodological choices matter, because even if the methodologist does not appraise what is going on, simply articulating the methodology implicit in what economists are doing may raise questions about why economists are behaving as they are. Such questions open the possibility that there may be other ways of proceeding that could be explored. It may also turn out that economists are behaving in a way that, whether or not it is desirable, is inconsistent with their explicit methodological statements. Understanding methodological choices, which brings in a historical dimension, raises even more clearly the possibility that alternative paths might have been chosen.

Appraising economic theories is clearly something that has to be done with great caution if it is not to be open to the charge of intellectual arrogance. Yet there is every justification for methodologists asking whether economics or its specific branches are succeeding in achieving various aims. These aims may be set by those engaged in the discipline, or they may be set by outsiders. In a society where economists are supported by public funds, there is every reason to ask whether the subject is achieving the ends that society desires. The result of such inquiries may be to question the presumed aims of the subject rather than economists' practices – it may be, for example, that particular aims are not achievable, or that to achieve them other, possibly unarticulated, aims would have to be abandoned, and that this would be undesirable.

Understanding what economics is about is perhaps the most controversial role of methodology, for it might be taken as implying that the subject is homogeneous. Perhaps economics is concerned with many different things, with different economists following different methods in order to achieve these different tasks. There may be no single answer to the question of what economics is about, but the question is still important. For good or bad, economists have rarely been able to refrain from trying to define their subject. Such definitions presumably play a role in the discipline and should therefore be examined critically. Such examination may reveal facets of the discipline that would otherwise remain unnoticed. The search for a generalisation, whether or not it is successful, may lead to greater understanding of what is going on in the subject.

Nancy Cartwright remarked that she has a happier and optimistic feeling about the very phenomenon Salanti described in his opening speech. There are periods when one needs general philosophical considerations, which are not highly detailed or immediately relevant to the actual scientific content, and there are different periods when one faces different issues, as was the case at the time when people sought to mathematise the social sciences. To be very detailed about the case studies shows a kind of assurance that one can leave the rest of the philosophy of science as it is in philosophy of physics, philosophy of statistics, philosophy of biology, and so on. It is enormously interesting what one discovers in the case studies, for example in sorting out the concept of involuntary unemployment. These are highly social issues and highly local issues on which both people trained in methodological departments and people trained in economics departments have something to offer.

Daniel Hausman noted that the conference has been very different from the sort of methodology conference that would have taken place thirty years ago. In contrast to what would have happened in the past, there is no evidence in the chapters presented here of anyone saying 'OK, we have the truth from some philosopher', and then looking for an issue suited to be approached in that way. This does not mean that the chapters have not employed tools, analyses and concepts drawn from philosophy, but the chapters are not mere applications of philosophical systems. This is a good thing, but there remains the question of what precisely discussion of these case studies accomplishes. If philosophers do not provide models that generate norms for the right kind of the science, then what good are they? Mäki and he wanted the conference to demonstrate how much philosophy matters and that methodology really had a lot to contribute. Has the conference done this? A great deal of philosophy enters into these particular case studies. But what has been learned? Have the philosophers here learned any general epistemological morals? Have economists here learned something in detail concerning the problems that concern them?

Maurice Lagueux observed that the task of methodologists is not so much to advance the understanding of economic problems as to clarify philosophical issues. In principle, the possibility of getting generalisations that can be applied to different topics cannot be excluded, but what has come out of this conference has instead been an awareness of the many philosophical problems raised by different concepts currently used by economists. The conference has employed the tools of philosophers, not of economists. For instance, people have discussed what is meant by 'progress' and whether there has been progress in monetary policy, what methodological individualism means or what externalities might be. In the discussion of Pierre Salmon's Chapter 2, it turned out to be very difficult to define a mechanism, probably because 'mechanism' is a metaphor suggesting that processes in economic or social life are similar to processes in mechanics. It would be highly desirable to have explicit definitions of such concepts, but very general concepts often cannot be defined in the same way as precise technical concepts are defined. To be aware of this is a positive thing which can help one to appreciate how difficult it is to do good economics and to contextualise some of the conclusions economists reach. All this is philosophy. Even when the discussions may appear negative, such clarification is quite positive.

Thomas Mayer said he appreciated Nancy Cartwright advocating a kind of methodology more concerned with very specific issues, because if methodologists want to do any good, they will have to talk not to themselves but to other economists. Instead of telling economists 'here is the philosophical system that approves the economics you do' it is more useful to tell them 'look, it is crucial to be careful about this type of definition'. In that case maybe, just maybe, somebody will listen.

Uskali Mäki responded to the opening remarks by Salanti and Backhouse. He interpreted the former to suggest that symposium consisted of case studies in recent history of economics rather than case studies in methodology. He agreed that in a sense this is true, but noted that the notion of 'recent history' appears to be ambiguous. The source of ambiguity is not so much the meaning of 'recent' (cases in a more distant past could have been discussed) as the notion of 'history', which has several connotations. One of them is that history is something actual, something that actually happened, etc. The very idea of a case study implies an interest in what actually happened. But there is another connotation concerning development and transformation across time. In the last two days of the conference there were four papers dealing with the formation of concepts and perspectives.

Mäki went on to offer some additions to what Backhouse said about the goals of methodological work. He agreed that those methodologists who are employed by economics departments are often apologetic about what they are doing. To some extent, this is unavoidable, because a number of people believe that methodologists should address their efforts to convince the economic profession (as Mayer said before). But Mäki pointed out that there are other audiences who are interested in what methodologists are doing and saying. Philosophers of science have an intrinsic interest in learning about economics, because philosophers of science are interested in science and the variety of scientific practices. And there are other social scientists (sociologists, political scientists and so on) who are considering borrowing ideas from economics. There are policy makers who are using tools that economists provide, and they have questions about these tools. In a sense, therefore, one may fully agree with Ariel Rubinstein that economics is a powerful social institution and has to be studied irrespective of whether the economic profession is interested in what methodologists discover or whether economics departments are willing to employ methodologists.

Kevin Hoover maintained that the borders that have been drawn between methodology and economics are arbitrary and that a pluralistic view of economic methodology may be most sensible, because there are a lot of different things that methodologists can do. Some of them are much more abstract and others are much more particular, so that one has to face the question of what can be done in order to foster mutual communication. In his own field, macroeconomics, he was delighted to hear the very reflective remarks of Mayer and McCallum – two people who have tackled controversial issues in trying to make macroeconomics more 'scientific'. To foster mutual communication is exactly to provide opportunities for such reflective exchanges to happen. In any case there is a difference in being a methodologist in a methodological home and being a methodologist among economists. He has certain obligation to maintain his macroeconomic proficiency that philosophers do not necessarily have and do not need to have. A continuum between pure philosophers and non-methodologically-minded economists is needed to permit communication. Regardless of their intrinsic interest and importance, many methodological debates in the past seemed irrelevant to practitioners simply because they were carried on at such high levels of generality. Methodologists with more detailed knowledge of economic practice might find lessons in such debates that would be relevant to practitioners. There is a need to build bridges at several different levels.

Cartwright asked if there is a good reason for talking about 'methodology' and economics rather than philosophy and economics. In philosophy departments inquiries get a lot of different names: one speaks of foundations of physics, philosophy of biology, and so on. In her department, she has reclaimed the label of a 'methodologist' because of the political climate in Britain, which makes one more likely to be funded if one is a methodologist than if one describes oneself as a philosopher.

Hoover replied that it is more common to hear people talking about methodology simply because economists are already accustomed to talk about 'methodology' construed as an account of statistical or theoretical practices. Those called 'methodologists' are certainly driven by philosophical considerations. Anyway, it is not more enlightening to be called a philosopher of economics instead of a methodologist, except that the term 'philosophy' perhaps suggests a little bit more distance from practice.

Lagueux observed that professional division is more a matter of sociology than of conceptual boundaries. Of course, people doing something different from the majority of the colleagues in their department might face special constraints, but this is another problem. In any case the content of this conference has been philosophy. Nobody at the conference has tried to make his or her point by using correlations, empirical studies, mathematical models and the like, which are the usual tools of the economists. It is unclear, however, why one should attach so much importance to whether such inquiries are carried out in economic departments or elsewhere.

Mäki, commenting upon what was said by Lagueux and Hoover, pointed out that the label 'economic methodology' looks like a kind of market ploy within economics. He suggested that three things may help to make some of the progress that is needed in economic methodology. First, one should welcome the continuum of communication Hoover defined with overlapping conversations between philosophers, philosophers of economics, methodologically oriented economists, practising economists, and so on. Secondly, one should foster mutual collaboration, that is joint projects where philosophers and economists work together on specific case studies. Thirdly, there is criticism: more serious, deep, careful, and detailed criticism is needed. But dismissive criticism is not needed – there has been too much of that.

Hoover pointed to what seemed to him a limitation in Mäki's idea of collaboration, which seems to run from economics to philosophy (if thought in terms of case studies). It runs a little bit the other way in the case of criticism, and one should not overlook the possibility that things learned at one level of generality can be brought down a level.

Philippe Mongin proposed, as a member of the Programme Committee, to make a case for what it intended to do with the conference. Many economists do not realise that economic methodology has become a largely self-referential field. It has become a very sophisticated field, losing sometimes any connection with economics and developing a philosophy of its own, which has some value but which is sometimes difficult to assess according to professional philosophical standards. One of the implicit aims in organising this conference was to break into this monologue, and from this viewpoint it has been successful at a rather non-trivial level. Such interaction between philosophy, methodology, and economics should be regarded as an important part of the output of this conference, which will emerge even better in the subsequent volume.

References

Hausman, D.M. (1992) *The Inexact and Separate Science of Economics* (Cambridge and New York: Cambridge University Press.

Rosenberg, A. (1992) *Economics – Mathematical Politics or Science of Diminishing Returns* (Chicago: University of Chicago Press).

Conclusions

Roger E. Backhouse and Andrea Salanti

1 THE AIM OF THE CONFERENCE

As Daniel Hausman and Uskali Mäki explained in their Introduction to this volume, the aim of the conference was to foster mutual dialogue between economists, economic methodologists and philosophers interested in methodological problems in economics. Following recent trends in economic methodology, notably the one which motivated the choice of discussing case studies instead of grand but old-fashioned general epistemological issues, all participants abstained from grounding their arguments on appeals to philosophical authorities, trying to focus their attention on the specific issues raised in each single case.

Such an attitude has two very important advantages. First, it forces us to avoid speaking about economics *tout court*, compelling us to recognise the specific methodological problems that economists have to face in different subfields in the discipline. These are often very different. Second, it guards against the temptation of approaching the philosophy of a social science like economics by simply re-styling one of the various descriptive or prescriptive epistemological analyses originally devised with reference to one or two disciplines (typically including physics) in the natural sciences. Economic methodologists have recently reached a remarkable consensus on these two points and on the importance of paying attention to economists' actual practices.

It remains to be seen, however, whether positive results can be obtained in this way. Of course we cannot expect to solve all the methodological problems facing us by simply looking at what economists actually do, or hearing from them several accounts of what they perceive to be their own task (in the same way in which we cannot expect to shape consumer theory simply observing consumer behaviour or interviewing consumers about the way they usually make their own choices). The need is for case studies either by outsiders to the discipline, informed by close dialogue with economists in the relevant field, or by insiders who are prepared to distance themselves from the immediate concerns of their discipline sufficiently to get a broader perspective.

2 THE CASE STUDIES

The case studies can best be classified in three ways: (1) the branch of economics covered; (2) the type of economics discussed; and (3) the type of case study.

(1) The papers were selected to cover a variety of areas within economics. Four out of the six case studies were on micro, and two on macro. This reflected a great unevenness in the numbers of micro and macro papers submitted: there were far fewer macro submissions than micro, and even fewer dealing with what Schumpeter termed 'the applied fields' and empirical techniques.

(2) Within various fields of economics we can distinguish, broadly between theoretical and applied economics.[1] Five case studies focused on theory, but only one (Mayer) on applied economics. Some of the economic theory case studies (for example, Hands and Mirowski) discussed empirical work but their focus was nonetheless sharply on economic theory.

(3) Two papers were concerned to analyse fundamental concepts within economics, two provided accounts of the way such concepts had evolved over time, and two were concerned with very specific episodes in the recent history of economic thought. This distinction is important because it has clear implications for the nature of the philosophical and other tools that are brought to bear on economics. There is some, though far from perfect, correlation between the types of case study and the tools that are relevant to analyse them. Oversimplifying to a considerable extent, one might distinguish between the tools of the philosopher, the historian and the sociologist. Analysis of fundamental concepts involves philosophical tools, whilst historical analysis is required to analyse both the evolution of concepts and specific episodes. Sociological tools were used extensively by the authors of one of the case studies on specific episodes (Hands and Mirowski) and by one of the discussants of the other (Wulwick on Mayer).

Ignoring the distinction between theoretical and applied economics, the resulting variety is summarised in Table C1.[1]

Table C1 Classification of the papers

	Fundamental concepts	*Evolution of concepts*	*Specific episodes*
Microeconomics	Janssen Salmon	Lagueux	Hands and Mirowski
Macroeconomics		De Vroey	Mayer

3 THE PARTICIPANTS

In classifying the participants the crucial issue is specialisation. Everyone knew some economics and some philosophy, but the mix was very different. However, the key distinction is rather between those whose main concern was to contribute to research in economics, and those who had chosen to specialise in reflecting on economics. Participants could be arranged along a spectrum, from philosophers and historians who have never contributed to economics, to economists whose publications have been entirely within economics.[2] This categorisation of the contributors is not without problems (the distinction between contributing to economics and reflecting on it is not clear-cut, with some participants, such as Hoover and Backhouse, finding themselves wearing different hats on different occasions), but it is useful in understanding the debates which took place. The authors of the case studies fell mostly into the latter category, though one, Mayer, had been a significant contributor to the episode on which he had chosen to reflect. The intention was that discussants would include one methodologist and one economist for each paper. In the event, however, some people proved impossible to pigeon-hole in this way. Zamagni and Mäki both criticised Salmon in a way that was philosophically too well informed to count as the reaction of a typical economist. Similarly, the differences in the perspectives on De Vroey's paper offered by Leijonhufvud and Hoover were very small. Though he was a major participant in the debate over unemployment, Leijonhufvud was historically sensitive, and hostile to much contemporary theorising. On the other side, though he was philosophically well informed, Hoover was in some ways closer to contemporary unemployment theory than Leijonhufud.

4 INTERACTION BETWEEN THE PARTICIPANTS

One hypothesis about the interaction between participants in the conference was that communication would be easier when people are closer together on this spectrum.[3] There is, however, more to the story than this. Where the case studies involved philosophical analyses of fundamental concepts, though methodologists and economists have different backgrounds, areas of expertise and experiences, they are talking on the same plane. The interaction between Janssen, Rubinstein and Mongin illustrates this well. Though all three approached the problem of individualism and game theory from three very different perspectives, they could engage with each other because they all focused on the same object of inquiry. Such interaction can result in a productive cross-fertilisation of ideas.

The situation is very different with historical case studies, for here economists and methodologists have different objects of inquiry. Though contemporary economists are still concerned with economics when they enter such discussions, the methodologists are concerned with the historical economists themselves, not simply with what the economists are studying. Economists' views are important not simply as a source of ideas for discussion, but as evidence concerning their objectives, the constraints they perceive and their arguments. There is also the possibility that, in the same way that an economist who uses a profit maximisation model may not care whether or not economic agents think of themselves as maximising profits, the methodologist may offer explanations of economists' behaviour that differ from the way in which the economists concerned may prefer to think of their own actions. This asymmetry was greatest in the Hands and Mirowski case study, which dealt with a story in which Hurwicz was closely involved. When Hands and Mirowski told their story, Hurwicz was able to respond by pointing out how it looked to the key participants. The same situation arose, though with roles of author and commentator reversed, when Wulwick discussed Mayer's case study. Mayer, like McCallum, was a participant in the episode under discussion, whereas Wulwick was analysing economists' behaviour using sociological tools. The same situation of an asymmetry between participant and observer would also have arisen had De Vroey chosen, as he might have done, to approach the problem of involuntary unemployment from a perspective closer to that Mayer adopted to monetary policy. However, because he focused on a conceptual analysis, it did not arise to the same extent.

A major difference between economists and some methodologists is that economists, entirely understandably, see the truth of economic ideas as relevant to understanding why certain ideas succeeded and others did not. Thus Hurwicz, McCallum and Rubinstein argued strongly that Slutsky's theory of demand was adopted by the profession because it

parison with the 'harder' natural sciences, but at the same time it appears to be 'hard' if compared with other social sciences. The distinction between supposedly 'hard' and 'soft' disciplines is admittedly open to question, and not all economics is equally 'hard' or 'soft', but it is sufficiently well defined to be usable here. In this view of economics relative to other disciplines, the supposed 'hardness' of economics is the result of economists having taken, at various stages of the subject's evolution, some strong methodological decisions about the boundaries of its subject matter and the proper way to analyse it. First, it was maintained that the ideal agent should be conceived as *homo oeconomicus* rather than as a human being driven by a variety of motives and instincts. Second, in order to describe the aggregate results of individual actions, economists relied more and more on mechanical analogies. Finally, it was postulated that economic men always act according to a strict principle of instrumental rationality and that any sound economic explanation should take full account of this.

These three, very strong, methodological constraints[8] have undoubtedly enabled economists to achieve impressive results, with the consequence that the great majority of economists perceives them as a boundary that cannot be crossed. This attitude means that though methodologists may interact with their fellow economists in many fruitful ways, they are doomed to lack of interest and reproach if they decide, for whatever reason, to cross this boundary and to question these methodological choices.

A further difference to emerge between economists and methodologists concerns the concept of a mechanism. Philosophers were predominantly uneasy about the use of the term 'mechanism' in economics, as was made very clear in the discussion of Salmon's chapter. Mechanisms were seen as involving causal relationships, and there was concern about using the term when the precise causal relationships could not be identified. In contrast, the economists were comfortable with using the term 'mechanism'. This may be simply because economists have become so accustomed to using mechanical analogies that they fail to see the problems involved.[9] There is, however, possibly a deeper reason, related to the way economists use models. The models used by economists have three characteristics:

(1) They frequently require assumptions that are clearly false, not simply in that they abstract from inessential detail, but in ways that are are relevant to the problem in hand.
(2) They are sometimes too complex for simply solving the model to provide a clear explanation of what is happening in the model.

(3) They are often incapable of giving precise predictions because the effect in which the economist is interested is the sum of two effects which work in opposite directions and nothing is known about their relative sizes.

The first characteristic means that models cannot be tested by considering whether or not they predict correctly (or any similar criterion), for they will fail. And yet, economists believe that the models are saying something important about the real world. They express this by arguing that the model is capturing a mechanism that is operative in the real world. Related to this is the second characteristic. Even if a model produces some result, economists will not consider themselves to have explained that result (and hence will not have confidence in it) until they can provide an intuitive explanation of how the model produces the result – unless they can tell a story about how the result occurs. These stories are, for economists, about mechanisms. Providing accounts of the 'mechanisms' that are operating within models is, therefore, a crucial part of any economic explanation. Sometimes the 'mechanism' may be a process involving agents' decisions; at other times a feature of the constraints faced by agents, such as the existence of a discontinuity or non-convexity in a revenue or production function. Thus although the causality underlying them may be very different, both free riding (in which the mechanism is the structure of the problem facing agents) and the market mechanism (which involves agents responding to incentives) are intuitive explanations or stories about what is going on within economic models.

The third of these characteristics implies that in some problems, more than one mechanism is at work. In such cases, mathematics is frequently an essential tool for solving the models, for correct conclusions cannot, in practice, be drawn using ordinary language alone. Nevertheless, even if the use of mathematics is essential, it is equally important to have a simple, intuitive description of the most important mechanism at work. (an example is provided by the presentation of the Keynesian multiplier and the IS–LM model in intermediate macroeconomics textbooks). Such intuitive explanations, however, are not only useful in teaching or as possible sources of heuristic suggestions for scholars, but they also play an essential role in channelling economic ideas towards policy makers and public opinion. It is not by chance that when an economic institution (in the widest sense of the term) is implemented, this is usually done in order to either foster or counteract some economic mechanism whose understanding has successfully crossed the boundary of economic profession. Regulations on takeover bids, or the design of contracts to deal with problems of free riding is a case in point.[10]

6 FINAL REMARKS

Economic institutions impinge continually on our daily life, and as a result much economic research is publicly funded. This means that, as Ariel Rubinstein pointed out, there is a strong case for monitoring economists' activities and the ensuing policy proposals. For this, if for no other reason, methodological studies in the field of economics ought to have a promising future. Such studies, however, can also serve a number of other purposes, pointed out by Backhouse in his introductory remarks to the final discussion.

In order to pursue all these goals, case studies have an important role to play. They can attract the interest of economists who would not be interested in discussions of abstract philosophical issues. Perhaps equally important, they are able to cover what de Marchi has called the 'somewhat neglected middle ground' between 'the notion of science as ideals with no traceable links to practice' and the proposal to consider 'interpretation [as] all there is, the only game in town'.[11] Methodological discussions cannot be completely reduced to a collections of case studies, but the examples included in this volume go a considerable way towards showing what can be achieved in this 'somewhat neglected middle ground'. Though there have been previous collections of methodological case studies[12] the present collection is different in that it does not focus on a particular methodological framework. This is important if economic methodology is to develop in response to the specific problems of economics.

Notes

1. This is a different distinction from that made in the previous paragraph, for 'applied fields' involve theory. It would, for example, be possible to have had a case study of the theory of economic development – of economic theory within an 'applied' field.
2. We resisted the temptation to quantify each participant's place in this spectrum by classifying and counting publications.
3. See the final discussion in chapter 7 (pp. 433–5), especially the contributions by Hoover and Mäki.

4. A much telling case in point is given by Hurwicz's comment and McCallum's interjections during the discussion on chapter 6 by Hands and Mirowski (pp. 428–6). Compare also Boitani's Comment and McCallum's statement in the discussion on Lagueux's attempt to show the vagueness of the notion of externality (pp. 173, 175).
5. Cf., for instance, Rubinstein's Comment on Janssen's chapter 1, as well as Zamagni on Salmon (chapter 2), and Leijonhufvud and Hoover on De Vroey (chapter 4).
6. McCallum's and Wulwick's comments and the following discussion on Mayer's chapter 5 about the debate between monetarists and Keynesians on the role of central banking provide a clear example of such a kind of interest.
7. See De Marchi and Blaug (1991); Blaug (1992); Hausman (1992).
8. The list could be articulated in various ways, but without affecting the substance of the argument.
9. Even though they share common roots, the notions of mechanism and mechanical analogy are not the same, but this is part of the problem.
10. Other relevant examples include institutions designed to achieve the benefits of competition. It is hardly necessary to ask whether these have been designed on the basis of general equilibrium proofs of the two fundamental theorems of welfare economics, or on the basis of less rigorous but more easily understandable partial equilibrium 'mechanisms'.
11. Cf. the Introduction to de Marchi (1992)
12. For example, Latsis (1976) and De Marchi and Blaug (1991).

References

Blaug, M. (1992) *The Methodology of Economics: How Economists Explain* (Cambridge and New York: Cambridge University Press).

Hausman, D.M. (1992) *The Inexact and Separate Science of Economics* (Cambridge and New York: Cambridge University Press).

de Marchi, N. (ed.) (1992) *Post-Popperian Methodology of Economics. Recovering Practice* (Dordrecht: Kluwer).

de Marchi, N. and M. Blaug (1991) *Appraising Economic Theories: Studies in the Methodology of Research Programmes* (Cheltenham and Brookfield, VT: Edward Elgar).

Latsis, S.J. (1976) *Method and Appraisal Economics* (Cambridge and New York: Cambridge University Press).

Index of Names

Subject Index